# HUGO!

Bart Jones is a reporter for *Newsday* and worked for eight years in Venezuela, mainly as a foreign correspondent for the Associated Press. He holds a master's degree in Social Studies from Columbia University. He has also reported for *The Atlantic City Press* in New Jersey, where he won awards from the Philadelphia Press Association. He lives with his family on Long Island. *Hugo!* is his first book.

Published by Vintage 2009

2 4 6 8 10 9 7 5 3 1

Copyright © Bart Jones 2008

Bart Jones has asserted his right under the Copyright, Designs
and Patents Act 1988 to be identified as the author of this work

First published in Great Britain in 2008 by The Bodley Head

Vintage
Random House, 20 Vauxhall Bridge Road,
London SW1V 2SA

www.vintage-books.co.uk

Addresses for companies within The Random House Group Limited
can be found at: www.randomhouse.co.uk/offices.htm

The Random House Group Limited Reg. No. 954009

A CIP catalogue record for this book
is available from the British Library

ISBN 9780099520528

The Random House Group Limited supports The Forest
Stewardship Council (FSC), the leading international forest
certification organisation. All our titles that are printed on
Greenpeace approved FSC certified paper carry the FSC logo.
Our paper procurement policy can be found at:
www.rbooks.co.uk/environment

Printed and bound in Great Britain by
CPI Bookmarque, Croydon, CR0 4TD

BART JONES

# Hugo!

The Hugo Chavez Story
from Mud Hut
to Perpetual Revolution

**VINTAGE BOOKS**
London

*For Elba and Frank*

# Contents

*"America is ungovernable.
Those who serve the revolution
plough the sea. The only thing to do
in America is emigrate."*

Simón Bolívar


*"Those who make peaceful revolution
impossible will make
violent revolution inevitable."*

John F. Kennedy

# Preface

Hugo Chávez and I were sitting alone on the second floor of the Miraflores Presidential Palace in Caracas, Venezuela. It was close to midnight on April 30, 2007. Venezuela was minutes away from making a small bit of history by taking majority control of four multibillion-dollar oil projects in the eastern Orinoco River basin from international companies, including ExxonMobil, Chevron, Conoco, and Total.

Chávez was overseeing the takeover from a table on a semi-enclosed outdoor patio. A thatch roof provided shelter. Several birdcages hung from it, and the birds occasionally chirped. It was tranquil. But in eastern Anzoátegui state, things were hardly placid. The situation was electric. Workers and executives from the state oil company, Petroleos de Venezuela (PDVSA), accompanied by Venezuelan troops, were to take control of the private oil companies' installations at the stroke of midnight on May 1, International Workers Day. Workers would hoist Venezuelan flags and change the names of the companies. Sincor, for instance, would become PetroJunin, named after a famous battle in Peru that had been led by Chávez's hero, Simón Bolívar.

Like many of Chávez's moves, the oil takeover was controversial. His detractors claimed it was another step in creating a totalitarian dictatorship modeled after Fidel Castro, his mentor. His supporters responded that he was proudly re-establishing national sovereignty over a strategic natural resource that had been exploited for years by foreign companies enjoying a virtual tax holiday.

I had a privileged view as Chávez coordinated the takeover. We were alone on the patio from 11:10 P.M. to 1:30 A.M. — prime time for the president. It was my second interview with him in two days — a rare opportunity to spend time with a man flooded with interview requests.

No one interrupted us save an attendant in street clothes who came in from time to time to ask if we wanted a cup of coffee or a glass of water.

The previous night I had flown back with Chávez on the presidential jet from the city of Barquisimeto to Caracas, interviewing him in his private office in the plane. Then he invited me to drive up to Caracas in his car, and finally took me for a short walk outside Miraflores.

Now, as midnight approached, Chávez got on his cell phone with Rafael Ramírez, the head of PDVSA. The president wanted to know which companies had not signed the contracts agreeing to turn over control to Venezuela. Conoco was the only company holding out, Ramirez told him.

A small television was attached to the thatch roof, and Chávez was keeping one eye on it. The president of the state television network was talking live on the screen from Anzoátegui, declaring that the country was about to witness a historic moment. "It would be good if you could make a statement to the country at twelve on the dot, maybe in a *cadena*," Chávez told Ramirez, using the word for a legally mandated broadcast all networks were required to pick up. "Call Willian Lara," the communications minister, Chávez said. "No, I'll call him right now. Let me order a *cadena* from here. Don't speak very long. Not like Chávez," he joked.

Within a few minutes Ramirez was speaking live on nearly every television station in the country. Chávez flipped the channels to make sure all the stations were complying. When he came to Channel 2 RCTV, he paused. The station was to lose its license to broadcast on May 27 and was engaged in a vigorous international campaign to denounce Chávez for crushing freedom of speech. The government contended that RCTV played an active role in a 2002 coup against the president, and its activities — such as journalists and politicians declaring on television that the president should be overthrown — would never be permitted in the United States. The Federal Communications Commission would have shut it down instantly. Nevertheless, when RCTV later did go off the air after the government refused to renew its license, Chávez came under worldwide attack; everyone from US Secretary of State Condoleeza Rice and President George W. Bush to human rights and free press organizations denounced his actions.

Chávez was pleased when he saw RCTV complying with the *cadena*. "So they get even angrier," he said, laughing as he imagined the reaction of RCTV executives being forced to broadcast the *cadena*.

Ramirez spoke on television, and everything seemed to be proceeding smoothly. The PDVSA head ceremoniously gave an oil worker a red helmet — the color of the Bolivarian Revolution — to replace his blue one. The crowd in Anzoátegui cheered wildly.

• • •

Getting to sit next to Hugo Chávez as he commanded the takeover was not easy. His aides told me in April 2007 they'd been flooded with more than a thousand requests for interviews — since January. Some said the best I could hope for would be a couple of quick questions in a hallway somewhere. In the process of researching this book, I spent nearly two years lobbying officials to be able to sit down with Chávez to discuss his life and his presidency. Many said they would do what they could — and then nothing happened.

It was a far cry from when I lived in the country from 1992 to 2000, covering the ups and downs of Chávez's rise to power. I had interviewed Chávez a number of times, and stood not far from him on an outdoor terrace the night he won the presidency in 1998. Yet before his triumph, Chávez at times practically had to beg for media coverage. Once, when he returned from a trip to Colombia and called a press conference, only a few reporters showed up.

Now, in early April 2007, my break finally came — or seemed to, anyway. Government officials called me in New York to tell me the interview with the president was all set. Wednesday, April 25, would be the day.

I flew down a couple days early, showed up at the palace on the appointed day — and got stood up. "*Se complicó la cosa,*" I was told — things got complicated. He couldn't do it.

Disappointed and miffed, I decided to take advantage of the day off by interviewing the two most powerful men in the government besides Chávez — his brother Adán and his longtime vice president, José Vicente Rangel, who had recently stepped down from his post. Government officials assured me they were doing everything possible to get me in to see the president the next day.

The following day, nothing happened — at least not until 3 P.M. By then I had given up hope and was mentally preparing to proceed with my scheduled flight back to New York the next day. But then a Miraflores aide called and informed me Chávez wanted me to accompany him on the presidential jet to Barquisimeto for a meeting with Bolivian president Evo Morales and Nicaraguan president Daniel Ortega, among others. I would be able to interview the president in the plane on the way back Sunday, or on Monday morning in the palace.

That Saturday morning we headed to Barquisimeto on the presidential jet. Only Chávez wasn't aboard. He missed the flight on his own airplane, which took some of his ministers, media people, security agents, and me to Barquisimeto, then turned around and went back to Caracas to get the president. I didn't talk to Chávez during the weekend — he was busy tending to Morales, Ortega, and others.

But as we headed back to Caracas on the Airbus 319 that Sunday night, I was summoned into the presidential office. I was getting a rare chance to spend extended time one-on-one with the man who was shaking up Venezuela and trying to spread his Bolivarian Revolution throughout the world.

After we landed in Caracas, forty-five minutes later, we spoke in his car during the twenty-minute trip to the palace and then talked some more at Miraflores. Finally we bid each other good night, and Chávez promised to see me the next day around noon to finish the interview. I doubted it would happen, since he had already spent more time with me than he had with most other journalists and had given me some unusual access on the plane and in the car. Moreover, Venezuelans are famous for making appointments they never keep.

Noon came and went with no word from Miraflores. Around 3 P.M. I started to prepare to head back to New York the next morning. But about 5:15 P.M. my cell phone rang with a call from the palace: Be there at 8 P.M. The president will meet with you.

I showed up at the appointed hour, and then waited three hours. It was just after eleven when I was summoned upstairs to see the president.

In conversations that night and the previous one we talked for nearly four hours. We covered a lot of territory, from Chávez's impoverished childhood to the 2002 coup in which he was almost killed . . . and at least one sensitive topic he had never spoken about publicly and that I feared might bring the interview to an abrupt end.

# ¡HUGO!

# Hurricane Hugo

Hugo Chávez's presidency was slipping out of his hands. Hundreds of thousands of protestors were marching toward the Miraflores presidential palace in Caracas, Venezuela, on April 11, 2002, demanding that he resign. "Get out Chávez, traitor!" some yelled. "We're going to topple the government!" "Chávez is going to pay!" It was one of the largest protest marches in Venezuelan history, a diverse coalition of men, women, and even children waving flags, blowing whistles, and banging pots. Many had their faces painted yellow, red, and blue, the colors of Venezuela's flag.

Three years into his presidency Chávez was a hated man among some Venezuelans. They believed he was a messianic demagogue, another Fidel Castro who was destroying the country with a half-baked experiment in communism. To the protestors, Chávez had divided Venezuela between rich and poor, pushing a peaceful nation to the brink of civil war. He dismissed the wealthy elites who led the opposition as "squealing pigs," "rancid oligarchs," and "the squalid ones." He denounced the Roman Catholic Church hierarchy in Venezuela as a "tumor" and "devils in vestments." Chávez was an embarrassment to the protestors, a crackpot *caudillo* who was inciting class warfare and plunging the country into economic chaos.

But as word spread in the capital city's teeming mountainside barrios that the protestors had illegally changed the route of their march at the last minute and were converging on Miraflores, several thousand of Chávez's supporters jumped on motorcycles and public buses to head to the palace. They vowed to defend the president to the death. To them, he was a messiah. He was the first president in Venezuela's history to stand up for millions of poor people who made up a majority of the population. Venezuela possessed the largest oil reserves in the world outside the Middle East and was one of the largest foreign suppliers to the United States, yet most of its population was mired in poverty. Many blamed a corrupt ruling elite for pillaging the oil wealth and amassing private fortunes. While bus drivers, electricians, and teachers lived in shacks, the elites jetted off to Europe and the United States for vacations and lived in gated mansions.

A few hundred of the Chavistas gathered on an overpass near Miraflores called Llaguno Bridge. To distinguish themselves from the protestors, many had their faces painted red, Chávez's color. Down on the streets, thin lines of Metropolitan Police and National Guardsmen tried to keep the groups apart. Clothing stores, coffee shops, and restaurants that sold corn bread *arepas* were closed, with metal gates pulled down to protect the windows. The hot Caribbean sun was beating down on the city. Tear gas choked the air.

At about 3:20 P.M. one of the anti-Chávez protestors, twenty-nine-year-old Aristóteles Aranguren, was standing on Baralt Avenue about seven blocks from Miraflores when the first shots rang out. He wasn't sure where they came from, but he assumed it was the Chavistas. The bald, freckle-faced former soldier and fifth-grade teacher flinched and ducked behind a tank-like vehicle called the Whale. It was owned by the Metropolitan Police and had suddenly turned onto Baralt from a side street. Aranguren started running backward and had gone just a few steps when a woman on the seventh floor of a nearby office building yelled out a window, "Watch out! They're bringing someone wounded!" A group of men came running down the street carrying the limp, bloody body of a man by the arms and legs. The man was slipping from their grasp, so they paused to get a better hold.

Aranguren ran over to see if he could help with some of the first-aid techniques he had learned in the military. The victim was about twenty and dressed in black — shirt, jacket, and dungarees. His body was limp, and his head was hanging to the side. A bullet had pierced it on the left side just above the ear, exiting on the right. It left an inch-wide hole through which Aranguren could see part of the man's gray, bloody brain. In his free hand one of the rescuers was carrying a bloody gray glob that looked like another part of the young man's brain. He was bleeding profusely. The back of his head was soaked through in blood, matting down his hair.

Aranguren was enraged at the sight of the young man, who appeared dead. The protestors had come to peacefully demand that Chávez resign. Aranguren had never imagined the march would turn bloody. Maybe some tear gas from the police. Maybe some fistfights with the Chavistas. But never gunshots.

Keeping a wary eye on the bridge, he retreated another twenty yards south on Baralt. More gunshots rang out. He could see the leaves shake on a tree in front of a McDonald's as bullets whizzed by. At the corner of University Avenue, he encountered a second revolting scene: a man lying faceup and unconscious on the sidewalk. A bullet hole left a gaping wound on the left side of his head. Five protestors stood around him in shocked silence. One held his head slightly off the ground and unsuccessfully pressed a handkerchief against the wound to try to stop the bleeding. The cloth was soaked with blood.

Aranguren quickly surveyed the ghastly scene, and was struck by a chilling thought. Both men were killed with a single bullet to the head. Were snipers taking people out? He'd undergone training in the military in how to neutralize snipers, and this seemed to fit the bill. He glanced at the rooftops of buildings up and down the street, but didn't see anything unusual. Then he took off running, turning his back to the overpass and yelling to the crowd, "There are snipers! Go back! Two people are already dead!"

He had gone about thirty yards when, on the other side of the street, he saw the head of a man running parallel to him jerk forward abruptly as if someone had pushed him from behind. The man then crumpled to the ground. He was thin, with a crew cut and no shirt. He had taken a bullet to the head, which now had a small stain on it. He lay on his right side on the sidewalk and did not move. It was the third person Aranguren saw with a bullet in the head. The shooting had started barely a minute ago.

Shots were still raining down on the crowd. About fifty people were in the immediate area around Aranguren. Half a dozen or so had bullet wounds to their feet, legs, torsos, or arms. People were walking, trotting, sprinting in all directions. Others just stood there, dumbfounded. No one knew where the shots were coming from or what was happening.

Aranguren kept running, turning his eyes quickly again to the street in front of him. Ten yards away he saw another man lying on his back on the sidewalk in front of a men's clothing store. A protestor running in front of Aranguren spotted the man at the last minute and leaped over his body. The man was motionless except for his lower left arm and hand, which were extended into the air and moving back and forth weakly in a sweeping motion. Just as Aranguren reached him, his arm fell to the ground and stopped moving.

Aranguren stopped in front of the man and looked down. He was about forty, had black hair, a white T-shirt, blue jeans, and white sneakers. His face was full of sweat from running in the tropical heat. On the left side of his neck was a gaping bullet wound. Blood was gushing out. He didn't look like he had much life left in him. His lips were white. His eyes were 90 percent closed. His head moved slightly from side to side.

Part of Aranguren wanted to leave the man and flee, since his own life was in danger. But he had seen his arm move a moment earlier, and thought he might still be alive. He couldn't just abandon him.

He dropped to the ground and straddled the man with one leg on either side. Then he did the only thing he could think of to stop the bleeding: He shoved the middle finger of his right hand into the warm, slippery wound, which swallowed his finger completely. The man's bleeding slowed but did not stop. The wound was near his artery. Aranguren could feel blood pulsing against his finger. Maybe there was a chance to save him after all, he thought. Another marcher came over, crouched down, and said, "How is he? Is he alive?"

"I think so," Aranguren responded. "Call the rescue squad. Call civil defense."

Luckily paramedics were in the area in case the protest turned violent. Two quickly came zooming up the sidewalk on a motorcycle from the south of Baralt, where most of the protestors were massed. One jumped off and shouted at Aranguren, "Don't take your finger out of there! Wait a second!" The paramedic was in his midthirties and wearing a bulky jacket that served as his medical kit. Its pockets were filled with bandages, needles, sutures, rubber gloves, splints, gauze, little bottles with liquid medicines. He was a walking emergency room.

He crouched down next to the man on the sidewalk, pulled out a needle and a small bottle of medicine, and told Aranguren he was going to inject the man with it. If he was still alive, he would respond, the paramedic said. He jammed the needle into the man's right arm, squeezed the lever, and pulled the needle out. Then he opened the man's eyelids and looked at his eyes. Nothing. "I'm going to put another injection in his arm," the paramedic said. "If he responds, he's alive. If he doesn't, he's dead, and I have to go to another victim that needs help."

Aranguren protested, "But he's alive. I can feel the pulse. You've got to do something." He told the paramedic he wanted to at least carry the man out of there, out of the line of fire, to a safe location where he could be treated.

The paramedic explained that Aranguren might simply be feeling the man's blood draining from his brain. He injected him a second time, looked at his eyes, and again saw no response. "This person can't be saved," he said. "He's practically dead."

Aranguren exploded with anger. "How is it possible you can't do anything?" he yelled. The two shouted back and forth, and the paramedic ordered Aranguren to back away so he could look at the wound. He pushed him against the chest, but Aranguren, instead of backing away, simply pulled his finger out of wound and stood up.

Just as he did, he felt something strike the back of his right leg. He turned around to see if someone was behind him, shooting, but didn't see anyone. He wasn't sure if he'd been hit by a bullet or a rock. It didn't hurt much. But as he reached around, he felt that his pant leg had been ripped open. Blood was on his leg, just below the buttock. He'd been shot. He realized to his horror that the spot he'd been hit on the leg was exactly where his head had been just a second earlier, before the paramedic pushed him. The bullet had been aimed at his head. He was in the sight of a sniper.

Panicked, adrenaline pumping, he took off running down Baralt. He had his eye on the Plaza Caracas, a football field or so away, where he thought he might be out of the range of the snipers. He ran diagonally across the street, desperate to reach the plaza. But as he ran, his leg felt strange, like it was asleep in the area where he'd been shot. It was getting harder and harder to move it, as if he had a weight attached to it. Then the part that was numb got bigger and bigger. By now he was practically dragging his leg. He made it across the street but only halfway to the plaza before collapsing onto a sidewalk. Terrified that the snipers were going to get him as he lay defenseless, he started screaming for help. "I've been shot! Get me out of the line of fire because there are snipers!"

Just a few minutes had passed since the first shots rang out.

• • •

One of the most extraordinary events in modern Latin American history was unfolding. The gunfire went on for several hours, and before long a television network owned by billionaire Gustavo Cisneros, the richest man in Venezuela and one of the richest in the world, was showing a video of Chavistas purportedly firing from the Llaguno Bridge at the marchers. In reality, they were firing at the Metropolitan Police, who were controlled by a Chávez opponent, and not at the protestors, who were too far away to be hit by their handguns. But it didn't matter. The world was soon blaming Hugo Chávez for the "Massacre of El Silencio."

Military officers appeared on television declaring that they no longer recognized Chávez as the head of state. Opposition political and business leaders came on, too, pronouncing Chávez an "assassin." Eventually Chávez gave in to threats by military rebels that they were going to bomb Miraflores Palace, surrendering himself to them while a general announced to the world that he had resigned. Then Chávez disappeared for the next two days. No one in the public knew where he was. In fact, he was secretly shuffled among four different locations, including a remote Caribbean island. At one point in the middle of the night, his captors took him to a dark, desolate road, where it appeared they were going to execute him.

Forty-seven hours after his disappearance, Chávez returned to power when tens of thousands of his enraged supporters took to the streets and loyalist military officers launched a countercoup to rescue him and bring him back to the palace. The two-day putsch was one of the most dramatic chapters in a life that has taken one remarkable turn after the other and transformed Hugo Chávez into a seminal figure in modern Latin American history — the most controversial and closely watched leader in the region since Fidel Castro.

Chávez's life story is the stuff of Hollywood, a Lincoln-like rise from poverty to power . . . with a Venezuelan twist. He was born in a mud hut on the Great Plains of Venezuela, delivered by a midwife because few doctors worked in the impoverished countryside. As a child he sold candies in school and on the streets to help his family survive. By the time he was seventeen he had entered the country's prestigious military academy, Venezuela's version of West Point, mainly to play on its baseball team and pursue his dream of pitching in the major leagues.

But the road to professional baseball took a detour in the academy when he discovered South American independence hero and Venezuelan native son Simón Bolívar and launched a mission to change his country's destiny. He later organized a secret conspiracy of fellow soldiers disgusted by the nation's rampant corruption and moral decay, creating a clandestine cell dedicated to studying the Liberator's teachings. He met secretly for years with former guerrilla leaders such as Douglas Bravo, arriving for clandestine encounters in a secret location in Caracas that became a "house of conspiracy." He cultivated an underground following of progressive and nationalist civilians who wanted to pursue his dream with him, operating under the noses of military superiors who failed to stop his expanding movement.

In 1992 the conspiracy burst into public view when Chávez led a failed coup against President Carlos Andrés Pérez. The paratrooper and his allies were enraged by Pérez's orders to troops three years earlier to mow down hundreds of people in the wake of food riots triggered by an International Monetary Fund–endorsed economic "shock package." It ended with one of the largest massacres in modern Latin American history, rivaling Tiananmen Square for the number of dead.

Chávez landed in jail for two years, but became a hero to millions of impoverished Venezuelans for standing up to a corrupt ruling elite. His detractors dismissed him as little more than a two-bit demagogue who was fomenting class hatred and hawking leftover 1960s Marxist economic policies.

After Chávez got out of jail, he spent several years "in the desert," crisscrossing the country in a mission whose ultimate goal not even he was certain of. Dead broke, he relied on friends and supporters to feed him and give him a place to sleep. The media wrote him off as a has-been, and he all but disappeared from the local and international press. Secretly, he was still weighing another coup attempt. The United States and others hailed Venezuela's "model democracy" as an island of stability during the 1960s, 1970s, and 1980s when civil wars and brutal dictatorships reigned in the region. But Chávez was convinced that this model democracy was a fraud controlled by a corrupt ruling class, and that it would never allow an outsider like him who wanted to destroy the status quo to take power via elections.

In 1997, after his fellow coup leader Francisco Arias Cárdenas won the governorship of oil-rich Zulia state, Chávez underwent a change of heart and launched a campaign to win the presidency. He was the quintessential outsider — a man who had tried to overthrow the system in a coup. Most of the nation's eyes were on his opponent, a former Miss

Universe: six-foot-one strawberry-blond Irene Sáez. Before Chávez, Venezuela was known for two things — beauty queens and oil. As a successful mayor in an affluent Caracas municipality, Irene, as she was universally known, was leading the polls.

But the contest between the beauty and the beast, as the campaign was dubbed, shifted ground as Irene's sugary platitudes revealed an alarming vacuousness and Chávez's fiery rhetoric captured the imagination of millions of shantytown residents seething over the nation's vast gap between poor and rich. In the end Chávez won the December 1998 election in a 56 to 40 percent landslide.

He started his presidency trying to take control of the state oil giant PDVSA (pronounced *pay-day-vay-suh*), which he dubbed an out-of-control "state within a state" that was serving the country's wealthy elites rather than its majority poor. He also played a leading role in reviving the nearly defunct Organization of Petroleum Exporting Countries, hosting the first summit of OPEC leaders in twenty-five years. By helping take world oil prices from rock bottom, when he assumed office, to record highs, he boosted Venezuela's income from $14 billion in 1998 to $40 billion in 2006.

In his first year in office he convoked a constitutional assembly, helped it rewrite the constitution, and then watched voters approve it by a 72 to 28 percent margin. The same day, a torrential downpour of biblical proportions wiped hundreds of communities off the map along Venezuela's Caribbean mountainsides, burying thousands of people under mud or washing them out to sea. The greatest natural calamity in Venezuela in at least a century, it took its heaviest toll among the poor.

Before long Chávez's policies set off a maelstrom of anger, fear, and resentment among Venezuela's ruling elites and their allies in the United States, provoking street marches, searing newspaper editorials, and ultimately the April 2002 coup attempt. It was followed eight months later by one of the most devastating strikes in modern Latin American history, when opponents shut down PDVSA for two months. The economy nearly collapsed, food and gasoline became scarce, and Chávez was on the verge of being forced to resign. Somehow he survived again.

With the opposition debilitated and discredited, Chávez was able to focus on governing. He instituted a series of New Deal–like "social missions" that became the hallmark of his first term as president, teaching a million and a half illiterate Venezuelans to read, subsidizing food markets, opening soup kitchens, distributing land to the landless, and inviting twenty thousand Cuban doctors into the poorest neighborhoods of the nation to live and work.

Chávez pursued his dream of implementing Bolívar's vision of a united Latin America, creating a television news network that spanned the region, selling cheap oil to his neighbors, and proposing a continentwide oil cartel — a Latino OPEC. He envisioned building a fifty-six-hundred-mile, $20 billion natural gas pipeline starting in eastern Venezuela, slicing through Brazil's Amazon jungle, and ending in Argentina, with trunk lines to Peru, Bolivia, and Chile. He even proposed creating a Latin American version of NASA and sending Latinos into space. To his opponents, it was all lunacy. To his supporters, he was a visionary in action.

Today Chávez is one of the most colorful, charismatic, and controversial figures on the world stage. He is widely depicted in the mass media worldwide as a kind of monster, a communist dictator-in-the-making who has destroyed Venezuela's economy, fomented class warfare, trampled on human rights, attacked the free press, and undermined democracy. But the reality about Chávez is far more complex. In many ways the media has missed the story by failing to explain why he is so popular and viewing Venezuela mainly through the lens of the light-skinned elites. As Venezuelan political scientist Edgardo Lander puts it, the international media "is presenting day after day grotesque distortions of what is happening in Venezuela."

Chávez won a landslide victory in an August 2004 recall referendum by a 59 to 41 percent margin in a free and fair vote in which voters had the unusual chance to toss him out of office before his term was up. He followed that with another landslide victory for reelection in December 2006, giving him a new six-year term. It was his tenth electoral triumph in eight years including a plethora of referendums, "re-legitimization" votes, and national and state elections. Like all governments, Chávez's is flawed. But for millions of Venezuelan slum dwellers and for a growing number of progressives around the world, he is waging the most radical social transformation in Latin America since at least the Sandinista Revolution in Nicaragua in the early 1980s.

For decades a forgotten Latin American backwater, Venezuela today is a hot destination for revolutionary tourists who are flying in from the United States, Europe, and other destinations to see the Bolivarian

Revolution in action. Chávez counts among his friends African American leaders, including Harry Belafonte, Danny Glover, and Jesse Jackson, who see a parallel between his Bolívar-inspired revolution on behalf of Venezuela's dark-skinned majority poor and black Americans' Martin Luther King Jr.–inspired struggle for social and economic justice in the United States. The Venezuelan leader delivers discounted home heating oil to impoverished neighborhoods in Harlem and the Bronx and as far away as Alaska, where Indian tribes benefit from the deal. When he visited New York City in September 2006, he traveled to Harlem and spoke at Cooper Union in the East Village, becoming the first foreign president to deliver an address in a hall where eight US presidents, including Lincoln, had given speeches. A few months earlier *Time* magazine had listed him among the one hundred most influential people in the world.

But Chávez is not universally loved. He has generated intense hatred, too. He has powerful enemies at home and abroad who see him as a reincarnation of his mentor in Cuba, a "Castro with oil," as some like to say, although in reality profound differences separate the two men. One of Chávez's most formidable opponents is media mogul and Cuban immigrant Gustavo Cisneros, whose fortune was estimated by *Forbes* at $5 billion, making him the 114th richest person in the world. Cisneros is a friend of former president George H. W. Bush, who has gone on fishing trips to Venezuela with him. Most of the rest of Venezuela's fabulously wealthy upper class also despises Chávez, as do the other interconnected power elites who used to control Venezuela. They include many members of the Catholic Church hierarchy, business leaders, union bosses, media barons, and heads of the traditional political parties whose organizations were annihilated by Chávez's string of electoral triumphs. Aligning itself with Venezuela's elites, the Bush administration has openly pushed for Chávez's demise. Top political leaders from both parties in the United States consider him a pariah, egged on by the mass-media depiction of him as a crazed leftist dictator and many of his own incendiary statements.

To Chávez's supporters, the opposition to him is driven by one basic fact: The poor have taken power in Venezuela for the first time in the country's history, and the moneyed classes who live in gated mansions and travel to Miami for weekend shopping excursions don't like it. While the opposition hotly disputes it, Chávez's government, his allies, and a number of organizations contend that life really has improved for poor people in Venezuela, who are less poor, fewer in number, and filled with hope for the first time in decades. Chávez has retaken control of the oil industry, implemented laws taking a larger share of profits from foreign companies, and instituted a historic shift of the revenues to the majority poor. A plethora of new Bolivarian schools and the social missions are providing the underclass with a fresh chance at health and education now and sustained prosperity down the line. A participatory democracy model has energized and incorporated millions of disenfranchised people into the political process in a way that promises to outlive El Comandante's presidency and spread to other countries.

Chávez is at the forefront of a new wave of leftists who are rising to power across Latin America with widespread support from the underclass, from Luiz Inácio Lula da Silva in Brazil to Néstor Kirchner in Argentina to Evo Morales in Bolivia to Rafael Correa in Ecuador. They are leading a backlash against free-market "neo-liberal" economic programs. Also known as the Washington Consensus, the programs swept the region in the 1990s and 2000s and were supposed to herald a boom in living standards and a reduction in mass poverty. That didn't happen. Latin America still has the most unequal distribution of wealth in the world — "gold medalists in inequality," as Chávez puts it. The result is leftists, reformers, and radicals led by Chávez who are seeking a new path, something between "savage capitalism" and failed communism. He calls it socialism for the twenty-first century.

Not surprisingly, Chávez's reform program is under attack from the Bush administration, which returned to power several key figures from the Iran-contra scandal and the "dirty wars" in Central America during the 1980s Reagan era. They include Otto Reich, Elliot Abrams, and John Negroponte, who brought with them what progressives consider a backward, retrograde view of Latin America and a willingness to distort facts and undermine democratically elected governments if they do not serve US interests as they perceive them.

Since the declaration of the Monroe Doctrine in 1823, the United States has considered Latin America its "backyard." For decades it engineered coups, backed dictators, and bankrolled governments charged with widespread human rights abuses. US Marines occupied Nicaragua from 1912 to 1933 to head off a leftist insurgency, while the CIA mounted a coup in Guatemala in 1954 that overthrew a democratically elected president and ushered in a thirty-year civil war that left two hundred thousand people dead. Since the early 1960s the CIA and the US government have waged a campaign to undermine, overthrow, and at times even assassinate Fidel Castro. In 1973 the CIA helped engineer another coup in Chile, deposing Salvador Allende, the first democratically elected Marxist president in the Western Hemisphere. His successor, General Augusto Pinochet, installed a bloody dictatorship that systematically killed, tortured, and "disappeared" Chileans, leaving three thousand dead. In the 1980s the United States supported a "death squad" government in El Salvador that regularly killed priests, nuns, peasants, and teachers, decapitating some victims and putting their heads on fence posts to terrorize the population.

By almost any measure the US history of intervention in Latin America is a travesty and a contradiction of the democratic principles that it espouses. This was a fact that did not escape Chávez and his supporters, who knew that history far better than most Americans — whose knowledge of the region tended to focus on its exotic climate and historical attractions, such as the Amazon rain forest in Brazil or the Inca ruins in Peru.

By the 1990s most dictatorships were gone in Latin America. The United States under Bill Clinton embraced a formula of free markets, democracy, and less intervention. But the Bush administration reversed that, openly encouraging Chávez's downfall. In contrast to almost every other country in the hemisphere, it endorsed the 2002 coup attempt against him. Officials ranging from Otto Reich to Condoleezza Rice repeatedly denounced Chávez as a threat to democracy. US-funded agencies including the National Endowment for Democracy (NED) and United States Agency for International Development (USAID) pumped millions of dollars into Venezuela for "democracy promotion." Most of the money went to Chávez opponents, including some who backed the violent overthrow of the government.

Chávez offered some of his own bombastic responses to the US attacks, calling Bush a "fool," a "drunk," and a "donkey." He made other controversial moves. He attacked journalists by name for their outrageously biased coverage, provoking his followers to physically attack some in the streets. He flaunted his friendship with Fidel Castro, paid a visit to Saddam Hussein in Iraq, and developed an alliance with Iran's Mahmoud Ahmadinejad. In Venezuela he came under criticism for failing to stem street crime and unemployment. His cabinet seemed to have a revolving door. Some government programs were disorganized. Critics accused him of running roughshod over opponents and politicizing the courts. His wildly popular social missions, while successfully meeting short-term needs and energizing Venezuela's impoverished masses, still left questions about their long-term viability, especially if soaring oil prices plunged. Even some supporters worried that an increasingly hard-line revolutionary environment was shutting down healthy internal debate of the movement's faults. Others wondered if Chávez was a one-man show whose "Bolivarian Revolution" would collapse without him.

But in the impoverished barrios and countryside of Venezuela, Chávez remained a hero to millions. He was the first president in the country's history to defend them, to talk their language, even to look like them with his coffee-colored skin and curly hair. He used street slang on national television, horrifying the upper class but endearing himself to the lower classes, who could scarcely believe one of their own was running the country. It was as if a poor man from Harlem had landed in the White House.

Chávez was a character unlike any the country had seen in Miraflores. Allergic to diplomatic protocol, he acted as president the same way he would act in the backyard on a Sunday afternoon playing dominoes or bocce. One Valentine's Day he announced in a seductive voice to his wife on national television, "Marisabel, tonight you're going to get yours." Venezuelans are among the friendliest and most outgoing people in the world, and love to make jokes. In the barrios many found Chávez's comment hilarious, although feminists overseas hardly chuckled.

He hosted a weekly television and radio program named *Hello, President*. It was the only program in Latin America and perhaps the world where ordinary citizens could call in and talk to their nation's leader about their problems, live and nationwide. His shows went on for hours, and so did many of his speeches. He sang songs on the program, cracked jokes, recited poetry, reminisced about his childhood, announced cabinet changes, launched policy initiatives, and quoted everyone from Jesus Christ to Simón Bolívar to John Kenneth Galbraith.

He trotted the globe. He threw out the first pitch at a New York Mets baseball game while wearing a warm-up jacket with Venezuela's national colors. He rang the bell at the New York Stock Exchange. He sprinted along the Great Wall of China. He played baseball with Castro in Havana. He disarmed world leaders such as Vladimir Putin, dropping into a karate stance the first time he met the Russian leader to show he knew Putin was a black belt.

He was a gifted communicator and storyteller. Even Michael Skol, former US ambassador to Venezuela and no fan of Chávez, acknowledged that "he has a charisma, an ability to speak and be impressive and empathetic, which I have never seen the match of anywhere in Latin America, or for that matter in the United States." He was a one-man whirlwind, "Hurricane Hugo," sleeping barely a few hours a night, working seven days a week, downing up to two dozen cups of espresso a day to keep the adrenaline pumping, running his aides and allies ragged with telephone calls at one or two o'clock in the morning. If New York was the city that never slept, Chávez was the president who never rested.

Beneath the jokes and the songs and the pranks and the outrageous comments was a profoundly serious man. He was on a mission to change Venezuela and the world in the name of social justice. Even his enemies could not doubt that his instinct to help was genuine, even if they thought his approach was misguided. He spent years reading voraciously and absorbing the thoughts of revolutionaries from Bolívar to Mao to Ernesto "Che" Guevara. He wasn't easy to define. He was a mix of many things: capitalism and socialism, conservative economics and liberal social programs. When asked to define himself, he once said simply, "I'm a revolutionary."

He gave an unforgettable performance at the United Nations General Assembly in September 2006, emerging onto the world stage for good. In an appearance that rivaled Nikita Khrushchev famously banging his shoe on the podium during an address in 1960, Chávez called George W. Bush "the devil." He accused Bush of "talking as if he owns the world," and suggested that a psychiatrist analyze his speech of the previous day. "Yesterday, the devil came here. Right here. Right here," Chávez said on the floor of the normally sedate United Nations, setting off titters. "And it smells of sulfur still today, this table that I am now standing in front of." He made a sign of the cross, which in Venezuela is a common practice not only to show one's Catholic faith but also to ward off evil spirits. Then he brought his hands together as if praying and looked up at the ceiling. The South American showman still wasn't finished. "Yesterday, ladies and gentlemen, from this rostrum, the president of the United States, the gentleman to whom I refer as the devil, came here, talking as if he owned the world."

The next day, invoking triumphant visits by his mentor Fidel Castro in 1960 and 1965, Chávez traveled to Harlem. He addressed a throng of cheering supporters in the Mount Olivet Baptist Church, announcing that he was more than doubling his program to provide discounted home heating oil to needy Americans. He also continued his tirade against Bush, calling him an "alcoholic" and "a sick man" who acted like he was John Wayne. He imitated what he called Bush's cowboy swagger, puffing out his chest and swinging his arms. The crowd broke up in laughter.

While he won over the throng in Harlem, Chávez's statements set off an uproar elsewhere in the United States. The incendiary comments and personal attacks, one of his Achilles' heels and a habit even some of his supporters opposed, opened him to criticism from detractors that he was little more than a buffoon, a crazy banana republic dictator who didn't know the bounds of decency. Secretary of State Condoleezza Rice called the statements "not becoming for a head of state." Representative John Boehner of Ohio, the Republican House majority leader, blasted Chávez as a "power-hungry autocrat." Senator John McCain of Arizona dismissed him as a "two-bit dictator." In an editorial, the *Los Angeles Times* mocked him as a "clown president" and "the clown prince of Caracas." *The Wall Street Journal* published an editorial calling him a "dictator" — three times. The New York *Daily News* published Chávez's photograph on the entire front page with a headline referring to an editorial inside: "*News*' Message to Crackpot Venezuelan Leader."

Even liberal Democrats and Bush critics attacked him. "Hugo Chávez fancies himself a modern day Simón Bolívar but he is an everyday thug," House minority leader Nancy Pelosi said. Former president Bill Clinton weighed in. "Hugo Chávez said something that was wrong yesterday — unbecoming a head of state." In a sign of how badly Chávez's performance went over in many sectors, even Representative Charles Rangel, a Democrat from Chávez's supposed US power base of Harlem, thundered: "We resent the fact that he would come to the United States and criticize President Bush . . . You don't come into my country, you don't come into my congressional district, and you don't condemn my president."

The governor of Maine announced his state would no longer accept Chávez's discounted oil. A businessman in Alabama launched a boycott of Venezuela-owned Citgo gasoline stations. In Boston a city council member called for tearing down the large neon Citgo sign visible over the left-field fence in Fenway Park that had for decades served as a city landmark. The 7-Eleven chain, inundated with angry callers, formally announced and hyped its separation from Citgo as the gasoline supplier at twenty-one hundred of its convenience stores, even though the decision had been made months earlier. The company blasted Chávez for his "derogatory" remarks about Bush.

The Venezuelan president, in short, took a heavy political hit in the United States for his attack on Bush, counteracting much of the goodwill and positive publicity he'd generated with the Citgo-run discounted home heating oil program he'd started a year earlier. But in a larger context his comments were not so crazy or ill conceived. In the United Nations, where more than half the member states are developing countries, they provoked laughter and cheers. When he ended his twenty-three-minute address, he received the largest ovation of any speaker. The wild applause went on so long — about four minutes — that UN officials had to cut it off.

During his speech Chávez waved a copy of leftist intellectual Noam Chomsky's 2003 book, *Hegemony or Survival: America's Quest for Global Dominance*, a diatribe against US empire building. He urged people to read it. Sales soared overnight, putting it atop Amazon.com's best-sellers chart.

The performance at the United Nations was quintessential Chávez: controversial, provocative, impulsive, devoid of diplomatic niceties, winning enemies and admirers alike, playing to his base and sending the rest to hell. He said what he believed and didn't care what others thought. Despite the outrage among American leaders, some people believed Chávez had merely verbalized what many other foreign leaders thought about Bush but were afraid to say publicly. Like Chávez, they were increasingly disturbed by the war in Iraq, the US government's role in Israel, unfair trade practices, and the US cowboy-style domination of the planet.

If Chávez had not called Bush a devil, would as many people have paid attention to him and his speech? As *Washington Post* columnist Eugene Robinson wrote, "Can anyone name the last president of Venezuela, or remember when a speech by any president of Venezuela made such news?" Even some critics of Chávez acknowledged that the speech won him political points around the world, if not in the United States. "Chávez's speech achieved a great deal, and it is foolish to pretend otherwise. He raised his own standing. He got the world to look at him," former Reagan speechwriter Peggy Noonan wrote in *The Wall*

*Street Journal.* "Everyone this weekend will be discussing what he said — exactly what he said and how he said it. He shook things up . . . He broadened his claimed base . . . He claimed as his constituency everyone unhappy with the uni-polar world."

At the time he spoke, Chávez was campaigning against the United States for a nonpermanent seat on the UN Security Council. In the end he failed to defeat the US candidate, Guatemala. Neither country gained the two-thirds of votes required to secure the seat. Some interpreted the results as a devastating loss for Chávez and evidence that his comments at the United Nations were over the top. But there was another way of looking at it: A Third World nation had battled the world's only remaining superpower to a tie. Not bad.

While Chávez's comments shocked many Americans, other US leaders and public figures traded similar insults without provoking anywhere near the same type of uproar. Rangel himself, the Democrat from Harlem, had called Bush "Our Bull Connor," referring to the infamous 1960s Alabama police chief who turned fire hoses and attack dogs loose on civil rights marchers. Rangel also called the president "a stone-cold alcoholic who found Jesus." In another case, during an introduction of Senator Charles Schumer at a college commencement in 2006, New York State controller Alan Hevesi said Schumer would "put a bullet between the President's eyes if he could get away with it." Hevesi quickly apologized, saying the comment was "beyond dumb." In the 1990s right-wing radio talk-show host Rush Limbaugh ridiculed Chelsea Clinton, then thirteen, as the "White House dog." In 2001 he routinely referred to Democratic leader Tom Daschle, literally, as "El Diablo" and carried on "at length about how Daschle may well be Satan in soft-spoken disguise," according to the director of the media watchdog group FAIR.

If Chávez was taking off the gloves with Bush, and if he wasn't apologizing, he had his reasons, no matter what the political cost in the United States. The comments didn't come out of nowhere. The United States was almost alone in the world in endorsing the 2002 coup to overthrow him. Its support was so blatant that following Chávez's ouster the US ambassador to Venezuela, Charles Shapiro, had breakfast with Pedro Carmona in the presidential palace on his first full day in office after he eliminated the Congress, the Supreme Court, the constitution, and every other vestige of democracy in the country. Declassified CIA documents later revealed that the Bush administration had advance knowledge of the coup but lied about the events, claimed it wasn't a coup at all, and blamed Chávez for his own downfall. Documents also disclosed that the US-funded National Endowment for Democracy, created during the Reagan era, was pumping nearly $1 million a year into Venezuela, largely to groups that supported or took part in the coup. The money flow kept climbing, with new agencies such as USAID stepping in with millions more, but the United States refused to divulge where much of the taxpayer money was going.

After the putsch failed and Chávez returned to office, Condoleezza Rice issued a warning to respect democratic norms. Stunningly, it was aimed not at the opposition that had tried to oust him, but at Chávez. As Chomsky noted, Chávez's anger at Bush wasn't hard to understand. "The Bush administration backed a coup to overthrow his government," he said. "Suppose Venezuela supported a military coup that overthrew the government of the United States? Would we think it was a joke?" Katrina vanden Heuvel, editor of *The Nation*, added, "To be fair, how much diplomatic tact does Chávez owe to a President whose administration supported a coup against him?"

Besides backing the coup, the United States engaged in a constant verbal war with Chávez. On July 31, 2006, Bush told Fox News in an interview that "I view him as a threat of undermining democracy," even though Chávez was freely elected and reelected by the Venezuelan people — unlike US allies such as Pakistan dictator General Pervez Musharraf. Bush's former point man for Latin America, Otto Reich, wrote a cover story in April 2005 for *The National Review* on "Latin America's Terrible Two." The cover featured a photograph of Chávez and Fidel Castro speaking closely in conversation and a banner that read, "The Axis of Evil . . . Western Hemisphere Version."

In February 2006 Secretary of Defense Donald Rumsfeld went so far as to compare Chávez to Adolf Hitler. "We've got Chávez in Venezuela with a lot of oil money," Rumsfeld told the National Press Club. "He's a person who was elected legally just as Adolf Hitler was elected legally and then consolidated power." Six months earlier the evangelical minister Pat Robertson, who had close ties to the Bush administration, had publicly called for Chávez's assassination.

After Chávez's speech, the US ambassador to the United Nations, John Bolton, who boycotted the talk, said: "You know, it's a phenomenon of the United States that not only can he say those things in the General Assembly, he could walk over to Central Park and exercise freedom of speech in Central Park, too, and say pretty much whatever he wanted. Too bad President Chávez doesn't extend the same freedom of speech to the people in Venezuela." The *Daily News* went even farther: "Back home, a Chávez critic who dared voice such colorful language about El Presidente would risk prison or, worse, a bullet."

It was typical of the US government and international media hysteria about Chávez. While like any world leader he had his flaws, accusing him of eliminating free speech at home was absurd. In Venezuela the media was rabidly anti-Chávez, with television stations running non-stop vitriolic propaganda calling him everything from a dictator to a madman. Along with most major newspapers, they openly supported the coup. When the political opposition went on strike, so did the newspapers, refusing to publish. Television stations preempted regular programming to run wall-to-wall coverage of the walkout. Chávez enemies regularly appeared on television calling for his overthrow, sentiments sometimes expressed by news anchors themselves. His opponents held protest demonstrations attracting hundreds of thousands. If this was a dictatorship, it was a strange one indeed. If people in the United States called for the military to overthrow George Bush, they would land in jail. In Venezuela they went free, even when they not only talked about overthrowing the president but tried to do it. Chávez's Venezuela was a far cry from Castro's Cuba.

While the mainstream media ignored them, Chávez made other points in his speech at the United Nations that many saw as worthwhile. He offered an innovative four-point program to reform the body. He also explained some of the source of his rage against Bush and his administration: The United States, he said, had blocked his personal doctor and his chief of security from entering the country, locking them inside the presidential airplane.

More gravely, Chávez noted that "the biggest terrorist of this continent," former CIA operative Luis Posada Carriles, was in the United States, where authorities refused to extradite him to Venezuela to face charges of bombing an airliner. An infamous anti-Castro Cuban exile, Posada masterminded the 1976 bombing of a Cuban airliner that left Venezuela for Cuba. No one survived.

Posada eventually spent several years in prison in Venezuela, and then, "thanks to the CIA and then-government officials, he was allowed to escape, and he lives in this country, protected by the government,"

Chávez told the United Nations. "The US government has double standards; it protects terrorism when it wants to." Posada had entered the United States illegally in 2005 and was detained in Florida. He was later transferred to an immigration jail in Texas. By May 2007 he was freed.

To Chávez, Americans were outraged by his calling Bush the devil, but unfazed that the United States was harboring a known terrorist with blood on his hands. What was worse? When Venezuela sought Posada's extradition, the United States refused. A judge claimed he would face torture.

Chávez is a Latin American original, a leftist firebrand destined to alter the landscape of the continent perhaps in a way Bolívar only dreamed of and reach even beyond Latin America. To the lighter-skinned elites of Venezuela who despise him, he is *ese mono* — that monkey. "The peon has taken over the farm," some like to say.

But to the millions of poor people languishing in Venezuela's barrios and to a growing number of supporters around the world, he is El Comandante — the man who is leading Venezuela out of its bleak abyss in the name of their nation's greatest hero and paving an alternative route for undeveloped nations around the world to emerge from centuries of exploitation and misery. His story echoes that of Latin America and the struggle of the underclass today, from Caracas to Harlem to Johannesburg to Bombay. As Venezuelan Jesuit priest and Chávez critic the Reverend Arturo Peraza once observed, "The man touches the souls of the poor."

## Roots of Rebellion

Hugo Chávez touched the souls of the impoverished because he was one of them. He grew up dirt poor at a time when Venezuela's oil wealth was creating fabulous fortunes for a fortunate few. He was born on July 28, 1954, in the mud house of his grandmother Rosa Inés Chávez. She lived in the rural village of Sabaneta in the state of Barinas. It was a forgotten little place of a thousand people and a few dirt streets that had to be watered in the hot, dry winter to keep the choking dust down. During summer monsoons they turned into seas of mud.

Sabaneta was located in *los llanos*, a vast expanse of sparsely populated grassy marshlands that were Venezuela's version of the Great Plains of the United States or the pampas of Argentina. Home to Venezuela's legendary cowboys, the llanos were a kind of Wild West, a remote and undeveloped region near the Colombian border that took up one-third of Venezuela's landmass. It was a world apart from the exclusive enclaves of Caracas, with their tuxedo-clad servants and elegant champagne parties.

Chávez's parents, Hugo de los Reyes Chávez and Elena Frías de Chávez, lived in a village called Los Rastrojos that was even smaller and more destitute than Sabaneta. It had no doctors, hospitals, or clinics. When it came time for Elena to give birth to her first son, Adán, and then Hugo Rafael a year later, the family traveled a couple of miles to Sabaneta. At least there they could find a midwife to deliver the babies in Rosa Inés's house. They had a total of seven boys, although one, Enzo, died at six months from leukemia.

It wasn't unusual in those days for older children in large, poor families to be taken in by grandparents who helped raise them. Chávez's parents, schoolteachers who traveled constantly by bicycle between Los Rastrojos, where they worked, and Sabaneta, asked Rosa Inés to care for Hugo and Adán. Abandoned by her husband and then widowed long before, she had time on her hands and motherly love to spare.

She lived alone in a simple house that was typical of the impoverished region. Its walls were made of mud and straw, its roof of palm leaves, its floor of dirt. When it rained, water poured through the ceiling. Rosa Inés scampered about placing pots on the floor in a fruitless effort to keep it from turning to mud. The house had no refrigerator, no fan, no running water, no indoor bathroom. Rosa cooked over a wood fire, fetched water from a well, and utilized an outhouse. Her single luxury was a small radio run by batteries. She was lucky to get a few hours of electricity at night from the village's small gas-oil-fueled power plant. Vehicles were rare. People got around on bicycle or walked, often making the hour-long trek to Los Rastrojos by foot. Half a century later, the streets of Sabaneta still teemed with bicycles.

After Rosa took Adán and Hugo into her home, she became more of a surrogate mother than a grandmother. She spent more time with the boys than did their parents, who came into Sabaneta on weekends when they could. In the early years of Chávez's life, they still maintained their home in Los Rastrojos. By the time Hugo and Adán started to talk, they didn't call Rosa Inés "Grandma," but rather "Mama Rosa." For her part, she called them "grandchildren-children." In many ways Hugo was closer to Rosa than to his own mother. At Rosa's side he learned to walk, to read, and to write before he entered first grade.

Rosa gave him and Adán all the affection and wisdom she had. She didn't have much else to offer. On the first day Hugo attended the Julián Pino elementary school down the block, he showed up wearing a ragged pair of rope sandals. Most of the other students wore shoes, and mocked him. He came home crying, prompting Rosa to break down into tears of shame and frustration. With the help of family and friends she scraped together the funds and bought Hugo a pair of shoes.

Money was tight. Rosa had to rely on the boys to help her survive financially. She ran a small business out of her house selling sweets and tropical fruits that grew in her backyard. Her specialty was sugar-coated *arañas*, spiders. She made them by cutting papayas into thin strips, cooking them in a pan, slathering them with sugar, and then fashioning them into spider shapes.

Every day Hugo took a jar of Rosa's highly popular products to school and sold them to classmates during recess. After school and on weekends, he roamed the village selling them to locals watching cock-fights or playing *bolas criollas* — a kind of bocce ball. He also sold them to people gathered at Sabaneta's Plaza Bolívar or near its sole extrava-gance — a movie theater that showed Mexican films. Unlike his brother Adán, Hugo enjoyed the job. It gave him a chance to get around town and talk to people. But it also underscored the precarious economic sit-uation of his family. These years of selling candies left a lasting imprint. Some of his classmates were even worse off. They had to drop out of ele-mentary school completely to help support their families.

Sabaneta didn't offer much in the way of entertainment, so Hugo had to invent his fun. Like many local youngsters, he was obsessed with baseball. The sport was introduced to Venezuela in the 1920s by American oil workers, who arrived in droves after the first major wells blew out. In contrast with the rest of Latin America — where soccer reigned — baseball became the national sport in Venezuela and an object of intense devotion by fans. Hugo and his friends played con-stantly. They used bottle caps or rolled-up socks for balls; sticks or broom handles were their bats.

Hugo was so obsessed with the sport that when he wasn't in school, he spent hours playing a game he made up. On a table inside Rosa's house he drew a circle and divided it up like pieces of a pie. Inside each slice he wrote the key events of a game — single, double, strike, ball, out, double play. He put a knife in the middle of the circle, spun it around, and played baseball with himself, Adán, or friends. He kept score in a notebook, jotting down every play inning by inning. Sometimes, playing alone, he leaped out of his chair and shouted, "Home run!" — startling his grandmother.

Despite the economic privations, Chávez recalled a joyful early life. "We were very poor children, but very happy." Rosa had a large back-yard filled with tropical fruits and plants. Hugo spent hours watering the plants and even singing to them — something Rosa insisted helped them grow. His favorite songs were Mexican rancheros and *llanero* bal-lads, melancholy tunes that dealt with frontier themes of romance or knife fights, hard drinking or skill in breaking horses. He learned to plant and harvest corn in the backyard. He ate the oranges, pineapples, grapefruits, and mangoes that grew there. He helped Rosa tend a garden of tomatoes, onions, and other vegetables. He also played baseball and other games with Adán and friends. "Ours was a backyard of dreams," he said, "an entire universe."

He loved drawing and painting, was fairly good at it, and eventually got a slightly less impoverished uncle in the state capital to buy him supplies. From a young age he also developed an astounding ability to quickly memorize and recite long poems, songs, or book passages, many of them about historical subjects or the llanos. It was a skill he would continue to exhibit as president.

Rosa was Chávez's first role model. A strict and upright Roman Catholic who prayed in her home, she brooked no foolishness and kept the boys in line. She also encouraged something common among Venezuela's lower classes — solidarity with the less fortunate. When a neighbor needed some food or clothes, Rosa was there to help, even though she possessed little herself. Her influence seemed to rub off. For a short time Hugo served as an altar boy in the local Catholic church. He also took part in a government-sponsored literacy program called *cadenas abajo*, or "off with the chains." He taught several adults to read and write even though he was only ten and eleven years old himself.

While Hugo was deeply attached to his grandmother, his relationship with his parents and especially his mother seemed more ambivalent. Elena and Hugo Chávez eventually moved from Los Rastrojos to a cement house on the same street in Sabaneta as Rosa's. But Hugo kept living with his grandmother. Again, this wasn't unusual for the times, but it did underscore his closeness with his grandmother. Often absent in the early years of Hugo's life, his mother was also a stern taskmaster. She didn't hesitate to pull out a strap to discipline the boys — another common practice in the era. Hugo and his brothers often ran to Rosa's house, where she hid them in a closet to ward off a beating.

While his family strongly denies it, by some accounts Chávez eventually had a falling-out with his mother, with the two reportedly refusing to speak for a couple of years and even ignoring each other when they passed on the street. The alleged conflict seems to have been rooted in bitter feelings from his childhood when she beat the boys and, by at least one account, erupted into open conflict in the late 1970s when she disapproved of the first woman he married, Nancy Colmenares, and they stopped talking. Chávez denies he suffered a falling out with his mother and that they did not communicate for two years — an assertion which appeared in *Hugo Chávez Sin Uniforme*, published in Venezuela in 2004 and later in the United States. In an interview in April 2007, he said "such a thing never happened." He said he and Nancy married in late 1977 while she was pregnant with Rosa, and that his mother was not overly enthusiastic about the marriage. But there was never a dramatic break in their relationship. "There certainly were not, let's say, good relations between my mother and Nancy," Chávez said. "But to arrive at a rupture of two years where we did not speak, no."

He said he always visited his mother with Nancy during vacations while they were still together, and noted that later the two women often visited him together when he was in jail. After Chávez became president, his mother managed a government-run children's foundation in Barinas, and Nancy worked with her for a time.

Chávez's brother Adán, in a rare interview in April 2007, also denied that Hugo and his mother stopped talking for an extended period and ignored each other on the streets.

Still, reports and rumors about the sometimes strained relationship between Chávez and his mother provided fodder for his detractors to speculate that he suffered from an unhealthy lack of maternal affection in his childhood that affected his personality. Of course, he had the unquestioned and constant love of Rosa, and many people emerged unscathed from far worse childhoods than his.

He seemed closer to his father than to his mother — at least when he got to see him. After his parents moved to Sabaneta, his father went to work at the Julián Pino elementary school and at one point served as Hugo's fifth-grade teacher. He dabbled with a leftist political party, the Electoral Movement of the People (MEP), but had a longer affiliation with the Social Christian COPEI, one of the two parties that dominated Venezuela for decades. When Chávez eventually won the presidency, his father became a state governor. His mother was Rosa Inés; he'd grown up selling *arañas* on the streets, too.

The younger Chávez often speaks publicly of Rosa and the impact his grandmother had on him. Of his four children, he named one Rosa and another Rosinés. He named his only son Hugo. "I adore my parents, but I have to recognize that the education Rosa gave me was very important for me. She was a pure human being ... pure love, pure kindness ... At Rosa's side I got to know humility, poverty, pain, sometimes not having anything to eat. I saw the injustices of this world ... I learned with her the principles and the values of the humble Venezuelan, those that never had anything and who constitute the soul of my country."

Her death in 1982 was one of the most painful moments of his life. Plunged into sadness, he wrote a poem of love and admiration, pledging never to forget her lessons or betray his roots in Sabaneta. He said he hoped to be buried beside her when he dies.

> *Perhaps one day*
> *My dear old woman*
> *I will direct my steps*
> *Toward your grave*
> *And then*
> *Only then*
> *At the end of my life*
> *I may come to look for you*
> *My Mother Rosa*
> *I may arrive at the tomb*
> *I may water it*
> *With sweat and blood*
> *And I may find comfort*
> *In your love of a mother*
> *And I may tell you*
> *Of my disappointments*
> *Among the mortals*
> *Then*
> *You may open your arms*
> *And you may hug me*
> *Like when I was an infant*
> *And you may lull me*
> *With your sweet song*
> *And you may take me*
> *To other places*
> *To release a shout*
> *That never stops*

Rosa encouraged another trait that turned into a cornerstone of Hugo's personality: a love of history. Starting when he was five or six years old, Rosa would sit in the house or backyard and spend hours telling him stories of the past. A favorite was the tale of how legendary nineteenth-century guerrilla fighter Ezequiel Zamora had ridden through Sabaneta with his men on their horses. They passed right in front of her family home, kicking up dust as a bugle blared. Rosa didn't see the scene herself, but was told the story by her mother.

Zamora was a revolutionary, a lesser-known heir to Simón Bolívar's dream of a more just society. He helped organize local peasants and slaves into an army that in the 1850s and 1860s waged a civil war against troops tied to the landowning oligarchy. Zamora harbored a passionate hostility to the elites and had a radical vision for reforming Venezuelan society. "There will be neither rich nor poor, neither slaves nor owners, neither powerful nor scorned, but brothers who disdaining leadership will treat each other equally, face to face," one of his slogans declared.

A man ahead of his time, Zamora offered a platform that included abolition of the death penalty, complete freedom of speech, and universal suffrage. He advocated an end to restrictions on the free movement of workers, who at the time could be arrested and sentenced to forced labor on haciendas if found idle on the streets. He even called for a kind of social security system that assisted people stricken by "incapacity or general scarcity." He also wanted large landowners to be forced to provide ten milking cows that would be farmed out on common land and provide "free milk each day to the homes of the poor."

Zamora remained committed to unconditional respect of property rights, but his egalitarian rhetoric alarmed even some of his allies. Popular myth has it that he was killed in 1860 not in battle but by some of his own troops, who shot him in the back. Some predicted that Chávez himself might someday meet a similar fate. In the end Zamora's crusade did little to transform Venezuela's unjust social structures, partly because his federalist forces did not offer a comprehensive program of economic and social reform. But he left behind a legacy as a progressive liberal with a strong sense of solidarity with the rural poor. It was a philosophy that was to fit neatly into Chávez's emerging vision for a new Venezuela.

Many of Zamora's battles were fought not far from Sabaneta, leaving intriguing memories for schoolboys like Chávez. But Hugo had an especially close link to Zamora. His great-great-grandfather, Colonel Pedro Pérez Pérez, was one of those men who rode off into the endless fields of the llanos to do battle at Zamora's side. Moreover, Pérez Pérez had a son, Pedro Pérez Delgado, who was Chávez's great-grandfather.

This relative, however, was hardly a source of pride for Chávez when he was growing up. Pérez Delgado was known as Maisanta. It was a sobriquet he earned from his battle cry — "Madre Santa, Virgin of Socorro." In his crunched *llanero* vernacular, the first two words became "Mai Santa." While his father had risen to the rank of colonel, Maisanta was known in Sabaneta and its environs as little more than a thief and an assassin. In one of the most notorious crimes attributed to him, he was said to have killed a colonel and fled for the hills. His unsavory reputation grew to the point that many believed he often tied people to trees and shot them, or even decapitated them in front of their children and stuck the severed heads on fence posts.

Hugo Chávez grew up half believing all this, since most other people seemed to. It wasn't until 1974 that he discovered another version of Maisanta. That year, a prominent doctor in Barinas, José León Tapia, published a book arguing that Maisanta was not an assassin but a freedom fighter. Like his father and Zamora before him, Tapia asserted, Maisanta had risen up in rebellion against social inequalities and oppression by joining a guerrilla movement. In this case, it was one aimed at overthrowing General Juan Vicente Gómez, a brutal dictator who ruled Venezuela from 1908 to 1935.

Maisanta, it turned out, had indeed killed a colonel when he was a teenager. But it was no simple case of cold-blooded murder. The colonel had gotten Maisanta's sister Petra pregnant and refused to marry her. Maisanta tracked him down and, following the Wild West tradition of the day to save the family's honor, shot him. Then he fled and joined the guerrillas fighting Gómez.

The book was a revelation to Chávez, who believed it vindicated Maisanta. He was convinced the oligarchy had twisted his predecessor's reputation the same way it had Zamora's. "The truth liberated me," he said. Maisanta and others "were leaders of a revolution that perhaps they did not understand well, but it was on behalf of those from below. An agrarian revolution . . ."

He wrote a poem in Maisanta's honor and set off on an investigation of him that turned into a lifelong pursuit. At one point several years into his career as a soldier Chávez retraced his great-grandfather's steps in the llanos, interviewing old-timers who still remembered him and inadvertently crossing over the border into Colombia. Armed with a tape recorder, a camera, military maps, notebooks, photographs of the region, two pistols, and a couple of hand grenades, Chávez was mistaken by the Colombian military for a spy. He was arrested and detained for three days until he convinced the Colombians he was engaged not in espionage but in a quixotic historical journey to recapture his roots. The Colombians finally accepted his unlikely tale. One officer shared a beer with Chávez and then gave him a brotherly hug at the midpoint of a bridge connecting the two countries as Chávez headed home.

While some still argue whether Maisanta was a courageous freedom fighter, a two-bit criminal, or something in between, he became one of Chávez's heroes, along with the more undisputed revolutionary heroes Zamora, Bolívar, and Bolívar's visionary tutor, Simón Rodríguez. As one of his mentors in the military put it, Chávez "carries in his soul the spirit of Maisanta." He eventually tracked down Maisanta's two long-lost children, by then elderly adults. When one of them, Ana Domínguez de Lombano, opened her door and Chávez informed her he was Maisanta's great-grandson, she said he didn't have to tell her that. It was obvious. Chávez was "the living portrait" of Maisanta with his broad forehead, thick nose, and deep-set eyes, she said. He would come to resemble Maisanta not only physically, but also in his "desire to struggle, his love of liberty."

Pedro Pérez Delgado and his legacy grew out of a long tradition of frontier rebellion in the llanos. Along with the pampas of Argentina and their gauchos, Venezuela's llanos were home to some of South America's finest horsemen. Fearless fighters, they made up the backbone of Bolívar's liberation army, turning the llanos into the scene of some of the bloodiest fratricidal battles of the nineteenth century. *Llanero* cowboys gained a reputation as hard-bitten, independent men with an egalitarian spirit forged from living in the wild. Even today, the region holds a special place in Venezuelan mythology and its sense of national identity. It is the setting for the country's most famous novel, *Doña Bárbara* by Rómulo Gallegos. For many people the still largely undeveloped region of half-asleep, dusty frontier towns embodies the "real Venezuela," in contrast with the Westernized capital city of Caracas with its gleaming skyscrapers, shopping malls, and American fast-food chains.

The llanos remain a place of haunting beauty, where the grassy plains seem to stretch on forever. Royal palms, zebu cattle, and sprawling ranches dot a landscape that teems with exotic wildlife in its more remote corners: jaguars, piranhas, freshwater porpoises, electric eels, fluorescent-colored birds, twenty-five-foot-long anaconda snakes, and even the world's largest rodent, the capybara — a watergoing guinea pig that is a delicacy among *llaneros*. Off in the distance from Sabaneta stand the majestic Andes Mountains, where rivers flow down into the llanos and eventually into the mighty Orinoco River in the Amazon rain forest. When he was a boy, on a clear day Chávez could see snowcapped Bolívar Peak. At 3.1 miles tall it is the highest mountain in Venezuela and higher than Switzerland's Matterhorn.

The llanos' legacy as a place of resistance, rebellion, and revolution was not lost on young Hugo Chávez. He grew up in a region where more than a few people viewed rebels such as Fidel Castro and Ernesto "Che" Guevara sympathetically. As a thirteen-year-old in 1967, Chávez listened to news reports pouring in over the radio as troops closed in on Guevara in Bolivia. The revolutionary icon was surrounded in the forests and almost alone. Chávez thought of it as a movie. He wondered why Castro didn't send in airplanes and his own troops to rescue Che as he made his final stand. "It was infantile," Chávez later remarked, "but it demonstrated an absolute identification with them, a point of view marked by the sympathies that I perceived in Barinas toward both leaders."

Like Castro's revolutionary movement against the dictator Fulgencio Batista in Cuba in the 1950s, the *llaneros* of Venezuela had plenty to rebel against. Bolívar had led his independence war in the early nineteenth century in the name of social justice and equality, but the battles left the unjust social structures intact and the country devastated. The landed oligarchy still presided over a primitive system of labor exploitation that treated workers like peons. Decades of dictatorship, bloodshed, and anarchy followed Bolívar's failed quest. The 1858–1863 Federal War fought by Zamora and others against the landed elite left sixty to a hundred thousand Venezuelans dead. It also decimated the cattle industry, with herds plummeting from 12 million to 1.8 million head. By 1888 Venezuela had suffered 730 battles and twenty-six major insurrections since Bolívar's war. As the twentieth century dawned, barely 19 percent of the population was literate. Venezuela was an impoverished, forgotten Latin American backwater.

By 1908 the country's most notorious dictator, General Juan Vicente Gómez, seized power. Self-educated, a teetotaler, unmarried but sexually promiscuous, Gómez was a mixed blessing. He brought order to a country racked by anarchy. He professionalized the military. He balanced the budget. He oversaw the birth of the oil industry, which put Venezuela on the map and attracted oil companies from all over the world.

But Gómez was also a notoriously corrupt and brutal dictator. He turned modest personal assets he acquired as a cattle feedlot operator in Táchira state into an immense personal fortune — up to $300 million in 1927 and $400 million when he died in 1935. The richest man and the largest landowner in the country, he stopped at nothing to maintain his grip on power. "Dissidents found themselves condemned to primitive jails where one of the dictator's sons supervised tortures. Some prisoners were hung by their feet or genitals; some had straps tightened by a tourniquet around their head until their eyes nearly popped out. Prisoners customarily wore hundred-pound leg irons around each ankle; one dissident editor languished for twenty years in this condition."

In the late 1940s Venezuela experienced a brief experiment in democracy, then returned to another period of dictatorship in the 1950s, this one led by General Marcos Pérez Jiménez. Like Gómez, the general was a study in contrasts. He was a master builder and a visionary full of grand dreams. He blasted tunnels through mountains. He paved thousands of miles of highways and created one of the best road systems in Latin America. He built a mammoth bridge across the largest lake in South America, Lake Maracaibo. He erected the world's longest and highest cable car in the picturesque Andean city of Mérida. He built a hotel on top of Mount Avila overlooking Caracas, ferrying supplies up the mountainside by mule and later by a cable car he also built.

But Pérez Jiménez was also another brutal, corrupt dictator. Bribes, kickbacks, and assassination were common. Pérez Jiménez modernized many of Gómez's methods of repression, employing phone taps, radio surveillance, and electric cattle prods on political opponents. The regime released four hundred political prisoners in January 1954 and acknowledged that it held at least three hundred more. Some believed additional thousands languished in jails including a notorious labor camp deep in the Amazon jungle. The dictator and his cronies, many of them from his native Táchira, also plundered the public treasury. They lavished money on luxurious officers' clubs and extravagant hotels and theaters. On weekends Pérez Jiménez flew to the small Caribbean island of La Orchila, where he romped on the beach with naked Venezuelan beauties.

Despite his brutal rule, the United States viewed Pérez Jiménez favorably. He was a loyal ally throughout the Cold War. In 1954, the year Chávez was born, President Dwight Eisenhower awarded him the nation's highest civilian award, the Legion of Merit. The honor outraged many Venezuelans who were trying to overthrow Pérez Jiménez, often risking their lives.

Pérez Jiménez's regime gave way to the formal establishment of democracy in Venezuela by 1959. But it did little to change the society's unjust social structures. The great masses still suffered in poverty. Leftist rebels who thought Venezuela's practice of democracy was a sham dominated by the elites for their own benefit mounted an armed insurgency in the 1960s to overthrow the government. The rebels included men and even a few women who were to become central figures in the nation's political life right into the Chávez era, among them Alí Rodríguez and Teodoro Petkoff. The Cuban-backed rebels turned into one of the strongest insurgencies in Latin America. They carried out a series of spectacular actions including train bombings, the kidnapping of foreign executives and US embassy personnel, and commando raids on cities. Petkoff gained fame for escaping twice from prison.

Many of the guerrilla fronts were based in the llanos. Chávez did not have any direct contact with the rebels as a teenager, but he did have his first significant exposure to the left through a neighbor. In the mid-1960s he and Adán left Sabaneta and moved with their grandmother Rosa Inés to the city of Barinas to attend the Daniel O'Leary High School. Named for an Irishman who joined the South American independence movement and became one of Bolívar's most trusted confidants, it was the only high school in the rural state.

The boys and their grandmother moved in across the street from a family whose patriarch was a small, erudite man named José Esteban Ruíz Guevara. A founder of the Communist Party in Barinas, Ruíz Guevara was a historian who owned an extensive library and the city's largest collection of books about Bolívar. He named his two sons for Friedrich Engels and Vladimir Lenin, although the latter's name was misspelled on his birth certificate as *Wladimir* and stayed that way. While communism was anathema in the United States, the party was vibrant in many parts of Latin America, where disgust for the Americans' support of dictatorships ran strong. Communists played a central role in the overthrow of Pérez Jiménez. Ruíz Guevara himself was jailed by the dictator for his political activities.

Chávez became best friends with the Ruíz brothers. By one account, the biography *Hugo Chávez Sin Uniforme*, their father played a key role early on in forming Chávez politically, with a decidedly leftist bent. The three teenagers "tossed themselves on the rug of the family's library every afternoon to listen to an impassioned communist" — the elder Ruíz Guevara. According to this account, Ruíz Guevera encouraged Chávez and his sons to read books such as Rousseau's *The Social Contract* and the works of Karl Marx. While not completely "catechized" in communism, Chávez was "inoculated" through this contact with Ruíz Guevera. By the time he entered the military academy at seventeen, the account contends, he carried one book under his arm: Che Guevara's diary.

In an April 2007 interview Chavez denied this suggestion that he was somehow indoctrinated in communism or Marxism starting when he was as young as thirteen. He said that he went to Ruíz Guevara's house mainly to get the brothers to play baseball or to hang out on the streets, and simply said hello to their father once in a while. "That as an adolescent at fifteen or sixteen I had sat down even one time to talk politics with Ruíz Guevara, no. With no one," Chávez said. He was, he said, "a normal boy . . . I didn't have any political motivation."

Chávez added that it was false that he entered the military academy with a copy of Che Guevera's diary, and that the assertion was part of black legends sprouting up to try to discredit him. "It's a lie," he said, laughing. "I had never read almost anything political."

He said it was true Ruíz Guevara may have indirectly influenced him politically early on through some general commentaries, but that the real influence occurred later when he was in his early twenties, after he graduated from the military academy and was stationed back in Barinas. "Then there was an intense exchange with Ruíz Guevara," he said. "He was a great moral, political, and ideological reference." Many of their talks focused on Bolívar, Zamora, Maisanta, and other historical Venezuelan figures.

Ruíz Guevara's son Wladimir concurred with Chávez's contention that his father was hardly out to convert them into adolescent communists. "My father didn't sit us down like a priest and give us classes in communism," he stated, noting that he himself did not read the *Communist Manifesto* until he was twenty-three, not thirteen as *Hugo Chávez Sin Uniforme* contends. "My father didn't set as a task converting Hugo Chávez to communism." At O'Leary High School, another one of Chávez's friends was the head of the Communist Youth Party, but Chávez never joined.

His mind wasn't on revolution. It was on his studies, girls . . . and baseball. He spent hours at night listening to the radio as longtime rivals Los Leones and the Magallanes faced off in Venezuela's professional winter league, which attracted many of Venezuela's top stars, including players from the US major leagues. During the day Chávez played baseball with friends or practiced pitching by throwing rocks against a can he set up in Rosa Inés's backyard. He jogged, lifted weights, and studied pitching techniques.

He was a talented left-hander. His hero was Isaías "Latigo" (Whip) Chávez. He picked him for several reasons. They shared the same last name, for one — although they were not related. Latigo was also on Hugo's favorite team, the Magallanes. And he was a pitcher, too. Hugo never actually saw his idol on the mound because televisions were scarce in rural, impoverished Barinas. Instead, he imagined him in action as he listened to the radio. Hugo was so good himself that locals called him "Latigo" and "Golden Lefty."

One Sunday morning in March 1969, Chávez received some devastating news about his hero. Rosa Inés was preparing breakfast in the kitchen when a radio announcer broke in with an urgent bulletin: Latigo Chávez had been killed the night before in an airplane crash. Chávez, who was fourteen, was shocked. He was so depressed he stayed home from school that Monday and Tuesday. In his mourning, he wrote a poem that he started repeating every night, swearing he would be like Latigo Chávez someday — a pitcher in the major leagues.

The problem was how to get there. No scout was going to discover him in the backwaters of Barinas and Sabaneta. He needed to be in a place with professional baseball. As he neared the end of his high school years, he contemplated joining his brother Adán at the University of the Andes in Mérida. He thought about studying mathematics and physics. But when he learned that Mérida had no professional baseball team, he dropped the idea.

Then one day a recruiter from the military academy visited O'Leary High School to give a talk. Chávez wasn't very interested in joining the military . . . but the location of the academy did attract his attention: Caracas, where the Magallanes often played. He started thinking that he could enter the academy, spend a year or so training, and then drop out to pursue his real passion. The academy would be "like a transit point," he later remarked, "a bridge."

Around the same time, a friend from Barinas who was a cadet came home to visit and urged Chávez to sign up. "I asked him if they played baseball, and he said, yes, and that José Antonio Casanova and Héctor Benitez Redondo were the managers. Casanova? Benitez? But that was the glory, like Olympus, and immediately I signed the papers." Casanova and Benitez Redondo were Venezuelan baseball legends. Casanova was a shortstop and later a manager of the Caracas Leones in Venezuela's winter league. Benitez Redondo had been a cleanup hitter in the 1940s and 1950s.

Chávez passed a preliminary entrance examination held at the local barracks in Barinas. Later he received a telegram instructing him to report to Caracas for more tests. He got on a bus and traveled to the nation's bustling capital for the first time in his life. It was another world compared with provincial Barinas. He passed that test, too. But after he returned to Barinas, he ran into a problem.

Chávez was generally a good student and an avid reader. But he could not get himself interested in one class: chemistry. He sat in the back of the room and asked few questions. His teacher, Manuel Felipe Díaz, thought Chávez was grasping everything he presented. Chávez wasn't. Díaz was a tough teacher. Students dubbed him *Venenito* — little poison. When it came time for the tests, Chávez's grades were poor. So Díaz flunked him.

That presented a problem for getting into the military academy. Applicants with a failed course generally were not accepted. There was one exception: If they played a sport well enough, they could get in and retake the course. That was fine with Chávez. At his next interview at the academy, instructors sent him to a nearby stadium for a tryout to "see if you can really play," as he recalled it.

When Chávez walked into the stadium, his jaw dropped. Casanova and Benitez Redondo were conducting the tryouts. The two stars told the young men that their first test would be to see who could put on their uniform the fastest. Those who couldn't put it on properly would be eliminated. Chávez had played on organized teams in Barinas, and he was among the first out on the field.

The coaches put him on the mound to see how he could pitch.

Chávez had thrown in a game in Barinas a few days earlier. With his arm still sore, he was wild. The coaches pulled him off the mound. He was one step away from losing his chance to get into the military academy. Luckily, Chávez also played first base and was a respectable hitter. The coaches sent him to the batter's box to see what he could do. A teenager from the city of Maracaibo was on the mound. He hurled three fastballs. Chávez smacked them against the outfield wall.

The performance saved him. Chávez was admitted to the military academy. His hitting arguably altered the course of Venezuelan history. If he had struck out, he probably never would have become president. After his ascent to power, his chemistry teacher, Díaz, spent years second-guessing himself, thinking he had failed as an instructor and nearly derailed Chávez's career. Chávez often made good-natured jokes about *Venenito* on national television and radio.

On Sunday, August 8, 1971, Chávez and 374 other aspiring cadets entered Fort Tiuna military base in Caracas. They lined up for the induction ceremonies on a sprawling courtyard surrounded by a glistening white, U-shaped building. Chávez had made it to Venezuela's version of West Point. Back in Barinas, Rosa Inés was horrified. She didn't think the military was right for Hugo, and she worried that his rebellious streak would get him into trouble. She took to lighting votive candles, praying to the patron saint of Sabaneta that he would come home.

Despite his initially lukewarm feelings about the military, Chávez soon felt comfortable. When he found himself "in uniform, with a rifle, on the live firing range, the close order drills, the marches, the early morning runs, the studies of military science, of the general sciences . . . in sum, I liked it, man. The courtyard. Bolívar in the background . . . I felt like a fish in water. As if I had discovered the essence or part of the essence of life, of my true vocation."

Chávez was finding a new calling — and leaving behind an old one. On one of his first leaves a few months after entering the academy, he bought a bouquet of flowers and went to the Southern General Cemetery in Caracas. He had read that Latigo Chávez was buried there. Dressed in his blue uniform and white gloves, he asked a gravedigger for his hero's tomb. When he found it, Chávez took off his gloves, cleaned the tomb, and lit a candle. He left the flowers on top of the grave.

He was doing penance. His dream of becoming a professional baseball player was shifting to new pursuits. "I went because I had a knot inside me, like a debt that had been forming since that oath, that prayer . . . I was forgetting it, and now I wanted to be a soldier . . . I felt bad for that reason . . . It was as if I was saying, Forgive me, Isaías, I'm not going to follow that path. Now I am a soldier."

When he left the cemetery, he said, "I was liberated."

# A Revolutionary Is Born

Hugo Chávez's arrival at the military academy in August 1971 at the age of seventeen coincided with a radical restructuring of the school by a group of nationalistic military officers. They wanted to give cadets a broader, more humanistic foundation than the traditional course of studies focusing exclusively on military sciences. They called it the Andrés Bello Plan, for the nineteenth-century Venezuelan poet and philosopher.

For the first time in the school's history, cadets were to receive university-level degrees and needed a high school diploma to be admitted. They were also to study the liberal arts along with military history and strategy. The school's directors brought in civilian professors to teach economics, political science, world history, constitutional law, physics, chemistry, engineering, medicine, and other subjects, including classes that looked at Venezuela's history and current reality. The soldiers could go on to graduate studies at civilian universities.

Paradoxically, cadets who were undergoing training to combat a fading leftist guerrilla movement also started reading the *Communist Manifesto*. Chávez delved into everything from Mao to Clausewitz to Napoleon to Claus Heller, a Prussian general who wrote about the military as an agent of social change. Some of the cadets' studies ran even further afield from the traditional course material of their predecessors. One who entered a year after Chávez and became a close ally, Raúl Isaías Baduel, specialized in Eastern philosophy and meditation. He eventually took to burning incense in his room, playing Gregorian chants, and reading Sun Tzu. Friends nicknamed him El Tao.

The Andrés Bello Plan marked a clear divide between the old guard and the new in the Venezuelan military. Unlike their predecessors, most of the new cadets did not study at US-run counterinsurgency institutions like the School of the Americas, then based in Panama and today at Fort Benning, Georgia. If they did attend, they went "well-fortified with progressive ideas." The school, dubbed the "School of the Assassins" by critics, was infamous for training some of Latin America's most notorious dictators and human rights abusers. They included General Hugo Bánzer of Bolivia and, later, many of the "elite" Salvadoran troops that massacred nearly a thousand elderly men, women, and children in El Mozote in December 1981.

Even before the Andrés Bello Plan, Venezuela's military differed significantly from many others in Latin America. There was no discrimination in Venezuela's armed forces — anyone could reach the highest ranks or enter the prestigious military academy. There was no "military caste" like those in Chile and Argentina, where the sons of the light-skinned elites dominated the upper ranks and elite units of the armed forces. In Venezuela many senior officers came from poor urban and peasant families, and knew from their own experience the difficulties their people faced in putting food on the table. That did not mean, of course, that all of them were "immune to the clever co-opting maneuvers of the oligarchy with whom they inevitably come into contact once they reach the higher ranks." But a large number of the new cadets who rose through the ranks — like Chávez, Baduel, and another classmate, Jorge Luis García Carneiro — never forgot their roots. Some were so poor, their families could not afford shoes.

The Andrés Bello Plan and the Venezuelan military's historical openness to all social classes combined to produce a new kind of soldier in the early 1970s — much different from the right-wing officers who were launching coups and installing bloody dictatorships elsewhere on the continent. "In sharp contrast to the archetypal, muscle-flexing neo-Nazis that comprised the Armed Forces in Argentina and Chile, in Venezuela a new type of soldier returned to the barracks with professional skills, civilian contacts and a fresh social sensitivity."

The Andrés Bello Plan had a tremendous impact on Chávez, who did not forget it or the men who created it. He was mesmerized by the classroom lectures of Lieutenant Colonel Jacinto Pérez Arcay, an author and historian who told tales of Zamora and the Federal War.

When Chávez reached Miraflores Palace three and a half decades later, he gave Arcay — by then a retired general — a small office next to his. He named the former director of the academy who conceived of the Andrés Bello Plan, General Jorge Osorio García, ambassador to Canada.

Arcay and other professors also spoke in the classroom about Venezuela's towering historical figure, Simón Bolívar. As a boy and a teenager, Chávez received a cursory education about the Liberator in school. "Instead of Superman, my hero was Bolívar," he once said. Now, spurred by Arcay and others, he delved more deeply into the life of the man who had freed six South American nations from Spanish rule and turned into an icon in Venezuela. A small, wiry man who stood five-foot-five and sported long sideburns and Napoleonic garb, Bolívar was George Washington, Abraham Lincoln, and Jesus Christ all rolled into one for Venezuelans, a "secular saint" in the words of political scientist Daniel Hellinger.

Chávez developed more than a passing interest in Bolívar. His fascination turned into deep devotion that bordered on obsession. He started reading everything he could about the Liberator. After the 9 P.M. bell rang at the academy calling for silence, he often headed back to the empty classrooms, where cadets were allowed to stay until 11 P.M. to study. Sometimes Chávez remained even later, occasionally falling asleep on a desk where someone would find him with his head down and a book open.

It wasn't surprising that the Liberator was captivating Chávez.

Simón Bolívar's life was a mind-spinning series of triumphs and defeats played out on the world stage. Born into one of the most aristocratic families in the New World, he was orphaned at a young age, inherited one of the New World's greatest fortunes at twenty-one, and then exhausted it pursuing a quixotic dream of first liberating and then uniting Latin America as the world's largest nation. Exiled from Venezuela twice and the target of numerous assassination attempts, Bolívar led some of the most audacious military campaigns in history. During one, he marched a ragged, starving army of twenty-four hundred men — many of them shoeless *llaneros* — across icy Andean peaks to launch a surprise attack on loyalist troops in Colombia.

Bolívar achieved part of his goal. He liberated Venezuela, Colombia, Panama, Ecuador, Peru, and the country named for him

— Bolivia. He was feted as a hero in all the capitals as he marched down pathways strewn with flowers in his honor. He declined repeated offers to crown him emperor. But in the end Bolívar's dream came crashing down as the nations he freed succumbed to squabbling among competing *caudillos*, strongmen. The brief union of Venezuela, Colombia, Panama, and Ecuador known as Gran Colombia fell apart. Bolívar was outlawed as a traitor in his native Venezuela, where the same crowds who had cheered him wildly just a few short years earlier now jeered him. He died in 1830 in exile in Colombia, penniless and nearly friendless.

Bolívar is now almost unknown to most people outside Latin America. But in Venezuela and other parts of South America he is a towering giant. Venezuelan schoolchildren memorize his sayings and speak of him in reverential tones. People hang portraits of him in their living rooms, something it is hard to imagine Americans doing with paintings of George Washington. Even the smallest and most remote villages have a Bolívar statue and plaza. Until the 1950s men could not pass through the plazas unless they were wearing a tie and jacket out of respect for the Liberator. Main streets, municipal buildings, airports, schools, hospitals, stadiums, tunnels, and even dams are named for him. His sayings are painted on walls all over the country. MORALITY AND KNOWLEDGE ARE OUR FIRST NECESSITIES appears in virtually every Venezuelan school.

Today few historians doubt Bolívar was a genius, although his detractors deride him as a reckless dreamer. They depict him as an arrogant, unpredictable, and sometimes cruel man who was also a notorious womanizer. Admirers lined up at a legendary country house he had outside Lima, Peru, eager to offer themselves. The shrieks from Bolívar's lovemaking reputedly made one cavalry officer move out of the residence because he couldn't sleep. Every time Bolívar triumphantly entered a new town, "local leaders chose the prettiest girl for the honor of delivering a crown of flowers. If she delivered more, well, he was the Liberator."

Bolívar was born in 1783. By the time he was nine both his parents were dead — his mother of a chest infection, probably tuberculosis, his father simply of old age and an indulgent lifestyle. Simón lived for several years with his tutor Simón Rodríguez, a brilliant and eccentric schoolteacher who was a visionary in his own right. Along with Bolívar, Zamora, and Maisanta, Rodríguez was to become one of the guiding lights of Chávez's "Bolivarian" project for Venezuela and Latin America.

Even less known outside of Latin America than Bolívar, Rodríguez was a young devotee of the French philosopher Rousseau. He espoused his own radical philosophy. To the shock of the city fathers, he publicly proclaimed that the school in Caracas where he taught the children of wealthy whites should also admit blacks and mixed-race *pardos*. His advocacy for the underclass got him into constant trouble, and eventually he was fired from the school. He then spent five years as Bolívar's tutor before finally fleeing Caracas in 1797, when he was implicated in one of the first revolts of the independence movement against Spanish rule.

Years later in the 1820s, he found himself in trouble again when he landed in Bolivia. He insisted that the children of Indians be admitted to the free public schools he was setting up. Before long authorities under pressure from white parents who did not want their children educated with Indians found an excuse to shut down the schools.

Before he fled Caracas, Rodríguez brought his revolutionary notions to the tutoring sessions with Bolívar, who while absorbing the calls for radical social change was at the same time protected by great wealth. After his formative years under Rodríguez's wing, Bolívar's uncles sent him to Spain in 1799 at the age of fifteen. He spent three years in Europe, where he was captivated by the revolutionary environment. A sprouting intellectual, he devoured the works of Voltaire and Rousseau. By now he was well read in the classics.

He was also falling in love. At seventeen he met the daughter of one of Spain's leading aristocratic families, Maria Teresa Rodríguez y Alaiza, who was two years his elder. They eventually married in May 1802 and returned to Caracas. But just eight months after their wedding, unaccustomed to the tropical climate, she contracted yellow fever and died. Grief-stricken and half mad, Bolívar vowed never to marry again — and never did. Instead, he was to throw himself into his dream of liberating South America.

A few months after Maria Teresa's death, a restless and disconsolate Bolívar headed back to Europe. He spent several years in France and Italy and was reunited with his mentor Rodríguez. In one famous encounter in August 1805, no doubt embellished in the telling, the two climbed the slopes of Mount Aventino in Rome where Bolívar took a romantic oath, swearing to God that he would not rest until his homeland was free. His words were immortalized and even today remain deeply ingrained in the psyche of the Venezuelan people, learned by schoolchildren and memorized by soldiers performing their military service. Chávez was to invoke them in 1982 when he organized a secret conspiracy in the military that led to the birth of his Bolivarian movement and eventually his ascension to the presidential palace:

> I swear before you, and I swear before the God of my fathers, that I will not allow my arm to rest, nor my soul to rest, until I have broken the chains that oppress us . . .

Three years later and after a trip through a United States of America basking in its freshly won independence, Bolívar was back in Venezuela to directly take up the struggle in Latin America. He immersed himself in the embryonic and clandestine independence movement. Despite his young age, he quickly rose to a leadership position. By April 1810 the movement was fully under way. A full-fledged uprising broke out against the Spanish in Caracas, where a revolutionary junta took over. Less than a year later, on July 5, 1811, Venezuela declared its independence. But a decade of bloody fighting still lay ahead.

Bolívar suffered defeat after defeat, some from human causes, others natural. On March 26, 1812, a powerful earthquake struck Venezuela, leveling entire towns, destroying much of Caracas, and burying complete corps of independence troops. In the city of Barquísimeto alone one regiment of fifteen hundred men was swallowed by a fissure and vanished. In Caracas, where ten thousand people were said to have died, Bolívar was helping dig out victims when a pro-Spanish acquaintance came by and remarked that nature had put itself on the side of the Spanish. A defiant Bolívar responded, "If Nature is against us, we will fight it and make it obey us."

It became one of his most famous sayings. Chávez invoked it in December 1999 when mudslides and floods devastated Caracas and the nearby Caribbean coast, leaving an estimated fifteen thousand dead in Venezuela's worst natural disaster of the twentieth century. In an echo of Bolívar's time when the pro-Spanish Catholic Church declared that the earthquake was evidence of God's displeasure with the revolutionaries, Caracas archbishop José Ignacio Velasco suggested from the pulpit that the floods were a punishment against Chávez.

Bolívar was not an entirely noble freedom fighter taking the high road during the war. He could be as cruel and vindictive as the royalists, whose lust for violence was legendary. They regularly executed captive patriot soldiers with no trial. One psychopathic commander known as the Butcher, General José Tomas Boves, personally supervised the massacre of entire villages. He often wandered through the ruins with a sinister smile. Once, after capturing the city of Valencia, his troops found a girl in the house of a former patriot commander, tied her to her hammock, gang-raped her, tore her tongue out, cut her breasts off, and then lit a fire under her so she would cook in her bed. It was a common practice of the Spaniards.

Bolívar responded to the Spanish mayhem with retaliatory violence of his own. During *La Campana Admirable* (the admirable campaign) after the earthquake, he declared a "war to the death." He ordered that any Spanish-born prisoner be shot and warned royalists in general that they would be killed. At one point in 1814 he ordered the execution of thirteen hundred prisoners, who were decapitated. His actions contributed to an atmosphere of rabid violence, drawing even more of the population into the conflict and leaving vast swaths of the country devastated. By the end of the war, one-third of the population had perished. Livestock numbers plummeted from 4.5 million to about 250,000. The treasury was bankrupt. Venezuela was the scene of some four hundred battles. Nowhere on the continent was the fighting more cruel and destructive.

As his military campaign continued to suffer setbacks, Bolívar was exiled once in Jamaica and twice in Haiti — countries from which he launched several failed attacks. But in 1817 his struggle reached a turning point. Returning again from Haiti, he sailed around the eastern coast of Venezuela and up the Orinoco delta, where he established a headquarters at Angostura (now Ciudad Bolívar). From there, he made contact with republican leaders in the llanos, most notably José Antonio Páez, a Herculean, illiterate cavalryman. At one point Bolívar was described as something of a wild, even half-crazed figure with huge sideburns and shoulder-length hair. His cast-off uniform included the helmet of a Russian dragoon. On a bamboo lance he carried a skull-and-crossbones flag with the slogan LIBERTY OR DEATH.

The *llaneros* had been fighting on the side of the Spanish, but now Bolívar convinced many of them to join the independence cause. They were a devastating, irregular cavalry force, and became the backbone of Bolívar's new army.

His forces spent part of the next two years doing battle in the llanos and other spots. Then, in 1819, he shifted strategy, giving up on Venezuela and turning his attention to neighboring Colombia. In one of the most audacious and desperate strokes of Latin America's independence struggle, Bolívar marched twenty-four hundred men through the Orinoco jungles during the rainy season and up into the frozen passages of the Andes. Passing the tree line at ten thousand feet, the troops hiked over narrow, treacherous, slippery trails, often shrouded in fog. Many of the *llaneros*, ill clothed, shoeless, and unaccustomed to the bitter cold, died of exposure. Pack and saddle animals succumbed, too. Bolívar, wrapped in a great scarlet cloak, was indomitable, but others wanted to give up. Still, the survivors made it over the towering peaks, descended the other side, and caught the Spanish off guard. Bolívar quickly won a series of battles that culminated with a major victory at Boyaca, where he defeated five thousand Spanish troops. Three days later he entered Bogotá triumphantly.

The thousand-mile march over a thirteen-thousand-foot-high mountain barrier nearly as impregnable as the Himalayas is considered one of the greatest military exploits in history. It left Bolívar in control of Colombia. He retraced his steps, climbing back down the slopes of the Andes and sailing down the Apure to the Orinoco and his base at Angostura. His victories came more quickly after that. By June 1921 he and his men had advanced north and defeated the Spanish at the bloody battle of Carabobo, opening the way to Caracas, where Bolívar arrived at night in triumph.

He did not linger long. He had wider ambitions. He soon set off to lead the liberation of Ecuador, Peru, and Bolivia. He and his troops did battle among the volcanoes near Quito, Ecuador, the Inca ruins of Cuzco, Peru, and the bleak altiplano beyond Lake Titicaca in Bolivia. His epic campaign ended in 1824. He "could now claim to rule one of the greatest empires of any military leader in history, some three million square miles in extent, the size of eastern and western Europe combined . . . In ten years, he personally had covered at least twenty thousand miles on horseback . . . and fought in some three hundred battles and skirmishes." His public appearances were greeted with wild applause and huge crowds. "Bolívar was just forty-two years of age, yet, the world, or at least the Americas, appeared to be at his feet."

It wouldn't last for long.

Barely two years later Gran Colombia was in danger of breaking up, racked by feuds among competing *caudillos* and by Bolívar's "inept, vacillating and autocratic style." José Antonio Páez, the *llanero* left behind by Bolívar to run Venezuela, was planning to lead the country to secede. Bolívar rushed back to Caracas to patch up the federation, but it was too late. After six months of trying to reorganize the government, authorities passed a resolution asking that he never return to his native land. He left for Bogotá, where he was equally reviled.

A final ignominy came in 1828 when he was nearly assassinated. In Bogotá he reunited with Manuela Sáenz, his beautiful and feisty longtime mistress. The two had met during Bolívar's triumphant entrance into Quito, Ecuador, on June 16, 1822. When she tossed him a laurel wreath from a balcony, so the story goes, Bolívar looked up to see who threw it — and their eyes met. She became the woman with whom he maintained the longest romantic relationship of his life.

Well read in the classics herself, Sáenz rose to the rank of colonel in Bolívar's revolutionary army. She accompanied him on long marches with his troops and was even present during the battle of Ayacucho in Peru — a battle the Liberator himself missed. She was awarded the Order of the Sun, the highest decoration conferred by the new Peruvian government. As one of Bolívar's most intimate and loyal confidantes, she earned a place as one of the most influential women in Latin American history.

Now, after reveling in Bolívar's most glorious days and suffering through some of his worst, Sáenz was still the faithful servant as he arrived in Bogotá seeking refuge. Rumors of plans to assassinate him were rampant. At about midnight on September 25, 1828, two or three dozen of Bolívar's enemies quietly entered his country estate, stabbed three sentinels, and broke down two doors as they made their way to the Liberator's bedroom.

Manuela was in bed with him. Hearing the commotion, she awakened Bolívar, lent him her boots, and helped him escape out a bedroom window. Bolívar hid under a bridge for three hours with one of his servants, whom he had met as he fled. Inside the house, the frustrated conspirators severely beat Manuela when she failed to help them find Bolívar. Her quick thinking and bravery prompted him to dub her "the Liberator of the Liberator."

Bolívar's dream of a united Latin America was crumbling, and so was his health. Peru was invading Colombia. Venezuela and Ecuador were leaving the union. Tuberculosis was ravaging Simón's lungs. He decided to abandon his native continent and seek exile in Europe. But he only made it to the small Colombian coastal town of Santa Marta. Moving in and out of consciousness, he was disoriented in his final, tortured days, which Colombian writer Gabriel García Márquez captured a century and a half later in his best-selling novel *The General in His Labyrinth*.

Bolívar died on December 17, 1830. Just forty-seven years old, he was bitter, penniless, and almost friendless. Before he died, in a letter to an Ecuadorean general he penned a bitter prophecy that would echo down through the decades of Latin American history: "America is ungovernable. Those who serve the revolution plough the sea. The only thing to do in America is emigrate."

Sitting in the military academy classrooms late at night nearly a century and a half later, Hugo Chávez was not nearly as pessimistic as Bolívar in his final days. Instead, he was inspired. Eventually he adopted the Liberator's life and thoughts as a blueprint for his own mission of reforming Venezuela's corrupt institutions and achieving a sovereign and united Latin America free of imperialist exploitation from abroad and social injustice at home.

He studied Bolívar's "open letters" and speeches, which were models of the advanced political thought of the time and to Chávez remained relevant. In his famous "Letter from Jamaica" in 1815, Bolívar outlined a visionary plan for the future of Latin America, from Argentina to Mexico. In an essay written for a congress gathered at Angostura in 1819, he warned against one individual harboring too much power for too long and called for repeated elections — even though his failure on these counts contributed to his own demise. "The most perfect system of government is the one that produces the greatest possible happiness, the greatest degree of social safety, and the greatest political stability," he wrote.

After he liberated the country named for him in 1825, Bolívar drew up a constitution hailed as the most liberal in the world. It called for civil liberty and equality before the law, freedoms of speech, movement, and the press, the abolition of slavery, and provisions for due process of law and trial by jury. In his final years Bolívar turned his attention and his wrath toward the United States, which by now had adopted the Monroe Doctrine declaring Latin America its "backyard." In another famous quote he wrote that the United States was "destined by Providence to plague Latin America with misery in the name of liberty."

Bolívar died a disillusioned and detested man. But decades later as historians and others reassessed his legacy, it became clear he had been a visionary. Generally he was devoted to democracy, equality, and freedom at a time when dictatorships, oligarchies, and social injustice reigned throughout Latin America. He was a figure unmatched in the region, as author Robert Harvey noted in his 2000 book *Liberators*:

> Simón Bolívar is a quasi-deity in Latin American today. He is the one non-controversial figure, the one continental leader, the man who freed millions of people from tyranny and did not then enslave them himself. His reputation transcends the bitterness of modern Latin American divisions — between left and right, between militarists and democrats, between oligarchy and revolutionaries. Among the educated and propertied classes, his radicalism has long since been quietly forgotten. To hundreds of millions of ordinary Spanish Americans, many of them illiterate, he was the leader who tried to overcome class and racial divisions, who tried to give rights to that vast swathe of humanity that remains so downtrodden . . .
>
> As soldier, statesman and man of common humanity, Simón Bolívar stands head and shoulders above any other figure Latin America has produced, and among the greatest men of world history. Small wonder that he remains a symbol of hope for millions of Latin Americans seeking liberation from poverty, ignorance and disease.

In Chávez's view, Bolívar had laid down the outlines of a formidable national project for Latin America. Zamora took up that project a quarter century after Bolívar's death, and Chávez — at least in his mind — was to inherit it in the late twentieth century.

He delved so deeply into Bolívar's life that over time he seemed to almost *become* Bolívar. "When he starts to talk about Bolívar, it seems like the Liberator is inside him," stated Milagros Flores de Reyes, a close friend and the wife of one of Chávez's military allies, Luis Reyes Reyes. "One feels that he was in those places, that he's able to see what Bolívar saw. He talks to you about the trees, the animals that were with him, the things that were around him. One day I told him, 'You incarnate him.' He smiled and said, 'Be careful, *co-madre*, what you say.'"

By the time Chávez attempted to take up Bolívar's mantle, Venezuelans had forgotten much of his revolutionary thought. It was watered down over the decades by elites who feared an uprising among the masses; the social injustices that plagued the country before the independence movement remained intact. In the words of Venezuela's most famous 1960s protest singer, Alí Primera, Bolívar had become "merely a saint for whom one lights a candle." In his classic "Canción Bolivariana," a Venezuelan boy holds an imaginary conversation with Bolívar, for whom the national currency is named, and informs him that Venezuelans are still not fully liberated:

> *Boy*: And what's worse is that my people are now without a
> Bolívar.
> *Bolívar*: They are without money? Terrible.
> *Boy*: Without consciousness, Liberator, without conscious-
> ness. The people have been fooled into believing the rich
> bourgeoisie who go to the National Pantheon to bring
> flowers on the anniversary of your death.
> *Bolívar*: Then why do they go, little patriot?
> *Boy*: To be sure that you are still dead, Liberator, truly dead.

It would become Chávez's mission to make sure that the Liberator was truly alive.

Chávez's passion to transform Venezuela was born not just from reading books about Bolívar. It was also forged by trips into the barrios of Caracas, where sewage trickled alongside the streets of some neighborhoods and people lived in mountainside *ranchos* stacked precariously on top of one another. In the status-conscious academy they still told cadets to head to the more affluent eastern part of the city, and to avoid taking public buses used by the masses. Chávez ignored the instructions and spent Saturdays visiting a friend of his father's in Catia. He wore his uniform, complete with white gloves, which surprised many residents.

He started to see the reality of the world of the *ranchos*, and to listen more to the songs of Alí Primera. Once he visited a family in the wealthy

Prados del Este neighborhood. When he left he had to walk for miles to get home because he had no money for a taxi and the family did not offer him a ride. That was a problem he never encountered in the barrios. "Among the poor there is so much love, so much solidarity. They share their bread," he related. "Among the rich, there is coldness."

By some indications, Chávez harbored dreams of succeeding Bolívar as Venezuela's savior from early on. After he marched in a ceremony honoring the new president, Carlos Andrés Pérez, he recorded in his personal diary thoughts of one day reaching the heights of power too. "After waiting a long time, the president arrived," he wrote on March 13, 1974, at the age of nineteen. "When I look at him, I wish that one day I will assume the responsibility of an entire country, the country of the Great Bolívar."

He showed other signs he was on a mission. The following September during a training exercise in the field he lamented how other young men his age probably were living it up in discothèques. "If they knew what we are doing they would say we're crazy," Chávez wrote. "But I'm not crazy. I know very well what I am looking for and what I am doing and why I'm sacrificing myself. I remember in these moments a thought of Che's: 'The present is the struggle. The future belongs to us.'"

By now he clearly possessed a well-developed social sensitivity borne of his own impoverished childhood in Sabaneta and what he continued to see all around him. In another diary entry he wrote of how "we passed by the house where we drank coffee last night. The woman came out, now with two children, and they put their hands out to say goodbye. I saw the little ones with tremendous sadness, with bloated bellies, without doubt full of parasites from eating so much dirt, barefoot, nude. With a scene like that, I feel the blood boil in my veins, and I convince myself of the need to do something, whatever it may be, for those people."

As he witnessed more and more of Venezuela's widespread poverty and immersed himself in the life of Bolívar, contemporary efforts at liberation in Latin America were sweeping other nations. One was Peru. Chávez had turned into a budding expert on Bolívar and was often asked to give talks to fellow cadets about his hero. He was among a group informally known as the Bolivarianos because of their devotion to the Liberator. They even named their class for Bolívar, the first one permitted that honor in decades. In late 1974 in his final year at the academy, superiors selected Chávez and a dozen others to travel to Peru for a special event: the 150th anniversary of the battle of Ayacucho, witnessed by Manuela Sáenz.

The day he learned he had been chosen for the trip, Chávez went to the academy's library to start studying what was happening in Peru. What he discovered caught his attention.

A nationalist military general named Juan Velasco Alvarado was leading a revolution called the Plan Inca. In a pattern Chávez and his allies would repeat two and a half decades later, a group of progressive Peruvian officers angry over widespread corruption and the deteriorating state of their country launched a coup in 1968. They overthrew the civilian regime of its leader, Fernando Belaúnde Terry. The officers were disgusted by and distrustful of the country's main political party, APRA, which he led.

Because of their experience fighting guerrillas in rural Peru, they were also keenly aware of the abject poverty in the countryside. While Velasco helped crush the guerrilla insurgency in the 1960s, he also adopted much of their political program once in power. He nationalized foreign oil companies and expropriated sugar haciendas. He implemented extensive land reform. He made Quechua, the language spoken by the dirt-poor indigenous population in the Andean altiplano, an official language of the country. He expropriated conservative newspapers and encouraged worker participation in the management of state industries. To the annoyance of Washington, he also reestablished diplomatic relations with Cuba and engaged in bilateral trade with the Soviet Union.

Chávez landed in the middle of Velasco's Plan Inca, immersing himself for several days in the revolutionary environment. He met cadets from Peru, Chile, Colombia, Panama, and other countries. He asked everyone he met about the Peru experience. He visited the homes of the Peruvian cadets and went to parties where he met local girls. He saw the impoverished conditions of the indigenous population when he traveled to Ayacucho.

Toward the end of the trip, he and the other Venezuelan cadets met Velasco himself at a reception for them at the government palace. Velasco gave the cadets two books. One was *The Manifesto of the Revolutionary Government of the Armed Forces of Peru*. The other was a small blue booklet of speeches by Velasco called *La Revolución Nacional Peruana*. The meeting made an impact on Chávez. "After listening to Velasco, I drank up the books, even memorizing some speeches almost completely," he recalled. For years afterward, he kept the little blue book with him. Authorities eventually confiscated it and others after he launched a coup attempt of his own seventeen years later.

Two years after Chávez's visit to Peru, Velasco's nationalist experiment collapsed. It lacked popular support and it lacked money — its foreign reserves were exhausted. Velasco had made two crucial mistakes. First, his government consisted entirely of military officers; it had no civilian presence. It also never reached beyond the immediate beneficiaries of his reforms. They were lessons that did not go unnoticed by Chávez. While the pro-leftist Velasco regime was derided by many journalists and scholars, it did provide Chávez with one thing: his first direct exposure to a progressive military regime, albeit one that differed substantially from the project he eventually pursued. It also did not escape his attention that Peru was a country where Bolívar's name was still held in esteem.

Peru was not the only country in Latin America where progressive military officers were leading revolutionary regimes. A similar experiment was under way in Panama, where General Omar Torrijos also had seized power in 1968. Chávez ended up studying with one of Torrijos's sons at the military academy in Caracas, where he was sent for training, since Panama did not have a university-level military school. The two played baseball and became friends on the field and off. Intrigued about the nationalistic experiment in Panama, Chávez asked him to bring books about his father. Torrijos's son also gave him some photographs showing the general giving a speech to peasants. Chávez was impressed. Before he graduated, Chávez visited Panama, met Torrijos, and saw the revolution in action.

Torrijos launched his rebellion for reasons similar to those that propelled the military officers in Peru and, years later, Chávez himself. Torrijos was disgusted by the corruption of the political elites and the income gap between a tiny upper class and the poor masses. He also despised the military's forced role in keeping the system in place and the virtual control exercised over Panama by the United States. The Americans still controlled the Panama Canal. It was sixty-five years after they had expropriated a sweeping swath of Panama in 1903 to build the canal and then turned large chunks of the country into US military bases.

In an interview in 1975 Torrijos explained why he launched the coup that brought him to power. The Panamanian National Guard that he led had turned into "the wage slaves of the oligarchy":

Our mission was to maintain the status quo, with blood and thunder, with timely military deployment, or with a coup d'état. I was forced to take part in acts of repression, indeed I got sick of so much repression. As a direct result, the National Guard decided to rebel, to decolonize the country. Above all, we wanted to solve the problem of the canal, which for Panamanians was almost a religion.

We were the sentries of the oligarchy until the mistakes of the politicians became so serious that there was no prospect of rectification. A generation of young officers, graduates of the Panamanian Military School, decided not just to organize a coup d'état, but to do away with the entire system of apparent "democracy" in the country. People had grown accustomed to mixing up politics with their economic activity, using their democratic freedom in much the same way women use cosmetics.

As leader of Panama, Torrijos pushed through a land reform program to try to benefit the peasants. He also won a pledge from President Jimmy Carter in 1979 to turn over control of the canal to the Panamanians two decades later. He didn't live to see his greatest achievement fulfilled, though. Torrijos was killed in a plane crash in 1981, thirteen years after he seized power.

But his radical program of reform, along with the project in Peru, served as a seductive example to the young Chávez. Torrijos and Velasco were progressive military officers who used their power to try to raise their country's living standards, regain their sovereignty from the United States, and address issues of mass poverty. "One began to see then that the military men weren't meant to massacre people, to wage bloody coup d'états, to sever the rights of the people, but that rather they could serve the people," Chávez told interviewer Agustín Blanco Muñoz in 1995.

Torrijos and Velasco stood in stark contrast to other military leaders who were also seizing power in Latin America while Chávez was in the military academy. On September 11, 1973, General Augusto Pinochet overthrew Chile's Salvador Allende, the first democratically elected Marxist president of a nation in the Western Hemisphere. The United States and the CIA backed the coup. Pinochet installed a regime that "disappeared" at least three thousand people and maintained its grip on power for seventeen years. In neighboring Argentina in 1976, General Jorge Videla overthrew the government of María Estela, the widow of Juan Perón. Videla imposed a junta that disappeared at least thirty thousand people. Soldiers drugged some victims, put them on military airplanes, and threw them from the air into the open sea.

At the time of the coup against Allende, Chávez was training in the mountains. He was horrified. Listening to the radio, he heard Fidel Castro come on and denounce the putsch. One comment stuck with him. "We recorded a phrase forever," Chávez recalled. "'If every worker, if every laborer, had had a rifle in his hands, the fascist coup in Chile would not have happened.' Those words marked us so much, they became a saying, a type of password that only we knew." After that, when he and some secret allies in the military met, one often would say, "If every worker, if every laborer . . ." The other would finish the phrase.

The military uprisings throughout Latin America in the late 1960s and early 1970s provided Chávez with a clear distinction between military men who launched rebellions to liberate their people and those who launched coups to oppress them. "We military men had the example of Pinochet, which of course we did not share," Chávez later stated. "He represented the military men who kill people, who destroy, who decapitate, while those Peruvian military men spoke differently, spoke of the people. Even though in the end that experience failed, unfortunately, perhaps for lack of strategic clarity, at least they spoke and acted differently."

As graduation day at the military academy approached in July 1975, Chávez was not thinking about launching a coup in Venezuela. He was simply restless about what he saw around him — a land rich in oil with millions of poor people and a corrupt political class in charge. His mind was filled with the thoughts of Bolívar and other revolutionaries. His soul was filled with increasing anger at the elites and sympathy for the underclass. In the academy he was instructed to combat the guerrillas, but now he was wondering if they were the real enemy.

"We studied antiguerrilla tactics, but I was already questioning everything," he recalled:

I think that from the time I left the academy I was oriented toward a revolutionary movement . . . The Hugo Chávez who entered there was a kid from the hills, a *llanero* with aspirations of playing professional baseball. Four years later, a second-lieutenant came out who had taken the revolutionary path. Someone who didn't have obligations to anyone, who didn't belong to any movement, who was not enrolled in any party, but who knew very well where I was headed.

# Testing the Waters

Hugo Chávez thought he was lucky when he got his first assignment out of the military academy. In July 1975 he had graduated seventh out of a class of sixty-seven who made it through the rigorous program. Most of the original class of 375 didn't survive. Now Chávez was going back to his home state of Barinas. He was named a communications officer at one of thirteen counterinsurgency units the military established in the early 1960s — "the violent decade" as it is known in Venezuela. By the time Chávez arrived in 1975, hardly any guerrillas were left to fight. He would have plenty of time to dedicate to other endeavors.

With his first paycheck he splurged and rented a room in a hotel near the Plaza Venezuela in Barinas. Then he bought a refrigerator, a new bed, some furniture, a fan, and a big radio for Rosa Inés. When he showed up at her house, she was thrilled by the gifts, if not by his new life as a soldier.

While he was pleased to be home, Chávez was not greeted with open arms by everyone. He was the first graduate of the Andrés Bello Plan at the military academy assigned to the Manuel Cedeno Hunters Battalion in Barinas. Some old-guard officers did not take kindly to the "college boy" Chávez. He clashed with one captain who refused to call him lieutenant. Instead, in a mocking tone he called him *licenciado* — the title used for college graduates. Chávez refused to respond to the captain until he used his military rank. Fresh out of the academy, the rebellious Chávez's troubles already were beginning.

Chávez was immersing himself in the military and coming to love it, but he had not abandoned his passion for sports. He still played baseball frequently. That was another thing the captain did not like. "He told me, 'Are you a solider or a baseball player?'" Chávez recalled. "I could never convince him you could do the two things at the same time. He told me to dedicate myself to sports with the soldiers. 'I am dedicated, Captain.' The team of the soldiers was good, but I wanted to play in an organized league."

One day the manager of the Barinas team that played in a national league called Chávez and invited him to play that weekend in a game against a team from Caracas that was coming to town. It was a big game: The team was inaugurating a stadium that was to be used for a national championship series later in the year. On top of that, the manager needed a left-handed pitcher. Chávez doubted his superiors would give him permission to play. So he went without telling them.

In the first inning in his first at-bat, Chávez cracked a hit. In his second at-bat the pitcher threw a curve and Chávez knocked it out of the park. It was the first home run in the new stadium. The crowd exploded in cheers. So did Chávez's soldiers back in the barracks. Unknown to Chávez, Radio Barinas was broadcasting the game live and his troops were listening in. The radio announcer even identified Chávez as the second lieutenant of the local battalion. It was after 9 P.M. The barracks were supposed to be silent.

The ruckus woke up the captain. He angrily marched down to the dormitory to see what was going on. "Turn on the light," he barked. "What's happening here?" "Captain, we're happy because our commander Chávez hit a home run," the soldiers said. What? Chávez Frías? The second lieutenant was supposed to be in the barracks, not out playing baseball.

The next day the captain tried to arrest Chávez for violating orders. He hauled him into the commander's office. Chávez tried to talk his way out of it. "Look, commander, here in this battalion there are some ten second lieutenants," he said. "If you go at night to the Guayanesa — a famous brothel in Barinas — you'll find them there with a bunch of women and a bottle of rum. Or if you go to the military club, they'll be there with their girlfriends, dancing and drinking. On the other hand, I like sports. I can't understand why they are going to arrest me for playing baseball, and for holding up high the name of the battalion that you command."

The commander was listening. Chávez was still in his early twenties, but he was charismatic and convincing. He continued. "Don't you think it's better that I'm involved in baseball rather than women and booze?" There wasn't much the commander could say. "You're right," he told Chávez. "I give you permission to play."

He kept on playing. A few times a week Chávez drove an old Volkswagen from the barracks to the ball field and changed in the dugout from his combat fatigues into his baseball uniform. He also got the chance to expand his passion for sports throughout the battalion. His unit often traveled to the Wild West–style border zone with Colombia to hunt for whatever guerrillas still existed. The movement had largely died off after Rafael Caldera assumed the presidency in 1969 and offered an amnesty to any guerrillas willing to give up the armed struggle. Most did. During the excursions to the border, as the officer in charge of communications Chávez often stayed with the battalion's commander or his top aide at the command posts. Chávez developed a good relationship with the commander.

One day he asked Chávez to organize a sports program for the battalion. In what he later described as a small-scale precursor to the "social missions" he launched in hundreds of barrios as president, Chávez contacted a friend of his who was the head of the National Institutes of Sports in Barinas and recruited trainers to coach the soldiers for free.

The program was a big success. For two years straight the Cedeño's soldiers were the interbattalion champions in baseball, soccer, volleyball, basketball, and track and field. Chávez turned the treeless plain where the men played baseball into an official-sized, snappy-looking diamond. He procured white and red sand for free, and a truck to transport it. The men chopped rectangles out of the grass for base paths. They erected two dugouts, two small changing rooms, and a fence made of poles. "When we finished, it was a tremendous stadium," Chávez later noted. "We inaugurated it with a party that seemed like a festival." Chávez believed it was the second best stadium in Barinas, outdone only by the one where he played in the local league. The soldiers invited the public to watch them play whenever they wanted.

His superiors also assigned the dynamic young second lieutenant the task of recruiting candidates for the military academy. Chávez regularly visited the high schools of sprawling Barinas state — all ten of them by now — giving talks to seniors and encouraging them to apply to the academy. He took his evangelization campaign to the airwaves, too, stopping by Radio Barinas to put in his plug. Military superiors in Caracas gave him and other recruiters a guide to read, but Chávez injected his own commentaries. "I never told them they would have a sure salary, but rather I spoke to them about Bolívar and what [Cuban independence hero José] Martí said about him." He took to painting the saying on the walls of the barracks. He got some soldiers to whom he gave painting classes to help.

Chávez also won permission to write a weekly column in the local newspaper *El Espacio* — the space. He wrote about history and his unit's activities — everything from playing sports to raising rabbits and tending a tropical fruit orchard. In another precursor of his presidency, Chávez wrote about a "civilian-military union." Besides the weekly column, Chávez even found time to call the numbers at bingo games and serve as master of ceremonies at the local beauty pageant. His energy was endless.

Chávez's unit was dedicated to combating guerrillas, but he never encountered any in Barinas. The closest he came occurred one day while he was assigned to a sleepy outpost outside the capital and found an abandoned car. It was a black Mercedes-Benz riddled with bullet holes. He learned that it had belonged to a group of guerrillas killed in a shoot-out with soldiers a decade earlier. Chávez pried open the trunk and found a stash of moldy books, almost all of them Marxist. He brought them to the military post, repaired them, and set up a small library.

He had plenty of time to read and think — the nights were long and lonely in the llanos. There were books by Lenin, Mao, and other leftists, but the one that interested him the most was *The Times of Ezequiel Zamora*. Chávez immersed himself in the books during the few months he spent at the outpost, deepening the foundation that began with his discovery of Bolívar in the military academy. "By the time I was 21 or 22, I made myself a man of the left," he later commented.

His two years in Barinas also served as a testing ground for his ideas about a new kind of soldier and a new kind of relationship with society — inspired by Bolívar, Zamora, Torrijos, Velasco, and other figures. "It was a very intense period, in which I was involved inside and outside of the battalion in sports, journalism, recruiting students and hosting the beauty pageants . . . The most important thing was that the Battalion of Hunters started to have another profile. It was no longer an antiguerrilla unit separated from the people, hated at times by the people, but rather one whose boys participated in the athletic and cultural life of Barinas."

With few guerrillas to fight against in Barinas, Chávez's unit was transferred in 1977. In the eastern Venezuelan state of Anzoátegui a fresh outbreak of guerrilla activity by the ultraleft Bandera Roja, Red Flag, was cropping up in the mountains. Chávez's new assignment soon provoked conflicts within him about the role of the military and some of its behavior.

Not long after his arrival he was left in charge of a remote command post. One night a retired colonel from military intelligence showed up with what he called "prisoners of war." They were three skinny *campesinos*, their heads bowed and their faces full of fear. The colonel wanted to spend the night, so Chávez sent them to an empty tent. At 9 P.M. he ordered a small electric plant turned off, and the camp went dark.

An hour later Chávez heard loud shouts coming from the tent. He walked over and found the colonel beating the *campesinos* with a baseball bat covered with a cloth. The colonel told Chávez to leave him alone, he was busy. Chávez grabbed the bat and ordered him to stop. He told the colonel to either end the torture or leave the camp. The colonel left. Later he filed a report accusing Chávez of impeding military intelligence work. Chávez had to fight off the threat of a court-martial for instigating a military uprising and failing to recognize authority.

Chávez had done the right thing, yet he was the one who faced punishment. The experience left him with questions about an institution that on the one hand he loved but on the other was racked by the same kind of corruption that permeated most of Venezuelan society. "That really affected me and I said to myself, 'Well, what kind of an army is this that tortures these men? Even if they had been guerrillas, there was no reason to torture them.'"

The seeds of Chávez's doubts about the military were planted back in Barinas. He saw firsthand how the generalized corruption of the political establishment was filtering into the armed forces. Ranking officers fiddled with budgets and pilfered equipment for their own use and profit. Even though their official salaries were modest, many lived the high life, flying off to the Caribbean resort island of Margarita on weekends, for instance. There were many ways to rob. One of the easiest was through the food budget, as Chávez described in an interview in 2004:

From the first days in Barinas I started to perceive the corruption, immorality and arbitrariness of some superior officers. And they wouldn't let you fight it in the barracks. One very vulnerable point, for instance, was the food for the troops. When I was on duty, I often went at 4 or 5 A.M. to the shack where they prepared the food. I waited until the supplier's truck came, with the cheese for breakfast and the meat for lunch. They put the food on the scale. "How much for each soldier?" "Eighty grams for cheese," they told me, for example. You calculated it and most of the time there was less than there was supposed to be. Or they delivered us mountain boots that broke on the first march . . .

There were a million ways to rob. Later came the abuses in the east against the supposed or real guerrillas. All this started to create in me a feeling of resistance against the negligence and arbitrary things I collided with in the barracks and that went beyond military life. I started to look at the country and try to find explanations for the contradictions I found myself in. Swirling around me were situations, daily conflicts, that were very far from the Bolivarian principles and the values we had been educated with. So this question appeared that was uncomfortable for the military and political elite, but someone obviously had to ask: What kind of a democracy is this that enriches a minority and impoverishes the majority?

Chávez was supposed to be fighting the guerrillas. But by the time he was sent on his first full-fledged counterinsurgency mission to hunt guerrillas in the mountains of Anzoátegui in October 1977, he was starting to feel some sympathy toward the people who were supposedly the enemy. He kept a diary during the mission between October 21 and November 18. It reveals a driven young officer drawn to Ernesto "Che" Guevara, resentful of US "imperialism," proud of Venezuelan indigenous culture, and convinced he is destined for greater things even though at the moment his work is tedious.

"It's the first time I'm in a guerrilla operation," Chávez wrote on October 22, 1977. "Here I am, fulfilling an insignificant role, that may be immensely larger and productive." Three days later, he evoked Che — "Vietnam. One and two Vietnams in Latin America." — and Bolívar — "Come. Return. Here . . . It could be." The next day, October 26, he continued in the same vein. "This war is for years . . . I have to do it. Even if it costs me my life. It doesn't matter. For this I was born.

How long can I be like this? I feel impotent. Unproductive. I must prepare myself. To act." A day later, he added, "My people are stoic. Passive. Who will light the flame? You can make a huge fire. The wood is wet. There aren't the conditions. There aren't the conditions. There aren't the conditions. Damn it! When will there be? Why not create them? There aren't the conditions. Subjective, yes. Objective, no. A huge excuse. We'll see each other there."

The wood in Venezuela was wet. Chávez wanted to light the flame of social revolt, but it wasn't possible. There weren't the conditions because the country's economy was soaring. Fueled by booming oil prices sparked by the rise of OPEC, the Arab–Israeli War of 1973, and the consequent Arab oil embargo, Venezuela was awash in petrodollars. The price of Venezuelan crude, which dropped to a nadir of $1.76 per barrel in 1970, recovered to $3.56 in 1973 and nearly tripled to $10.31 in 1974. Between 1973 and 1983 oil earned Venezuela's sixteen million people more than $150 billion. They enjoyed the highest standard of living in South America.

Drunk with oil money, the country's middle class went on a binge. Lawyers, doctors, teachers, real estate agents, and others routinely flew to Miami for weekend shopping sprees and became famous for the saying *Está barato. Dame dos.* — It's cheap. Give me two. The bonanza the country reaped from the 1974–1981 "oil crisis" earned it the nickname "Saudi Venezuela." The intoxicating mood was captured by a book with the same name. Splashed across its cover was a depiction of President Carlos Andrés Pérez in the robe and headdress of an Arab prince.

Politically, Venezuela was one of the most stable countries in Latin America. At a time when bloody military dictatorships reigned throughout the region, Venezuela was an oasis — a "model democracy." It held presidential elections every five years, passed power back and forth peacefully between two parties, and enjoyed a vigorous press, albeit one largely controlled by the oligarchy. Those in the lower classes who missed out on the oil boom dreamed of getting some.

In 1976 Pérez made history by nationalizing the oil industry. Venezuelans were taking control of their country's principal resource — at least in theory. While a vast swath of the population remained mired in poverty, the oil riches and the crumbs thrown to the underclass were enough to extinguish the possibility of a massive social uprising. The guerrillas were all but dead. Most Venezuelans did not want to see a return to the "violent decade."

Sitting in the mountains of Anzoátegui on a forlorn mission he sympathized with less and less, Chávez was a frustrated man. His mind turned to a local woman from Barinas, Nancy Colmenares, whom he would soon marry and start a family with. Chávez had apparently become involved with her during his assignment in Barinas, and now after his transfer hundreds of miles away thought of her with nostalgia. He dreamed of them fighting the revolution together like Bolívar and Manuela Sáenz or even dying together like Romeo and Juliet, although in reality Colmenares shared little of Chávez's budding revolutionary consciousness and by some accounts was partly the object of a falling-out between him and his mother, who disapproved of the marriage. A humble woman from the working class, Colmenares has kept a low profile over the years and is almost unknown to Venezuelans. She and Chávez were to have three children together — Rosa Virginia in September 1978, María Gabriela in March 1980, and Hugo Rafael in October 1983. The couple's marriage eventually ended in divorce in the early 1990s; Chávez later remarried just before he ran for president in 1998, although that union also dissolved.

That October 1977, eleven months before Colmenares gave birth to their first child, Chávez wrote warmly of his future first wife in his diary — although with thoughts of revolution and romance all mixed together. "My little black one is far away," Chávez wrote, using a common Venezuelan term of endearment. "If I could be with her, feel her warmth. Be happy with her. The truth is I love her. It's very hard to live without her. Mami, everything is going to be OK. Wait for me. Maybe one day I will bring you with me. And you can learn with me. And triumph with me. Or die with me. This war is for years . . ."

Beyond the separation from the current love of his life, Chávez was morose because even his favorite baseball team, the Magallanes, had lost a game. The man who entered the military academy in the hope of reaching the major leagues was now experiencing mixed emotions about a sport imported by the imperialists:

I lost that fanaticism. This baseball isn't ours. It's also from the North Americans. Over there I hear a "joropo" song. That's our music. It's also trampled on by the foreign music. The Venezuelan has never been able to find himself. With his land, with his people. With his music. With his customs. We lack an identity. We import

everything. We have "dough." We are "petroleum producers."
That's all we care about: getting "dough." Having the latest model
car. Being tourists. Having "status." It's the consciences of these
people, corroded by "petro-dollars." "Gold corrupts everything."
Once again Simón José Antonio [Bolívar]. We can't avoid him.
It's the only real and beautiful thing that we have left, those of
us who love this land: to hold fast to that heroic past and its men,
constructors of its history. What else?

Chávez was increasingly disgusted by the Venezuelan middle
class's American-style consumerism at a time when many people
struggled to get by. The abuses by the military and the government
also disturbed him. But he didn't think the guerrillas were the answer
to Venezuela's woes, either. He saw things with them he didn't like.

On a trip to the city of Barcelona one day to pick up supplies, Chávez
was at the local military base when a helicopter landed. It unloaded several soldiers. Some were injured, others dead. Chávez walked over to
the helicopter to help. One of the soldiers still alive recognized him. He
grabbed Chávez's arm. "Lieutenant, don't let me die," he pleaded . . .
but it was too late. He expired a short time later in the hospital.

Chávez learned that the soldier and his unit had been ambushed
by guerrillas linked to Bandera Roja. The soldiers had taken a long
hike in the mountains. Half asleep, they were returning in a truck
coming down a country road. The guerrillas were waiting for them.
When the truck came around the corner, the guerrillas opened fire.
The soldiers did not even have time to defend themselves.

The incident left Chávez wary of both the counterinsurgency
campaign by the military and the guerrilla warfare by the rebels. "I
said to myself, 'I am neither in favor of torturing these farmers because
they might be guerrillas nor of the guerrillas massacring those soldiers
who were innocent guys just doing their jobs.' Moreover, this was a
guerrilla group that had already been defeated, that no longer had any
kind of popular support; these were small isolated groups."

Chávez didn't see much hope in either path. So he decided to pursue
his own. At the age of twenty-three, he formed his first subversive cell
within the military. It was made up of several soldiers, including two
sergeants from the llanos who were also stationed in Anzoátegui. They
called their group the Venezuelan People's Liberation Army (ELPV).

They had no specific agenda or plan of action. They were simply outraged by the abuses they saw. Their vague goal was to somehow combat the injustices of Venezuela. "What were we going to do?" Chávez asked rhetorically in an interview in 1995. "We didn't have the slightest idea what we were going to do at that moment." He later commented to the author Gabriel García Márquez that "we did it to prepare ourselves in case something should happen."

As their first action, they secretly dug a hole in the ground and buried a few grenades. It was their "arsenal," Chávez later joked. The cell didn't go very far. It died off not long after. But it marked an important step in Chávez's evolution. It was his first concrete act of rebellion in the military. It was 1977, fifteen years before he launched his coup.

Outside the armed forces, Chávez also was taking tentative steps to find allies for his embryonic struggle. He maintained close contact with the Ruíz brothers back in Barinas and their father, the historian and founder of the local Communist Party. As a cadet in Caracas and a second lieutenant in Barinas, Chávez visited them when he could. The Ruíz brothers were pursuing their own activities. They helped found the left-wing La Causa R (the Radical Cause) workers' party. It was an offshoot of the Communist Party and grew out of the union movement in the industrial powerhouse of Ciudad Guayana — Venezuela's Pittsburgh. In time the Causa R turned into one of Venezuela's major political parties and a serious threat to the traditional parties that dominated the corruption-filled democratic era.

Its founder and leading light was former guerrilla fighter and Communist Party cadre Alfredo Maneiro — a charismatic, legendary figure on the left. In 1971 Maneiro published *Notas Negativas*, a document outlining his vision of a left-nationalist group that would abandon socialist dogma and embrace grassroots "radical democracy." It helped lead to the birth of the Causa R not long after.

By 1978, with Chávez's restlessness growing, the Ruíz brothers helped arrange a meeting between Maneiro and the young second lieutenant. The brothers also invited Pablo Medina, another Causa R leader. Medina spent years working in the factories of Ciudad Guayana in eastern Venezuela and clandestinely organizing workers. He even published a workers' newspaper between shifts. Medina was to turn into a major figure in La Causa R and the left in Venezuela.

The secret meeting between Chávez and Maneiro took place in an apartment Chávez rented in front of a military base in Maracay, a ninety-minute drive west of Caracas. The encounter did not last long — fifteen minutes or so. Chávez was in awe of Maneiro. He said little. Maneiro did most of the talking. He was interested in meeting with Chávez. He was looking for what he called the "fourth leg" of a figurative table to complete a revolutionary alliance.

The alliance would comprise workers mainly from Ciudad Guayana and residents of the sprawling Caracas barrio of Catia. It would also include progressive middle-class university intellectuals and, finally, the military. "I remember Maneiro quite clearly," Chávez later stated. "He said, 'We have the fourth leg for the table.' . . . And he added: 'I am only going to ask one thing of you. You have to agree that whatever we may do, it is not for right now. It is for the medium term, ten years from now.'" Revolution was not going to break out anytime soon in Venezuela. Chávez would have to remain patient. The wood was wet.

It was the only time Chávez met Maneiro, who died five years later in 1983. Chávez did not see Medina again, either, until they met at Maneiro's funeral. But the initial meeting served as a seed that later yielded an important element in Chávez's rebellion — his link with the civilian left.

During the same period, Chávez ran into one of his classmates from the military academy, Jesús Urdaneta Hernández. They met at a military base in Maturin in Anzoátegui state. One night when Urdaneta was on duty Chávez approached him. He confided in him about the formation of his tiny revolutionary group, the Venezuelan People's Liberation Army. Chávez said he was disappointed by his experience in the military. It wasn't what he had expected. Why don't we create something entirely different? he suggested. We're not going to join the guerrillas. That's over and done with. Anyway, our outlook and education don't fit with theirs.

What Chávez had in mind was another path, a movement within the armed forces. Urdaneta was receptive. He was frustrated with the corrupt government and military, too. He was also imbued with the ideals of Bolívar. He agreed to join in the embryonic project. He said he would contact two other officers, Felipe Acosta Carles and Miguel Ortiz Contreras, to see if they wanted to participate. It was little more than a vague idea at that point. But Chávez was reaching an important turning point.

That night he told Urdaneta, "I'm not going to go on like this in the army all my life."

# 5

# A Sacred Oath

William Izarra's plan to bring revolution to Venezuela was born at Harvard University. In 1978, around the same time Chávez was forming his first subversive cell in the military and starting the tentative search for revolutionary allies, Izarra won the chance from Venezuela's military to study at Harvard for a year. Ensconced in the university's library, he delved into the teachings of Mao Tse-tung and other revolutionaries. He came back to Venezuela with a plan to overthrow the system.

Izarra was an air force pilot, but he harbored the same kinds of doubts about the military and Venezuelan society in general that Chávez soon developed. As a freshly minted pilot in 1967, Izarra was assigned for about six months to antiguerrilla "theaters" where Marxist rebels still thrived.

Like all soldiers, Izarra underwent intense ideological training depicting the guerrillas as bloodthirsty communistic subversives bent on destroying Venezuela's "model" democracy. But like Chávez years later, Izarra started to feel sympathy toward the people he was supposed to be fighting.

One day he was handed the assignment of interrogating a captured Cuban guerrilla leader who was aiding the Venezuelan rebels. Izarra encountered not a thug but an intelligent officer who provided compelling arguments about why rebels were rising up in Latin America to fight social injustice. The next day the Cuban officer showed up dead — supposedly shot when he tried to escape. Izarra saw his mangled face and was horrified.

Eventually he started holding informal talks with other disgruntled officers. He also made contact with a legendary Venezuelan guerrilla leader, Douglas Bravo. By 1978 Izarra reached a turning point when he was sent to Harvard to study full-time for a year. "My goal at Harvard was just one: to finish shaping my revolutionary thesis for the Armed Forces . . . In Harvard my political project was born, conceiving of a different social system."

By now imbued with Trotskyist leanings, Izarra came back to Venezuela in 1979 convinced that provoking change in Venezuela through electoral means was not feasible. He believed a combination of ballot-box fraud and patronage handouts by the two main parties, AD and COPEI, made it impossible for anyone outside the two-party system to win the presidency.

Venezuela was a democracy on paper but run mainly for the benefit of the elites, who maintained a tight grip on power through political surrogates. Besides controlling the national budget, the president and his party appointed state governors — amazingly, they were not elected by popular vote until 1989. The president and his party also controlled posts all the way down to mayors and councilmen in tiny villages. Congressional members were not elected by name or district; voters simply selected a *plancha* or slate put up by the party, which then named the person to fill each seat. Senators and Congress members were virtually unaccountable to the public, who often did not even know the name of their representative.

The ruling party handpicked the members of the Supreme Court, which almost never decided against party interests. The party also appointed judges throughout the court system. Law firms known as "tribes" that were well connected to AD and COPEI could assure anyone with the money to pay for it that they would get the ruling they wanted. Those poor and unconnected were out of luck.

The hands of the two parties reached into seemingly every aspect of society. If you wanted a job as a teacher, you needed a connection with one of the local party heads. Some schools even divided up the spoils — the principal of the morning session was an Adeco and the afternoon session a Copeyano. If you belonged to neither party, you weren't likely to get hired.

The genius of the system was that it provided just enough patronage and handouts to a keep a resentful underclass at bay. Each electoral season AD and COPEI threw barrio dwellers a crumb by handing out free buckets of paint to spruce up the fronts of their cement shacks. For a few weeks, people were grateful. The government also passed out thousands of low-paying, make-work jobs. Some employees stood around all day at the entrances of government buildings that sometimes had eight or ten doormen for a single door. Or they didn't show up at all. It created one of the most bloated, inefficient government bureaucracies in Latin America. But it also created a loyal class of party devotees. Some swore they would be Adecos until the day they died.

Izarra concluded that the only way to break the monolithic grip of AD and COPEI on Venezuela's corrupted political, judicial, economic, and educational institutions was a civic-military uprising. He envisioned something akin to the revolt that had overthrown the dictator Marcos Pérez Jiménez in 1958. Returning from Harvard, Izarra formed a revolutionary cell in the air force. He called it R-83. The R was for "revolution," 83 for the year he optimistically thought they would triumph.

Izarra's goal was to replace Venezuela's practice of "democracy" with something that met the needs of the majority. "The R-83 was based on the implementation of a socialist system — possibly different from the ones already existing, but a socialist system," he stated. He gathered like-minded officers and started holding clandestine discussion groups. He even devised an oath to swear in new members. They took it late at night in front of the National Pantheon in Caracas where the remains of Bolívar and other founding fathers were entombed.

Izarra resumed the contact he'd entered into several years earlier with Douglas Bravo. The former guerrilla leader was hunting again for disgruntled military officers to help with a revolutionary project of his own.

Short, dapper, and barrel-chested, Bravo was a legend on the left in Venezuela and throughout Latin America. For a time some believed that after Che Guevara and Fidel Castro, he was the man highest on the CIA's most wanted list. The son of a landowner, Bravo joined the Venezuelan Communist Party in the 1950s as a teenager and participated in the movement to overthrow Pérez Jiménez. Joining the Soviet-influenced communists in those days was not unusual. Between 1928 and 1968 they were the second most powerful party in Venezuela, overshadowed only by Democratic Action. In the 1950s they played a leading role in overthrowing Pérez Jiménez, who was enthusiastically supported by the United States.

By backing a string of dictators and oppressive regimes in Latin America, from the Somozas in Nicaragua to Fulgencio Batista in Cuba, the United States had sown ill will across much of the region throughout the twentieth century. The Americans quickly recognized Pérez Jiménez after he seized power in 1952. Dwight Eisenhower's decision to award him the Legion of Merit two years later added to a bitter taste.

Bravo and his cohorts in the Venezuelan Communist Party launched an initiative in 1957 to draw military officers into an alliance to overthrow Pérez Jiménez. The next year another sector of the military aligned with civilians beat them to it. But Bravo and the others kept building their ties to the barracks — they believed the new government installed by Democratic Action was anything but revolutionary. "There has always been a link with sectors of the armed forces in the revolutionary processes of Venezuela," according to Bravo. He found Venezuela's military to be fertile recruiting ground. Most Venezuelan soldiers were from poor or working-class families. They had little interest in maintaining the status quo. Neither did Bravo.

By February 1959 AD's Rómulo Betancourt replaced Pérez Jiménez as the nation's leader, ushering in Venezuela's return to democratic rule. Before long he found himself under siege by both the left and the right. On June 20, 1960, he was nearly killed in a car bomb attack authored in part by rightist Venezuelan officers. At the same time, small *focos* of leftist guerrillas were forming, and frequent street protests were breaking out. By 1962 leftist naval officers had led two failed coup attempts against Betancourt.

The president cracked down on dissent, ordering troops to fire on marchers and jailing communists, including some congressmen. Eventually he outlawed the entire Communist Party and MIR (Left Revolutionary Movement). The MIR was created in 1960 after some of the more radical and youthful members of AD became disillusioned with Betancourt for turning his back on the country's admirers of Fidel Castro and moving closer to the foreign and domestic bourgeoisie. Many young AD members had worked closely with Venezuela's communists to help overthrow Pérez Jiménez. The nickname for party members reflected the tie: *Adeco*. The *Ade* came from Acción Democratico, the *co* from communist.

Amid the upheaval, Bravo's Communist Party and the MIR were convinced an armed, broadly backed insurrection similar to Castro's revolt in Cuba was inevitable in Venezuela. Besides cultivating support among leftist military officers, they began to train guerrilla cadre. Soon after, the PCV, MIR, and other leftist groups formed a centralized guerrilla command structure. The Armed Forces of National Liberation (FALN) handled military operations. The National Liberation Front (FLN) took care of political affairs and organizing.

They launched a series of audacious, bloody, and controversial attacks between 1962 and 1964. Their offensives often provoked pitched battles with the military. With many residents caught in between, the guerrillas won scant public support.

By 1965 some of the Communist Party and FALN leadership had decided to abandon the armed struggle. But Bravo refused. He still believed it was the only way to change Venezuela. The Communist Party ejected Bravo, who kept fighting in the hills with the FALN. At the same time, he formed the Revolutionary Party of Venezuela (PRV) as the political arm of his movement. For years Bravo lived clandestinely with an arrest warrant hanging over his head. He frequently traveled incognito to Europe, where his group enjoyed support from leftist intellectuals and others. Alienated from the Russians and Cubans, he made trips to Iraq, Libya, China, and other nations seeking financial and military assistance. He didn't get much.

Bravo was not simply a crazed rebel bent on senseless, wanton violence. His goal was creating a utopian world where social divisions were erased and justice reigned. He was a dreamer, envisioning a society where people worked five or six hours a day and devoted the rest of their time to writing poetry, painting, or reading. Part of Bravo's project aimed at preserving the environment, especially the Amazon rain forests. He also wanted to rescue the indigenous population's culture, which was under assault from the North American consumerism invasion. He sought to resurrect the images of Simón Bolívar, Simón Rodríguez, and Ezequiel Zamora as well. He believed the trilogy could provide the ideological foundation for a new Venezuela. His embrace of Bolívar was another reason for his separation from the Communist Party, which remained loyal to Soviet orthodoxy and considered Bolívar anathema.

By the late 1960s the armed revolutionary movement was dying out. In overwhelming numbers Venezuelans were taking part in presidential elections every five years. President Rafael Caldera, who took office in 1969, all but finished off the rebels by offering an amnesty. Most accepted, but Bravo refused, saying he would not accept a pardon because he had done nothing wrong. He became the best-known guerrilla leader never to accept the amnesty. He continued working underground, creating urban guerrilla cells and maintaining some armed fighters in the hills, although they undertook few violent actions. The political wing, the PRV, operated in major cities across the country. One was the picturesque Andean town of Mérida, where the city's liberal University of the Andes (ULA) proved a fertile recruiting ground.

One of the students at the ULA was Hugo Chávez's brother Adán. The oldest of the six Chávez boys was the most politically precocious. While Hugo's mind was mainly on baseball as a teenager and he never joined any political movements, by the time Adán was sixteen he had joined the MIR. He described it as a "Marxist-Leninist organization. There I started my political and revolutionary education." To this day Hugo jokingly refers to his older brother as "the communist in the family."

Adán spent a few years in the party, into the early 1970s. But it "started to degenerate, becoming a revisionist party which even split into two factions: one which continued to call itself the MIR and the other called New Alternative. I decided not to join either of the groups. I did not agree with revisionism and I was of the opinion that we needed to build a genuine revolutionary party in contact with the masses. We were a group of youngsters, doing work in the university. We spent more or less a year and a half like that, until we joined another party."

The party was the PRV. Adán joined Ruptura, a legalized political arm of Bravo's struggling armed revolutionary movement. To Adán Chávez, it seemed to be the most promising vehicle for revolutionary change in Venezuela. As he graduated from the ULA and landed a post there as a physics professor, he also moonlighted as an organizer for the PRV-Ruptura, engaging in "urban guerrilla work." His job was mainly to recruit students for the movement. It was not an easy task. Even though Ruptura was a legal party, it still faced persecution from the government because of its ties to Bravo. Ruptura members operated semi-clandestinely because they might be arrested or even "disappeared" by the government. "Because of its clandestine character this party did not have contact with the masses," Adán Chávez said. "Furthermore, they were very dogmatic and sectarian."

Hugo Chávez knew very little of his brother's secret political activities during this period, although he was aware of his increasingly radicalized political ideology. When he was studying at the military academy in the first half of the 1970s, Adán occasionally showed up in his sandals and long shaggy hair to call on the clean-cut cadet. Other times, when

Hugo went home to Barinas, Adán came in from nearby Mérida, and they went out with some of his hippie-like friends. They talked politics. "Adán was one of the ones who most influenced my political attitudes. He has a great responsibility for my formation," Chávez said in a 2004 interview. "My brother was in Mérida and was a member of the MIR. I didn't know it, it just drew my attention that he and his friends went around with long hair, some of them with beards. Apparently I was out of place with my short hair, my uniform. I felt good with this group. We'd go to a young guys' bar, near my mother's house. Especially to one that was called Nights of Hungary . . ."

It was a time when another offshoot of the Communist Party founded in 1968, the Movement to Socialism (MAS), was growing into an important political force, led by former guerrillas including Teodoro Petkoff. Chávez's high school friends the Ruíz brothers were also involved in the nascent Causa R. "We were friends, and they accepted me with the uniform and everything," Chávez recalled. "There was also a lot of discussion, of course. One time one of these guys, a young man, told me, 'This soldier must be one of those parasites.' We almost traded punches, but the group defended me. 'Respect him, man, this is Hugo Chávez, our friend.' There was a lot of political discussion and a lot of reading. I was getting more and more interested in social issues. However, if I look back, since childhood I always had sympathy for the rebels. That area of Sabaneta was an area of insurgents."

By Christmas 1977, as Chávez's disillusionment with the military was growing, he went home to Barinas for the holidays and confessed his frustrations to Adán. He told his brother that he was thinking of resigning. He asked if he could find him a job at the ULA. Adán counseled his brother to stay in the military. For the first time he revealed his own clandestine activities with the PRV.

At the time, Bravo's group was in the midst of a transition from the heyday of guerrilla warfare in the 1960s. They had long ago concluded that this strategy was unfeasible in Venezuela, and in 1975 they completely disbanded the FALN. They instituted what they called the *Virage Tactico*, tactical turnaround. Largely ending the rural insurgency in part because many *campesinos* were flocking to the cities, they refocused their work on urban centers.

They also implemented a strategy dubbed the *tres patas*, three legs. It was similar to the four legs espoused by La Causa R's Alfredo Maneiro.

Bravo's first leg was *el pueblo* — union members, farmers, students, barrio dwellers, cultural and community organizations. Organizers such as Adán Chávez worked on this segment, trying to build support among the masses. The second leg was the church. To advance that agenda, Bravo's people conducted a series of secret meetings with progressive Roman Catholic priests including the Reverend Arturo Sosa, a bright young Jesuit from a well-to-do family who years later became head of the religious order in Venezuela.

The third leg was the armed forces. PRV leaders met with Izarra in the air force, with a subversive cell in the navy, and with Hugo Trejo, one of the main military leaders of the civic-military movement that toppled Pérez Jiménez. Bravo envisioned all three legs eventually uniting to participate in a similar civilian-military uprising to overthrow the AD-COPEI hegemony. He dreamed of some kind of socialist system distinct from the Soviet and Cuban models he abhorred and infused with a nationalistic, Bolivarian flavor.

After Hugo Chávez poured out his frustrations that Christmas season, Adán informed him that PRV members had already been talking about him. Hugo heeded the advice dispensed by his brother and by José Esteban Ruíz Guevara, the old communist from Barinas. He returned to the barracks and kept his eyes open for ways to advance the cause of transforming Venezuela.

One soon presented itself. He was transferred from the antiguerrilla unit in the east to a military base in the city of Maracay in central Venezuela. He was still a communications officer. But when he arrived in Maracay and saw an array of tanks, he realized how much more useful they could be to his plans someday. "As a soldier, little by little I realized that as a communications officer I would not have much power or capacity for action. So in Maracay when I saw the French AMX 30 tanks I asked for a change to tanks. That was the power." A year later, his request was granted.

He kept talking to Adán. By early 1979 Adán broached the idea of meeting with Bravo. Hugo "was immediately ready to make the contact," according to Adán.

The encounter would not be a simple task. Bravo was still a wanted man. He was living clandestinely in the Montalban section of Caracas. To avoid being recognized and arrested, he rarely left his apartment during the day. When he did go out at night, he often wore disguises including wigs, hats, and dark glasses.

The PRV assigned the sensitive task of arranging the meeting between Bravo and Chávez to one of its most trusted operatives, Nelson Sánchez. When Douglas Bravo had hoped to accelerate his attempts to infiltrate the armed forces in the late 1970s, he'd picked Sánchez to lead the creation of a new "career military front" of officers willing to align themselves with the PRV with the goal of overthrowing Venezuela's political system. Sánchez spent much of 1976 through 1978 studying Venezuelan military history and everything else about soldiers, from how they talked to how they thought to what they ate. "Since 1976 we were studying the psychology and class composition of the members of the armed forces, their likes, their customs, their worries. It was a truly scientific study, since conspiracy and insurrection is not exactly a game." He discovered that one way to reach the hearts and minds of many soldiers was by talking about topics like corruption in the armed forces and border conflicts with Colombia and Guyana.

Sánchez took on another code name for his contact with the military — Harold. He met with Izarra and other members of his R-83 movement. By 1979 he received the name of another promising officer who might be willing to join the conspiracy: Hugo Chávez. By then Chávez was on the road to being promoted again, eventually winning an assignment to teach at his alma mater, the military academy in Caracas. His superiors had no idea of his growing restlessness.

Sánchez set in motion the plan to connect Chávez and Bravo. He instructed Adán Chávez that the first contact would take place at Fort Tiuna, where the military academy was housed. They established a password so that when the PRV activists met Hugo, he would know it was them. Gaining access to Fort Tiuna was not simple — Sánchez could not just drive onto the base and ask for Chávez. So he contacted a cousin of his, Elizabeth Sánchez, who was divorced from a soldier and had a special military identification card that allowed her onto the base.

With Sánchez posing as her chauffeur, they drove late one morning to Fort Tiuna. They entered and had a guard call Chávez. He came down to meet them. When he asked who'd sent them, they said Adán, and gave him the password. They met for about ten minutes in a parking lot near some gardens. It was a brief but important encounter. Chávez was entering into a relationship with Douglas Bravo and his forces. It would play an influential role in forming the ideology behind a revolutionary movement that eventually turned Venezuela upside down.

• • •

One week later Chávez and Bravo met. Separately, they were secretly shuttled to Elizabeth Sánchez's house in the middle-class Altos Prados de María neighborhood. It was a good location for clandestine meetings. Cars could pull into a concealed driveway and let their passengers enter directly into the house without neighbors seeing them. Besides, it was night.

The two men met for about an hour. This time Chávez was far more loquacious than in his meeting with Causa R leader Alfredo Maneiro. He and Bravo spoke about current political events in Venezuela, the idea of recruiting rebels in the military, the notion of a possible civilian-military uprising. Chávez made a good impression on Bravo and Sánchez — sure of himself and determined to reform the country. "I understood that he was a very daring guy, very intelligent, and strong-willed," Bravo said two and a half decades later and after a falling-out with Chávez. "He was prepared to carry out this work over the long term . . . From that moment on we started a long-term project."

Chávez and Bravo initiated a series of meetings that lasted for several years, with "Harold" serving as the go-between. They sometimes met as often as once a week, although the frequency of the encounters varied. The rendezvous point often was Elizabeth Sánchez's house. They developed code names of their own. Bravo was Martín; Chávez was José María. The *José* came from independence war general and Bolívar ally José Antonio Páez, whom Chávez admired. The *María* came from Maisanta and the "Madre Santa" he shouted each time he headed into combat.

The two men developed a close relationship, albeit one the Venezuelan public still knows little about. Even some of Chávez's co-conspirators in the military did not know about it. Chávez realized that if they discovered his alliance with the communist Bravo, they would be repulsed. He was forced to live a double life not only within the military, but within the conspiratorial movement itself, concealing relationships from those who would be alienated if they found out who else he was aligned with. He did this by forming small "rings," cells whose members did not know the identity of the members of other cells. Many such soldier-members had no idea Chávez was cavorting with a communist like Douglas Bravo. One founding member of Chávez's movement in the military, Jesús Urdaneta Hernández, did not discover Chávez's link to Bravo until the early 1990s. "If I had learned he had these ties, I never would have accompanied him" in the movement, Urdaneta said in 2005. "Chávez is an astute man from this point of view. He played games with us — he knew who was who. He navigated through those waters."

Likewise, Bravo would have wanted nothing to do with soldiers such as Urdaneta, whom he viewed as a stereotypical right-wing military gorilla. To appeal to his cohorts in the military, Chávez framed his movement not in terms of Bravo's Marxism and communism, but in terms of Bolívar's nationalism and Latin American unity. Bolívar they could accept; Bravo, never.

He got the message clearly one day when he told a close ally in the military he was going to meet with Bravo. "His reaction was to ask me if I was crazy, that he was a communist, a guerrilla, that he killed soldiers. Right away I told him no, that it was a lie" — he was not going to meet with Bravo at all. "Later I spoke with another who didn't have the years of the guerrillas so fresh in his memory to have a negative idea about Douglas Bravo. But he also rejected him just like my other closer friends . . . So I maintained a relationship with the movement [and Bravo] more on a personal level. I continued working with a nationalist Bolivarian profile, and realized this got through to the armed forces, this fell like a seed on fertile ground. On the other hand, if you spoke about ex-guerrillas it became very difficult to advance, to discuss. There was a natural rejection, above all because of their military formation."

Chávez's incipient movement was neither purely communist nor purely Bolivarian. It was a mix of things, and would continue to add new elements as it developed. It eventually incorporated everything from Tony Blair's "Third Way" in England to Mao's thoughts in China, although Chávez's central underlying motivation was to correct the social injustices of Venezuela. Urdaneta, who later broke bitterly with Chávez partly because he believed the president was betraying the Bolivarian roots of the movement and giving too much power to discredited civilians, described him — perhaps harshly — as a "sugar cane crushing machine. He grabs you, he sticks you in, he squeezes you, he takes out everything he has to take out, then he throws you in the garbage."

As Chávez's movement began to take shape in the early 1980s, Venezuela's oil boom days were coming to a crashing and, for him, fortuitous end. While the country took in a whopping $150 billion between 1973 and 1983, much of the oil money disappeared. Government corruption and inefficiency were rampant. By 1978 the

Pérez administration "undertook the first fateful step toward the crisis of the 1980s, when it contracted several large, short-term loans to cover the balance of payments deficit and to continue industrial expansion projects." Venezuela's external debt started to balloon. A wide range of government ministries and institutes took out international loans, often without congressional approval. For several years the true size of the debt was not even known. As it later turned out, half of it was not recorded or approved.

When COPEI's Luis Herrera Campins ran for president in 1978, his slogan was "*Donde Estan Los Reales?*" — where is the money? He won, and in his inauguration speech in February 1979 declared he was receiving a "mortgaged country." He pledged to scale back spending. But between 1978 and 1981 the Iranian revolution triumphed, war between Iraq and Iran broke out, and oil prices took a second jump, from $13 to the breathless figure of $34 a barrel. Herrera ended up spending as much in the first three years of his administration as Pérez had in five.

His fiscal laxness came back to haunt him. In the early 1980s oil prices collapsed. Revenue from petroleum exports plummeted from just below $20 billion in 1981 to $11 billion in 1983. At the same time, large short-term debts were coming due. Herrera Campins resisted devaluing the previously rock-solid bolivar from its exchange rate of 4.3 to every US dollar to compensate for the changed economic reality. But by February 18, 1983, he could no longer postpone the inevitable. That day became known as "Black Friday."

Herrera Campins announced a new, three-tiered exchange system. By the end of the year the free-market rate for the bolivar, once widely regarded as the blue-chip Latin currency, tripled. By the end of the following year, unemployment in the urban sector nearly doubled, from 7.8 percent to 14.3 percent. The external debt — finally revealed to the public — stood at $34.2 billion. That was nearly double the figure for 1978. It made Venezuela the fourth largest debtor in Latin America, after Brazil, Mexico, and Argentina. The party was over. Things would only get worse.

Two months before Black Friday, the Venezuelan armed forces were preparing their annual ceremonies marking the death of the nation's leading light, Simón Bolívar. At the military base in Maracay that was home to the heart of the air force, they needed a speaker. Chávez, who was taking a course there, was an obvious choice. He was a budding expert on

Bolívar and promoted him every chance he got, handing out books and painting his image on barracks walls. At about 1 P.M. on December 17, 1982, the troops assembled on a patio. Chávez got up to talk.

His speech was not the typical ceremonial pabulum expected at such patriotic events commemorating the dead forefathers. Instead, he delivered a fiery, rebellious talk that grabbed the attention of his superiors and fellow soldiers. Bolívar was still alive, he said, and angry over the mess Venezuelans had made of their country and Latin Americans of their region. It was a not-so-subtle call to revolt, as he later stated:

> I started remembering [Cuban independence hero José] Martí. "There is Bolívar in the heavens of America, vigilant and frowning . . . because what he didn't do, still has to be done today." And I tied in the situation of that moment. "How can you say Bolívar still doesn't have anything to do in America, with so much poverty, with so much misery? How can you say Bolívar has nothing to do?"
>
> When I finished the speech after about half an hour . . . I immediately felt the enormous tension of the officers. The formation broke up and we left running, one along side the other. Major Flores Gilán ordered everyone to stop and stand at attention, and told me in a very hard tone, "Chávez, you seem like a politician." During that time calling someone a politician, especially someone in the barracks, was an offense. Politics had degenerated so much it was like calling someone a liar, a demagogue . . .

A colonel broke the tension by ordering everyone to remain silent. The night before, he continued, Chávez had informed him of everything he was going to say. "No one believed him, but it saved the situation for the moment," Chávez recalled. They returned to the barracks. A friend of Chávez's, Felipe Acosta Carles, suggested they go for a run to relieve the tension. They invited along two colleagues — Urdaneta and Lieutenant Raúl Isaías Baduel, who was a year behind Chávez and his classmates at the academy.

Chávez changed out of his uniform, but couldn't find his sneakers. So he put on his baseball shoes with plastic cleats. It was about 2 P.M. They took a slow, six-mile run toward a place known as La Placera and a famous tree called the Samán de Güere. Simón Bolívar was said to have slept beneath it with his troops before the crucial battle of Carabobo in 1821. Chávez was seething with anger. As they jogged it occurred to him to ask his colleagues to formally create an organization that would rescue the values of the fatherland, dignify the military career, and fight corruption.

When they reached the tree, Chávez made his proposal. The men accepted. Chávez improvised an oath to swear them in. He invoked the pledge Bolívar had made in 1805 in Rome before Simón Rodríguez when he swore to devote his life to liberating Venezuela from the "Spanish yoke." Chávez added three of Zamora's key slogans to the new oath:

> I swear by the God of my parents, I swear by my nation, I swear by my honor that I will not allow my soul to rest, nor my arm to relax, until I have broken the chains that oppress my people through the will of the powerful. Free elections, free land and free men, horror to the oligarchy.

It was a historic moment. Chávez was finally creating a serious, secret political conspiracy within the military. He was twenty-eight years old. It was five years after his initial and short-lived attempt to create a tiny conspiratorial cell in eastern Venezuela. They named the new group the Bolivarian Revolutionary Army-200, or EBR-200 in Spanish. The letters were a play on the names of the heroes who were to serve as the guiding lights of the movement: Ezequiel Zamora, Simón Bolívar, and Simón Rodríguez. Borrowing a page from Douglas Bravo, they became the "three roots of the tree" of Chávez's movement. They added the 200 to mark the yearlong celebrations taking place to honor the two hundredth anniversary of the birth of the Liberator in July 1783.

Chávez's movement was not clearly defined. He hardly had a concrete plan to overthrow the government or launch a coup. "At that moment, the Bolivarian movement that was being born did not propose political objectives," he said. "Its goals were imminently internal. Its efforts were directed in the first place to studying the military history of Venezuela as a source of a military doctrine of our own, which up to then didn't exist . . . There we formed a movement that was essentially democratic. There we discovered the teacher Simón Rodríguez, the leader Simón Bolívar and the fighter Ezequiel Zamora."

Urdaneta, who eventually became one of Chávez's chief critics, said the initial goal of the movement was not "to topple the government . . . The purpose was to become conscious of the reality of our country. In some ways they want to stick the soldier between the four walls of the barracks and isolate him from what is a reality, which is his country. And that is impossible . . . We detested the corruption and we realized that one corrupt officer came with a group of officers who were also corrupt. They went around together and were a combo. That's why we called them combos of corruption. So we said, the vagabonds unite and on the other hand the honest men are isolated and stepped on by the vagabonds. Why don't we unite, too, to confront them? That's how we started to organize."

The movement was amorphous enough to mean different things to different people. To Urdaneta, a staunch anticommunist, it was a democratic, nationalist movement based on Bolívar's ideals, neither of the left or the right. To Chávez, who was meeting secretly with Douglas Bravo, the idea was to take the best of all systems and merge them under the central unifying banner of Bolívar. The Liberator was the trunk; Rodríguez and Zamora were the main roots to the side; other thinkers and ideas were welcome to help nourish the tree. "This tree has to be a circumference, it has to accept all kinds of ideas, from the right, from the left, from the ideological ruins of those old capitalist and communist systems," Chávez said. "There are elements or ruins that are gigantic, and they must be taken."

While Bolívar was the central unifying force of the tree, Zamora offered a key element to Chávez's ideology. A long-forgotten nineteenth-century radical and revolutionary, Chávez brought him back to life. In some ways he could identify even more with Zamora than with Bolívar. The Liberator was a landowning oligarch and a white Creole — one born in Latin America but of Spanish descent. His aristocratic family in Caracas could afford to send him to study in Europe as a teenager. Zamora, in contrast, came from the llanos, was of humble origins, and had a direct connection with the *campesinos* of Barinas.

Zamora dreamed of uniting civilians and soldiers in his project. In a famous portrait of the warrior-hero made after his victory at Santa Inés, Zamora is depicted wearing two hats, one atop the other in an unusual way: The first is an ordinary bowler, the second a military cap, together symbolizing his desire to unify the armed forces and civil society. As a young man Chávez, still an avid painter, often painted copies of the portrait. Years later he sent out Christmas cards adorned with a drawing of Zamora's face. His devotion was so intense he suggested to friends that if reincarnation were possible, he might have been Zamora in an earlier life.

After taking the oath that day in Maracay, Chávez and the three others started jogging back to the barracks, although he and Baduel later jumped on a public bus to finish the long trip. Back at the military base, they kept talking about their plans at the officers' club. They discussed how they would organize themselves, how they would recruit new members, who would carry out each task. They discussed setting up a security system. They agreed they would bring no new soldiers into the movement without first consulting the others.

Eventually they developed the system of "rings" of security. The first circle comprised the "supersafe" members of the movement who formed its inner core and could be trusted completely. The others included a secondary group of trusted members, neutral soldiers, and "enemies" — intelligence agents or traitors who could infiltrate and betray the movement.

The group also developed an elaborate communications system. They carried around a book about Bolívar by Augusto Mijares and devised a set of code words based on the text. "If you called me and told me the telephone of your sister or your mother is 258342," Chávez recalled, "the 42 was the number of the page, and there were the code words that we wanted to say." The security systems worked well. Chávez and his cohorts were to operate their clandestine subversive movement inside the military for a decade with superiors unable — or in some cases unwilling — to stop it.

The day after they took the oath under the great tree, Chávez was in his office at the base when the impetuous Acosta Carles pulled up in his car and ran in excitedly. He blurted out that he had his first recruit for the movement. Chávez was pleased and angry at the same time. They needed to exercise supreme caution. But they also needed new members. Acosta assured him the new recruit was a good find: At least come out and see him. He's in the car. Chávez walked outside. Sitting in the vehicle was Ronald Blanco La Cruz, a promising young soldier. He was to become of one of Chávez's key allies.

Chávez's recruiting efforts were soon to take off — right in the heart of the military. His superiors had made the mistake of naming him an instructor back in his alma mater, the military academy. Chávez would have direct access to Venezuela's best and brightest cadets.

# 6

# The Conspiracy Deepens

Chávez turned the military academy into his chief recruiting ground. His appointment as an instructor in 1981 could not have been a luckier stroke. He had at his feet a platoon of impressionable young cadets, including many who came from humble families and shared his disgust over Venezuela's corroded political and military institutions. They eagerly ate up the rebellious talk of the charismatic captain who spent hours extolling the thoughts of Bolívar, Zamora, and Rodríguez.

"We knew the enemies of Venezuela were hunger, corruption, misery, unemployment and the handing over of the nation's immense abundance of riches," remembered Pedro Carreño, one of the cadets who two decades later won a seat in Congress as part of Chávez's coalition. "In the military academy we spoke about this, because the topic of security and defense is preponderant."

At the beginning Chávez was completely alone. It was some four years after he had formed the ephemeral cell in eastern Venezuela where he and a few other soldiers buried grenades in the ground. At the academy "I started it in silence, with a lot of discipline, with a lot of attention to the boys" — the cadets.

He began his recruiting efforts, he stated in April 2007 interviews, by focusing on the one hundred or so cadets directly under his command at the military academy. Then he turned to the approximately three hundred he taught in classes. He said he tried to obtain as many hours as possible in the classroom so he would have maximum contact with cadets and possible recruits for his movement. He also ran sports programs, which became another venue for attracting candidates. In addition, he organized cultural activities, such as theatrical shows that reenacted historical events. He would assign cadets the roles of various historical figures, including Bolívar and Zamora. He also talked to many individual cadets during guard duty and other solitary activities. "It was a combination" of methods, he said, adding that the cadets "were the backbone of the revolutionary movement in the army."

Chávez meticulously studied each one to determine who might be inclined to join his secret movement. He pored over their personnel files. He learned about their families, their social status, their roots. He automatically ruled out anyone who came from the upper classes. Even those who came from poor families had to show they had the proper outlook to be considered. "One error would have been fatal," he said, noting that fortunately he never committed one in eleven years of recruiting inside and later outside the academy.

When he was confident they would join and remain loyal to the movement, he moved to incorporate them as members. They replicated the oath-taking of December 17, 1982. Often they gathered at night on the academy's patio to swear in new members.

Chávez spoke with the recruits alone and in small groups. They talked in the academy, in an apartment Ronald Blanco La Cruz had in Caracas, or in the small room above the garage at Elizabeth Sánchez's house. Chávez spread his rebellious message at the academy under his guise as professor of history and military doctrine. On billboards he posted the sayings of Bolívar, Zamora, Rodríguez, and Maisanta, along with other information about them. At times his efforts were hardly subtle. Like other officers he took his troops out jogging at 4:30 A.M. But instead of traditional war songs he had them sing a hymn from the era of the Federal Wars that paid homage to Zamora:

> The overcast sky warns of storms to come,
> While the sun behind the clouds loses its bright shine
> Oligarchs tremble, long live freedom!
> The troops of Zamora, at the bugle's sound
> Will destroy the brigades of the reactionary scoundrels.

The contact with the young soldiers reenergized Chávez and pumped life into his fledgling organization. He was operating under the noses of his superiors, yet few suspected he was building a subversive movement. He often talked with or even acted like the "enemy" in the military to fool higher-ups, he stated in April 2007.

"In my notebook I can demonstrate how we functioned in the classrooms of the Military Academy, during normal class hours, on the patios and when we jogged," Chávez once noted. When he arrived there, "I still had my doubts . . . this dilemma, what am I doing here. I felt this impulse for politics. I felt this thing inside me and lived with this contradiction." But the cadets "stimulated me and erased the dilemma . . . It gave me an extraordinary force and I forgot for good about requesting a discharge or any other alternative . . . Every day with them, I returned to being just another cadet. You live the pureness of youth there. That was the seed bed of the rebellion . . . That's why I call it my second graduation class. I was with them almost all four years."

Carreño calculates that by the time he and his classmates completed their studies, at least 30 out of 133 graduates were sworn members of the movement. Before they left and were assigned to posts all over the country, they pledged to maintain contact with at least two cadets back at the academy so the movement would not die. The class of 1985 produced some of the key members of Chávez's movement and comrades in arms. They included Diosdado Cabello and Florencio Porras, who two decades later were to become state governors as Chávez rose to power.

Besides the classroom, Chávez had another recruiting tool — baseball. He organized a team at the academy. On weekends he sometimes took the cadets in a military academy bus to Sánchez's house, where they celebrated team victories and eventually held meetings of the Bolivarian movement. Chávez was a regular at the house, where he continued his secret meetings with "Martín" — Douglas Bravo.

Amid all the conspiring, Chávez was a family man, too. He and Nancy Colmenares were busy with their three young children, Rosa Virginia, María Gabriela, and Hugo Rafael. Even by the accounts of people who later became his political enemies, Chávez was a doting and tender father. He spent as much time as he could with his family amid his numerous activities. He made sure the children had school uniforms, books, and other necessities. Even in fatherhood, however, thoughts of revolution were not far from his mind. As his children grew older, he helped them draw Christmas cards. They featured a depiction of Simón Bolívar.

The children sometimes seemed mystified by Chávez's unorthodox lifestyle and the mysterious mission that consumed his time. In 1995 his second oldest, María Gabriela, by then fifteen, wrote him a moving letter about their relationship. "Since I was a girl, I've been trying to understand you, Dad," she said. "There were things I didn't understand and now I understand. 'It was and is the struggle,' and that love of country, of humanity." She recalled how he would take them to a farm with an inviting river — but they didn't have bathing suits to swim because of "that mystery." She remembered him reading them poems about Bolívar and how he once tore up a piece of money the two girls were fighting over, saying, "Money isn't worth anything, only love is." She ended the letter by saying, "You are my great love, my teacher, my brother, my best friend, my father. I ask you, please, don't let your boat get far from mine."

María Gabriela and Chávez's other children from his first marriage largely shun the public light. So does their mother, Nancy Colmenares. Chávez rarely mentions her in public. While by some accounts she was a humble, hardworking, and well-liked woman in her native Barinas, she did not share Chávez's passion for history, his obsession with Bolívar, or his growing restlessness over Venezuela's future.

In 1984 he met someone else who did. Herma Marksman was a history professor who was going through a difficult divorce. She was moving to Caracas from the eastern city of Ciudad Bolívar to start a new life. She hoped to teach in a high school and pursue a postgraduate degree in the economic and social history of Venezuela. Her sister Cristina was living in Elizabeth Sánchez's spacious, three-story house in Caracas. Herma and her two children joined her temporarily until she could find permanent housing. She was in transition, shuttling back and forth between the capital and Ciudad Bolívar.

One night in April 1984 Marksman and Sánchez were on an upper floor of the house when a car pulled up outside. Out stepped Hugo Chávez. Sánchez asked Marksman to greet him at the door and ask what he wanted, since she was getting ready to go out.

Chávez was with his brother Argenis and had come to ask if he could borrow Sánchez's house the following night. His baseball team was finishing a championship series the next day. He wanted to celebrate if they won. It was fine with Sánchez, Marksman told him, and the two sat down to chat a bit. They found they had some things in common. "That night we started to talk like anyone would. He showed a great concern about the armed forces, about the deterioration of the country, while I spoke about education . . . and the need to come up with correctives, to implement reforms." As he got up to leave, Chávez gave Marksman his business card. If you ever need anything, he told her, give me a call.

By the next day Marksman had forgotten all about him. She went out to dinner with friends and was surprised when she came home about midnight and saw a military bus parked out front. Chávez and his teammates were inside celebrating. Marksman went in, said hello, went to the kitchen to get a glass of water, and then returned to bid him good night. She had to get to bed since she was taking an early flight to Bolívar. But Chávez wouldn't let her go so easily, as she recounts the story. "He told me, 'No, let's talk. What we spoke about yesterday was very interesting. Stay awhile with us.' So I stayed, and that's how we started to get to know each other."

She flew to Bolívar in the morning to continue preparing her move to Caracas. Chávez — according to her recounting — kept asking her sister Cristina about her and requesting her telephone number. Cristina told him he would have to wait until Herma returned. She finally moved to Caracas for good in August 1984, and started to bump into Chávez more and more at the house. "At first I thought he went to that house only for reasons of friendship, because there was a very beautiful relationship with that family, with Elizabeth, her children and him. But it bothered me that sometimes he came and asked, 'Did Martín call? Has Martín come?' And one time I asked Elizabeth, Who is Martín? Well, he's a friend of Nelson [Sánchez] who comes sometimes to talk with Hugo."

Martín was a mysterious figure to Marksman. Every time he was to arrive at the house, strange things happened. Herma had a room on the second floor, and Elizabeth Sánchez would instruct her to stay there. A meeting was going to take place in a room downstairs, Sánchez told her, and no one should open the door. Marksman could not imagine what was happening.

The mystery deepened one day when Elizabeth traveled out of town. Marksman decided to clean up a cobwebbed storage room at the back of the house where Sánchez often washed clothes and hung them to dry. The room was full of magazines, books, and documents. As Marksman started dusting, they caught her attention. Among them were the magazine *Ruptura* from Bravo's group, Mao Tse-tung's *Red Book*, and other leftist literature.

When Sánchez returned, Marksman confronted her. I want you to tell me what is going on in this house, she said, because I'm here with my two children and my sister, too. Sánchez was caught off guard. She could no longer hide the truth. She told Marksman what was going on. The materials belong to my cousin Nelson, Sánchez said, and, you know, he has leftist ideas. He's a member of the PRV. And I am going to tell you who Martín is. I think it is time to tell you the truth. Martín is none other than Douglas Bravo. My cousin Nelson is the right-hand man of Douglas and he's involved in forming a civilian-military group. "She explained to it to me, and I understood why he [Chávez] came on a regular basis, and sometimes brought the boys from the academy," Marksman later recalled. "That's how I started to get to know him little by little."

Marksman was intrigued more than alarmed by the revelation. She and Chávez began to see more of each other. On her thirty-fifth birthday that September, Chávez showed up at the house with a big bouquet of flowers to celebrate with some other friends who were there. As the evening ended and he went to say good-bye, he said he wanted to have a "serious" conversation with her. He invited her to go out for a cup of coffee away from the house.

The following Monday he swung by and took her to the commercial district of Sabana Grande in eastern Caracas. As they sat in a café sipping coffee, Chávez confessed everything. By Marksman's account, he said he liked her and that he was going to be "frank." I am a person with a double life, he told her. In the day I am an officer in the armed forces. I belong to the army. I try to fulfill my duties. But I also have another, dangerous activity. The rest of my time I dedicate to a conspiratorial movement called the EBR — the Bolivarian Revolutionary Army. It's made up of military officers, but we also need to recruit civilians. I want you to accompany me in this struggle to the final days. "From that moment," Marksman said, "I started to help him prepare the meetings."

Chávez had something of a reputation as a ladies' man, which was not unusual in Venezuela, where few marriages were exclusive arrangements. Marksman was not unaware of it when she met him. EBR-200 co-founder Jesús Urdaneta joked that "when Chávez was young, he couldn't see a broom stick in a skirt because he would fall in love."

Still, the relationship with Marksman was to be different. She was a serious woman, an intellectual. She and Chávez were brought together by a common passion for Venezuelan history and a desire to reform the country. Marksman was hardly attracted to him for his looks — Chávez was skinny and far from handsome. Instead, she was drawn in by his interests and the Bolívar-inspired mission that propelled him. He was also a charming *llanero*. He engaged in spirited conversation for hours, telling stories, cracking jokes, singing *llanero* songs.

Before long Marksman turned, in a way, into Chávez's Manuela Sáenz, the well-read, longtime companion of Bolívar who aided the Liberator in his independence struggle and whom some consider one of the most influential, though overlooked, women in Latin American history. Marksman helped organize meetings of the Bolivarian conspirators. She served as a key contact between Chávez and his military cohorts, and alerted them when military investigators were hot on their trail. She functioned as a bridge between Chávez and civilian groups. She took notes at meetings, maintained an archive of Chávez's secret documents, and burned some when authorities were closing in. She stored many of his personal effects for safekeeping, including his first clip of hair, family photographs, diaries, letters, newspaper articles, and certificates.

An apartment she bought in the middle-class section of El Paraiso in Caracas in 1985 turned into a refuge for Chávez, who often ate, slept, read, and met with co-conspirators there. Marksman sometimes accompanied Chávez as he ran around the country secretly rallying the troops in his free time. There were days when she would drive for hours as the normally indefatigable Chávez, who slept as little as three hours a night, collapsed in exhaustion in the passenger seat.

Much more than a chauffeur or a secretary, Marksman was a respected partner for Chávez, who listened to her opinion and sometimes heeded it. Like Sáenz with Bolívar in his bleakest moments, at times she was nearly the only one at Chávez's side when the movement seemed on the verge of collapse. She became so integrated into the conspiracy, she earned own nom de guerre — Comandante Pedro.

It wasn't a typical romantic relationship. Before he entered into it, Chávez once confessed to Marksman, he sent some friends to investigate her and her background to make sure she wasn't a spy and wouldn't betray him and the movement. But Chávez could be tender and romantic — he often brought her flowers or chocolate, serenaded her, and brought her medicine when she was sick.

But he was also Chávez. The first present he gave Marksman was a copy of the book about Maisanta by the Barinas doctor José León Tapia that first revealed to Chávez the other side of the story about his great-grandfather. On another occasion when she fell down some stairs and cut open her forehead, Chávez came to visit her every day as she recovered. One night he showed up with some tapes of a narrator reading speeches and documents by Bolívar. The idea, Chávez told her, was that she could play them while she was asleep so she could have the Liberator ever-present.

Chávez didn't have time for frivolous activities — he was on a mission to save Venezuela. "He said the purpose of his life was his project," Marksman later said. "He feels he has a mission to fulfill and he is going to fulfill it . . . This preoccupation he has for those who have nothing has always marked his life — the excluded ones. Perhaps because he comes from a situation where he lacked so much."

In the nine years they were close, Chávez and Marksman almost never had time to see a movie together. She remembers only one: *Fatal Vision*. They didn't even go to the movie theater. It was on television. But they got along well. Neither was inclined to spend time in bars or at the beach like many Venezuelans. They preferred to stay home and read, something Chávez often did at her house. "The image I have of Hugo Chávez is of a man who was always reading," recalled Marksman, who later broke bitterly with him. He read everything, but especially enjoyed tales of history and great leaders. He even had a book about how to give talks on different occasions — funerals, Masses, political events. From the moment she met him, Marksman believed Chávez was going to go far. "He had an indefatigable tenacity. He knew what he wanted and where he was going."

When Marksman met Chávez, his movement was on the upswing. It was in the middle of a period of expansion that lasted from about 1982 to 1986. The group held regular meetings, mostly in private homes or apartments, usually with just a few people present for security reasons. They assigned tasks to members who made five-minute presentations on different topics. Marksman, for instance, was assigned the topic of Simón Rodríguez at one point and had to research him and give a short talk. Others might be sent to investigate the problems of Venezuela's educational system or economy, then report back to the group. Chávez wanted to prepare them in case one day they took power. The military officers did not know about his meetings with Bravo on the side, and he told Marksman to keep it quiet. He knew most of them would not accept it.

Besides his success in recruiting cadets at the military academy, Chávez was also resuming his contacts with the Causa R. He was a different man from the day in 1978 when he'd secretly met Alfredo Maneiro and barely opened his mouth. Now Chávez was far surer of himself and where he was headed. He had met briefly with Causa R leader Pablo Medina in 1983 after Maneiro's death, although nothing came of it. But two years later he decided to contact Medina again.

It could not have come at a better time for the Causa R leader. His group was in disarray after the 1983 passing of central figure Maneiro. It had suffered a string of defeats. The nation's largest union, the CTV, which was controlled by Democratic Action, had intervened with the workers' union in Ciudad Guayana, firing three thousand workers and undermining the Causa R's influence. The group barely existed outside Ciudad Guayana. In Caracas its membership numbered no more than half a dozen. "We had to raise it from nothing," according to Medina.

Chávez's reappearance was more than welcome. He and Medina established code names. The Causa R leader baptized him *luz* — light. For Medina, Chávez potentially represented the light at the end of the tunnel for his beleaguered party. From that point on, Causa R leaders and Chávez established a close working relationship. Medina in particular played a significant role in the logistics of Chávez's movement. He arranged apartments or houses for meetings. He came up with money to fix his car. He even sent an airplane to pick up Chávez when he was stationed in remote parts of Venezuela to take him to clandestine meetings in other parts of the country. Marksman served as the contact between the two men.

Chávez had plenty to do. By now a captain, he was racing all over the country in his free time to stay in contact with members and recruit new ones. According to Medina, at one point Chávez wanted to convoke a meeting of one hundred committed officers. Medina thought the idea was crazy. Military intelligence probably would detect them and put them in jail. He counseled against it and, according to Medina, Chávez accepted the advice. Douglas Bravo also was worried the movement was growing too rapidly: With so many new members coming in, he felt, intelligence agents could easily infiltrate. He advised Chávez to stop expanding and close the circle. But in those days the up-and-down movement was decidedly up.

Chávez's conspiracy was becoming so successful that starting in 1985 they launched a series of five national "congresses" held around the country. The first took place on November 9, 1985, in Catia La Mar near the Simón Bolívar International Airport on the Caribbean coast about half an hour's drive from Caracas. They arranged to use the house of a friend of Ronald Blanco La Cruz for the weekend. They invited about two dozen people — mainly soldiers and a few progressive civilians. They held a cookout complete with barbecue, beer, and music. But the party was just a cover. The real goal was to recruit new members, discuss the group's project, and analyze the national political situation. Most met in a room inside the house, while some stayed outside in the yard to maintain the appearance of a fiesta. A few even danced to the salsa music.

Chávez got the idea of holding congresses during a discussion with a Communist Party leader in Mérida whose son, Ruben Avila, was a cadet in the military academy. Borrowing their model, he came up with an agenda, handed it out ahead of time, and assigned topics for members to present. They kept the materials camouflaged in case they fell into enemy hands.

By now Chávez had moved beyond his initial stage of mainly analyzing Venezuela's sociopolitical situation and Bolívar's thoughts. He was more actively weighing some kind of civil-military uprising, acts of sabotage, or even a coup. He didn't believe forming a political party would work — AD and COPEI held a death grip on the electoral system through fraud and patronage. It wasn't clear when would be the moment to act to overthrow the system. The wood was still wet, although it was drying out.

Five months later, in March 1986, Chávez convened another congress. This one had a special purpose: to fully incorporate Francisco Arias Cárdenas into the movement. Arias graduated from the military academy a year ahead of Chávez. In the late 1970s and early 1980s Arias was in contact with William Izarra's clandestine group based mainly in the air force. Izarra eventually changed the name of the group to ARMA (Alianza Revolucionaria de Militares) since R-83 didn't fit anymore — 1983 came and went with no revolution in sight. Arias also was in contact with "Harold" — Nelson Sánchez, the PRV's liaison to the military. Sánchez would stop by every so often to go out for a cup of coffee or a beer.

Chávez had a good impression of Arias Cárdenas. He was a respected and cerebral officer who had his own following within the military. Chávez wanted him to become more active in the EBR-200.

A native of the western oil city of Maracaibo, Arias Cárdenas had spent ten years in a minor seminary as a boy and teenager during the 1960s. He passed hours poring over documents from Vatican II, the seminal 1968 meeting of Latin American bishops in Medellín, Colombia, where they declared a "preferential option for the poor," and other progressive materials of the period. He eventually left the seminary because he thought the priests he met were too confined to the chapel and the classroom. They were not out in the community and on the streets enough. But Arias departed imbued with the ideals of Vatican II, liberation theology, and social justice for the poor.

Still in his late teens, he figured he had two options. He could enroll in the university, or he could join the military. His family didn't have money for the university, so he applied to the military academy. He was a good student and, like Chávez, embarked on a promising career as an army officer coming out of Venezuela's West Point. But he was racked by the same kind of anxiety over the corrupt political establishment and the suffering of the impoverished masses that troubled Chávez. Short, slight, and soft-spoken, Arias was a soldier but looked and talked more like a priest.

In March 1986 Chávez invited Arias to a congress he was organizing in the city of San Cristóbal in Táchira state on the Colombian border. Arias was stationed nearby. It was to be a small group that included one woman — Marksman.

Chávez and the others were worried intelligence agents were on their trail, so they took extra security precautions. They prepared both for a raid of the apartment that would require a fast escape, and for a siege where they would be forced to fight it out. They met in an apartment on the fifth or sixth floor of a building, bringing with them ropes they planned to use to rappel down the side of the building if they had to flee. A bemused Marksman listened as they instructed her how to use them. She figured there was no way she was going to lunge out a window and slide down a rope. She would simply have to surrender.

The rebels also packed the apartment with assault rifles, grenades, and a week's worth of food, bracing themselves for a prolonged standoff. Chávez even drove a small tank all the way from the remote village of Elorza hundreds of miles away in the llanos, where he had been transferred several months earlier, to just outside San Cristóbal. It was one way of showing that the movement was gaining force. Strikingly, no one in the military stopped him. Most of his superiors seemed blind to his activities, although — as he was learning — not all of them.

Chávez was intent on making a good impression on Arias. He prepared meticulously for the meeting. He came armed with a series of plastic sheets he placed on an overhead projector outlining his Bolivarian project. He and the others talked about the three roots of Bolívar, Rodríguez, and Zamora, the rot in the armed forces, and the pathetic political situation. They spoke about the need for a civilian-military movement and uprising to break the oligarchy's grip on the country through its political surrogates.

Arias agreed with most of the points. By about 3 A.M., six or seven hours into the meeting, discussion turned to how to achieve their goals. Chávez said he believed the group had to spark an insurrection by desta-bilizing Venezuela. He wanted to blow up bridges, electric towers, and oil wells. He wanted to help leftist civilians launch assaults on barracks to steal weapons, and organize urban and rural guerrilla-style units. His proposal was along the lines of Douglas Bravo's ideas of accelerating the "objective situation" to provoke a mass rebellion.

Arias did not like what he was hearing. He thought Chávez's pro-posal was nothing more than a throwback to Bravo's failed guerrilla tactics of the 1960s. Distrustful of civilians in general and of Bravo in particular, Arias opposed letting the PRV take the lead in the move-ment and the rebellion. For one thing, he sensed mutual distrust. Some of the leftist civilians suspected some of the soldiers were right-wing military gorillas similar to the thugs who'd overthrown governments in Chile and Argentina. They wanted the civilians to control the revolt.

But Arias had little confidence in them, either. They seemed stuck in a 1960s paradigm, not realizing that most Venezuelans wanted nothing to do with the guerrilla violence of that era. He also believed that they did not grasp the fundamental difference between Venezuelan soldiers and those from elsewhere in Latin America. If we are the ones who might die or go to prison for years, he thought, we are the ones who should be in charge of the rebellion.

"The same thing that we felt, Douglas and his people felt: lack of confidence," Arias Cárdenas later stated:

> We thought we were putting the meat in the grinder while those people were flying kites and playing around with ecology. We were risking our lives every day . . . I thought we had to be more autono-mous and that we ourselves should control the movement and the process. At times the interventions of Harold tended to cloister us

in a pre-conceived project that did not allow us to think, that did not allow us to create, that limited the horizon a lot . . . We knew that to grow within the armed forces we could not run the risk that the proposals be linked with a Marxist vision of history, of man, of the economy.

Arias rose to his feet at the meeting and declared that he would not accompany "failures." If we as a group want to take power and produce real changes, he continued, we can't abandon the role of the armed forces by turning ourselves into quasi-guerrillas. We're going to lose legitimacy if one of our members is caught blowing up a bridge or helping civilians steal weapons. Let the civilians agitate on the outside, and we'll be ready to join them at the end when the time comes for a revolt.

By now Chávez was getting frustrated. The meeting got heated. Chávez tore into Arias, accusing him of being afraid to act. The problem with you, he said, is that you arrive at a certain point in the revolution, but you have a Social Christian stuck inside that keeps you from taking the final step. Others picked up on the theme, as Arias recalled. "Ronald Blanco, who very much agreed with the theory of Chávez, came over to me and said, 'Look, major, we have to go for it. Don't be afraid.' I responded, 'It isn't fear. What I have clear is that the method that's being proposed here is wrong. I think that if we accumulate more military power, we are going to be a lot more effective than if we let ourselves get discovered and we reduce our possibilities of growing inside.'"

As tensions simmered, Major David López Rivas tried to break the impasse. He walked over to the overhead projector, took one of the plastic sheets, and drew a picture of Zorro on it. He placed it on the projector, and the room broke up laughing. It relieved the tension, and the discussion continued more calmly. As a condition for inserting himself more fully in the movement, Arias wanted Chávez to distance himself from Bravo. Chávez agreed, although he had other reasons, too. The PRV was splintering. Amid the bickering, he did not want disgruntled members revealing his clandestine activities.

Still, his meetings with Bravo did not stop completely. The men remained in sporadic contact until a definitive rupture came five years later. As Chávez's relationship with Bravo and the PRV dwindled, his contacts with the Causa R intensified. The group came to play an important role in the movement, producing the man who later became

Chávez's oil czar, Alí Rodríguez, although the military remained its heart. To Chávez, the Causa R was closer to the pulse of the masses and was not out flying kites.

"My meeting with Maneiro and, why not come out and say it, my certainty that Douglas Bravo's direction was not the right one, pushed me closer to the Causa R, especially because of its work with the popular movements, which was vital to my still developing vision of the combined civilian-military struggle," Chávez said. "I was very clear on the idea of the role of the masses, which Douglas's group was not; on the other hand, in the Causa R I felt this presence."

As dawn drew near in San Cristóbal, Arias took the Bolivarian oath and was formally sworn in as a full member of the EBR. It was a decisive moment in the movement's history. Arias was to play a key role, rising to a level of co-leadership and offering a contemplative balance to Chávez's sometimes impetuous nature. The two were to fall out later in a bitter public dispute, until Arias finally returned to the fold dramatically in 2006 when Chávez sent him to the United Nations as Venezuela's ambassador.

Four months after the congress in San Cristóbal, Chávez and his cohorts organized another one in Maracay. The central Venezuelan city was teeming with military. It was home to the nation's main air force base and other important barracks. The Bolivarianos had to take extra precautions to avoid detection. As he drove west from Caracas with Marksman, López Rivas, the major who had eased the tensions at the meeting in San Cristóbal, pulled out a woman's wig and sunglasses. He put them on and paid his fare at a tollbooth acting like a woman. He also had a dress in the car. When they arrived at the zoo in Maracay where some conspirators were to meet, he slipped into a bathroom and put it on. His disguise was complete. He even tried walking like a woman. He was fairly convincing, at least to Marksman.

Marksman was the contact person for some of the conspirators. They would know her by the red hat she always wore for the rendezvous. Usually she would meet them in the Bolívar Plaza of whatever city or village the group was gathering in — they all had a plaza honoring the Liberator. She would set a time — 8 A.M., for instance — and wait exactly ten minutes before leaving. They could not linger around and risk detection by intelligence agents.

In Maracay the group decided to make the popular zoo their initial contact point. Marksman and López Rivas picked up some of the others and made their way to an apartment building in the city. When they walked in Chávez laughed at López Rivas's disguise. Marksman recalled the meeting for one of the most emotional oath-takings she witnessed. At the encounters all the participants, including those already sworn in, usually gathered in a circle, took hands, and repeated the oath again along with the newcomers. That day in Maracay one of the original founders of the EBR-200, Felipe Acosta Carles, brought his two young children — a boy and a girl — to the meeting. When it came time for the oath, he propped them on each of his knees, held one of their hands in the air, and repeated, "I swear by the God of my parents . . ."

As the meeting in Maracay ended, Chávez was sick and checked into a hotel for the night. The next day he departed for Elorza in southwest Venezuela while Marksman returned to Caracas. The movement was on a roll. New members were flowing in, congresses were becoming regular events, Arias was on board, and spirits were flying high. So many people were joining that the leadership decided to put a temporary freeze on recruiting. They were afraid the movement was getting too big; word would leak out.

At the San Cristóbal meeting, the members had decided to organize Comandos de Areas Revolucionarias (CARs). They divided up the map of Venezuela, assigned teams of civilians and soldiers to organize activities, and named each section for a Venezuelan Indian tribe — Jirahara, Guajira, Piaroa, Cumanagotos. Some of the civilians even pledged to start publishing a newspaper. They called it *Alianza Patriotica*, patriotic alliance. Chávez was excited. A newspaper was a concrete sign of progress. The movement was consolidating itself. The man who struggled for years to find a voice and create an organization to channel his angst was optimistic. The Bolivarian movement and his dream of transforming Venezuela were coming together.

The good times, though, were about to hit their first major setback. At least one man in the military was on Chávez's trail.

# 7

# First Betrayals

Carlos Julio Peñaloza Zambrano had barely assumed his new post as director of the military academy in 1984 when he heard the rumors that Hugo Chávez was organizing a conspiracy. Peñaloza wasn't surprised. For at least a year he'd been hearing talk of a subversive cell among junior officers in the armed forces; he just didn't know who was leading it. The supposed rebels called themselves the *comacates* — Spanish for colonels, majors, captains, and lieutenants.

In September 1984 the academy held a ceremony marking the first time newly arrived cadets were granted permission to leave the grounds. At the event Peñaloza ran into an old high school friend whose son was one of the cadets. The friend pulled Peñaloza aside. "He told me, 'Look, my son says there is a captain here by the last name of Chávez who is talking about'" rebellion and coups, Peñaloza recalled years later. "This was the first time I connected Hugo Chávez with conspiracy."

It was almost an open secret in the military that groups of soldiers were conspiring. Chávez's was not the only one. There was William Izarra's ARMA, which was dying off as its leader was forced out of the military. There were also others. Officers with a higher rank than Chávez knew about the movements and, in Peñaloza's view, let them thrive. Disgust over Venezuela's political and economic decline was widespread in the armed forces. So was a leftist indoctrination instilled in part by the Andrés Bello Plan.

Peñaloza investigated Chávez's activities. He strongly suspected Chávez was indoctrinating some cadets and organizing a conspiracy.

But he could not prove it. Chávez and the others were clever. They weren't going to let themselves be caught easily.

Peñaloza's investigation did not lead to any conclusive findings, but it was enough that superiors made sure Chávez was transferred. The village of Elorza was located deep in the llanos in Apure state near the Colombian border — about as out-of-the-way as you could get. Until 1941 it wasn't even clear whether the area belonged to Colombia or Venezuela, as Chávez once remarked. It was a no-man's-land.

Elorza was reachable by a twelve-hour trip south from Barinas over a crumbling highway. It featured shops run by Syrians, restaurants owned by Colombians, and a couple of indigenous tribes who lived on the outskirts of town. The mighty Arauca River thundered nearby.

Chávez arrived in Elorza in August 1985. He was heartbroken by the move. The class of 1985 at the military academy had produced some of the star recruits of his movement; they would later play key roles in his government. He called them *Los Centauros* — the centaurs. He wrote a mournful poem the day they graduated.

> *The Centaurs are leaving*
> *My soul fills up*
> *With a profound pain*

The graduates also were dispersing throughout the country. They planned to spread the movement, Chávez wrote, like seeds sprinkled across Venezuela.

> *But it doesn't matter*
> *The seed will soon bear its fruits*
> *And will germinate throughout Venezuela*
> *Each one is going to be*
> *What he must be in whatever place he goes.*

Chávez might have sunk into a depression in Elorza. He was cut off from his cohorts in the Bolivarian movement and far from the action of Caracas and other cities. Instead, though, he threw himself into local life. He played baseball with the locals. He helped organize annual patron saint festivals, sack races, piñata parties, historic storytelling events, running races, tree plantings, commemorations, Little League baseball, medical treatment days, and children's folkloric festivals.

Elorza became another experiment for Chávez's ideas of merging soldiers and civilians into a common force to transform Venezuela. He turned himself into a kind of local mayor and a leader unlike any the village had seen. He was wildly popular. He became so well liked, villagers named him head of the prestigious local patron saint day organizing committee. Two years in a row. Students at the local high school twice honored him by naming him *padrino*, godfather, of the graduating class — even though he never taught a single class there.

Some military superiors may have thought they were punishing and isolating Chávez by sending him to Elorza. But Peñaloza believed it was a mistake. "I was surprised when they sent him to a command post where he was isolated, where he was the commander. For me it was a barbarity, a tremendous error, because if someone is suspected of conspiring the last thing you want to do is send him to a place where he is alone and the top superior."

More than anything else, what drew Chávez's attention in Elorza were the indigenous tribes living in the wilderness outside the village. The Cuiva and Yaruro peoples were among half a million Indians in Venezuela who had survived centuries of exploitation. Shortly after he arrived in Elorza, Chávez spoke with a local priest who told him about the abuses the local Indians often endured at the hands of large landowners who grew wealthy off their labor. "Look, Captain, a lot of those gentleman that you see here now, that have ranches and are rich, twenty years ago they used to go out and kill Indians like someone killing deer," Chávez recalled the priest telling him. "They massacred them and threw them in the ground. He even told me how they burned them alive."

Chávez's first contact with the Indians came one day when an impoverished woman arrived at his command post complaining that Indians had stolen her two pigs. Chávez often received complaints from cattle owners, but he usually told them to contact the police. "The cattle owners started to say that I didn't collaborate, because they were used to the army abusing the Indians, and I always told them this wasn't my job," he recalled. In the case of the woman, though, Chávez decided to investigate.

He selected fifteen soldiers from his troops and contacted an expert tracker who was a former soldier and spy in the troops of Marcos Pérez Jiménez. The old man was skilled at finding Indians, as he soon showed

Chávez. He could pick up the scent of urine left behind by travelers and differentiate whether it was a man or a woman — "women leave little puddles while the men sprinkle it all over," he told Chávez.

Before long the old man advised Chávez that the Indians were nearby.

Chávez took out his binoculars and spotted them under a mango tree. They were eating the tropical fruits. Naively, he told a sergeant he wanted to surround the tree and talk to the Indians. The old man told him he would never be able to reach them. But Chávez insisted. He stuck his pistol in his belt with the barrel pointing down. He told his men no one was to fire unless ordered.

As soon as they saw Chávez and his men, the Indians were galvanized. "They improvised an extraordinary and immediate defensive action," Chávez said. "It was like twenty rays of light had come shooting out of the mango tree. They dispersed like a mass of clouds in the thicket, including the women with their children. In a blink of the eyes the men opened battle against me. They pulled out their knives and a rain of arrows fell down on us. One passed me so close it almost hit my head."

Thinking quickly, Chávez grabbed his pistol out of his belt and fired in the air. He ordered his men to pull back, although not before two soldiers and an Indian scuffled. Luckily, no one was hurt.

The Indians left, but Chávez soon heard a shout in the dense thicket. They headed over to the Cano Caribe River. It was at its rainy-season peak, raging with water. In the middle of the river Chávez saw a woman trying to cross. She was carrying her infant son in a shawl with one hand; in the other she held a knife and was trying to swim. She kept dropping below the water with the boy and coming up again for air.

Chávez thought she might drown. "I will never in my life forget the eyes of that woman who shot me a look, a flash of hatred, and it impacted me," he said. "I was anguished. 'She's going to drown.' You know what the tracker told me? 'Captain, shoot her.' And he wasn't a bad man as far as I knew him. He surprised me. 'What?' 'Kill them, they're animals, and that kid when he grows up, he is going to shoot arrows, too.'"

Chávez didn't shoot. He made sure the woman crossed the river safely and joined the others. Then he returned to his command post. He had survived his first encounter with the indigenous tribes, but it left him unsettled. "Two things shook me up that day. First, the response of the Indians when they saw me in uniform, and that 'Kill them, they're animals.' I was reflecting over that for several days."

Chávez's musings prompted him to investigate the tribes more deeply. He traveled to the state capital of San Fernando de Apure, and visited the library of the regional office of the Bureau of Indian Affairs. On a map he located where they lived. He started to study more about their history, their culture, their beliefs. He contacted Arelis Sumavila, a sociologist from the Central University of Venezuela who had studied the Cuivas and the Yaruros for twenty years.

Chávez and Sumavila became friends. Eventually she invited him along on one of her field expeditions. Chávez let his cropped military-style hair grow out, put on civilian clothes, and joined Sumavila as she trekked deep into the llanos. She presented Chávez and two other people she invited as students doing an investigation.

Chávez spent several days with the Indians, eating with them, sleeping with them in their community, "trying to understand their world." The Indians accepted him warmly. Two weeks after the expedition, he returned on his own to see the tribe. He was dressed in his uniform. The Indians did not recognize him, and at first they were afraid. Chávez took off his hat and called the Indian captain by his name, Vicente. The Indians "stood there paralyzed," realizing that the anthropology student they had befriended was actually a soldier. They sat down to talk. "There started a process of mutually drawing closer to one another, which ended with mutual adoration," Chávez said.

His soldiers were soon visiting the Indians like old friends. Chávez was to win their affection and trust to the extent he was able to persuade them to take part in some of Elorza's cultural activities, participating in sack races and the like. The Cuivas could never pronounce Chávez's name correctly. So they called him "Chivas Frías." It was a term of affection.

His friendship with the Indians had a profound impact on him. It led him years later to implement some of the more progressive policies in the hemisphere directed at indigenous tribes. They included provisions in the constitution recognizing their languages, cultures, and economic systems. "I felt their pain in the depths of my soul," Chávez recalled in a 2004 interview. "I learned to love them. At their side I lived terrible experiences and also beautiful ones. The Indians were abused all their lives and I knew it but I really became conscious of it there, when I was a captain in their territory, living at their side."

• • •

While Chávez was integrating himself into the world of the Indians and life in Elorza, he continued trying to clandestinely build the Bolivarian movement. He held meetings, traveled the country to stay in contact with his cohorts, and kept studying. He delved more deeply into the life of Maisanta, who was still remembered by some of the older residents of Elorza. Chávez retraced Pedro Pérez Delgado's steps, arming himself with maps and notebooks and making the aforementioned trip into Colombia in which he was detained by military officers who thought he was a spy.

When he'd first arrived in Elorza, Chávez had met a woman who told him she remembered seeing Maisanta when she was a girl. She recounted how he arrived one day to find her mother and grandmother in mourning because a colonel in the army of dictator Juan Vicente Gómez had kidnapped one of the girls of the house. As Chávez recounts the story, Maisanta asked which way they headed and took off on his horse. He rescued the girl and brought her back a few days later. When the woman in Elorza told the story decades later, she cried in gratitude for Maisanta's actions. When Chávez informed her he was a descendant of Pérez Delgado, she said her family had adored his great-grandfather for generations. "Sixty years or so later," Chávez recalled, "I found in that land the traces of the battles and hopes of Pedro Pérez Delgado. I feel that in Elorza I finished finding myself."

Chávez's search for Maisanta's roots might have appeared to be an innocent, if unorthodox, activity for a soldier in a remote outpost. In reality, it was feeding Chávez's subversive movement. So were other endeavors. About a year after he arrived in Elorza, he decided to reenact a famous march General José Antonio Páez had made from the depths of the llanos north to Carabobo state for the critical independence war victory on June 24, 1821. The 165th anniversary of the battle of Carabobo was approaching in June 1986. Chávez sent Marksman to a store in Caracas to find a book that illustrated the rebel flag Páez and his troops used to fly. The flag was black; in the upper left-hand corner were a skull and crossbones, beneath which was written LIBERTAD O MUERTE — liberty or death.

Using the book as a guide, Chávez asked Marksman to make two large copies of the flag out of cloth. She sent them to Elorza. Chávez put one up to fly at his military base and another at the spot of a key battle Páez had won decades earlier, yelling *"Vuelvan caras!"* — turn around! — to his troops in a move to outmaneuver the Spanish. Chávez had to research to determine where the site was located. He proudly called Marksman the day he found it and hoisted the banner.

A few months later he came up with an even more grandiose plan. He asked Marksman to make about one hundred smaller copies of the flag. Then he gathered some soldiers, outfitted them in the clothes of peasants from the Páez era complete with straw hats and pants cut off at the knees, and mounted them on horseback. They set off on a week-long journey through the llanos, retracing Páez's path. They stopped at villages along the route, making their way to each Plaza Bolívar, where Chávez made floral offerings to the Liberator and gave incendiary speeches. He attacked the government and hailed Bolívar as a revolutionary who would be repulsed by the current state of Venezuela.

If Chávez's superiors had heard the speeches, they undoubtedly would have considered them subversive. Instead, when he finally reached Carabobo, reenacting Páez's triumphant entrance into the state, the general in charge of the parade commemorating the day was so impressed that he made Chávez one of the stars of the event. He instructed Chávez to give a speech at the beginning of the parade explaining what he and the men were doing. Then he had them ride proudly down the street as the closing act, their black flags waving in the breeze as they sat atop their horses. It was a minor sensation, carried live on national television and featured in the next day's *El Nacional* newspaper with a full-page spread including photographs. Chávez was cultivating his Bolivarian movement right before the eyes of his superiors, who apparently didn't notice or feel inclined to stop him.

But only apparently. Two months later, in September 1986, the movement suffered its first serious leak. After his transfer to Elorza, Hugo Chávez ordered the Bolivarians to stop recruiting new members because the group was growing too rapidly. He feared that authorities would discover the movement and dismember it. But with Chávez's approval a lieutenant named Valera Querales continued his efforts, trying to finish off a recruiting job that was close to success.

One potential recruit, however, apparently got spooked at a meeting in which Chávez was not present in San Juan de los Morros when the conversation turned to the possibility of a coup against Carlos Andrés Pérez if he won the next presidential election. Someone even made an offhand remark about killing him if he resisted. The nervous recruit alerted his commander, giving him Chávez's name among others. Word quickly reached Peñaloza and other military chiefs at Fort Tiuna in Caracas. They convened a meeting, instructed a secretary to pull out Chávez's file, and launched an investigation. Chávez had been promoted from captain to major just two months earlier.

Luckily for him, a fellow member of the military academy's class of 1975 was assigned to the office of the military heads. The generals asked him to accompany them to Miraflores Palace, where they went to meet with President Jaime Lusinchi. When they left him alone in the car for a few minutes he glanced inside an envelope at the classified report they had outlining the allegations against Chávez and his colleagues. He managed to see a few of the names mentioned. Later he called Marksman's house, reaching her sister Cristina. He gave her a brief message in code: "*Peligro. La vieja esta grave. HCHVQCHR.*" Danger. The old lady is in serious condition. *HCH* was Hugo Chávez; *VQ*, Valera Querales. The *CHR* wasn't clear. Something strange was happening.

Chávez was on vacation, and had come to Caracas to have minor surgery on his eye. He was leaving the hospital that day. When he arrived with Marksman at her house around noon with a patch over his eye, they encountered a nervous Cristina and the message. A few hours later they got a second, equally cryptic call from the classmate with the same information. Chávez told Herma Marksman she needed to find Ronald Blanco La Cruz, who was stationed at Fort Tiuna, so he could locate Chávez's classmate and find out what was happening.

At about 7 P.M. Marksman took a taxi to Blanco La Cruz's house in La Valle. She spoke to his wife, Guadalupe, who told her Ronald was on duty at the military fort. Guadalupe drove the short distance to the base, and told Ronald he needed to come home to talk with Marksman. When he did, she told him what was happening. He instructed Marksman to wait in the house while he looked into matters back at the base. A few hours later he returned with the news: Officials had uncovered evidence that Chávez, Valera Querales, and another officer named Chacon Rojas were possibly involved in a conspiracy. You need to put everyone in the movement on alert, he said.

Marksman returned to her house in El Paraiso, a fifteen-minute drive away, and informed Chávez. He instructed her to burn all the incriminating documents they possessed. They had plenty: notes from meetings, documents compiled by the group, an agenda with a list of the movement's members.

Chávez and Marksman threw the materials into a box and doused it with kerosene. Then about 1:30 A.M. Marksman and her sister drove to La Guaira on the Caribbean coast, half an hour away. They found a remote spot on the beach in the Macuto section. Marksman scrambled over a rock jetty, dropped the box into a crevice, and tried to get a fire going using some candles and matches. The wind kept extinguishing it, and she ran out of matches. She had to walk back up to the road to try to find an open store where she could buy more. She had instructed her sister to remain close by in case they had to make a quick getaway. But when Marksman arrived at the road, Cristina was parked so far away she could barely see her. She was terrified the authorities were going to find Herma and arrest both of them.

Chávez had some documents of his own to burn back in Elorza. Fearing authorities were going to detain him, he tore the patch off his eye, got into his car, and started driving. He passed through Maracay, about ninety minutes away, where he alerted one of the movement's members. He continued on another half hour to Valencia, where he gave the same message and instructed the Bolivarians to go underground. Then he made the long trek to Barinas, another seven hours away.

In a village outside the city, he contacted some civilian members of the movement. It had a significant presence in the area including in Chávez's hometown of Sabaneta, where some residents had joined the guerrillas and leftist movements in the 1960s. He connected with two of his closest friends there, the Orta brothers, who agreed to drive their truck down the bumpy road to Elorza. They alerted some of his underlings at the military post, used a key Chávez lent them to enter his room, and took out and burned all the incriminating books, documents, and agendas he had stored there. "They went through everything, because we suspected intelligence was going to take it all," Chávez said. "And in fact the day after a plane arrived with people from intelligence. They looked, and didn't find anything."

Chávez went on to Barinas to his mother's house, and with his eye swollen called his commanding officer in San Juan de los Morros to report that he was convalescing. He alerted his brother Adán, who spread word about the leak to other civilian collaborators. In the end, despite strong suspicions that Chávez was involved in something, military authorities couldn't prove it. The Bolivarians had managed to elude the first serious breach in their security.

•••

But Chávez did not escape unscathed. When he returned from his vacation, authorities took away his troops in Elorza, telling him it was part of a reorganization. They ordered him to create a new unit of "frontier development." Chávez saw it differently: "They left me with nothing, with no budget, no land, nothing, in the loneliness of the *Cajon de Aracua,* conversing with the ghosts of Lorenzo Barquero" — a character in the famous Venezuelan novel *Doña Bárbara* whose life is destroyed by misfortune and vice and who lives in misery in a shack in the llanos. "In the end we made a unit of ten soldiers and some Indians. They kept watching me. There is even a report from the DISIP [political police] that links me with the Colombian guerrillas and says that I was preparing an Indian rebellion!"

Chávez and the soldiers dedicated themselves to reviving a nearby abandoned Colombian hacienda called Santa Rita. They planted some crops and even tended to some pigs a neighbor gave them. They hoisted the Venezuelan flag and alongside it Páez's big black flag, only this time with the words SANTA RITA O MUERTE. By Chávez's account, they turned into something of a ragtag outfit lost in the wilderness.

One day a general named Arnoldo Rodríguez Ochoa decided to pay Chávez and his men a visit. It was midmorning. Chávez was still asleep, since he had arrived late from a trip to Capanaparo in the llanos. A helicopter appeared in the sky and approached the base. A soldier knocked on Chávez's door. Major, a helicopter has arrived! Chávez and his outfit were not exactly ready for a visit from a high-ranking commander. His troops

> looked more like guerrillas, with rubber boots because the combat boots had worn out, with ragged uniforms, some with blue jeans, me with long hair and a beard . . . I put on a green t-shirt, a pair of dirty pants, some boots full of mud. When I saw the general I thought, "I've got myself into a problem." It didn't seem like a military unit. There was no discipline. Some soldiers on horseback. So the general stands there looking at me, like he was surprised. He has a special subtle humor, and alongside his high command he says to me real seriously:
>
> Are you Chávez? That captain from the military academy?
> Yes, general, I'm Chávez.
> Jesus, and that black flag? And what are you doing with those soldiers that they don't salute a general?

> Welcome general . . . . I didn't know what to say to him . . . You
> want a cup of coffee?

They went inside the house, which was filled with smoke from the woodstove in the kitchen. Wandering nearby were some of the pigs. Outside was a small field of corn. The general asked Chávez what he was doing there. They sent me here, Chávez responded. They say I am going around conspiring. And is it true? the general asked. No, General, what happens is that I'm like that, you know me, I talk, I say things. I'm a Bolivariano.

Chávez convinced the general he was not conspiring, and they stayed in touch. Rodríguez Ochoa liked him. Eventually, in 1988, Rodríguez Ochoa invited Chávez to become his personal assistant. He spent a few months with him at his command post in San Juan de los Morros. Then one day he made an announcement: Rodríguez Ochoa was being named head of CONASEDE, the national security council. He was going to the Miraflores presidential palace in Caracas. And he wanted to take Chávez with him.

It was another stroke of luck for Chávez. No one in the military blocked the move to Caracas. Before long Chávez found himself working in the Palacio Blanco across the street from Miraflores. Its main occupant, President Jaime Lusinchi, was coming to the end of presiding over another five debilitating years of the country's history. It was the "Lost Decade" of mounting debt, spiraling inflation, and economic retrenchment in Latin America. Venezuela was no exception.

Lusinchi had taken over the country back in 1984, one year after "Black Friday" when the once rock-solid bolivar was devalued, shocking Venezuelans. Voters had thrown out of office the man who'd ordered the devaluation, COPEI's Luis Herrera Campins, and brought back the more populist party of Carlos Andrés Pérez, Democratic Action. Its new standard-bearer was Lusinchi.

When he took over, the full amount of Venezuela's mounting debt was unknown even to the government because so many government agencies and institutes were contracting loans on their own without congressional approval. As it turned out, it had doubled since 1978, to $34.2 billion — with a high proportion of it short-term.

Lusinchi managed to pay not only the interest due on the debt but the principal as well. He also stoked economic growth at a time when oil prices were plummeting. It all seemed like an act of economic magic. How did he do it? In essence, he devalued the bolivar twice and raided the national piggy bank. The country's noncommitted foreign reserves dropped from $8.98 billion in 1985 to $1.77 billion in 1986. A positive balance of payments of $1.7 billion in 1985 turned into a deficit of $3.8 billion in 1986 and $4.4 billion in 1987. An economic disaster was brewing, although few Venezuelans knew it.

Adding to it was a scandal known as RECADI, for the national office in charge of currency exchange. Lusinchi created the office to handle a three-tiered (four-tiered from 1984 to 1986) exchange rate and currency control system that provided dollars at preferential rates for certain imports. It turned into a massive money-laundering scheme for Venezuela's elites. They could make tremendous profits merely by buying the dollars at the preferential rate and then converting them back to bolivars at the free-market rate.

Several businessmen and politicians associated with the scheme were charged and detained, but the highly politicized Supreme Court eventually annulled their arrest warrants on a technicality. It wasn't surprising to most Venezuelans. If a journalist asked the man and woman on the street "Do you think anything will come of this?" — referring to the allegations of corruption — the common reply was "Aqui no ha pasado nada." Nothing has happened here.

RECADI wasn't even the biggest scandal of Lusinchi's administration. Not long after he moved into Miraflores, it became apparent to the nation that he was having an affair with his personal secretary, a much younger woman named Blanca Ibáñez. A petite redhead who had risen from an impoverished family in the Andes to a private office in the presidential palace, Blanca Ibáñez fancied herself a Venezuelan version of Eva Perón, although she lacked Evita's charisma.

Ibáñez accumulated tremendous power, was implicated in several corruption cases, and usurped the role of first lady, even using her position to harass Lusinchi's wife, who had filed for divorce. "Blanquita," as she was known, often attended state functions and even accompanied Lusinchi on official trips overseas. On one to Spain their illicit relationship provoked a public scandal. Officials refused to allow them to stay in government facilities and sent them packing to a hotel.

As Lusinchi's presidency drew to a close in 1988, the financial system was on the verge of collapse. His rob-the-piggy-bank policies gained him popularity points for the moment, but left a disaster looming for the next president. Hoping to return to the good times of the 1970s oil boom years, Venezuelans turned again to Carlos Andrés Pérez, *el gocho*, who promised a "great turnaround" in the nation's fortunes. As political scientist Daniel Hellinger has noted, "Lusinchi's policies probably helped his fellow *adeco* win the December 1988 elections, but he left Pérez an economic time bomb to dismantle."

Hugo Chávez arrived in Caracas as the time bomb was ticking. Unfortunately for him, his Bolivarian movement had reached one of its low points. Arias Cárdenas had left for two years of study in Colombia shortly after the 1986 meeting in San Cristóbal in which he formally joined the movement. He had not played a key role in developing the group, which by now had changed its name to MBR-200 thanks to the growing incorporation of civilians like Marksman.

For his part, of course, Chávez had been isolated in Elorza. He found it difficult to maintain his contacts. Even the newspaper the civilians at the meeting in San Cristóbal agreed to publish turned out to be a disappointment. A couple of months later, a package of two hundred copies arrived in Elorza for Chávez. When he opened it he was horrified. The newspaper was supposed to emphasize Bolívar, Rodríguez, and Zamora. Instead, staring out from the cover was an image of Ernesto "Che" Guevara. Inside, the articles had a similar bent. Chávez admired Che, but knew the Cuban revolutionary hero would never be accepted in the armed forces or even among most of the general population. He took the newspapers out back and burned them.

As the 1980s came to a close, Chávez thought his movement might die out completely. "The process went advancing from 1982 with ups and downs until 1991, and there were times I thought it was going to end." The rebels needed a dramatic event to revitalize the conspiracy. One would not be long in coming.

# 8

# The Massacre

Carlos Andrés Pérez wanted to make his inauguration an unforgettable affair. He won the December 1988 presidential election decisively, riding a wave of expectation that he would return the country to the heyday of the oil boom years he'd presided over during his first term in the 1970s when billions of petrodollars seemed to fall out of the sky like rain. After a decade of economic retrenchment, "Venezuela Saudita" was making a comeback, or so millions of Venezuelans hoped. CAP, as he was known, was the first president elected to a second term in Venezuela since democracy had been established in 1958.

Chávez was a front-row witness to his comeback. He was now stationed at the Palacio Blanco, across the street from Miraflores presidential palace, working in the national security office. But he was to miss the traumatic events that soon followed Pérez's swearing-in and changed the country forever. While Caracas was burning, Chávez was confined to bed with the chicken pox.

Until Chávez came along, Pérez was the principal figure of the country's democratic era. A charismatic and demagogic politician who at sixty-six could still stir crowds at campaign rallies into a frenzy and make women faint, he wasn't popular because of his good looks. "Tall, balding, and with a spreading nose and a receding chin, he is no movie star," *The Atlantic Monthly* said in a profile. "Nor is he a great orator. CAP's appeal is CAP himself."

Like Chávez, he was a workaholic who slept no more than four or five hours a night. Up before dawn every day for another dizzying round of meetings, phone calls, and trips, Pérez was a globe-trotting whirl-wind of activity. At rallies he flailed his arms overhead like two wind-shield wipers and could work crowds into near hysteria with phrases as mundane as "Let's Get to Work! Let's Get to Work!" A political animal, his lust for the limelight was legendary.

He hailed from the small border state of Táchira, which had two principal products: coffee and autocrats. It produced all three mili-tary dictators in twentieth-century Venezuela; all told, they ruled the country for forty-six years. Pérez entered politics at fifteen, landed a job eight years later as private secretary to the patriarch of Venezuelan democracy, Rómulo Betancourt, and fled into exile in 1949 for nine years after General Marcos Pérez Jiménez seized power. He served as interior minister in the early 1960s when Betancourt became the coun-try's first popularly elected president, and eventually took the country by storm during his own 1974–1979 presidency. He nationalized the oil industry, established diplomatic relations with Cuba, lobbied the US Congress to turn over control of the Panama Canal to Panama, and supplied the Sandinistas with guns as the US-backed Somoza regime wobbled in its final days.

Surrounded by a group of high-rolling cronies dubbed "the Twelve Apostles," Pérez saw his presidency end in scandal when he was accused in a kickback scheme. It involved a frigate, the *Sierra Nevada*, bought for twice its value and given to landlocked Bolivia. The ethics com-mittee of his own Democratic Action Party sanctioned him and tried to toss him out of the party.

But a decade later, after Venezuela's descent into economic morass, all that was long forgotten, or at least forgiven. So was the healthy bank account he had somehow amassed on modest government sala-ries. Pérez blew across the country during the 1988 campaign like a human tornado, striding through barrios as he shook hands, kissed old women, and promised prosperity. His slogans were "The Man Who Really Walks" and "The Man with Energy."

He'd spent fifteen years crossing the globe on behalf of Third World causes. Like Chávez years later, he envisioned himself a modern-day incar-nation of Simón Bolívar, uniting Latin America to take on the crushing foreign debt crisis of the 1980s Lost Decade and becoming the official spokesman for the Third World in general. As he prepared to assume the presidency again, he wanted to mark the day with a spectacle heralding his emergence as a full-fledged world leader and savior of Latin America.

Critics dubbed it a "coronation." The guest list included twenty-four heads of state, half a dozen ex-presidents including Jimmy Carter and Julius Nyerere of Tanzania, five OPEC oil ministers, and hundreds of foreign dignitaries. Fidel Castro came, ending intense speculation over whether he would make his first appearance in Venezuela since his triumphant visit thirty years earlier after taking power in Cuba. The United States dispatched Dan Quayle, making his maiden diplomatic trip overseas as vice president. Both Nicaraguan contra leaders and the country's Sandinista president Daniel Ortega — still at war with each other — flew in. Middle Eastern oil sheiks rubbed elbows with Latin American guerrilla leaders from the Faribundo Martí National Liberation Front. The shining Hilton Hotel in central Caracas where many of the high-powered guests checked in was transformed into a "gun-bristling militarized zone," with Soviet KGB officers, US Secret Service agents, and Cuban security agents staking it out along with hundreds of Venezuelan soldiers. Some seven hundred journalists from around the world flocked to the city to witness the spectacle.

They weren't disappointed. Pérez and his cronies put on a show not often seen in the region — "one of the grandest celebrations Latin America has ever known," *The New York Times* reported. By some accounts it was the largest assembly of foreign leaders ever in Latin America. A total of ten thousand guests invited to ostentatious inaugural parties reportedly drank twelve hundred bottles of scotch and consumed 650,000 hors d'oeuvres, twenty sides of beef, and 209 sides of lamb, washing it down with champagne. "It's like a coronation, something an emperor would do," one South American diplomat said. "You would think he was Hirohito or something."

The crowd of special guests invited to the swearing-in was too large for the congressional building. So for the first time it was moved to the elegant Teresa Carreño Theater, the city's largest performing arts center, located across the street from the Hilton.

The invitations to Castro and Ortega had fueled speculation that Pérez, who had nationalized foreign oil companies in 1976, was going to make a radical announcement about Latin America's ballooning foreign debt. It was provoking what many economists and political analysts called the worst crisis in the region's history. Many expected Pérez to announce the creation of a debtors' cartel to pressure foreign banks and the United States to grant the countries relief.

At 10:30 A.M. on February 2, 1989, Jaime Lusinchi finally passed Pérez the presidential sash. Venezuela's new president launched into a forty-minute address, invoking Bolívar's dream of a united Latin America and appealing to its leaders to form a common front against the "onerous" debt burden. He didn't refer much to Venezuela specifically, but did hint at something to come.

Two weeks later the country and the world found out what he was talking about. Even as Pérez was publicly denouncing foreign capital in the weeks leading up to his inauguration while he crisscrossed the globe, he had been privately sending a message to the International Monetary Fund and the World Bank that Venezuela would comply with their stringent requirements for a desperately needed $4.3 billion in loans over the next three years, including $1.5 billion immediately.

The conditions were part of what was known as the Washington Consensus. Viewed as the bible of the emerging "neo-liberal" free-market economic policies sweeping Latin America in response to the debt crisis, the Washington Consensus called for reducing the government's role in the economy, slashing state spending and subsidies, lifting price controls, reducing government bureaucracy, privatizing state-owned enterprises, opening economies to foreign investment, floating currency exchange rates in the free market, reducing trade tariffs, and deregulating the economy. In sum, unfettered free-market capitalism with little of the social safety net of European-style socialism.

On the staff of Pérez's new administration were two young US-trained economists well versed in the disciplines of the Chicago School of neo-liberal economics: Moisés Naím, the trade and industry minister, and Miguel Rodríguez, the minister of planning — whiz kids from MIT and Yale. They helped put together an economic "shock package" that other countries in Latin America, such as Bolivia, had already implemented to try to tame hyperinflation, stoke economic growth, and attack foreign debt.

The idea was simple: Short-term pain to correct "economic imbalances" would lead to long-term prosperity. No matter that Pérez had denounced the IMF package as an "atom bomb that kills only people and leaves buildings standing" and IMF economists as "genocide workers in the pay of economic totalitarianism." In his mind, he now had little choice. The debt-saddled country was close to broke thanks to Lusinchi, who had raided the foreign reserves to pay the debt service and left Pérez with almost nothing. His predicament was captured in a scene by Venezuela's leading playwright, José Ignacio Cabrujas, who imagined a conversation between Pérez and banker Pedro Tinoco, who has just informed the president-elect, "There are $200 million":

*Pérez:* To buy paper clips, Tinoco?
*Tinoco:* No, no. In general, Mr. President.
*Pérez:* I assume you're referring to the petty cash box, Dr. Tinoco.
*Tinoco:* No. No. I'm talking about the general treasury. That's all we have. There's nothing else.
*Pérez:* But Jaime . . . he didn't . . . he didn't tell me anything about this . . . Call Jaime!
*Tinoco:* Jaime is in Miami, Mr. President.

On February 16 Pérez announced the new *paquete*. He didn't call it a "shock package." Instead, he declared it part of *El Gran Virage* — the great turnaround — that would return Venezuela to prosperity. It was an orthodox IMF austerity package, along with a few specific measures aimed at Venezuela's economic peculiarities. Gasoline prices, for instance, among the cheapest in the world at 13¢ a gallon, were to nearly double, followed by two more increases in subsequent years. The idea was to bring them to world market levels.

The government didn't think it had to prepare the population for the measures, which included drastic hikes in the price of bread, milk, pasta, and other subsidized foods. Naím, Rodríguez, and the others simply assumed people would accept them as commonsense steps to correct economic imbalances.

The package went into effect the weekend of February 25–26, as workers quietly changed price signs at gas pumps. The country was already tense. During the electoral campaign, Democratic Action's Lusinchi had kept price controls on a wide variety of products intact to ensure his own popularity and boost Pérez's chances of winning in early December. Anticipating that the controls would be lifted, the bolivar would be devalued, and prices would rise after the new president took office, merchants hoarded rice, black beans, corn flour, pasta, powdered milk, soap, toothpaste, shampoo, deodorant, even cars.

For weeks, the country was hit with food shortages. People who went to small neighborhood bodegas or larger supermarkets to buy commodities that made up the standard Venezuelan diet were told *No hay* (there isn't any), even though many of the items were hidden in storage rooms. Unable to buy even the most basic necessities, Venezuelans' patience was wearing thin. In mid-February isolated food riots started breaking out in Caracas and sections of the interior.

On Monday morning, February 27, the dam broke. While Pérez's new shock program called for boosting gasoline prices by 100 percent, it restricted increases for bus and jeep fares to 30 percent. The drivers were unhappy. That morning they simply ignored the new regulations, doubling their fares to match the gasoline hike and refusing to accept 50 percent student discount cards.

The increase was a shock to millions of poor people who relied on the buses and jeeps to get to work. Many woke up at 4 A.M., left their hillside shacks by 5, and then stood in long lines for an hour or two to get a place on vehicles so packed, passengers often hung out the doors or shoved one another to get on. In the evening they repeated the same humiliating routine, arriving home around 8 or 9 P.M. Bus companies that monopolized the business refused to put more vehicles on the road to reduce the lines because it would cut into their profits.

For frustrated commuters barely scraping by economically, an unannounced, overnight doubling of transportation fares was too much to take. In some outlying areas of the capital, the new fares ate up a quarter of the typical worker's monthly salary.

The first signs of trouble broke out in Guarenas, outside Caracas. As dawn broke and commuters lined up at bus stops, they were hit with the 100 percent fare hikes. They argued with drivers, tossed stones at the vehicles, and took to the streets to protest. By 7:30 A.M. two cars were ablaze. About the same time, disturbances erupted in Caracas near the Nuevo Circo (new circus) bus terminal.

A few hours later protestors moved from Nuevo Circo to the six-lane Avenida Bolívar. They built a barricade, cutting off one of the main traffic arteries of the capital. Nervous store owners lowered their *santamarias* (holy Marys) — the corrugated steel curtains or iron gratings businesses normally used at night to protect their shop windows. Others left their *santamarias* half down and their stores partly open, not sure what was happening.

That morning similar protests broke out in nineteen cities across the country. Television networks broadcast images of the disturbances in the capital, helping to spread the unrest.

Shortly after noon in Caracas, a crowd of students gathered in front of the Central University of Venezuela. They denounced not only the transportation hikes but also Pérez's entire shock package. They placed cars across the road to the Plaza Venezuela and Plaza Las Tres Gracias, blocking traffic at another of the city's nerve centers. By about 2 P.M. they descended on the nearby Francisco Fajardo Highway, the capital's main roadway, and blockaded it with branches, empty crates, and other objects. They stopped food trucks, unloaded the cargo, and ordered the drivers to park the vehicles across the road.

For the most part police were nowhere to be seen throughout the city; others stood by idly, overwhelmed by the protestors. Part of the force was on strike in a wage dispute. Complicating matters, government leaders were caught off guard. Pérez was in Barquísimeto, one hundred and seventy miles away. He apparently was either unaware of the mayhem in Caracas or dismissed it. In Barquísimeto authorities called out the National Guard around noon, so that city was not as hard hit.

By late afternoon in Caracas, though, public buses and jeeps had vanished. The subway system was shut down. Hundreds of thousands of people were walking miles to get home from their jobs while cars and buses burned in the streets. As Caracas descended into a state of almost complete anarchy, a final barrier was passed: Mass looting broke out.

It started downtown sometime around 4 P.M. The first targets were bodegas, supermarkets, and stores stocked with people's most critical needs — food and clothes. Looters smashed windows or broke down doors and metal gates, and rushed into the businesses. To their astonishment, they found that many of the products that had been missing from store shelves for weeks were hidden in back storerooms. In an orgy of pillaging, they grabbed anything they could get their hands on: pasta, rice, corn flour, powdered milk, bread, butter, ham, cheese, meat, chicken, pants, shoes, diapers. Many people ran down the street with their booty. Others pushed it in shopping carts. Some even lugged sides of beef almost as big as a man on their backs.

The riots spread like wildfire. The sprawling barrios of Catia in western Caracas became engulfed. So did Petare in the east. Businesses owned by Chinese, Portuguese, and Lebanese immigrants were attacked with special viciousness because many residents blamed them for hoarding products and creating shortages. While they trashed the businesses, rioters also built bonfires in the streets, setting tires, cardboard boxes, and other debris on fire, blocking traffic. They stopped cars, ejected drivers, and burned the vehicles. Television networks broadcasting the mayhem live helped spread the disturbances by showing where the latest break-ins were and emboldening people to loot. Hundreds of motorcycle messengers who usually spent the day delivering packages, checks, or letters also helped spread the word, zooming from hot spot to hot spot with the latest news.

It was the dinner hour. Caracas was in a state of unprecedented pandemonium.

As night fell, the looting turned massive, and more organized. Residents and overwhelmed police had the looters line up outside stores, and then let women and children enter first. The men followed. Some looters waved Venezuelan flags and sang the national anthem. Others shouted slogans or scribbled them on walls: THE PEOPLE ARE HUNGRY. THE PEOPLE ARE ANGRY. NO MORE DECEPTION. Many people joined in because they feared there would be nothing left for them.

After the bodegas and supermarkets were largely cleared out, the rioters turned their attention to appliance outlets, furniture stores, and other businesses that dangled big-ticket items in their windows and on television. The throngs carted away televisions, stereos, refrigerators, washing machines, stoves, beds. For many, with prices soaring and salaries stagnant, the riots represented what might be a last chance to grab a new bed, sofa, or TV. Residents carried the goods down the streets or pushed them in shopping carts or wheelbarrows stolen from hardware stores. Some pulled up with cars or station wagons. Others lugged refrigerators on their backs. One television reporter called it "collective madness."

Police could identify with the pillaging residents. Most came from the barrios themselves, received meager wages, and had not been paid in weeks because of a labor dispute. Badly outnumbered, they let the hordes loot. But as the hours passed, they became looters, too. Armed groups including some in police uniforms with their faces covered by handkerchiefs arrived in trucks or even police vehicles and hauled away the entire stock of some stores. News reporters saw some police fire tear gas at crowds to keep them away from establishments they were raiding. They also fired indiscriminately at looters running away from them. As Charles Hardy, then a Roman Catholic priest working in a barrio as a Maryknoll missionary, put it: "Stealing spaghetti suddenly merited the death penalty."

That night the looting spread from the main commercial avenues at the foot of Caracas's valley into the hillside barrios themselves. Hoping their businesses would not be entirely trashed, some owners simply threw open their doors to the crowds, who often respected the buildings but carted away the goods. In the barrio of San Augustin, residents stole fifty cow carcasses from a butcher shop. They took the scales, too. In middle-class Palo Verde and La Urbina, "pistol-armed mobs" descended from nearby Petare, sacking grocery stores and a Portuguese restaurant, and burning its furniture in the street. Some protestors yelled, "We prefer to be killed by bullets than to die from starvation."

The orgy of pillaging became known as "the day the poor came down from the hills." It turned into an escape valve for the long pent-up anger of a massive underclass. For years they had watched impotently as a tiny group of elites grew ever wealthier while they struggled to eat. Although the rioters left the wealthy neighborhoods untouched, the rich were terrified. In exclusive sections of eastern Caracas, residents formed armed defense brigades, roaming the streets with submachine guns, rifles, pistols, and machetes. To the elites of Venezuela, the country was descending into a state of barbarity.

But to many in the barrios, the spontaneous upheaval was an act of social justice. Just eleven days earlier, newspapers had run front-page accounts of the "Wedding of the Century," an ostentatious affair put on by two of Venezuela's richest families. It featured a reception for at least thirty-five hundred guests including two hundred flown in at their hosts' expense from as far away as Tahiti. The marriage of Mariela Cisneros Fontanals, the daughter of Oswaldo Cisneros, and Gonzalo Fernández Tinoco y Zingg put the nation's high-class life on full display. Oswaldo Cisneros was president at the time of Pepsi-Cola's Venezuelan subsidiary and a member of one of the richest families in the world. Tinoco y Zingg was the scion of a prosperous business family. *El Diario de Caracas* ran a front-page story and nine more pages inside detailing the lavish affair. According to news reports, the guests imbibed imported scotch, thousands of bottles of vintage French champagne, and "the finest delicacies from abroad" including a buffet overflowing with caviar, lobster, and salmon.

On top of Pérez's "coronation" two weeks before that, the IMF-backed austerity package, which called for little sacrifice from the wealthy, was more than the country's underclass could stomach. For years the elites and the government "had kept telling us we had to tighten our belts. But there were no holes left," commented community organizer Xiomara Tortoza. Like Hardy, she was working with Maryknoll in Nueva Tacagua, where people lived in tin shacks, defecated on newspapers they tossed into the hills because they lacked toilets, and drank parasite-infested water out of barrels that got filled by trucks as infrequently as once a month. "The poor and the working classes had been putting up with it and putting up with it and putting up with it until that day arrived and we said, 'Enough,'" Tortoza recalled. "This was how the people expressed their rage. A person who could not even afford to eat a piece of meat, that day could eat for free, that day could dress for free, that day could get their capitalist dream for free."

The looting raged on the night of February 27 and into the morning of February 28. By noon it petered out in many areas. Downtown Caracas turned into a ghost town. Schools, banks, and stores were closed. Public buses and taxis were nonexistent. Radio stations warned people to stay inside.

Up in the hillside barrios, people spent the rest of the day either locked up in their homes in fear or enjoying their booty. In Tortoza's barrio in Catia, a massive fiesta broke out. Residents in Isaías Medina pulled grills out onto cement patios, and the smell of broiling steaks wafted through the air. Neighbors shared or traded their loot with one another, bragged about what they had grabbed, and drank beer, whiskey, and even champagne. It was a day of triumph, a day of justice.

But it soon turned into a night of terror. Pérez had arrived back in Caracas from Barquísimeto at about 8 P.M. on February 27. Apparently he was surprised by the mayhem he encountered in what until that day was known as Latin America's model democracy. He spent the night trying to figure out what to do. At one point he flew over the city in a helicopter to see the anarchy for himself. The government was in a state of shock.

It wasn't until 2 P.M. on Tuesday, February 28, that an official, Interior Minister Alejandro Izaguirre, finally appeared on television. He appealed for calm and declared — obviously too late — that violence would not be tolerated. In the middle of his address the elderly minister grew ill, and the transmission was cut. It left the public even more rattled. Two hours later he returned to finish.

Two hours after that Pérez finally appeared, accompanied by his cabinet. He gave a rambling and angry address. It was shortly before 6 P.M. Even though most of the looting was over, Pérez announced he was declaring martial law, imposing a 6 P.M. to 6 A.M. curfew and suspending a raft of constitutional guarantees including freedom of speech and assembly. In effect, it meant the military had the right to detain anyone on sight without any particular cause. Those detained had no right to see a lawyer or relative. All bets were off.

Earlier that day Pérez had ordered federal troops into the streets to "restore order." Now he was in the process of flying in nine thousand more from around the country. It was a fatal decision. During Betancourt's administration, Pérez had served as interior minister and brutally repressed the leftist guerrilla movement backed by Fidel Castro. He had to know that sending troops into the streets of Caracas with instructions to restore order was risking a bloodbath. They were trained for war, not to establish public safety and order, and had never been in the city to control disturbances of this magnitude.

After Pérez announced the suspension of guarantees, rumors started flying in many barrios that inhabitants of other barrios were going to invade their neighborhoods and steal their looted goods. Gang members and ordinary residents organized self-defense brigades. Pistols, rifles, shotguns, even machine guns and bazookas appeared on the streets seemingly out of nowhere. Others produced knives, clubs, sticks, and machetes, or concocted Molotov cocktails. The armed groups gathered on street corners or hid on roofs or behind abandoned vehicles, waiting for the enemy.

The outsiders soon arrived. But they weren't rivals from other barrios. They were soldiers. The first trucks full of them rumbled up the hills and into barrios such as Isaías Medina in the middle of the night, followed by tanks. Their orders were simple: Shoot anything that moved, and shoot to kill. "They didn't say raise your arms or anything," Tortoza recalled. "But everything that appeared, they killed." Some of the young men who had pledged to defend Tortoza's neighborhood were on the streets or hiding on roofs. Like many Venezuelans, they didn't fully understand the curfew or think it was serious — one hadn't been imposed in Venezuela for decades.

Down the street from Tortoza's house, soldiers started shooting like crazy, "like they were in a war." They mowed down several young men and left them dead in the street. Even closer to her home, a twenty-two-year-old neighbor was shot dead and left in the street for a day. It was illegal to move a corpse; you had to wait for authorities to take it away. The only thing neighbors could do was cover the body with a sheet and light some candles around it.

In the San Martin barrio near downtown Caracas, bookstore worker Wolfgang Quintana was standing on his second-floor balcony near a window overlooking the street. He was holding his three-month-old daughter Estefania in one hand and a glass of lemonade in the other. Suddenly he felt a stinging pain just below his heart and said, "Ayy!" He dropped the glass on the floor, put the baby in a stroller, and started to walk toward a stairwell heading down to the first floor. He was still talking, but when he reached the stairwell and put his hand on the handrail, it was full of blood. He made his way down the steps, reached the last one, and fell on his knees. Then he collapsed onto the floor.

His wife, Iris Medina, ran out of the house screaming and looking for help. Relatives who lived nearby rushed Quintana to a hospital, but it was too late. He was dead.

The indiscriminate repression went on like that for three days after Pérez suspended the constitutional guarantees. It turned into the worst massacre in Venezuela in the twentieth century and one of the worst in modern Latin American history. Soldiers and police operated without restraint, filling the air, especially at night, with the terrifying sound of automatic gunfire. Red Cross workers who ventured into the hills of Catia near Tortoza's house to try to rescue the wounded and ferry them to overwhelmed hospitals saw one victim slumped on the street. The top of his head was blown off.

Hugo Chávez had barely avoided being among those ordered to repress the population. On Sunday, February 26, he was working in Miraflores and went to see the palace's doctor because he had a fever. The doctor diagnosed him with chicken pox and ordered him to go home immediately so he didn't infect the rest of the palace staff with the contagious disease.

Others in the Bolivarian movement were not so lucky. Francisco Arias Cárdenas was taking an advanced training course at Fort Tiuna in Caracas and was among those sent out to the *ranchos* to suppress the uprising. He had little choice — he had to obey orders. But he resolved to keep the men under his command from firing indiscriminately on people who were "unarmed, hungry, long-punished and condemned to suffer the consequences of a package of economic measures that were unjust and perverse from every point of view."

He was assigned to a barrio in Catia. When he got there, residents were seething at the military. One tossed a toilet out of a high-rise; it smashed to bits on a tank. If one of Arias's soldiers had been sticking his head out of the tank, he could have been killed. Arias was appalled at what he found in Catia, where some apartments were riddled with scores of bullet holes:

> As soon as I arrived at the place that was to be my center of operations, I realized that the officer from whom I had taken over had already been firing against the tower blocks, in an irresponsible and inhuman fashion. I also heard stories of the excesses committed by the political police, the DISIP.
>
> Immediately I gathered my troops together and said: "Hands up those who belong to the County Club!" I looked at their expressions of surprise, and saw that they all remained motionless and silent. I repeated my request: "Hands up all those who live in Alto Prado, in Lagunita Country Club or in Altamira [the wealthiest and most exclusive sectors of Caracas]!" Nobody moved.
>
> Then I said, "Well, that means that we all come from the barrios and the poor sectors like this one. The people who live here are like us, they are the people, our brothers. That means that no one must fire without authorization. No one must shoot unless we are attacked."

Most of the mayhem ended by Saturday, March 4, five days after the first protests broke out in Guarenas. By the time it was over, at least a thousand businesses were burned and looted in Caracas alone, twenty-nine hundred nationwide. The pillaging left an estimated $1.5 billion in losses to businesses. The official death toll stood at 277, the government later grudgingly conceded, although Venezuelan human rights organizations eventually identified 399 by name. Others believed the figure was far higher. One anthropologist from the University of Chicago cited medical personnel who estimated a thousand to fifteen hundred dead in Caracas. A reporter for the Caracas daily *El Nacional* summed up the mayhem when he wrote, "Yesterday, Caracas was Beirut."

But the suffering still wasn't over. Many victims were missing. Rumors soon spread that the government dumped them in a secret mass grave in a remote section of the Southern General Cemetery called La Peste (the plague). The government denied it, but by November 1990 a new human rights group named COFAVIC won a court order to search the cemetery. Accompanied by the judge, prosecutors, human rights workers, nuns, priests, and relatives of the missing, they found to their horror what they were looking for: black plastic garbage bags containing corpses. Many were mutilated, with arms, legs, and hands chopped off so they could fit in the bags. Others, young men, had their hands tied behind their backs and gunshot wounds to their heads, apparently executed by authorities.

Within weeks, they found a total of sixty-eight bodies believed to be victims of the Caracazo. Three were identified by name and turned over to their grieving families. Then the government stopped the investigation. The remaining sixty-five bodies were stored in individual niches in a concrete mausoleum several hundred yards above La Peste. To this day the unidentified bodies remain there. Their anguished relatives still don't know their fate.

**9**

# Waiting in the Wings

The Caracazo left Venezuela traumatized, and its image as Latin America's model democracy in tatters. It marked the beginning of the end of the ancien régime. Venezuela's elites, who imported not only scotch whiskey but water from the Scottish Highlands to go with it and who helped give the country the highest per capita consumption of scotch in the world, had "been living in a fool's paradise," one foreign economist observed. In a post-riot document, the hierarchy of Venezuela's Roman Catholic Church, among the most conservative in Latin America, put it another way: "The luxury of the few has become an insult to the misery of the masses."

The Caracazo also marked a turning point in the history of Chávez's Bolivarian conspiracy. It served to stiffen the rebels' resolve to overturn a system they considered corrupt and evil, and provided a jump start to a movement that had fallen into one of its lulls. "For us it was a real trauma to fire at unarmed people who were robbing because they were hungry," Arias Cárdenas commented nearly seven years later.

When Chávez returned to his job at the Palacio Blanco across the street from Miraflores Palace a few weeks after the Caracazo, he was stopped one night by a young palace guard traumatized by the repression. The officer had an inkling Chávez was involved in a subversive movement and wanted to join in. Chávez was returning from classes at Simón Bolívar University, where he was studying for a master's degree in political science. The two went to his office to talk.

The young officer told him that nearly a week after the riots broke out, he was sent on patrol near Miraflores and detained a group of young men who were sacking a store. He ordered them to sit down on a basketball court, told them they shouldn't be looting, and promised to release them. But before he could, he was ordered to turn them over to the DISIP political police. They took the young men away. Half an hour later, as the officer and his troops patrolled the neighborhood, he found the young men. They were lying on a street, dead. There were twelve to fifteen of them.

Now he sat in Chávez's office, horrified. "He was saying his heart couldn't take it and ended telling me, 'Look, major, if you have a movement, tell me. Because if you don't I'm leaving here. I'm not cut out to be in this army.'" The encounter with the young officer was telling. So were similar ones with others, part of President Pérez's honor guard, who told him, "We're not prepared to go on killing people." These were elite soldiers in charge of protecting the president and trusted by the government. Even they were turning in revulsion against the crackdown, as Chávez recalled:

> The truth is that was a horror. People protesting in the street against neo-liberalism, against the shock programs of the International Monetary Fund, against the privatization of everything, against unemployment, hunger. And they send us to spray them with bullets in the chest. And the political leaders, the supposed democrats, talking about justice and democracy. That was no democracy. It was a dictatorship of the parties and the elite, using the armed forces and using the media to brainwash and confuse people. Here there was never democracy.

> The members of the MBR-200 realized we had passed the point of no return and we had to take up arms. We could not continue to defend a genocidal regime. The massacre was the catalyst for the MBR-200. We began to accelerate our organizing, our search for civilian contacts and popular movements.

The uprising hit Chávez's movement close to home for another reason: One of its founders was killed. In an unexplained incident, Felipe Acosta Carles, one of the four men who jogged to the Samán de Güere on December 17, 1982, and took the famous oath creating Chávez's Bolivarian organization, was shot dead. The thirty-six-year-old major was killed in the working-class neighborhood of El Valle while leading a group of soldiers who were pursuing snipers in a secluded hut near the Pan-American Highway. When they got to the hut, a burst of gunfire erupted.

President Pérez himself referred to Acosta Carles's death, describing it emotionally as an ambush and an example of the wanton violence unleashed by irresponsible radicals he insisted sparked the riots. But some people including Chávez believed the government itself was behind the killing. They suspected that the DISIP knew of Acosta Carles's participation in the Bolivarian conspiracy and took advantage of the chaos of the uprising to kill him, knowing his death could be blamed on rioters. They also felt that if Chávez had not been at home sick, he could have met the same fate.

Devastated by both the loss of Acosta and the bloody upheaval, Chávez wrote a long poem to his fallen comrade and classmate from the military academy, using the Venezuelan term of affection *catire* — "the blond, white one" ("the black one" is likewise a term of affection). He also invoked a plethora of Venezuela's historical leading lights, from Bolívar to Simón Rodríguez to Francisco de Miranda.

> *Ay, they killed the blond one Acosta*
> *The blond one Acosta Carles*
> *Acosta Carles*
> *The storm of the people*
> *Let loose on the streets*
> *Nothing was left standing*
> *From Petare to La Valle.*
> *And Caracas was thirsty*
> *And the thirst was for blood.*
> *Ay, a bullet in just one instant*
> *Took you away my compadre.*
> *They killed Felipe Acosta*
> *Felipe Acosta Carles*
> *I didn't want to believe it*
> *I swear to you before my mother*
> *That just before yesterday*
> *I saw you there in the alma mater*
> *With all your being*
> *You entered the classroom*

> *And we shouted like always*
> *Maisanta, there are so many!*
> *You are still here with us*
> *They didn't kill you, compadre.*

The wake and funeral for Acosta Carles was held at the military academy. It attracted many members of the Bolivarian conspiracy as well as new recruits who wanted to join. As they stood over their dead comrade's body, seething with anger over his killing and the massacre of the Caracazo, they silently repeated the Bolivarian oath and swore to take action against the country's sick government and society. Venezuela's facade of democracy had collapsed. More upheaval was on the way.

After a rocky start, Carlos Andrés Pérez's second presidency and his neo-liberal economic "shock" package bounced back, in a way. It ended up producing impressive macroeconomic growth rates. By 1991 the economy was growing at an annual rate of 9.2 percent, the fastest in the Americas.

But the protest rate was also probably the fastest in the Americas. Little of the new wealth trickled down to the masses. The economic model created a "scandalous concentration of wealth," as one of Pérez's political opponents, COPEI congressman and onetime presidential candidate Eduardo Fernández, put it. Daily protests by students, teachers, workers, and others became the routine in one of the most tumultuous presidencies of Venezuela's democratic era. The first three years of Pérez's tenure saw five thousand street protests — an average of nearly five a day. Some 2,068 of them ended violently. Police and National Guardsmen often opened fire on demonstrators. More than a few died. Pérez's presidency was, in effect, over before it ever really started. The Caracazo killed it.

The food riots and the ongoing political discontent and repression provided an ideal incubator for Chávez's secret movement. Just like the economy, it boomed. New recruits joined, and the group regained some of the strength it had lost in the late 1980s. Military authorities continued to investigate reports that Chávez was conspiring against the government.

The most serious probe occurred in December 1989, nine months after the Caracazo. General Carlos Peñaloza, one of Chávez's main nemeses, uncovered new information that Chávez and his cohorts were plotting a coup that by some (exaggerated) accounts included plans for assassinating Pérez during the annual Christmas dinner at Miraflores Palace. Peñaloza and other officials hauled in a dozen Bolivarians for a nightlong interrogation. It became known as "the night of the majors" for the rank of Chávez, Urdaneta, and others who were questioned.

Chávez denied everything, but Peñaloza remained unconvinced. According to Peñaloza's account, he had at least one spy inside Chávez's movement who was delivering information to him. Peñaloza was especially angry that the plot was said to include a plan to capture him and, if that failed, to kidnap his son. "I told him, 'Look, Chávez, you can be conspiring all you want, and it's my duty to stop you from conspiring. But at the same time when you get involved with my family, then the problem is personal.'"

Livid, Peñaloza challenged Chávez to go outside and settle their difference in a duel. Chávez declined. He denied again he was plotting to overthrow the government.

Peñaloza failed to prove anything. Chávez was set free. But his troubles were not over. During 1990 and 1991 he took a mandatory course in preparation for assuming direct command of a battalion for the first time. He failed part of the exams and was forced to retake them. Chávez believed superiors suspicious of his activities were purposely flunking him to derail his career.

But while some like Peñaloza were convinced Chávez was leading a subversive movement, many others were not — or chose to allow him to conspire. Among those who didn't believe it was Carlos Andrés Pérez. Peñaloza repeatedly told him about Chávez's activities. The skeptical president didn't want to hear it. "CAP said don't talk to me again about the topic," according to Peñaloza.

In the end Chávez passed the course. By the summer of 1991 he was due to receive direct command of troops. But July 5, Venezuela's Independence Day and the traditional date for new assignments, came and went. Chávez, by now a lieutenant colonel, was empty-handed. So were two of his MBR-200 cohorts, Urdaneta and Joel Acosta Chirinos. Eventually the defense minister, Fernando Ochoa Antich, intervened to help Chávez and Urdaneta land posts. Acosta Chirinos got one, too. They all ended up in charge of elite paratrooper units in Maracay. It was an amazing stroke of luck.

Ochoa's intervention later prompted widespread suspicions he was aiding the rebels. Chávez denied it. He believed Ochoa had little choice but to promote him. He was a charismatic, high-profile young officer who'd graduated from the military academy high in his class and had a large following. Passing him over would have provoked unrest in the barracks. Chávez also thought the high command was simply inept and didn't realize what he and his comrades were doing. "What other explanation could there be that we were working right under their noses for years? . . . We even openly sang the songs of Zamora while jogging" at the academy, where Ochoa also was posted in the mid-1980s.

For his part, Ochoa believed that while suspicions abounded over Chávez's conspiratorial activities, little concrete proof existed. He could not lightly derail a promising officer's career. Others concluded that the promotions implicated Ochoa, whose brother Enrique was a leader of the leftist political party MAS, in the conspiracy. Yet another theory was that the military high command did not take seriously the idea that young officers were planning a coup. This was Latin America's "model" democracy. Coups didn't happen anymore.

Whatever the reason, it was a decision Ochoa came to rue. "We made a mistake. We didn't think they were going to launch an insurrection . . . There was a penetration of the left in the armed forces. They had tricked us."

Chávez's assignment was nonetheless an odd one. He hadn't jumped out of an airplane in ten years. He had little experience in parachuting. His specialty was tanks. His superiors told him he could accept the assignment or wait for the next round. Chávez knew that must not happen. It was imperative that he and the Bolivarians immediately take command of troops. "Truly you felt the movement was galloping ahead and you had to have a command in hand," Chávez recalled. "It didn't matter if it was paratroopers or artillery or tanks. The important thing was to have the military force in hand."

It was a critical turning point for the rebels. At last they had soldiers they could unleash against Pérez and the corrupt system he symbolized. Within weeks Chávez and his cohorts were plotting their first coup attempt: Plan Ezequiel Zamora.

**10**

# Rebellion of the Angels

Rising political tensions in Haiti gave the rebels their first opening to launch a coup against the hated Carlos Andrés Pérez. Rumors were flying that right-wing military rebels might try to overthrow the Caribbean island's newly installed leftist president, Jean-Bertrand Aristide. Officials from the United States, France, and Venezuela discussed sending troops to the island in a preventive show of force to try to dissuade the rebels. Pérez, who fashioned himself a champion of Latin American democracy, eagerly joined in the plan.

At the time, Chávez was in Cojedes state. Superiors summoned him to Maracay. He feared they had discovered his plans to overthrow the government again. Instead they told him to prepare to go to Haiti. His assignment was to take the airport at Puerto Principe. His cohort Acosta Chirinos would handle a nearby beachhead. They began preparing for the assault. But Chávez had no intention of going to Haiti. If he got the order to fly overseas, once in the air he would go to Caracas instead. He and the others would launch a coup of their own and try to capture the president. But Pérez's plan was never enacted. The order for Chávez to depart never came.

The rebels kept hunting for openings. On December 10 they were scheduled to take part in an air show in Maracay. The president and military high command were to attend. It seemed like a good opportunity. They could use the cover of preparing for the spectacle to prepare for a coup instead. On the day of the show, they would leap out of their airplanes, land on an open field, and storm the presidential reviewing stand — kidnapping Pérez and the high command. Then they would call on other barracks across the nation who didn't know about their movement to rise up with them.

But as they prepared their plan, they faced problems. Communications were difficult, since the intelligence services were on their trail. They had to limit their contacts. They were also trying to convince their allies in the air force to join them in the revolt. But the pilots told them they didn't think they had enough support in the air force. Another complication was that Arias Cárdenas was tied up with a trip to Israel to buy replacement parts for missiles. Chávez told him to cancel the trip, but after a heated argument Arias went anyway.

The rebels' never-easy relationship with some of their civilian allies also was deteriorating. Some members of the Radical Cause Party, afflicted by their own internal divisions, had pulled out of the conspiracy. Even more seriously, members of the radical leftist group Bandera Roja, Red Flag, had infiltrated the Bolivarian movement. They were urging two young captains, Ronald Blanco La Cruz and Antonio Rojas Suárez, to launch the rebellion themselves since, according to them, Chávez had betrayed the movement. By some reports, the captains even flirted with killing Chávez and Francisco Arias Cárdenas. He and Arias Cárdenas had to work vigorously to deter them from launching the coup independently. At one point they drove Blanco La Cruz and Rojas Suárez around Caracas for hours to dissuade them.

With the problems mounting, Chávez and his cohorts suspended the December 10 plan. By the day of the show it appeared authorities suspected something was afoot. They took extraordinary security measures, sending F-16s soaring overhead for hours, encircling the base with troops, and letting the public in for free. That assured a large crowd of what were essentially human shields. "If we had launched that operation there, a great number of people would have died," Chávez told an interviewer — making the rebels cold-blooded murderers rather than heroes trying to overthrow a corrupt political system. "December was a black month for us. We had the enemy within and serious internal problems that threatened to create a rupture."

Another plot targeted for December 16 also was put off. By now their plans were hardly a secret in some circles. At the Central University of Venezuela in Caracas, a hotbed of leftist activity, every week seemingly brought a spate of fresh coup rumors — fed possibly by Bandera Roja or state intelligence agents who had infiltrated Chávez's group. So many *hora ceros* — zero hours — came and went, it almost became a joke. Some suspected Chávez had backed down and betrayed the movement. Bandera Roja spread the word that he and Arias Cárdenas were sellouts to the oligarchs and transnationals.

Even among many people on the street, coup rumors were swirling, although almost no one had heard of a lieutenant colonel named Hugo Chávez. "Everybody talks about it," a hot dog vendor in Caracas told one reporter. The country was on edge. In late November the education minister canceled classes nationwide at public schools and universities for two days after violent student protests. Then he canceled them indefinitely for weeks more. Pérez dismissed the unrest and scoffed at the rumors of a coup. He called it "an offense to Venezuelan society" to even mention the word.

While the rebels faced problems in December that prevented them from launching a coup, they would also encounter problems if they did *not* act soon. With military intelligence closing in on them, the chances were growing daily that they would be detected and arrested. They had another problem: Military superiors were sending some of the troops led by Chávez and Acosta Chirinos all over the country on training missions. The only time they would all be back in Maracay together was in late January and early February. As 1991 drew to a close, Chávez knew time was running out. He figured he had about a two-week window in which to act.

One promising opportunity fell in the middle of it. Pérez was heading to Davos, Switzerland, for a meeting of world leaders to discuss economic issues. After he returned, the president, Ochoa, and other high-ranking officers were scheduled to attend another air show on Tuesday, February 4, at El Pao in Carabobo state. The units of Chávez and Acosta Chirinos were to participate. Chávez figured they could move troops and arms as if they were preparing for the event when in reality they were preparing for a coup.

Chávez's conspiratorial group had expanded to the point that he had contacts inside Miraflores Palace among the presidential honor guard. They were going to leak word to him about Pérez's specific plans for the trip to Switzerland — most importantly the date and time of his return. The plan was to capture him at the airport.

In the last week of January, seeking a final psychological boost for his rebellion, Chávez traveled to La Guaira on the Caribbean coast near Caracas. He met with one of his old mentors, retired colonel Hugo Trejo, who had helped lead the 1958 civic-military rebellion that overthrew the dictator Pérez Jiménez. Then, on Thursday, January 30, Chávez met briefly with Arias Cárdenas and Urdaneta. The rebels shifted into high alert, waiting for the final signal from Chávez.

The word came that weekend. Chávez's contacts informed him that Pérez would be coming back from Switzerland on Monday night, February 3. That Saturday, February 1, Chávez sent a messenger to Maracaibo to inform Arias Cárdenas. Calling was too risky — their telephones were probably tapped.

The following day, Sunday, Chávez met with two air force pilots who were sympathetic to his movement, Luis Reyes Reyes and General Francisco Visconti Osorio. It was a last-minute attempt to bring the air force into the rebellion. Rendezvousing at about 9:45 P.M. at a gas station on the Pan-American Highway outside Caracas, Chávez told them the revolt was hours away. He explained that air support was crucial to back up the troops on the ground. Reyes and Visconti wanted to help, but told him they couldn't. The best they could offer was "active neutrality" — seizing control of the Maracay air base and preventing airplanes from taking off to attack the rebels. Visconti, who had been active in the by-now-defunct conspiracy cell ARMA, wanted to delay the insurrection altogether to allow them to build more support in the air force. But Chávez said it was too late.

Two hours into the meeting, around midnight, he received a telephone call confirming the president's arrival. Speaking in code, a contact at Miraflores told him that "the uncle" — Pérez — would be landing at Simón Bolívar International Airport on the Caribbean coast near Caracas at 10:30 P.M. The phone call was the final piece needed to trigger the revolt.

The rebels had a clear set of plans. A commando team was to go to the airport, kidnap Pérez as he got off his airplane, throw him in a truck, and whisk him to Caracas, where he would be turned over to Chávez alive. If that failed, they had a Plan B: They would seize the president inside a highway tunnel on his way back to Caracas, grabbing him in the midst of a traffic jam they planned to provoke by setting a car on fire. If Plans A and B fell through, there was Plan C: They would nab him at Miraflores Palace or La Casona presidential residence, which they planned to seize along with Fort Tiuna military headquarters in the capital and other military bases across the country.

With the aid of civilian allies, they hoped to commandeer television and radio stations and proclaim that they had overthrown Pérez. They wanted to display the captured president on television and install a civilian-military junta to temporarily guide the nation until they could hold elections and write a new constitution. Pérez was to be put on public trial for crimes against the state. They ranged from corruption to mass poverty to the killings of protestors to the surrender of the nation's riches to transnational companies as part of a "false" nationalization of the oil industry.

Using radio equipment that would allow him to communicate with rebels on land and in the air across the nation, Chávez would command the operation Bolívar-like from a military museum on a hilltop overlooking Miraflores Palace, where he hoped he and the other Bolivarians soon would be installed, running the country themselves.

It was an audacious plan. Chávez knew part of the price was that even though the orders were to avoid violence as much as possible, some of his brother soldiers — loyalists and rebels alike — would likely die. In his mind, there was no choice. The country was in a state of ruin. Radical, revolutionary action was required to break out of the misery and oppression. It was a decision that would make his detractors question his democratic credentials forever since, despite his flaws, Pérez was a legitimately elected president. To them, Chávez would have the blood of fellow Venezuelans on his hands.

But to the fiery lieutenant colonel, this was not a traditional coup by stereotypical right-wing Latin American gorillas. It was an insurrection by young, progressive officers against an unjust, failed, and brutal system. It had more in common with the leftist guerrilla uprisings against repressive regimes in places such as El Salvador in the 1980s than it did with coups by generals like Pinochet in Chile. Venezuela had reached the tipping point. The Caracazo, the mass grave, the blatant corruption, the mass poverty — it was all too much. The country held up by officials in Washington as a "model democracy" was little more than a closed system where a small circle of elites controlled everything, leaving a few crumbs for the masses and violently repressing them when they rebelled.

Chávez believed he was following in the footsteps not of Pinochet and Somoza, but of Torrijos and Velasco, Bolívar and Zamora. Because in Venezuela, very little had changed from the days of Pérez Jiménez or even Juan Vicente Gómez dating back to 1908. As Chávez later put it:

Everything has basically remained the same; it's been the same system of domination, with a different face — whether it's that of General Gómez or of [former president] doctor Rafael Caldera. Behind this figure, this *caudillo*, with a military beret or without it, on horseback or in a Cadillac or a Mercedes-Benz, it's been the same system — in economics and in politics — the same denial of basic human rights and of the right of the people to determine their own destiny.

Venezuela was suffering a terminal crisis, ruled by a dictatorship dressed up in democratic clothing, a dictatorship that took a people living on a sea of oil, with huge navigable rivers and millions of acres of agricultural land, to abject poverty and limitless political and moral corruption.

Arias Cárdenas, the former seminarian deeply influenced by Vatican II, liberation theology, and its "preferential option for the poor," harbored similar sentiments. Like Camilo Torres, the Catholic-priest-turned-guerrilla in neighboring Colombia in the 1960s, Arias saw the use of force in certain extreme circumstances as a tool not for oppression but for liberation. It wouldn't be the first time in history. In the United States rebels led by George Washington waged the Revolutionary War against the British because of grievances such as "taxation without representation" that paled in comparison with the mass killings of the Caracazo.

It was not a decision Arias came to lightly. He had long advocated finding peaceful ways to provoke change in Venezuela.

On many occasions I thought we had to make a gesture. One time I made a proposal to some colleagues. I told them, "Why don't we go — a complete battalion or even two — and place our rifles at the foot of the statue of the Liberator Simón Bolívar and demand that the politicians take the situation of the country seriously, the situation of poverty, the situation of corruption, the situation of anarchy, the situation of an absence of true democracy." And they looked at me and they said, "Yes, go ahead and do that, and they'll take you to the fifteenth floor of the military hospital [for the insane] and tell you you've gone nuts, and nothing will happen. You have to act with force" . . . We are going to have deaths, but they are necessary to make the changes happen.

By early 1992 that was a point of view shared by more than a few Venezuelans, who while opposed to dictatorships and violence were disgusted by the country's corrupt political establishment. Arias knew the sentiment on the street. "The perception that we lived in a system of injustice, of oppression, of abuse, of corruption — all of us Venezuelans had this stuck in our heads and we wanted to break with this. So it was very simple."

After the meeting with the air force officers ended early that morning, Chávez drove to his house in Maracay to say good-bye to his children, Rosa Virginia, María Gabriela, and Hugo Jr., and to his wife, Nancy. They were all in bed. On a table he left Nancy a check and some cash he got out of the bank. He didn't know if he would return. Pumped with adrenaline, full of hope and fear, he was unable to sleep and uncertain what the next crucial hours would bring — a new revolutionary Venezuela or, perhaps, his own death. "I didn't sleep that night, going over documents, having the kind of feeling of arriving at the end of a chapter of my life and not knowing if another chapter would begin, or if everything would end there. I went through a lot of memories, looked at the kids sleeping, and finally I left."

Dressed in a T-shirt and blue jeans, he drove toward the air base in Maracay. He stopped near the Tapa-Tapa tollbooth at about 7 A.M. and called some of his co-conspirators. "OK, let's play ball," Chávez said, using a prearranged code. "Yesterday we played the game we had planned, and the score was 2–1." The code called for adding up the score to indicate the day the rebellion would take place — February 3. Chávez kept driving, then stopped at the Aragua Park Plaza and made some more calls to other rebels. By 9 A.M. he was at the air base mobilizing his troops. The men were packing parachutes, preparing uniforms, gathering in formation.

Only a handful of officers knew the Bolivarians were preparing to take part not in an air show, but in a coup. As for the troops, they were completely in the dark. As Chávez has told it:

> I had my battalion, they were twenty officials and more than five hundred soldiers. Of them, only a very small group of the officials knew what we were going to do that night. The troops didn't know anything. I had a dilemma: I had been trained to be a leader and I felt like if I was their leader, then I couldn't take these guys to

Caracas and ask them to risk their lives without telling them what it was all about.

So first I called together the officials and explained the military operation. And I told them that if any of them were not in agreement, they could give me their pistol and lock themselves in their rooms until I left with the battalion for Caracas and they would be free to go home or wherever they liked. Before then, however, I could not let them leave. One of them started crying and said to me: "Don't think I'm a coward, but it's my wife, the kids . . ." "It's OK, go home, but you can't leave until after I do." And that is what he did, and afterward he submitted his resignation, he couldn't deal with the pressure. He was the only one who had asked to stay behind. Later I brought the soldiers together and gave them the same pitch.

Other troops never found out they were taking part in a coup until they were about to engage in combat to take the objectives in Caracas and elsewhere around the country. That morning Chávez and others scrambled to find transportation to take the troops to the capital. They found a private bus company at the local terminal, hired thirty drivers, and told them to show up at 8 P.M. That would give them enough time to get to Caracas before the *hora cero* of midnight. They planned simultaneous attacks on Miraflores, La Casona, and nearby La Carlota military air base.

Later, at about 1 P.M., Chávez went over to Los Palos air base in another part of the city to speak with Visconti and deliver a radio for the operation. Visconti again pleaded with Chávez to hold off on the revolt, saying the air force wasn't ready. But Chávez insisted there was no turning back.

The first troops to leave from Maracay were under the command of Major Francisco Javier Centeno. He loaded 250 soldiers into buses and trucks that also were carrying cooking equipment and other supplies to set up an advance camp for the air show at Carabobo Field. Supposedly they were going to spend the night there. Instead their secret plan called for quietly departing for Caracas later on. At about 6:30 P.M. Centeno and his men left the air base. Within half an hour they made their way to neighboring Carabobo state and the park that was the site of the famous battle of Carabobo led by Bolívar.

By about 7 P.M. Urdaneta and Acosta Chirinos took control of San Jacinto barracks in Maracay. Urdaneta called Chávez, indicating by code that their first move was a success: "The bird is in the cage." Chávez was busy seizing the Páez barracks where his unit was located across town. Meanwhile, outside Caracas a commando team was preparing to descend on the airport to seize Pérez. The plan seemed to be progressing, although Chávez received unsettling news in code from several barracks. Some rebels were backing out. The stakes were high. They could lose their military careers. They could lose their lives.

"I can't make it."
"The party's today. Send me the whisky."
"No, we can't send the whisky. We couldn't get the money."
"OK, don't send me anything."

While the problems seemed surmountable, in reality the plot already was imperiled. Hours earlier, a captain whose mission was to take over the military academy in Caracas where he was stationed was having last-minute doubts. Captain René Gimón Álvarez had a personal conflict. He was dating the daughter of the new director of the military academy. Eventually he would marry her. Guilt-stricken, late that morning he approached his future father-in-law and revealed some details of the plot in Caracas. He did not disclose the full scope of the nationwide operation or the identities of its leaders. But his decision alerted the government for the first time to a concrete plan. By early afternoon military superiors were meeting in Caracas to determine what was happening and try to head it off. As a precaution they ordered troops at Fort Tiuna confined to their barracks. They also disabled tanks and other vehicles by removing ammunition, radios, and batteries.

The "head of the snake," as Chávez called it, since Caracas was the centerpiece of the revolt, was getting chopped off. But he and the other coup leaders knew nothing about it. Chávez received a single call from a collaborator in the capital, at about 4 P.M., but the informant did not know of the leak or the move to corral the rebellion.

Blind to events unfolding in Caracas, Chávez and his men left Maracay at about 10 P.M. in the civilian buses they rented. They departed with the excuse they were headed to the Liberator air base across town to prepare for the air show the next day. They divided into three columns taking three different routes to the capital. If any of them were stopped, they figured, the others would still make it. On at least one bus rebels placed a Carl Gustav anti-tank gun near the front. If loyalist troops attacked them on the way to Caracas, they would open fire.

As Chávez and his troops prepared to depart, Defense Minister Fernando Ochoa Antich was in the air on his way from Maracaibo to Caracas. Ochoa had spent the day in the western oil state of Zulia. The hierarchy in Caracas did not advise him of the reports of a possible coup. It was a mystifying decision. Ochoa later figured they might have had several motivations. Maybe they thought they had it under control. Maybe they didn't believe a coup attempt was really occurring. Maybe they didn't want to upset Pérez.

Whatever the reason, Ochoa did not learn of the coup reports until he stepped off an airplane at Simón Bolívar International Airport outside Caracas at 8:30 P.M. He received a telephone call from a National Guard commander, who told him rumors were flying that Pérez was going to be the target of an attack that night. Ochoa took the information half seriously. Coup rumors had become routine.

He got into his car to head back to Caracas. But as he reached the first tunnel five minutes later, he found himself blocked from entering. Inside, a car was on fire. For the first time he thought something might be afoot. Ochoa turned around, headed back toward the airport, and stopped at a National Guard barracks. Personally assuming command, he ordered the soldiers to take over the airport. He also summoned the DISIP political police for added security. Soon some four hundred soldiers swarmed the airport, lining the landing strips, clambering on top of roofs, occupying the control towers, standing guard at the power plant to prevent sabotage.

As Ochoa was springing into action to safeguard the airport, Arias Cárdenas was preparing his troops for their assault on the heart of the nation's oil capital, Maracaibo. At about 9:30 P.M. he called thirty-five officers into his office. Half of them already knew about the revolt and were committed to taking part. The rest didn't know, but had been prepared ideologically by Arias. He often talked to them and handed out books and articles about Venezuela's infirm democracy, the historical role of the military as defenders of *el pueblo*, and the legacy of Bolívar and other leading fathers.

That night, "I told them this is what's happening in the country, that we need to stop being the guard dogs for the politicians, that we have to resolve the misery, the poverty, the abuses, and construct a real democracy." When Arias concluded by announcing that he wanted his unit to take part in a nationwide coup attempt in the next few hours, every officer agreed to join in — even one of Ochoa Antich's nephews.

Arias swore them in with the oath of the Bolivarian rebels. Then he went over the details of the operation. They planned to take over fifteen key locations, including military bases, police stations, National Guard headquarters, the governor's mansion, and oil installations. Arias had ordered five days' worth of C-rations for the unit. He thought combat might be extensive.

With his officers on board, Arias walked over to the barracks. He ordered his seven hundred soldiers to assemble on the courtyard and gave them a similar talk. The soldiers knew nothing about the coup plot against Pérez. As Arias revealed the plan, they erupted into cheers. They hated Pérez as much as anyone. The time of *el pueblo* has finally arrived! some of them shouted. We're going to leave the misery behind! No more humiliation! No more oppression! Some of the soldiers were so excited, they started to cry. Others hugged. Their moment had finally come to strike back at a system that left their own families in misery. The outburst became so effusive Arias finally had to step in to call them to order. Gentlemen, he said, this is a military operation. We are going to have the celebration after we finish fulfilling the mission.

By 10 P.M. they moved out from the military base to prepare for the attack.

Ten minutes later the presidential jet touched down in Maiquetia. It was twenty minutes early. Favorable tailwinds sped up the trip. When the aircraft pulled up to Ramp Number Four reserved for the head of state, Pérez was met with an unusual sight. A dozen yellow DISIP cars surrounded the ramp. On the tarmac, Ochoa Antich and Interior Minister Virgilio Avila Vivas waited to greet him.

As he came down the airplane's stairs to a presidential car ready to whisk him away, Pérez demanded to know what was going on. Ochoa said there were rumors of an uprising. But he assured the president everything was under control. He added that he would fill him in more on the trip back to Caracas. He wanted to get the president out of there as quickly as possible.

They sped off, and the rebels' Plan A was foiled. With so many soldiers guarding the airport, the commando team was helpless. As Pérez and the others climbed the mountain highway toward Caracas, Ochoa supplied more details about the reports of a coup or even an assassination attempt. Pérez wasn't alarmed or worried. He was angry. He was sick of hearing about coup rumors. He thought they were undermining his administration. These rumors are what damage the government, the irritated president told Ochoa in the car. I'll wait for you at seven tomorrow morning in Miraflores so we can investigate what is going on.

As they reached the first tunnel, one side was still blocked because of the burning car. Soldiers stopped traffic on the other side to let the presidential caravan by. They passed through without incident. The rebels' Plan B had failed. Pérez's car made it through the capital city smoothly. By 10:45 P.M. he arrived at La Casona presidential residence in eastern Caracas. Pérez was so assured no revolt was going to take place, he went into the colonial mansion, put on his pajamas, and went to bed.

Before long he was deeply asleep, exhausted after a three-day trip during which the sixty-nine-year-old president barely slept. He had little reason to rest easy, though. One of the columns from Maracay was about to arrive.

At about 11:15 P.M. on the other side of the country, Arias Cárdenas issued the order to attack in Maracaibo. His operation had to be moved up half an hour or so. Authorities had detected unusual movements of rebel tanks at a military base outside of the city earlier in the night. Arias was worried authorities would realize that his unit, too, was preparing to act. So he plunged into action ahead of time before they could stop him.

Rebels stormed police stations, the National Guard headquarters, the DISIP secret police office, the governor's mansion, and the oil installations. They met little resistance. The city of two million people — home to one of the world's largest oil reserves and operations — fell into their hands almost effortlessly. The authorities were caught so off guard, they had almost no time to react. Barely a shot was fired. Almost no one was injured. By midnight the rebels controlled the city.

In Caracas, Ochoa Antich had gone to his home at Fort Tiuna. As he was turning in for the night at about 11:30, he received a call from a Democratic Action congressman, who told him he was hearing reports of a military uprising in Maracaibo. He gave Ochoa the name of a commander to call. The commander confirmed the report. The news set off alarm bells for Ochoa. He realized the revolt was not confined to the rumors of trouble in Caracas. He immediately called La Casona and ordered the operator to put him through to the president. But Pérez was sound asleep. After several failed attempts to rouse him, Ochoa called one of Pérez's daughters, Carolina, and told her to wake the president. It was urgent. When she did, Ochoa told him soldiers in Zulia were revolting. A rebellion really was under way. They might want to kill the president. A groggy Pérez responded that he would head to Miraflores Palace right away.

Pressed for time, Pérez didn't bother to take off his pajamas. He simply put the shirt, pants, and suit jacket he'd worn on the trip back from Switzerland over them. He rushed out of the residence, jumped into a car with a driver and a bodyguard, and pulled out. He barely missed the rebels, who were just arriving. They didn't shoot or try to stop him. They might not have known it was the president. Instead of departing with his typical large entourage of cars and motorcycles, he'd left in a single vehicle. With luck on his side, he slipped through the rebels' fingers again.

He had barely departed when the Bolivarians attacked. In a bloody blaze of bullets, soldiers, police, presidential guards, and rebels shot it out in the normally quiet, leafy residential neighborhood. Startled residents jumped out of their beds. First Lady Blanca Rodríguez Pérez huddled inside with other family members. They gathered in her bedroom as the building shook and bullets chewed up the white wall surrounding it.

Half a mile away rebels led by Acosta Chirinos unleashed an attack on La Carlota military air base. They captured the base's commanders and blocked airplanes from taking off. It was a critical move. It would protect the rebels on the ground from air attack. Across town, the Bolivarians were closing in on Miraflores. They had a column of tanks.

As Pérez's car barreled down the highway, his guards got a call on their radios that La Casona was under attack. Pérez was shocked. At two minutes past midnight, he pulled into the palace. His car sped through a large metal gate that separated the palace grounds from Urdaneta Avenue, raced one hundred yards up a paved driveway, and screeched to a halt at the *puerta amarilla*, yellow door. It was a special, ceremonial entrance reserved for the president and visiting dignitaries. Palace soldiers in colorful dress uniforms usually guarded it. But now the gleaming white century-old palace was quiet. Many of the presidential troops were asleep in their barracks across the street.

Pérez jumped out of the car, dashed up the stairs to the *puerta amarrilla*, and turned left into a small waiting room that led to his office. Waiting inside were Senator Luis Alfaro Ucero, a leader of the Democratic Action Party, and Virgilio Avila Vivas, the interior minister in charge of domestic security. They had gotten word of the troubles and rushed to the palace. Pérez was enraged with both of them. How was it possible that a coup attempt was being planned for months, if not years, and neither the government nor the party knew anything about it? Why didn't you warn me? he shouted, pacing around the room and waving his arms. Pérez said he suspected a lieutenant colonel named Hugo Chávez was behind the revolt. Carlos Peñaloza and others had told him all about it.

As the president vented at the two men, the head of his security team, Vice Admiral Mario Ivan Carratú, was pulling into the palace. Jumping out of his car, Carratú bounded up a set of ornate marble stairs to his own office on the other side of the palace. He bumped into one of the president's bodyguards, Romel Fuenmayor, who looked like he was ready for war. He had a machine gun and a pistol in his hands, a revolver stuck in his belt, a knife strapped to his leg, hand grenades lashed to his chest, a combat helmet on his head, and a bulletproof vest across his torso.

Fuenmayor, Carratú, and the number two man on his security team, Colonel Rafael Hung Díaz, made their way to the small waiting room outside Pérez's office. A presidential bodyguard, Colonel Gerardo Dudamel, stood at the entrance. Carratú waited for a break in Pérez's ranting to talk to him.

About thirty seconds later they heard a loud crash outside. They dashed out of the waiting room and through the *puerta amarrilla*. Pérez darted over to a window behind his desk. What the men saw shocked them: A tank had smashed through the metal gate by the street and was coming straight at them. More tanks were following. Behind them soldiers were running in, faces smeared with camouflage paint. Despite the lockdown at Fort Tiuna, about two hundred rebels had managed to escape. They were led by Blanco La Cruz and Rojas Suárez, the young captains who had nearly betrayed Chávez in December by launching a coup themselves.

A few seconds after the first tank smashed through the gate, flashes of light flickered from a machine gun on one tank in the rear. It sprayed the palace walls with bullets. Pérez flinched and backed away from the window in his office. He might have been hit if not for the bulletproof glass. A handful of loyalist soldiers who were across the street in towers at the barracks opened fire, creating a blistering crossfire.

The first tank braked abruptly in front of Carratú and the others, and a soldier gripping a FAL assault rifle leaped down. "We're going to kill you like dogs!" he shouted. "Fatherland or death!" When the soldier landed on the ground, Fuenmayor grabbed his weapon. Shots rang out as the two wrestled. Caught by surprise and overwhelmed by the assault, Carratú and the others fled inside to take cover.

In the waiting room Dudamel had run inside Pérez's office, slammed shut the heavily fortified bulletproof metal door, and locked it with a key. Carratú and the others ran through the *puerta amarrilla*, passed the waiting room, and sprinted twenty-five yards to his office on the other side of the palace. Carratú fumbled for the keys to his safebox to get out his pistol. Amid the attack and his nervousness he couldn't open the safe. Pérez's car was parked outside, but his chauffeur had run inside to protect himself. Carratú shouted at him to go back and retrieve the weapons inside the car: two mini Uzi submachine guns. The driver got them, handing one to Carratú and the other to Hung Díaz. His heart racing, the vice admiral quickly got on the telephone to call for reinforcements. Hung Díaz and Fuenmayor stood near the door, arms ready.

The rebels quickly attacked, charging through the *puerta amarrilla* with their guns blazing. Hung Díaz, Fuenmayor, and a few other guards poked their heads out from behind the door and some large potted plants and returned fire. The Bolivarians kept storming in, turning left into the waiting room with the door to the president's office ten yards in front of them. Before long the floor and even the door were bathed in blood. At one point during the combat, a bullet grazed the head of Blanco La Cruz, who crumpled to the ground and passed out as blood poured. Some of the rebels thought he was dead. They dragged him away, threw him on a tank, and later took him out of the area.

With the sound of gunfire exploding outside his door, Pérez walked over to his desk, picked up a small black executive-style suitcase that was lying next to it, and opened it. Inside were two pistols and an Uzi submachine gun. Pérez's guards carried the suitcase wherever the president went for his use in case of emergency. Pérez knew how to handle the weapons well. He often practiced at the presidential retreat on the Caribbean island of La Orchila and other places. He removed the Uzi from the suitcase, turned off the safety, and prepared to defend himself.

He decided his best chance of survival was to flee his office. He opened a concealed door at the rear. The president, Alfaro Ucero, Avila Vivas, and the bodyguard Dudamel darted through the door to the adjoining office of Pérez's private secretary, and then to a stairwell. It led to the president's private quarters upstairs — a bedroom, kitchen, and small office. Pérez made it halfway up the stairs, and froze. He couldn't go any farther. Bullets were coming through the windows and the roof on the second floor. He stood paralyzed on the stairwell, clutching the Uzi and trying to figure out where to go. He was trapped.

Down the hall Carratú was trying to get help. He was calling frantically for reinforcements. He tried the defense minister but couldn't get through. He called the head of the president's honor guard in the barracks across the street; the commander told him that rebels had taken the tunnels connecting the barracks with Miraflores. He called the local head of the National Guard, who said he couldn't do anything immediately: He had to regain control of the troops and of the city first. Carratú hung up and realized there was only one option. He had to get Pérez out of the palace.

He waited for a break in the shooting and then sprinted down a hallway. As he passed a ten-yard open stretch where the rebels had a shot at him, he fired his Uzi. He found Pérez inside the stairwell and told him the situation was hopeless. Mr. President, we have no time, he said. We can't defend ourselves. The tunnels are taken. We are surrounded by tanks. There is no possibility of help from the army. There is no help from the National Guard. The rebels have taken the palace militarily. We don't have the capacity to resist. We have to leave.

But Pérez did not want to leave. He wanted to fight back. We have to defend the palace, he told Carratú. We have to defend the country and defend democracy. Carratú insisted they would be killed if they stayed; they had to leave. Pérez finally relented. If that's the case, he said, then get me out of here immediately.

Carratú took off running about four hundred yards through secret tunnels. He reached a heavy glass door that led to the parking garage housing the presidential motor fleet. The door was locked. He didn't have the key. So Carratú took the butt of his Uzi and smashed it. He pounded the door at least a dozen times, carving out a jagged waist-high opening large enough to climb through. He slipped through the gap, ran over to a guard, and shouted for him to prepare the president's car. He told him he wanted a gray one. Most presidential cars were black. He didn't want to give the rebels any clues.

Rebels were inside the palace, outside the palace, and had all the exits covered — all except one: the huge metal door that opened from the parking garage onto the street at the rear of Miraflores. Carratú raced back to the stairwell, told the president he was ready, and led him and others through the tunnels. Still clutching his Uzi, Pérez climbed through the hole in the door, made his way to the car, and jumped in.

They were ready to leave, but now there was another problem. No one had the key or the electronic device to open the gate. Two parking garage guards were lying on the floor injured and yelling for help. They'd been shot by rebels firing on the palace from outside. The only option was to try to hot-wire the cables in the control box. Carratú jumped out of the car, ran over to the box, and tore it open. Splicing wires together, he got the door to open. It wasn't a second too soon. Tires squealing, they roared out of the garage and swung wildly to the right. Fifty yards up the hilly street to the left, a tank and soldiers were descending on them. The president barely escaped again.

Pérez's entourage had no idea where to go. They swung onto grimy Baralt Avenue and climbed a mile up an incline toward Mount Avila. They turned onto Cota Mil Highway, which ran along the foot of the mountain. They were safe for the moment, but Pérez was livid. He was yelling about the disloyal military hierarchy and Chávez, the man he was convinced was behind the plot.

The president told Carratú he wanted to get to a radio or television station to show the nation he was still in control and that the rebels had failed. He thought his appearance might demoralize them and prompt them to give up. Picking up a car phone, Carratú called the operator at Miraflores. The rebels had smashed a tank through the metal gates outside the Palacio Blanco across the street from Miraflores and climbed halfway up the stairs with it. But they had failed to reach the fourth floor where the government's main switchboard was housed. Carratú told the operator to get him in touch with the first radio or television station he could. Thirty seconds later the operator called back. He had Venevisión, one of the country's major networks, on the line.

It was the network's nighttime head of security, and Carratú knew him. Carratú said he needed to go on the air. He didn't mention he actually wanted the president to speak. The guard told him to come. Pérez's car exited the highway, sped through the middle-class La Florida neighborhood, and screeched to a halt at the television station headquarters.

The men ran in and were rushed upstairs to the office of the network's president, Gustavo Cisneros. He was the richest man in Venezuela and a friend of President George H. W. Bush. To the side of Cisneros's office was a small, plain broadcast studio. Pérez walked in and got ready to go on the air. The president was flustered. He had just escaped from a palace under siege. He knew the rebels were hunting for him. He still had on his blue pajamas under his suit. Part of the shirt was sticking out from under his collar. Carratú mentioned it. Pérez shoved the pajama top back inside.

A couple of minutes after they arrived, at about 1:15 A.M., Pérez went on the air. His hair was mussed. He was nervous. Speaking rapidly, he told the Venezuelan people that a coup attempt had been launched — but he remained in charge of the country. "The subversive antipatriotic movement is being brought under control," the shocked president said. "I ask all of you for confidence and faith in the democratic system . . . Be confident. Democracy will win."

The message lasted just a few minutes, but the station kept repeating it so the nation would see it as word of the revolt spread and people turned on their televisions. It was about an hour after the rebels had first attacked Miraflores. Pérez's claim that the rebellion was under control was false. Major barracks around the country were under siege. Pitched battles were raging at La Carlota and La Casona. Rebels were swarming through Miraflores. The city of Maracaibo was under Bolivarian control. The state governor was a prisoner in his own mansion.

But Pérez's appearance gave the impression he was in charge, shaky as it was. It would soon help turn the tide in the government's favor by demoralizing the rebels, whose chief objectives included capturing the president. He would make more appearances as the night went on.

The man in charge of the rebellion nationwide, Hugo Chávez, had missed the early action. By the time the battle broke out at Miraflores, he was just arriving in Caracas. By his own account, he pulled in somewhere between 12:30 and 1 A.M., initially with just a few fellow officers. Chávez headed to the Museo Histórico Militar on a hilltop a mile from Miraflores. He could see the palace from there. He expected to be met by soldiers who were to leave Fort Tiuna about 10:30 P.M., take over the museum, and install the communications equipment he would use to direct the rebellion.

But the soldiers had never left the fort because superiors had them confined to the barracks. Instead of fellow rebels, machine-gun fire greeted Chávez, as he recounted the story. Loyalist soldiers sent at the last minute by the government were occupying the museum. When Chávez arrived they had no idea who it was, so they opened fire. The bullets barely missed Chávez, who — employing deception and some quick thinking — shouted that he had come to reinforce the loyalist troops amid reports of a possible social uprising. They fell for it, letting Chávez and his colleagues in.

But it was the first sign for Chávez that something had gone wrong. There were no rebel troops, no communications equipment, no way of knowing what was going on in the rest of the country or even in the capital. He was cut off. "I was almost a prisoner starting the operation . . . We arrived to a vacuum. There was almost nothing, no one to back up, no one to connect with. The page of Caracas was ripped out of the notebook. Some fragments remained that we couldn't put back together or connect. It was a terrible confusion."

Before long, the colonel in charge of the museum turned on the television and saw Pérez talking, according to Chávez's account. The president spoke of an elite paratrooper unit from Maracay leading the rebellion. The colonel turned to Chávez suspiciously and confronted him. Chávez's ruse was up. Yes, this is a coup d'état and you are surrounded, Chávez told him. Hand over the weapons, because if you don't, a massacre will start.

It was a lie, of course. The one who was surrounded was Chávez. Luckily for him, Major Centeno, the commander who was supposedly camping out at Carabobo Field that night with his troops, was pulling up with two busloads of soldiers. He shouted out to Chávez. There are my men, Chávez told the colonel. Hand over the weapons and put your men under my command. The colonel relented, and Chávez won his first small victory of the night. It was about 2 A.M.

Then he waited. Incommunicado and blind to what was happening in most of Caracas and the country, he didn't think he had much choice. In hindsight, his detractors accused him of lacking the courage to attack the palace. Years later the defense minister, Ochoa Antich, still contended Chávez could have emerged victorious if he had sent his troops from the museum to help Blanco La Cruz and Rojas Suárez at Miraflores. He believed they could have captured the country's symbolic seat of power, prompted more barracks around the country to rise up, and turned the tide of the revolt. "No one understands why Hugo Chávez didn't attack," Ochoa stated. "He knew what was happening, he could see it. He lacked personal courage to attack Miraflores." Others speculated that Chávez didn't head to the palace because he was worried Blanco La Cruz and Rojas Suárez planned to kill him as part of a Bandera Roja plot.

But to Chávez, that had nothing to do with it. He had little idea of what was happening on the ground and no contact with the rebels at the palace. His principal mission, as he has told it, was to command the entire operation nationwide from the museum and provide support to the troops assaulting Miraflores if he could. Now, amid the confusion and uncertainty, he needed to employ common sense and good judgment.

> Any action there . . . would have been like stopping in the middle of this dark room, without knowing where the wall was, and launch a coup, senselessly. Kill a few people and die, a senseless and fratricidal fight. Any operation there would have been blind. There was no information of any kind, there was no information about what was happening below, absolutely nothing, not even communication with our forces. The thing to do was wait for events to develop . . . That is to say, to launch an attack with one hundred men against a regiment is a suicidal thing, and without knowing what was happening, it's craziness and they taught us not to do crazy things.

So Chávez waited in the dark "for events to develop." At Miraflores the shooting slowed. Hung Díaz negotiated with the rebels by radio to try to get them to surrender. When he advised them that the president had left the palace, they didn't believe it. So he told them to turn on the television. When they did, their spirits sank. In the meantime the government was regrouping. Ochoa Antich ordered troops and tanks from Fort Tiuna and La Guaira on the Caribbean coast to reinforce loyalists at the palace. They were set to arrive by 2:30 A.M.

Pérez's appearance on television shocked members of Venezuela's political and business establishment. Many flocked to Venevisión to support him. Some, including COPEI's Eduardo Fernández, went on the air themselves. They denounced the coup and voiced their backing for the unpopular but democratically elected president. At about 2:30 A.M., Pérez went on for a second time. This round was smoother. Instead of the barren background shown the first time, someone moved a Venezuelan flag next to the president. Accompanied by supporters who eventually numbered two hundred, Pérez appeared more self-assured. The rebels tried to "launch a coup to kill me," he said, but "I have counted on the support of the entire nation."

Word of the shocking coup attempt was starting to spread around the world. Two hours after initial reports of it were received in the United States, Assistant Secretary of State Bernard Aronson called Pérez, "who offered assurances that loyalist troops would prevail." Still, shortly before 2 A.M. (3 A.M. in Venezuela), Aronson called Secretary of State James Baker III, who awakened President Bush minutes later. Bush called Pérez to express his support for Venezuelan democracy.

By about 2:45 A.M. the rebels at Miraflores surrendered. Pérez was gone. Chávez was nowhere to be seen or heard from. Loyalist reinforcements were descending on the palace. It was the first major crack of the rebellion. About fifteen minutes later Pérez and his team left the television station and returned to Miraflores. Ochoa Antich joined them there. Pérez soon went on the air for a third time, transmitting live to the nation from behind his desk. He assured the nation again that he was in charge.

While the government had retaken Miraflores, in reality rebels were still battling soldiers at La Casona and La Carlota. They also controlled important barracks in Maracay, Valencia, and Maracaibo. And the leader of the revolt, Chávez, was still on the loose. The first order of business was getting him to surrender.

Ochoa Antich got the palace switchboard operator to put him through to the Museo Histórico Militar. At about 4 A.M. he spoke to Chávez. The insurrection is over, Ochoa told him. You've lost. You are surrounded. We have recovered the palace. The president has spoken to the nation. All you have left are a few units supporting you.

Chávez refused to concede. Instead, he asked Ochoa to come to the museum to talk. It was a ruse — Chávez would try to kidnap him if he came. Ochoa did not fall for it, so Chávez suggested they meet at a halfway point. The defense minister rejected that, too. As they spoke, another general, Ramón Santeliz Ruíz, came into Pérez's office. Santeliz was friendly with Chávez. Some even believed he was sympathetic to his movement and had dabbled with groups such as ARMA. Ochoa figured Santeliz could help mediate. He offered to send him to the museum.

When Santeliz arrived, Chávez learned for the first time details of what was happening around the country. Santeliz told him rebels were in control of Maracaibo, and that a column of tanks was on its way from the city of Valencia. But Caracas was lost, and the media were lost. Chávez told him he still wasn't going to surrender. Santeliz returned to Miraflores with the message.

In reality, Chávez knew he was in trouble. Most of the troops in Caracas — the nerve center of the operation — had failed to appear, dealing a heavy blow to the rebellion.

> I was like a tiger in a cage. I didn't know how to confront this, how to direct it . . . In Caracas nearly three thousand or four thousand men were committed, and of these barely five officers, two lower-level officers and some fifty soldiers, in twelve tanks without ammunition and without radios, left in a suicidal action against Miraflores. That's why you see the image of the tank crashing against the wall. It was the impotence of the man who made a commitment and an oath and wants to fulfill it. And the tank goes up the stairs, that's why one sees the figure of this tank arriving to crash against Miraflores Palace, it's the dignity of the man, almost like a desperate Kamikaze.

With the crucial operation in Caracas a failure, Chávez was by now stalling for time. As dawn approached, he was hoping for two things that might turn the tide: General Visconti and the air force arriving at daylight, and the people of the slums rising up in revolt. But Visconti never came. As for the civilians, they were an equal disappointment.

By Chávez's account, civilians especially from the Causa R Party were to play an important role in the uprising. They were supposed to show up at prearranged points and receive weapons from the rebels. They were even given secret passwords. But in the end, according to Chávez, few came. It left him bitter and distrustful.

> We were working together on the popular component and the military component of the military rebellion that we were planning. A few days before it all came together, in a meeting of the national

directors, they decided to withdraw their support from the rebellion. But the worst thing was they didn't tell us about their decision although we had already committed to action, to plans of combat. We had previously agreed that they would organize their people to go to pre-arranged points where we were going to distribute weapons, but only [Causa R congressman] Alí Rodríguez was there waiting with a small group, trying in vain to fulfill their responsibility. But as a party the Causa R didn't show up. They publicly hung us out to dry . . .

Later, when they told me about the decision they had made, I didn't want to believe it, because I was still new to politics and I was a soldier, and for me, my word was my honor . . . The experience made me lose my political virginity — if you will excuse the expression — what with politics, and commitments, and broken promises.

Some of the civilians including the Causa R's Pablo Medina have told a different story, contending that Chávez and the others never showed up with the weapons. Several months before the revolt, former guerrilla leader Douglas Bravo met with Chávez in an attempt to resolve their long-simmering differences and collaborate in the rebellion. The meeting ended in failure, and their relationship broke off definitively. Bravo argued that civilian action should precede military action but, according to him, Chávez was not interested:

We met to talk about the plans for the uprising . . . We said that first of all there should be a civil action, like the general strike organized by the Patriotic Junta on January 23 [1958]. The military action would come later. This was so that civil society should have an active participation in the revolutionary movement. But that was exactly what Chávez did not want. Absolutely not! Chávez did not want civilians to participate as a concrete force. He wanted civil society to applaud but not to participate, which is something quite different . . . No one can give an opinion at his side . . . He doesn't allow dissidence or a different opinion.

As Chávez debated what to do, back at Miraflores Palace a livid Pérez considered bombing the museum to end the standoff. Some of his aides suggested buzzing it first instead. At about 6 A.M., with dawn breaking, Ochoa ordered several F-16s at the air base in Maracay to fly over the Museo Histórico Militar. He wanted to send a clear message to Chávez. Ochoa called him again. He informed him that fighter jets were in the air, most of the rebellious barracks had surrendered, and marines were on their way from the coast to Caracas to attack the museum. It was going to be a bloodbath.

Using the information he got from Santeliz, Chávez responded that the rebels were in control of Maracay and the governor of Zulia was a prisoner. We have tanks on the way from Valencia, he added, and control of that city, too. "This is just beginning," Chávez boasted. It was a false bravado: He knew the revolt was collapsing. Desperate for air support, he was able to reach Jesús Urdaneta in Maracay. But the news was not good. Compadre, send me air support, Chávez said. Urdaneta told him the airplanes had left, "but they are going to fire on you. We've lost control of the base."

Losing patience, Pérez instructed Ochoa to inform Chávez that if he did not surrender, the bombing would commence. Ochoa called Chávez for the third time. He told him the F-16s were going to bomb the museum in ten minutes if he did not give up. In reality, Ochoa was not anxious to bomb the museum, which was surrounded by the sprawling 23 de Enero barrio of high-rise apartments. Any bombing would kill and injure scores of civilians.

It was close to 7 A.M. Chávez hung up. A few minutes later he spoke with Santeliz again. He was ready to surrender. He wasn't anxious for a bloody showdown, either, especially one he had little chance of winning.

> I had perceived that the plan wasn't going anywhere. There was no contact with any unit. I didn't know what was happening, only that the president had recovered the symbolic position of power, that the tanks had arrived to Miraflores supporting the president, that the air force [rebels were] tied down to ground, and that we had lost the situation of neutrality in the air and that the F-16s were coming against us.
>
> How can you continue operating so dispersed, so disarticulated, without knowing what was happening in Maracay, in Maracaibo, not even in Caracas? It was impossible to fight blindly. It would have been a disaster for us and for the people, a battle with the high-caliber arms we had [at the museum] in

La Planicie, surrounded by barrios, and without a chance of achieving our objective. You can keep fighting when you have a chance of achieving your objective, but to fight hopelessly, to die or kill, isn't right. .

Chávez told Santeliz his conditions for surrendering. The government had to respect the lives of the rebels and the people in the barrios. It also had to allow him to visit strategic spots around the city to tell his cohorts it was time to end the struggle. Santeliz agreed, and Chávez hung up.

He prepared to turn himself in. He instructed his troops to line up and hand over their weapons. Then he hugged the officers, saluted the soldiers, and got ready to leave. He kept his own pistol, assault rifle, and hand grenades. He figured the loyalists had orders to kill him; he wanted to protect himself. After Santeliz arrived about 8 A.M., the two left quickly. They spent about two hours driving around Caracas so Chávez could tell his cohorts that the rebellion was over. At each stop, he gave a short speech. He said the men had fought valiantly in the name of Bolívar, but it was not possible to attain their objectives at the moment. He called on them to lay down their arms.

Chávez and Santeliz arrived at the Defense Ministry about 10 A.M. A crowd of soldiers was out front awaiting his arrival. As he went inside and entered an elevator, some saluted him. He took it as tacit approval of his actions. He reached the fifth-floor office of Ochoa Antich, who was still at Miraflores, saluted an officer, and said he had come to surrender. He handed over his pistol, assault rifle, hand grenades, and radio, and sat down on a couch. He asked a soldier to get him a cup of coffee and some cigarettes. He was nervous. He was also depressed. "Surrendering is worse than death. When I gave up, I told my men, I would have preferred death, that is, I broke into pieces and I was breaking into pieces."

As he dragged on a cigarette, he listened to the generals and other officers in the room debate how to finish off the last of the resistance. Some were shouting orders into the telephone. They wanted to end it by noon. Chávez learned some of the details of what was happening around the country. Arias had left Zulia to fly to Caracas to take part in the negotiations. Acosta Chirinos had given up at La Carlota. But Urdaneta was still fighting in Maracay, refusing to abandon the struggle. Chávez remembered his words ten years earlier when they had founded the EBR, which he repeated the day before they launched the coup: "If we fail, I'm not giving up. I'll fight to the death." Now Urdaneta had cut the telephone lines in Maracay, apparently determined to keep his word.

The generals in Ochoa Antich's office were shouting into the telephones for the fighter jets to begin bombing the military base at Maracay. Chávez protested. How can you bomb them if we have surrendered? he said. He asked if he could call Urdaneta to tell him to lay down his arms. But the telephone lines were cut. He asked if he could fly to Maracay to speak to Urdaneta personally. The generals ruled that out, too: So many aircraft were in the skies, they would probably be shot down. Chávez had another idea: Could he go on a radio station and issue a call for his comrades to lay down their arms? He even knew which one to use, Radio Apolo, a local station in Maracay popular among soldiers in the barracks.

The officers thought it was a good idea. They even suggested using television, too. They checked with Ochoa, who consulted with Pérez. The president agreed. But he insisted Chávez write out what he was going to say and that the television stations tape it so officials could censor anything they didn't like before it aired. Pérez also wanted Chávez presented as a prisoner in handcuffs and out of uniform. Ochoa sent the word back to Fort Tiuna. But Chávez refused to write out his statement. He insisted he was only going to call for his comrades to surrender. The authorities thought there was too little time to tape it, anyway. The situation in Maracay was critical. The message had to go out live. Ochoa allowed them to proceed. He didn't have time to inform Pérez.

As the military heads summoned the press corps and television stations, Chávez thought about General Manuel Noriega when the Americans captured him after the December 1989 invasion of Panama. Noriega was unshaven and wore a wrinkled T-shirt. He looked like a felon. It was precisely the appearance Chávez wanted to avoid. I'm going to appear with dignity, he thought to himself. He went into a bathroom, washed his face, and straightened his uniform. He even put on his red paratrooper beret. The officers didn't make him change out of his camouflage combat uniform as Pérez had ordered. Chávez then walked into a room full of reporters and looked into a bank of television cameras. Repeating a version of the short speech he delivered earlier, he spoke in a confident tone for seventy-two seconds:

First of all, I want to say good morning to all the people of Venezuela. This Bolivarian message is directed to all the courageous soldiers who are in the paratrooper regiment in Aragua and the tank regiment in Valencia. Comrades: Unfortunately, for now, the objectives we had set for ourselves were not achieved in the capital city. That is, those of us here in Caracas did not seize power. Where you are, you performed very well, but now is the time to reflect. New opportunities will arise and the country has to head definitively toward a better future.

So listen to what I have to say, listen to the Comandante Chávez, who is sending you this message. Please, reflect and put down your arms, because in truth, the objectives that we set for ourselves at a national level are not within our grasp. Comrades, listen to this message of solidarity. I am grateful for your loyalty, for your courage, for your selfless generosity. Before the country and before you, I accept responsibility for this Bolivarian military movement. Thank you very much.

He walked out of the room and back to Ochoa's office. He was depressed. He thought he was a failure. "I was very broken up and I felt very defeated. That is, I thought I had carried out the fiasco of the century. Besides surrendering and the plan not working, I had to call on the others to give up. Santeliz sat down on my right side and shook my hand. 'That was great, man, what you said!' I told him, 'What do you mean good, if I called for surrendering?' 'You said, 'for now.' I didn't realize it. It just slipped out. I remember I told him, 'Maybe they will erase that.' 'No, that already came out. That was live.'"

Chávez's appearance was a bombshell. The gallant young officer in the dashing red beret instantaneously captivated millions of people who had never heard of him and were wondering who'd led the stunning rebellion. Chávez started by invoking the sacred national icon of Simón Bolívar. Then he did something almost inconceivable in a country where seemingly everyone dodged accountability: He took responsibility for a failure. "I accept responsibility for this Bolivarian military movement."

He also indicated the rebellion wasn't over yet. Two words — *por ahora*, for now — sounded to many people like a pledge that the rebels would be back someday. They had not achieved their objectives "*por ahora*." The two words instantly turned into the most popular slogan on the streets. In time they became part of Venezuelans' permanent lexicon.

Chávez appeared out of nowhere, giving a face to a faceless rebellion. For years many Venezuelans had been waiting for someone to come to their rescue, a modern-day Bolívar who would avenge the crooked politicians and set the country on a path to prosperity. Now, it seemed, their man had arrived. "Hugo Chávez entered our hearts that day and never left," stated Lisa Sullivan, a longtime Maryknoll Catholic missionary from the United States who was married to a Venezuelan and lived in a barrio in Barquísimeto.

Ochoa Antich had made a terrible miscalculation, one he would regret for years to come. "The most serious mistake was to allow Hugo Chávez, instead of being presented as a military felon who had betrayed the institutions and had been defeated, to be presented in a way as a hero who had risen up against an unjust government that was corrupt, which wasn't true. Rather, it was a constitutional government that had made mistakes like all governments but was classified within what was the democratic evolution of Venezuela . . . It was a political mistake to allow him to go on live. I never imagined it would have the political impact it did."

In Maracay rebel soldiers were tuned in to the television in the barracks when Chávez came on. They summoned Urdaneta, who was stunned and angry as he watched. He didn't want to surrender. But he knew he had no choice. He soon gave up. The attempted coup d'état was over. It was barely noon. An hour later Arias landed in Caracas, only to learn that Chávez had already surrendered and called on the others to lay down their arms. A decade in the making, the Bolivarian uprising had come and gone in twelve hours.

Not everyone was cheering Chávez and the rebels. The oligarchy and most foreign governments were horrified. Venezuela's Congress convened an emergency session that morning. The politicians blasted Chávez and unleashed a stream of fiery rhetoric about the need to defend democracy.

In one of the most dramatic speeches of the day, a prominent Democratic Action congressman named David Morales Bello declared, "Death to the *golpistas*!" Outside Venezuela, the sentiment was not much different. President George H. W. Bush praised Pérez as one of the great democratic leaders of the hemisphere. "To have this outrageous, illegal military coup should certainly be condemned by all countries, not just in our hemisphere," he said. Even Cuba's Fidel Castro, who had never heard of Chávez but was later to become his mentor, joined in the criticism and defended Pérez.

One Venezuelan politician took a different tack. Former president Rafael Caldera, himself an architect of the *Punto Fijo* system, all but endorsed the coup. He rejected the notion that the rebels were attacking democracy. Instead, he said, it was Venezuela's practice of democracy that had failed the people. He blamed Pérez and his neo-liberal economic program for the troubles with the armed forces. He noted that the masses were not pouring into the streets to defend democracy the way they had recently in Eastern Europe, the Philippines, the Southern Cone of South America, and Tiananmen Square in China. Chávez's brief appearance was the speech of the day, but Caldera's was a solid second.

> It is difficult to ask people to self-immolate for freedom and democracy when they think freedom and democracy are not capable of feeding them and stopping the exorbitant rise in the cost of living. When it has not been able to put a stop to the terrible round of corruption that has eroded the institutional legality of the country, as everyone has seen with their own eyes. This is something that cannot be hidden.

Caldera's speech resuscitated his fading political career overnight. Nearly two years later he abandoned the party he founded, COPEI, ran with the support of a splinter party, and was reelected president. He broke the AD-COPEI grip on Miraflores for the first time. Another politician who gave a speech that day along the same lines, Aristóbulo Istúriz of the Radical Cause, was elected mayor of Caracas — the first black to hold that post.

In just over a minute, Chávez had given one of the most remarkable performances in Venezuelan history. "Many specialists have analyzed those words," a leading Venezuelan journalist wrote a decade later. "Never before did so few words have so much influence on the opinion of Venezuelans and the future of events." Chávez became an instant hero. Days after the coup attempt, the most popular costume for children during Carnival celebrations was an imitation of his military fatigues and red beret. By October a best-selling book came out depicting Chávez and the others as courageous avengers of injustice and defenders of democracy. Its title was *La Rebelión de los Angeles — The Rebellion of the Angels*.

The coup left fourteen soldiers, five police, and one civilian dead. Dozens were injured. Some 1,089 soldiers — including 130 officers — were detained and faced charges of sedition and criminal violence. Some military units were left entirely leaderless because all of their officers were involved in the uprising.

The attempt to overthrow Pérez failed, but it managed to catapult a wholly unknown lieutenant colonel to national prominence. From the jaws of military defeat, Chávez seized an unlikely political victory. While his actions left him open to the criticism of detractors who doubted his democratic credentials, Chávez had taken a major step forward in his struggle to transform Venezuela. The country would never be the same.

As he headed off to jail, he would contemplate the next move to propel the Bolivarian movement ahead. Because in the barracks, the plotting was not over yet.

# 11

## Jail

Hugo Chávez thought he was a failure. After surrendering, he and some of the other coup leaders were whisked to military intelligence headquarters. They spent two weeks locked up in cells in the basement as investigators interrogated them. They were cut off from the rest of the world. The lights burned twenty-four hours a day. A video camera filmed their every move. Guards confiscated their shoelaces and belts to prevent suicide attempts.

The rebels had little idea of what was happening outside. They had no newspapers, no television, and for the first week no visitors. Chávez tried to keep up his spirits by singing in his cell. But he was depressed. He thought a decade of conspiring had gone down in ignominious defeat. Worse, some of his comrades — including Urdaneta and Ronald Blanco La Cruz — were seething. They blamed Chávez for the coup's collapse, since he had failed to take Miraflores Palace.

A week into his captivity Chávez received his first visitor and the first hint that outside he was anything but a failure. "The first human being who entered my cell was a priest, a chaplain of the military prison," Chávez later told an interviewer. "This priest secretly gave me a small bible. He hugged me and whispered in my ear. I thought he was going to tell me something spiritually uplifting. But he told me, 'Cheer up. In the streets you're a hero.'"

Seventeen days after authorities dumped the rebel leaders in the basement, they transferred Chávez and the others to the San Carlos military stockade in central Caracas. There they joined hundreds of lower-ranking officers and soldiers who had taken part in the revolt. The trip was a revelation to Chávez and the others. Cheering supporters filled the streets. "When we left military intelligence for the San Carlos jail was when we realized we had produced a true impact, that we had shaken up the bases of the system itself," stated one of the leaders, Joel Acosta Chirinos. "When we were transferred in a caravan and we saw all the people in the streets . . . well, we said, we are like stars. The thing didn't fail like we thought."

The government was still politically tone-deaf. They sent Chávez to a jail just down the street from the National Pantheon, where his hero Simón Bolívar was buried. Chávez did not miss the symbolism. From the start of his captivity, he invoked the Liberator as the guiding light of his rebellion. "The real author of this liberation, the authentic leader of this rebellion is General Simón Bolívar. With his incendiary words he has illuminated the path," Chávez told a journalist from *El Nacional* who managed to interview him in San Carlos. He described how he often gazed out his window toward the Pantheon and Bolívar's remains. The journalist snapped a photograph of Chávez standing serenely before his window.

His popularity spread like wildfire. Newspapers, television networks, and radio stations were full of reports of what could not be hidden: Chávez was a hero. "The soldiers took up arms to fight for us," a nineteen-year-old student told *El Nacional*. "My aunt wept when they gave up. Everyone applauded because they are heroes. I don't think they should be punished. They should be given a medal."

Carlos Andrés Pérez tried to stem Chávez's soaring popularity by eliminating the positive media coverage of him. Two days after the coup, on Thursday, February 6, Pérez dispatched six agents from the feared DISIP political police to search the offices of *Zeta* magazine. Its latest edition featured a photograph of Chávez on the cover in his red beret. Inside a story declared that "a substantial percentage of Venezuelans . . . hoped for victory by the insurgents." Agents confiscated thousands of copies of the magazine.

Later that day Information Minister Andrés Eloy Blanco appeared on television to warn that the news media should "contribute to public tranquility" by imposing temporary self-censorship or face "severe sanctions." The media ignored the threat. On Friday they put out more reports depicting widespread support for the rebels and criticizing Pérez's corrupt government.

Pérez intensified the crackdown. The government seized twenty-five thousand copies of another magazine, *Elite*. Its cover also featured a photograph of Chávez. This one showed him with Pérez and his wife, Blanca. In a move not seen since the dictatorship of Marcos Pérez Jiménez, Pérez stationed censors in newsrooms. Their orders were that television networks, newspapers, and magazines were not to broadcast or print Chávez's picture or put out stories critical of the president.

Police agents allowed the Saturday edition of *El Nacional* to come out only after ensuring that paid advertisements attacking the government were pulled. Political police also raided *El Diario de Caracas*. The newspaper had told readers its Saturday issue would carry a full-color supplement with exclusive photographs of the military uprising. Agents ordered the paper to remove the photographs. Then police confiscated most copies of the supplement.

Pérez appeared at a press conference on Saturday to defend the crackdown. "You should not forget that just four days ago my own life was in danger and our democracy was on the verge of perishing," he said. "Don't exalt the man who attempted the military coup. Let's not make a starring figure out of a felon who betrayed the armed forces and caused death and damage."

That night, government censors ordered *El Nacional* to delete a story about a retired general. He was arrested after a group of sixty-two retired high-ranking military officers ran full-page advertisements in Friday's papers attacking the government and supporting the rebels. Patrol cars from the secret police blocked delivery trucks from leaving the newspaper's printing plant until 1 A.M., after the censors gave their final approval.

The next morning *El Nacional* appeared on newsstands with a gaping white space on the front page where the article was supposed to go.

Late that night the government decided to shut down *El Nacional* completely. Just as the newspaper was going to print, twenty political police stormed into the newspaper's offices and ordered editors to stop the presses. The newspaper managed to print about 2,000 of its normal run of 120,000 copies before the agents halted production. The copies that got out had blank spaces with the word CENSORED where the government ordered stories removed. All other newspapers in the city also were censored.

With criticism of the censorship mounting, Pérez later that day promised to lift the restrictions. Political police withdrew from *El*

*Nacional*, which had been surrounded for about twelve hours. On Tuesday morning the newspaper was back on newsstands with more articles criticizing Pérez. Other newspapers also circulated freely for the first time in four days.

But journalists were seething over the crackdown in Latin America's supposed bastion of democracy. That morning more than one hundred marched through downtown Caracas to Congress shouting "Democracy with censorship is dictatorship!" Pérez's move to quell Chávez's growing popularity had backfired. As much as government censors tried, hatred of the president and admiration for Chávez could not be concealed. "Nearly everyone interviewed on the streets of Caracas expressed negative opinions about Pérez and his free-market reform program," the Associated Press reported that Tuesday. "Chávez appeared to be shaping up as a popular hero."

A few lone voices, mainly in the upper class and in diplomatic circles, came to Pérez's defense. Michael Skol, the US ambassador who had praised Venezuela's 9.2 percent economic growth in 1991, agreed "with the president's portrayal of the coup plotters as a small group of arrogant right-wing fanatics with opinions far removed from the mainstream," *The Christian Science Monitor* reported.

Carlos Peñaloza, the army general who pursued Chávez for seven years, told another reporter he was worried by the rebel leader's "messianic personality." Chávez, he said, "considers himself a God-chosen man, somebody whose destiny was signed by Simón Bolívar, and is not ready to share power with anybody." Peñaloza claimed that the rebels had published a twelve-page manifesto opening with a quote attributed to Thomas Jefferson: "The tree of liberty should be irrigated from time to time with the blood of patriots and tyrants." He also claimed Chávez and his cohorts planned to hang civilian politicians in public squares or execute them by firing squads in sports stadiums. Pérez was at the top of the list.

"The level of hate especially caught my attention," Peñaloza told a television interviewer before government censorship cut off discussion of the rebels. "They were convinced that the only way to wash the honor of the humiliated fatherland was through a ritual bath using the blood of corrupt men who had put our nation on its knees. Chávez Frías was our Saddam Hussein."

But the Bolivarians denied they were going to execute anyone, and few Venezuelans were stirred by Peñaloza's remarks, at least not in the barrios. One economist told *The New York Times* in hushed tones that he was shocked when "the day after the coup, my secretary complained that they failed to kill the president."

A month after the coup, elation over Chávez's rebellion was still burning bright. In an evening demonstration organized by anonymous leaflets and word of mouth, Venezuelans across the nation hung out their windows or stood in their doorways and banged pots and pans. Denouncing Pérez and hailing Chávez, the demonstration spread beyond the slums to some wealthy areas. "Viva Chávez!" one resident yelled in the upscale Las Mercedes district. "The people of Venezuela are with you!"

By now the few working telephone booths in Caracas were spray-painted with messages like CHÁVEZ TO POWER. At the Pantheon, admirers lit candles in Chávez's honor near Bolívar's tomb. One even invented a prayer based on the Our Father, dubbed "Chávez Nuestro": "Our Chávez, who art in jail, blessed be thy coup," was the first line. The last was, "Save us from so much corruption, and free us from Carlos Andrés Pérez. Amen."

By early April, eager to tamp down the hysteria over Chávez, officials transferred him and nine other rebel leaders to a more remote prison in Yare about two hours outside Caracas. The day they moved the rebels, supporters lay down in the streets of the capital to try to block the armored vehicles from leaving.

The transfer did little to dampen the commotion. The crowds of admirers simply followed Chávez to Yare. They were like mesmerized worshippers pursuing their messiah. People wanted to see him, touch him, confirm that he was real. Some trembled in his presence. Others grabbed at his clothes, or passed him notes of admiration or pleas for help. They brought him flowers, clothes, food, a small refrigerator, a microwave, a bookshelf. Long lines of women willing to throw themselves at him fought with one another to be first in line on visiting day. Others sent him letters from all over the country. Chávez was turning into a rock star, a movie star, and a sex symbol, signing autographs as if he were Rock Hudson, Herma Marksman ruefully noted. Except this rock star wanted to overturn Venezuela's political establishment in the name of a nineteenth-century revolutionary.

Authorities helped Chávez cultivate the myth. They allowed him to keep his uniform and red beret. He donned them for clandestine interviews with journalists who snuck in. The authorities kept him and the others in a special part of the jail normally reserved for conjugal visits between inmates and their wives. Each rebel got his own small, private room with a toilet. Outside was a courtyard with a statue of Bolívar. Chávez visited it every day.

The wild adulation he was receiving didn't sit well with all the rebels, though. Frictions invariably set in. Ten headstrong men were living on top of one another in cramped quarters. Arias Cárdenas, who had his own large following among the Bolivarians and was a co-leader of the movement by the time of the coup, was left out of the limelight as Chávez soared to stardom. Serious conflicts erupted between the two in a struggle for leadership and the path the movement should take.

Jesús Urdaneta, one of the founding members of the movement, was back at San Carlos, wallowing in anger at Chávez over the failed coup and the prospect of spending decades in jail. Before he was transferred to Yare, Ronald Blanco La Cruz, the fiery young captain who had nearly split from Chávez in December and launched a coup on his own, spoke of convening a military tribunal in San Carlos to judge Chávez for the failure of the February 4 putsch.

Still, the jailing of the rebels served to consolidate the Bolivarian movement and put them on the national stage. Chávez filled his tiny room with books. On the days visitors weren't allowed he buried himself in study. With plenty of time to read and think, he considered more deeply the nationalist foundations of his political philosophy. Some of the leading lights of the left soon aided him.

After the Caracazo, a group of leading civilians formed a "Patriotic Front" to try to take advantage of widespread dissatisfaction with the state of the country and set it on a different path. It was a device that had historically played an important role in Venezuela at crucial moments. A Patriotic Front of civilians working in conjunction with soldiers helped lead the overthrow of Marcos Pérez Jiménez in 1958. Another front was formed as far back as the days of Ezequiel Zamora in the mid-nineteenth century.

The newest one was presided over by Luis Miquilena. A former leader of a bus drivers' union, Miquilena was one of the great survivors of the Venezuelan left. He split from the Venezuelan Communist Party in the 1940s, founded his own radical anti-Stalinist Communist Party in 1946, and spent most of the Pérez Jiménez dictatorship in jail. He was tortured so horrifically that the late writer Miguel Otero Silva made him the central character of *La Muerte de Honorio*, a novel about the resistance movement against Pérez Jiménez. In the mid-1960s Miquilena disappeared from public politics and went on to become a successful businessman.

By the time Chávez burst on the scene, he was largely unknown by most Venezuelans. Intrigued by Chávez's insurrection and his calls for a constitutional assembly, Miquilena contacted Chávez and visited him in jail. He was to turn into a key political mentor and father-like figure who also helped bankroll Chávez's revolutionary aspirations. His front included Douglas Bravo, the former guerrilla leader; Manuel Quijada, an intellectual with an Italian law degree who was jailed for his involvement in the civil-military rebellions of 1962; Lino Martínez, a former guerrilla fighter who later became a minister in Chávez's administration; and William Izarra, the Marxist revolutionary who'd founded ARMA and had recently retired from the air force after years of harassment by superiors.

Chávez's older brother, Adán, served as a go-between with some of the Patriotic Front members, including Bravo, who could not visit the jail for security reasons. Adán smuggled messages into the prison by rolling up small pieces of paper, sticking them inside a pen, and slipping the pen in between his sock and his shoe.

About the same time the Patriotic Front was forming, progressive professors at the Central University of Venezuela in Caracas created their own study group. They had heard the conventional wisdom that Pérez's neo-liberal shock package was the only path Venezuela could take to rectify its economic woes. They didn't believe it. They started to search for alternatives. After the coup, they decided to seek out Chávez, believing they shared common goals. The group included Héctor Navarro, who was to become Chávez's education minister; J. J. Montilla, later his minister of agriculture and land; Adina Bastidas, who became his vice president; and Jorge Giordani, who assumed the post of planning minister and became one of Chávez's principal economic advisers.

A tall, cerebral man with glasses and a white beard who looked to some like an "anorexic Santa Claus," Giordani became the most regular visitor to Yare of the group. He was a development economist trained at the University of Sussex and was the economic guru of the leftist Movement to Socialism (MAS) Party. Giordani established a close relationship with Chávez. The rebel leader asked the professor to become his tutor for a master's degree in political science he was pursing at the well-regarded Simón Bolívar University in Caracas. The only thing Chávez needed to finish was his thesis. The coup had interrupted work on it. The UCV group was to turn into a kind of shadow cabinet for Chávez during his time in jail and after. They accelerated work on their book project, *The UCV to the Country: An Alternative Proposal.* It became a blueprint for some of Chávez's early plans.

While Chávez and the others received some special privileges in Yare, they were hardly in a honeymoon getaway. The section they were confined to was on the first floor. Above them three floors full of inmates lived in horrendous conditions. A lack of functioning toilets forced them to defecate on newspapers. They tossed the soiled papers out the windows onto the ground. They also relieved themselves in jars and dumped the urine out the window. The waste fell near the rebels' quarters. Foul odors and flies filled the hot, stagnant air.

Venezuela's jails were lawless *Midnight Express*–style places. Guards wielded little control. Inmates executed their own style of justice. Often free to roam the cell blocks, they carried large homemade knives called *chuzos*. Drug dealing, rape, extortion, beatings, and murder were common. One night Chávez and his colleagues heard noises above them. "Ay, ay, ay," an inmate yelled. "No, no, no." Other prisoners were raping him. After a while the prisoner started to yell, "Don't kill me, don't kill me." To shut him up, the inmates slashed his throat, prompting him to start "squealing like a pig," according to Francisco Arias Cárdenas. Not long after, the rebels heard the sounds of the inmates plunging knives into their victim. Then silence. Later, Chávez and the others heard the prisoners throw something out the windows. The next morning, they saw the knives on the ground.

During the attack Chávez, Arias Cárdenas, and the others yelled at the top of their lungs for the guards to intervene. "Help! Run! Come and save this man! They are going to kill him!" No one came. The next day Arias Cárdenas angrily complained to a guard. The guard responded that it was "internal justice" of the jail. There was nothing he could do. Arias was livid.

Chávez and the others tried to make the best of the situation. They imposed military discipline. They read, they held political discussions, they smuggled out communiqués to journalists. They even held occasional prayer groups, played soccer or volleyball on the patio, and cultivated a small garden with peppers, tomatoes, and cucumbers. The tireless Chávez often stayed up late into the night, reading or answering the thousands of letters he received. Ronald Blanco La Cruz, who had studied at the School of the Americas in Fort Benning, Georgia, and Troy State University, organized English classes.

A large amount of Chávez's studying and discussion centered on the rebels' idea of convoking a constitutional assembly to rewrite Venezuela's constitution. He drew the idea partly from the French Revolution and its notion of constitutional power, or revolutionary power as Chávez saw it. It was a concept most Venezuelans were unfamiliar with, but eventually it would help upend the country's political establishment. The rebels relied on some of their lawyers to smuggle in blank cassette tapes and take them out with Chávez's recorded messages. They distributed copies to his political allies, who played them on public buses. By now the elite-controlled commercial media had reversed themselves and were blackballing Chávez. They viewed him as a dangerous radical and a threat to the system.

The rebels faced even larger dangers than censorship by the media. They feared their enemies might try to kill them. Allies smuggled weapons into the prison for their protection. The rebels hid the guns in their beds or amid their clothes. Guards frequently harassed them. They tossed tear gas into their cells, conducted searches, and hauled away their books and documents, forcing them to start from zero.

Despite the harassment, Chávez felt free in prison to pursue and deepen his revolutionary movement:

> I've always said the jail was a school. In the first place, because it feeds the soul, it consolidates your conviction and deepens your conscience. All those days and nights in jail, we advanced ideologically, above all because we were prisoners of conscience, prisoners of dignity, prisoners conscious of why we needed to be there . . . I never felt like a prisoner really, neither desperate nor closed in. I felt free in that small space, because above all I was taking advantage of the time.

Almost from the time he entered jail, plots were under way to free Chávez. One of the first visits he received in San Carlos was from an army lieutenant who entered with a false identification card. He told Chávez about a plan to overthrow the government and liberate him from prison. Helicopters were to swoop in from Maracay sixty miles away, the lieutenant told him, and whisk Chávez out of San Carlos. Chávez convinced him to hold off. His movement was in a state of upheaval after the coup. The chances of another rebellion succeeding were unclear.

Not long after, Chávez received another visit from retired army colonel Higinio Castro. He offered Chávez his services. This time Chávez told him to see what he could organize with the Bolivarian rebels who had avoided prison or with other dissidents in the army. They soon planned several rebellions. One plot even called for killing President Pérez on July 5 during a parade marking Venezuela's independence day. But the army rebels were still not sufficiently organized to launch a rebellion, and none took place.

They needed help from other sectors of the armed forces. About the same time Chávez was making Castro his emissary to the army, he received a message from Luis Reyes Reyes, the air force pilot who had tried but failed to get allies in the air force to fully participate in the coup. On a jail visit, Chávez's son Hugo Jr. slipped him a small piece of paper from Reyes Reyes. "Be tranquil. We're working," it said. "The chatter of the parrots has grown." The parrots were the air force. While Chávez's movement in the army had suffered a heavy blow with the failed February 4 coup, rebels in that branch of the service had escaped relatively unscathed.

Chávez put Colonel Castro in touch with Reyes Reyes, who contacted fellow pilot Brigadier General Efraín Francisco Visconti Osorio. Chávez had met with Visconti and Reyes Reyes a day before the February 4 coup, but could not convince Visconti to join the revolt on such short notice. He and Chávez, though, shared a common desire to overthrow Venezuela's political system.

Visconti had spent much of the 1970s and 1980s immersed in William Izarra's subversive air force group ARMA. He also met with civilians such as Douglas Bravo and organized his own secret cell of pilots. Now, with the failure of the February 4 coup and Pérez's grip on Miraflores slipping, he saw an opening for another revolt.

Officers in the navy including Admiral Hernán Grüber Ódreman had the same idea. Not long after Visconti and Reyes Reyes made contact with Higinio Castro and the remnants of Chávez's MBR-200, they also got in touch with Grüber. Visconti ceded overall command of the operation to Grüber since he was the senior officer. In contrast with the February 4 revolt carried out by young lieutenant colonels and captains, this rebellion was to be led by experienced generals and admirals.

Chávez stayed in touch with them, receiving letters or cassettes of meetings the groups held to plot the coup. He left the planning to the others since he was confined to jail. "We collaborated with some ideas, but we always felt they had sufficient military capacity to plan and execute the operation," Chávez told interviewer Agustín Blanco Muñoz. "Until that date in July [of the aborted coup against Pérez] there was contact between the two groups, the ones outside and us, but after that we let go of the reins . . . I never handled details of the plans. I never had access to them."

Chávez's support for another coup did not receive unanimous support from his comrades in jail. Arias Cárdenas vigorously opposed the idea. He believed the time for a military uprising had passed, and the rebels now should pursue a peaceful political path rather than armed insurrection. He thought the rebels no longer had enough strength in the military to pull off another coup. Chávez disagreed. He still believed Venezuela's political system was a fixed game controlled by the political elites. Only a civic-military uprising could break their grip on power.

It was the most serious dispute they had in prison, and underscored their differences about the direction the Bolivarian movement should take. The two fought bitterly. Tensions also built between them since Luis Miquilena, Chávez's emerging alter ego, was advising the group that El Comandante had to be the star of the group to focus public attention. The others had to take a backseat. At one point he issued an edict for Arias Cárdenas to remain silent with the media.

The new conspiracy fell into a "cold period" in August and September 1992. But the rebels could not wait forever. Elections for state governors and local mayors were coming on December 5. A week before that, on November 25, practice sessions were to begin for an annual air show on December 10. Most of the air force's jets would be concentrated at the Liberator air base in Maracay. The rebels decided it was their moment.

On the night of Thursday, November 26, Chávez received word that the uprising was imminent. His son had smuggled a piece of a communications radio into the jail. Reyes Reyes's son snuck in the other part. The prisoners put them together, contacted some relatives, and got confirmation of the revolt. Expecting the rebels to pluck them from jail, Chávez, Arias Cárdenas — by now resigned to the coup's inevitability — and the others in Yare put on their combat uniforms. They established a nighttime guard to alert one another when the rescuers came. "I remember that Arias and I almost did not sleep," Chávez said. "And about 5 A.M. we heard on the radio that the rebellion had already started."

The November 27 rebels had learned some lessons from the failed February 4 insurgents. Instead of launching the rebellion at midnight, they waited until 4:30 A.M. The air force was to play a key role. They needed daylight to see their targets and give civilian supporters a chance to flood the streets. They also moved quickly to seize control of the media. They took over the antennae that sent out the signal for three major television stations. They also bought expensive communications equipment so they would not be stranded incommunicado like Chávez at the military museum.

The revolt started off well. The insurgents seized control of major air bases including Liberator in Maracay. They were largely in control of the skies. At one point Reyes Reyes thundered into the valley of Caracas in an F-16, breaking the sound barrier for the first time in the capital and shocking residents who heard their windows rattle and shake as the jet fighter passed just three thousand feet overhead. The usual minimal safety level was ten thousand feet.

Down on the ground, rebels took over the state-run channel 8 in eastern Caracas during a bloody battle. But a video Grüber had taped announcing the rebellion and calling on the nation to rise up never got played. Instead, one Chávez had recorded a few months earlier in jail came on. Worse, another video of masked men bearing arms and talking in crude, violent language appeared. They urged Venezuelans to haul out clubs, bottles, and homemade arms to overthrow the government. Few did. The images of the thug-like figures merely frightened the public, which was still terrified of the violence from the Caracazo. To this day, the rebels don't know how the video got on the air.

While rebel pilots took quick command of the skies, the army was almost nowhere to be seen. Ground support was crucial, since the insurgents couldn't take Miraflores and other targets with airplanes alone. But the army was fractured. At least three different rebel tendencies existed, and they could not coordinate their actions.

Even the air force suffered problems. When the rebels took over the air base at Maracay shortly before dawn, one pilot led a minor defection and took off with two F-16s. He flew to Barquísimeto in the interior of Venezuela. Operating under orders of the government, he engaged in midair dogfights with rebel planes as shocked residents below looked on.

By about 9 A.M. the air force insurgents realized they were alone in battle. About the same time, loyalist forces shot down the first rebel air-plane in Maracay. The pilot ejected himself to safety. But the insurgents realized the government orders were to engage in combat and kill.

Infuriated, they changed their original plans. They started to bomb some targets. They fired rockets at the DISIP political police head-quarters in Caracas. They dropped bombs on Miraflores presidential palace, blowing a sixty-foot-wide hole in the wall of the white, colonial-style structure and leaving craters in surrounding streets. At the height of the bombing the seventy-year-old Pérez reportedly crawled on his hands and knees to an underground bunker, from which he rallied loyal units. They responded by attacking more rebel airplanes.

Part of the coup plan called for liberating Chávez and his cohorts. Some army officers accompanied by civilians went to Yare that morning to try to free them. They rode in on a tractor, with others following close behind. A much larger and more powerful force of guards and soldiers turned them back. At one point they fired a rocket at them, tearing off the face of one would-be liberator.

The rebels in this coup had done a better job than Chávez's forces of controlling the media. But they left Pérez with one opening: They failed to take over Televen channel 10. Pérez made his way to the sta-tion. In a repeat of February 4, he declared that he was in control of the country; the rebellion had failed. Grüber soon followed at midday by announcing that he was surrendering. By around noon the govern-ment took over La Carlota air base in Caracas. By 2 P.M. it seized Base Mariscal Sucre in Maracay. By about 3 P.M. rebel leaders at the nearby Liberator base realized they were next.

Government ground troops were surrounding the air base with tanks and preparing to take it. The insurgents piled into two C-130s inside a hangar and took off down an emergency strip. They left behind helicopters that were still running but had no pilots inside. The rebels had no idea where they were going. Up in the air, Visconti decided Peru was the best destination. Its government had broken diplomatic relations with Pérez and was most likely to grant the ninety-three rebels political asylum. They headed for Lima but landed prematurely in the Amazon jungle city of Iquitos because of engine trouble.

Despite the precautions and the array of forces lined up — air force, navy, army, National Guard, even significant groups of civilians including the Patriotic Front, the UCV professors, Douglas Bravo's Third Way, the Causa R, and the ultraleftist Bandera Roja — the coup attempt had turned into a bloody fiasco. The death toll reached 171. It was far worse than the February 4 putsch.

After the second coup attempt in ten months and with the country on edge, Pérez defiantly rejected demands that he resign. "My presence in the government has been a guarantee of democratic stability," he declared, although the opposite was true. When he led reporters on a walk around the bullet-pocked palace, several bystanders shouted: "Pérez, get out of here!"

The winds of change were evident in elections a few days later. Little-known geography teacher and anticorruption crusader Aristóbulo Istúriz of the leftist Causa R Party won the mayor's election in Caracas, breaking Democratic Action's and COPEI's decades-long grip on the post. "His passionate speaking manner and appearance alone — he is black — sent shock waves through the political system and the generally white Venezuelan elite, which is still comfortable with racist jokes."

Venezuelans were so desperate for change, they elected a former beauty queen as mayor of the upscale Chacao district in eastern Caracas. In a typically vacuous post-victory statement, Irene Sáez, a six-foot-one bleached-blond former Miss Universe who ran as an independent, told supporters, "You will always have a friend in me." But in beauty-queen-crazy Venezuela, she quickly became one of the most popular politicians in the nation.

As newcomers like Sáez and Istúriz took power, Pérez's once dominant Democratic Action Party suffered one of its worst electoral setbacks in decades. Opposition control of powerful state governorships increased from one-half to two-thirds. Even though on paper 1992 was a "banner year" for the country with 7.3 percent economic growth and $2 billion in new foreign investment, little trickled down to the masses. From his exile in Peru, coup leader General Francisco Efrain Visconti captured the national sentiment: "There is no human being in the country that does not feel beaten down by the effects of the brutal economic policy imposed by the IMF."

With hatred of the president intensifying, a new breed of antiestablishment politicians on the rise, and Democratic Action mired in the deepest crisis in its five-decade history, party leaders decided that if Pérez would not go out on his own, they would get rid of him themselves.

The seeds of his destruction were planted two weeks before the November coup. Muckraking journalist José Vicente Rangel reported in his newspaper column that the politically influenced judicial system was investigating charges that the president and two ministers had enriched themselves through a currency speculation scheme. Pérez allegedly withdrew 250 million bolivars from a secret government account earmarked for national security just days after he was sworn in during his "coronation" in February 1989, exchanging them for $17.2 million. Then two weeks later, after the government devalued the bolivar by 88 percent as part of the *paquete* that provoked the Caracazo, Pérez and the ministers allegedly changed the dollars back into the national currency at the new, higher rate. The scheme allegedly netted anywhere from $3 million to $10 million. Some speculated that Pérez had used the money to pay for the lavish inauguration ceremonies.

In May 1993 the Supreme Court ruled that Pérez could be tried on the charges and prepared to begin his trial. The next day the Senate suspended him from office. The half-century-long career of one of the grand old men of Latin American politics was for all intents over.

The political demise of Pérez was a badly needed boost for the rebels in jail and particularly for Chávez. He was going through roller-coaster rides that ranged from basking in unalloyed adulation to deep depression. The rebels were demoralized by the failure of the second coup, and racked by infighting. Some in the November movement blamed Chávez for the coup's failure, claiming that he had prevented the video of Grüber Ódreman from appearing on television and replaced it with the one of himself. They believed he was trying to wrest control of the rebellion. Chávez insisted he had nothing to do with the botched videos.

In Peru, Visconti bad-mouthed him, and word spread in Yare and San Carlos. "Arias himself became contagious with it," Chávez told interviewer Agustín Blanco Muñoz. "In one of many letters he wrote, he pointed to me as the one responsible for the failure. One sector of the November twenty-seventh rebels started to see in us and especially in me the cause of all their problems. And they instilled this in some of the officers from February 4th, who came to believe it . . . After this defeat they pointed their cannons at me in an unjustified manner." It turned into some of the lowest moments of his time in prison. "In the months of December 1992, January 1993, I was a solitary figure in the jail, where for the first time I felt the ice of bitterness. I'd never felt it before, not even with the surrender of February 4th, the pain of the bitterness of being pointed to by my friends as the one responsible for the failure."

He'd seen better times in prison, when his comrades exulted in his newfound stardom and hailed him as a courageous leader. Chávez's image of himself as the heir to Bolívar, Zamora, and Maisanta, entrusted with the historic mission of rescuing Venezuela, could reach dizzying heights. Herma Marksman thought it bordered on messianic delirium at times. Shortly after he arrived at San Carlos, the grandson of Maisanta whom Chávez had met in 1983 brought an original medallion that Pedro Pérez Delgado had worn and was handed down through the family. In an impromptu ceremony in the jail, the grandson presented the medallion to Chávez and told him he now "incarnated" Maisanta. Chávez put on the medallion and never took it off again.

One night months later in Yare, he and some of the coup plotters were drinking rum and whiskey and smoking cigars that had been smuggled in. Chávez had spent weeks arguing with Arias over whether the group should support an outside candidate against the two traditional parties in the upcoming 1993 presidential election or simply call on Venezuelans to abstain from the election, which was Chávez's position. The night before they decided, he was trying to win over the other rebels. When Arias walked into the room Chávez told him they were "invoking the spirits." With Maisanta's medallion hanging around his neck, Chávez started to tremble and talk like an old man. "How are you, boys?" he said. One jumped up and said, "My General Bolívar!" Chávez responded, "I'm not General Bolívar. Don't put me up so high." Ronald Blanco La Cruz then interjected: "My General Maisanta!" Chávez responded, "Of course, my son, I am here."

The next day Chávez insisted the liquor-fueled incident was all in fun and designed to persuade his younger charges. It did. Arias thought he had a six-to-three advantage going into the vote, but he lost by the same margin. The rebels issued a communiqué calling on Venezuelans to boycott the "illegal and illegitimate" elections. Arias refused to sign it. Beyond that, the Maisanta incident seemed to underscore Chávez's belief that he was the vehicle his trilogy of heroes was using to refound the country.

While Chávez was wrestling for power with Arias, another one of his key relationships was also undergoing a shift. His relationship with the secret comandante was ending.

12

## Secret Comandante's Good-Bye

Herma Marksman didn't care for all the adulation and attention Chávez was receiving. She thought his ego was ballooning out of control and he was turning into a person she barely knew. She also didn't like many of his new friends. She believed that some, like Luis Miquilena, were nothing but communist leftovers who were betraying the nationalist and Bolivarian roots of the movement she had helped Chávez build over a decade.

On the other hand, Chávez's new allies didn't always appreciate Marksman's presence. She believed some of them, in particular Miquilena, wanted her to disappear from Chávez's life. She represented an inconvenient and potentially embarrassing liaison that could hurt the rising star's reputation. That was especially so since Chávez presented himself as the antidote to the immorality and corruption of political leaders such as Carlos Andrés Pérez, who had two daughters by his mistress Cecilia Matos, and Jaime Lusinchi, whose mistress Blanca Ibáñez was nearly running the country in the late 1980s. "I think that if they could have dug a hole and put me in it and covered me up forever, they would have done it," Marksman commented years later.

People like Francisco Arias Cárdenas didn't think there was any comparison to Matos or Ibáñez. Marksman was a serious woman, a well-read historian who played an important role in the clandestine Bolivarian conspiracy starting in 1984, risking her job and throwing herself into the movement. If anything, she was Chávez's Manuela Sáenz, the sharp-witted intellectual and revolutionary who had stood by Bolívar in his bleakest moments and even went into battle with independence troops, earning the rank of colonel.

Chávez had indirectly admitted as much to people who knew the story of their secret relationship — which really wasn't a secret at all to the members of the movement, who often received messages from her, saw her at meetings, and called her on the telephone. According to Chávez interviewer Agustín Blanco Muñoz, Marksman "wasn't just the sentimental companion of Hugo Chávez for ten years . . . She was his principal and at times only collaborator . . . She was the key person for the meetings, the contacts, the discussions, the resolutions, to process the conflicts, to resist the actions of the leaks, to clean up fingerprints and to put together the archive of that time."

One leading rebel who was imprisoned for two years with Chávez in Yare, Luis Valderrama, has contended that Marksman played a "key role" in the decade-long Bolivarian conspiracy, serving as a "guide" and "teacher" for Chávez. During the time in jail, Yare turned into a focal point for the movement, attracting everyone from leftist intellectuals to priests to relatives of the rebels, and it became more difficult to conceal the fact Chávez had two women. "Remember that Chávez had his wife, Nancy, who lived in San Joaquín, and at the same time had the woman of his dreams, who was Herma," Valderrama has recalled. "Herma is the woman who along with him serves as the motor for everything having to do with that crazy conspiracy. She's the one who serves as his handkerchief, the one who helps him, including psychologically, who gives him encouragement."

After gaining access to the rebels in Yare, former guerrilla Ángela Zago published her best-selling book *The Rebellion of the Angels* in October 1992. She dedicated the glowing account of Chávez and his comrades "especially to Comandante Pedro, a person who one day we will discover and who in a meticulous and responsible way, with profound love, has collected, archived and saved every little paper that takes us through a history that goes beyond the nine years since the movement was founded."

Comandante Pedro was Marksman. She was unknown to the nation and even today remains largely a mystery to most Venezuelans. Zago wrote that Comandante Pedro "during two months was busy gathering any document that showed who 'his boys' are. Comandante Pedro believes profoundly in the philosophy of his comrades and feels a profound respect and affection for Comandante Chávez. Only a person who admires the other is capable of — at whatever hour, in whatever place — leaving their job with all the risks that entails and following the path the rebels followed in these past years. To this secret Comandante, my thanks, admiration and respect."

Marksman even wrote the prologue to the book, signing it by her nom de guerre. After entering the MBR-200 eight years earlier, she wrote, she set herself to collecting, putting in order, and saving the letters, work papers, and documents that were produced in the rebels' meetings. In the clandestine gatherings they "not only deepened the study of the historic roots of our movement, Simon Rodríguez, Simón Bolívar and Ezequiel Zamora — the tree of the three roots — but discussed and analyzed the national problem, the deepening of the crisis, and the moral deterioration in all the institutions that make up the country, proposing possible solutions without, of course, detaching ourselves from international events." The Bolivarians' ultimate goal, she added, was "to rescue the dignity of the Venezuelan people."

A month after the book came out, Chávez himself indirectly acknowledged Marksman's contribution to the movement in a handwritten dedication he wrote to Zago in a reprint of the best-seller. Calling it a "marvelous book," Chávez started his dedication by stating, "In the name of dreams, of comrades alive and dead, of Felipe Acosta Carles . . . and Comandante Pedro, who inhabits Yare."

In the later editions, Zago gave further hints of the identity of the secret comandante. On a separate page from the dedication, she wrote, "Some people exist who have the capacity to understand that history is constructed in every moment. To this group of people belongs Herma M. Marksman B., professor of history, post-graduate in economic-social history of Venezuela, a degree she received magna cum laude." Zago added that without Marksman, "this book would have been very difficult to achieve."

But Herma Marksman seemed destined in ways to repeat the history of Manuela Sáenz. Venezuelans had a conservative streak when it came to demigods like Bolívar. For decades his lover and partner was erased from the country's official history. Historians left her out of books. Authorities destroyed or hid old documents that referred to her. Barred from her native Ecuador and from Colombia after the Liberator's death in 1830, "Manuelita" spent her last twenty-five years despised and destitute. She sold tobacco in a seedy port town in northern Peru and translated letters North American whale hunters wrote their lovers in Latin America. In 1856 she died in disgrace during a diphtheria epidemic. Authorities dumped her body in a mass grave, and burned her belongings — including most of Bolívar's love letters.

The demonization of Sáenz lasted decades. Even as recently as the mid-1980s, a proposal to erect a bust of her in a square in the Andean city of Mérida provoked fierce opposition from the Roman Catholic Church. It wasn't until the late 1980s and the 1990s that Venezuelans and South Americans began to reassess "the Liberator of the Liberator" as one of the continent's greatest heroines. A series of newspaper articles, movies, and books came out, including one by Colombian writer Gabriel García Márquez, who wrote warmly of her in his 1989 novel *The General in His Labyrinth*. Today she is considered a national heroine in her native Ecuador and is gaining respect in Venezuela.

The end of Chávez's relationship with Marksman came on his birthday, July 28, 1993, as she has told the story. That day, Chávez gave a radio interview from jail. Speaking on a cell phone that was smuggled into the jail and presenting himself as a model family man, he went on at length about how his wife, Nancy, whom he would divorce the following year, had supported him wholeheartedly throughout the years he conspired, playing an important role in the movement. Not a single mention of Marksman, his true love and co-conspirator.

Zago heard the interview on the radio. She called Marksman, hoping she could head her off from listening. But Marksman heard it all. She was both crushed and livid. On top of the pressure from Chávez's advisers to squeeze her out, the long lines of women anxious to throw themselves at El Comandante, and what she thought was the dramatically changed personality of a man who had turned into a messiah, it was more than she could take. "For me, he died July 28, 1993," Marksman told interviewer Agustín Blanco Muñoz. She felt like she'd become a widow.

The interview — and the end of the relationship — was devastating for another reason. By Marksman's account, Chávez's attachment to her had become so deep that in the late 1980s and early 1990s he had told her he wanted to divorce Colmenares, marry Marksman, and have a child together. At one point she became pregnant, but lost the baby prematurely. Their plans for marriage never materialized.

Chávez has never publicly spoken about Marksman or recognized their relationship — at least not until an interview in April 2007. "I was very fond of her," Chávez confessed, using the verb *querer*, which could also be translated as "love" but is not as strong as the verb *amar*, meaning a much deeper love. Chávez said Marksman was a "fighter" who played an "important" although not "definitive" role in the conspiracy, mainly on the logistical rather than ideological side. Marksman demonstrated "great loyalty and a great capacity for work," he said, helping prepare places for meetings, preparing and archiving documents, and assisting with other tasks.

He dismissed any comparisons to Manuela Saenz, saying "I'm Bolívar?" with a laugh. "It would never be comparable. Bolívar is the giant. I am a tiny soldier. I don't think the comparison is valid. There are not grounds for comparison in this case. Manuela Saenz accompanied Bolívar in war, in battle, in the campaign. She accompanied him in his final days, until his death. She was loyal until death. There is no comparison possible here on any side."

He also provided a different account of possible plans to have a child together and Marksman's assertion she became pregnant at one point but miscarried. "She at one time had the desire to have a child," Chávez said simply. "We were never in agreement."

In contrast to Chávez's acknowledgement of the relationship during this 2007 interview, Blanco Muñoz noted that in fourteen extensive conversations he conducted from March 1995 to June 1998 for his 643-page book of interviews, *Habla El Comandante*, Chávez never mentioned Marksman once. Marksman was to remain invisible to the public for the next decade, nursing her wounds, until she finally granted several interviews to television and newspaper reporters on the tenth anniversary of the February 4 coup. She later collaborated with Blanco Muñoz and Alberto Garrido for her own books of interviews. By then she'd become a bitter critic of Chávez, whose supporters wondered how much of her anger was stoked by their failed romance. Despite the occasional bursts of publicity, she remained a largely unknown figure to most Venezuelans.

As Chávez's nine-year relationship with Marksman was ending in 1993, the presidential electoral campaign was revving up. Former president Rafael Caldera was roaring back to political life. After leaving office in 1974, Caldera had faded away to the point that by the early 1990s journalists joked that the aging patriarch of COPEI was a "political cadaver." But with the speech he delivered in Congress the day of Chávez's coup, Caldera "left the grave," according to Zago. As the December election neared, the seventy-seven-year-old Caldera was in the midst of a heated four-way race.

Whoever won, Chávez believed the rebels stood a good chance of gaining their freedom. Pressure was building in the streets to release them. Besides, Caldera had won fame in his first term by "pacifying" the guerrilla movement, offering them amnesty if they laid down their arms. On the night of the presidential vote, December 5, Caldera — who was running as an independent backed by a coalition of small parties nicknamed the *chiripera* for small insects that make a noisy racket when they chirp together — squeaked out a victory. It was marred by allegations of fraud from Causa R leader Andrés Velásquez. He finished fourth, but many people believed he had really won. Ballot boxes containing results favorable to him turned up in garbage dumps.

While Caldera was a political relic who had started his political career when Franklin D. Roosevelt was in his second term in the White House, he was also one of the few politicians in the nation seen as honest. In a country where presidential mistresses were so well known that they were called by their first names, Caldera had been happily married to the same woman for half a century. He attended Roman Catholic Mass every Sunday. He campaigned on a pledge to reverse Pérez's free-market austerity program. He promised a low-key inauguration, in contrast with Pérez's ostentatious, self-glorifying bash. After the recent shocks of the Caracazo, two coup attempts, an economic austerity package, and the impeachment of a president, Venezuelans wanted the stability of the past that the reassuring grandfatherly figure of Caldera offered. The night he won, Chávez spoke with him on a cell phone smuggled into Yare, congratulating him on his triumph. Caldera told him to avoid provocations while he prepared to assume the presidency.

He soon had other problems to deal with. Even before he was elected, rumors were circulating in Venezuelan financial circles that the country's second largest bank, Banco Latino, was in trouble.

Banco Latino was partly a creation, phenomenon, and symbol of Pérez's presidency. It quickly rose from a middle-of-the-pack institution to a high-flying financial operation with executives living the good life. Many were close to Pérez, which led critics to dub Banco Latino "the Bank of the Twelve Apostles" — the name for the president's kitchen cabinet. Shortly after Pérez was sworn in for his second term in February 1989, he named Banco Latino's president and major shareholder, Pedro Tinoco, head of the Central Bank of Venezuela. Other bank "apostles" included Ricardo Cisneros of the powerful and wealthy Cisneros family, and the president's brother Francisco.

As part of the neo-liberal free-market *paquete* Pérez implemented shortly after his inauguration, he deregulated the banking industry. But he failed to put in place the beefed-up supervision a deregulated system requires. The result was rampant mismanagement.

Three months after Banco Latino held an extravagant bash for clients and directors, flying them to Paris in a Concorde and putting some up in the Ritz hotel, the bank collapsed and authorities padlocked its doors. Its spectacular failure in January 1994 sent shock waves through Venezuela and set off a chain reaction of failures at more than half the nation's banks. By the end of 1994, the government had spent $10 billion propping them up — more than half that year's entire budget. Authorities issued arrest warrants for two hundred bankers, but most had fled the country, taking millions of dollars with them.

It was a prime example of the corruption, mismanagement, and rot that permeated Venezuela and propelled Chávez to launch his coup. Meanwhile, a popular nighttime soap opera was sweeping the country with an amazingly true-to-life depiction of the rot. *Por Estas Calles* (*Through These Streets*) was the first television program to expose the corruption and moral decay afflicting the nation. It also gave the rich their first realistic view of what life was really like in the barrios where Chávez was a hero.

One of the main characters was Governor Don Chepe Orellana. His character bore a striking resemblance to former president Jaime Lusinchi, who in real life had of course been manipulated by Blanca Ibáñez. On the show, Don Chepe and his mistress Lucha pocketed public money with one sleight-of-hand move after another, doled out favors to campaign contributors, developed all kinds of illegal schemes to hold on to power, and ruthlessly eliminated political enemies.

Another character was Dr. Valerio, a physician and "caricature of the upper-middle-class scoundrel." He ran a private clinic and spent most of his time developing schemes to obtain more money and power. Dr. Valerio was what is known in Venezuela as *un vivo* — a "clever one" who knows how to get one over on the system. Like many white-collar criminals, he proudly bragged about his exploits. In contrast, people who have a chance to steal or take advantage of a situation for their own personal benefit and don't do it are known as *pendejos* — fools.

The series even featured a fourteen-year-old *malandro*, barrio thug, who represented the new gangs that were terrorizing residents with their guns and street violence. There was also a schoolteacher in a poor neighborhood who denounced the corrupt, paternalistic government. The program touched on subjects few others bothered with, such as the shortage of water. In Venezuela, mismanagement by the government utility company meant water might come to people's homes and apartments as infrequently as once a month. When it did, they dropped everything to fill up storage tanks or barrels.

In one memorable episode of *Por Estas Calles*, the schoolteacher manages to pull together community activists for a meeting. Just as they pledge to work together, the group scatters from the room in a dozen directions. "Did I say something wrong," the teacher asks a friend as they stand almost alone in the meeting room. "No, the water's back on," a student answers. "We have to fill our buckets." In another scene, after days of trying two lovers finally find the time to be alone. Then the water starts flowing, and they run out.

It was all a perfect summary of why Venezuelans were so disgusted with the system and clamoring for a rebel like Chávez to clean it up.

A few months before *Por Estas Calles* ended its two-year run, President Rafael Caldera was preparing to release Chávez from prison. He had little choice. Much of the public was demanding it. Caldera figured the rebel leader was more dangerous in jail than out. Once out on the street, the thinking went, the myth of Chávez would deflate. But Caldera made one mistake. He failed to bar Chávez from future political activity. Chávez's opponents would never forgive Caldera for the misstep.

On February 23, 1994, the president released Francisco Arias Cárdenas and nine other officers, with the only condition that they resign from the military. Little by little Caldera released the rest until only Chávez and a few others were left. Chávez insisted on staying behind bars until all the others were freed. As the end neared, he asked to undergo eye surgery, which authorities had until then denied him. Caldera approved his transfer to a military hospital. He underwent the surgery and spent two weeks in the hospital. By late March, as Holy Week approached, marking the death and resurrection of Jesus Christ, Chávez was set to be freed.

He had one last demand before he went. He wanted to sign his discharge papers at Fort Tiuna and visit the military academy one last time in his paratrooper uniform. General Raúl Salazar, a heavyset friend of Chávez's who was in charge of handling his discharge, told him he was asking for trouble with military superiors. He pleaded with him not to insist. But Chávez wouldn't back off. A part of his life that he loved and that had served as the incubator for his rebellion was ending. He wanted to say good-bye the right way, in his own style. Salazar finally ceded to the request on the condition that no media would be present; they would keep it secret.

Early in the morning of Saturday, March 26, Salazar snuck him out of the hospital through the kitchen and a back door, avoiding the reporters, photographers, and television cameramen gathered out front. They hustled him into the car of the general's daughter to avoid drawing attention, then whisked to him Fort Tiuna. As they pulled into the military base, a tremendous nostalgia washed over Chávez:

> I hadn't been to Fort Tiuna since the day they took me prisoner, and it's very difficult to explain what was happening to me. I felt like I was dying a bit, because the truth is I loved my entire military career. When we got to Salazar's office, I felt I was crying. The Fat One, who is a really good guy, realized it and moved away for a bit. He left me alone. I went out on a patio and I looked at areas where I had worked. After a while, Salazar asked me, "Chávez, are you OK?" "Yes, general, I'm ready."

Chávez was to be released late that morning. Before he departed, Salazar let him pay his final visit to the military academy on the other side of the Fort Tiuna campus. He drove Chávez over to the gleaming white academy building, which was empty because the cadets and professors were on vacation for Holy Week. Chávez walked onto the patio, "to a place that is like magic. I stayed there, and walked toward a statue of Bolívar. I cried again . . ." He spoke to himself alone until Salazar finally called him and they departed. Back at the general's office, Chávez took a shower, changed into civilian clothes, and got ready to leave. It was the day before Palm Sunday.

Outside the military base, journalists and admirers clamored to see him. A crowd of hundreds of people, mainly women, was gathered, waving Venezuelan flags, holding flowers, donning red berets. Their hero was free after two years and two months in prison. He could have faced thirty years.

At about 12:30 P.M. Chávez finally appeared. Pandemonium broke out. The throng swarmed around him, clambering over a table full of microphones and even knocking him down. One ally, Nicolas Maduro, watched as people tried to touch him, or hand him their children so he could hold them. If they managed to press a hand on El Comandante for a moment, they would then place it on their children's heads, "as if he were a saint," Maduro said. Others fell to their knees, cried, and shouted that Chávez was Simón Bolívar. "That day I heard for the first time something we heard many times during the trips throughout Venezuela: 'Chávez, you are Bolívar reincarnated.'"

Chávez planned to give a formal press conference, but it was impossible. He managed only a few statements. "This military generation that chose the road of sacrifice and was forged at the military installations of Fort Tiuna, is going to show Venezuela's hack politicians what it is to lead a nation and restore its true destiny," he told reporters.

As he got ready to leave, one journalist shoved a tape recorder at him and shouted out amid the tumult, asking where he was going next. Without thinking, Chávez turned to the reporter and responded instinctively:

"To power."

**13**

## On the Road

The next day, Palm Sunday, Chávez visited the tomb of his hero Simón Bolívar. It was just down the street from the San Carlos jail where he had spent several weeks after the February 4 coup. He placed a wreath at the Liberator's grave inside the National Pantheon, emerging from the building to a cheering throng. Many were getting their first live glimpse of Chávez since the day he'd appeared on television giving his famous *por ahora* speech. He'd spent the morning giving a long press conference for local and international reporters. Outside the Pantheon he waded through the crowd, then headed down the street and into the barrios of Catia in western Caracas, where more fans mobbed him. People followed him on bicycle, on motorcycle, and on foot, jogging behind him as his entourage advanced and made stops along the way. Chávez's new life in the outside world had begun. He was a star. Everyplace he went crowds flocked to him. "I could not feel alone, because where I went it would produce the same avalanche of people as when I left the jail. After I left Yare, I could not walk one hundred meters alone . . . I don't know the word solitude. I don't know what it is to be alone."

Chávez spent a few days visiting the barrios of Caracas, basking in his newfound freedom and the adulation of his supporters. Then he headed to his hometowns of Sabaneta and Barinas, where he spent the rest of Holy Week, and got ready to embark on a one-hundred-day tour of Venezuela. He and his allies called it the "Bolivarian Hurricane." It was to take him to nearly every corner of the country, from the snow-capped Andes to the sultry Caribbean coast to the Amazon jungle.

Their slogan was, "The Hope Is in the Streets." Chávez wanted to meet many of his admirers face-to-face for the first time, and build support for the MBR-200 and his proposal for a constitutional assembly.

With a few of his military and civilian allies in tow, he hit the road. They traveled in a four-wheel-drive jeep he dubbed *la burra negra* (the black donkey). Chávez met with teachers, union leaders, *campesinos*, fishermen, indigenous tribes, "people from the right, people from the left, people from the extreme right, people from the extreme left, apolitical people, everyone, but who in some way identified with the change," he recalled. At one point he even climbed into one of the precarious holes gold miners in the Amazon jungle blasted in the earth with powerful water hoses searching for their El Dorado. "I don't think that we skipped a single city, town, encampment, Indian village or neighborhood. We went from town to town with the flag of the constitutional assembly, building the organization, strengthening it."

His appearances created a sensation almost everywhere he went. Women kissed him, smearing his cheeks with lipstick. Children donned imitations of his paratrooper's combat fatigues and red beret. Men formed makeshift security details in case any of his adversaries tried to physically attack him. Chávez didn't have to talk to provoke cheers. He simply raised his arms in triumph and the crowds went wild. After the rallies, autograph seekers and small-town reporters gathered outside his room hoping for a minute of his time. In some places such as his hometown of Barinas, graffiti messages adorned walls: BOLÍVAR LIVES AGAIN.

While Chávez and his supporters were so stretched financially that they sometimes lacked money for gas and other basics, food was not a problem. They had far more dinner invitations in each town than they could possibly accept — often dozens. They slept in the homes of supporters honored by the visit. When they heard El Comandante was coming to town, residents — many of them dirt poor — pooled their money and rented out a sound system or a hotel conference room for Chávez's appearance. Others gave him clothes.

In an Andean village dotted with coffee fields, Chávez was dressed in a rugby shirt, blue jeans, and his trademark red beret one day in May 1994 as he stood in a central plaza before a crowd of admirers. A torrential spring rain poured down, rattling tile roofs, but Chávez and the crowd in Humocaro Alto were undeterred. "The crisis is so deep," he boomed to the shivering but enthusiastic audience, "the gangrene is so profound, as Bolívar used to say, that it can't be cured by palliatives. The only way is revolution."

Later, residents packed the village church, where the smell of wood smoke mingled with farmers' sweat. Cheers and waving baseball caps greeted Chávez's calls for a clean government and "a revolution to raise our country from the swamp." One sinewy farmer wearing a red beret watched admiringly from the back. "He's the only one who could put the country back together, who could throw out the *corruptos*," the farmer commented. After the rally, the village priest explained why he opened the church to a man who spent two years in jail for trying to overthrow the government: "Chávez is always in favor of the people, against the *corruptos*." As he left the town in his motorcade, Chávez rubbed his cheeks clean of the lipstick left by adoring female fans.

A few weeks later at another rally in the city of Valencia, one admirer, hairstylist Gladys Núñez, took the morning off when she heard El Comandante was coming to town. She bought a 30¢ pamphlet of his essays and waited three hours just to watch him walk by.

Diplomats and Venezuelan elites dismissed the adoration as a passing and overblown fad. One diplomat suggested Chávez was getting far more attention than he deserved. "He's a little weird, you know . . . This is not the voice of reason." A retired National Guard general, Enrique Prieto Silva, predicted Chávez was a mirage that would soon vanish. "In a certain way, he's blind . . . Before the next elections, he'll be forgotten."

Chávez's first tour out of jail was so successful, he was to repeat it several times over the next few years. The trips were exhilarating but grueling. Pedro Carreño, one of Chávez's military academy recruits who eventually joined his entourage, and two other former soldiers often took turns driving through the night while Chávez read or studied documents. When they were exhausted, Chávez took over, sometimes driving at 3 or 4 A.M. To pass the long hours traveling, he told jokes or stories of his days in Barinas. They listened to music by the Venezuelan protest musician Alí Primera. "We started our agenda early in the day and Chávez would do his rally even if there were only five or six people," according to Carreño. "He would get down from the car and get up on the back of the truck and give a speech as if there was a multitude like the ones that fill Avenida Bolívar today." After they finished their day's activities, they would drive through the night to the next town or village, arriving in time for a morning event.

At one point a retired air force colonel who joined Chávez's inner circle, Luis Alfonso Davila, obtained a flatbed truck for the tours. They turned it into a mobile office and home complete with bedrooms, a bathroom, and loudspeakers. On the side they painted a huge picture of Chávez. They dubbed it the "Chávez mobile." After pulling into a town, Chávez would get up on the back and give a speech preaching revolution.

While Chávez was free to roam the country, he was also broke. He was nearly forty. He had no job, no bank account, no place to live. He owned almost nothing. His military career was finished. His only income was a monthly pension from the army of about $170. He sent it to his three children and his wife, Nancy, whom he was in the process of divorcing. Their relationship, while not hostile, had long since withered.

After their release from jail, some of his comrades decided to make ends meet by joining the system they had tried to overthrow two years earlier. Arias Cárdenas accepted a job from President Caldera running PAMI, a government milk program for pregnant women. Urdaneta happily took a post as Venezuela's consul in Vigo, Spain, where he stayed the next five years. Chávez would have nothing to do with it. Unlike Urdaneta, who was relieved at avoiding twenty-five years in jail, Chávez refused to thank Caldera for signing his pardon. He would not even meet with him. Instead he denounced the administration as more of the same corrupt elitist rule that had destroyed the country.

Barely six months out of jail, Chávez publicly warned Caldera of more violent outbursts unless he addressed the nation's deepening social problems. After the arrest of four MBR-200 sympathizers, Chávez accused the president of trying to crush his movement. He challenged Caldera to put him in jail, too. "I'd bet to see who lasts the longest, Caldera at Miraflores or me in any prison cell in the country," Chávez boasted.

With no place to live, the newly freed coup leader accepted the offer of an architect in Caracas to move into a guest cabin in his backyard in the middle-class neighborhood of La Floresta. The architect, Nedo Paniz, was a parachuting aficionado who had befriended many soldiers — the military was the only setting in which he could practice his hobby when he started out in the 1960s. Some of them turned out to be rebels such as Jesús Urdaneta. Eventually Paniz, a tall, athletic, youthful-looking man, became a supporter of the clandestine Bolivarian movement. He missed out taking part in the February 4 coup because he didn't bother returning a telephone message from a contact who called hours before the revolt hoping to tip him off.

Besides giving Chávez a place to live, Paniz lent him his nearby office in Chuao for meetings. The guest cabin and the office turned into beehives of activity. Former soldiers streamed in and out of the cabin at all hours of the day and night. When Paniz complained, Chávez responded, "That's how I operate." He was a night owl, often going to bed at 3 A.M. or later. He ate when he could, and whatever he could, leaving the cabin strewn at times with chicken bones. At the office, visitors flocked to see Chávez. Some out-of-towners slept on a sofa at night. Many mornings one of the first guests to arrive was Jorge Giordani, the bearded economics guru from the MAS. He and Chávez spent hours developing documents, statements, and plans.

Chávez was an emerging leader for many Venezuelans, but he had nothing suitable to wear. Friends bought him three sets of *liqui liquis*, a traditional Venezuelan outfit from the llanos with a Mao collar and buttons down the front. It gave Chávez a look of elegance when he went for interviews with the media or businessmen. It also accentuated his nationalist outlook. He had three colors: blue, gray, and olive green, his favorite.

While most of Chávez's activities were focused on Venezuela, he also wanted to broaden his perspective. He hoped to build support for his movement in other countries and shoot down the negative image of him promoted by some of the media. He'd barely been out of Venezuela. He did not even possess a passport. Paniz and others helped him obtain one. By July 1994 he had embarked on a tour of several South American nations including Argentina, Uruguay, and Chile. He also visited Colombia, where he met with former members of the M-19 guerrilla movement and with some of the organizers of that nation's recent constitutional assembly. In December he realized one of his greatest dreams: He traveled to Cuba.

As Chávez recounted the story, although he met with Cuban embassy officials in Caracas before the trip, he was simply expecting to take part in a cultural exchange and conference honoring Simón Bolívar during a two-day visit to the island. But when the plane landed in Havana at about 9:30 P.M., it taxied to the other side of the airport to a spot reserved for the reception of dignitaries. The pilot came back and told Chávez and his personal assistant, Rafael Isea, that they were to debark. By then Chávez had figured out that something was up. But he was still stunned when he walked down the stairs in his green *liqui liqui* and saw who was waiting to greet him: Fidel Castro.

Flashbulbs lit up the night air as the Cuban leader embraced Chávez with a bear hug. After a short exchange, they made their way to the Palace of the Revolution. They stayed up talking until 3 or 4 A.M., even though Chávez and Isea had to be up at 7 A.M. for the next day's activities. Castro fired question after question at Chávez — everything from how many men he'd had for the February 4 coup to what kind of arms they'd carried. Chávez eventually asked his own questions, especially about the death of Ernesto "Che" Guevara that had so worried him as a boy in Barinas. Chávez, himself a history buff, was amazed by Castro's knowledge not only of world history but also of Venezuela's past. He brought up topic after topic, from Zamora's attack at Santa Inés to the story of Maisanta, only to find that Castro knew all about it. When he discovered that Castro knew the history of Pedro Pérez Delgado intimately, "I said to myself, 'I give up, I give up. I'm not going to try any more. This man is invincible.'"

By the time Chávez and Isea woke up a few hours after the encounter with Castro, the morning edition of the Communist Party daily *Granma* was out with a front-page photograph of Castro and Chávez embracing. The newspaper quoted Chávez saying the warm welcome from Castro was "an honor that in truth I do not yet merit." But Castro wanted to send a message to Cubans and others who had barely heard of Chávez and might be skeptical of a former coup leader from Latin America: This was a man to be watched and respected. "Never was there a more opportune or more fitting time to come to the airport to receive a visitor like Lieutenant Colonel Hugo Chávez," he said in a statement published in *Granma*.

They spent two days locked in each other's company. Castro, who had telephoned Carlos Andrés Pérez with a message of support during Chávez's 1992 coup, had rethought the matter. He accompanied Chávez throughout his trip to Havana, walking through Habana Vieja, placing a wreath at a statue of Simón Bolívar, visiting the house where the Liberator passed through when he came to Cuba at the age of sixteen. Chávez gave a speech there, with Fidel sitting in the front row. Later the two made their way to the University of Havana, where both delivered speeches to student leaders. In his address Chávez declared the island a "bastion of Latin American dignity" and confessed, "It's the first time I have come physically to Cuba, but in my dreams I have come many times."

Besides giving the speech at the university, El Comandante also visited Cuba's armed forces academy, walked through the underground tunnels that hid tanks poised to repel an attack by the United States, and inspected a room with models of the major military battles in world history. Before he left, he and Castro sat on a sofa together and pored through a photo album that the Cuban leader gave him as a memento of the trip.

Chávez's opponents would use the visit against him for years to come. They cited it as evidence he planned to impose a Cuban-style dictatorship in Venezuela. When he ran for president, a video of his speech at the University of Havana surfaced and was widely circulated. It was true Chávez admired many aspects of Castro's revolution, including an educational system that gave Cuba a higher literacy rate than the United States and a health system that the World Health Organization cited as a model for Third World countries. Chávez himself would later compare his relationship with Castro to that of a father and son. The Cuban leader would help guide Chávez through some of his bleakest moments, including when his presidency and even his life were on the line — with the United States lurking in the background.

But he also seemed to recognize that installing a Castro-style regime in Venezuela was impossible. Venezuelans held a deep antipathy to communism, especially after the bloody guerrilla wars of the 1960s. Chávez himself was skeptical of many Venezuelan leftists, saying they had spent so many years in the hills engaged in armed conspiracy and isolated from the masses that they had lost touch with the average Venezuelan. Beyond that, a new century was dawning. Castro's model implemented forty years earlier with its heavy state control of the economy, the media, and the electoral apparatus — albeit in the face of US hostility and numerous attempts to destroy his revolution and assassinate him — was out of date and heavily criticized. While Chávez clearly admired aspects of Castro's revolution and the man himself, he would follow his own leftist path. Venezuela was not Cuba, and he knew it. The world had changed.

After his return to Venezuela, Chávez kept up a frenzy of meetings, tours, and discussions with community leaders, advisers, and Bolivarian sympathizers. While his constant forays into the capital's barrios and the villages of the countryside were open affairs, he was also quietly meeting with small groups of community leaders in unpublicized private sessions. He wanted to win their support, broaden his movement to include more civilians, and explain his proposal for a constitutional assembly. His slogan was "Constitutional Assembly Now!"

He faced challenges even among those on the left. Many were skeptical because he was a former soldier. Others didn't know how to react. A few months after his release from jail when he showed up for a low-profile meeting at the community organizing center where Xiomara Tortoza worked in Catia, some of the local leftists called Chávez "comandante" and gave him a military salute. Tortoza was horrified. She'd traveled to the Southern Cone countries during the so-called dirty wars of the 1970s and 1980s and thought the last thing Venezuela needed was another "military gorilla" trained to order people around, or worse. Indeed, when Chávez traveled to Uruguay, Eduardo Galeano, the leftist author of one of his favorite books about exploitation, *The Open Veins of Latin America*, refused to meet with him.

On another occasion Chávez showed up at a meeting of leftists in Caracas's Parque Central. He walked in, and no one on the dais bothered to recognize him. "I never forgot that . . . Imagine, I was trying to present myself to the political left. I was being watched, persecuted, defamed, etc. and the leaders treated me like that . . . The official bourgeois discourse infected and destroyed the left. I don't deny my mistakes, I have certainly made some, but those groups rejected and condemned me."

At the meeting in Catia with Tortoza's group, Chávez was low-key, informal, modest, and accessible — a regular guy from the barrio. He wore a colorful beach shirt and patiently answered questions. He made a good impression. Tortoza's doubts eased a bit. Maybe this was a different kind of soldier.

While Chávez's popularity was booming in the barrios and among community groups and he was slowly building organized bases of support, he disappeared from most of the Venezuelan mainstream news media and the international press. Major Venezuelan newspapers, television networks, and radio stations had fought the Pérez government to report on the popularity of Chávez and his coup in the days after the revolt. The coup leader was still an unknown entity then, and Pérez was virulently hated.

But now Chávez's radical nationalist views were well known. Media barons hostile to his calls for revolution tried to eliminate him from their coverage. When he returned from his trip to Colombia in July

1994 and held a press conference, for instance, most major newspapers didn't report a word about it. "I was barred from TV, from the press and from the radio. They even fired some journalists for interviewing me and putting out a taped interview on radio, or they [the authorities] would come and close a radio station because it interviewed me." At one point, as Chávez recalled it, someone remarked on television that he didn't even exist. Many editors and reporters considered Chávez *caliche*, Venezuelan slang for someone who is not news but tries to be. When he visited newsrooms, editors scattered and hid so they wouldn't have to meet with him.

But the boycott by the elite media merely added to Chávez's mystique in the barrios. He got around the snubs partly by going to local media in the regions he visited. He'd been told by a journalist friend that people in the interior read the local papers a lot more than they read the big-city dailies like *El Nacional* trucked or flown in from Caracas. Many of the local editors were delighted, giving Chávez hours of their time and pages of their newspapers. After a three-hour chat at one paper, Chávez finally told the editor he had to go.

Operating below the mainstream media radar line, Chávez was tapping into working-class Venezuelans' growing frustration with the government. Pérez's administration had been a disaster. But Caldera's wasn't turning out much better. By now nearing his eighties, the grand old man of Venezuelan politics spoke with a tremulous voice and had a frail appearance, walking stiffly and slowly. One of the authors of a landmark labor law in the 1930s, he came into office for his second term promising to undo many of the neo-liberal measures imposed by Pérez.

He inherited one of the worst banking debacles in Latin American history. After the fall of Banco Latino in January 1994 provoked a nearly systemwide collapse, angry depositors milled outside the doors of barred banks, frantic to withdraw their deposits. At the federal agency that insured the banks, small groups stood vigil, sharing whatever news they could get and reading missives left by other depositors. One listed the names of sixty-three officials accused of theft, including Presidents Pérez and Lusinchi. "Don't let the guilty escape," it said. Underneath, someone wrote in red: "Execute them. Now!"

Under pressure to act, Caldera merely exacerbated the problems. "The government panicked. Desperate to avoid further bank failures, it simply printed money, sparking a sharp rise in inflation and a plunge in the value of the bolivar." Caldera tried to limit the damage by imposing price controls on food, medicine, foreign exchange, and even movie theater tickets.

He also suspended some constitutional guarantees. The decree allowed the government to seize private property, make arrests without the usual legal safeguards, and restrict travel. When Congress restored the guarantees a few weeks later, Caldera simply suspended them again. He threatened a referendum in which the loser, himself or the legislature, would have to resign. Congress backed off. Underscoring an authoritative streak, Caldera also started sending out police to interrogate critics of his government, from academics to media men.

In his first year in office, the doddering president still enjoyed a high level of popularity. His reputation as a man of personal honesty and integrity was unblemished. One analyst said he had "more moral authority than any living Venezuelan." In contrast with Pérez's ostentatious "coronation" in 1989, Caldera assumed office with a simple ceremony in Congress rather than the glittering Teresa Carreño Theater. Unlike CAP's invitation to hundreds of dignitaries from all over the world, Caldera invited almost no foreigners. "There will be no party . . . just some refreshments," Caldera's son Juan José, a newly elected senator, told reporters.

But Caldera seemed incapable of resolving the nation's mounting problems. A string of constantly changing economic plans — eight in the first year and a half of his administration — was doing little to ease the economic woes. Inflation soared to 71 percent in 1994 and 57 percent in 1995, the highest in Latin America. By April 1996 Caldera did what he swore he would never do — he "got down on his knees" before the International Monetary Fund. He implemented the same kind of economic shock package Pérez had imposed.

To carry out the distasteful task he recruited the most unlikely of neo-liberal free marketers: former Marxist guerrilla Teodoro Petkoff. The son of a Bulgarian communist exile and a Polish physician mother, Petkoff, with his trademark bushy mustache, acerbic style, and caustic wit, was a legend of the left. An economist who graduated with honors, he helped lead one of the most powerful guerrilla movements in Latin America in the 1960s. He joined in spectacular antigovernment actions including the kidnapping of a US Army colonel.

He spent three years in jail, and escaped twice. Once, he and several comrades fled San Carlos military prison in Caracas by digging a 230-foot tunnel with their hands. They crawled through and climbed up into a store jammed with their delighted Marxist comrades, taking off amid the chaos of Carnival celebrations. No one had ever escaped from the prison before. The second time, he swallowed and then spit up smuggled cow's blood to convince authorities he was sick, then slid down a rope of knotted sheets from a seventh-floor military hospital window.

A brilliant and charismatic student leader in the 1950s, Petkoff joined the Communist Party and fought to overthrow the dictator Marcos Pérez Jiménez. He took to the hills in the 1960s when he and other leftists felt the democracy that replaced the strongman was "bourgeois" and didn't represent the poor masses. But by 1969 he and other rebels surrendered, accepting an amnesty from Caldera as their armed insurrection failed to catch on.

Petkoff and others split from the Communists in 1971, saying the Soviet model was dictatorial. Three years earlier, he had earned a public scolding from Soviet president Leonid Brezhnev for writing a book condemning the 1968 Soviet invasion of Czechoslovakia that had crushed the "Prague Spring" democracy movement. The dissidents formed the Movement to Socialism party, which turned into Venezuela's third largest. Petkoff won a seat in the Senate and ran for president twice, losing badly both times. During his first campaign, Colombia's Nobel Prize–winning author Gabriel García Márquez lauded him with an essay about his daring escapes, love of literature, and bold politics. Eventually Petkoff migrated to the center, and then to the right.

Caldera's move to make Petkoff the point man for his free-market turnaround was a stroke of genius, although his former communist comrades called him a sellout and an "instrument of savage capitalism." Caldera named Petkoff planning minister in March 1996. A month later, the president announced his new economic program, dubbed Agenda Venezuela. Wall Street was thrilled. If a famous former communist guerrilla was endorsing the package, it had to be good. Petkoff argued that there was little choice, and that the world had changed. A week before the announcement, he described Venezuela as a "house on fire."

He became the administration's chief apostle for free-market economic measures, landing on the front page as much as Caldera himself. He was certainly more colorful. When he underwent minor knee surgery, the daily *El Universal* splashed a photograph of him in his hospital bed across the front page with the headline, "The Economy Will Not

Limp." By some accounts, Petkoff became even more orthodox than the US-educated technocrats who carried out Pérez's *paquete*. He negotiated a new labor law, privatized subsidized state industries, forged a lending agreement with the IMF, tried to lure foreign investors to the country, heralded an opening of the nationalized oil industry to international companies, and handed out pink slips to 80,000 of Venezuela's 1.4 million public employees.

But even Petkoff's charisma and credentials as a former card-carrying leftist could not convince most Venezuelans of the merits of the program or lift Caldera's fortunes. The package did little to improve life for average workers. Inflation in 1996 leaped to a record 103 percent in a nation that had never known soaring inflation until the 1990s. Caldera's popularity ratings plummeted over two years, from 66 percent in May 1994 to 33 percent in September 1996. Venezuela sank deeper into economic recession.

As criticism picked up, Caldera cracked down. In March 1995 he ordered the third raid in less than a year against leftists suspected of fomenting a plan to destabilize the government. Political police raided one hundred offices and homes, and arrested 150 people including dozens of Chávez supporters. Among them were former policeman Freddy Bernal, the coup leader's brother Adán, and even a former featherweight boxing champion, Antonio Esparragoza. The government did not dare arrest Chávez himself. They knew that this would provoke widespread unrest amid a precarious political situation. Instead the people around him were targeted. Chávez repeated his challenge to Caldera to put him in jail and see who lasted longer: the rebel in prison or the president in Miraflores. In the end police quickly released those detained. No charges were filed, creating the impression again that it was more of a political witch hunt than a serious investigation.

The detentions were part of an ongoing campaign of harassment against Chávez and his supporters. Political police from the widely feared DISIP followed him around the country and in Caracas. Chávez had to be constantly on the alert against agents who might try to discredit him by planting drugs or illegal arms. A physical attack was not out of the question, either. Davila, the retired colonel, carried a gun or kept one on the seat next to him in the truck. Police agents maintained permanent surveillance of Paniz's office in Chuao where Chávez conducted many of his meetings. He sometimes held them in cars as they drove around the city to avoid the DISIP's spying. On more than one occasion Chávez donned wigs, hats, and even fake mustaches so agents would not recognize him.

Political police also tapped the telephones of Chávez and his key supporters, and stole some of their cars. Héctor Navarro, the Central University of Venezuela professor who formed part of Chávez's "shadow cabinet" of leftist academics that by now was meeting with him almost every Tuesday, figured he was about the only one in the group whose car was not stolen. Authorities knew Chávez and his backers had little money. Leaving them without vehicles was one way to trip up the movement. Eventually the "Chávez mobile" itself was attacked and destroyed. Someone set it on fire one night while it was parked in the Propatria section of Caracas.

Caldera's crackdown on dissent reached absurd proportions. In October 1996 the feared DISIP arrested an astrologer who had predicted Caldera's "death" the following year. They held him incommunicado for two days in DISIP headquarters, where he slept on a cement floor in a cell. The rotund, bearded José Bernardo Gómez was the president of the Venezuelan Astrologers Association. He was also a university philosophy professor with postgraduate degrees in history, education, psychology, and philosophy from three Venezuelan universities. After his release, he told reporters that when police asked him where he'd gotten his information about Caldera's possible death, he'd responded that the president's astrological charts showed trouble on the horizon. "Uranus is over the sun, Pluto is in ascendancy, and Mars is going behind its moon." Caldera's "death," he noted, might be symbolic, such as leaving office. "I wish the president good health," Gómez said, adding that he voted for Caldera in 1993. "I'm not betting on his sickness, much less on his death. It's just that from an astrological point of view, 1997 looks dark for Caldera."

Embarrassed government officials tried to play down the incident. "He's not accused of anything," Interior Minister José Guillermo Andueza said tersely. Political police merely wanted to know "what basis he has for making this kind of statement."

Gómez, who had many accurate predictions to his credit, had declared that if Caldera was still alive or at least in office by the following June 8, he would give up astrology for good. When the date arrived and Caldera was still in place, the government hailed it as a triumph. Officials took steps on several occasions to beat down rumors that the seldom-seen octogenarian president with ailing health was no longer among the living. A few months earlier he'd walked from Congress to the presidential palace to scotch rumors that he was dying, or even dead. On another occasion the administration arranged front-page photographs in newspapers showing Caldera playing dominoes on a Sunday afternoon.

Caldera's elected predecessor, Carlos Andrés Pérez, was suffering his own problems. A year after his impeachment in May 1993, the Supreme Court ruled that the investigation into corruption charges indicated that Pérez and two aides engaged in the misappropriation of funds. They decided to put the former president on trial. In an unprecedented move, they also ordered his arrest and detention. It was the first time in Venezuela's democratic era that authorities jailed a president, and was a rarity in Latin America in general. The Venezuelan establishment pointed to it as evidence that the system was working. Critics said the system had no choice: The elites had to sacrifice one of their own to keep the whole structure from crumbling.

Pérez showed up at the Supreme Court that morning for the announcement. He denounced the case again as a political witch hunt. Armed with a suitcase full of books, he departed for El Junquito jail in Caracas's Catia section, scene of some of the worst repression of the Caracazo. Pérez was spared the worst of Venezuela's squalid and dangerous jails: El Junquito was among the most comfortable. His former interior minister Alejandro Izaguirre was his new cell mate. Another aide also ordered to jail, Reinaldo Figueredo, had fled the country.

Pérez's new world was a twelve-by-nine-foot cell. Cashing in on his years of globe trotting, he received an outpouring of support from leaders overseas outraged by his imprisonment. At home he was reviled. Citizens in the streets cursed him, blaming him for the country's ills including the banking collapse. Within hours of Pérez's arrest the executive committee of his own party, Democratic Action, voted to toss him out of an organization he'd helped found more than five decades earlier, in 1941. The meeting turned into a melee, with flying metal chairs and thrown fists — Pérez still had some supporters.

Taking a cue, his sixty-eight-year-old predecessor, Jaime Lusinchi, resigned from the party a few weeks later, ending a lifelong membership. Lusinchi was under investigation for allegedly diverting five hundred thousand dollars in secret national security funds in part to purchase sixty-five jeeps used during Pérez's 1988 presidential campaign.

Authorities were also investigating allegations that he allowed his then private secretary and mistress, Blanca Ibáñez, to use $1 million in government funds to throw lavish parties and import twenty-four white horses from the United States for her daughter. By July, Lusinchi, increasingly unnerved by Pérez's fate, slipped out of the country on a yacht.

Shortly after Pérez's imprisonment, Venezuela's attorney general expanded the allegations against the former president. Jesús Petit Da Costa claimed Pérez funneled huge amounts of stolen government funds through his mistress Cecilia Matos, whom he charged had at least $200 million in Swiss bank accounts the government could not touch. Congressional investigators were making similar allegations. Matos, a former government secretary who earned barely a couple of hundred dollars a month, had landed in an apartment on exclusive Sutton Place in Manhattan. She ended up working with the Venezuelan clothes designer Carolina Herrera, and had two children by Pérez.

The former president, who grew up poor, spent his life in politics, and by most accounts amassed a sizable fortune, denied all the allegations. Ten weeks into his imprisonment he got a reprieve. The Supreme Court freed him from jail. They placed him under house arrest while his trial went on. Pérez, by now seventy-two, took advantage of a law that permitted anyone over seventy to await trial at home. He returned triumphantly to La Ahumada, the walled hilltop estate on the outskirts of Caracas where his estranged wife, Blanca Rodríguez de Pérez, was living.

Pérez settled into a routine as if he were still an important head of state. He received journalists, political allies, and the occasional ambassador. He took phone calls from foreign leaders. Photographs of him with George H. W. Bush, Jimmy Carter, and others filled the walls of his study. Two glass cases showed off dozens of medals bestowed on him by foreign heads of state. A rifle from the Nicaraguan contras saluted his role in that nation's transition from war to peace in the late 1980s.

He woke up every morning before dawn after a few hours' sleep, worked out for ninety minutes, and then slipped into an impeccable suit and tie for another day of business. He still exuded the magnetism that used to make women faint at campaign rallies. But he couldn't go anywhere. So he started communicating with people by Internet.

With Pérez under house arrest, Caldera's administration crumbling, and few promising alternatives for the nation in sight, Chávez struggled with his political future. For several years he advocated abstaining from Venezuela's elections. He believed they were a fixed game, a farce that outsiders had no chance of winning. In Yare in October 1993, of course, he and some of the other rebels issued a communiqué calling on people to boycott that December's elections for president, Congress, and state assemblies. "To take part in an election like this one, which has been controlled by the elites, would be to make oneself an accomplice in a deliberate mockery of the popular aspirations of a movement like ours," they wrote. They called the elections "illegal and illegitimate" and ended the communiqué with a quote from Bolívar: "All history indicates that gangrenous politicians will not cure themselves with palliatives."

The communiqué and the debate over boycotting the elections produced one of the most serious fissures among the rebels during their time in jail. Arias Cárdenas firmly opposed Chávez's position. The two fought bitterly. Arias believed the system would allow outsiders like themselves to participate and win, and he was to soon show Chávez how. Their dispute grew so acrid, Arias split from Chávez's Bolivarian movement.

During his first year or two out of prison, El Comandante was still thinking about a coup. He envisioned a civic-military uprising followed by a constitutional assembly that would overhaul the established order. "In those first years, 1994–95, we hadn't ruled out the possibility of reverting to the armed struggle. But we wanted to evaluate the possibilities in terms of real force, and we concluded we didn't have what it would take . . . The situation at the time was not ripe for another armed movement . . . Once we analyzed the situation we realized that another military insurrection would have been crazy."

With the prospects of success for another coup appearing dim, some of Chávez's advisers, notably Luis Miquilena, urged him to reconsider his opposition to Venezuela's elections. Miquilena thought Chávez could win so overwhelmingly that even the elite-controlled electoral machine could not deny him victory. To find out, Chávez and his comrades decided to conduct a poll. They knew from the reaction in the barrios that he had support in the streets, but they wanted to find out in a more scientific way how much.

They organized teams of psychologists, sociologists, university professors, and students to carry out the survey. They included people from outside their movement to try to maintain some measure of objectivity.

They divided the country into three zones — east, west, and center — and called on grassroots members of the Bolivarian movement to poll residents. They questioned tens of thousands of people. There were two main questions: Do you support Hugo Chávez's candidacy for the presidency? Would you vote for him?

Chávez, Jorge Giordani, Héctor Navarro, and other allies pored over the results on a computer. They appeared clear: The response to the first question was 70 percent yes and 30 percent no. "That result was totally clear: the people wanted me to run for president," Chávez later told an interviewer. The results to the second question indicated he might actually win: 57 percent said they would vote for him. The numbers were revealing because in polls conducted by private firms — many of them linked to Venezuela's elites — Chávez was almost invisible.

He had another reason to reconsider his opposition to taking part in elections run by the establishment. With the backing of the Causa R and other groups, Arias Cárdenas ran for governor of Zulia state in the December 1995 elections. On the campaign trail, it was evident he was stirring up support, even though Chávez had eclipsed him as the more charismatic coup leader. On one campaign swing through rural towns outside Maracaibo, "mothers with their hair in curlers, young men swilling beer and gray-haired retirees waved and cheered the noisy caravan of trucks and cars accompanying Arias. 'Vote for the Comandante!' blared the music from a truck. 'This is what we need in the country!' cried a woman in a white-and-yellow house dress, as she rushed up to the pickup truck where Arias stood."

Despite lacking the support of Chávez's MBR-200, which was holding hard to its abstention campaign, Arias won. Two months later, he moved into the same governor's mansion he had seized during the February 4, 1992, coup. He was now in charge of the state that accounted for at least half of Venezuela's economic output with its oil, minerals, and cattle.

The Bolivarian movement spent a year debating whether Chávez should run for president. They held local assemblies, regional assemblies, national assemblies. Often the sessions started in the morning and lasted into the middle of the night. While many of the Bolivarians supported the idea, Chávez also faced resistance. Some segments opposed the electoral route and "accused us of having abandoned the revolution because we had discontinued the armed struggle . . . We knew taking the electoral path was a strategic decision that could be catastrophic, that we could walk right into the trap that the system set for us, that it could lead us into a pit of quicksand." It was possible Chávez would not have an adequate electoral machine in place and go down in defeat, destroying his political aspirations.

But he wanted to take the risk. By early April 1997 he was telling reporters the MBR-200 would probably put up a candidate — with Chávez the obvious choice. On April 19, the anniversary of Venezuela's declaration of independence, he and the Bolivarian movement convened a special national congress to make a final decision. After a meeting that started about 9 A.M. and ended about 2 A.M. the next day, they decided to launch Chávez's candidacy. They thought too much was at stake. Not only the presidential race but regional and municipal elections nationwide were to take place the same day. Not everyone supported the decision. Some key members of the movement who opposed the campaign resigned.

Three months later, in July, Chávez officially registered his new party, the Fifth Republic Movement (MVR), with the National Electoral Council. He and his supporters had to change the name of their group because Venezuelan law prohibited the use of Simón Bolívar's name for political parties.

Two thousand supporters cheered Chávez outside the board's offices that day. El Comandante was embarking on a road that would make him famous worldwide and a force to reckon with. But the international media hardly noticed. They made brief mention of the developments, or ignored them. Even those that did report Chávez's candidacy dismissed it as almost irrelevant. "Few Venezuelans think the retired lieutenant colonel has a serious chance of winning, since his once sky-high popularity has plummeted . . . Critics say he talks too much about South American independence hero Simón Bolívar and too little about concrete solutions to the country's problems, such as unemployment, poverty and corruption." One report cited a recent poll giving Chávez 8 percent of the vote.

Instead of the former coup leader, the establishment's eyes were fixed on Irene Sáez.

**14**

# Beauty and the Beast

A former Miss Universe, Irene Sáez was the mayor of the glitzy Chacao section of Caracas. In a nation that worshipped beauty queens, Sáez was the most popular politician in the land, according to the polls. A six-foot-one strawberry blonde who referred to herself as a political "atomic bomb," she was sweeping the imagination of the public, the media, and the establishment with her clean-government agenda in Chacao and the good looks and manners she'd learned to cultivate as Miss Venezuela. It was a combination that seemed hard to beat.

In Venezuela beauty pageants were a religion. On the night of the Miss Venezuela contest, the country came to a halt, with millions of people glued to their television sets. The four-hour extravaganza was the highest-rated show of the year, attracting at least two-thirds of the viewing audience. It was the same routine the night of Miss Universe if Venezuela's representative was in the running. She almost always was. By the time Sáez rose to prominence in the political arena, Venezuela was the undisputed beauty-queen capital of the world. Between 1979 and 1997 its women won ten major international titles. That was more than any other country, even though Venezuela accounted for just 0.4 percent of the world population.

To some people Venezuela's obsession with beauty and beauty pageants was a troubling sign of superficiality, of a tendency "to settle for appearance rather than substance, and to avoid serious thinking." Clearly, it was a nation virtually untouched by feminism. With an average tropical temperature of eighty-two degrees in Caracas, and even hotter in the interior, women dressed scantily to display their charms. Skintight pants, blouses with plunging necklines, and open-back or short dresses were standard attire for everyone from secretaries to lawyers. It created a "strange city, with an aura of sexuality bordering on the absurd." Men were free to voice their admiration; they were almost expected to.

A national institution almost off limits to criticism, the Miss Venezuela pageant produced a string of successful actresses and prosperous business women. Irene Sáez chose a different route: politics. When she first ran for office in 1992, most people thought it was a joke. She was a mindless Miss. Or so they believed.

The youngest of six children of businessman Carlos Sáez and his wife, Ligia, Irene was three years old when her mother succumbed to cancer. Her death at forty devastated Irene and left a lasting mark. "I used to look at the night sky and see my mother as the brightest star. Since then, she's my guardian angel, my inner voice," Sáez told *People* magazine in a glowing portrait titled "Not Just Another Pretty Face." After her mother's death, two older sisters helped raise her in a well-off, conservative household. By the time she was nineteen and a university engineering student, Irene's inner voice spoke to her. It told her to compete for Miss Venezuela. Though she'd never had much interest in pageants before, she entered at the last minute, just two weeks before it took place.

With no dieting, no plastic surgery, no modeling experience, and little preparation, Irene won. Shortly after she went on to take the Miss Universe title. "I just knew in my heart and soul that I'd win," she told *People*. "I only wish that my mother had been with me to share the moment." She spent a year traveling the world, meeting everyone from Ronald Reagan to Margaret Thatcher to Augusto Pinochet. After her reign ended, she reportedly gave up a multimillion-dollar contract to star opposite John Travolta in a movie. Hollywood, she said, "didn't attract me."

Instead, she switched majors and took up political science at the Central University of Venezuela, one of the country's top public universities. She went on to serve for a year as Venezuela's cultural representative to the United Nations. Sáez cultivated a reputation as a devout Catholic who attended Mass almost every day, opposed abortion, and volunteered in a church group. Still, she wasn't merely a Girl

Scout trying to do good for herself and her country. For nearly a decade she "enjoyed something of a playgirl existence. She had a prominent Venezuelan banker for a lover and traveled the world on behalf of his bank," Consolidado, where she was employed as a spokeswoman.

By the early 1990s Sáez had turned her energy to electoral politics. She was motivated by a "vocation of service" and believed she could use her fame, her worldwide contacts, and her training in political science to improve life in the oil-rich but impoverished nation. She won the race for mayor of Chacao a week after the November 1992 coup attempt. She quickly shut up critics who thought she was nothing more than a brainless blonde. She cleaned up Chacao.

With its Baskin-Robbins stores and drive-in McDonald's, Chacao seemed in ways like a slice of the United States in Venezuela. Nestled in the foothills of verdant Mount Avila, it was Caracas's richest section and home to many of the capital's diplomatic missions. But it had fallen into disrepair. Crime was rampant, making it dangerous to head out at night. Hold-ups by armed bandits in fancy restaurants were common. The streets were dirty. Public plazas were falling apart.

Irene's first attack focused on the crime wave. To make the streets safe again, she professionalized the police force. She hired university graduates as officers, hiked their pay dramatically, and outfitted them with the kinds of white pith helmets she'd seen British bobbies wearing when she'd visited London as Miss Universe. She put transit officers on golf carts dubbed "Irene-mobiles" — an idea she imported from the Far East. She sent out other police on roller skates, mountain bikes, and motorized children's scooters. She also bought a fleet of shiny new police cars that cruised tree-shaded streets.

Crime plummeted. The streets filled with pedestrians at night again. Restaurant-goers could eat out in peace. Sáez also spruced up public squares, including Plaza Altamira, where old people took to sitting on benches under trees sparkling with lights at night and children roller-skated past gushing fountains that for years had been dry. The attractive young mayor offered early-morning tai chi classes for senior citizens, set up a paramedic team that made house calls, and improved garbage collection. She hired top-notch administrators and listened to their advice about everything from setting the budget to running public services. Chacao turned into an oasis of safety, cleanliness, and cultural life in a city where most people locked themselves in their homes at night, the streets were filthy, and culture consisted mainly of watching maudlin soap operas on TV. It bordered on the miraculous. People dubbed it "Irene-landia."

Sáez was so popular by the time she ran for reelection in December 1995 that she didn't bother to mount a campaign organization. The only person who dared to run against her, lawyer Paulo Carillo, was scolded by his own mother and the high school he graduated from. About the only thing Carillo could attack was Sáez's well-coiffed, stylishly dressed figure. "She's a plastic doll," he sniffed. Sáez crushed him, taking 96 percent of the vote. It was the most lopsided victory in Venezuela's thirty-seven years of democratic rule.

Not long into her second term, people were talking about Irene for president. She was seen as that rarity in Venezuela — an honest and efficient public servant. Besides, she was young, beautiful, and had a performer's sense of how to win admirers. She donned Indian headdresses, swiveled to salsa music, rode to ceremonies on the back of police motorcycles, and planted kisses on old men's cheeks. Former president Luis Herrera Campins called her "capable." *The Times* of London ranked her among the one hundred most powerful women in the world. At number eighty-three, she beat out Jodie Foster and Mother Teresa.

Sáez flirted with the presidential rumors, although she kept her distance from the traditional parties Herrera Campins represented. She didn't join any party, or form one of her own. Instead, she created a "movement" her followers could join. She called it Integration, Renovation, and New Hope. In Spanish, the initials spelled out *IRENE*. As the presidential campaign entered the defining year of 1998, she was the odds-on favorite to win, at least in the mainstream polls.

Hugo Chávez was off the establishment's radar screen. The major media mostly ignored him, or lambasted him. He made some missteps that provided them ammunition. One was his relationship with the Argentine sociologist Norberto Ceresole. An intellectual with an interest in progressive military regimes who later moved to the far right, Ceresole was intrigued by Chávez's coup in 1992. He sent some of his books and a card with his telephone number on it to El Comandante in Yare. When Chávez was released and traveled to Argentina a few months later, he called.

Ceresole was controversial. He claimed he was a member of the Montoneros, the radical leftist and nationalist Peronist guerrilla group that carried out a series of spectacular assaults, assassinations, and kidnappings in the 1970s. He later argued in favor of the military coup that overthrew Juan Perón's widow Isabel Perón in 1976 and led to a bloody dictatorship under General Jorge Videla. Ceresole claimed human rights organizations that criticized the abuses during Argentina's 1976 to 1983 dirty war — when the military regime killed or disappeared at least thirty thousand people — were part of a "Jewish plot" against the nation. He also cast doubt on whether the Holocaust had really happened.

Despite some of Ceresole's unsavory, even bizarre viewpoints, Chávez was attracted to him for a number of reasons. One was his early interest in progressive military leaders. A radical Peronist, Ceresole had written books in support of the Peruvian general Juan Velasco Alvarado, whose reformist government sparked Chávez's interest when he was a cadet at the military academy in the early 1970s and traveled to Peru. Ceresole also wrote favorably about Panama's General Omar Torrijos, another figure who inspired the young Chávez as he sought a way to fuse his emerging social conscience with his career as a soldier.

Ceresole considered Peronism "the most important dignifying movement in the history of mankind." Recalling his own humble roots, he told interviewer Alberto Garrido why:

My family did not have shoes before Peron. When Peronism ended, we had our own house, with the loans completely paid off. My parents had never gone on vacation. I had never been to the sea. I was able to see it when I was ten or twelve years old. There were vacations. They were free, absolutely free. Well, this is called dignity.

The middle-class and the upper-class hate populism because this means sharing. But we who come from the lower class say, "Long live populism!" That dignifies us. When I was ten years old I had never seen a soccer ball. I saw them in photos and Eva Peron and the Eva Peron Foundation gave us soccer equipment, a soccer ball, a real one. It was leather, an authentic soccer ball. And she gave us shirts . . . and shoes.

We're talking about the people and of course, it is the mortal enemy of the oligarchies, naturally. That's why they created the black image of Peron, as if Peron were the son of Hitler . . . Every dollar that we give to the people is one dollar that we won't give the to International Monetary Fund. That's why, long live populism. There's no other form of revolution in the Americas than that.

Chávez was attracted to Ceresole for other reasons, too. Much of the left in Uruguay and Argentina, wary of another coup-leading military officer after right-wing military dictatorships had devastated their nations, closed the door to Chávez during his trip to the Southern Cone in 1994. Ceresole was one of the few willing to meet with him. He also had other ideas that interested Chávez, such as integrating business and transport along some of South America's major rivers including La Plata, the Amazon, and the Orinoco.

Most importantly, however, Ceresole offered Chávez a vision of how to achieve and maintain power by going around the discredited traditional political parties. It was Ceresole's celebrated triangular notion of uniting the *caudillo*, the military, and the people. "The caudillo would transform the military into the armed wing of a nationalist revolutionary project and enlist the poor as its popular support base." Ceresole believed that

> the leader of such a political project would provoke a strategic confrontation between a unipolar and multipolar world, in which the caudillo would face down the global hegemony of the United States by rallying all factors hostile to US power. A multipolar axis would emerge, involving left-wing guerrillas, progressive social movements, and nonaligned governments in Europe, Latin America, and the Middle East. Ceresole described his ideas as "post-democratic," as the caudillo would sweep aside parliament, courts, and other institutions that slowed down decision-making processes and reined in ambitious presidential projects.

After Ceresole met with Chávez in Argentina, they reunited later that year in Colombia. Ceresole remembered the second meeting more for Chávez's desperate financial situation than any profound intellectual exchanges. "He didn't have anything. There wasn't a single cent. It was so bad we had to change hotels several times because there was no money to pay. I'm talking about low-level hotels where we slept three to a room . . . What Chávez was looking for at that moment was financing, which he couldn't find anywhere."

Ceresole accompanied Chávez as he returned to Venezuela, crossing the border by land since he didn't have money for an airplane ticket. The Argentine joined Chávez on some of his tours around the country and then left for Madrid. Eventually he returned to Venezuela in 1995. By now the government of President Rafael Caldera had reached its limit with the controversial sociologist, and expelled him from the country.

Chávez thought it was hypocritical, since Ceresole had met privately during his trip with some of Caldera's cabinet members, including Border Minister Pompeyo Márquez, a former guerrilla leader and MAS member. Still, Chávez did not buy into all of Ceresole's ideas. "Of his theses and opinions, some I share, others I don't," Chávez told an interviewer. "But he was never an advisor, a mentor. He's an intellectual, a writer." And Ceresole did not agree with all of Chávez's positions. According to political scientist Daniel Hellinger, "Chávez's admiration for Fidel Castro, his refusal to disavow liberal democratic norms and civilian control over the military, and his pragmatic attitude toward the United States alienated Ceresole." The self-exiled Argentine turned up in Venezuela again after Chávez took office in 1999, but soon Chávez, like Caldera, threw him out of the country.

Even after Chávez's announcement, Irene Sáez seemed to some like the candidate to beat. Newspapers referred to her as the "aircraft carrier," capable of carrying other candidates along with her to victory in Congress and other offices. The Social Christian COPEI Party led by former president Herrera Campins — a big Sáez supporter — was seriously debating the idea of joining forces with the former Miss Universe and backing her bid for president. Irene started preparing herself for the nation's highest post. Consultants drilled her in economics, constitutional rights, oil industry politics. On her desk in the mayor's office she displayed a copy of Margaret Thatcher's book *The Path to Power*.

But as potential presidential timber, she was beginning to look less than sturdy by early 1998. In contrast with Chávez's tough talk about destroying the status quo, convoking a constitutional assembly to rewrite the constitution, and unleashing a "peaceful revolution" on behalf of the poor masses, Irene was full of sugary platitudes. She spoke about her love for "my people" and the need to make politics more "human." In a country suffering a severe crisis of corrupt politicians, soaring inflation, and plummeting oil prices, her mushy, sentimental statements didn't seem to cut it. She still spoke like a beauty queen anxious to avoid offending anybody in any way in anyplace. People wondered if her success in affluent Chacao — the "Disneyland" of Caracas — would translate to the rest of the impoverished country with its deep-rooted problems.

She made moves that were outright silly. In late 1997 she banned kissing in public plazas in Chacao. Alarmed by complaints from neighbors that exhibitions of affection were going far beyond smooching in public parks and plazas, Sáez dispatched her smartly dressed police to crack down on couples whose embraces surpassed what she deemed acceptable limits. Armed with whistles, they watched for couples who squeezed too tightly, embraced too ardently, or kissed too long. Five seconds could be too long. "Kissing in itself isn't a problem," one police official explained. "The problem is when they do it in a way that goes beyond normal." He acknowledged that defining such a kiss wasn't easy, but "when you see it, you should know it." Some lovers said they were arrested and briefly thrown in jail. As he sat with his girlfriend on a bench under a vine-covered canopy in Plaza Altamira one night, a man in his twenties remarked, "Whoever invented this law must not have a girlfriend."

The campaign seemed especially ludicrous in a country where presidents openly shacked up with their mistresses. During his 1984–1989 term, Jaime Lusinchi even installed a bedroom in Miraflores presidential palace for his mistress and personal secretary, Blanca Ibáñez.

About the same time Sáez was cracking down on kissing in public plazas, press reports were linking her to real estate tycoon Donald Trump, whose empire included the Miss Universe pageant. Irene said they were only good friends, but some reports breathlessly spoke of a "steamy romance" and predicted that marriage was imminent. "Friends of Irene are saying she has captured his heart just like she has captured the hearts of the Venezuelan people," the Caracas daily *El Nuevo Pais* wrote. The paper then quoted an unnamed friend of Sáez: "Irene is Donald's dream girl. She has beauty, intelligence and ambition. All in one very sexy package."

While Sáez was batting away rumors of a romance with Trump and cracking down on kissing, Chávez was preaching revolution. His message was catching on. He was gaining in the polls. Some said the election was shaping up as a contest between "the beauty and the beast."

Chávez's new political group, the Fifth Republic Movement (MVR), had grand visions. Its goal was to create a new republic, with Chávez leading the charge as president. Venezuela's first two republics were formed during the wars of independence. The third emerged at the time of the formation of Gran Colombia in 1819. A fourth came eleven years later, in 1830. Founded by one of Bolívar's generals, José Antonio Páez, it lasted the longest. But Chávez insisted that it was never a true democracy, contending it was built by "a class of oligarchs and bankers, on the bones of Bolívar and Sucre." His movement would give the country its first new beginning in a century and a half, recovering the ideals of the Liberator and throwing out the villains who had pillaged the nation. While small at first, the MVR absorbed a number of civilians with extensive experience from Venezuela's old left. They included Luis Miquilena, economist José Rafael Núñez Tenorio, and attorney Omar Mezza Ramírez. What Chávez lacked in political experience, they could help fill in.

At the same time he and his allies created the MVR, they kept the MBR-200 intact. Some MBR-200 leaders had feared that a flood of new members who did not share the ideals of the Bolivarianos would join Chávez's bandwagon, blurring the movement's ideological roots. So this separate entity, the MVR, was created to run the campaign activities. It could absorb independent personalities and other groups with distinct ideologies and political positions, while the MBR-200 would remain the true bastion of Bolivarian beliefs. The MVR was "not conceived to be a party, but rather an electoral front controlled by the MBR-200." It also was not designed to be a democratic organization given to drawn-out decision making by consensus like the MBR-200. Rather, it would make rapid and hopefully good decisions related to the election. It would be run by people Chávez had confidence in and whom he appointed himself.

Like Chávez's early cells in the military, MBR-200 members continued to meet in small study circles throughout the country to read together and discuss politics and ideology. When they joined a local "Bolivarian Circle," they took an oath pledging to be "honest, hardworking, humble and exercise solidarity." The MBR-200 included a large number of retired military officers, although the movement tried to erase hierarchies between civilians and soldiers — with mixed success. Its national directorate, for instance, comprised two former military officers, Chávez and Luis Davila, along with a former police officer and two civilians.

The MBR-200 and the MVR coexisted for several years, with membership, activities, and ideology often overlapping. The initials of the groups even sounded alike, in Spanish as well as English. The organizations' novel use of the symbols and images of Venezuela's national heritage represented by the three roots of a tree — Bolívar, Rodríguez, and Zamora — were to play a key role in Chávez's political success. Eventually the MVR was to win so many victories in the political arena that it overtook the MBR-200, which disappeared.

As Chávez built his own political organizations, existing parties on the left began to take notice and migrate toward him and his presidential campaign. The most significant leftist political party, the Causa R, was in the process of dividing. In April 1997, the same month Chávez and the MBR-200 decided to seek the presidency, former Causa R presidential candidate Andrés Velásquez expelled a number of leaders from the party. The fiery former union leader wanted to pursue a more moderate, centrist path. Aristóbulo Istúriz, Alí Rodríguez, Pablo Medina, and others wanted to step up the party's anti-neo-liberal, nationalistic stance in solidarity with the working class. The Causa R split, and the Medina faction formed their own party, Patria Para Todos (PPT) — fatherland for all.

By the end of 1997 it was apparent that PPT and MVR shared a similar political outlook. Early the next year the party formally endorsed Chávez, bringing considerable political experience both in the streets and in the nation's institutions. The PPT and the MVR formed the core of what was to turn into Chávez's Polo Patriotico (Patriotic Pole), an amalgam of parties and movements that latched on to the former coup leader's candidacy. Velásquez's Causa R, meanwhile, endorsed Irene Sáez.

Venezuela's other major leftist party, the MAS, was also a significant force, controlling four state governorships. Most party leaders, including Caldera's planning minister and neo-liberal convert Teodoro Petkoff, opposed backing the former coup leader. Some even wanted to go with Irene. But many in the party's base favored Chávez. The debate dragged on until June 1998, when the MAS finally decided to join Chávez's Patriotic Pole. Of course, by then he was riding atop the polls.

By early that year the tide was beginning to subtly shift. Chávez's candidacy was official, and people were starting to take notice. Chávez believed he always had the support of the masses — it just wasn't reflected in the establishment's polls. The joke in Venezuela was that pollsters would conduct their work by standing outside the subway station in affluent Altamira and ask people what they thought. They never ventured into the barrios. By late February the leading daily *El Universal* reported that even establishment polls showed Chávez quickly catching up to Sáez. His support had increased from 4.6 percent the previous September to 11 percent. Other polls put him at 16 or 17 percent. Sáez was holding steady at 18.1 percent, the newspaper reported. A few other candidates were behind them.

Chávez's support was growing for a number of reasons. Even his opponents acknowledged that his blistering diagnosis of Venezuela's institutional ills was right on target. And now that he was an official candidate and attracting sizable crowds to his rallies, the media could no longer ignore him. On top of that, his critique of Caldera's neo-liberal economic policies was resonating with many. After the trauma of the 1989 riots and crackdown, two coup attempts in 1992, the impeachment of Carlos Andrés Pérez in 1993, and the bank collapse the next year, Caldera had brought some sense of political peace to the country. In 1997 the economy even showed some signs of reviving. The GDP grew 5.12 percent, inflation dropped to 50 percent from 99.97 percent the previous year, and the reserves grew to $17.745 billion.

But Caldera had done little to resolve the institutional problems of the country, and left it open to the vicissitudes of the oil market. By October 1997 oil prices started to drop, ushering in another economic debacle outmatched only by the banking crisis. Prices were to fall by 34 percent during 1998 compared with the previous year, reaching their lowest point in years by December, at just $7.66 per barrel. It caused a loss of $7 billion in oil income, prompted the government to slash $2.3 billion in spending, and fueled a fiscal deficit of at least 5 percent of the GDP. As Caldera's term was coming to a close, accumulated inflation was 800 percent — the highest of any administration in Venezuela's nearly forty years of democracy.

The economic mess played into the hands of Chávez, who was the only candidate attacking Caldera's neo-liberal policies. Above all, he was a charismatic, dynamic, and colorful leader and showman who was talking the language of the poor and vowing to topple an establishment that had destroyed the country. His status as a former coup leader not only didn't hurt him in the eyes of the massive working class, but actually helped. At a rally in July 1998 launching his candidacy after the official start of the campaign, Chávez donned his trademark paratrooper's red beret and pumped his fist in the air before a cheering throng of ten thousand supporters. He made no apologies for trying to overthrow the government six years earlier. "Go ahead, call me a coup leader," he bellowed. Then he added: "Raise your hands if you think the coup was justified." A sea of hands went up.

As Chávez established himself as the genuine outsider and defender of the poor, Irene caved in to pressure from the political elite. Her floundering campaign increasingly took on a Hollywood-style, image-driven look. A campaign kickoff party in May featured the salsa star Oscar de León. Slipping in the polls, she tried changing her hairdo, tying up her flowing blond curls in a bun that made her look to most people like a Venezuelan imitation of Eva Perón. She denied she was trying to evoke Argentina's revered champion of the poor. At the same time, Irene tried to discredit Chávez and win back voters to her camp. At some rallies her team mounted a cinema-sized screen and showed images of the bloody 1989 street riots and Chávez's failed coup attempt. It backfired.

Worst of all, she accepted the support of COPEI. She needed the help of a party with an established electoral structure that could get out the vote. But the offer from COPEI was a "poisoned chalice." The traditional parties in Venezuela were so deeply despised that accepting their support was tantamount to political suicide. Sáez's poll numbers plummeted. By August the Causa R withdrew its backing. "We simply feel betrayed," party leader Andrés Velásquez stated. "Irene is no longer an option for change. She's lost her status as an independent."

Venezuela's other major traditional party, Democratic Action, was equally adrift. It nominated a political dinosaur to run for president. Luis Alfaro Ucero was seventy-six years old and a relic from AD's past. Short, mustachioed, and sporting a gray crew-cut, AD's secretary general was an old-time *caudillo*, strongman, who ran the party with an iron fist. As a candidate, he was about as uncharismatic as could be. A lifelong backroom bureaucrat, he stumbled in public speech and inspired almost no one. Few outside the party apparatus had even heard of him. He had one advantage, though. Despite its loss of prestige, AD remained one of the largest parties in Latin America. More towns in Venezuela had an AD outpost than a church, a significant accomplishment in the heavily Roman Catholic country. AD was famous for its skill in using public funds to entice voters through pork-barrel spending or gifts. This was the party whose members handed out buckets of paint at election time, for instance, so people could spruce up their homes and promote AD at the same time. But even the party's well-oiled political machinery could not salvage Alfaro's candidacy. It was a lost cause from day one. He never got beyond single digits in the polls.

With the traditional parties floundering and Chávez on the rise, the United States stepped into the fray. The State Department announced in April that it was denying Chávez a visa to visit the United States, citing his 1992 coup attempt. It was telling, since the United States had let numerous other coup leaders into the country without hesitation. Several months later, former US ambassador to Venezuela Michael Skol revealed what many other US officials may have been thinking but could not publicly state: "I'm shocked and terribly disappointed that somebody whose only actions to date have been terroristic, anti-constitutional and anti-democratic has been able to reach this point. I've got real problems with the evidence that he's going to be a good leader of Venezuela and that he's going to be democratic."

Chávez made light of the US rejection. Appearing on a popular national TV comedy program, he said the decision didn't bother him because he already had a visa. Then he pulled out a Visa credit card from his pocket and flashed it for the camera.

Chávez hoped to address businessmen, academics, journalists, and Wall Street investors in the United States to try to offset what he called a "black legend" his adversaries were spinning around him. Some of the Venezuelan media made a tentative pact with Chávez as he appeared headed for victory and sought some degree of objectivity in their coverage in the hope of favors in the future. But others unleashed a vicious smear campaign. Newspapers published a barrage of editorials attacking him as a demagogue, a criminal, a dictator-in-waiting. Television stations ran advertisements with crazy music, swirling pinwheel colors, and the face of a deranged-looking person. The message was clear: Chávez is *un loco*. One newspaper publisher, Rafael Poleo of *El Nuevo Pais*, warned that "Chávez's messianic aim is to establish a pseudo-religious reign of terror that would make every tyranny that Latin America has known since the nineteenth century pale in significance."

Some of the international media joined in, too. One newspaper seemingly with a particular distaste for Chávez, *The Miami Herald* — dubbed by critics the "oligarch's daily" — published a long front-page news article that referred to "unconfirmed reports of secret connections with rogue Middle Eastern states like Libya, and rumors that Cuba may have helped train Venezuelan militias" organized by Chávez. The reports were unconfirmed, but that didn't stop the newspaper from publishing them. Other newspapers mentioned reports that Chávez had a list of journalists deemed "shootable" if he won.

Much of the media emphasized the fears of the small upper class that Chávez was a dangerous demagogue who was going to destroy Venezuela's democracy and provoke civil war. They played down his support among millions of poor people who made up the majority of the population and saw him as a beacon of hope. As one official at the US embassy, hardly a bastion of Chávez admirers, later put it: "The smear campaign promoted by Chávez's opponents was picked up by US journalists passing through here on assignment, who portrayed Chávez as a wild-eyed radical and played up the possibility of violence."

At one point the anti-Chávez propaganda in Venezuela was so fierce, Chávez felt it necessary to issue a statement denying he "was in the habit of drinking blood or eating fried babies for breakfast." He called the attacks part of a "psychological war lab" mounted by his well-heeled adversaries. "A lot of people say I am Hitler combined with Mussolini," he remarked. "Others say I am Gadhafi with a bit of Castro."

In one famous episode, television networks ran spots of him declaring he was going to "fry the heads" of members of Democratic Action and COPEI in a pot of boiling oil. The remark was widely reported in the local and international media, provoking images of a bloodthirsty Latin American military gorilla like Augusto Pinochet exterminating his opponents once he got into power. Chávez later alleged it was a fabrication, made with the help of an actor imitating his voice. The actor eventually confirmed it, saying he was unaware his work would be appropriated for anti-Chávez propaganda purposes.

Still, Chávez made enough incendiary statements on his own to give opponents ammunition to stir up fears he was a new Fidel Castro who was going to set off a climate of terror leading to civil war. He declared at one rally he would "sweep AD from the face of the earth." At another he said those opposed to a constitutional assembly would go to jail.

Yet even when Chávez stumbled, his opponents failed to take advantage. After the "fry the heads" episode, AD ran television commercials showing images of poor people in front of a sizzling frying pan. One woman remarks that Chávez will have to fry all of Venezuela, because "we're all Adecos." The ad backfired, provoking numerous jokes, earning the censure of the electoral commission — which pulled it off the air — and merely reminding people how much they despised the Adecos.

To combat the onslaught of negative publicity, Chávez tried to soften his image. He traded his combat fatigues for a pullover sweater or suits and ties. He hit the TV talk-show circuit and granted interviews as fast as he could. He darted from meeting to meeting with officials of Citibank, J. P. Morgan, Morgan Stanley, and other investment companies to calm their fears. He said he would welcome foreign investment, meet Venezuela's foreign debt obligations, and respect private property. He likened himself to Tony Blair and said he wanted to pursue a more humane "third way" between hard-line socialism and "savage capitalism."

He also pulled out a new secret weapon: a woman.

Chávez had first come into contact with Marisabel Rodríguez in 1995 during one of his whirlwind tours around the country. He was passing through Carora, a stifling hot city in the interior near Barquísimeto, Marisabel's hometown. She tried to fight her way through the crowd and pass him a handwritten note with her name, her telephone number, and her offer to help in his revolution in any way she could. She didn't know Chávez, but she already admired him.

The note never made it into Chávez's hands, but by January 1996 they were formally introduced by a radio announcer in Barquísimeto. Telephone calls and notes followed until finally, according to Marisabel, they started dating on January 14, 1997, the day of a huge procession in Barquísimeto honoring the Divina Pastora, the city's patron saint. Marisabel ended up pregnant — it might have been that very night — and by that December, two months after the birth of Rosinés, the couple married.

With baby in tow, Marisabel hit the campaign trail the following year with Chávez. She was an attractive figure. Young, blond, bright, with blue eyes and a background herself in the media, she was an asset to El Comandante. Along with Chávez's pullover sweaters, she helped soften the image promoted by his opponents of a bloodthirsty former coup leader. Chávez, who had been living in Luis Miquilena's small apartment in Altamira after a disagreement with Nedo Paniz, moved into his own place with his wife. On his daughter's first birthday, he beamed for newspaper photographers at her party.

The couple's honeymoon lasted throughout the campaign season, but rough times were ahead. At home, Marisabel was an argumentative, mercurial, and complicated figure. Adding in Chávez's own unorthodox lifestyle, headstrong personality, and obsession with transforming Venezuela made for a combustible combination.

• • •

As Chávez emerged as the clear front-runner in the campaign, his opponents became desperate. Fearful that he was going to pull off a clean sweep in the congressional and regional elections along with the presidency on December 6, the AD- and COPEI-controlled Congress took the unprecedented step of separating the votes. They moved up the other elections by a month. They thought that might help their chances in the congressional and state votes. But they still lacked a strong opponent against Chávez for the presidency. For months, they talked about throwing their support behind a single candidate in a last-minute "all against Chávez" front. With Irene and Alfaro fading, they set their sights on one put forth by another new party, Proyecto Venezuela.

That party's candidate, Henrique Salas Römer, was a classic Venezuelan elitist and oligarch. Born in Venezuela, he was educated at exclusive Lawrenceville Prep outside Princeton, New Jersey, and then at Yale, from which he graduated in 1961. His three brothers were Yalies, too. Salas went on to a career as a successful businessman in Venezuela, and by 1989 was elected governor of Carabobo state, an agricultural and industrial powerhouse. A neo-liberal preaching governmental efficiency in a land of waste, he claimed widespread success. He slashed the payroll at the Puerto Cabello port from 5,300 to 190 workers, computerized highway tollbooths to avoid theft by collectors, and created the only police emergency telephone system in the country. Chávez's advisers scoffed at his boasts, painting him as an elitist who governed for the richest 10 percent of the population and ignored the rest. But Salas's campaign prompted interest as far way as New Haven, Connecticut, where at his alma mater the *Yale Daily News* predicted in late September that he was poised to win.

He had some problems to overcome first. In contrast to Chávez's charisma, the sixty-two-year-old, gray-haired former COPEI member was dry and staid on the campaign trail. To puff up his image, his managers put out a series of nationwide television advertisements showing him galloping on a white stallion. The idea was to make him seem less elitist and more like Bolívar or Venezuela's rugged, earthy *llaneros*. Salas even took to leading hundreds of supporters, including former Miss Universe Alicia Machado, on a twelve-mile march on horseback that ended with a run through the streets of Caracas. To many people in the street-tough barrios, the scene was laughable and simply underscored how completely

Salas was out of touch. Chávez belittled him, referring to him dismissively by the name of his horse, Frijolito (little bean).

As the two battled head-to-head and the November congressional and regional elections approached, a surprising candidate emerged in one of the races for a Senate seat: Carlos Andrés Pérez. The former president's trial on corruption charges had come to an end in July 1996 when the Supreme Court convicted him of misusing $17.2 million in secret national security funds but dropped the more serious embezzlement charge. Pérez hailed it as a vindication. His lawyers argued that his only "offense" was to send about three dozen bodyguards to help protect Nicaraguan president Violeta Chamorro in 1990 as she took power after the defeat of the Sandinistas.

The court sentenced him to two years and four months of house arrest. He'd already served most of it, and by that September he was a free man. He quickly hit the campaign trail. A few months earlier, he had become the first Venezuelan president to lose his lifetime seat in the Senate. His colleagues voted to bar him because of his conviction. Now at the age of seventy-three he wanted it back — and the parliamentary immunity that came with it.

He traveled triumphantly to his home state of Táchira, where he planned to run for a national Senate seat in November 1998, and swung through ten more states. Even his enemies acknowledged he stood a good chance of winning the seat in Táchira, one of the few places in the country where he was still popular.

By April 1998, though, his campaign had hit a stumbling block. A judge charged him in a new case: This one involved allegations that he and his mistress Cecilia Matos deposited illicit funds in several joint US bank accounts. Pérez claimed it was another ploy to derail his bid for the Senate. Authorities placed him under house arrest again. But he simply campaigned from home, conducting interviews with journalists and making television and radio ads.

A week before the election, a federal court granted his request to shift his residence temporarily to a cousin's house in Táchira for the final days of the campaign. When he showed up in the state capital of San Cristóbal, the city went wild. People cheered from balconies and ran out to greet him.

A week later Pérez won. He was freed from house arrest and got his parliamentary immunity. His "crucifixion and persecution" were over, he told reporters. Now he would devote himself to stopping the man who'd tried to overthrow him as president from reaching Miraflores Palace himself.

But Chávez was on a roll that could not be slowed. Pérez's victory in his home state was one of the few bright spots in the congressional and regional elections for the forces opposed to Chávez. Many viewed the contests as a first round in the presidential vote. Chávez's Patriotic Pole took eight governor's seats, including Barinas state, where his father pulled off a surprising and emblematic victory. The coalition matched the number of triumphs by a stunned Democratic Action. AD had figured that in the worst-case scenario they would retain the eleven governorships they'd won in 1995. They thought even gaining fourteen was possible. The party's disappointing showing of only eight victories was a sobering message that change was coming. On top of their triumphs, the Patriotic Pole also placed second in ten of the thirteen gubernatorial contests they did not win, showing they were clearly a force to be reckoned with. In total votes nationwide, the PP nearly doubled those of Democratic Action: 1,096,116 compared with 564,391. In the House and Senate, where no party won a majority, the Patriotic Pole took about one-third of the seats.

As the days ticked down to the presidential vote, the opposition forces got desperate. Their campaign to paint Chávez as a monster had failed among the country's millions of peasants and shantytown dwellers, as he noted. "They've called me everything — terrorist, dictator, killer, coward. Yet my popularity keeps going up." Now they decided their only chance of victory lay in combining forces.

On Friday night, November 27, just over a week before the election the following Sunday, Democratic Action leaders met. In a session marked by an outbreak of fistfights, they voted to dump Alfaro Ucero as their candidate. The next day they ordered their followers to vote for Salas Römer. It was laughable on many levels, for one because the party had spent months attacking the governor from Carabobo. For his part, less than two weeks earlier Salas had sworn he would not accept the support of the traditional parties.

Alfaro Ucero, who had devoted a lifetime of service to AD, did not take kindly to its decision and refused to abide by it. So the next day AD leaders threw him out of the party. They asked the National Electoral Council to transfer any ballots marked for him to Salas Römer. Under Venezuelan law, this could be done only if the original candidate resigned, died, or was declared incapacitated. But that didn't seem to matter. The council granted AD's request anyway.

Two days after AD ejected Alfaro, on Monday, November 30, Venezuela's other leading party, COPEI, dumped its candidate, too: Irene Sáez. They also called on backers to vote for Salas Römer. Like Alfaro, Irene refused to drop out of the race, and said she would soldier on with or without COPEI's support. The opposition's efforts were turning into a circus. It seemed obvious they could do little to head off Chávez's victory. "Chávez will not be beaten by any earthling," former Caracas mayor and Chávez ally Aristóbulo Istúriz stated a week before the vote. "Someone would have to come from another planet. Let them fabricate a Martian to see if he could do it."

Venezuela's elites were terrified of Chávez's seemingly imminent triumph; rumors of a right-wing coup to prevent it ran rampant in the final days. While legitimate questions existed about whether a former coup leader might usher in an authoritarian government, the opposition campaign bordered on hysteria. They turned Chávez into a cartoon figure. "He's nuts. He's completely out of his mind," one university architecture professor said. Salas himself joined in. He claimed that not only the presidency was at stake in the vote, "but liberty."

Chávez won in a landslide. He took 56.20 percent of the vote to Salas's 39.97 percent. Chávez's share was the same figure his movement's polls had predicted two years earlier. Out of about 5.2 million cast, he garnered 3,673,685 — about 1.2 million more than Salas. Irene was so far back, she was nearly out of sight: 184,568 votes. Alfaro barely managed to register a blip on the screen: 27,586. Most of Caracas exploded into celebration, with people dancing in the streets, setting off fireworks, and honking their horns. In wealthier neighborhoods the streets remained eerily quiet. One resident in upper-class Altamira summed up the mood when she cast her vote earlier that day: "He's a crazy man on the loose, a communist."

That night after the results were announced, Chávez appeared on a terrace outside the Teresa Carreño Theater where Pérez had held his "coronation" nearly a decade earlier. It was almost midnight. Floodlights lit up streets jammed by a throng of his wildly cheering supporters. A huge Venezuelan flag flapped below him. It was a historic and electric moment. A new era was dawning. AD and COPEI were all but dead. "The resurrection of Venezuela has begun," Chávez bellowed, "and nothing and no one can stop it."

Many analysts and journalists interpreted Chávez's victory as a blow to the conventional wisdom that democracy and free markets were inescapable in Latin America. They were right about the second point. Venezuelans and Latin Americans were disillusioned with the "free-market revolution" pushed throughout the region over the last decade by the International Monetary Fund, the World Bank, and the US government. The wealth had not trickled down. Latin America still suffered the widest gap between rich and poor in the world.

Venezuela had one of the most unequal income distributions anywhere. Nearly half the country's income went to the richest 20 percent of the population, according to the United Nations Development Program. It was a country where the poor scrambled to eat, while the rich lived in large mansions protected by towering walls, barbed wire, and private security guards. They employed legions of servants to meet their domestic needs and took personal jets for shopping sprees to Miami or vacations on remote Caribbean islands. Venezuela had one of the largest numbers of private jets per capita in the world. To many, the country's reality of two separate worlds was captured by the phrase *social apartheid*.

While the pundits were right about Venezuelans' anger over the failure of neo-liberal economic policies to improve their lives, however, they were wrong about their supposed antipathy to democracy. Most wanted a democracy — but one that worked and served the interests of the majority, not just a tiny, fabulously rich elite. For decades Venezuela's democracy had functioned as a racket designed to enrich the wealthy. In 1998 Transparency International ranked the country one of the ten most corrupt in the world. One US-born analyst who was not sympathetic to Chávez and moved in elite circles in Venezuela described the country's practice of democracy as a fixed network that would be illegal in the United States. It encompassed businessmen, judges, lawyers, police, journalists, politicians, priests, and even soldiers. "This interlocking system of privileges and graft that runs through Venezuela wouldn't last a half-hour with a RICO grand jury," he said, referring to the American law for prosecuting organized crime. "It's a racket and has been run like a racket for a very long time."

Chávez was the man who was going to break up the racket and the mafia that ran it. Shortly after his triumph, he declared, "Venezuela is a ticking time bomb, and I have been elected to defuse it." The oligarchy was terrified. Their game might be over. But the poor masses and even a few in the moneyed classes were cheering in streets. In the president-elect's home state of Barinas, a twenty-four-year-old market worker summed up the sentiment: "Democracy is infected," she said. "And Chávez is the only antibiotic we have."

## 15

## To Power

Hugo Chávez started his presidency by shocking Venezuelans. On February 2, 1999, he stepped to the dais in the ornate congressional building to be sworn in by Luis Alfonso Davila, his ally who was now Senate president. Outgoing president Rafael Caldera, ordinarily the indicated oath-giver, could not bring himself to do it. He stood between the two men with a dour look on his face. Venezuelan politicians and dignitaries from sixty countries filled the hall, among them Fidel Castro and Carlos Andrés Pérez, now a senator from his home state of Táchira. Chávez raised his right hand in the air, placed his left hand on the constitution, and promptly broke with the traditional pledge repeated by every president during forty years of democracy. "I swear in front of my people that over this moribund constitution I will push forward the democratic transformations that are necessary so that the new republic will have an adequate magna carta for the times."

The crowds of his supporters inside Congress and out erupted into cheers. His opponents gasped. Chávez's message was unmistakable. The constitution of Caldera's generation was moribund, on its deathbed. The Bolivarian revolution had arrived.

With the blue, yellow, and red presidential sash draped over his shoulder, he delivered a one-hour-and-forty-five-minute address lambasting the oligarchy for turning Venezuela into an "immense and putrid swamp." Proclaiming it a "mathematical mystery," he asked how a country so blessed with natural resources could have so much poverty. "So many riches, the largest petroleum reserves in the world, the fifth largest reserves of gas, gold, the immensely rich Caribbean Sea. All this, and 80 percent of our people live in poverty." Turning to the observing heads of state, he asked, "Who can explain this? What scientist can explain this?"

Chávez compared the nation to a "social time bomb" of hunger, disease, and malnutrition that was going "tick tock, tick tock." Quick and dramatic action was required to disarm the bomb before it exploded. Surprising his opponents, he announced that he planned to issue his first decree the same day. It would call for electoral authorities to schedule a national referendum within sixty to ninety days on whether Venezuelans wanted to convoke a constitutional assembly to write a new constitution. He wasn't going to wait for the opposition-laden Congress to decide the issue. "The constitution, and with it the ill-fated political system to which it gave birth forty years ago, has to die; it is going to die, sirs — accept it," he said.

It was nearly seven years since Chávez had launched his coup. Far from apologizing, he took the opportunity to praise his comrades in arms. "The Venezuelan military rebellion of 1992 was inevitable," he said, "just like the explosion of volcanoes." He announced that the military, rather than repressing the people, was to be sent into the streets to help rebuild the country. At the end of his speech, he shocked the country again by walking over to the first row and shaking the hand of the man he had tried to topple, Carlos Andrés Pérez. The normally hyperkinetic and loquacious CAP stood dumbfounded.

Chávez's first performance as an elected official and Venezuela's youngest president ever at forty-four was electrifying, as even his critics had to admit. He weaved in blistering critiques of Venezuelan democracy with quotes or references ranging from Walt Whitman to Pablo Neruda to Galileo. At least thirty times the audience interrupted with applause. He was off to a good start. Opinion polls pegged his approval ratings at an astronomical 90 percent. He had the country at his feet and a golden opportunity to transform what *The New Republic* called "one of the region's most inexcusable basket cases." As one middle-class Venezuelan journalist who came to despise the president but was disgusted by the country's corruption put it, "We all had a little Chávez in us."

Chávez was clearly a gifted and brilliant speaker. He wrote his own speeches, although most of what he said was extemporaneous. He was so good and so smooth, he simply made it up as he went along. Not long after the inauguration, Jorge Olavarria, a prominent historian and journalist who turned into one of Chávez's fiercest critics, called him "the most important orator Venezuela has had this century."

Even the United States, which denied him a visa during the campaign, was coming around. After Chávez's victory, it reversed course and not only granted him a visa but arranged a meeting with President Bill Clinton and other top administration officials, including national security adviser Sandy Berger. Chávez met with Clinton for about twenty minutes on January 27, albeit in Berger's office and not the Oval Office. The United States wasn't ready for a full-fledged embrace quite yet. The meetings a few days before Chávez's inauguration went well. White House spokesman Jim Dobbins proclaimed that Chávez and Clinton established "good chemistry." Clinton "expressed broad support to the direction President Chávez is going," Dobbins said. He added that Chávez "impressed everybody. He was vital, articulate and saying the right things." Chávez convinced the North Americans that he was "clearly not the person he was in 1992" and that "he would pursue change through a democratic and constitutional framework," Dobbins said.

For his part, Chávez praised Washington, Jefferson, Lincoln, and "the land of democracy." He called previous tensions over the visa "a thing of the past."

Relaxed after his meetings, he declared, "We have begun this relationship between Venezuela and the United States on a good footing."

It only got better after his inauguration. The United States sent Energy Secretary Bill Richardson as its official representative. He was full of praise after Chávez's swearing-in. "I think Chávez is a potential leader in the hemisphere," Richardson told reporters. "He is a bright, street-smart individual who is developing a lot of political skills . . . He is off to an excellent start . . . It's a good start in the American–Venezuelan relation."

The US decision to engage Chávez rather than isolate or try to topple him led to a kind of peaceful coexistence between the two nations initially, albeit with some tensions. US ambassador John Maisto led the engagement faction, becoming famous for his oft-repeated statement, "Watch what Chávez does, don't listen to what he says." The rhetoric may be radical, he suggested, but the actions are not. And as he started off his presidency, Chávez's actions — while bold — weren't radical. He operated within the bounds of democracy.

Although Chávez was wildly popular at home, not everyone was cheering his ascent to power. The elites saw disturbing signs. He was, after all, a former coup leader. Some worried that Chávez had "little respect for the rule of law and even less understanding of the importance of checks and balances." His penchant to don his red paratrooper's beret, and his admirers' tendency to follow suit, created a militaristic image his detractors found troubling. On other occasions he wore combat fatigues or a medal-studded officer's uniform. His language was laced with military jargon like *battlefronts* and *taking to the trenches*.

At the same time, he brought significant numbers of retired and active military officers into the government. He appointed them to help run everything from the state oil company to the tax collection agency to the secret police — a job he gave fellow MBR founder Jesús Urdaneta. Chávez also named Hernán Grüber Ódreman, one of the leaders of the November 1992 coup, governor of the Federal District of Caracas. Meanwhile, Francisco Arias Cárdenas had won reelection as governor of oil-rich Zulia state with Chávez's backing. Two days after his inauguration, during a military parade marking the anniversary of his February 4, 1992, coup attempt, Chávez reinstated many of the coup participants into the armed forces. He called them "heroes."

Chávez's critics wondered whether he was militarizing the government and installing an old-style Latin American authoritarian regime. The night before he was sworn in, he talked into the wee hours with his friend Fidel Castro.

Some of his first comments as president ramped up the worries. When the Supreme Court received eleven lawsuits challenging Chávez's assertion that he would decide how members of the constitutional assembly would be chosen, the president warned that his supporters "will take to streets" if the court tried to block his decree. Some interpreted it as a veiled threat of violence and an attempt to bully the court. "About the only thing he didn't do was call on the people to lynch the judges if the Supreme Court annuls his decree," commented Henrique Salas Römer, who had lost the December presidential race.

Chávez also called for the Congress and Supreme Court to be dissolved, raising fears among opponents he wanted to install a dictatorship. Hundreds of his supporters surrounded Congress for a couple of days in April, blocked lawmakers from leaving or entering, and shouted

"Dissolve Congress!" Chávez called opposition political leaders "a nest of dying venomous vipers" and "worm-eaten and decadent." He also indicated he hoped to eliminate a ban on immediate reelection and serve for ten years.

His supporters viewed his high-voltage statements as the rhetorical give-and-take of democracy — a bargaining tool to get what he wanted and to get people out to vote. He wasn't going to wipe out the Congress and Supreme Court, but replace the discredited institutions with new ones that would be more responsive to the people. They also noted that mass street protests were a political tool frequently used by the US civil rights movement. They saw Chávez's red beret not as a sign of danger but a sign of hope that change was coming. Reelection, they argued, was common in countries around the world including the United States. In the end, when the Supreme Court ruled against Chávez on the issue of his decree, he accepted the decision and tried to make the decree conform to the court ruling.

Nonetheless, as time passed he would have to prove to skeptics in the elite and in the media who pounced on every misstep that he was a true democrat. To Chávez, the same held true: The oligarchy would have to prove they would permit a true democracy that benefited the majority and not only a small minority.

Chávez spent the weeks before his inauguration on a whirlwind tour of Latin America, Europe, and the United States, trying as he put it "to convince anybody out there that still believes Chávez is the devil or a cross between Hitler and Mussolini" that he was really a committed democrat. Some of his moves were outright conservative. In mid-January he announced the reappointment of Caldera's economy minister, Maritza Izaguirre, a longtime technocrat at the Inter-American Development Bank. The day before his inauguration, he named Roberto Mandini president of the huge state oil monopoly, Petroleos de Venezuela (PDVSA). A respected businessman, Mandini was vice president of Citgo, a PDVSA subsidiary and one of the largest gas station chains in the United States.

Chávez made other clever moves "to neutralize opponents and pacify followers." He recruited two of the nation's most prominent journalists, José Vicente Rangel and Alfredo Peña, as foreign minister and chief of staff. He also named a Wayuu Indian, university professor Atalá Uriana Pocaterra, environmental minister. Many of his allies from the

Central University of Venezuela, the Patriotic Front, and his days in Yare and touring the country also joined the government. They included Jorge Giordani, Héctor Navarro, Luis Miquilena, and Manuel Quijada. At the same time, after the controversial Argentine sociologist Norberto Ceresole resurfaced in Venezuela around the time of Chávez's inauguration, the president quietly ordered him to leave.

On February 20 Chávez announced his first major initiative besides the constitutional assembly. He planned to pull 70,000 of the nation's 120,000 soldiers out of the barracks and send them into the streets and countryside. They were to repair roads and hospitals, conduct medical campaigns, clean up trash, and sell meat, cheese, chicken, pasta, and other food out of the backs of trucks at rock-bottom prices. He called it Plan Bolívar 2000. With the nation's treasury empty, its governmental institutions collapsed, and the "social time bomb" ticking, the plan was an attempt to bring immediate relief to the most desperate Venezuelans. Chávez also called for eighty thousand civilians to join in the effort, with some receiving small salaries. Two days later five thousand people in tattered clothes and even on crutches lined up outside Miraflores presidential palace, clamoring to sign up.

Plan Bolívar officially kicked off on February 27, the tenth anniversary of the Caracazo riots. Chávez picked the date intentionally. "My order to my men was, 'Go house to house combing the land. Hunger is the enemy.' And we started on February 27, 1999, ten years after the Caracazo, as a way of redeeming the military. I even made the connection when I said, 'Ten years ago we came out to massacre the people. Now we are going to fill them with love. Go and comb the land, search out and destroy poverty and death. We are going to fill them with love instead of lead.' And the response was really beautiful."

The response was, in fact, largely positive. Shantytown dwellers and peasants were shocked and delighted to see soldiers out helping improve their communities. "I never thought I would ever see the army doing this, but it is welcome," one teacher remarked as she waited in line to buy food in a Caracas barrio. "Just the presence of the military here inspires order and discipline, and that is exactly what this country needs." The soldiers — from the army, navy, air force, and National Guard — did everything from running medical clinics offering pediatric, gynecological, and dental care along with surgery and vaccinations for children, to helping fishermen repair boat motors or form cooperatives. They flew residents in and out of remote villages and ventured into isolated Indian communities in the Amazon jungle accessible only by boat along rivers, bringing doctors and medicine. In cities National Guardsmen stood on street corners in an effort to reduce crime. In rural areas soldiers helped farmers develop agricultural projects. They even gave people haircuts.

By Chávez's reckoning, the plan dramatically altered the public perception of the Venezuelan military. "This represented quite a change, because after the February 27th massacre, for instance, to go to a poor neighborhood a soldier had to dress as a civilian," he said. "He was taking a risk because the army had massacred the people. Today, when a soldier shows up, people greet him with enthusiasm and happiness."

The plan was not without its critics. Some saw it as another dangerous intrusion of the military into civilian life, opening the door to authoritarian rule. The Venezuelan newsmagazine *Primicia* ran a cover article warning of a surge of "military nationalism." Others worried that the military's civic activities would undercut efforts to strengthen civilian and governmental institutions. Some believed Plan Bolívar was shifting the armed forces too far away from their traditional role of military defense. For their part, butchers and bodega owners complained that the military-run "people's markets" were undercutting their business. Others simply saw it as a Band-Aid that didn't get at the country's root problems.

But to Chávez and his supporters, the plan was a pragmatic first step to address Venezuela's pressing problems, at least short-term. Some compared it to Depression-era public works programs in the United States under Franklin Delano Roosevelt such as the Civilian Conservation Corps, which included paid work for the unemployed. Others noted that the US military itself plays a role in civilian life, with the Army Corps of Engineers helping with flood control, wetlands management, and beach erosion projects. The National Guard is often called in to help during emergencies and natural disasters. Many Venezuelans saw the military as one of the few institutions in the country that worked.

Chávez didn't think he had much choice but to implement the plan. "Imagine February 2, 1999, with almost all the state and municipal governments opposing us," he recalled:

> The Congress against us; the Supreme Court against us; a budget written by the previous regime; a government almost without resources to pay the salaries; the price of oil down to seven dollars a barrel; on top of this, pressure from the high expectations our

electoral triumph had generated. Around the palace there were lines of thousands of people asking for jobs, with their sick kids, sleeping there, on the ground, not letting my car pass. "We are not leaving until Chávez sees us." . . . So I decided to turn to the armed forces.

It was his first effort as president at creating a "civil-military union." The program was not an unblemished success. Months later accusations of corruption emerged, with critics charging that high-ranking military officers were skimming off thousands of dollars from what turned into a loosely supervised $1 billion program. By December 2001 Chávez, to his credit, removed the general in charge of the program, Victor Cruz Weffer. But the battle against corruption, one of the pillars of Chávez's 1998 campaign, was to remain a weak flank in his early presidency. Few major figures ended up in court or behind bars.

Chávez argued that it wasn't easy dismantling an ingrained culture of corruption where many people believed it was their right to take whatever they could get their hands on. It was, he said, like "a cancer that has metastasized in all directions." Some people called it the "piñata culture," where the "candy" or the money from oil revenues spills to the floor after the piñata is broken open and everyone grabs what they can in a free-for-all as they elbow others aside. Those who didn't take what they could were considered *pendejos*, fools.

A best-selling book, *The Dictionary of Corruption in Venezuela*, cataloged some of the most infamous pillaging. It was three volumes long. It picked apart three hundred cases of graft among the high and mighty between 1959 and 1989. The series didn't even go into the second term of Carlos Andrés Pérez, considered a gold-medal contender in the category, or mention his mistress Cecilia Matos. One of the most vile cases in the book was known as the six-year milk scandal. Venezuela imported powdered milk from Belgium and other countries supposedly to be distributed to poor children. "Instead, government employees sold it at inflated prices. Worse, the milk had been contaminated in the wake of the 1986 Chernobyl nuclear disaster. But instead of following orders to destroy the milk, employees repackaged and sold it."

As Plan Bolívar kicked into high gear and tended to Venezuelans' daily needs, Chávez focused on his initiative to transform the country long-term — the constitutional assembly. The Supreme Court settled the dispute between the president and the Congress, which contended that he did not alone have the power to decree a referendum asking Venezuelans if they wanted to convoke a constitutional assembly. The vote was set for April 25. Chávez considered it a triumph of democracy, and proof that he was a democrat. It was the first time in Venezuela's history that the people would be allowed to vote on a major public issue.

Most Venezuelans considered the result a foregone conclusion. Chávez was wildly popular, and he saw a constitutional assembly as the centerpiece of his new administration. Many of his moves since assuming the presidency had simply elevated his popularity. While skeptics predicted that the political neophyte who'd never before held public office would crumble once he took over the nation's top post, Chávez was turning out to be a master politician. He had a common populist touch that was softening the hearts of even some of his most ardent opponents.

He gave up his $1,200-a-month salary as president, donating it to a scholarship fund instead. He dispensed with the presidential limousine. A virtual insomniac, he paid surprise visits to decrepit public hospitals at 3 A.M. and fired doctors he found asleep on the job. On other occasions he stopped the presidential convoy after midnight to chat with stunned garbage collectors. At Miraflores he served guests decidedly lowbrow fare — *arepas*, the tortilla-like corn patties that are the national dish. He ran his entourage ragged with eighteen-hour days, making himself a teetotaling role model of hard work in a fiesta-intoxicated nation. He launched an attack on waste, too. When he found out the government owned 128 civilian aircraft, he put the entire fleet up for sale. He cracked down on tax evasion, which was a national sport.

An open, friendly, and informal man given to breaking protocol, Chávez disarmed some of his most bitter opponents with charm. The same newspaper editor and opposition senator who had warned during the campaign that Chávez would unleash "a reign of terror" — Rafael Poleo — declared after meeting with the president, "He treated me very affectionately."

Chávez was the most popular president in Venezuelan history and one of the most popular in Latin America. A couple of months later, in June, he was to take his show to New York. He banged down the closing gavel at the New York Stock Exchange and charmed one thousand bankers and businessmen at meetings aimed at attracting foreign investment. He threw out the first ball at a New York Mets game at Shea

Stadium. Then he wandered up to the broadcast booth and provided color commentary in Spanish for the audience back home. He won over the investors and financiers in part by enlisting the help of Frank Sinatra, paraphrasing in English from one of the crooner's trademark songs: "If I can make it in New York, I can make it anywhere."

A host of one the meetings, Susan Kaufman Purcell, director of the Americas Society, commented that "Chávez put those financiers in his pocket. I don't know if they will actually invest their money in Venezuela . . . but they were enchanted with him. He seduced them all." Citibank president William Rhodes, who was leading a group of sixteen US banks with an interest in Venezuela, said his bank planned to increase its investments, and others did, too. Chávez finished off his whirlwind tour with a stop in Houston, where he met with US oil executives and attended a breakfast hosted by former president George H. W. Bush and another person with whom Chávez was to cross paths down the road — his son George W., then the governor of Texas.

Despite Chávez's popularity, the international media painted him as a "Dr. Jekyll and Mr. Hyde" or — as one economist linked to the oligarchy put it — "President Jekyll and Colonel Hyde." They questioned whether he was a democrat or a dictator. While Chávez was donating his salary for scholarships and turning over Venezuela's version of Camp David to the homeless, he was also threatening the Supreme Court with a popular uprising and generally looking "the part of the Latin American strongman."

Some reporters referred to a famous comment by Colombia's Nobel Prize–winning author Gabriel García Márquez. In an article titled "The Enigma of the Two Chávezes," he recounted a conversation with Chávez aboard a flight from Havana to Caracas. While impressed with Chávez's charm, his intellectual restlessness, and a "supernatural" memory for the poems of Walt Whitman and Pablo Neruda, the left-leaning writer also echoed fears about the former coup leader. "I was struck by the impression that I had traveled and talked delightfully with two opposite men," García Márquez wrote. "One whom good luck had given the opportunity to save his nation. And the other, an illusionist, who could go down in history as just another despot."

Chávez did make statements that could make it hard to pin down where he stood or what he believed in. In reality he was a mix of many things. He was a Latin American original, an iconoclast not easily defined as simply another Juan Perón or Fidel Castro or Salvador Allende. He famously told interviewer Agustín Blanco Muñoz in May 1996: "I am not Marxist, but I am not anti-Marxist. I am not communist, but I am not anti-communist." Three years later, he made a similar comment to *The New York Times*. "If you are attempting to determine whether Chávez is of the left, right or center, if he is socialist, Communist or capitalist, well, I am none of those, but I have a bit of all of those."

He was socially progressive but fiscally conservative, with a bit of a strong-arm streak thrown in. After all, he was trying to break up a mafia, a bankrupt political system that had helped turn Caracas into what *The New Republic* called "a paved-over monument to urban chaos and mismanagement." He deployed the military in Plan Bolívar to meet social needs, but followed an orthodox free-market economic plan in his first year by paying the foreign debt, imposing new taxes, and reining in spending as the country faced economic decline. Izaguirre, his conservative finance minister, described Chávez as eager to learn the most arcane details of state spending. What was the one overarching constant in all his efforts was that they gave priority to Venezuela's majority poor.

In the early months of Chávez's presidency, the media also pounced on his relationship with Norberto Ceresole and a letter he sent that April to Carlos the Jackal, the Venezuelan-born international terrorist whose real name was Illich Ramírez Sánchez. Ramírez masterminded the 1975 seizure of OPEC ministers in Vienna, Austria, and the 1976 hijacking of an Air France jet to Uganda. He was serving a life prison term in Paris for murder. In an unwise public relations move, Chávez sent him a letter of "human solidarity." He later explained that "I was in prison for two years, and know it is heartening when one receives a letter. This does not imply political solidarity. It is simply human solidarity. Every human being deserves respect."

Many of Chávez's supporters felt the media's emphasis on his missteps and its drumbeat of Chávez the dictator-in-waiting was unfair and failed to capture the real story of what was happening in Venezuela at the grassroots level — a breakthrough in democracy. They thought reporters were writing about Chávez's revolution from the comfortable perch of their five-star hotel balconies or their penthouses in exclusive neighborhoods while failing to delve into the trenches in the barrios where the majority of the people lived.

That fall eight men from a group called the Congress of Venezuelan Artists and Intellectuals occupied the Caracas office of the Associated Press and AP–Dow Jones to protest the international media's treatment of Chávez. The peaceful eight-hour sit-in ended when Interior Minister Ignacio Arcaya called the AP bureau late that night and told the protestors' leader that Chávez, who was visiting Washington, DC, considered the takeover illegal and counterproductive. Moments later Caracas governor Hernán Grüber Ódreman, the Caracas police chief, and four members of the secret police arrived to escort the protestors out.

Chávez got around what his supporters saw as biased international reporting and even worse local coverage by creating his own media outlets. In May he launched his own Sunday-morning radio show, *Hello, President,* on the state radio network. That was followed by his own Thursday-night television program, *Face to Face with the President,* on the state television channel. Then in July came his own newspaper, *The President's Post.* Chávez was editor in chief. He also convoked frequent *cadenas,* or nationally broadcast addresses that commercial television networks were obliged to run, preempting regular programming. They often ran for hours.

*Hello, President* was Chávez's most successful media venture. There wasn't anything quite like it in Latin America or, for that matter, the world. Every Sunday morning Chávez went on the air live. Anyone who wanted to could call in and ask the president a question. Most called about problems they wanted him to resolve. They ranged from getting help collecting a pension to obtaining a job transfer to fighting government bureaucracy. One listener even wrote in asking Chávez to denounce her husband on the air for having an affair. Chávez listened patiently to the callers and assigned aides to tackle their problems.

But he also used the show to discourse about everything imaginable, citing famous thinkers, singing songs, making policy announcements, outlining his agenda for the coming week, firing and hiring officials, reminiscing about his childhood in Barinas, speculating on the health of Atlanta Braves slugger Andrés Galarraga. In one typical two-hour program that July, he blasted free-market economics, read a section of the Bible, gave a mother advice about a rebellious teenager, declared war against corruption, announced he was the target of a possible assassination plot, sang a religious hymn, criticized Colombia's foreign minister, and swore his love for the Venezuelan people. He also made a man who entered the studio weep when he told him he would help pay for an operation for his seriously ill daughter.

The show was a smash hit. Within a few months its reach went from a handful of state-run stations to more than sixty, including three in Mexico, Spain, and Miami. It was the highest-rated program in Venezuela in its time slot, attracting 90 percent of listeners. Telephones at the Radio Nacional de Venezuela started ringing at 5 A.M. on Sundays, four hours before the show began. Crowds carrying signs asking Chávez for help gathered outside the studios before dawn.

Chávez eventually merged his radio and television programs into one show on Sundays, transmitted from locations around the country — farms, schools, fishing villages, oil fields. It ran for seven or eight hours at times and became required viewing for millions of Venezuelans, including his ministers. If they were not on the set with him, they tuned in to find out the latest policy initiatives.

Some opposition politicians complained that Chávez, with his own television show, radio program, and newspaper, was creating his own small media empire. "The only thing he lacks is his own movie," cracked the president of Democratic Action, Carlos Canache Mata. But Chávez was merely trying to counter the onslaught of negative coverage from the much more powerful corporate media both in Venezuela and overseas. The state-run channel 8 television station, for instance, was a small fry compared with the commercial networks of Radio Caracas Television (RCTV) or Venevisión. That station was owned by media mogul Gustavo Cisneros, who was on his way to becoming one of the richest men in the world. While the poor generally loved Chávez's show, the upper class dismissed it — and Chávez — with disdain. To them, he was *ese mono* — that monkey.

On April 25 Chávez breezed to an overwhelming victory in the referendum on the constitutional assembly, with 88 percent voting "Yes" to rewrite the nation's magna carta. Abstention was 60 percent, leading some critics to call it an "outright defeat for Chávez." But that was a hard case to make. Abstention in US presidential elections was commonly 50 percent. Many voters stayed home during the referendum ballot because little doubt existed about the outcome. Opponents didn't bother to campaign, knowing the result was unalterable. Chávez, said one pollster, was "superman."

A few weeks before the vote, Congress buckled under his pressure and granted him emergency powers to rule by decree for the next six months on economic issues. Critics called it another step toward dictatorship. It wasn't the most democratic of methods, but it was also something many other presidents had done, including Rafael Caldera and Carlos Andrés Pérez. Chávez felt he needed the temporary fast-track authorization to combat a worsening economic crisis. The economy was to shrink 7.2 percent in 1999, the fiscal deficit was to balloon to 3.1 percent of GDP, and unemployment was to reach its highest level in four decades — 15.4 percent. Despite all that, Chávez remained stunningly popular.

The one positive piece of economic news was oil prices, which soared from $8.43 a barrel in February when Chávez took over as president to $23.34 barrel in January 2000. Many attributed the increase partly to one of Chávez's first decisions as president — cutting back production and complying with OPEC quotas.

With his longtime dream of a constitutional assembly close to becoming a reality, Chávez set his sights on the next election — to choose its members. In what was to turn into a dizzying series of events in his first year, the date of the next vote was set for July 25, one day after Bolívar's birthday. The campaign turned into a frenzy of activity, with everyone from street vendors to policemen to sports celebrities to astrologers to lawyers and doctors weighing a run for one of the 128 seats in the assembly. Three more were designated for representatives of Venezuela's half million indigenous people, who were to elect them in tribal councils. Chávez may have been a dictator-in-waiting, but Venezuela certainly seemed like a beehive of democratic activity. The country was alive with debate about the constitution, from Indian villages in the Amazon rain forest to the barrios of Caracas. Potential candidates put together proposals and walked the streets trying to recruit voters. One street vendor who hoped to run commented, "It's the first time in five hundred years that the people have been asked what they want."

The stakes were high. Chávez believed a constitutional assembly controlled by his supporters was the major breakthrough the country needed to end the traditional parties' stranglehold on power. The oligarchy, the traditional parties, and much of the media feared it was the final step to establishing a one-man dictatorship. Chávez pulled out all the stops to win. Five cabinet members, including Luis Miquilena, resigned to run. His wife, Marisabel, threw her hat in, too. So did his brother Adán, and Chávez's personal psychiatrist, Edmund Chirinos. Former coup leaders, including Joel Acosta Chirinos and Francisco

Visconti, ran. Even the wife of legendary folk singer Alí Primera, Sol Mussett, became a candidate.

The electoral council prohibited the use of political party names on the ballot. So Chávez came up with a device to make sure his candidates won. He created a card called the *kino*, the name of the Venezuelan lottery card. Each card contained the names and photographs of some of his candidates, who in some cases were unknown to many in the public. Supporters simply had to enter the voting booth with their kino and pull the levers.

More than 900 of the 1,171 candidates who qualified to run for the assembly by collecting enough petition signatures did not belong to Chávez's Patriotic Pole. Yet his forces won an overwhelming victory. They took 125 seats including the indigenous spots, or 95 percent of the total. The opposition managed just six seats. The top vote getter was Chávez's former chief of staff, journalist Alfredo Peña. Number two was Chávez's wife. The wife of the late Alí Primera also won a seat. So did the others the president supported, including a popular *llanero* singer, a horse race announcer, and Maisanta biographer José León Tapia. Some weren't exactly constitutional experts. But it didn't matter. The new constitution would be in the hands of *el pueblo* rather than the elites. Enough experts would be on hand to guide them.

The night of his victory Chávez was delirious with delight. He opened the grounds of Miraflores again and appeared on the balcony. This time he was with Marisabel. It was a scene straight out of Evita's Argentina as she stood with him in the tropical night, illuminated by a spotlight with the adoring masses at their feet. Chávez called his triumph a "home run with the bases loaded." Then in an unusual public gesture for him, he kissed his bride. The crowd went wild. Chávez capped off the unforgettable night by announcing that he would ask the constitutional assembly to change the name of the country. He wanted to call it the Bolivarian Republic of Venezuela.

The overwhelming victory of the Chávez forces made it clear a showdown was coming. For months Chávez had urged the incoming assembly to temporarily shut down Congress and the Supreme Court until new institutions were created. He argued that the constitutional assembly would be the supreme power in the nation, above even the president himself. Many constitutional experts agreed. The Supreme Court and the opposition did not. Chief Justice Cecilia Sosa warned

Chávez against closing the Supreme Court, arguing that the assembly's job was to draw up a new constitution, not supplant existing institutions or govern the country. With a constitutional crisis looming, Congress went on vacation.

When the constitutional assembly convened the night of August 3, its newly elected president, Luis Miquilena, promptly declared that the body had an "originating character." He meant it could shut down Congress, the Supreme Court, and other institutions. The crowd at the magna aula of the Central University of Venezuela burst into applause. The fight was on. Chávez urged quick action. "Venezuela is a sinking ship," he told reporters. "We can't wait too long to do something before it sinks completely."

They didn't wait too long. Nine days later, on Thursday, August 12, the assembly voted to give itself far-reaching powers to abolish government institutions, dismiss officials, and intervene in other ways. A week later, on Thursday, August 19, it declared a "judicial emergency," giving itself the power to overhaul the courts. The next day it appointed a nine-member panel with the power to suspend or dismiss nearly half the country's forty-seven hundred judges, clerks, and bailiffs because of pending accusations of corruption, incompetence, or other irregularities. Even Supreme Court justices could be removed.

It was a breathtaking move. To its supporters, it could force reforms that had been blocked for years by corrupt politicians and judicial authorities. To its critics, it was an overreach of power and a threat to democracy. The stage was set for a confrontation with the Supreme Court.

No one disputed that the judicial system needed cleaning up. Corruption was rampant. A best-selling 1995 book, ¿Cuánto Vale Un Juez? — How Much Does a Judge Cost? — filled 144 pages with story after story of crooked judges. Finding material wasn't hard. The previous year, a judge was caught throwing bribe money out of her office window. Another was taken into custody with bribe money stuffed in her underwear. The book's author, journalist William Ojeda, ended up spending a year in jail after another judge found him guilty of defamation.

The entire system was susceptible to bribery and influence peddling. For decades most judges, including Supreme Court magistrates, were appointed by the majority party in Congress — either Democratic Action or COPEI. Only one-quarter of Supreme Court justices held permanent posts; the rest could be dismissed at will. That made moving against politicians, well-connected businessmen, or other members of the power elite unlikely. The system was dominated by interlocking judicial *tribus*, tribes, comprising law firms, politicians, judges, and other powerful figures who could get clients any decision they needed for the right price or the right connection.

The Supreme Court held up corruption charges against President Jaime Lusinchi for years even though the investigating magistrate recommended putting him on trial. CAP himself was finally indicted, not because he was corrupt but mainly because he was politically unpopular. After winning a seat in the senate in the November 1998 election to represent his home state of Táchira, he suffered a humiliating defeat in the constitutional assembly race when the same voters dumped him in favor of a Chavista.

If all that wasn't enough, the judicial system was also notoriously backlogged. Only about ninety-seven hundred of the nation's twenty-three thousand prisoners had actually had their day in court and been convicted. The rest were awaiting trial, often for years.

While few doubted the system needed fixing, the disagreement was over whether the constitutional assembly had the right to do it. Stepping back into the fray, on Monday, August 23, the Supreme Court reversed its earlier ruling that the assembly's sole mission was to write a new constitution. Instead, it ruled eight to six that the assembly did not act unconstitutionally in assuming judicial powers. The decision provoked a crisis on the court. The next day Chief Justice Cecilia Sosa resigned. In a live, nationally televised news conference, she declared: "The court simply committed suicide to avoid being assassinated. But the result is the same. It is dead."

It was a dramatic appearance. Her resignation and rapidly ensuing events provoked an uproar among Chávez's opponents and consternation in the United States. "We regret that she has chosen to leave public service for she is a person of great ability and integrity and has been a true leader in Venezuela's efforts to reform the judicial system," State Department spokesman James B. Foley said.

But Chávez's allies noted that Sosa was implicated in the delay of a number of high-level corruption cases. They called her a symbol of a court system gone amok. While the constitutional assembly's actions were bold and controversial, they argued, it was not a time for timidity. A revolution was under way. US-born political analyst Eric Ekvall, a former adviser to high-level, old-regime politicians and no Chávez fan, put it this way: "He's come in to clean up town, and that doesn't happen without a showdown. He's not here to fine tune. He's here to tear things down and build them up again." The Reverend Raúl González of the Jesuit think tank Centro Gumilla added that Chávez was merely implementing what his supporters demanded. "Chávez was elected in order to carry out the coup d'état that he left unfinished in 1992, that is, to bury one political system and give birth to another."

Chávez argued that he was carrying out peacefully what in most countries would require a civil war, a bloody coup, or other violent action, like the guerrilla war that led to Castro's triumph in Cuba in 1959. He dubbed it a "peaceful revolution." He argued moreover that if the reforms were not enacted, the country might indeed erupt into a civil war. The majority poor were seething with anger.

The constitutional assembly did not skip a beat after declaring a judicial emergency and watching Sosa resign. The next day, Wednesday, August 25, they declared a "legislative emergency." This time they had their sights on Congress. The assembly all but dissolved it. Congress could no longer pass laws. The only duties it was left with were things such as budget oversight and granting the president permission to travel outside the country. Chavista congressional members, a minority in the chamber, didn't oppose the move — they thought it needed cleaning up, too.

Opposition congressional members immediately announced they were cutting short their vacation and would reconvene that Friday. They would head to the congressional building, which they had ceded to the constitutional assembly for their meetings. If the assembly wanted to fight, they would fight back. They pledged to refrain from approving budget outlays or presidential trips abroad. Chávez was scheduled to visit Brazil and Panama over the next ten days. The stage was set for another showdown. "Democracy is dying," COPEI lawmaker César Pérez Vivas declared. "The coup d'état against Venezuela is being consummated."

The opposition legislators and their supporters showed up at Congress that Friday morning burning red berets and shouting "Democracy!" and "No to Dictatorship!" Chávez supporters rushed to the scene to stop the lawmakers from entering Congress. The gates around the building were locked shut. National Guardsmen and police stood vigil. Militants on both sides were armed with sticks.

Chaos erupted. Some lawmakers broke through the crowd of Chavistas and National Guardsmen. Identification cards clenched in their teeth, they tried clawing their way over the spiked fence and onto the congressional grounds. Supporters helped push them over. Fistfights broke out amid the stick-waving crowd of a few hundred people. The National Guard and police fired tear gas, rubber bullets, and water cannons to try to control the brawl. Images of the legislators climbing the fence went around the world.

That afternoon the Catholic Church negotiated a truce between the two sides. But the truce broke down that night when the opposition returned to Congress to try to get in again. Chávez called it all a "provocation" and a "macabre show" intended to "cause a tempest in a teapot."

The following Tuesday, August 31, the assembly voted to effectively shut down Congress. It usurped the few remaining powers Congress still had, arguing that it was interfering with the assembly's work. It left Congress technically alive, saying it would perform the legislature's remaining functions only if it refused to do so itself. One opposition delegate to the assembly compared the pared-down Congress to an "invalid."

The standoff provoked officials in Washington, DC, to express growing worries about the process of writing a new magna carta. "Our concern is that its democratic essence in substance as well as form be preserved, both for the people of Venezuela and for the people of the hemisphere," State Department spokesman Foley said. Nine days earlier, *The New York Times* had run an editorial titled "Emergence of a Venezuelan Potentate." It warned that while "Venezuelans overwhelmingly supported radical reform, they should be very wary of the methods Mr. Chávez is using. [He] has so far shown little respect for the compromises necessary in a democracy."

But not everyone overseas believed Chávez was a rising threat to democracy. *The Economist*, hardly a bastion of leftist thought, wrote that "the fears of his opponents that he would quickly be metamorphosed into an authoritarian dictator have so far proved misplaced . . . By and large, change has happened without infringing democratic rights and freedoms." Chávez, the magazine added, had managed "the peaceful abolition of a corrupt and privileged elite," possibly sparing Venezuela "a worse fate."

Chávez believed he was under siege because he was attacking the interests of the oligarchy. He argued that leaders of the traditional parties were trying to "spread a dirty war" of misinformation that much of the US and international media was gobbling up and spewing out for millions of readers and listeners around the world. Referring to Hitler's minister of propaganda, Joseph Goebbels, he said the campaign was "based on a Goebbels strategy . . . They have repeated lies so many times that they believe it is the truth."

Four assembly members, including one opposition delegate, announced in mid-September that they were traveling to New York and Washington, DC, to meet with political and business leaders to present a more accurate picture of what was happening in Venezuela. "There is no dictatorship here," declared Claudio Fermín, one of six opposition delegates to the assembly and Democratic Action's presidential candidate in 1993. He blamed "political infantilism" by both anti- and pro-Chávez factions for producing "verbal shootouts."

Despite the shootouts, on Thursday, September 9, the assembly and the Congress reached an agreement to resolve their impasse. With the Catholic Church mediating, the assembly agreed to reverse its order virtually shutting down Congress. It would be allowed to resume its normal activities, including reconvening as a full body. Congress, in turn, would not interfere with the assembly's work or Chávez's activities as president, such as his trips overseas.

Chávez had indicated as early as August 5 that, reversing his calls for immediate abolishment, he didn't expect the assembly to dissolve the Congress and Supreme Court until a new constitution was approved. But he added that it could abolish any branch that tried to block reform.

To some, the move demonstrated Chávez's brilliance as a political tactician. He would threaten adversaries, then back off and announce his willingness to compromise. The opposition would generally go along, and Chávez would get what he wanted. He was playing with them like puppets.

Two days before reaching the agreement for a limited "co-existence" with Congress, the assembly launched its first move of the assault on the judiciary. It fired eight judges suspected of corruption. Appearing at a nationally broadcast news conference, Manuel Quijada, the lawyer and head of the assembly's Judicial Emergency Commission who had befriended Chávez in Yare, also read out the names of fifty more allegedly corrupt judges. Their fate would be decided in the next few days. They probably would also be fired.

The timing could not have been better. Four days earlier, on Friday, September 3, two judges threw out the charges against two dozen bankers accused in the notorious financial scandal during Rafael

Caldera's government. The public was outraged. Two hundred bankers had fled the country after the 1994 collapse. Most were living overseas as fugitives, some in the United States. When one of the judges went on television a few days later to vigorously defend the decision letting the bankers go free, Quijada and his commission suspended him and the other judge, too.

The assembly had another mission: to clean up the nation's prisons. In the first week of October it declared a "prisons emergency." While the court system was notorious, the jails were even worse. Amnesty International called them the most dangerous in Latin America.

Built to hold 15,500 inmates, by the mid-1990s they overflowed with 25,000. Prisoners slept elbow-to-elbow on concrete floors in cells, or in hallways, beneath stairwells, two or three to a bed or even in makeshift outdoor tents. Bathrooms didn't work or were too dangerous to walk to, so inmates relieved themselves into plastic bags or newspapers and tossed them out barred windows into courtyards. The stench of human waste and rotting garbage choked the air.

Drinking water from corroded bathroom pipes was rife with bacteria and parasites. AIDS, tuberculosis, and typhoid were common. The food was repugnant. Breakfast was typically a cup of weak coffee and a small piece of bread, lunch an unappetizing bowl of spaghetti or rice and beans. There was no dinner — the Justice Ministry's food budget of about 81¢ a day per prisoner didn't allow it.

Knife fights, shootings, even massacres — some replete with beheadings — were common. Inmates carried the sharpened slivers of metal called *chuzos* everywhere they went, for protection. Badly outnumbered, guards rarely ventured into the cell blocks, where inmates roamed freely.

Medical care was minimal. Prisoners stitched their own wounds. New inmates had to defend themselves or find someone to protect them. Those who didn't could be gang-raped or killed. To survive, some became "slaves" to gang leaders, cooking, cleaning, and providing sexual favors in return for protection. Some gang leaders branded their "property" on their buttocks or backs with electric hot plates.

By October 1999 the constitutional assembly made its first move to clean up the prisons. It decided to process thousands of prisoners who had never been to court, often languishing for years. In July, Chávez had issued a new penal code by decree. It was aimed at modernizing the judicial system short-term until the new constitution was ready. It provided for the presumption of innocence and allowed inmates to be released until their court date. Some inmates could be freed for good because of time already served. Others might participate in a day-release program.

On October 3, Chávez announced that teams of judges, prosecutors, human rights activists, and priests were heading into four of the most dangerous jails to accelerate justice for inmates awaiting trial. The team hoped to clear six thousand prisoners by the end of the year. Chávez also wanted to segregate inmates by alleged crime. Accused pickpockets and minors as young as sixteen shared cells with alleged rapists and murderers.

The assembly and the government were to have mixed success in attacking the prison problem. Like Chávez's government in general, they were not going to achieve miracles overnight. The problems were too intractable to solve quickly. But no one could doubt his will to overturn the system.

With the conflict with Congress largely resolved, and the assembly getting down to the work of hashing out a new constitution, Chávez decided to hit the road. He had handed in his own proposed constitution to the assembly. Thousands of citizens also submitted their suggestions. Indigenous groups pushed for official recognition of their native languages. Even street peddlers pressed their interests. They gathered in front of the capitol and agitated for their inclusion in social security and other worker programs.

The assembly was broken up into commissions to address the various sections of the proposed magna carta. They held regional meetings around the country to listen to citizens. Chávez may have been a rabble-rousing demagogue like his critics said, but Venezuela was buzzing with political participation among the masses. As the debate sizzled, Chávez climbed into the presidential jet and headed for Asia. The battle to repair his battered international image was far from over.

**16**

# A Birth and a Tragedy

Hugo Chávez was giving Carlos Andrés Pérez a run for his money as the most traveled Venezuelan president. As president-elect, by some accounts, he broke the record. He traveled to twelve countries in six weeks, including Brazil, Argentina, Mexico, Spain, France, Germany, and the United States, where he met with Clinton and gave him a copy of the book *Bolívar Forever*. In France, Chávez said his tour of Europe was "aimed at showing I am not the devil, this mix of Mussolini and Hitler that they've said. I am not a tyrant."

He had a similar motive with his trip to Asia, and also wanted to drum up interest in foreign investment to help Venezuela's ailing economy. To critics, the expensive globe-trotting was hypocritical for a man who that February had denounced the luxuries he was inheriting at the presidential residence La Casona, including a pool, a gym, and an outdoor movie theater. He declared then that he "couldn't sleep at night" in the colonial-era twenty-five-bedroom mansion thinking about the Venezuelan street children who didn't have enough food to eat and slept with newspapers covering them instead of blankets.

But Chávez also believed his political project had global reach. This was not just about transforming Venezuela. It was about creating a "multipolar" world free of domination by the United States — one that brought social justice to the underdeveloped nations of the world so that children wouldn't sleep in the streets with newspapers for blankets. Chávez needed allies in his struggle. The only way to get them was to meet face-to-face.

He landed in China on October 10 to full state honors. Cannon shots reverberated through Tiananmen Square, and a military band played Venezuela's national anthem. In Beijing's Great Hall of the People, Chinese president Jiang Zemin lifted a champagne glass and proclaimed "*Salud!*" — Spanish for "to health!" The two leaders signed six agreements bolstering bilateral ties. In an important economic coup for Venezuela, the Beijing government agreed to buy two to four million tons a year of a special tar-based Venezuelan fuel called Orimulsion, a coal substitute.

Chávez was a curiosity for the Chinese public. People lined the streets to see the colorful, controversial Latin American leader as his motorcade passed. Chávez stopped often along the streets to talk to ordinary people. He did not hide his enthusiasm for them or for China's success in combining capitalism and socialism. "We are witnessing the triumph of the Chinese revolution," he declared, calling China "a true world power."

He expressed admiration for Mao Tse-tung, buying a white porcelain statue of the revolutionary leader and visiting his tomb where he wrote a eulogy to the "great strategist, great soldier, great statesman and great revolutionary." He told reporters that "I've always been very Maoist, in the sense that the people to the army is like water to fish." Critics seized on it as an endorsement of the excesses of the Chinese Revolution and a warning of things to come in Venezuela. But Chávez more likely was referring to a model that fit his own vision of a union between *el pueblo* and the military.

He saw the China of the late twentieth century with its mixed economy as a model that could serve as a counterweight to the dominance of the United States. "Soviet power has collapsed," he said, "but that does not mean that neo-liberal capitalism has to be the model followed by the peoples of the West. If only for that reason, we invite China to keep its flag flying, because this world cannot be run by a universal police force that seeks to control everything." He told Chinese minister Zhu Rongji that just as China had "stood up" fifty years earlier "under the leadership of its great helmsman," Venezuela, too, was beginning to "stand up."

Chávez's whirlwind two-week tour took him on to Japan, South Korea, Hong Kong, Malaysia, Singapore, and the Philippines. He made an impression everywhere he went. He was not your typical visiting head of state. In a region of restrained gestures, he was flamboyant, spontaneous, even outrageous. He was a master of the unpredictable. When he visited the Great Wall of China, he broke into a Rocky-like sprint, leaving bodyguards and Venezuelan businessmen accompanying him on the trip breathless trying to keep up. At the official guest house in Beijing where the government housed him, he jogged around lakes and gardens. Then he began pitching baseballs.

In Japan he broke protocol and caught the emperor's bodyguards by surprise when he gave Akihito a bear hug as he bid him good-bye. The bodyguards were less than pleased, but judging from the smile on the emperor's face, he seemed to enjoy the almost unheard-of gesture. Chávez became famous for similar stunts on other trips. On his first visit to Russia, he broke into a karate stance as Vladimir Putin approached. The two had never met. Putin seemed confused for a few seconds until he realized it was a joke. Chávez then changed his position and made like he was hitting a baseball. "I've heard you are a black belt in karate," he said with a big smile. "I'm a baseball man myself." Once he sang the Venezuelan song "Rosario" to Mexican foreign minister Rosario Green, whom he'd only recently met. The minister was surprised by the performance, to say the least. Later, at a summit meeting of Caribbean leaders, he snuck up behind her, put his hands over her eyes, and said, "Guess who?"

Chávez's proclivity to break protocol was partly a product of his personality and partly a product of the Venezuelan character. Venezuelans are famous for their warmth, gregariousness, informality, and quick embrace of people they just meet. Some say they are among the friendliest and happiest people in the world. They love fun, jokes, and other people. At midnight on Christmas Eve and New Year's Eve, millions of people pour into the streets to greet, hug, and kiss neighbors as well as complete strangers. Beyond that, Chávez's personal psychiatrist once noted, the president grew up in Sabaneta, "a village, humble, simple, where there is no protocol."

Chávez often used his spontaneity, charm, and sense of humor to his political advantage, catching world leaders off guard and leaving many of them impressed if not enchanted, although some also thought he was a bit wacky. He had a prodigious memory for names and faces, and would take the time to talk with everyone from presidents to cooks and cleaning people. He always made it a point to shake the hand and thank every head of state's bodyguard he met on his trips. "He plays this game of affection to disarm people," noted Venezuelan chef Helena

Ibarra, who accompanied the group on the tour. "He may achieve it or not, but you can never forget it . . . It's a mechanism to seduce the people. And it gets results."

Chávez's trip to Asia ended with a mishap. A wheel on his aging Boeing 727 fell off during takeoff in the Philippines. He made it to Bombay, India, where the eight-wheel airplane landed safely. The Boeing suffered more problems in later trips in 2000. Eventually Chávez decided he needed a new airplane. He bought an Airbus 319 for $65 million. His critics called it an outrage that contradicted his calls for austerity. But Chávez saw it as a necessity. In his first three years in office, he spent 170 days outside the country, or about five months total. He visited seventy-one countries on four continents. Chávez was taking his revolution to the world.

In November 1999 he headed to Cuba. Leaders from twenty-one Latin American nations along with Spain and Portugal were convening for a summit meeting. Chávez wasn't a big fan of such encounters. "We go from summit to summit," he said, "and the people go from abyss to abyss." But he wasn't going to miss this one. He stayed on after the meetings ended and turned it into a love-fest with his mentor Fidel Castro.

The highlight was a baseball game organized by the two countries. Seventy-three-year-old Castro managed the Cuban squad. Forty-five-year-old Chávez pitched and played first base for the Venezuelans. Retired all-stars made up the rosters, although Castro hinted he had a "surprise" in store. He was decked out in the national team outfit, a red baseball cap and a blue windbreaker he wore over his customary military fatigues. Chávez wore his country's national colors of red, yellow, and blue.

Fifty-five thousand screaming fans in Havana's Latin American Stadium greeted Chávez with thunderous cheers as he trotted around the track for a warm-up. Castro provoked an even louder, shrieking outburst. Millions of television viewers from around Latin America tuned in to the historic sporting event. Latin America's oldest and most famous revolutionary was cementing his friendship and political alliance with "the new kid on the block," whom some saw as his heir apparent.

Venezuela's first lady, Marisabel Chávez, blond hair tucked under a baseball cap, threw out the first ball. The game was underway. Her husband was a little wild on the mound, and almost beaned several Cuban batters. But he improved as the game went on. He even retired Cuban slugger Antonio Muñoz three times, once on strikes. Chávez switched over to first base after five innings with the score tied at four–four. At the plate he managed a sacrifice run batted in and a single — which he capped off by hugging Cuban first baseman Agustín Marquetti. The game was stopped for a minute.

In the bottom of the sixth Castro pulled out his surprise. He sent in a string of substitute batters who were introduced only as "reserves from the Cuban team." Several bearded, white-haired, beer-bellied players limped to the plate. The crowd roared. They were actually active members of Cuba's national team wearing wigs and with their shirts stuffed. As they faked being over the hill, Castro laughed from the dugout.

The ringers made several hits and Cuba pulled ahead five–four, with Chávez watching happily as his team lost. It didn't matter.

The game was about much more than baseball. It was about cementing an alliance between Latin America's two most charismatic leftist leaders, one an established star, the other a newcomer. A few hours before the game, Chávez returned to the University of Havana where he'd given a speech in 1994 after his release from prison. "Here we are, four years, ten months and twenty-seven days since I last visited Havana," Chávez said in an impassioned ninety-minute talk. "Fidel and Hugo. Cuba and Venezuela. More alive than ever." Then, in a remark heard around the world, he added that he had "not the slightest doubt" that Venezuela's politics were marching "in the same direction, toward the same sea of happiness that the Cuban people are marching toward."

Chávez's critics seized on the comment as proof he wanted to turn Venezuela into another Cuba. Taken in isolation, it certainly seemed to say that. But most of the media did not report the rest of what Chávez said. While both leaders were looking to build societies of "happiness, true social justice, of true peace and true dignity," he said they also had different policies. Chávez, at least up until then, was not another Castro.

The men did have some things in common. Both led armed revolts in their countries that eventually turned them into national heroes — Castro in 1953 with his failed attempt to take the Moncada barracks in Santiago de Cuba, Chávez with his failed coup in 1992. Both served time in prison after the rebellions. Castro rose to power in January 1959 after a two-year guerrilla war, while Chávez rose to power through the ballot box forty years after that. Both looked to national patriots from the nineteenth century for inspiration — José Martí for Castro, Simón Bolívar for Chávez. They shared Bolívar's dream of a united Latin America and were critical of what they viewed as a long history of US imperialism and exploitation in Latin America. They were gifted speakers known to give speeches lasting hours. They donned military garb — Castro his combat fatigues, Chávez his red beret — slept barely a few hours at night, and preached a virulent brand of radical nationalism that critiqued the free-market conventional wisdom sweeping Latin America. They provoked wild adoration among their fans and deep hatred among their foes. They both loved baseball. They were pitchers and aspiring professionals when they were young. They still loved the sport as grown men. It was ironic. Baseball was an American import. Cuba, Venezuela, the Dominican Republic, and Nicaragua were the only countries in Latin America where it was more popular than soccer.

The two men were leftists without doubt, but sharp differences also separated them. Chávez was not going to order the state to take over the entire economy like Castro did after his triumph in 1959, although by early 2007 Chávez did order the nationalization of some companies in key sectors, such as telecommunications and electricity. Private property was generally respected and owners compensated if the government took over their businesses. The media was free, too. Critics said anything they wanted to about the president, accusing him of everything from beating his wife to installing a dictatorship. That in itself was a contradiction — in a real dictatorship such a statement would land a person in jail, or worse. Elections were free and frequent. For the first time in Venezuela's history, citizens were voting on major initiatives such as the constitutional assembly. There were no political prisoners. There was no systematic state-sponsored torture. There were no kangaroo courts where corrupt or brutal officials from the previous regime were summarily judged, condemned, and lined up in a stadium to be shot. On the contrary, some of Chávez's supporters thought he was soft on an old regime that had pillaged the country.

One reporter called him "a Castro without calories, with no anti-American rhetoric, no expropriations of private property and no squelching of domestic dissent." Wayne Smith, former head of the US Interests Section in Havana, saw Chávez as "a social reformer. His objectives are social justice, a more equal distribution of income, a better shake for the downtrodden." Even so, he added, "I don't see any indication Chávez is going to follow the path that Cuba did in terms of massive nationalizations. They may have very similar goals . . . but different ways of achieving it."

While Chávez and Castro were playing baseball on the diamond, Venezuelan businessmen were busy exploring opportunities for investing in the country. Three hundred accompanied Chávez on the trip. Cuba wanted Venezuela to invest $200 million to help revive a dilapidated Russian-built oil refinery in the province of Cienfuegos. They didn't get that amount, but Venezuela did eventually agree to sell Cuba fifty-three thousand barrels a day at preferential prices. The deal was similar to one signed by Venezuela and Mexico in 1980 when they agreed to sell oil to eleven Central American and Caribbean nations at discounted prices.

Chávez's budding friendship with Castro was to provide ample fodder for the elites in Venezuela and opponents elsewhere to paint him as a dictator in the making. For weeks, Venezuelan newspapers printed his "sea of happiness" comment nearly every day. Castro himself summoned Venezuelan reporters to Cuba for a ten-and-a-half-hour meeting to deny Chávez was a closet Marxist.

When Chávez returned to the palace after his trip to Cuba, the vote on the new constitution was just a few weeks away. It was, admittedly, a rushed job. Chávez needed to get it done before his political capital wore out and the opposition regrouped. The constitutional assembly worked frantically in the final weeks, laboring seven days a week. The new magna carta they produced was progressive and impressive in some ways, and lacking in others. Its main import was that it marked a definitive and symbolic break with the old regime.

The constitution improved human rights guarantees and for the first time recognized indigenous and environmental rights. The Indian tribes' collective ownership of properties and collective economic systems were enshrined in the document. It also officially recognized housewives as workers eligible for government benefits like social security. It gave soldiers the right to vote; it took military promotions out of the hands of Congress — where past presidential mistresses such as Blanca Ibáñez dictated many appointments — and put them into the hands of the military and the president. It created an office called the "Defender of the People" to ensure that citizens' rights were protected.

It also established public selection processes for judges that called for input from human rights organizations and other groups. That moved the process out of the cigar-filled back rooms of the past, where congressmen appointed politically connected judges who were easily controlled by the political parties. The constitution replaced the Senate and the House with a single body, the National Assembly, and created the post of vice president. It extended the presidential term from five years to six, and permitted immediate reelection. It also for the first time in Venezuelan history created a mechanism to recall elected officials midway through their terms. These officials included everyone from village mayors to the president.

The constitution was praised by some for making bold initiatives like the recall referendum and criticized by others for concentrating power in the hands of the president. Chávez's detractors were suspicious of the provision extending his term by a year and allowing for reelection, although the latter put Venezuela in line with many other countries. They also worried that an enhanced "enabling law" gave Chávez too much power to fast-track legislation. Giving the vote to soldiers raised fears he was "militarizing" the government, although soldiers in the United States had the same right. Businessmen and neo-liberals argued that the new magna carta allowed excessive state intervention in the economy. It also changed the name of the country — something many Chavistas including Chávez's own brother Adán thought was not Venezuela's most pressing need. But the president insisted, and the name change made it in.

In the end the vote on the constitution was more a plebiscite on Chávez's year-old administration than on the document itself. Some polls indicated that only 2 percent of the population had actually read it by December 15, although it would become a well-thumbed and heatedly debated little book as time passed. Vendors sold them on the streets. Chávez often pulled one out of his shirt pocket during nationally broadcast talks. He called it the most advanced constitution in the world.

The campaign leading up to the vote turned nasty. Critics including the Catholic Church hierarchy warned that the constitution would help Chávez usher in a dictatorship. The country's former apostolic nuncio, Cardinal Rosalio Castillo, even compared Chávez's tactics to those employed by the former Italian dictator Benito Mussolini.

Chávez fired back, accusing the cardinal of condoning "immorality," branding Bishop Baltazar Porras a "pathetic ignoramus," and threatening to "exorcise" what he called "devils in vestments." He suggested the Son of God was on his side. "If Jesus Christ were resurrected in Venezuela, he would be walking the streets and calling on Venezuelans, without doubt, to vote 'Yes,'" for the referendum, he said.

Chávez let loose his high-voltage attacks on other sectors of the opposition. He called his detractors a "truckload of squealing pigs" and "vampires," and referred to the elites as a "rancid oligarchy." He labeled one newspaper publisher a "degenerate." Miguel Henrique Otero, publisher of *El Nacional*, the country's leading daily, returned the compliment. "No one in Venezuela can trust Hugo Chávez's democratic credentials," he said. Chávez seemed to win the battle of words. Within a week after he started actively campaigning for the constitution in early December, support for it went up by 11 percentage points, to 67 percent.

The vote on December 15 was the nation's fifth in a year. Like the others, the outcome was a foregone conclusion. Chávez romped to victory. Some 71 percent of voters approved the new constitution. It should have been a night of celebration, the culmination of one of Chávez's greatest dreams. But as the votes were being counted, tragedy was unfolding on the verdant mountainsides of Mount Avila overlooking the azure Caribbean Sea.

Mount Avila rises almost straight up from the shores of the Caribbean. Its tallest point, Naiguata Peak, is 1.7 miles high. Clouds often cover it and other peaks. Hundreds of shantytowns blanket the mountainside. Luxury apartment buildings where Caracas's elites often spend their weekends sit closer to the sea.

"Winter" or the dry season in Venezuela usually starts in December. But for two weeks prior to the vote on the constitution, a steady rain fell in the capital and around the country. It was unusual. Still, no one could have predicted what came next. Starting the evening of December 15, a downpour of biblical proportions drenched Mount Avila. In two days it dumped double the amount of rain that normally falls in a year.

The results were catastrophic. With Mount Avila already saturated from the previous rains, the mountain collapsed on itself. Boulders, trees, mud, and water came rushing down and crashed into the villages. The debris had been building speed and collecting mass from as far up the mountain as Naiguata Peak. By the time they reached the villages, the trees were like flying torpedoes. The boulders were even more horrifying. Many were the size of a truck or small house; one was thirty-three feet high and weighed an estimated 840 tons. The boulders crushed everything in their path. The wave of mud and debris was ten to twenty feet high in places. It was like a tidal wave coming down the mountain.

By the time it was over, anywhere from five to twenty thousand people were dead. Officials would never know the real figure. Most of the dead were buried under ten feet of rubble, or washed out to sea. Some residents carried away dead bodies on the only thing they could find — a broken door. In the little village of Carmen de Uria, the raging wave carved a thirty-foot-deep trench through the middle of town, wiping out everything in its path. It hurled cars into living rooms, tore buildings in half, and swept scores of victims out to sea.

The government quickly launched a massive search-and-rescue effort. Some twelve thousand soldiers and sailors flew helicopters, manned ships, and drove vehicles into the disaster zone to pull residents out, provide food and water, patrol streets, and search for bodies. In the first four days they plucked more than 140,000 people from the flooded coast to safety. Even US officials, who sent troops, airplanes, and equipment to help, said they were impressed.

Chávez took personal command of the rescue operation. He donned his combat fatigues, flew into the disaster zone, and visited stadiums and military posts where survivors were temporarily staying. Plan Bolívar 2000 had turned out to be perfect preparation for the military to handle the relief effort. The mudslide was a horrifying tragedy, but in ways it was Chávez's finest hour as president. He made a nationally broadcast address each night, stoically providing Venezuelans with an update on the rescue efforts and urging them to keep the faith. He worked tirelessly, sleeping just two hours a night as he turned the operations into a personal mission.

The recovery effort was grim. Authorities often did not find entire bodies but pieces: heads, arms, legs. Three weeks after the disaster, dozens of victims were found floating in the sea one hundred miles away off Venezuela's western coast. Many were dismembered.

The government's reaction to the tragedy was energetic, but that did not stop the opposition from trying to find fault. Chávez did not appear on television the night of December 15 as the referendum results came in and the mudslide began, prompting rumors picked up by the media that he was on La Orchila island getting drunk with Fidel Castro and other foreign leaders to celebrate his win at the polls. In reality, Chávez later explained, he had spent the night in Miraflores in a cabinet meeting. Around noon the next day, risking his life, he flew by helicopter over Mount Avila to reach the worst-hit areas. He overruled pilots who warned him it was too dangerous to fly in the near-zero-visibility weather and with the rains still falling. He barred journalists from the flight because it was too risky.

His detractors also seized on a report they said proved the government was warned about the impending disaster but did nothing because it didn't want to stop the vote on the constitution. But the heavy rains were at a minimum a once-in-a-century event, as experts later stated, and the national weather service was caught as off guard as anyone. "At no time did we warn people about how bad this event could be," stated the service's Alvaro Palache.

The attacks against Chávez even came from the Catholic Church hierarchy when Archbishop José Ignacio Velasco claimed from the altar that the tragedy was a punishment from God aimed at Chávez.

The president believed the cause was more earthbound. He thought many of the people died because previous governments had irresponsibly allowed entire villages to sprout up in mudslide zones. As for the luxury apartment complexes, payoffs to corrupt officials often speeded the permit process.

In the aftermath of the tragedy, Chávez came under attack for his handling of relations with the United States. Two days after the mud and rockslides, the first of 120 US soldiers started arriving in Venezuela to assist in the rescue-and-recovery effort. Black Hawk helicopters, a Hercules C-130 transport plane, a DC-8, and $3.4 million in aid also came. By December 23 an enormous C-5 Galaxy — the largest airplane made in the United States — touched down at Simón Bolívar International Airport carrying water-purifying machines.

But the smooth coordination hit a bump in mid-January 2000 when the United States dispatched two ships to Venezuela to help rebuild the main road along the coast at the foot of Mount Avila. The ships carried bulldozers, tractors, engineering equipment, and 450 marine and navy engineers. Chávez's defense minister, General Raúl Salazar, had requested the help in a letter sent December 24.

In what was a case of either miscommunication with Salazar or second thoughts by Chávez, the day after the USS *Tortuga* left Norfolk, Virginia, Chávez abruptly announced that the help of the Americans was not needed, although he would take the equipment. The United States ordered the USS *Tortuga* to turn around. It also held back the

USS *Nashville* in Morehead City, North Carolina. US officials were miffed and mystified. They said they could not send the machines without the men.

Chávez was in a delicate position politically. While his relations with the United States were still relatively good, the colossus to the north had a long history of subverting leftist governments and movements in Latin America. To allow 450 US soldiers and two ships to come ashore would be like giving the American "imperialists" a practice landing on beaches half an hour from the capital. It wasn't exactly the type of thing a self-styled revolutionary government did. Citing national sovereignty, earlier in the year Chávez also prohibited US airplanes from flying over Venezuelan territory in anti-narcotics reconnaissance flights. Chávez's detractors said they just wanted the disaster recovery help no matter where it came from.

He also came under fire for alleged human rights abuses in the aftermath of the disaster by soldiers and police dispatched to stop rampant after-dark looting. On January 3, 2000, human rights groups issued a report charging that security agents may have killed, beaten, and looted in the disaster zone. An intrepid reporter for *El Nacional*, Vanessa Davies, published a series of articles about the alleged abuses based on firsthand although anonymous accounts.

Chávez reacted defensively. He called the human rights report "suspicious and superficial." He attacked Davies' credibility, saying government investigators had found "not one single piece of proof" to back up her allegations. The DISIP political police subpoenaed Davies to come in for questioning.

On January 11 Chávez's own government contradicted him. State Ombudsman Roger Cedeno said he believed security forces had killed more than sixty people between December 17 and December 30 in Vargas state on the coast. Foreign Minister José Vicente Rangel, himself a former highly respected journalist, criticized the DISIP for subpoenaing Davies. He added that he wasn't surprised some security forces may have committed abuses, since it was nothing new in Venezuela.

To his credit, Chávez shifted his position. In a stunning move, he called Davies and invited her to accompany him to Vargas and visit the families she spoke to who described the abuses. The two got into a jeep with the uniformed Chávez behind the wheel and headed into the disaster zone on a Saturday night, January 22. One man they met took the president and his entourage to the site of an alleged mass grave.

He told Chávez soldiers had lined people up and shot them. Chávez said authorities would exhume the site; no bodies were ever found. He pledged to improve Venezuela's human rights record. "We have a terrible culture here," he said, "and that is not going to change overnight."

Human rights groups praised Chávez's turnaround. But one man was not happy. He felt the DISIP was being turned into a scapegoat. His name was Jesús Urdaneta, one of the founding members of the MBR-200. He was the first person Chávez had appointed to his government, taking over as head of the DISIP in December 1998 before Chávez was even sworn in.

Urdaneta believed officials and the media were scapegoating his agency by focusing the accusations on the DISIP, which had only a handful of agents in Vargas compared with thousands of soldiers and police. "There were eight thousand men there, and supposedly my sixty were the ones who violated all the human rights," he later stated. There was also a power struggle raging within the administration and between Chávez and his old military comrades. Some of the Bolivarians believed he was aligning himself too closely with political figures like Luis Miquilena and José Vicente Rangel, whom they considered part of the old regime. Urdaneta was disgusted and ready to quit.

Chávez was about to suffer the first major defections of his presidency, with the comrades who were once his blood brothers deserting and — in his eyes — betraying him.

**17**

# First Defections

As Chávez wrapped up his first year in office, he was still immensely popular. To the underclass he remained a messiah who was going to save the country from the corrupt oligarchy. But the first major signs of discontent also were cropping up. A couple of weeks before the vote on the constitution, residents in affluent Caracas neighborhoods opened their windows during one of Chávez's nationally televised speeches and banged pots and pans to protest against him and the proposed magna carta. Pot banging as protest was made famous in Latin America by middle-class housewives in Chile in the early 1970s before President Salvador Allende was overthrown in a US-backed coup.

Chávez's opponents also held candlelight vigils. They handed out pamphlets. They honked car horns. They were sick of his virulent language, of his calling them "a truckload of squealing pigs" and a "rancid oligarchy." Many of them had nothing to do with the oligarchy. Far from blue bloods born with silver spoons in their mouths, they were middle-class citizens who felt they had worked hard to get what they had. Chávez's revolution didn't promise much for them. Caracas mayor Antonio Ledezma of the discredited Democratic Action party vowed to keep up the pot banging if the president kept hijacking the airwaves for hours with his high-voltage attacks.

Chávez's speeches were driving his opponents crazy. He seemed ubiquitous, giving two or three speeches a day and frequently showing up live in prime time with talks that lasted an average of two hours. He kicked off the month of February with a 171-minute televised prime-time speech marking his first year in office on February 2. He came on again February 5 for another 39 minutes, February 11 for 100 minutes, February 14 for 104 minutes, February 15 for 88 minutes, and February 16 for more than an hour.

The speeches were cutting into popular nighttime soap operas, as well as television networks' profits since they were commercial-free. Many of Chávez's detractors and even some of his supporters thought it was overkill. "I can't take it anymore," one hairdresser complained. "He talks morning, noon and night on all channels. It's like living in a dictatorship."

Still, Chávez was an entertaining figure. No politician in the United States or most other countries could match his ability to tell jokes. One show in 2001 included a video of him visiting a rural town and assisting military doctors during an operation — Chávez held a flashlight. He turned to the audience and quipped, "You see? Now I can even do surgery!" Poor people loved it. Chávez was a born story-teller with "a great sense of timing," as Gabriel García Márquez put it. With the cadences of a Baptist preacher, he drew in millions of viewers, sipping a cup of coffee between rhetorical flourishes and pulling out a copy of the ever-present new constitution. His ruminations ranged from tales about his childhood to reflections about the meaning of love to thoughts about why one of his relatives was nicknamed the Rifleman. He quoted everyone from the German philosopher Friedrich Nietzsche to Thomas Jefferson to Mao Tse-tung. He was part historian, part philosopher, part statesman.

To his detractors, Chávez's long speeches before millions of viewers were proof that his ego was dangerously out of control. Without doubt, he had a sizable one. Even some supporters such as his spiritual guide, the Reverend Jesús Gazo, acknowledged that Chávez was something of a know-it-all who didn't always listen. Some people wondered whether he would turn into a Castro-style all-knowing potentate issuing orders from on high to the less enlightened masses or even his less enlightened ministers. His enemies insisted he already was.

But millions of people loved his talks and clamored for more. In his mind Chávez was leading a revolution, and that required a constant indoctrination to change the evil ways of the past. Many supporters viewed him as a teacher or the head of a family keeping the nation informed of what was going on — a rarity in Venezuela. Some compared the talks to Franklin Delano Roosevelt's "fireside chats" during the Great Depression and World War II. Chávez was also from the llanos, whose loquacious inhabitants would think nothing of droning on for hours at a time. In Venezuela time and punctuality were irrelevant. The personal relationship was what counted.

Chávez's public talks provided a measure of transparency to his government. People knew what was going on. He interrogated and sometimes even scolded ministers in the audience. He announced appointments and firings. He pulled out graphics and maps to illustrate his latest plans or trips overseas. To many Venezuelans with barely a grade school education, it was an informal geography class. He offered pocket histories of the countries, and described the people he met. Other talks focused on Venezuela's history or his government's economic policies. His informal, entertaining manner made it easy to swallow. He spoke the people's language. He was a regular guy from the barrio.

Chávez was a live wire, especially compared with his moribund predecessor Rafael Caldera, who rarely addressed the nation and had to bat down rumors he was dead. "He's the only president we've had who is interested in the people, in resolving our problems," a clothing salesman commented. Chávez himself was not concerned about the time people lost watching mindless television dramas. Just the opposite. "Soap operas, no, no!" he told reporters. "We need more speeches to explain to the people" what is happening in Venezuela.

His critics said his frequent speeches on television weren't filling anyone's stomach. The elites mocked and made jokes about his appearances. To them, he was an uncouth, indiscreet, long-winded embarrassment. "Did you see our Clown Prince last night?" was a typical remark. Others commented that *"el peon ha tomado la finca"* — the peon has taken over the farm. A former State Department official offered one explanation for why Chávez was isolated from most Venezuelan business leaders: "I don't think they know how to talk to him. They've probably never met anybody like him before, except maybe their houseboy." The elites were tired of hearing about Chávez's grandmother Rosa Inés, or listening to him compare world events to baseball games. Instead of talking incessantly, they thought, Chávez ought to shut up and run the government.

They accused him of running a mediocre one. In January the former comptroller issued a scathing report alleging that the government was paying too much attention to politics and not enough to the economy, crime, and corruption. Eduardo Roche Lander charged that Plan Bolívar 2000 had turned into a hotbed of corruption. He noted that the country's economic performance was dismal: The economy had contracted by 7.2 percent since Chávez took office, foreign investment had fallen by $1.7 billion, capital flight had reached $4.6 billion, and 500,000 jobs had been lost.

Chávez's government dismissed the report as an act of political revenge since the constitutional assembly had recently fired Roche Lander. Foreign Minister José Vicente Rangel noted that under Chávez the country had carried out the unprecedented act of firing two hundred corrupt judges, with more to follow. The economy was weak, but they'd inherited a fiscal disaster from Caldera. They also had to deal with the aftermath of the December floods.

Some US officials joined in the criticism of Chávez. Peter Romero, the State Department's top official for Latin America, told a newspaper in Spain that "we've extended our hand to Chávez. But you don't see a government operating, only plebiscites, referendums and more elections. They tell us 'wait,' but we gringos aren't exactly known for our patience." The comment sparked a minor diplomatic row.

It was the first open conflict between the two countries. Up until then, the general US approach with Chávez — advocated chiefly by Ambassador John Maisto — had been to seek engagement rather than conflict. They wanted to avoid confrontation that could endanger oil imports or the millions of dollars foreign oil companies were earning in Venezuela. As José Vicente Rangel explained, "The State Department has shown great caution toward Chávez because of what I call the Cuba syndrome: the fear that US inflexibility will push Chávez to the extreme left, as it did with Castro." He was talking about efforts by the United States to undermine Castro in the early years of his revolution, from the Bay of Pigs invasion to the economic embargo.

As Maisto argued to Romero and others in the State Department, it made sense to engage Chávez. He was tremendously popular at home and had won a string of free and fair elections. His polices especially on the economy up until that point were not radical. After pushing for a moratorium on the foreign debt as a candidate, Chávez as president stayed within the bounds of the agreement negotiated by Caldera with the IMF. He paid the debt and kept the bankers happy. As a populist, Chávez thrived on "us versus them" confrontations. He took on Venezuela's corrupt political elite, businessmen, media moguls, and

Catholic Church hierarchy. Maisto did not want the United States to join the enemies list.

The incident with Romero passed. But more were to come. The United States would have a new president by the turn of the year. It was destined to repeat the mistakes it made with Cuba.

Chávez and his forces made more than a few missteps that provided ammunition for his opponents and provoked the ire not only of his detractors but the president himself. After voters approved the new constitution on December 15, Congress and the Supreme Court were automatically eliminated. A week later the constitutional assembly officially declared the bodies defunct. In backroom dealings it named members of a newly created Supreme Tribunal of Justice, the nation's highest court, along with an attorney general, national comptroller, public defender, and National Electoral Council. It also appointed a twenty-one-member "mini Congress" of Chávez allies to replace the old body until elections could be held for the new National Assembly. The elections originally were scheduled for February, but were postponed for months because of the mudslides and technical problems with voting machines.

In contrast with the pronouncements of Chávez that the days of backroom appointments by political elites were over, the constitutional assembly did not consult civil society groups or other members of the public on the moves. Luis Miquilena, the head of the constitutional assembly and the mini Congress, handpicked many of the new appointees. One was Chávez's brother Adán. Critics accused the government of taking advantage of the chaos of the mudslides to push through the appointments. Chávez himself criticized the missed chance for departing from "the old way of doing politics." Miquilena publicly admitted the closed-door appointments of the electoral council members were a "mistake." Opponents said the entire arrangement and the delayed elections left power concentrated in Chávez's hands.

The opposition was frustrated, angry, and losing Venezuela's political battle.

For them, hating Chávez had become a national pastime. But they were finding comic relief in one place. A show called *La Reconstituyente*, the reconstitution, was the hottest theater ticket in town. Its name was a play on words of the pro-Chávez assembly that rewrote the constitution. During performances, an actor romped around the stage with a baseball mitt in one hand and a red beret on his head. He mercilessly lampooned Chávez, imitating his speech and his habit of interrupting speeches to greet friends he saw in the audience. One night one of the actors, comedian Laureano Márquez, told the audience he'd like to see more of Chávez's long-winded speeches. "While he talks, he's not governing, and that's a strategic advantage," he joked.

Besides the jabs in *La Reconstituyente*, one of the opposition's most articulate and energetic voices belonged to Teodoro Petkoff. The former 1960s Marxist guerrilla leader who had turned into Caldera's czar for the neo-liberal economic reforms had a new reincarnation. In this latest role he was a newspaper editor, heading the afternoon daily *El Mundo*. He was well suited for the post. He was something of a permanent dissident. He had engaged in disagreements and suffered fallouts with everyone from the Communist Party in the Soviet Union after the invasion of Czechoslovakia in 1968 to his colleagues in MAS when they endorsed Chávez for president in 1998.

Petkoff brought the mundane *El Mundo* back to life, editing the paper with flair, brilliance, and imagination. He put a large, scathing editorial on the front page every afternoon. It became required reading for Chávez opponents and even some supporters. The government often did not know how to respond. Despite the large number of prominent journalists in its ranks, it "proved notably poor at public relations, and found it difficult to rebut the attacks of the overwhelmingly hostile press" including Petkoff's operation. Chávez was so dominant that few other voices in the administration blossomed or got their chance at the microphone.

Petkoff left his job at *El Mundo* after what he alleged was pressure from a senior government official involving a pending legal case with the owners of the paper, the Capriles family. In April 2000, at the age of sixty-eight, he founded his own newspaper, *Tal Cual*. It quickly raised a ruckus. The day after its debut on April 3, its front-page editorial featured a headline that said, "The Official Line." Next to it was a photograph of Chávez and a story. The entire text read, "Bla, bla, bla."

The biggest blow to Chávez at the start of his second year did not come from Petkoff's newspaper, though. It came from his former comrades in arms. On the eighth anniversary of the February 4, 1992, revolt, Francisco Arias Cárdenas, Jesús Urdaneta, and Joel Acosta Chirinos, three key leaders of the rebellion, stunned the nation by holding a news conference in the western city of Coro to denounce Chávez and his inner circle. They believed his "peaceful revolution" was losing direction and betraying the Bolivarian ideals they had all risked their lives for. They thought it lacked internal democracy, was run by *caudillos* or strong-arm bosses, and was fostering corruption. They accused Chávez of selling out to the corrupt oligarchy that had led to the creation of the Bolivarian movement in the first place. They called on him to fire Foreign Minister José Vicente Rangel, former interior minister and recently appointed United Nations ambassador Ignacio Arcaya, and Luis Miquilena. Miquilena had turned into something of a kingmaker in the administration. He was the president's closest adviser. Chávez called him a father figure.

Arias Cárdenas, once Chávez's closest collaborator and co-leader of the 1992 coup, had another opinion. "We were cheated, and this is a grave disappointment to the nation," he said. Some of the president's civilian aides "appear to have turned into criminals." Arias added that "an organization that doesn't allow contrary opinion, that doesn't debate, that doesn't discuss, in my opinion doesn't exist."

Urdaneta echoed the doubts about the president's top civilian aides. "These men have put a blindfold on the president and are leading him to the cliff," he said. For his part, Acosta Chirinos complained that the Chávez government was turning into a replica of the old Democratic Action regimes that operated in almost a Stalinist manner, with backroom deals engineered by *caudillos*. "The party has turned into a kind of clandestine organization where, it seems, decisions are made in a style reminiscent of the Fourth Republic," he said. "The president is surrounded by a group of servants who simply bow their heads and say, 'Yes, master.'" The three men said they were not breaking with the president definitively. They were giving him a chance to "rectify" first.

The attack on Chávez was a shocker. It was coming from three of what were once his closest and most powerful allies. Arias Cárdenas was governor of oil-rich Zulia state. Urdaneta was Chávez's chief of intelligence, the man who kept the secrets. Acosta Chirinos was the national head of the MVR. Their protest threatened to pump life into a nearly nonexistent opposition movement and open the first major fissure in Chávez's government. Members of the all-but-defunct old regime were gleeful.

A week after the press conference in Coro, the comandantes upped the ante. Urdaneta, the former DISIP head who felt his agency was unfairly scapegoated for the human rights abuses in the aftermath of the mud-slides, showed up at the national prosecutor's office. He handed over files he said contained evidence of corruption against forty-six government officials including Miquilena. It was another bombshell. Chávez seemed stunned. Breaking a week's silence on the rupture, he gave a nationally broadcast address. He said he was "pained" by the split but that the revolution must march on. Many interpreted his statements as a final good-bye to his former comrades.

Lying beneath the complaints and accusations lodged by the former coup leaders, however, were petty jealousies, hurt feelings, and an internal power struggle within the MVR between civilians and military men. Some believed Arias and the others lashed out because they felt sidelined in the administration and were jealous of Chávez's success. Arias Cárdenas had been passed over recently for the newly created post of vice president. Urdaneta was fired as head of the DISIP. Acosta Chirinos lacked real power as head of the MVR. He was in the process of losing the post, anyway, as Chávez announced that he was personally retaking control of the party after "letting them do what they want" for the last year.

The men also had differences, some of them long standing, with Chávez's civilian aides. Back in Yare, Miquilena had ordered Arias Cárdenas to remain silent and out of sight from the media. He believed the coup leaders had to make Chávez the star around which the movement would coalesce. Arias resented it, and resented the overwhelming power Miquilena had assumed in the government. Urdaneta had his own feud with José Vicente Rangel, who accused him and the DISIP of intimidating and trying to silence the journalists and human rights groups investigating the killings in Vargas. Urdaneta believed Rangel had convinced Chávez to bar him from responding publicly to the accusations. He also thought he was forced out of his post because Chávez did not want cases of corruption he was presenting to be investigated, although the president did pledge to look into them.

Chávez was in a difficult position. He was under attack for his past as a coup-monger and for appointing too many soldiers to his government. To counter fears he was creating a military regime, he had brought in generally respected, high-profile civilians from the left such as Rangel and Miquilena to fill top posts. They could provide political experience to help run a government where many officials, including the president himself, were holding office for the first time. On the other hand, Arias,

Urdaneta, and Acosta Chirinos were his old comrades. Without them, he never would have become president in the first place. But he could not have it both ways. As one newspaper columnist put it, Chávez had two choices: cutting off his left hand or his right. In the end, he went with the civilians.

Rather than petering out, the mudslinging got worse. Urdaneta's accusations against Miquilena included charges that he was a shareholder in a printing company that won a noncompetitive contract from the National Electoral Council to print one million copies of Venezuela's new constitution. He also claimed Miquilena helped a friend win insurance contracts with eleven different state agencies, and that Miquilena pressured him to get the DISIP to sign one, too.

Miquilena fired back. He claimed Urdaneta was building an eight-bedroom, four-level chalet in an exclusive district of Caracas with slush funds taken from the DISIP before he was fired. Eventually, the attorney general opened investigations against both men. In the end, neither was convicted.

As the mudslinging intensified, Chávez's three former military comrades decided the president was not going to "rectify" and that they would break definitively with him — at least for now, since politics in Venezuela was a funny game of constantly revolving enemies and allies. On March 10 they held another press conference in the city of Maracay. They were joined by other rebels from the 1992 coup attempts, including retired General Francisco Visconti Osorio and Captain Gerardo Márquez. William Izarra, the air force pilot who studied at Harvard and founded the rebel cell ARMA, also came.

The former soldiers released a "Declaration of Maracay" criticizing Chávez's government. They pledged to fight corruption, bureaucracy, and demagoguery, and curb attempts to politicize the military. They vowed to protect private property and decentralize power. They said their "sea of happiness" would be built here in Venezuela, and not be modeled after Castro's Cuba.

Then Arias dropped another bombshell: He would run for president against Chávez. The new constitution had reset the clock on all public offices, requiring elected officials to revalidate their term in office in a nationwide "mega election" scheduled for late May. In all, sixty-two hundred public posts from president to local mayor were to be decided. Arias issued a blistering attack on the man who was once his soul brother, was now his opponent, and would later become his ally again. He accused him of demagoguery, of getting in bed with the corrupt elites, of encouraging poor people to rob instead of work. He warned that Venezuela could become another Cuba.

> We do not believe we rebelled or suffered deaths and injuries so that a person could disguise himself in Fidel Castro's shirt, and we want to say it clearly. We respect Fidel, but on his island. We can negotiate with Fidel and with the Cubans, respecting their revolution, but our revolution we will construct here, without advice from abroad . . . No one can give us an example from that sea of happiness . . . We don't believe in authoritarianism. We don't believe that you can repeat in Venezuela that tendency to concentrate power and remain in power. No revolution can be tied to a single person. That has been the dilemma, friends, what to do about this. The president doesn't listen.

It was a devastating attack by the man who helped lead the February 4 rebellion. Chávez did not take it passively. The two men engaged in a bitter electoral campaign. Arias ran ads showing chickens, implying Chávez was a coward because he'd never left his post the night of February 4 to attack Miraflores while his comrades were under fire and dying. Chávez shot back, mocking Arias's decision to accept a post in Caldera's government distributing milk to pregnant women. It was a job for a woman, he implied, not a real man.

The real debate, though, was not about who was more macho but about where Chávez was taking the country. Was he heading down the road to another dictatorship like Cuba, as Arias and others charged? Or was he creating a truly participatory democracy that served the needs of the poor majority for the first time in Venezuela's history?

Chávez provided plenty of ammunition for his detractors who believed he was simply another authoritarian *caudillo*, a classic Latin American strongman with little patience for democratic niceties. He was a former coup leader who palled around with Fidel Castro, wrote letters to Carlos the Jackal, wore his combat uniform, employed military metaphors, pressed to extend the presidential term, and appointed military men to his government. The spectacle of congressional members clawing their way over the fence the previous August created the impression there was no Congress. The temporary mini Congress that replaced it in December lacked opposition members. Chávez added fuel to the fire a few months later when he visited Saddam Hussein, becoming the first world leader to visit the Iraqi dictator since the end of the Gulf War.

Yet to argue that Chávez was installing a dictatorship was far-fetched. Unlike Castro's Cuba, it simply lacked the characteristics of a totalitarian state.

He was elected in free and fair elections, and won three more referenda to write and approve a new constitution. The jails held no political prisoners. No opposition parties were outlawed. No newspapers, television networks, or radio stations were censored, even though the majority were virulently opposed to Chávez. Private property was respected. The government for now was not nationalizing entire industries the way Castro did, although Chávez did start moving to nationalize a few companies in early 2007. "Not even his staunchest critics can impugn the democratic foundation of Chávez's power," reported *Newsweek*, which named him "Latin American of the Year."

Even the US ambassador, John Maisto, contended that Chávez's revolution was taking place through democratic channels. "Whether or not President Chávez's 'revolution' has been good for Venezuela, no one can question its democratic legitimacy," he said. An article Maisto wrote was titled "Democracy Standing Tall in Venezuela."

Still, it did not mean Chávez was treading lightly. He was on a mission to break up a mafia. It was not a job for the weak-willed. Chávez played hardball, and his opponents didn't like it. A typical example of how he sought to dismantle a corrupt political and economic apparatus and remain within the bounds of democracy was his relationship with the media. Chávez did not hold back in blasting what he considered biased coverage. He claimed the media rarely reported anything positive or balanced about his government. He complained of an "international smear campaign."

His critiques often were justified. In an article published nearly two years after it had declared Chávez "Latin American of the Year" with a government of unquestionable democratic foundations, *Newsweek* ran another article titled "Is Hugo Chávez Insane?" It quoted a political opponent from the discredited Democratic Action Party asserting that "he's a psychopath." The *St. Petersburg Times* picked up the theme. Its story, "Venezuelan Leader's Sanity in Question," described Chávez as "a man many of his countrymen regard as being dangerously unhinged."

The media's coverage of Chávez gave Venezuelans and the world a distorted, one-sided picture. As Venezuelan political scientist Margarita López Maya put it: "The national print media and television opinion programs reflected . . . a reality almost diametrically opposed to that expressed by the elections and polls. The criticism of Chávez was ferocious, the rejection permanent."

Despite the media's unbridled, all-out attack on Chávez, international media watchdog groups accused him of threatening freedom of expression. They charged that a provision in the constitution guaranteeing citizens the right to information that is "opportune, truthful and impartial" was a recipe for government censorship. The government contended it was aimed at curbing outrageous abuses and fostering more honest and ethical journalism in a country that essentially lacked libel laws.

The conflict left its casualties. That May, Venevisión, owned by media mogul Gustavo Cisneros, yanked its popular morning program, 24 Hours, off the air. Its host, Napoleón Bravo, was an acerbic critic of Chávez's government and previous administrations. Venevisión initially replaced 24 Hours with cartoons.

Bravo's wife was Ángela Zago, the former communist guerrilla and constitutional assembly member who wrote the best-selling book The Rebellion of the Angels about the 1992 coup. By the time of the 24 Hours controversy, she had split with Chávez and was working briefly on Francisco Arias Cárdenas's campaign.

Venevisión said it was promoting Bravo, who moved temporarily to Miami to work on the network's cable channel. The government denied it pressured Venevisión to fire him. But his transfer provoked an uproar among journalists, politicians, and television personalities. Five hundred staged a protest march in Caracas. Eventually Bravo and Zago returned to Venezuela and were linked to the opposition to Chávez.

A month earlier, the president faced more protest from the media. When he showed up at a news conference in Maracay, reporters refused to ask him questions. Instead radio journalist Amira Muci stood up, looked directly at Chávez, and said, "In view of your repeatedly disrespectful attitude, and your assessment of our questions as irrelevant, we, as serious professionals of the media . . . have decided not to pose

Hugo Chávez and his brother Adán in their hometown of Sabaneta.

Chávez grew up half believing his great-grandfather Pedro Pérez Delgado (on the right), also known as Maisanta, was a blood-thirsty outlaw. But a book by a Barinas doctor and his own investigations later revealed another depiction of Maisanta, who became one of his heroes.

As a cadet in Venezuela's military academy with a growing admiration for Simón Bolívar, Chávez was chosen for a special trip to Peru in 1974 to mark the 150th anniversary of the battle of Ayacucho. The sojourn provided his first direct exposure to a social experiment launched by a progressive, although dictatorial, military man, General Juan Alvarado Velasco. Chávez, third from right, enjoyed a dinner out with other cadets from around Latin America.

Besides delving into the life of Simón Bolívar, Chávez found time for a plethora of activities as a cadet and young officer, including serving as master of ceremonies for beauty pageants. This one took place in 1975 during his final year as a cadet.

Chávez holds a Venezuelan flag during a ceremony at a plaza in Barinas in 1976.

Chávez on a training mission in 1982.

The Caracazo food riots on February 27, 1989, and subsequent repression by government troops left more than one thousand people dead and galvanized Chávez and his Bolivarian comrades into action. Three years later, they emerged from secrecy and launched a coup against the man who ordered the repression, President Carlos Andrés Pérez. (Francisco Solorzano)

In his heyday President Carlos Andrés Pérez could make women faint at rallies, but he became despised after the bloodshed of the Caracazo, one of the worst massacres in modern Latin American history. Yet even after the killings and his impeachment as president, his home state of Táchira remained a bastion of support. In 1996, fans mobbed him. (AP/ Wide World Photos)

Chávez, then a lieutenant colonel, shocked the nation by leading a coup on February 4, 1992, and became a hero to millions for trying to overthrow President Carlos Andrés Pérez. His famous seventy-two-second speech, in which he declared live on national television that the rebels had not achieved their goals *por ahora,* for now, catapulted him to stardom. Still, Venezuela's traditional political class was horrified by the revolt, and foreign governments condemned it. (AP/Wide World Photos)

A day after the coup, photographers caught a glimpse of military officials transferring Chávez at the Fort Tiuna military base. Ever the voracious reader, he carried that day's newspapers and other material. (AP/ Wide World Photos)

5

Rather than villains, Chávez, Francisco Arias Cárdenas (second from right) and other rebels were seen by many Venezuelans as dashing heroes while they spent two years in prison for launching the coup. Newspaper reporters and photographers were able to sneak in with their equipment and photograph the rebels in heroic, wholesome-looking poses.

After his release from prison in 1994, Chávez hit the road to drum up support for his Bolivarian movement. Far from apologizing for the coup, he celebrated it. In 1997, while still debating whether to turn to electoral politics in Venezuela's corruption-ridden system, he marked the fifth anniversary of the uprising by holding a rally in Caracas. (AP/Wide World Photos)

Former Miss Universe Irene Sáez, a six-foot-one strawberry blonde who had a successful run as mayor of an upscale section of Caracas, was the odds-on favorite to win the 1998 presidential race — until she started opening her mouth and gushing platitudes. Chávez, in contrast, came soaring in from out of nowhere — at least in the eyes of the establishment — and catapulted to the top of the polls with his fiery calls for revolution. (AP/Wide World Photos)

Political analysts, diplomats and pollsters didn't give Chávez a chance of winning in early 1998, but before long he was attracting massive crowds. When he asked people at this rally to raise their hands if they agreed with his 1992 coup attempt, a sea of hands went up. (AP/Wide World Photos)

As a boy, Chávez dreamed of playing major league baseball. He never made it, but achieved the next best thing in 1999, when as Venezuela's newly elected president he threw out the first ball at a New York Mets game at Shea Stadium. Chávez took the Big Apple by storm, seducing Wall Street investors and providing play-by-play commentary for Venezuelans back home during the game. (AP/Wide World Photos)

Ever the master of the spontaneous, unpredictable gesture, Chávez left bodyguards and businessmen accompanying him on a trip to China in October 1999 breathless as he took off jogging up the Great Wall of China. Chávez later disarmed Vladimir Putin by dropping into a karate stance when they first met to show he knew the Soviet leader was a black belt. (AP/Wide World Photos)

A master communicator, Chávez quickly sought to exploit his talents by starting his own weekly, live radio program, *Hello, President*. Before long he expanded the Sunday program to television, and by 2007 turned it into a two-night-a-week affair. (AP/Wide World Photos)

While Venezuela's upper-class despised and mocked Chávez, the massive underclass worshipped him. In dirt-poor barrios such as Nueva Tacagua, where North American Maryknoll missionaries worked and residents lived in tin shacks, Chávez was a demigod. People hung portraits of him on their walls and vowed to defend him to the death. (Noah Friedman-Rudovsky)

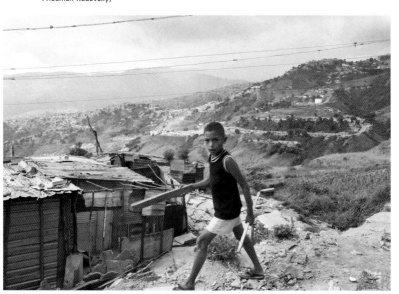

Mudslides in December 1999 on the Caribbean coast near Caracas left an estimated fifteen thousand people dead in the worst natural disaster in Venezuela in at least a century. Yet in many ways it was one of Chávez's finest hours as president. He took personal command of the rescue and recovery operation in Vargas state, gave nightly updates to the mourning nation on television, and barely slept. The navy sent in ships to pull thousands of people out of the disaster zone. (Agencia Bolivariana de Noticias)

Three days after the tragedy struck, Chávez personally gave instructions to paratroopers before they were sent into the disaster zone. (Agencia Bolivariana de Noticias)

Fidel Castro turned into Chávez's main mentor, provoking worries among Venezuela's upper classes that Chávez planned to turn the oil giant into a twenty-first-century version of the Communist-run island. But while Chávez and Castro were allies, sharp differences separated their social experiments. (AP/Wide World Photos)

When floods hit the frontier town of Guasdualito in Apure state in 2002, Chávez visited to listen to residents' concerns and help direct relief efforts. (Agencia Bolivariana de Noticias)

Chávez's empathy with Venezuela's majority poor was legendary and flowed naturally out of his own upbringing in poverty in Barinas state. He hugged an old woman on Margarita Island in 2001. (Agencia Bolivariana de Noticias)

Chávez reached out to Venezuela's five hundred thousand indigenous people, pushing for a new constitution that recognized their languages and economic systems, and reserving three spots in the Constitutional Assembly for representatives from their tribes. Still, his environmental policies early in his presidency did not please some indigenous leaders. In 1999 he visited members of the Piaroa tribe in Bolivar state. (Agencia Bolivariana de Noticias)

Chávez provoked rabid hatred among many people in Venezuela's moneyed classes who believed he was destroying the country with a half-baked experiment in communism. A protestor painted herself in the colors of Venezuela's flag in the days before a recall referendum in August 2004, during which Chávez's presidency was on the line. (Noah Friedman-Rudovsky)

In Venezuela's barrios and in the impoverished countryside, Chávez generated wild enthusiasm. Fans cheered him in August 2004 as he went to cast his vote in the recall referendum. (Noah Friedman-Rudovsky)

After opposition leaders illegally changed the route of a massive anti-Chávez protest march on April 11, 2002, protestors closed in on Miraflores Palace and clashed with National Guardsmen. While most protestors were peaceful, some tossed bottles, rocks, chairs, tubes, watermelon rinds, and pieces of brick they tore off the nearby Fermín Toro High School. National Guardsmen responded with tear gas and in some cases bullets. On nearby Baralt Avenue and Llaguno Bridge, both opposition marchers and Chávez supporters fell injured or dead — many from shots fired by snipers during the most controversial and defining moment of Chávez's presidency. (Agencia Bolivariana de Noticias)

After Chávez disappeared from public view for nearly two days during the 2002 coup, thousands of his supporters streamed down from Caracas's barrios and surrounded the Miraflores Presidential Palace to demand his return. Some hung a sheet on the gates outside the palace asking, "Where is Chávez? Let him speak." Chávez would soon make a miraculous return to the palace and the presidency. (Gustavo Frisneda/Cadena Capriles)

Chávez disappeared for two days during the April 2002 coup, and made a miraculous return to the Miraflores Presidential Palace early in the morning of April 14, 2002. For his supporters, it was as if he had risen from the dead. (AP/Wide World Photos)

Chávez opponents paralyzed the oil industry in December 2002 in an attempt to strangle the economy and force him out of office. Massive oil tankers like the *Pilín León* dropped anchor and refused to transport oil. Chávez had to pull captains out of retirement to get the ships moving again. (AP/Wide World Photos)

Chávez in a thoughtful moment during a *Hello, President* program in 2001. (Agencia Bolivariana de Noticias)

Simon Bolívar was never far from Chávez's thoughts. During a *Hello, President* broadcast in 2003, a portrait of the Liberator gazed down on the man who hoped to fulfill his dream of a united and more just Latin America. (Agencia Bolivariana de Noticias)

any questions this afternoon." The president was left speechless. He got up and stormed out.

Muci and the head of the press workers' union, Gregorio Salazar, later acknowledged there was no direct censorship by Chávez. No media outlets were closed or reporters jailed. But they believed Chávez was trying to intimidate them. They asserted that his pointed attacks on journalists and media owners could incite his enraged followers to physically attack reporters and cameramen on the streets — which eventually some did.

Chávez consequently directed more of his attacks against the media owners themselves and urged his supporters not to attack reporters. "Our criticism is against manipulation by the owners of the media," he said. "I will not accept aggression against any journalists who are only doing their job."

As Chávez's battle with the media intensified, the presidential campaign heated up as well. The two former "blood brothers" went at each other mercilessly. Chávez, with a healthy lead in the polls, refused to debate Arias. So Arias took as many shots as he could. He declared that Chávez's "unpleasant, thoughtless comments" sometimes gave the impression he suffered "problems of mental equilibrium."

Chávez fought back. He called Arias a "traitor" who was bought off by "the rancid oligarchy." On his Sunday radio program he suggested that Arias was angry because Chávez had not selected him as his vice president. "It's a good thing I didn't pick him. Can you imagine, having a traitor for vice president?"

The media painted Arias as the more moderate of the candidates. Pro-business and pro–United States, he was depicted as the man who would lure foreign investment, decentralize power, distance the country from Castro, end Chávez's rich-versus-poor class warfare, smooth relations with the Catholic Church, bring good management to government, and provide Venezuela with mature leadership minus the president's antics.

But even though he publicly distanced himself from the traditional parties, in the eyes of many Arias was the candidate of the oligarchy who was going to roll back the Bolivarian Revolution. Even Carlos Andrés Pérez endorsed him. More introverted and distant in a Caribbean land where emotions ran hot, Arias lacked Chávez's charisma and thundering rhetoric. He was an ineffective campaigner and orator. Polls put

Chávez ahead by as many as 20 percentage points. He had not one iota of doubt he was going to win. "Even a rock knows that," he said.

His candidacy was not without problems. His Patriotic Pole was suffering internal divisions. Angered by Arias's candidacy and the decision by Urdaneta and Acosta Chirinos to run for governor in Aragua and Falcon states, Chávez named his own slate of candidates for seventeen of the twenty-three governorships up for grabs. His former colleagues were not among them. The Movement to Socialism and Homeland for All (PPT) were angry Chávez did not endorse some of their gubernatorial candidates, and pulled out of the coalition — although some members would eventually be back.

Chávez was also vulnerable because of the economy's weak performance despite a quadrupling of oil prices since his election. He blamed his predecessors and asked Venezuelans for more time. He argued that he had inherited the controls of a "plane with the engines burned out." He promised to usher in a "Venezuelan golden age." Most Venezuelans believed him. There was only one problem: The voting mechanism was a mess.

The "mega-election" called for a breathtaking vote unprecedented in Venezuelan and probably Latin American history. Some sixty-two hundred posts, including president, congressmen, governors, local mayors, and thousands of delegates to local assemblies, were on the ballot. The number of candidates was astonishing: thirty-five thousand. It was so complicated, Chávez and his allies came up with a yellow rectangular "key" listing the names of candidates they backed. Most supporters had no idea who many of them were.

Three days before the scheduled vote on Sunday, May 28, the Supreme Court suspended the elections. Computer glitches were hobbling a new electronic balloting system. The decision was an embarrassment for the government. Chávez and others contended that the Omaha, Nebraska–based company in charge of the machines was part of a "destabilizing campaign." The company said it was overwhelmed by eleven thousand requested changes to the ballots. Some international observers praised the postponement, saying it would help ensure a fair vote.

Chávez's detractors charged that the National Electoral Council, handpicked by Miquilena, was incompetent. Its ten members and alternates included Miquilena's daughter and former personal secretary. They openly admitted they had no experience organizing an election, which they saw as an advantage in Venezuela with its past corruption-tainted votes. The day after the mega election was supposed to take place, the entire council resigned in disgrace.

The election was rescheduled for July 31. The campaign started again.

The extra time did not allow Arias and the opposition to make up ground in the polls, as some had predicted. Chávez romped home to victory — again. He took 59.8 percent of the vote, even higher than the 56.2 percent he'd garnered in 1998. He won in every state except Zulia, an even better performance than 1998 when he won in eighteen of twenty-four states. His allies made a strong showing in the governors' races, too. The Patriotic Pole took fourteen out of twenty-two races outright and seventeen in all, including victories by the PPT and MAS, which were to return in part to Chávez's side. AD, in contrast, saw its number of governorships drop from eight to two. COPEI fell from five to one. Proyecto Venezuela and Caldera's Convergencia clung to one each.

Chávez's forces did well in the National Assembly races too, although they did not completely dominate. They took 105 of 165 seats. That was less than the two-thirds majority needed to approve appointments to posts including the Supreme Court and the attorney general, pass the budget, and approve other items. The Chavistas would face real opposition and be forced to negotiate at times. "A balance of power has been restored," declared *Tal Cual* editor Teodoro Petkoff. "Now we have to see how Chávez responds."

That night a euphoric Chávez appeared on the Balcón del Pueblo at Miraflores. Speaking to thousands of ecstatic supporters, he quoted the late Chilean poet Pablo Neruda as saying "Simón Bolívar awakes every hundred years." Then Chávez added: "You, the Venezuelan people, have awoken as a result of this process of revolutionary change." It was a stunning victory. The economy was a mess — unemployment was 18 percent, and the recession, in place since the start of his presidency, showed few signs of easing. Yet Chávez won by 3 percentage points more than his victory in 1998. It was a remarkable achievement to maintain his popularity amid such a difficult backdrop.

Legitimate concerns about Chávez persisted among the opposition and even some of those sympathetic to him. He was largely a one-man show, with the coalition that supported him lacking well-defined, long-term goals. Given his military background and the large number of officers he appointed, some feared he was going to militarize the government and turn his back on democratic rules. Others worried he might "limit himself to an aggressive discourse in favor of social change, while doing little to alleviate the lot of the poor in concrete ways." The Plan Bolívar 2000 was useful as a temporary emergency measure. But now Chávez had to move beyond that and the focus on dismantling the corrupt political establishment. He needed to turn his attention to the economy and pursue more long-term, structural solutions to mass poverty.

His supporters were hopeful and gave him their full backing. "I have nothing to lose but hunger," one man said as he stood outside a market to vote for Chávez that Sunday. But more sinister forces in Venezuela were already looking for a way to derail the president.

The new constitution gave soldiers the right to vote in Venezuela for the first time. It also assigned the army the role of "active partic- ipation in national development," although soldiers were to refrain from "acts of propaganda or political proselytizing." Chávez himself encouraged soldiers to speak out in public if they discovered evidence of wrongdoing in public institutions. It was an unprecedented liberty in Latin American militaries.

Some soldiers took up Chávez on his offer, only not in a way he expected. A few weeks after Chávez made his announcement, a National Guard captain, Luis García Morales, asked for an interview on the tele- vision station Globovision. Instead of airing the interview, the station sent it to the defense minister. In it, García Morales called for Chávez to resign. He also announced the formation of a military-civilian "Venezuelan Patriotic Junta." He insisted the junta favored peaceful civil disobedience and not a coup, but acknowledged that the group had discussed overthrowing Chávez. It had even considered killing him. "A comrade of ours, a sniper, argued that it would be easy to shoot him, and that would be the end of the problem," García Morales said.

Other voices warned of Chávez's presidency ending prematurely through unconstitutional means. Retired general Fernando Ochoa Antich, the defense minister during Chávez's failed February 4, 1992, coup, was one of them. "I don't discount the possibility that there could be a violent outcome," Ochoa Antich said. "I am among those who feel the possibility is high."

In the United States, Elliot Abrams, one of the central figures of Ronald Reagan's dirty wars in Central America in the 1980s, was watching Venezuela and Chávez closely. He didn't like what he was seeing. "The criticisms of him, which so many people in Washington think are obvious, are not obvious to all that many Venezuelans — yet, anyway," said Abrams, who had been Reagan's assistant secretary of state for Latin America. "I don't think his policy is going to change, including his economic policy. At the same time, I don't see how it can possibly succeed. It seems to me that bad days are ahead."

Before long, Abrams would be back in power in Washington, DC.

**18**

# Oil Man

Barely a week after his latest electoral triumph, Chávez set off on his next mission: reviving the Organization of Petroleum Exporting Countries. He wanted a "fair" price on the world market for the product that accounted for three-quarters of Venezuela's exports and provided more than half the country's income. Boosting oil prices and bringing OPEC back to life were two of Chávez's chief goals and, as it turned out, chief successes during his first eighteen months in office.

When he first won the presidency, the world petroleum market was suffering its worst price collapse in at least fifty years. Venezuelan crude was selling for as little as $7.66 a barrel in December 1998. The eleven-member OPEC was beset by internal bickering and a failure to adhere to quotas. Iraq and Iran had even gone to war against each other. Venezuela was one of the worst quota busters. Many believed it might simply drop out of OPEC. Since its founding in 1960, the organization had held only one summit in its forty-year history. That was in 1975, some twenty-five years back. OPEC was on the brink of collapse.

One of Chávez's first moves as president was to shore up the price of Venezuelan crude. He dispatched his energy and mines minister, former leftist guerrilla and Causa R congressman Alí Rodríguez, to negotiate a deal with Saudi Arabia and Mexico. He wanted them to cut back on production and reverse the slide in prices. Saudi Arabia was the world's biggest producer of petroleum, pumping out 7.4 million barrels a day. Mexico was not an OPEC member but was nonetheless a major oil producer. Venezuela was the top foreigner supplier to the United States after Canada, and the third largest exporter in the world after Saudi Arabia and Iran. Its oil reserves were the largest in the world outside the Middle East. The state oil company, Petroleos de Venezuela, had six refineries in the United States. It also owned Citgo, which had the franchise for 14,500 American gas stations.

After an OPEC meeting in March 1999 Rodríguez convinced Saudi Arabia and Mexico to cut production by two million barrels a day. Venezuela contributed half a million barrels' worth of that reduction. The move would bring it back in line with its OPEC ceiling of 2.72 million barrels a day. The agreement by the three countries encouraged other OPEC members to follow suit and adhere to quotas. Prices quickly started rising.

By one year later, March 2000, Venezuelan crude hit a nine-year high of $34.37 a barrel. The boost in prices gave the country a windfall of $4.5 billion for 1999. Exports surged 33 percent to $16 billion. The soaring prices helped offset some of Venezuela's economic troubles. After shrinking 7.2 percent in 1999, the nation's economy began to show signs of reversing the decline in 2000. It had grown by 1.5 percent by the middle of the year and 3.2 percent by the end of the year. Inflation dropped to 14.2 percent, the lowest figure in fifteen years.

Chávez also hoped to avoid the vagaries of the world oil market by enhancing an economic stabilization fund established by Caldera's government. The idea was to bank money when prices were high and use it when they plummeted, providing the government with a steadier source of income. The previous government had established a benchmark of $14 a barrel. Any time prices rose above that figure, extra revenue was channeled into the fund. Rodríguez took an even more conservative approach, dropping the benchmark to $9. As the world oil market boomed, millions flowed into the fund.

With prices solidifying, Chávez set his sights on his other goal: unifying the nearly collapsed Organization of Petroleum Exporting Countries. He had a grand vision. He wanted to organize the second summit in the group's history. And he wanted to hold it in Caracas. He prepared to make another breakneck world tour, this time to personally invite the head of each OPEC nation to the meeting. The list included Saddam Hussein, the dictator of Iraq. He was, after all, an OPEC member.

Reviving OPEC was a crucial component to Chávez's plans for transforming Venezuela. Oil was the lifeblood of the country — for better or for worse. Some people called it the "devil's excrement." It had brought great riches to the country. It had also brought corruption, distorted values, dependency on a single product, and an economic roller-coaster ride as the price of a barrel fluctuated wildly. Some people thought it infected Venezuelans with a sense of easy money. "Venezuelans lost their values," remarked a US native who spent years working as a translator for an oil company in Venezuela. "It's much better to be street smart and cunning than to be hard working and honest." One of Venezuela's most famous writers and intellectuals, Arturo Uslar Pietri, believed historians might one day sum up his country's history in nine words: Columbus discovered it. Bolívar liberated it. Oil rotted it.

When Spanish explorers first showed up on the shores of Lake Maracaibo in Zulia state in western Venezuela, they barely noticed the thick black stuff oozing from the sandy earth. Local Indians used it to caulk canoes, to make candles, and even for medicine. It wasn't until the advent of the twentieth century and the mass production of automobiles that Venezuela's potential reserves of oil attracted much attention.

While Venezuelans were carrying out scientific studies of oil to promote its development as early as 1839, the first major deposit was discovered and the first well was drilled in 1914. The companies initially on the scene were foreign: John D. Rockefeller's Standard Oil of New Jersey (later Exxon) and Shell. The boom in oil came eight years later, in December 1922, when a Venezuelan subsidiary of Shell "blew out" a well on the east coast of the lake. Dozens of foreign companies flocked to the country. Hundreds of Christmas tree derricks soon rose from the water, providing the image most of the world had of Venezuela. Boomtowns sprouted up amid a "black gold rush." Engineers from Texas and Oklahoma provided the technical expertise. Venezuelans provided the muscle. It was a frontier environment of makeshift towns. Brothels outnumbered food stores in some places. Prostitutes earned nicknames like "Pipeline" or "Four Valves."

By 1928 Venezuela was the world's second largest oil producer and its top exporter. Standard Oil and Shell remained the major players, controlling 85 percent of oil extractions in Venezuela by the late 1930s. The Americans brought not only their expertise in extracting oil but also their culture. They introduced baseball. The oil companies were so integrated into Venezuelan society, some people even named their children *Esso*, Exxon's trade name.

Still, much of the profits remained in the hands of the foreigners, who were given major tax breaks by the dictator Juan Vicente Gómez and other leaders who followed him. To regain control of the industry, President Carlos Andrés Pérez nationalized it in 1976. It was a major event in the nation's history, and a source of immense pride for most people. The new state oil company, Petroleos de Venezuela, took over eleven thousand oil wells, eleven oil refineries, and fourteen oil tankers. It also obtained pipelines, port terminals, and numerous office buildings.

The money poured in. Between 1973 and 1983 alone, Venezuela earned more than $150 billion from oil, a staggering amount for a country of sixteen million people. Yet despite the boom in prices in the 1970s and early 1980s, and the transfer of the industry to the government, the bulk of the money never seemed to trickle down to the masses. Venezuelans did enjoy the highest standard of living in Latin America, and even working-class families could afford to eat out in modest restaurants once a week. But the elites commandeered most of the profits, accruing fabulous fortunes. Decades earlier, Uslar Pietri had urged the nation to "sow the oil" by diversifying its industries and spreading the wealth. This never happened.

By 1975 Juan Pablo Pérez Alfonso, the Venezuelan energy minister who was a founding father of OPEC, wrote a visionary book titled *We Are Sinking in the Devil's Excrement*. As oil prices plunged during the 1980s and 1990s and one crisis after the other hit the nation — from Black Friday in 1983 to the Caracazo in 1989 to the coups in 1992 to Pérez's impeachment a year later — his warnings seemed especially prescient.

By the time Caldera took over the presidency in 1994, a proposed *apertura* — opening of the oil industry — was gaining momentum. Venezuela was inviting private international companies back in. There was even talk of disbanding PDVSA and privatizing the entire industry. Nationalization, critics argued, hadn't worked.

The night Chávez won the presidency in December 1998, he charged in his first press conference that PDVSA, the company that was supposed to help "sow the oil," had instead turned into a "state within a state" — an entity unto itself that was beyond the control of the government. It fostered a "gold card culture," he continued, among an elite corps of executives and managers who were out of touch with the masses and enjoyed a lifestyle far removed from most Venezuelans. He vowed to take control of the company and subject it to the oversight of the

Ministry of Energy and Mines as originally intended. Alí Rodríguez was his point man. The answer to Venezuela's woes, Chávez believed, was not the oil opening but rather regaining control of PDVSA, redirecting its resources to benefit the majority poor, and resuscitating a moribund OPEC.

By August 2000 Chávez had set off on his mission to remake the organization. He planned to personally visit each of the ten other OPEC members and invite their heads of state to a summit in Caracas in late September. The visit to Hussein attracted the most attention. Chávez was the first head of state to enter Iraq since the United Nations had imposed sanctions as punishment for its 1990 invasion of Kuwait and aimed at ridding the country of weapons of mass destruction.

The United States, which waged war against Iraq a decade earlier, was aghast. Ending its policy of public restraint regarding Chávez, the State Department called his visit "particularly galling." State Department spokesman Richard Boucher said it "bestows an aura of respectability upon Saddam Hussein which he clearly does not deserve." He questioned why Chávez would want to elevate the prestige of a dictator "who has invaded neighboring countries, occupied neighboring countries, persecuted his own people and violated human rights." Chávez was unfazed. Before the trip, he said almost gleefully, "Imagine what the Pharisees will say when they see me with Saddam Hussein."

While the United States was livid, the Venezuelans argued that Chávez was on a geopolitical tour to strengthen OPEC and that he could hardly bypass one of its key members. They also accused the Americans of hypocrisy. The United States had long maintained cordial relations with military and communist regimes such as China when it suited their purposes. In Latin America, it had even helped create or bankroll some of the most brutal regimes throughout the twentieth century, such as General Augusto Pinochet's in Chile or the Somozas' in Nicaragua. The United States, in fact, was an ally of Saddam Hussein during the 1980s, when he received a visit from Donald Rumsfeld. It also maintained close ties to oil-rich Saudi Arabia, hardly a bastion of democracy. In Afghanistan in the 1980s, Osama bin Laden worked alongside CIA-backed forces as the United States and the Soviet Union clashed in the Cold War using surrogates. Realpolitik, as Henry Kissinger knew well, could be a rough business.

Chávez did not underplay the trip to Baghdad. He took two helicopter rides from Tehran and then crossed the Iraqi border in a limousine provided by Iran since flights into Iraq were prohibited under the sanctions. Then he was flown by helicopter to Saddam International Airport in Baghdad, where he met with Hussein. The Iraqis rolled out the red carpet for Chávez, taking full political advantage of the breach in the embargo. A large headline in a state-run newspaper trumpeted, "Welcome President Chávez." Another government daily devoted more than half a page to a story praising Chávez's "courageous decision to visit Iraq." The newspaper added that "the Venezuelan president challenges sanctions and decides to visit Iraq even if he had to do it riding a camel." Saddam himself gave Chávez a tour of the city. A photograph of him behind the wheel and Chávez riding shotgun flashed around the world.

The US and international media made much of the twelve-hour visit, and never let the world forget it in subsequent stories about Chávez. It became part of the boilerplate paragraphs about him, along with his friendship with Fidel Castro. Yet besides the US government, few other countries seemed perturbed, including Kuwait itself.

In Venezuela it was not even front-page news. The country was more preoccupied with the installation of the new National Assembly. Some of Chávez's most vociferous critics failed to raise a protest. "I think if the trip is seen as being for purely commercial interest there is no problem," opposition Congressman Gerardo Blyde said. "Chávez can go to Iraq and not be supporting its political regime." Teodoro Petkoff, whose front-page editorials normally blasted Chávez, commented that "the only reason the visit has been a problem is because the United States doesn't like it and that is not a reason. I don't think this trip worries Venezuelans much."

Chávez even picked up some support during his next stop on the itinerary, Indonesia, when he called for an end to the sanctions against Iraq because he believed they were simply hurting innocent civilians. He described how his son Hugo, who accompanied him on the trip, visited a mosque and saw a naked child who was dying from cancer and could not get the drugs needed for treatment. "Who has the right to really let an innocent child die there?" Chávez said in an emotional plea. "Let God have pity on the soul of those who act that way."

After meeting with Chávez, Indonesia's President Abdurrahman Wahid said he now planned to visit Iraq, too, and he also believed the embargo should be lifted. They joined other high-profile critics of the trade sanctions, including the Vatican and former weapons inspector Scott Ritter. Ritter contended Iraq was essentially disarmed and had no weapons of mass destruction. That fact would be borne out after the United States invaded Iraq in 2003 to destroy Saddam's weapons of mass destruction — and couldn't find any.

Despite the controversy over the Iraq visit, many observers saw Chávez's trip as a major international political success. He visited ten countries in as many days, including Saudi Arabia, Kuwait, Qatar, United Arab Emirates, Libya, Nigeria, and Algeria. He convinced all the OPEC nations to send representatives to Caracas, although Hussein and Libya's Moammar Gadhafi had to dispatch stand-ins because of fears their enemies might infiltrate Venezuela and try to kill the two leaders. Chávez had taken a major step toward revitalizing OPEC. His country had already been rewarded for its renewed leadership by members who gave Venezuela the presidency. One US political scientist commented that "in geopolitical terms, the OPEC tour was masterful. It demonstrated that Venezuela was not just a Latin American backwater." Despite the State Department complaints, "more people in the Third World now know about Chávez than they do about any other Latin American leader except Fidel Castro."

That September the summit gripped Caracas for three days. In a scene reminiscent of Carlos Andrés Pérez's "coronation" in 1989, princes, presidents, and sheiks descended on the city from around the world. Central Caracas, notorious for its chaotic traffic jams, fell quiet. Authorities closed off streets around the glittering Teresa Carreño Theater and removed street vendors. Some three thousand soldiers and police patrolled the capital and the winding mountain highway that connects Caracas and the international airport on the Caribbean coast. Helicopters and motorcades ferried delegates back and forth from the theater to their hotels.

The Iranian delegation rented out three floors of the elegant Eurobuilding hotel. They left two empty as a security precaution. Some guests and journalists complained of half-hour delays at metal detectors, but they all gawked as President Mohammad Khatami walked by. He wore a flowing robe, a black cape, and a black turban that signified his descent from Islam's seventh-century prophet Muhammad. Saudi Arabia had the largest delegation, with 380 people. They took over the entire sprawling Melia Hotel.

Intelligence agents with bomb-sniffing German shepherds combed hotel hallways. OPEC had been obsessed with security ever since its oil ministers were kidnapped at the first and only previous summit in 1975 in Vienna, Austria. The kidnapping was orchestrated by Carlos the Jackal, the Venezuelan-born international terrorist Chávez had written to in 1999 as he sat in a Paris prison.

The Venezuelans took pains to make the visitors feel at home. For those from Iran, Saudi Arabia, and other Muslim nations, they rearranged hotel furniture, shifting beds to face away from Mecca, the holy city in Saudi Arabia that Muslims face in prayer five times a day; some observant Muslims never let their feet face Mecca when they sleep. The hotels also prepared food according to Muslim guidelines. The Tamanaco Inter-Continental Hotel offered up an "Arabian Nights" theme in its Cacique restaurant. At night, the government lit up the sky with fireworks to celebrate the historic meeting.

At the summit itself delegates debated the rising oil prices. They blamed taxes, middlemen, and bottlenecks, although OPEC cutbacks in production were also a major factor in the tripling of prices in the past fourteen months or so. The more militant Muslim nations, including Iran, Iraq, and Libya, favored keeping production down and prices up. Pro-US Saudi Arabia advocated the opposite. Chávez stepped into the debate, promoting a "band system" in which prices would be allowed to oscillate between $22 and $28 a barrel but remain relatively stable. Producers would increase or scale back output to keep prices within the band.

Chávez defended the prices set in the band, saying, "What we are asking for is justice." As Arab sheiks, princes, and presidents listened patiently, Chávez, the cartel's only leader of a non-Muslim nation, elaborated on the relationship between oil producers and industrialized nations. "What would they do without oil?" he said. "Where would they be?" The delegates' patience turned to smiles and applause. Chávez pushed on, comparing the cost of various consumer goods including suntan lotion and shampoo with oil. "A barrel of Coca-Cola: $78.80. Milk: $150. Ice: $1,105. Good wine: $1,370." Many of the heads of state nodded and laughed approvingly at the comparison. Several were still chattering about it as they filed out of the auditorium. Days earlier, Chávez told listeners to his call-in radio show, "How nice it would be if they also lowered prices for the things they sell us — computers, medicine, cars, and the interest on foreign debt."

Chávez was working his rhetorical magic on the OPEC delegates, just as he did with Wall Street financiers, shantytown dwellers and anyone else he corralled. But his proposals went beyond a price band for oil. He had a larger vision for OPEC. He wanted the organization to address global poverty, foreign debt, terms of trade, and other issues facing developing nations. He proposed establishing an OPEC bank as a substitute for the IMF. A "Declaration of Caracas" drafted by the delegates urged "developed nations to recognize that the greatest environmental tragedy confronting the world is human poverty."

While some of Chávez's detractors dismissed the summit as little more than talk, many people viewed it as a major success in solidifying an organization that two years earlier seemed on the verge of collapse amid rock-bottom oil prices. The day after it concluded, Iran's president met with Iraq's vice president in the Iranian leader's suite at the Eurobuilding to try to repair frayed relations dating from their 1980–1988 war. It was the highest-level meeting between the two countries since 1997.

To some, Chávez emerged from the summit with enhanced status on the world stage. The Parisian daily *Le Monde* wrote that he passed from being an advocate of "a peaceful revolution against his nation's oligarchy and corrupt political class to the main spokesman for an offensive — this time at the planetary level — against savage capitalism." Days before the summit, rising oil prices forced the United States to tap its strategic reserves for only the third time in its twenty-five-year history. It was preparing to release another one million barrels a day starting in November.

Back in March, President Clinton called Chávez from *Air Force One* while en route to India to ask the Venezuelan leader to increase output. Besides the fact that half of Venezuela's production went to the United States, it was tacit acknowledgment that Chávez was a driving force behind the resurgence of the cartel, which produced 40 percent of the world's crude oil.

His relations with the United States, though, would never be the same after his visit to Iraq. It was the beginning of the end of the US policy of flexibility and constructive engagement. The same month Chávez met with Saddam Hussein, the US ambassador to Venezuela and the chief proponent of the engagement policy, John Maisto, ended his tenure. He was replaced by hard-liner Donna Hrinak, the former ambassador to Brazil. Then, barely a month after the OPEC summit ended, Chávez gave the United States more reason for worry. Another world leader paid a visit to Venezuela.

It was Chávez's budding mentor, Fidel Castro.

Castro had attended Chávez's inauguration in February 1999, but he was among scores of foreign dignitaries traveling to Venezuela for that event. This was to be an official state visit, his first to Venezuela in forty years. The last one he made was in 1959, shortly after the triumph of his revolutionary battle to overthrow Fulgencio Batista. Castro would have Chávez to himself this time, one-on-one. A friendship that began with Chávez's visit to Cuba in December 1994 after his release from prison and deepened with their unforgettable baseball match in November 1999 would be cemented during five days in which the men did everything from play baseball again to sign a crucial oil deal. Chávez said he hoped to "give oxygen to Cuba" with the pact.

Castro arrived on October 26 to a hero's welcome. He and Chávez visited Simón Bolívar's tomb near the San Carlos jail where Chávez had been briefly imprisoned in 1994. Castro also received the keys to the city, and visited a home used by Cuba independence hero José Martí in 1881. Hundreds of admirers waved Cuban and Venezuelan flags and shouted "Welcome Fidel!"

The pair set off for the llanos, lunching with Chávez's father in Barinas and traveling to Chávez's hometown of Sabaneta. Castro visited the small blue-and-white concrete home where Chávez had lived with his grandmother Rosa Inés after they'd eventually moved out of the mud hut across the street. The two leaders walked down the block to Bolívar Plaza, where Castro mounted a stage draped with a banner portraying Cuba revolutionary hero Ernesto "Che" Guevara. He called Sabaneta the "cradle of the Bolivarian revolution" and told a cheering crowd of three thousand that "just like people go to Caracas to visit the house of Bolívar, one day people will come to visit Sabaneta, where Chávez was born."

On a trip to nearby Guanare, Castro impressed farmers with his questions about the minutiae of potash fertilizer and soil ratings. That night, a Saturday, he and Chávez arranged a rematch of their baseball game in Havana, this time in the city of Barquísimeto. Chávez played first base for Venezuela. Castro managed the Cuban squad of retired players until inserting himself as a pinch hitter in the last inning. Oddly dressed in sneakers, a red helmet, and a blue warm-up jacket with his military fatigues underneath, Castro managed a three-and-two count. When the umpire called a third strike, he disputed the call and simply walked to first base. No one argued. Cuba won seventeen to six.

The two spent Sunday on Chávez's radio program *Alo Presidente*. To mark the occasion, producers added an *-s* to the name. The men gabbed for five hours and even sang a song together. They showed signs they would have gone on all day if not for other commitments. Castro praised Chávez for helping to revive OPEC. He also offered indications he viewed the younger leader as his ideological and spiritual heir. "I have confidence in you," Castro said. "At this moment, in this country, there is no one who can substitute for you." He gave Chávez some advice on governing, suggesting that the thousands of Venezuelans who pressed notes into his hands or sent him letters could not look to him to personally solve each of their problems. He had to delegate. "Chávez can't be the mayor of all of Venezuela," Castro said.

He'd given Chávez more advice when he'd addressed the National Assembly a couple of days earlier, urging the younger man to protect himself. "There is no doubt that his enemies here and abroad will try to eliminate him," Castro said. He knew something about the topic. He'd been the target of numerous assassination attempts, most launched by the CIA and Cuban exiles in Miami.

The highlight of the trip in terms of concrete actions came on the final day, when they signed an energy accord. Venezuela agreed to provide Cuba with fifty-three thousand barrels of oil a day on favorable terms. Cuba would be allowed to pay with a mixture of money, goods, and services. It already had 450 doctors living and working in the mudslide disaster zone of Vargas. That would be extended nationwide and turned into one of the hallmarks of Chávez's presidency, *Mision Barrio Adentro* (Inside the Neighborhood). It entailed placing doctors in urban shantytowns and rural villages where few Venezuelan doctors would dare tread. To many poor Venezuelans, that was a revolution in itself.

Cuba could also pay for the oil by treating Venezuelan patients in Cuba, providing vaccines, medical equipment, and aid in producing medicines, and exporting physical education teachers, sports coaches, tourism advisers, and agricultural experts to Venezuela. Or it could pay for some of it with cash, and up to a quarter of it under preferential financing terms. It had fifteen years to pay, with a two-year grace period, a 2 percent interest rate, and prices as low as $20 a barrel — significantly better than the $30 current at the time. The entire deal was worth about $500 million a year. It would supply Cuba with a third of its oil needs. It was a lifesaver for the embattled Cuban regime.

Critics called it a giveaway — and to a human rights abuser, no less. They said the money could be better used building schools, repairing roads, investing in decrepit public hospitals, and paying off the foreign debt. But Venezuela had just re-signed similar agreements with twelve other Caribbean and Central American countries. The pacts dated back to the 1980s when oil giants Mexico and Venezuela offered their poorer neighbors cut-rate oil deals.

Ten months after Castro's visit, he decided to mark the historic occasion of his seventy-fifth birthday not in Cuba but in Venezuela, alongside Chávez. When he landed in Caracas on August 11, 2001, he declared that he "wanted to celebrate my seventy-five years in the land of the Liberator." A beaming Chávez draped his arm around Castro and said, "We welcome our brother, we welcome our friend, we welcome our revolutionary soldier who has been an example of dignity for all the continent."

They took off for Ciudad Bolívar, the "cradle" of South America's independence movement from Spain. It was the eastern Venezuelan city where Simón Bolívar had planned and then launched his famous march across the steamy llanos and up the ice-capped Andes Mountains into Colombia. In the city's central plaza thousands of people laughed at Castro's jokes, cheered his speech, and sang "Happy Birthday." Then he and Chávez flew deep into the Amazon jungle to Canaima National Park. They flew past spectacular Angel Falls, the world's tallest waterfall at 3,212 feet — fifteen times higher than Niagara Falls. They also passed by the mysterious, ancient flat-topped mountains called *tepuis* that inspired Sir Arthur Conan Doyle's classic adventure story *The Lost World*.

Castro called it the best birthday he'd ever celebrated. Still, his friendship with Chávez was complicated, a double-edged sword. Many Venezuelans remembered Castro's support for Marxist Venezuelan guerrillas in the 1960s and still resented it. They wanted nothing to do with a Cuba-style regime in Venezuela. While turning out crowds of supporters, his visit also provoked protests. Other Venezuelans, especially among the underclass, admired him for standing up to the United States. He was a David who had survived forty years of subversion, attempted invasions, and failed assassination plots. Still, even many Venezuelans who viewed Castro as a hero didn't want a communist regime in Venezuela.

Castro had taken pains during his earlier trip in October to ease fears that his Venezuelan ally was going to replicate the Cuban revolution in Venezuela. "It's a lie that Chávez wants to implement the Cuban model in Venezuela," he'd insisted. Some observers believed Castro's talk was not just empty rhetoric or a cover for Chávez. Janet

Kelly, a US-born political analyst and prominent commentator in Venezuela who was not sympathetic to Chávez, believed Venezuela's leader was carving out an independent path despite seeing Castro as an older brother or father figure. Chávez took obvious delight in poking the United States in the eye by flaunting his friendship with the Cuban revolutionary, visiting the pariah Saddam Hussein, or carrying out other provocative acts. But he was not another Castro.

"There is an admiration for Fidel, but it is linked not so much to Cuba's domestic system, which I do not think Chávez is interested in trying out, as it is to adopting some of Fidel's style, such as the David against Goliath stance and the sense of humor that galls the other side," Kelly said. "He is more a student of Fidel the defiant than Fidel the Communist."

In Washington, DC, that was not the view among a new administration about to take office. George W. Bush had squeaked past Al Gore in a disputed presidential election a week after Castro visited Venezuela. To run his Latin America policy, Bush soon recruited several discredited figures from the Iran-contra scandal and the US dirty wars in Central America in the 1980s. Some despised the Cuban leader almost obsessively and were convinced Chávez was the new Fidel Castro. They were alarmed by his open friendship with the Cuban revolutionary, his seeming sympathy for leftist guerrillas in neighboring Colombia, and his criticism of Washington's $1.3 billion Plan Colombia aimed at eradicating drugs and rebels who — like much of Colombian society — benefited from the world's largest cocaine industry. Their sentiments were summed up in a *Washington Post* editorial about Chávez that ran November 2, 2000: "The Next Fidel Castro."

Publicly the Venezuelans maintained a semblance of diplomacy, given the anti-American sentiments many top administration officials harbored over the long and atrocious history of US intervention in Latin America. Foreign Minister José Vicente Rangel, for one, had deep ties to Chile. He would never forget the US-backed coup in 1973 that ended with the overthrow and death of President Salvador Allende. In a statement issued as 2000 drew to a close, Rangel characterized relations between Venezuela and the Clinton administration as "normal and cordial." He added that "the start of relations with the new US administration . . . is seen with optimism and confidence by the government of President Chávez."

That optimism would not last long.

**19**

# First Revolts and the Return
# of the Iran-Contra Crowd

Venezuela's public school system was in a state of collapse when Chávez
took over the presidency. Schools lacked books, paper, and pencils.
Paint peeled off walls. Ceilings leaked. Classrooms overflowed with
children. The dropout rate was alarming — half the students never
finished high school. One in ten never got through elementary school.
Many teachers and principals showed up for work when they felt like it.
Nationwide strikes often shut down the schools for weeks. Even when
they were open, the level of instruction was questionable. "I don't know
what's worse," commented one longtime US Maryknoll missionary,
Lisa Sullivan. "When the schools are on strike, or when they're open."

Chávez made attacking the decay a top priority. One of his first
acts was banning the "registration fee" many public schools improperly
charged parents to enroll their children. The first year the fee was eliminated, an estimated four hundred thousand children who should have
been attending school, but were not, signed up, according to the government. The second year that figure grew to a total of one million.

Chávez also attacked the quality of education. He established five
hundred "Bolivarian schools" during his first two years in office that
served as pilot programs. The schools offered a full eight-hour day as
opposed to the half-day shifts in most public institutions. They provided
students a free breakfast, lunch, and snack every day, free uniforms and
books, and sometimes even computers in the classroom. Many also

offered health care teams of pediatricians, social workers, nutritionists, and psychologists. Chávez poured money into the Bolivarian schools and the system in general. Spending on education grew from 3.3 percent of gross domestic product in 1999 to 5.2 percent in 2001. Teachers' salaries doubled. Libraries filled with books. Government workers or Plan Bolívar 2000 soldiers plugged holes in leaky roofs.

The Bolivarian schools weren't perfect, but they were a vast improvement over most public schools. At one Bolivarian school established on the Fort Tiuna military base in Caracas and initially overseen by an army colonel in a khaki uniform decked out with medals, parents were knocking down the door to get their children in. After its first year of operation, it was at full capacity and had a waiting list of more than sixteen hundred families.

Like most of Chávez's initiatives, this one quickly came under attack from the middle and upper classes and the media. They charged that Chávez wanted to "Cubanize" the schools — including the private ones most of their children attended — and use them to impose a leftist ideology. Their fears were heightened when a former Marxist guerrilla and sociologist named Carlos Lanz helped produce a proposal for the government to overhaul the system and update the curriculum.

By October 2000 Chávez had stepped up his attack on the system. He issued a decree creating a corps of senior-level supervisors empowered to inspect public and private schools and recommend dismissals of teachers and directors in public ones. Chávez's plan, known as Decree 1,011, set off a firestorm among the moneyed classes, who incorrectly claimed that the recommended dismissals could extend to private schools. Along with the supposed "Cubanization," they viewed the decree as a direct intervention in the lives of their children. They adopted a slogan: "Don't Mess with My Kids!"

The government insisted it was not trying to Cubanize the schools, just as it was not trying to Cubanize the economy or political system. Education Minister Héctor Navarro said the government was simply looking to crack down on abuses, like the teacher he discovered in one school who regularly had sex with his teenage students. Navarro believed other reasons also lurked behind the clamor. The corrupt party machines of AD and COPEI still controlled the schools, which they used as a patronage trough to appoint inept, no-show, or abusive teachers and principals.

The opposition to Decree 1,011 coalesced on January 19, 2001. Five thousand parents and teachers marched to protest the reform project.

It was the first major street protest against Chávez and the first time in years — maybe ever — that well-to-do Caraqueños took to the center of grimy downtown Caracas with megaphones and signs. Two weeks later, the marchers were back. This time they headed to the Supreme Court, where they demanded justices strike down Decree 1,011.

Chávez responded two days later by leading his own march of five thousand parents, teachers, and students who supported the reforms. He blasted those opposing the project as a well-off elite who looked upon the majority poor as "scum." The decree, he pledged, "is going to be carried out, and I will be supervisor number one."

In the end Chávez was not supervisor number one. Amid the uproar, the government backed off. It implemented a less controversial reform program, although it kept the Bolivarian school concept and continued to open more. Still, withdrawing Decree 1,011 was Chávez's first major defeat after a string of overwhelming victories.

He was facing growing criticism on other fronts, including his attempted intervention in Venezuela's largest union, the Confederation of Venezuelan Workers (CTV). Long controlled by Democratic Action, the CTV was a bastion of corruption and thuggish tactics. Many workers felt it represented the interests of business owners more than employees. In December 2000 Chávez's forces won a nationwide referendum calling for democratic internal elections in the CTV. But international labor organizations accused the government of illegally intervening in a private union, and of trying to substitute for it a government-controlled organization. Voter abstention in the referendum was high — 77 percent.

CTV leaders abided by the referendum results, and stepped down to make way for direct elections among the rank and file. But they sought revenge against Chávez, launching a series of strikes by oil workers, steel workers, and teachers in early 2001. By October the CTV held direct elections. That in itself was an achievement for the Chávez government. But its candidate, Aristóbulo Istúriz, lost badly to AD's candidate, Carlos Ortega, who headed the oil workers' union, Fedepetrol. The old CTV may have been corrupt, but it also won some benefits for workers over the years. The Chavistas alleged fraud amid high abstention and widespread irregularities, but the results stood.

Instead of unions, Chávez looked to the MBR-200 to focus his political organizing efforts. In June 2001 he announced that he was relaunching the movement. He called on women, peasants, students, "honest" journalists, and other supporters to form "Bolivarian Circles" to defend and propel his peaceful revolution. The move was aimed at revitalizing the MBR-200 and better organizing his disorganized mass of supporters. Some believed he was concerned that the MVR, increasingly under the influence of Luis Miquilena, was engaging in the backroom, Fourth Republic politics his movement was pledged to destroying. Their suspicions increased when Miquilena resigned as minister of the interior in early 2002.

Based loosely on the original study circles Chávez instituted when he started his conspiracy in the army, the Bolivarian Circles were made up of small groups of neighbors, ideally between seven and eleven people. They studied the new constitution, formed sewing cooperatives, ran job training programs, cleaned streets, organized children's sports programs, and conducted literacy classes. Chávez encouraged the groups to apply for government funding for local projects like buying playground equipment or improving roads and bridges. It was part of his notion of active "participatory democracy" as opposed to "representative democracy." By some estimates, a million and a half people, or nearly 10 percent of the country's adult population, eventually joined a circle.

While Chávez saw the circles as democracy in action, his opponents and the media depicted them as the armed and violent shock troops of Chávez's revolution. They compared them to Cuba's Committees for the Defense of the Revolution, neighborhood watchdog groups aimed at stamping out dissent. After Chávez announced the formation of the circles, the opposition blamed them for every incident of street violence that broke out.

In reality, the vast majority of circles were busy filling potholes or studying the thoughts of Simón Bolívar. Some participants were armed, but so were members of the middle and upper classes. Thugs existed on both sides.

While Chávez was encouraging the growth of the Bolivarian Circles, he was also turning his attention to Venezuela's indigenous population. He won praise for helping set aside three seats in the constitutional assembly for representatives of the nation's five hundred thousand Indians, and for helping to pass a constitution that enshrined their rights in unprecedented ways. They included recognition of communal landownership and implementation of bilingual education. He also for the first time in Venezuela's history named an indigenous person to the cabinet with his appointment of Wayuu Indian Atalá Uriana Pocaterra as environmental minister.

But while Chávez was winning accolades, he also had a problem. His predecessor, Rafael Caldera, had opened up half of the pristine Imataca rain forest reserve in southeastern Venezuela to large-scale logging and gold and diamond mining, as well as signing an agreement with Brazil to construct a 470-mile high-voltage electricity line to carry power from the Guri hydroelectric dam in Venezuela into northwest Brazil.

The line was to cut through the nine-million-acre Imataca reserve, home to several indigenous tribes. Twice the size of Switzerland, Imataca was a modern-day Eden boasting a variety of wildlife few places in the world could match: jaguars, pumas, red howler monkeys, neon-colored butterflies, and the world's largest eagle, the endangered harpy. It was also home to Canaima National Park.

The Caldera government saw Imataca as a potential source of vast untapped wealth. It held gold deposits thought to be worth billions of dollars. Over the centuries it had attracted explorers including Sir Walter Raleigh looking for the legendary golden city of El Dorado. The government envisioned dozens of mining companies flocking to the region. It even proposed constructing a five-hundred-room hotel on sacred Pemon lands in Canaima.

By mid-1998 bulldozers and workers with chain saws had started carving a swath through the forest, leveling some of the Pemons' yucca, corn, banana, and pineapple crops. The Pemons reacted quickly. With some wearing red loincloths and their faces streaked with warpaint, they rolled huge logs across the only highway cutting through the region. When workers erected massive steel towers, tribe members snuck out in the middle of the night and knocked some down. As the project progressed, they toppled at least thirty. The government had to send in troops to protect the towers.

Chávez inherited this mess, and in October 2000 said he was willing to talk to the tribes. He also appointed a commission to ensure that the Indians' concerns were acknowledged. But he declared that "the project does not cause ecological damage" and must go forward. Venezuela and Brazil had a legally signed contract that would heavily penalize Venezuela if it was not fulfilled.

The following August, with Fidel Castro at his side, Chávez and Brazilian president Fernando Henrique Cardoso inaugurated the $400 million power line. Business interests were pleased. Environmentalists and some indigenous leaders declared that Chávez had betrayed them.

Less than a month later, events two thousand miles away shook the world.

Muslim terrorists flew airplanes into the World Trade Center in New York City and the Pentagon in Washington, DC. The attack was to dramatically impact relations between the United States and Venezuela.

Two days after the attacks, in a nationally broadcast address Chávez condemned the terrorists' actions and called for a minute of silence in commemoration of the victims. But the following day he also urged the United States not to launch the "first war of the twenty-first century" in response. Two weeks after that, he urged world leaders to search for the causes of terrorism rather than merely hunt down terrorists and punish them.

The United States, of course, was preparing to launch the first war of the twenty-first century. On October 7 it commenced bombing in Afghanistan after the Taliban refused to hand over Osama bin Laden. The United States enjoyed widespread support for the action. But Chávez was disturbed by the civilian "collateral" damage inflicted by the bombings.

He went back on television Monday, October 29, and held up what purportedly were photographs of dead children in Afghanistan. Chávez was sickened. "We must find solutions for the problems of terrorism. We must find the terrorists," he said. Then, lowering his voice, he added: "But not like this." He paused as the camera focused on the grisly photographs. "Look at these children," Chávez continued in a quiet voice. "These children were alive yesterday. They were eating with their parents and a bomb fell on them." He went on: "This has no justification, just like the attacks in New York didn't, either. The killing in Afghanistan must stop . . . You cannot fight terror with terror." He called the United States bombing campaign a "slaughter of innocents."

The US government was enraged. The State Department called Chávez's comments "totally inappropriate." President Bush expressed "regrets" over the statements. That Thursday the United States ordered its ambassador, Donna Hrinak, to Washington for "consultations." Two days later Chávez tried to repair the damage, asserting on his radio program that his comments were misinterpreted. "I want to be your friend," he said in English.

His comments did not repair the damage. The incident marked a turning point in his relationship with the United States. In the eyes of the Bush administration, he was violating one of the president's principal doctrines in the war on terrorism: "Either you are with us, or you are with the terrorists." Even some of Chávez's supporters complained that his comments were inappropriate. "Public relations–wise, he's been screwing up," commented Congressman Cass Ballenger, a Republican from North Carolina who hosted Chávez for a barbecue in his hometown. "I told him the feeling of the American people is that we are at war. I told him you have to watch what you say."

Hrinak spent a week in Washington, where officials convened an unusual interagency review of US relations with Venezuela. Officials from the National Security Agency, the State Department, and the Pentagon met November 5 to November 7. When Hrinak returned to Caracas she asked for a meeting with Chávez. Behind closed doors at Miraflores Palace she started to read a letter sent from Washington. According to Chávez's account, it asked him to publicly and officially retract his statements on the Afghanistan bombings. As Chávez has told it, before Hrinak got far he interrupted her. "You are talking to the head of state of this nation. You are an ambassador in my country. You are out of line. Please leave my office now." Hrinak was shocked; she hadn't expected such a reaction to a request from the most powerful nation on earth. She apologized and asked if she could at least finish reading the letter. Chávez agreed, but when she was done the meeting was over.

The era of the US "watch what Chávez does, not what he says" approach was clearly over. In reality, its demise was inevitable from the day Bush had taken office the previous January. He temporarily named the architect of the engagement policy, John Maisto, as his top envoy to Latin America. But he really had his eye on a hard-line Cuban exile and Cold War warrior who had gained fame during the Central American wars and Iran-contra scandal of the 1980s, was obsessed with overthrowing Fidel Castro, and saw Hugo Chávez as his heir apparent.

Otto Reich had been out of government service since the late 1980s, after the Iran-contra scandal broke. He was a native of Cuba, where his Jewish father had fled from Austria in 1938 to escape the Nazis, and later saw ominous parallels to Hitler as Fidel Castro rose to power. Reich's family soon fled to the United States, where Otto eventually wrote his master's thesis on the totalitarian trademarks of dictatorships.

His credentials as an ultraconservative anti-Castro and anticommunist activist helped land him a series of jobs in President Ronald Reagan's State Department. From 1983 to 1986, at the height of the US-sponsored wars in Central America, Reich served as head of the Office of Public Diplomacy. The office was created in 1983 to counter heavy criticism of Reagan's policies in Central America. One US newspaper described it as essentially a "propaganda and disinformation outfit." Its mission was "gluing black hats on the Sandinistas and white hats" on the US-created and funded contras, a guerrilla army that was trying to overthrow Nicaragua's leftist government and raped, murdered, and pillaged along the way.

Officially his office was part of the State Department, but in fact it reported to the National Security Council, where Lieutenant Colonel Oliver North was running a covert anti-Sandinista program that arranged for the secret sale of weapons to Iran and diverted the profits to the contras — circumventing the Boland Amendment that prohibited US funds from going to the right-wing rebels. Reich left the Office of Public Diplomacy in 1986 just as the Iran-contra scandal broke. Reagan sent him to Venezuela as the US ambassador. He was never convicted of breaking the law, but the comptroller general of the United States determined that his office engaged in "prohibited, covert propaganda activities."

Reich remained in Venezuela through Carlos Andrés Pérez's "coronation" and the February 1989 Caracazo riots and mass killings. After that he left government and went into lobbying for US companies, including rum maker Bacardi-Martini — which paid him more than $600,000 — and weapons manufacturer Lockheed Martin. Both had business interests in Latin America. Controversy dogged him about his alleged help as ambassador in gaining entrance into the United States for a terrorist named Orlando Bosch. A former pediatrician, Bosch helped mastermind the bombing of a Cuban airliner in 1973, killing all seventy-three passengers aboard. He had been in jail in Venezuela, where the airplane had departed.

By March 2001 George W. Bush had proposed Reich as his assistant secretary of state for Western Hemisphere affairs — the number one official in the State Department for Latin America. Leading Democrats, human rights groups, and progressive Latin America advocacy organizations were aghast. They viewed Reich as a loose cannon and an embarrassment. Many saw his proposed appointment as a payoff to the Miami Cubans for helping hand Bush the presidency.

Senator Christopher Dodd, a Democrat from Connecticut, a former Peace Corps volunteer in the Dominican Republic, and the chairman of the Senate Foreign Relations Subcommittee for the Western Hemisphere, refused to allow the committee to give Reich a confirmation hearing. Meanwhile Reich gave up his lobbying activities and went to work at the State Department without salary. The standoff lasted nearly a year. Finally in January 2002 Bush used a "recess appointment" while Congress was not in session to circumvent Dodd and his allies and give Reich a one-year appointment to the post.

The Cuban exile community in Miami was elated. With Castro still entrenched in Cuba, his protégé Chávez digging in in Venezuela, the former leftist labor leader Luiz Inácio Lula da Silva poised to be elected president of Brazil in October, and neo-liberal "model student" Argentina suffering a financial meltdown after defaulting on its $312 billion foreign debt, Reich seemed the perfect candidate to turn back — or least slow down — the rising tide of leftist politicians in Latin America. "South America is burning up, and we are looking the other way," commented Congresswoman Illeana Ros-Lehtinen, a Florida Republican and standard-bearer of the Cuban exile community. "Otto is going to be a great fire extinguisher."

Reich was not the only fire extinguisher Bush was bringing back into power from the disgraced Iran-contra crowd. As Ronald Reagan's assistant secretary of state for Latin America, Elliot Abrams was one of the principal architects of the US dirty wars in Central America in the 1980s and a key player in the Iran-contra scandal. A "pit bull" for the administration's "better dead than red policy" in Central America, he was known for his "snarling appearances at [congressional] committee hearings, defending death squads and dictators, denying massacres, lying about illegal US activities in support of the Nicaraguan contras," one newspaper columnist wrote.

Abrams vigorously defended the US support for the "death squad" government of El Salvador, where soldiers and paramilitary forces often beheaded their victims and stuck their heads on fence posts to terrorize the population. The war left seventy-five thousand people dead, most of them victims of the US-financed military or death squads.

Along with other US officials, Abrams tried to cover up the worst massacre of the war. In December 1981 elite US-trained Salvadoran troops surrounded the isolated mountain village of El Mozote and killed nearly a thousand women, children, and elderly men. They tossed babies in the air and speared them with rifle bayonets. They raped and then killed teenage girls. They forced some of the men into a church and set it on fire. Less than two months later, on February 8, 1982, Abrams told a Senate committee that front-page stories in *The New York Times* and *The Washington Post* describing the massacre "were not credible." He suggested the reports were a propaganda exercise by leftist guerrillas to win sympathy.

Abrams once declared that "the administration's record in El Salvador is one of fabulous achievement." He said the United States was fighting communism.

Abrams worked closely with Oliver North on the contras' offensive in Nicaragua. He repeatedly told Congress he did not know about the arms exchange with Iran and diversion of profits to the contras. In 1991 he pleaded guilty to two misdemeanor counts of misleading Congress. But President George H. W. Bush, in his last days in office in 1992, pardoned him on Christmas Eve.

He was a disgraced figure. But that didn't prevent Bush's son from resuscitating his government career and bringing him back to a high-level post. A few months into his administration, Bush hired Abrams at the National Security Council, where his job was to promote democracy and human rights worldwide. A *Newsday* columnist noted that "the appointment was made with a straight face. The post does not require Senate approval. All it takes is a president willing to appoint a convicted criminal and unrepentant liar to high public office."

Rounding out the gallery of returned rogues from the Iran-contra era was John D. Negroponte, Bush's nominee to serve as the US ambassador to the United Nations. Bush sent up Negroponte's name in March 2001. Six months later it was still languishing in a congressional committee. Questions were surfacing about Negroponte's past as ambassador to Honduras from 1981 to 1985.

In the 1980s the United States provided extensive training and financing to the military in Honduras, which served as a key base for the contra rebels who were attacking the Nicaragua government. The CIA provided training to one covert unit in particular, Battalion 316, which allegedly kidnapped, tortured, and murdered left-wing sympathizers including one US citizen, Jesuit priest Joseph Carney. They tossed some of their victims into secret graves and others allegedly out of airplanes. In 1995 a Pulitzer Prize–winning investigation by *The Baltimore Sun* exposed the activities of the military and Battalion 316.

The *Sun* asserted that Negroponte, as the all-powerful US ambassador, must have known about the abuses. But the newspaper said he tried to suppress evidence of them. If Honduras was shown to be a human rights violator, it could not receive US military aid. If it did not receive US military aid, it could not serve as a launching pad for the contras.

The controversy over Negroponte's past in Central America, however, was quickly forgotten when the September 11, 2001, terrorist attacks struck. Three days later the Senate quietly approved his appointment to the United Nations. *Los Angeles Times* columnist Frank del Olmo wrote that "by putting Negroponte in a key foreign policy post, Bush has rewarded a US diplomat whom many Latin Americans consider a terrorist — albeit of the well-bred, Ivy League variety."

Bush didn't simply appoint contra sympathizers to high-level government posts — he appointed an actual contra. Rogelio Pardo-Maurer worked closely with the contra political leadership during the 1980s, serving as chief of staff at an office they established in Washington, DC. Bush named him deputy assistant secretary of defense for inter-American affairs, making him the top Pentagon official for Latin American affairs. He was Otto Reich's counterpart in the US military.

In late 2001 and early 2002, still waiting in the wings for confirmation was Bush's nominee to replace Hrinak as ambassador to Venezuela: Charles Shapiro. The Augusta, Georgia, native served in the US embassy in El Salvador as a political officer from 1985 to 1988. At one point in 1986 he testified in US District Court in Los Angeles, defending US policies in El Salvador against a lawsuit by immigrants who were seeking political asylum. The United States rejected nearly every application for political asylum filed by Salvadoran refugees. If it approved them, it would in effect be admitting that the government it was supporting in El Salvador with $1 million a day at the height of the dirty war was committing gross human rights abuses. After denouncing the Salvadoran government in the United States, the refugees who lost their political asylum cases faced a less-than-friendly reception when they were deported home.

A decade after Shapiro left El Salvador, the Clinton administration appointed him in 1999 head of the State Department's Cuba desk, where he continued the US policy of trying to undermine Fidel Castro. If confirmed to his newest assignment in Venezuela, Shapiro would report directly to Otto Reich.

The return of the Iran-contra crowd to Washington was shocking and repulsive to many left-leaning congressmen, church leaders, and Latin American policy groups — not to mention to Latin Americans themselves. "The resurfacing of the Iran-contra culprits has been nothing short of Orwellian in this administration," stated Peter Kornbluh of the National Security Archives, a Washington, DC–based research institute that specialized in declassified government documents. "These are not twenty-first century appointments. They are retrograde appointments, a throwback to an era of interventionism when the United States was the big bully on the block."

Robert White, who served as US ambassador to El Salvador in the early 1980s and watched grimly as the bodies of four murdered US churchwomen were pulled from their clandestine graves, said: "There isn't a single democratic leader in Latin America that doesn't reject and deplore the role that our government played in Central America during the 1980s. To choose men like Elliot Abrams and Otto Reich is an insult." The media watchdog group FAIR went farther. "Negroponte and Abrams have blood on their hands," it declared. "Reich's are mostly smeared with ink. Negroponte and Abrams coddled torturers, protected death squads and helped kill peasants in Central America. Reich messed with the media."

The United States started to play a covert role in shaping events in Venezuela even before Reich officially assumed his post in January 2002. By the later part of 2001 a parade of Venezuelan politicians, businessmen, journalists, and military officers opposed to Chávez started passing through Washington, DC, and the US embassy in Caracas to meet with American officials. One Venezuelan general, Lucas Romero Rincón, chief of the Venezuelan army, met with Pardo-Maurer on December 18, 2001, in Washington. Another of the visitors was a diminutive businessman named Pedro Carmona. He was the head of Venezuela's national chamber of commerce, Fedecámaras. He and a delegation of seven business leaders met with Reich, Maisto, and other officials in November. Carmona insists the meeting was to discuss including Venezuela in a group of Andean nations that received preferential trade treatment.

Others contend that the trips by the Venezuelans had another purpose: to sound out the United States about support for a coup. US officials later were to claim that they "explicitly made clear repeatedly to opposition leaders that the United States would not support a coup," in the words of White House spokesman Ari Fleischer. But a Defense Department official offered a different version, telling *The New York Times* that "we were not discouraging people. We were sending informal, subtle signs that we don't like this guy."

About the same time Pedro Carmona was traveling to Washington to meet with Reich and the others, back in Caracas lame-duck ambassador Donna Hrinak took the unusual step of ordering the embassy's military attaché to end his frequent meetings with dissident Venezuelan military officials. One of them, Rear Admiral Carlos Tamayo Molina, was a leading Chávez opponent who was contemplating a coup. A State Department official later explained that Hrinak prohibited the meetings because US officials had learned the attaché's contacts were "involved in illegal activities or what would be illegal activities."

While US officials were quietly meeting with Chávez's critics, the US government and allied agencies were also pumping hundreds of thousands of dollars into organizations opposed to him. One group was the Assembly of Education headed by Leonardo Carvajal. He was leading the protests against the education reforms and the largest street protests to date against Chávez. The principal channel for the money to be delivered to his and other opposition organizations was an outfit called the National Endowment for Democracy.

For decades, the Central Intelligence Agency sought to influence events in foreign countries in directions perceived as favorable to the United States — namely, heading off "radical" movements and governments in favor of more moderate, pro-free-market ones. It covertly supported political parties, unions, newspapers, book publishers, student groups, and civic organizations around the world. But in the mid-1970s scandal erupted when congressional investigations including the Church Commission and agency defectors such as Philip Agee revealed that the CIA was also employing other techniques to shape world events. These techniques included assassination, economic sabotage, coups, and the installation of dictators. The CIA mounted and ran the 1954 coup that overthrew the democratically elected reformist government of Jacobo Arbenz in Guatemala and backed the 1973 coup that ousted Chile's Salvador Allende, the first democratically elected Marxist president in the Western Hemisphere.

The 1970s scandals accelerated a search by policy makers in Washington to find a way to carry out some of the same political work of the CIA but without the baggage left by the exposés. Their answer was the NED. It was designed to do overtly what the CIA used to do covertly, minus the assassinations and other direct bloody endeavors. "The NED was created to supplement the activities of the CIA," according to Kornbluh, an expert in US covert activities. In a September 22, 1991, interview with *The Washington Post*, Allen Weinstein, who helped draft the legislation establishing the NED and was the group's first acting president, said, "A lot of what we do today was done covertly twenty-five years ago by the CIA." The NED's stated mission was to "promote democracy," but its ultimate mission was to promote US interests abroad — which might or might not coincide with the pursuit of democracy. Some of its work was praiseworthy, such as supporting Lech Walesa's Solidarity movement in Poland in the 1980s. Other projects were far more questionable.

The NED was created in 1983 at the height of Reagan's anti-communist crusade in Central America. Reagan was a major supporter of the organization, as George W. Bush was to become as well. The group insisted it was an independent and private operation, but almost all its funding came from the US Congress. It was essentially a quasi-governmental organization. Congress channeled its funds to NED through the United States Information Agency and the United States Agency for International Development, which both were entities of the State Department. NED had to submit its grants to the State Department for approval. US embassies abroad often handled the logistics and coordination of NED programs.

One of the NED's first major successes, as outlined by William I. Robinson in *A Faustian Bargain*, was helping to overthrow the Sandinista government in Nicaragua. In a single year it pumped a whopping $10.5 million in grants into the small, impoverished Central American nation of three and a half million people. The money went to groups opposed to the Sandinistas. Already weakened by nearly a decade of the US-led economic sabotage and contra war, they lost the 1990 election to the US-supported candidate, Violeta Chamorro. In a country with an economy barely the size of Rhode Island's, the massive US military, economic, and political intervention created a badly tilted playing field that left the Sandinistas with little chance of survival.

As Reich and the other Iran-contra figures settled into their posts in early 2002, most Venezuelans were unaware that the NED was rapidly infiltrating their society in a way reminiscent of the Nicaragua experience. Grants were escalating quickly as US power brokers grew increasingly wary of Chávez. As 2001 rolled into 2002 the money nearly quadrupled, to $877,000. Most of it went to anti-Chávez "civil society" organizations including one called *Sumate*, Join Up. Its leader, María Corina Machado, an English-speaking fashion plate who had attended boarding school in Wellesley, Massachusetts, was to land an interview in the Oval Office with President George W. Bush — something Chávez never achieved.

Chávez and most of the rest of the country would not become aware of the extent of the NED's intervention until 2004 after a Venezuelan American attorney from Brooklyn and a muckraking journalist from Washington, DC, filed Freedom of Information Act requests to force the NED to release details of its operations in Venezuela. The revelations set off a national uproar among Chávez and his supporters. The lawyer's book about the NED became ubiquitous on sidewalk newsstands and its author, Eva Golinger, a darling and celebrity of the Chávez revolution.

As 2001 drew to a close, Chávez shifted his Bolivarian Revolution into high gear, sending the opposition into a frenzy. Until now, most of his moves were aimed at dismantling the corrupt political establishment. With the traditional parties all but annihilated, he turned to implementing a series of reforms aimed at everything from the oil industry to the fishing business. On November 13, using an "enabling law" that was about to expire, he issued forty-nine decrees.

They covered everything from requiring banks to provide some loans to small farmers to extending the area where industrial fishing was banned from five to ten kilometers offshore, to protect the interests of small fishermen and the environment. In general the measures were aimed at consolidating for the first time and enshrining in law his reform program on behalf of the majority poor. They were a direct challenge to the elite.

Two decrees in particular set off a firestorm. One dealt with the oil industry. Chávez had begun to wrest control of the state oil monopoly, Petroleos de Venezuela, from what he called a "state within a state" that he believed was selling out Latin America's largest company to foreign interests and a domestic elite. He had reversed PDVSA's practice of busting its OPEC quota, and played a leading role in revitalizing the organization. Now he wanted to complete the reforms.

The new law guaranteed PDVSA at least a 51 percent stake — and thus control — in joint ventures with foreign oil companies. It also raised royalty rates from 16.7 percent to 30 percent. To offset the increase, the government would slash income tax rates, from 67.7 percent to 50 percent. In addition, the law strengthened prohibitions in the new constitution against privatizing the company.

Critics, including former PDVSA head Luis Guisti and the company's well-oiled public relations department, painted the move as another step toward destroying a model company and discouraging foreign investment. Others disputed that, contending that PDVSA was actually one of the *least* efficient major oil companies. It cost PDVSA about three times as much to extract a barrel of oil as it did other major oil corporations such as ExxonMobil, Shell, Chevron, or Texaco, according to a ranking by the magazine *América Economía*. PDVSA also used transfer pricing to overseas affiliates to lower the royalties it paid to the Venezuelan state. The amount fell from 71¢ per dollar of gross earnings in 1981 to 39¢ by 2000.

The other decree that provoked the opposition's ire centered on land reform. No one in Venezuela could seriously argue that land reform was not needed. Between 1 and 2 percent of the landowners possessed 60 percent of the arable land. Many landowners had obtained their property through corruption and lacked legal titles. On top of that, they were not using it. Two million landless peasants were living in poverty, Chávez complained, while great swaths of the interior lay fallow with their owners living in Caracas.

He also argued that Venezuela needed to achieve "national food security" by producing most of its own food. Venezuela imported an estimated 70 percent of its food. It was the only net importer in South America. In the previous four decades most of its residents had moved from the country to the cities, which now held 87 percent of the population, nearly reversing the previous ratio. Between 1960 and 1999, agriculture's share of the GDP dropped from 50 percent to 6 percent — the lowest figure in Latin America.

The last land reform attempt, in 1961, ended in disaster. The government gave forty-four thousand square miles to peasants, but didn't give them the means to work the land. Most of it eventually ended up in the hands of large landowners.

Chávez wanted to rectify Venezuela's dismal land distribution. He proposed limiting the legal size of farms to areas ranging from one hundred to five thousand hectares, depending on productivity. To help dismantle portions of large unused *latifundios* or make them productive, he wanted to impose a special tax on land left more than 80 percent idle. He proposed distributing unused land, mainly owned by the government, to peasant families and cooperatives. His measure did permit limited expropriation of uncultivated and fallow land from large, private estates. But the government would take only a portion of the idle land, depending on its quality, and would compensate the owners at fair market rates. The law clearly stated that large landowners were generally entitled to most of their land.

The plan was not nearly as radical as the mass expropriations of the Cuban and Mexican revolutions. Some compared it to Abraham Lincoln's landmark Homestead Act of 1862, which helped develop an agrarian-based middle class and played an important role in the development of democracy in the United States. The Venezuelan government figured it could meet most of the peasants' needs by distributing state-owned property and would not have to touch many privately owned holdings.

But the decree set off a revolt among landowners. Many complained that the president was unfairly depicting them as thieves by questioning the legitimacy of their land titles. They contended his incendiary statements were prompting a wave of invasions by squatters. They feared they were going to lose their livelihoods. They believed the government would force them to give up the lucrative business of milking cows, for instance, because the new regulations required them to sow plantains on the most fertile soil. Others charged that even productive estates could be seized. They called the program a threat to private property and a throwback to communist-style economies.

Chávez kicked off the program with great fanfare on December 10, the anniversary of Ezequiel Zamora's famous battle at Santa Inés in 1859. Chávez traveled to the exact spot of the battle in Barinas for a ceremony marking the program's official start.

It didn't take long for violence to erupt. Landowners in the border region complained the government was not protecting them from Colombian rebels and invading peasants. They formed private militias reportedly trained by bloody right-wing Colombian paramilitary organizations. Soon they were assassinating land reform activists. One, Luis Mora, was killed a month after Chávez's announcement. Two men drove up to his house in the rural state of Mérida, pulled out pistols, and shot him in front of his two young sons. Over the next year the government National Land Institute calculated that another fifty popular leaders were assassinated. By the middle of 2005 the figure was up to at least 130.

Despite the violence, the land reform program advanced. By early 2005 the government had distributed 2.2 million hectares of idle, state-owned property to 130,000 families. No private property was expropriated — although a few controversial cases where that was under study would later arise. Peter Rosset, co-director of the Institute for Food and Development Policy think tank in San Francisco and an expert on land reform programs, singled out Venezuela's initiative as highly unusual. "Venezuela right now has the only serious government-administered land reform in Latin America," he said. "In the United States, Chávez is often painted as a villain or crazy, but this land reform, small and incipient as it is, shows that he is much more on the side of the poor than other presidents in the region."

But as Chávez launched his land reform in November 2001, the opposition was anything but enamored of it — or anything else he did. They sensed he was weak, and wanted to go in for the kill. His government suffered from a lack of experience in governing. Chávez had never held an elected office before suddenly catapulting to the presidency. Many of his ministers were newcomers to government, too. Sometimes they came and went at a dizzying pace. One of the most important ones, Luis Miquilena, was soon to join the ranks of the departed.

But Chávez's inner circle of advisers still included many of the other civilian leftists and progressives he met while he was in prison. Among them was the team of Central University of Venezuela professors including Jorge Giordani, his planning minister, and Héctor Navarro, his education minister.

Perhaps the most influential cabinet figure was to become José Vicente Rangel, the former journalist who served as foreign minister, defense minister, and eventually vice president. A former presidential candidate for the leftist party MAS, Rangel shared Chávez's anti-imperialist outlook, his commitment to overturning Venezuela's corrupt order, and his desire for a more just society. More a socialist than a communist, he had won widespread respect as a journalist for his bare-knuckled reports exposing corruption. He was old enough to be Chávez's father and turned into a mentor — along, of course, with Chávez's main guide, Fidel Castro. With Chávez's three old military comrades in arms now alienated from the administration, his civilian brain trust took on greater importance: Although the strong-minded president remained the towering figure, other military men hovered nearby, and Castro was always just a phone call away.

Chávez was facing a mounting series of protests and strikes — oil workers, teachers, steel and aluminum workers, telephone company employees, doctors and nurses, transportation workers. He had inherited a staggering $21 billion debt to state workers alone for back wages and pensions. Oil prices, after soaring in 1999 and 2000, were on the decline. By early December 2001 they dropped to $15.30 a barrel. The 2002 budget was based on a price of $18.50.

The attacks on Chávez went beyond legitimate concerns and debates over his policies, veering into hysteria and a smear campaign. Democratic Action leaders asked the Supreme Court to appoint a board of psychiatrists to determine whether Chávez was suffering from "mental incapacity" so he could be removed from office based on Article 233 of the new constitution. "He's a psychopath," declared AD's secretary general Rafael Marin. "Our psychiatrists have compared the psychiatric profiles of people like Hitler, Mussolini, Idi Amin and Ecuadorean President Abdalá Bucaram" — the latter of whom was ousted from office in 1997 on grounds of mental incompetence. The media eagerly picked up on the theme. *Newsweek* quoted Marin in its infamous article titled, "Is Hugo Chávez Insane?"

With the demonization of Chávez in full tilt, the Venezuelan opposition mobilized to attack him in a mass organized way for the first time. On Monday, December 10, the same day Chávez presided over the ceremony enacting his land reform law, Fedecámaras, the nation's most powerful business group, and the Confederation of Venezuelan Workers (CTV), its largest union, called a twelve-hour general strike to protest the forty-nine decrees. They didn't quite paralyze the country, but they brought large swaths of it to a standstill, aided by business owners who locked their doors. While shops in poor neighborhoods opened, much of downtown Caracas and the city's affluent eastern sector were ghost towns. Newspapers did not circulate. Schools, the stock exchange, malls, factories, and banks closed. The Francisco Fajardo Highway, normally packed during rush hour, was mostly empty.

The opposition was ecstatic. They convinced themselves that Chávez's support had all but vanished. "It's a great success," declared an ebullient Carlos Fernández, the first vice president of Fedecámaras. "Everything is completely paralyzed." He claimed 90 percent of the country shut down. Chávez refused to concede defeat. He rallied supporters in the Plaza Caracas to celebrate the passage of the agrarian reform law.

But the opposition had momentum. It was coalescing into a more cohesive protest movement. Chávez was at his weakest moment since assuming the presidency. The conventional wisdom hammered home by the opposition and the media was that his days were numbered. He would leave office prematurely — one way or the other. Former COPEI presidential candidate Oswaldo Álvarez Paz, among many others, was already calling for military action. "There is no legal solution, so what can we do?" he said. "In my opinion, military intervention is inevitable." *Euromoney* gushed that "no one in the country can imagine Chávez staying on for the remainder of his presidential term." It all sounded eerily reminiscent of the 1954 smoke-and-mirrors campaign against Jacobo Arbenz in Guatemala or the 1973 campaign against Salvador Allende in Chile.

The *St. Petersburg Times* noted that Chávez's new term was due to expire in February 2007, but "analysts say there's no way he'll survive that long. Various scenarios for his departure include discontent in the military and mass civil unrest." The newspaper then quoted the writer Alberto Garrido: "It all points to Chávez leaving power. How that happens is daily less important."

**20**

# The Coup

The coup against Hugo Chávez began to unfold in early 2002. In the space of three weeks in February, four ranking military officials including a general and a rear admiral publicly attacked the president and called on him to resign. One labeled him a "tyrant." In one of the most stunning denunciations, Rear Admiral Carlos Molina Tamayo appeared on television in full navy whites, medals across his chest, and said that if Chávez didn't step down voluntarily, the courts and the legislature should impeach him.

The officers had a litany of complaints. Chávez was alienating the United States by cavorting with Colombian rebels and international outcasts like Saddam Hussein. He was threatening free speech. He was undermining democracy. He was distorting the role of the armed forces by sending soldiers to build schools and distribute food instead of defending the country's borders.

Chávez and his allies saw other motives for the dissent. One rebel, air force colonel Pedro Soto, a former adviser to Carlos Andrés Pérez, had been passed over for a promotion to general. A report in *The Washington Post* later alleged that he and Molina Tamayo received $100,000 each from Miami bank accounts for denouncing Chávez. Molina Tamayo, in fact, was already involved in talks with other officers to plot Chávez's removal from office.

Two days before Soto's dramatic appearance on February 7, Secretary of State Colin Powell expressed concern about Chávez's "understanding of what the democratic system is all about . . . We have not been happy with some of the comments he has made with respect to the campaign against terrorism . . . And he drops in some of the strangest countries to visit," Powell said in an apparent reference to Iraq, Libya, and Cuba. "I'm not sure what inspiration he thinks he gets or what benefits he gets for the Venezuelan people, dropping in and visiting some of these despotic regimes."

The next day, CIA director George Tenet added that he was "particularly concerned" about events in Venezuela. He predicted the "crisis atmosphere is likely to worsen" at a time when Latin America is becoming "increasingly volatile."

The comments by Powell and Tenet were front-page news in Venezuela. US officials acknowledged opposition figures they met with in Washington, DC, and in Caracas were floating the idea of a coup. Publicly the officials insisted they condemned the idea. But the opposition interpreted the comments by Powell, Tenet, and others made in private differently. As two analysts put it, "They were perceived as coordinated signals. The opposition felt it had the green light to remove Chávez from power."

Molina Tamayo certainly felt that way. "We felt we were acting with US support," he later said. "We agree that we can't permit a communist government here." Two days after he denounced Chávez, two staff members of the International Republican Institute, Michael Ferber and Elizabeth Winger Echeverri, approached Molina Tamayo in the Hotel Tamanaco. Their organization, one of four core institutions of the National Endowment for Democracy, had its own office in Caracas. The IRI staffers wanted to talk about "human rights, democracy, their operation in Washington," Molina Tamayo recalled.

Chávez was under pressure on other fronts. By late January his closest political adviser, Luis Miquilena, resigned. Miquilena urged Chávez to negotiate with business and labor leaders and revoke the forty-nine decrees. Chávez believed there was no turning back. His government had to make a radical break with the past. Before long Miquilena was working with the opposition.

Amid a mounting series of street protests by the opposition, Chávez also faced problems at PDVSA. In February he moved to cement the plans outlined in his oil decree setting increased royalties, respecting OPEC quotas, and guaranteeing Venezuela a 51 percent share in joint ventures with foreign companies. He fired the man he had appointed fifteen months earlier to run PDVSA, Brigadier General Guaicaipuro

Lameda. He fired five of the seven members of the PDVSA board of directors, too.

Lameda and the old board wanted to continue the Caldera-era *apertura* or opening that called for increasing participation of foreign oil companies and dramatically boosting production — from 3.3 million barrels a day in 1997 to 6 million by 2006. Chávez disagreed. He believed cutting production would raise prices and bring more revenue to the country. He also believed the *apertura* crowd ultimately wanted to privatize the company.

As he moved to take control of the company, Chávez lambasted PDVSA directors for enjoying "obscene salaries that go beyond the imagination" — pensions of $24,000 a month in a country where most Venezuelan workers earned $180 a month. He complained of "luxurious chalets" in the Andes "where they hold bacchanals and where the whisky runs." Chávez wanted to divert the company's benefits to the majority poor. "PDVSA has long been the hen that lays the golden egg," said his foreign minister, Luis Alfonso Davila. "But today it is eating more than half of the eggs it is producing."

Chávez replaced Lameda with leftist economist Gaston Parra, who pledged to pursue Chávez's oil policy and launch a full investigation of PDVSA's accounting practices. The new board of directors backed him.

The appointments set off a firestorm. PDVSA executives charged that Chávez was "politicizing" a model company — undermining its cherished independence from the government and destroying a decades-long tradition of promotions based on merit. By late February a series of walkouts and work slowdowns began.

The protests were shocking in a country where PDVSA generally operated like clockwork. To some people, the combination of heightened tensions at the oil company, military dissidents denouncing the president, and a media that demonized him at every turn was starting to feel like the days before the overthrow of Salvador Allende in 1973. Coup rumors swirled. Blood-red graffiti calling for Chávez's death popped up on highway walls. Television stations ran nonstop talk programs lambasting Chávez. Beautiful middle-class women in tight jeans and blouses showed up at military bases and tossed panties at soldiers. They implied the men were pansies for failing to stand up to Chávez, and that it might be worth their time to try.

Turning up the verbal attacks, Caracas mayor Alfredo Peña, a Chávez-ally-turned-foe, suggested that the president was possessed by evil spirits. He called for the Catholic Church to perform an exorcism. "He has demons in his body and is making a hell of everything," Peña said. "The street is going to take Chávez out. He is an autocrat."

James Petras, a State University of New York at Albany professor who lived in Chile in the early 1970s, thought he had seen the same scene before. "The tactics used are very similar to those used in Chile," he stated that March. "Civilians are used to create a feeling of chaos and a false picture of Chávez as a dictator is established, then the military is incited to make a coup for the sake of the country." Venezuela's hostile media was also reminiscent of Chile's right-wing press during the pre-coup period, putting out "poisonous stories questioning Chávez's sanity."

At least one branch of the US government shared Petras's belief that a coup was brewing: the CIA. On March 11 it issued a top-secret "Senior Executive Intelligence Brief" to two hundred top-level US officials, stating that "the military may move to overthrow him." By April 1 the CIA said "reporting suggests that disgruntled officers within the military are still planning a coup, possibly early this month."

Five days later a new brief was titled "Venezuela: Conditions Ripening for Coup Attempt." It stated that "dissident military factions, including some disgruntled senior officers and a group of radical junior officers, are stepping up efforts to organize a coup against President Chávez, possibly as early as this month . . . The level of detail in the reported plans [CENSORED] targets Chávez and 10 other senior officials for arrest — lends credence to this information, but military and civilian contacts note that neither group appears ready to lead a successful coup and may bungle the attempt by moving too quickly."

The April 6 brief then laid out how the coup might occur. "To provoke military action, the plotters may try to exploit unrest stemming from opposition demonstrations slated for later this month or ongoing strikes at the state-owned oil company PDVSA." But it added that "prospects for a successful coup at this point are limited. The plotters lack the political cover to stage a coup, Chávez's core support base among poor Venezuelans remains intact, and repeated warnings that the US will not support any extra-constitutional moves to remove Chávez probably have given pause to the plotters."

The plotters were lacking "the political cover to stage a coup." They needed a convincing reason to show the world they were justified in overthrowing a democratically elected president. Some were working on finding one. As the CIA predicted, they would exploit the unrest at PDVSA and a strike opposition leaders were planning.

The day before the CIA issued its April 6 brief, the resistance to Chávez at PDVSA shifted into a more radical phase. Executives and administrative workers started to shut down the company. Thousands of white-collar workers stayed home, closed gates to facilities, and slowed gasoline and oil tanker deliveries. Two out of five main export terminals for crude oil and refined products were paralyzed.

The next day, the mainly white-collar walkout continued, while the nation's largest union, the CTV led by Carlos Ortega, announced a twenty-four-hour general strike to support the PDVSA protestors. The following day, Sunday, April 7, the nation's largest chamber of commerce, Fedecámaras led by Pedro Carmona, said it was joining the strike, too. It was a reprise of the December 10 work stoppage — management and workers banding together. They had cemented their partnership a month earlier with the blessing of the Catholic Church when they'd signed a "governability pact" at the Andrés Bello Catholic University in Caracas. Carmona and Ortega stood on a stage as the head of the Jesuit university, the Reverend Luis Ugalde, raised their arms into the air as if they'd both just won a boxing match.

The CTV and Fedecámaras set the strike date for Tuesday, April 9.

But Chávez swung back. That Sunday, April 7, he fired seven executives who had led the monthlong protests and strikes at PDVSA, and forced twelve others into retirement. Speaking on his weekly television program, he pulled out a whistle, blew it, and, imitating a soccer referee, declared, "Offsides!" Then he announced the firings. He warned of a "subversive movement in neckties" trying to sabotage his government and said, "It doesn't bother me if I have to throw the whole lot of you out." He insisted that politics had been behind PDVSA appointments for decades, and listed past company presidents who belonged to the ruling parties of their eras. "PDVSA has always been managed by a political elite," he said. "The plan is to return the oil industry to Venezuelans."

The CTV had a different interpretation of the dismissals. It responded that Chávez's government had just "committed suicide."

That night Chávez convened his cabinet and military high command to discuss how to respond to the strike. The government and military already had a general plan in place to restore public order in moments of chaos or conflict. Known as Plan Avila, it called for the military to take strategic points such as Miraflores presidential palace, Congress, and the Supreme Court as a dissuasive show of force. That night, Chávez asked the military commanders including the man in charge of Plan Avila, General Manuel Rosendo, if they were prepared to put it into action if needed. They assured him they were.

The strike kicked off on Tuesday, April 9. Oil workers slowed production at the crucial Paraguana plant. Newspapers refused to publish. Television stations preempted regular programming and ran continuous coverage of the strike. They canceled regular commercials and ran their own hastily composed, anti-Chávez ads as free "public service announcements." A string of politicians, businessmen, and analysts spewed nonstop vitriolic attacks against Chávez. On the bottom of the screen, some stations ran a slogan: NI UN PASO ATRAS — not one step back.

Fedecámaras and the CTV declared the strike an outstanding success. The government disputed their claim and contended that the strike was mainly an owners' lockout not supported by most workers. Chávez ordered a series of *cadenas* or mandatory transmissions on television to give the government's version. They showed workers unloading fruit at markets or walking in droves into office buildings.

That Tuesday night Ortega and Carmona announced they were extending the strike another twenty-four hours. Protestors gathered at PDVSA offices in Chuao, waving Venezuelan flags and chanting "Chávez Out! Chávez Out!" On the other side of town, Chavistas gathered in front of Miraflores for a counterprotest. Some camped out overnight to protect the palace, even bringing tents.

The next day, April 10, the strike started to peter out. Many schools resumed classes, more businesses opened, traffic increased. But the television networks kept up their nonstop coverage. Chávez intervened with *cadenas* to counterbalance the one-way reporting, but this time the television networks split the screen, showing the president on one side and scenes of the strike on the other. It was illegal — the president had the right to convoke *cadenas* — but that didn't stop them.

That night Ortega and Carmona announced they were extending the general strike — this time indefinitely. It seemed illogical. Who would indefinitely extend a fading strike? They called on people to attend a march the next morning from the Parque del Este to the

PDVSA offices in Chuao, where the march would culminate with a rally. Secretly, they had another idea. They would announce it the next day at the rally as a "spontaneous" decision prompted by the crowd's enthusiasm. They planned to change the route and descend on Miraflores Palace to force the president to resign.

Earlier in the day Brigadier General Néstor González González had become the latest active military officer to demand Chávez's resignation. Speaking to reporters and a bank of television cameras at a news conference staged at a hotel in Caracas, González González said, "Mr. President, you have betrayed the country. Respect the armed forces." Then he laid down an ultimatum: "The military high command has to say to the president, Mr. President, you are the cause of all this. It's time you stepped down. The military high command will have to take this stand, because if they don't, someone else will for them." As he finished and got up to leave, a reporter said, "General, do you mean a coup?" González González slipped on his military cap, let a small tight smile emerge from his lips, said nothing, and left.

González's statements had a specific purpose. Chávez was scheduled to fly to Costa Rica the next afternoon for a summit of the Organization of American States. The plotters needed him in Venezuela for their plan to work. Sufficiently alarmed by the march and the insurrectionary calls by González, Chávez canceled the trip.

By some accounts the government was already getting wind of the secret plan to change the route of the march. They had infiltrated the meeting where Carmona and the other leaders discussed it. Publicly, Defense Minister José Vicente Rangel called the decision to extend the strike indefinitely "insurrectionist." The opposition was looking to take down the government.

In Washington, DC, meanwhile, a State Department official who did not want to be named told reporters he believed Chávez's days as president were numbered. "It's really difficult to see him holding on until February 2007" when his term was due to expire, the official said.

After Carmona and Ortega announced the march for the next day, the media went into overdrive promoting it. They ran makeshift ads every ten minutes. "Venezuelans, everyone to the streets, Thursday at ten in the morning," one boomed. "Let's march together for Venezuela, from the Parque del Este to Chuao. Bring your flag. For liberty and democracy. Venezuela won't surrender. No one is going to defeat us." Another said, "Not One Step Back! Out! Leave now!"

• • •

That Thursday morning, April 11, Aristóteles Aranguren turned on his television. The light-skinned, freckle-faced schoolteacher at a private middle-class school was as disenchanted with Chávez as anyone. He couldn't get out of his mind Chávez's famous statement about Venezuela and Cuba heading for the same "sea of happiness." Aranguren had traveled to Cuba twice. He thought he knew what kind of sea the Cubans were swimming in. It was more like they were drowning. He remembered walking the streets of Old Havana and seeing people begging for clothes, soap, toothpaste, anything. He remembered the bare apartments with empty refrigerators. He didn't want any part of it.

As he flicked on his television about 10:30 A.M., he saw people massing at the Parque del Este and heading toward Chuao. It was an impressive showing. By some counts it eventually grew to half a million people — maybe even more. It appeared to be the largest protest march in Venezuela since the overthrow of Marcos Pérez Jiménez in 1958. Aranguren slipped on his blue jeans and sneakers, grabbed a textbook to read on the subway, and dashed out the door.

When he arrived at Parque del Este, it was like stepping into a huge outdoor fiesta. People were jubilant. They waved small Venezuelan flags or had their faces painted with its colors — red, yellow, and blue. They blew whistles or carried signs that said VETE, get out. Parents pushed children in strollers or walked hand in hand. Complete strangers hugged one another.

Pedro Carmona was shaking hands and smiling. He had emerged as a key figure in the opposition. A diminutive man with a bald head, he would soon be described in the international media as "mild-mannered." He was an economist with a postgraduate degree from Brussels Free University who spent thirty years in Venezuela's diplomatic corps before joining the business world at a petrochemical firm. The previous July, Fedecámaras elected him their leader. Now many people were thinking of him as Venezuela's next president.

In Miraflores Palace, Hugo Chávez was trying to maintain a normal schedule of activities after canceling his trip to Costa Rica. He had a meeting planned in the palace with a group of state governors. His father was coming in from Barinas to attend. It was also his older brother Adán's birthday. He'd be stopping by, too. Chávez's mother, Elena, was worried about her second oldest son and decided to tag along with Hugo Sr. The president knew the opposition was in an insurrectionist mode. But he figured he had the support of the armed forces to control any disturbances. He assumed the National Guard would stop the marchers from reaching the palace if they tried. Plan Avila was ready to go.

In Fort Tiuna, Defense Minister José Vicente Rangel was in his fifth-floor office analyzing the situation with the military high command. They had televisions tuned to the march. They were on high alert. The government suspected the opposition was plotting something. They just didn't know exactly what. Rangel later came to believe the intelligence services failed the government in part because they were infiltrated by the opposition.

Across town, media mogul Gustavo Cisneros was engaged in his own activities. He was hosting a luncheon at his mansion for some of the nation's business, political, academic, and media elites. The guest of honor was Charles Shapiro, the new American ambassador. Cisneros and the others wanted to welcome him to Venezuela. Shapiro had arrived in late February and met with Chávez the previous week. While accounts vary as to whether Shapiro mentioned the CIA warnings of a coup, he believed it was at any rate a moot point. All you had to do was turn on the television or open a newspaper to realize Chávez's opponents were plotting a coup.

"There were people extremely unhappy with that government and trying to overthrow it," Shapiro told an interviewer two years later. "Everybody knew it. Clearly, there were conspiracies going on and not one but multiple conspiracies . . . There were so many conspiracies going on that you weren't quite sure which one was the serious one and, often, which one were three guys getting together in a bar and talking."

At Cisneros's reception that day, as tuxedo-clad waiters served the guests, the main topic of conversation was Chávez and how to get rid of him. According to Shapiro's account, he told the guests the United States would not support a coup.

By late morning the marchers were massed at the PDVSA office in Chuao. They cheered wildly as speakers lambasted the president and waved their arms in unison, shouting "Out! Out!" Then, before noon, some speakers began calling on the crowd to head to Miraflores. It was a surprise to many. Rear Admiral Carlos Molina Tamayo shouted, "Come on, we're going to Miraflores!" Carlos Ortega accused Chávez of stealing "the resources of the state." Then he added, "I do not rule out the possibility that this crowd, this human river, marches to Miraflores to expel a traitor of the Venezuelan people."

The crowd roared its approval and took off for the palace, six miles away. They chanted slogans: "Chávez, you're fired!" "Go to Cuba!" "He's leaving! He's leaving!" They waved flags. They blew whistles. They carried signs that said, GET OUT! DEATH TO CHÁVEZ. BIN LADEN AND FIDEL CASTRO = HUGO CHÁVEZ.

The decision to illegally change the route of the march at the last minute without official permission set off alarm bells in the government. "They've gone crazy!" exclaimed José Vicente Rangel in his office. Thousands of Chavistas were already at the palace. A violent confrontation could occur if the two sides clashed. Caracas mayor Freddy Bernal went on state-owned channel 8 and called on Ortega and other leaders to halt their plans to head to the palace. "It is irresponsible of you to be calling for a demonstration in front of Miraflores when you know there are thousands of people already gathered there," he said. Bernal then called on Chavistas to head to Miraflores to defend the president. "Today," he said, "there is a conspiracy in progress."

Rangel got on the telephone to some of the television media moguls to ask them to stop the march from reaching Miraflores. They told him there was nothing they could do. General Lucas Romero Rincón, the nation's highest-ranking military official, called Carmona once and Ortega three times on their cell phones to try to dissuade them. When he reached Carmona, the Fedecámaras leader told him there was nothing he could do either, and that the time for dialogue had run out.

In the mountainside barrios of Caracas, word spread that the marchers were heading to the palace. Hundreds of Chavistas jumped on motorcycles or public buses and made their way to Miraflores. In the neighborhood of Guarataro one mile from the palace, unemployed baker Pedro Linares took a shower, got dressed, and walked out the door to go help defend the president. He'd barely gone fifty yards when he turned around and went back home. He summoned his six children into the living room. "I'm going, but I don't know if I'm going to return," he said.

A tall man with a beard and bushy eyebrows, Linares was forty-two years old and a devoted Bolivarian Circle member. He had gone to the PDVSA offices in Chuao that Tuesday night when a group of Chavistas clashed with anti-Chávez demonstrators and his best friend, Pastora Peña, got some of her teeth knocked out. Now Linares told his children that if anything happened to him, he wanted them to behave well for their mother and respect her. Then he walked out the door.

The march snaked its way down the six-lane Francisco Fajardo Highway, turned at a bend near the Hilton Hotel, and spilled onto six-lane Avenida Bolívar that led up to the Palace of Justice and — less than a mile beyond that — Miraflores. Helping lead the way were Rear Admiral Molina Tamayo and Guaicaipuro Lameda, the general whom Chávez had fired as head of PDVSA. At about 2 P.M. a television reporter stopped Lameda. "Despite the situation, you are insisting on going all the way to Miraflores?" he asked. The general responded, "Up to now, the call has been to reach Avenida Bolívar. If the people ask for it, we will carry on to Miraflores. This is a peaceful march." The protestors shouted and cheered in the background. Lameda shrugged, as it to say, How can I stop them?

Rumors were already swirling on television that Chávez had left the palace and resigned. At 2:10 P.M. General Rincón appeared to refute the reports. Flanked by some of the high command, he said, "It has been mentioned that the president of the republic is detained in Fort Tiuna or in Miraflores, which I categorically reject. Mr. President is in his office." Rincón also denied rumors that the military high command had resigned.

Chávez, in fact, was in his office and had not resigned. But he knew the situation was turning grave. Only a handful of police and National Guardsmen were in the streets around the palace to hold back the approaching march. The police were controlled by the city's anti-Chávez mayor, Alfredo Peña, and were helping the protestors move along. Shortly after noon Chávez decided to implement Plan Avila. He tried calling General Manuel Rosendo by telephone and radio, using a system of code names they'd established. Chávez was *Tiburon Uno* — shark number one. But Rosendo did not respond. He was a trusted Chávez ally, or so the president thought. Now he was nowhere to be found.

Another Chávez ally, General Jorge Luis García Carneiro, overheard the president trying to reach Rosendo and cut in after he failed to answer. García Carneiro offered to implement Plan Avila on his own. He was in charge of the Third Division of the army, the largest military unit in Caracas. García Carneiro graduated from the military academy with Chávez in 1975 and, although he did not take part in the 1992 coup, was sympathetic to the president's reform program.

But now, as he offered to help Chávez implement Plan Avila, something strange was happening at Fort Tiuna where his unit was based.

Soldiers blocked the Pan-American Highway with large trucks and diverted traffic into the fort. Buses, trucks, and cars flooded the base. García Carneiro's troops could not get out. Chávez had no way of stopping the marchers from surrounding the palace.

They passed by the Palace of Justice a little after 2 P.M. and swarmed onto the streets leading into the historic El Silencio section of white- and blue-painted buildings. They were a stone's throw from the gleaming white palace, which was up a small hill on Avenida Urdaneta. The crowd made its way to the towering white marble stairs of El Calvario park, where hundreds of protestors rested. Others tried to advance closer to Miraflores. A line of Metropolitan Police wearing bulletproof vests and anti-riot helmets with plastic face shields stood across the road with their motorcycles to block them.

A few streets away, hundreds of Chávez supporters stood on the Llaguno Bridge overpass at the intersection of Avenida Urdaneta and Avenida Baralt. Many had their faces painted red, the color of Chávez's famous beret. They shook their fists in the air and shouted as the marchers crossed Baralt a few blocks and several hundred yards below them, heading the back way to the palace near El Calvario. Some Chavistas had sticks, rocks, or bottles. Linares's friend Pastora Peña bought a hot red pepper from a local store. She figured she could smear it in the face of the enemy to blind them if hand-to-hand combat broke out. Most of the crowd still wasn't expecting much more than that. While tense, the atmosphere was also strangely festive. Street vendors were selling popcorn, hot dogs, and bottled water. One woman set up a stand to sell *empanadas*.

Thin lines of Metropolitan Police and National Guardsmen were separating the two groups, who were now barely one hundred yards apart at some points.

Tempers were at a fever pitch. Anti-Chávez demonstrators massed near the Fermín Toro High School a few hundred yards below the palace. They could see the high walls surrounding Miraflores.

Around the corner at El Calvario, the Metropolitan Police held back the marchers for a few minutes. But then the protestors walked right past them, knocking down some of the motorcycles and advancing up a palm-tree-lined boulevard toward the palace. The police did nothing. The protestors were led by Lameda and Molina Tamayo, who kept calling on them to surge forward for a direct assault on the palace about two hundred yards away. At the other end of the boulevard about fifteen National Guardsmen held back a group of Chavistas. The National Guard fired tear gas to keep the opposition marchers away. The demonstrators fell back, kept trying to advance, and then fell back again as they gagged on the gas. Molina Tamayo yelled to the crowd through a megaphone, "We must get past the gas. The wind is blowing this way . . . We have to run to the other side. Pass the message on — as soon as they throw tear gas, move forward quickly. We must overcome the tear gas."

At about 2:30 P.M. the anger of some protestors at Fermín Toro spilled over. They started throwing everything they could get their hands on at the National Guardsmen and Chavistas a block away: bottles, rocks, chairs, tubes, metal rods, mangoes, apples, plantains, watermelon rinds. They broke off pieces of clay block from the high school and threw them, too. The National Guardsmen tossed some of the objects back. The marchers and the Chavistas exchanged insults.

Protestors were still pouring into the city center. Aristóteles Aranguren was somewhere in the middle of the march. By the time he approached Avenida Baralt he was surprised authorities were letting them get so close to the palace. He thought the National Guard would have stopped them at the Avenida Bolívar before they reached the city center. Up ahead, tear gas clogged the narrow side streets. Recalling his military training, Aranguren shouted for the crowd to get down on their knees and crawl to avoid the gas. Some people covered their mouths with vinegar-soaked handkerchiefs. Others turned around and ran.

Aranguren reached Avenida Baralt and stood in the middle of the street wondering what to do next. Maybe he should turn back, too. As he raced through his options in his mind, someone suddenly shouted, "Watch out! Here come some guys on motorcycles!" Aranguren thought it was the Bolivarian Circles coming to attack the marchers. But when he saw them, they were actually Metropolitan Police. They were speeding north up the street, pushing the crowd toward the overpass and the Chavistas. Aranguren took off running toward Llaguno.

He'd barely gone a hundred yards when the anti-riot police tank dubbed the Whale swung onto Avenida Baralt from a side street and turned north toward the Chavistas. The first shot rang out. More followed. Aranguren ducked behind the tank and watched in horror as a group of men came running down the street carrying one of the first victims. He was dressed in black. Some of his brains were spilling out of a hole in his bloody head.

Aranguren took off running and saw a second victim on the ground with a bullet to the head. He looked up at the buildings lining the block and didn't see anything, but was convinced snipers were taking people out. The shots were coming from above. He sprinted south on Avenida Baralt and yelled for the people to go back. "There are snipers!"

A couple of blocks away Henry Rodríguez was walking back with a group of Chavistas from the Fermín Toro High School toward Miraflores. He was passing the Casa de Espagueti — the house of spaghetti — on a side street when he saw four men come running down the block carrying a heavyset man with no shirt. He was limp. His chest was covered with blood.

It was about 3:20 P.M. For the next few hours bullets rained down on both opposition marchers and Chavistas. Puffs of smoke were coming out of the windows of the Hotel Eden on Avenida Baralt. Red laser-like lights flashed with the sounds of gunfire. Shots seemed to be coming from other buildings, too, including the Hotel Ausonia across the street from Miraflores and La Nacional government office on Baralt. Aranguren watched as people scattered in all directions. They weren't sure where to go, or where the shots were coming from. They seemed to be coming from all over.

A photographer for the newspaper 2001, Jorge Tortoza, was shot in the head and later died. A bodyguard for Vice President Diosdado Cabello, Tony Velásquez, was hit and gravely wounded. A protestor named Malvina Pesate was shot in the head, but somehow survived. The attack was caught on horrifying videotape as her head snapped forward and she collapsed to the ground. Yesenia Fuentes, a Chavista selling empanadas on Llaguno Bridge, was hit in the face by a bullet. Like Fuentes, many of the victims had bullet wounds to the head or neck.

Back in the television studios, some newscasters initially were not certain what was happening since they could not see the entire scene. At 3:40 P.M., as one network showed Velásquez being carried away toward Miraflores Palace, a newscaster said she thought he might have fainted from the heat.

Five minutes later, as the situation on the streets was spinning out of control, Chávez took to the airwaves. It was a last-ditch effort to appeal for calm and head off what he believed was an insurrection. He called a cadena, cutting off images of the scenes on the streets. The president broadcast his message from the underground Salon Ayacucho and apparently was unaware of the violence breaking out up above. He spoke for about ninety minutes, pleading for peace and outlining the accomplishments of his administration.

But half an hour into the speech the networks split the screens in half again. They showed Chávez speaking on one side and the mayhem outside on the other. They also disrupted the audio, making it difficult to hear the president. An aide made hand signals to Chávez to indicate what was happening. The angered president announced he was ordering the government to jam the signals of the networks because they were inciting an insurrection. The networks receive licenses from the state to operate, he said, but "they can't use that right to attack the state itself, to instigate violence or, knowing there is an insurrectional plan, support it . . . This insurrectional plan has arrived at an extreme, to craziness . . . to bring people, some Venezuelans — even lied to — telling them that Chávez is already a prisoner, we have to go to Miraflores . . . that we're going to throw him out with a little push."

While the government cut off their transmissions, the networks had a contingency plan. They started transmitting through satellites, allowing anyone with a satellite dish to receive their broadcasts. To them, a horrifying news event was unfolding, and they needed to report it. They believed Chávez was trying to cover up the violence. As he continued speaking, an army officer handed him slips of paper with a list of the dead. Chávez was confused by it, but pushed on with his speech as the split-screen television images showed the bloodshed in the streets. He mentioned everything from his new program for subsidized vehicles to the price of oil. "The situation isn't serious," he concluded. "The situation is under control." It was a bizarre statement. The television screens showed the opposite. Chávez had committed his biggest mistake of the day by ordering the networks off the air and contradicting the reality of what was happening outside.

When he finished speaking at 5:15 P.M., the violence was so close to the palace that bodyguards made him walk back to his office through a tunnel instead of on the palace grounds. It was too dangerous to step outside. Now he learned the full extent of the violence on the streets. He made his way upstairs, slipped out of his suit and tie, and put on his combat fatigues and red beret. Then he strapped a pistol to his leg and grabbed an assault rifle. He believed the rebellion was entering a second stage. Military rebels were going to attack the palace. He called Brazilian president Henrique Cardoso. It was his first call of the day outside the country. He wanted the president of Venezuela's biggest neighbor to know what was happening.

He called Rincón at Fort Tiuna and told him to come to Miraflores with the high command to analyze the situation. They took off in a helicopter about 6:30 P.M. for the short ride. General Manuel Rosendo, who had vanished when Chávez called him earlier in the day to implement the Plan Avila, had reappeared and climbed aboard the helicopter. So did García Carneiro and Defense Minister José Vicente Rangel. But the head of the army, General Efraín Vásquez Velasco, was nowhere to be seen. Meanwhile, Chávez ordered one of Carneiro's underlings at Fort Tiuna to send tanks. He needed protection. A few arrived, but Vásquez Velasco later ordered them back to Fort Tiuna. He was no longer with the president — he had joined the coup.

As Chávez scrambled to respond to the rapidly unfolding events, the opposition moved quickly to take advantage of the violence. They blamed it on him. They depicted Chávez as a cold-blooded killer who ordered the repression to stop peaceful marchers from removing him from office — and then tried to cover it up by yanking the networks off the air. Lameda, Molina Tamayo, Carmona, Ortega, and other opposition leaders had fled from central Caracas on motorcycles a few minutes before the shooting began. Many rendezvoused at Venevisión, the television station owned by Gustavo Cisneros, who had been hosting the luncheon for US ambassador Charles Shapiro that afternoon. At 5:20 P.M., five minutes after Chávez stopped speaking, Lameda and Tamayo went on the air. "To all the armed forces, please do something," Tamayo said. "This government is now illegitimate. Not one step back."

An hour later Carmona, a string of opposition leaders, and even Chávez's former top adviser, Luis Miquilena, also started appearing and denouncing the president for the killings. Around the same time, the country was stunned when ten previously unknown high-ranking military officers appeared on the screen and said they no longer recognized Chávez as the chief of state. Dressed in his navy whites, Vice Admiral Héctor Ramírez said, "We have decided to address the people to announce we are removing our support for the government and the authority of Hugo Rafael Chávez Frias and the military high command for violating the main democratic principles and guarantees, and violating the Venezuelans' human rights . . . The president of the Republic has betrayed the trust of the people, he is massacring innocent people with snipers. Just now more than six people were killed and dozens wounded in Caracas."

The crowning blow came around 7:30 P.M. Venevisión started airing video that seemed to condemn Chávez beyond doubt. Earlier that afternoon, the network had stationed a cameraman and a reporter on the rooftop of a building on Avenida Urdaneta between Llaguno Bridge and Miraflores. They had a clear shot of the bridge, although not of Avenida Baralt below it where some of the violence was taking place. The Venevisión crew captured video of clearly identifiable Chávez supporters dressed in red berets or MVR T-shirts poking their heads from around a corner building at the side of the bridge and firing pistols. The implication was clear: The Chavistas had killed the marchers.

In one scene a man who turned out to be Chávez supporter and municipal councilman Richard Penalver was shown crouching down and peeking out from the corner of the building next to the overpass. Then he extended his right arm and squeezed the trigger of the pistol repeatedly. Standing behind him were a dozen Chavistas, including one in a red beret and another holding a gun. It was an outrageous scene: an elected official mowing down peaceful protestors.

Venevisión started playing that scene and others like it from the bridge repeatedly, juxtaposed with separate footage of dead or wounded protestors. A newscaster in the studio provided the interpretation of what had happened. "Now pay attention," he said. "Look at this man in the MVR T-shirt and the gray jacket, how he fires the gun, how he empties it. This man has just fired against marchers who came here peacefully, who are absolutely unarmed . . . They shoot the hundreds of defenseless demonstrators again and again."

As the screen showed people carrying some of the victims toward Miraflores, the newscaster added, "Here you can see those wounded by bullets arriving at Miraflores. It appears they had foreseen this. They had absolutely foreseen this because they had already set up a small mobile hospital in Miraflores, where they were treating as you have seen this afternoon those wounded by gunshot, victims of the armed MVR supporters and the Bolivarian Circles."

The newscaster then accused the Chávez supporters of planning an armed ambush against the marchers. While showing footage of the Chavistas lying on the street by the overpass, behind a metal rail, he said, "Look, here they are already in attack position. These are the Bolivarian Circles, firing rockets to disorient and attempt to somehow camouflage the action they are about to take with firearms."

It was a shocking piece of television journalism. The nation was outraged. Even avid Chávez backers were disgusted and decided they could no longer support a president who ordered his armed supporters to massacre peaceful marchers. The video was so impressive and horrifying that several months later the Venevisión news team won the prestigious King of Spain Journalism Award.

There was only one problem with the video footage. It was manipulated.

As later investigations and documentary films proved, the Chavistas on the bridge probably did not kill anybody. When they were captured on film shooting, they were not firing at the marchers, but at the Metropolitan Police and snipers who were firing at them. They were defending themselves and the hundreds of unarmed Chávez supporters on the bridge, who were lying facedown on the street to avoid the bullets coming at them — not to launch an "ambush." The Venevisión video never showed what the Chavistas were shooting at on Avenida Baralt. It only showed them firing.

As the documentary film *Llaguno Bridge — Keys to a Massacre* later demonstrated, using videos and digital photographs with the current time recorded, the bulk of the opposition marchers who were killed were shot between 3:20 P.M., when Tony Velásquez was wounded, and 3:55 P.M. The Chavistas filmed on the bridge did not start shooting until 4:38 P.M. Nearly forty-five minutes passed between the two events. But Venevisión combined them, to make it seem like the Chavistas had killed the marchers.

On top of that, most of the opposition marchers who died were at least three hundred yards away from the bridge — too far to be killed by the Chavistas with pistols. Some victims, such as the news photographer Jorge Tortoza and opposition marcher Malvina Pesate, were actually on a side street just off Avenida Baralt. They could not physically be reached by bullets fired from the overpass because there was no angle. Another victim, Juan David Querales, was even farther away from the bridge, and completely out of sight of the shooters on the overpass because he was not standing on Baralt.

Moreover, it turned out that many if not most of the nineteen people who died were not opposition marchers but Chávez supporters. Three of them were standing in front of Miraflores Palace two blocks away from Llaguno Bridge. They almost certainly were shot by snipers. The mobile hospital the Venevisión newscaster ominously pointed to had in fact been erected three days earlier to treat heatstroke victims during the pro-Chávez rallies. At least three Chavistas, including Pedro Linares, were killed on or near the bridge. In the media's version, they did not exist. They were never mentioned.

There was also another problem with the pronouncement made by navy vice admiral Ramírez and the others. It was taped. Otto Neudstadl, a correspondent with CNN en Español, later said at a public conference that when Ramírez and the others summoned him to an office in Caracas earlier in the day to tape the announcement, it was before any shots had been fired at the marchers. The military officers seemed to have advance knowledge that people were going to be killed. They even offered a number up to that point: at least six, with dozens injured.

It seemed clear that many of the victims were shot by snipers on rooftops or the upper floors of surrounding buildings. Many were killed or wounded by shots to the head or thorax. The trajectory of the bullets was downward. Government agents, in fact, soon arrested seven armed men who were found in the Hotel Ausonia, but they were to be freed amid the chaos caused by the coup. Investigators later found empty shells in the Hotel Eden. It was next to impossible that the Chavistas on the bridge had inflicted such precise injuries on so many victims who were so far away. It had to be highly trained snipers with high-power weapons, not Saturday Night Specials. It was certainly theoretically possible that some rogue Chavistas who were weapons experts climbed onto roofs and decided to take out the marchers, or even that the government ordered them there. It was also possible some Chavistas on the streets as well as National Guardsmen shot and injured some opposition marchers. But it appeared most likely that the mayhem started when snipers shot at both sides in order to create chaos and bloodshed, and to provoke armed Chavistas into responding. The killings begged the question: Who benefited? Clearly, Chávez did not. But now, with the streets of Caracas bathed in blood and the nation's television screens filled with horrifying reports of the massacre, the opposition had "the political cover to stage a coup" that the CIA reported they lacked five days earlier. Chávez was a cold-blooded murderer. Who could blame the military for stepping in and removing him?

The international media ran with the local media's version of the killings, almost preconditioned to unquestioningly accept the opposition's version of events and dismiss the government's point of view as absurd. They sent the infamous videotape of the Llaguno Bridge shooters around the world and repeated the opposition's statements blaming Chávez for the massacre.

Freelance reporter and *Miami Herald* contributor Phil Gunson told National Public Radio listeners in the United States that "the deaths and injuries appear to have been caused by snipers, apparently from the government's side, apparently from a roof of a building that's in the hands of government supporters, and also from the presidential guard." When a studio host asked about the government response to the accusation, Gunson replied, "Well, I spoke to somebody in the palace just a little while ago who told me that the version that they were being given there was that the killings had been carried out by the Metropolitan Police, which is in the hands of the opposition. That's certainly totally false from what I know." Chávez has "done precisely what he said he would never do," he added, "which is to have his security forces fire on the demonstrators in the streets."

Most of the rest of the commercial media took the same angle. CBS news reporter Anthony Mason told millions of viewers, "In the end, this is what triggered the overthrow of Hugo Chávez: Armed gangs loyal to the Venezuelan president fired on thousands of anti-government protestors." The *St. Petersburg Times* reported that "as protestors neared the palace, government troops opened fire with live rounds and tear gas, according to eyewitnesses." The paper quoted one Venezuelan journalist as saying, "It was an ambush." *The New York Times* said Chávez "was obligated to resign" after "at least 14 people were killed by gunmen identified as his supporters." *The Miami Herald* reported that "pro-Chávez soldiers and civilians opened fire on a massive street march called to demand the president's resignation." Viewers of PBS's respected *NewsHour* heard a host undoubtedly relying on international news reports state that "Chávez ordered National Guard troops and civilian gunmen to fire on the nearly two hundred thousand protestors to stop them from reaching his palace."

That night, not long after the Llaguno Bridge tape first appeared on Venevisión, the head of the army, Efraín Vásquez Velasco, came on television and delivered what seemed to be the final blow to Chávez.

Flanked by other high-ranking officers, he said, "Today, all the human rights consecrated in our Bolivarian Constitution of Venezuela were violated. Venezuelans died because of the incapacity of the government to dialogue." Stating that it was not the job of the military to hurt or "combat" civilians, he apologized to the Venezuelan people and ordered all troops to remain in their barracks. "This isn't a coup d'état. It isn't insubordination. It's a position of solidarity with the people of Venezuela." Then, in a phrase that echoed through the country like a jail cell door slamming shut, Vásquez Velasco said, "Mr. President, I was loyal to you until the end. But the violation of human rights and the deaths of today can't be tolerated." He turned his attention to the rest of the high command, and said, "Fulfill your duty. You are honorable men."

Chávez was in serious trouble. He wanted to get the government's word out about what had happened that afternoon, but the opposition controlled the media. No Venezuelan television station would interview him or other government officials. Police led by Miranda governor Enrique Mendoza stormed the state-run channel 8 and took it over. Mendoza announced that "this garbage of *Canal* 8 will be going off the air in the next few hours." Employees threw one last tape on before they fled — an old nature documentary about ducklings. It played over and over while the country was on the verge of going up in flames.

On the grounds of Miraflores, several of Chávez's top allies, including Education Minister Aristóbulo Istúriz, used a mobile unit to try to broadcast a message. Istúriz looked at his watch and said it was 9:20 P.M., as if to show the message was live and not taped. Congressman Juan Barreto tried to present the government's version of events. He addressed the military, where the coup plotters were trying to convince other officers to join the revolt — principally by making them watch the scenes of bloodshed on television and listen to the reports that Chávez ordered his followers to massacre the marchers. "Officers who may be confused by this type of media lies," Barreto said, ". . . it was the other side that massacred us." But a few minutes later the screen went blank. Channel 8, Chávez's last lifeline to the Venezuelan public, was dead.

Less than an hour later he ordered his wife, Marisabel, and their four-year-old daughter, Rosinés, evacuated out of the capital by airplane. He also ordered his other three children, Rosa Virginia, María Gabriela, and Hugo Rafael to abandon Caracas. He feared for their lives. Unknown to Chávez, his parents were inside the palace, where they remained. His oldest children fled for a house on the Caribbean coast. Marisabel and Rosinés flew to Barquísimeto. The activity at La Carlota military base in eastern Caracas, where flights normally are prohibited after dark, provoked hope among Chávez's opponents that he was preparing to leave the country. Reenacting a scene from 1958 when Marcos Pérez Jiménez's regime collapsed and the dictator fled, anti-Chávez protestors lit candles outside the airport in anticipation of his departure. They also wrote the names of Chávez's top allies on a wall. They were wanted — dead or alive.

While Chávez was cut off from the media and even his own state-run television station, the opposition had full access. By now they had regained their regular transmissions. Carmona came on the screen again. "What is important now is that the president must take respon-sibility . . . and resign now without a fight," he said. Lameda, the fired PDVSA head, appealed directly to the military. "Colonels. Officers. Lower-level officers. Troops. Those of you who are in the barracks. Because I know the armed forces I know you're watching this right now and you're not sure what to do. Take advantage of this message, think, and make the right decision."

By 10:20 P.M., National Guard general Alberto Camacho Kairuz came on to declare that Chávez had "abandoned" his office. "All of the country is under the control of the national armed forces," Camacho said. "The government has abandoned its functions." Adding to the myth created by the media that the marchers were killed by the Chavistas and were "martyrs of the democracy," Camacho blamed Chávez and said the demonstrators "were massacred from the rooftops." Ramón Escovar Salom, a former attorney general under Carlos Andrés Pérez, pounded home the allegation. "This is state terrorism," he said. "The interna-tional community must condemn these killings. This government is criminal." Caracas mayor Alfredo Peña joined in. "Chávez has shown his true face. This dictator's apprentice brutally ordered the repression of a peaceful demonstration." Because the allegations were repeated nonstop and the Venevisión tape played over and over, it was hard to doubt that it was the truth.

Chávez in reality had not "abandoned" the presidency. He was holed up in his office. He was trying to figure out his next move. He wanted to bring in the Catholic Church to help mediate a solution as the situa-tion got out of control. He tried calling Archbishop Ignacio Velasco, but couldn't reach him. Then he called Bishop Baltazar Porras, who agreed to come to the palace but in the end never did. Chávez contacted the ambassadors from France, China, Mexico, Cuba, and other countries. He wanted to inform them of what was happening and seek their help as mediators.

Around midnight, Fidel Castro called from Havana; Chávez was surprised he'd gotten through. Castro urged Chávez not to "self-immolate." He warned him against waging a senseless military resistance against the rebels or ending the crisis with the military the way Salvador Allende had in Chile in 1973. "I phoned Chávez because I knew he was defenseless and that he was a man of principle, and said to him, 'Don't kill yourself, Hugo! Don't do like Allende! Allende was a man alone, he didn't have a single soldier on his side. You have a large part of the army. Don't quit! Don't resign!'"

Chávez was too young and too important a figure to the left in Latin America to allow himself to be killed in a coup. The advice from Castro played an important role as Chávez debated what do while his presidency and his life hung in the balance. José Vicente Rangel, who accompanied Chávez most of the night, later commented, "The call from Fidel was decisive so that there was no self-immolation. It was the determinant factor. His advice allowed us to see better in the darkness."

Stuck in the darkness in an environment of overwhelming tension and confusion, Chávez got another call from General Raúl Baduel. One of the founders of the MBR-200 in 1982, he was now in charge of Chávez's old paratrooper unit in Maracay. Baduel wasn't surprised by the unfolding putsch. On April 5 he'd written in his diary, "The coup is imminent." He made a note to himself to call the president and warn him. But he never got through. Now he was calling to pledge his full support, "until death." He wanted to storm Caracas. Chávez thanked him for his loyalty. He was receiving calls from other commanders around the country pledging their support, too. Like Castro said, he wasn't alone. Chávez told Baduel his support and that of the others was serving as a "factor of contention so they don't come to attack us here in the palace and kill us." If Chávez wanted to fight back, he had the firepower. But according to Baduel, the president ordered him to hold back. "Brother, I order you, and more than ordering you, I beg you that neither you nor your unit become a factor in a bloodbath." Miraflores was surrounded by thousands of Chavistas. If the two forces clashed at the palace, carnage was inevitable.

• • •

Chávez designated two generals, Manuel Rosendo and Ismael Hurtado Soucre, to serve as emissaries to the rebels, now holed up in Fort Tiuna. He dispatched them to the fort to see what the rebels wanted and to open negotiations to find a way out — possibly by Chávez resigning or abandoning his post. Not long after, he also sent General Lucas Rincón Romero, the top-ranking military officer, to Fort Tiuna to inform him of what was happening.

On the fifth floor of the army headquarters in Fort Tiuna, even as the streets of Caracas were still wet with blood, the coup leaders were celebrating wildly. They believed their plan to oust Chávez had worked. They thought he was cornered and on his way out. Nearly the entire nation was convinced he had blood on his hands, thanks to the stunning Venevisión footage. High-ranking officers were hugging and congratulating one another. They downed whiskey and champagne. They were half delirious, as if it were New Year's Eve. Among the group was General Enrique Medina Gómez, Venezuela's military attaché in Washington, DC. He had flown in to Caracas earlier in the day.

Around midnight, a civilian showed up to join the military officers: Pedro Carmona. As the Fedecámaras head has told the story, the officers called saying they needed him to form the new government. Carmona responded to their call. He left Venevisión and headed over to Fort Tiuna. It was all part of a spontaneous reaction to the horrifying events of the afternoon, according to Carmona and the rebels. The military officers also said they were rebelling because Chávez had ordered them to implement the Plan Avila, which they now described as a macabre scheme to massacre innocent people.

Other evidence suggested that there was little spontaneous about the day's events at all — that they were part of a carefully planned and orchestrated rebellion aimed at overthrowing Chávez. One plotter, Colonel Julio Rodríguez Salas, went on television a little after 11 P.M. that night and stunned viewers when he told opposition journalist Ibeyise Pacheco, "Nine months ago a movement started to organize itself more firmly, a serious movement, and fortunately it has come to fruition today."

Chávez's ally Jorge Luis García Carneiro, the general who tried unsuccessfully earlier in the day to implement the Plan Avila, had returned from Miraflores to Fort Tiuna, and was taken prisoner by the rebels on the fifth floor after midnight. Some, including Medina, told him their plot to oust Chávez had been in the works for months, if not longer, and that they planned to have people killed to justify the coup against him. "They told me this was planned from years back, because it was the only way there would be fewer deaths," García Carneiro later told an interviewer. "They had even planned some deaths as actually occurred. They had the snipers in the sector where they [the plotters] never passed. They wanted to kill people on both sides to create confusion . . . That is where I convinced myself that, in fact, everything was well organized and that they had planned a massacre on the Llaguno Bridge to justify the participation of the armed forces against the president."

It was a version of events the plotters were to vigorously deny, but when Lucas Rincón showed up at Fort Tiuna after midnight, he heard similar stories, according to testimony he later delivered before the National Assembly. Navy vice admiral Héctor Ramírez, the officer who made the dramatic taped announcement at 7 P.M., told Rincón he had been involved in the plot for six months. Ramírez said a junta would be named and presided over probably by a businessman.

Carmona and other civilians who joined him went to work finishing off a decree making him the next president. The civilians included Daniel Romero, a lawyer and former political secretary to Carlos Andrés Pérez. In reality, Carmona already had a draft of the detailed document. It was written ahead of time and shown a day earlier on April 10 by Romero to Chávez critic and leading intellectual Jorge Olavarria for his comments. Surprised by the contents of the document, Olavarria told Romero it would violate democratic norms and provoke an international reaction.

Besides the revelations about the plan, García Carneiro was also surprised by two people he said he saw with the plotters: officers from the US military mission. They were later identified as Lieutenant Colonel James Rogers and Colonel Ronald McCammon. The Americans still had an office in Fort Tiuna, although the Venezuelan government had requested they leave nearly a year ago. It would be like Venezuela maintaining an office inside the Pentagon. The presence of Rogers and McCammon, along with reports of American ships and helicopters off Venezuela's western coast, were to raise questions about the role of the United States in the revolt. The United States later said that Rogers and McCammon simply drove to Fort Tiuna that afternoon to check on reports of troop movements and were in no way involved in any revolt. The American ships were participating in routine training exercises, the government said.

The rebels and Chávez launched into a confusing series of negotiations. Rosendo and Hurtado traveled back and forth between Miraflores and Fort Tiuna and spoke to Chávez on the phone. The negotiations were complicated because the rebels were fighting among themselves over what post each one would get in the new government, and over what to do with Chávez. Some were willing to let him leave the country and go into exile. Others wanted him to remain and be put on trial for the killings that afternoon.

Sometime after midnight Chávez's ministers and top allies huddled in his office to debate what they should do. They figured they had three options. They could try to move the seat of the government to Maracay, where Chávez had the support of Baduel. They could remain in the palace and resist — fight it out militarily with the rebels when they attacked. Or Chávez could cede to the rebels' demands and resign.

Chávez's new environmental minister, Ana Elisa Osorio, and his higher education minister, Héctor Navarro, among others, favored the first option. "Let's go to Maracay, we have strength there," Navarro said. But Chávez didn't think it was feasible. He thought they would be captured by the rebels as they tried to make their way to Maracay ninety miles away. They had no tanks to accompany them — the ones he had ordered to Miraflores were ordered back to Fort Tiuna by General Efraín Vásquez Velasco.

José Vicente Rangel, Chávez's brother Adán, and others favored the second option. Rangel had been exiled to Chile during the Pérez Jiménez dictatorship and was a friend of Salvador Allende. He didn't want Chávez to become another Allende. He wanted to at least go down fighting. His son, José Vicente Rangel Avelo, a local mayor, was with him in the palace. At one point the elder Rangel told him, "Get out of here, because we are going to die." The son refused. Rangel also called his wife, Anita, and told her, "I'm giving you the bad news that you're going to be a widow and without a son."

But there were also thousands of Chavistas outside the palace in the streets. If fighting broke out, there would be numerous deaths. According to Rangel's son, Chávez spoke serenely to the group and said, "There will not be a bloodbath. I'll never permit innocent people to die."

The only way to avoid such a bloodbath seemed to be to give in to the rebels' demand that he step down. Chávez told the group he would consider resigning if the rebels granted four conditions. The first was respecting the physical safety of his top government officials, his family, and himself. Second, they had to respect the constitution, allowing him to resign before the National Assembly and be succeeded in office by the vice president as the magna carta called for until new elections were called. Third, he wanted to address the nation live on television. Finally, he wanted safe passage out of the country for his cabinet, his bodyguards, his family, and himself. He considered heading to Cuba and the safety Castro could offer.

After the meeting with his ministers ended, Chávez asked the group to leave him alone. He needed time to think. As they got up to leave, he took the revolver off his leg strap and put it on a table. It was one of the most difficult moments of his life. Dozens of people were dead or injured after the afternoon's events. Some of his most trusted allies in the military were betraying him. He was cut off from the media. His presidency seemed over, drowned in a sea of blood on the streets outside the palace. As Chávez's allies walked out of his office, some braced for the sound of a gunshot. They feared Chávez might choose to end the crisis with the military the same way Allende had in 1973: by killing himself.

Rosendo and Hurtado eventually returned to Miraflores from Fort Tiuna, and informed Chávez that the rebels had agreed to his four conditions. They wanted him to step down as quickly as possible. They needed a signed resignation letter so the revolt would not appear to be a coup but a voluntary departure performed within "constitutional norms." They faxed a prepared resignation letter to Miraflores. At one point three rebel leaders brought the original copy to the palace for Chávez to sign. As the minutes ticked by, they were losing patience. With daybreak a few hours away, they started threatening to bomb the palace if he did not give up. They said the bombs would start falling in fifteen minutes.

With his back against the wall, Chávez called Rincón at Fort Tiuna a little before 3 A.M. He told the general he was accepting the rebels' demand that he step down. He had no choice. Half an hour later, Rincón went on national television and dropped a bombshell. Most of the country was glued to their television sets or listening to radios; no one really knew what was going on. Rincón seemed to end the confusion. In a grammatically twisted statement, he said, "The military leadership abhors today's events. In light of these events, it was requested of the president that he resign his post, which he accepted." He also announced that the high command was resigning.

It sounded to most people like Chávez had quit and left what opponents quickly called a *vacio de poder* — a power vacuum. Middle-class residents celebrated, leaning out the windows of their high-rises to cheer and shout. People stopped their cars on highways and got out to yell their jubilation. Television networks started playing Rincón's message every twenty minutes for the next thirty-six hours. The news went around the world that Chávez had resigned.

But according to Chávez's account, it wasn't that simple, as he told interviewer Marta Harnecker. For one thing, he was forced to resign with a gun pointed at his head.

> I had authorized General Rincón, who had been with me the whole evening and night, to go to Fort Tiuna to find out what those people really wanted. In the middle of these events he called me and said: "President, they're demanding your resignation and they're putting pressure on me to resign as well. But I've said that I'll follow whatever decision you make." Then I told him: "Look, Lucas, Rosendo and Hurtado have arrived and they've told me that they accept the conditions that I am demanding for my resignation. Tell them that yes, I will resign." I gave him the green light. He leaves saying what I told him. What he said was: "The President has accepted the demand for his resignation and so have I. My position is at the disposition of the high command." Therefore, I'm completely sure that he said what I had told him by phone.
>
> What happened ten, twenty minutes later? He declares my resignation and leaves, but a few minutes later we receive word that they no longer accept the four conditions. I was almost certain that they were not going to accept; it was a way to stall for time. Next they demanded that I go there as a prisoner. If I refused they threatened to attack the palace . . . And that was the end — I left as a prisoner.

Outside Chávez's office, his ministers had not seen him for nearly two hours. They wanted to know what was going on. They were confused by Rincón's announcement. They started banging on the door to be let in. A guard finally opened it. Chávez was sitting in a chair when they walked in. He seemed serene. He explained the situation. He said he wasn't going to resign. He was going to surrender himself as a "president prisoner." He had no choice. The rebels were going to start bombing at any moment. He followed the advice of José Vicente Rangel, who urged him not to sign any resignation letter. "Don't sign so it's a coup, Hugo," he said.

Osorio, the environmental minister, came out of the president's office to inform the crowd what was happening. "Politically, it's clear this is a coup," she said. "It's not that the president resigned. He didn't resign. He's being taken a prisoner because it's a coup." Then, her voice rising and tears welling in her eyes, she said, "Let the world know: It's a coup!" The crowd started clapping and yelling in defiant defense of Chávez. "It's a coup!" Osorio shouted. "It's a coup against the people, against the people of Venezuela who love him!" She wiped a tear that was running down her cheek. The crowd broke into shouts of "Hugo! Hugo! Hugo!" People clapped their hands above their heads. Others pumped their fists in the air.

Inside his office, Chávez prepared to say good-bye to his ministers. Hurtado told them to hurry. The rebels were threatening to commence the bombing. The president embraced each one of his ministers. They wanted to go with him, to protect him. They believed it would be harder for the rebels to kill fifteen ministers than to eliminate Chávez by himself, blaming it on a suicide or an airplane accident. But the rebels refused. "I gave [Jorge] Giordani and [Héctor] Navarro hugs and I said goodbye to my dispatch, saying, 'The strategic window has closed.' They did not respond. I thought I was going to die. That ominous feeling crossed my mind for a few moments. I said goodbye to everyone who was with me there in the palace."

He handed over his pistol to the interior minister, Ramón Rodríguez Chacin, and walked out the door of his office. When he appeared in the hallway, his supporters started singing the national anthem. "*Gloria al bravo pueblo,*" they intoned. Glory to the valiant people. Chávez slowly made his way through the crush of people, hugging them and shaking hands. He seemed serene, at peace with his decision. To Navarro, Chávez was making a heroic decision. "The president opted to sacrifice himself and not produce a bloodbath."

As Chávez pushed through the crowd, it was almost like the reception line at a funeral. People didn't know if they were going to see him alive again. Tears streamed down many of their faces. Jacinto Pérez Arcay, one of his instructors from the military academy, thrust a small blue cross into his hands. "Take it with you, and God bless you," the elderly general said. "This isn't ending here." Chávez saw José Vicente Rangel leaning against a wall. He wanted to hug him, but could only reach his hand. Rangel looked at the president with an enigmatic smile, somewhere between hope and despair, as if to say, We'll see each other here again — but not convinced they would. A sobbing Noheli Pocaterra, one of three indigenous leaders elected to the constitutional assembly, said to him wistfully, "What are we Indians going to do without you?"

The young men of Chávez's honor guard got on their knees and asked for Chávez's blessing. Many were crying. They wanted to fight back, to turn the palace into a bunker and defend the president. But Chávez told them no, you are too young, with too many years ahead of you. As he neared the door leading outside the palace to a car that was going to take him away, the crowd broke into applause. "I'll only be away for a short time," he said. "We will return."

His mother, who had remained in the palace throughout the ordeal, broke through the crowd, grabbed the car door, and tried to get in. Someone stopped her and said "Ma'am, we're going now."

The president left Miraflores about 4 A.M., sitting between Rosendo and Hurtado in the backseat. Istúriz and some of his other ministers followed in a vehicle of their own. They wanted to go into Fort Tiuna with him, although soldiers stopped them. Chávez spoke little during the trip. They drove through Caracas, passing the Southern General Cemetery where his childhood baseball idol Isaías "Latigo" Chávez was buried, before turning into the familiar grounds of Fort Tiuna. They pulled up to the military headquarters building on the sprawling campus, and Chávez got out. A phalanx of soldiers met him. A television camera showed the back of his head and his red beret as he slowly made his way through the crowd and toward the entrance. Then he disappeared into the building.

Half an hour later, at 4:50 A.M., Pedro Carmona came on the television. He announced that he was taking over the country.

**21**

# The President Is Missing

The room at Fort Tiuna, packed with celebrating military officers, turned quiet when Hugo Chávez walked in. Rincón had announced his resignation an hour earlier, and to the rebels Chávez was no longer the president. But they still felt compelled to treat him with some deference. Waiting in the room with them were Bishops Baltazar Porras and José Luis Azuaje. "I sat down beside them, greeted them and we sat there for a while in silence," Chávez recalled.

Now that he was back in Fort Tiuna and among his military comrades, Chávez thought he might be able to resolve the crisis. He noticed that many of the officers were arguing among themselves. He knew Carmona was inside the building. General Romel Fuenmayor León moved to the front of the room, held out the resignation letter the rebels had prepared, and spoke on their behalf. Chávez recalled the scene:

> He made an analysis of the situation and said that in the name of all those present he was asking for my resignation in view of what they regarded as a situation of ungovernability. I told them, with a serene voice that was a little louder than usual so that they all could hear, that they should think long and hard about what they were doing, and what they planned to do — the responsibility that they were assuming with regard to Venezuela and the outside world — and I told them I was not going to resign. They had a piece of paper for me to sign, and I said that I was not going to so much as look at it.

Chávez reiterated that before signing any resignation letter the officers had to meet his four conditions. The officers did not respond.

> I told them that I was not sure that they would be able to control the military, and that I had talked to various commanders who had assured me that they would not accept a coup d'état . . . I could see that I was catching their attention, since, clearly, some of them had been manipulated. Others began to take notice.

General Néstor González González, the bald-headed officer who had held the press conference on April 10 and implied a coup was coming, interrupted Chávez. González could see that the deposed president was making an impact and did not want to let him continue. "We have not come here to discuss anything," González angrily told the gathering. "We know what we have to do. I ask you to move into the room next door."

The officers left, arguing behind closed doors about whether to grant Chávez's conditions. He stayed behind with the two bishops and a guard. They were alone for about an hour. Chávez asked Porras why he never showed up at Miraflores as he had promised. The priest simply said he couldn't. Chávez, who had called Porras one of the church's "devils in vestments," asked him for forgiveness. But he also reminded the bishops of their role in the conflict. He told them he felt at peace "because whatever my destiny is, whatever happens to me, I am here for being loyal to the people who elected me to respond to their interests and not the interests of the minority. I didn't let those powers, the economic powers, the media powers, twist my arm."

Porras recalled Chávez as something less than a portrait of tranquility. He had been betrayed by once loyal allies, feared for his life, and was no longer sure whom to trust in the military. "He was truly a shaken up man, reflective, he could do little more than evoke a series of scenes from his childhood, of the various military posts he had served in." At times Chávez seemed near tears, according to the bishop.

When the officers returned to the room, Vice Admiral Héctor Ramírez Pérez took over. He told Chávez the officers would not accept his conditions and that he could not leave the country. He would have to remain in Venezuela to "answer to the people for the crimes he committed." Chávez responded that he would not sign the resignation and they would have to arrest him. "But don't forget that you are taking the president of the Republic prisoner, and do whatever you feel is necessary."

They took Chávez to a small bedroom at the end of a long hall, ordered him out of his uniform, and had him put on jeans, sneakers, and a T-shirt aides had packed into a small suitcase for him before he left Miraflores. The rebels brought him some breakfast, and he asked for a chair and a small table. He had not slept in two nights, but he didn't feel tired. He also asked for a television.

When he clicked it on, he was incredulous at what he saw on the morning news programs. Television commentators, political analysts, opposition figures, even his former comrade in arms Francisco Arias Cárdenas were stating that he had resigned and Carmona was filling a "power vacuum." They described Chávez as an "assassin" for ordering his supporters to open fire on a peaceful march. The bottom of Venevisión's screen ran a message: VENEZUELA RECOVERED ITS LIBERTY. CHÁVEZ RESIGNED.

Napoleón Bravo's popular Venevisión program 24 Hours produced eye-opening statements from gleeful guests who suggested the ousting of Chávez was anything but the result of a spontaneous uprising by the military — and that the media had played a critical role. Victor Manuel García, director of the statistical institute Ceca who was at Fort Tiuna during the coup, said: "We were short of communications facilities, and I have to thank the media for their solidarity and cooperation in helping us to establish communications with the outside world and pass on the instructions that General González González gave me." García thanked Bravo for letting them use his house to record a call to rebellion by González. That prompted a laughing Bravo to respond, "I'm just a journalist!"

García explained the importance of Gonzalez's declaration to the media the previous Wednesday, April 10: "When we decided that General Néstor González was going to go public, it was because Chávez was going to Costa Rica, and we had to have Chávez in Venezuela. This pronouncement of General González González was so that Chávez would not go to Costa Rica, that he would stay in Venezuela. And that is when we activated the definitive plan."

And what was the plan? Bravo asked.

Rear Admiral Carlos Molina Tamayo answered. After leading the charge against Miraflores the previous afternoon, he was now dressed in his navy whites. "The original plan was that when the previous support of the civil society arrived at its maximum point, this support of the democratic society in general, to pass to the use of the armed forces."

Meanwhile, the morning newspapers also were filled with diatribes blaming Chávez for the previous day's bloodshed. "A grave has been reserved for you next to the Venezuelan presidents who are remembered for their atrocities," *El Nacional* said in a front-page editorial. "Now you have your own massacre." *Asi es La Noticia* ran a headline in large red letters: "The Assassin Fell." *El Universal* columnist Roberto Giusti, a former aide to Carlos Andrés Pérez, wrote an "analysis" piece titled "The Last Crime of a Dictator."

> If anyone at any time had any doubts about the fascist and assassin character of this regime, they should have cleared up yesterday . . . After years and years of solemnly swearing that as president he would never order shots to be fired at the people, yesterday Hugo Chávez once again stained his hands with blood. In the end he removed the mask of democracy and revealed his true nature of a killer without scruples who ordered his supporters to fire against a peaceful and unarmed crowd. Relentless, he was ready to preserve power over a mountain of cadavers, if necessary, while he spoke nonsense on radio and television.

As Chávez watched the television news programs blame him for the "massacre of El Silencio" and reiterate that he had resigned, he became alarmed. The thought occurred to him that the only way the rebels could keep him from telling the world that it was a lie that he had resigned was by killing him. They could say it was a suicide, like Salvador Allende in Chile twenty-nine years earlier. "I see that [on television] and I think: 'I'm dead. I'm dead. The only way that I will never refute that is they are going to kill me' . . . I was sure they were going to kill me. I even said to myself, 'I'm not going to make it past tonight.'"

Chávez needed to make contact with the outside world. He asked a guard for a telephone, saying he wanted to talk with his family to make sure they were all right. The guard agreed. As president, Chávez never phoned them directly himself, so he had to ask the guard to call Miraflores and get the numbers. The guard came back with a slip of paper.

Chávez could not get through to the governor's mansion in Barinas, but he did reach his wife, Marisabel. It was about 9 A.M. He spoke quickly. "Look, Marisabel, this is what's happening. I need you to find me a journalist, some media, from here or international, and that you, the First Lady of the country, tell them that the president has not resigned, that he's a prisoner. I think they are going to kill me. Tonight I am sure they are going to take me out of here and it's to kill me, if we don't denounce this beforehand. Move quickly."

Chávez was also able to reach his daughters María Gabriela and Rosa Virginia, in hiding on the Caribbean coast. Rosa, at twenty-four the eldest, answered the phone. Overcome with emotion, she started to cry. She could not speak. She passed the phone to María, who tried to maintain some calm as her father spoke. "Look, my love, listen to what I am going to tell you. Are you OK? Take it easy. I don't have much time. I just need you to talk to someone, call someone, call some journalist. See how you can do it. It could be through Fidel. Make an effort, one way or the other, so that the world knows I have not resigned. Tell them with your own voice that your father told you he's a prisoner, and that I am not going to resign."

They hung up, and María called the vice president, Diosdado Cabello, who was also in hiding. Then she called Miraflores Palace. Her telephone could not call outside the country. She needed the workers at the palace to help put her through.

The rebels had not removed the Miraflores staff from their positions. The switchboard operators were still loyal to Chávez. "This is María Gabriela and I need to call Fidel Castro, in Cuba," she told one of them.

When I heard that they had connected me with the office of Fidel, I started to cry. I fell apart. As soon as he heard my voice, he told me, "María, how are you?" His voice was very soft. "Fidel, help us, please." "Calm down, María." I was desperate. "My father asked me to tell you that if he dies today, it will be because he was faithful to his convictions until the last moment. He expressly told me I should tell you." I told him about the entire conversation. As I spoke, I felt like an enormous weight was lifted. I knew Fidel would not abandon us.

Two hours later, at 11 A.M., Castro had María on the telephone with Cuban journalist Randy Alonso, the host of a Cuban television program called *Mesa Redonda*, Roundtable. Live on Cuban television, María recounted what was happening.

Two hours ago we were finally able to speak to my father. He called us on the phone and told us to please tell the world that he had not resigned at any time, that he has never signed a presidential decree to depose Vice President Diosdado Cabello and let alone resign. Basically, a number of military officers went in, detained him and took him to Fort Tiuna, the army's headquarters. He is currently being held at the military police's regimental headquarters in Fort Tiuna. They are holding him incommunicado. They have only permitted him to speak to us, his children . . . He never actually resigned. It is simply a coup d'état, which they are trying to cover up with an alleged resignation.

A far-right dictatorship is being instituted in the country and they are looking to cover it up with an alleged resignation. It is all a lie. They are searching for all those who sympathize with the government in order to arrest them. So they are all in hiding.

After María's interview, Castro called her every half hour to offer support. But her declarations that Chávez never resigned and was being held incommunicado never reached the Venezuelan public — at least not through the local mainstream media. Besides lambasting Chávez and blaming him for the massacre, they were also imposing a blackout on all things pro-Chávez. One news director at Radio Caracas Television, Andrés Izarra, the son of ARMA founder William Izarra, recalled getting the order from his bosses. "There was a very clear directive, drawn on Friday the 12th, and the directive was, on the screen, zero pro-Chávez, nothing related to Chávez or his supporters, his congressmen or his ministers," Izarra said. "The idea was to create a climate of transition and to start to promote the dawn of a new country."

The next day, disgusted by the violation of journalistic ethics, Izarra quit. He eventually joined Chávez's government as a spokesman after the Venezuelan media blacklisted him.

After Chávez spoke to his daughters that morning, two women from the military's legal department arrived to interview him. Chávez told them he had not resigned and was still the president of the republic. The women checked his health, filled out a form, and had Chávez sign it. He noticed they made no mention of his statements. But after the women left and were out of the guard's sight, they added a few words in small letters at the bottom of the paper: "He said he has not resigned."

The women faxed a copy of the statement to Attorney General Isaías Rodríguez, who immediately recognized its importance. He wanted to publicize it, but he knew the Venezuelan media would not allow him to do so on television or radio. So he tricked them. He said he was convening a press conference to announce his own resignation. He summoned the media to his office in Caracas and sat down behind his desk. It was 2 P.M., and he was appearing live nationwide on television and radio. But what he started to say was not what the reporters expected. Instead of lambasting Chávez, he announced the president had never quit.

> We have information from military attorneys who interviewed him that the president has not resigned. In fact, the president has not resigned and at no time has written proof of this resignation been shown to the attorney general's office. President Chávez continues to be president of the Republic of Venezuela.
>
> But in the supposed case that the president has resigned, the resignation of the president must be before the National Assembly. Only when the National Assembly accepts this resignation can it be considered valid. Therefore, even in the supposed case that the president has resigned, in fact he continues to be president of the Republic because no act has been carried out in the National Assembly to validate the supposed resignation of the president.

A journalist tried to interrupt Rodríguez's statement with a question, but he pushed on. He stated that Chávez was being illegally held incommunicado, with not even the attorney general's office permitted to see him. "If he is deprived of liberty, what crime did he commit? The crime of resigning? Resigning is a crime? . . . The situation is truly grave from the constitutional point of view . . . There is no constitutional state."

Most of Rodríguez's statement never got out. The Venezuelan networks cut him off before he finished and returned to the studios. Flustered news hosts like one at Venevisión stumbled with lines such as, "Well friends, how are you? I wish you all a good afternoon." But combined with María Gabriel Chávez's statements on Cuban television, word was slowly leaking out overseas that the opposition and Venezuelan media's version of events were at a minimum questionable.

Despite that, the coup quickly won backing from the US government. Nearly two hours after María Gabriela Chávez spoke on Cuban television, White House spokesman Ari Fleischer addressed reporters during his daily briefing. He blamed Chávez for the bloodshed and all but endorsed the putsch: "Government supporters, on orders from the Chávez government, fired on unarmed, peaceful protestors, resulting in ten killed and one hundred wounded." The State Department issued a similar statement through spokesman Philip Reeker:

> The Venezuelan military commendably refused to fire on peaceful demonstrators, and the media valiantly kept the Venezuelan public informed . . . Though details are still unclear, undemocratic actions committed or encouraged by the Chávez administration provoked yesterday's crisis in Venezuela . . . The Chávez government attempted to suppress peaceful demonstrations. Chávez supporters, on orders, fired on unarmed, peaceful protestors, resulting in more than one hundred wounded or killed. Venezuelan military and police refused orders to fire on peaceful demonstrators and refused to support the government's role in such human rights violations. The government prevented five independent television stations from reporting on events.

The statement was remarkable on many levels, including the allegation that Chávez "provoked" the crisis. The top-secret CIA briefs delivered to high-level government officials clearly warned before the revolt that a coup was brewing. The April 6 brief said opposition figures might "provoke military action" by exploiting "unrest stemming from opposition demonstrations slated for later this month or ongoing strikes at the state-owned oil company PDVSA." It even mentioned plans for arresting Chávez.

Inside the State Department building that Friday, April 12, Otto Reich, President George W. Bush's point man on Latin America, was working to convince other Latin American nations to accept the new government in Venezuela. Reich, who had Venezuelan television networks piped into his office and was getting updates from Venevisión owner Gustavo Cisneros in Caracas, summoned ambassadors from around the region to his office. He tried to make the case that Chávez had violently suppressed the march and voluntarily stepped down. He urged the ambassadors to recognize the new government led by Pedro Carmona.

"The Bush administration could hardly contain its glee Friday over the overthrow of President Hugo Chávez," one reporter wrote. Michael

Skol, the former US. ambassador to Venezuela, told National Public Radio listeners that "the White House was delighted, I'm sure, to see Chávez ousted, and even more delighted that the US had nothing to do with it." Republican senator Jesse Helms of North Carolina said, "The tragic deaths of a number of Venezuelans notwithstanding, Hugo Chávez's resignation as president of Venezuela early this morning can only be seen as a blessing and as the will of the people."

But the Latin American ambassadors Reich summoned did not all see Chávez's removal as a "blessing" or "the will of the people." The presidents of many Latin American countries, gathered in Costa Rica for the summit meeting Chávez never made it to, issued a declaration condemning the break in constitutional order.

Despite that rebuff, the new junta in Venezuela received support from another sector in the United States — the International Republican Institute, one of the four core groups of the National Endowment for Democracy. IRI president George A. Folsom issued a press statement praising the uprising against Chávez and boasting that his organization served as a "bridge" to many groups that opposed him:

Last night, led by every sector of civil society, the Venezuelan people rose up to defend democracy in their country . . . Several hundred thousand people filled the streets of Caracas to demand the resignation of Lieutenant Colonel Hugo Chávez. Chávez responded with sharpshooters and his paramilitary Bolivarian Circles killing more than twelve civilians and wounding more than one hundred others. In contrast, IRI commends the patriotism of the Venezuelan military for their refusal to fire on their countrymen.

IRI also applauds the bravery of civil society leaders . . . who have put their very lives on the line in their struggle to restore genuine democracy to their country.

As the United States worked to legitimize the new regime in Venezuela, Carmona's interim government launched a witch hunt for Chávez supporters. They started rounding up leading Chávez allies, who were allegedly complicit in the massacre in downtown Caracas. Television stations joined in the search. They flashed the manipulated video footage of the Llaguno Bridge shooters on the screen and said authorities were looking for them. "If you recognize any of these criminals and assassins, they are wanted because they are accused of mass murder," Napoleón Bravo stated on 24 Hours. The stations also said arrest warrants were out for Chávez allies including Caracas mayor Freddy Bernal and Education Minister Aristóbulo Istúriz. Radio Caracas Television said Istúriz was wanted dead or alive.

A mob outraged by the "massacre of El Silencio" surrounded the apartment building of Interior Minister Ramón Rodríguez Chacin in Caracas. Opposition-controlled police hauled him out in handcuffs. The horde tried to grab, punch, and yank him by the hair as police wrestled him into a patrol car to take him away. The minister "was nearly lynched," one news report stated.

Another Chávez ally, Congressman Tarek William Saab, a long-time human rights activist known as "the poet of the revolution," had spent the night hiding with other congressmen and fleeing opposition-controlled police. The next day he went home at about 9 A.M. He was worried about his wife and children. When he arrived, a note was taped to the door: "The government junta is looking for you, assassin."

Heavily armed police soon arrived and blocked off both ends of the street. Before long a hundred neighbors had surrounded the house waving sticks, throwing rocks, pounding on the door, and yelling insults. Saab's three-year-old daughter Sofia was confused. She thought the people had come with sticks to strike a piñata, since her birthday was soon. Saab had a different thought; he believed they might all be killed.

He surrendered to police, who hauled him away in a police van. Television stations captured the scene live, with Saab denouncing his illegal detention and pleading for help. The incident alarmed even some of Chávez's critics. The "interim government" was starting to look like a fascist dictatorship. Saab disappeared from public view.

Meanwhile, another mob was surrounding the Cuban embassy. The crowd of about one thousand people believed that Chávez government officials including Vice President Diosdado Cabello were hiding inside. They demanded they be turned over. Even if they were inside, embassies enjoyed diplomatic immunity. They were sacred safe havens were people could seek refuge from political attacks. That didn't matter to the mob. They smashed the windows of three cars with diplomatic license plates, punctured the tires, and jumped up and down on the vehicles. They pelted a wall outside the embassy with eggs, cut off the electricity and water, and threatened to storm the building. They smashed the surveillance cameras outside.

It was an outrageous attack, but opposition-controlled police at the scene did almost nothing to stop it. Mayor Henrique Capriles Radonski of the opposition party Primero Justicia showed up and spoke to the Cuban ambassador inside the embassy. But he did not disperse the crowd. The horde held the embassy staff including some of their children hostage into the night, without food. "Gentlemen, those who are inside, Diosdado Cabello and your friends," one protestor shouted. "You are going to have to eat the rugs. You are going to have to eat the chairs and the tables that are inside, because we are not going to allow food to enter." Around midnight they finally let some food in, but on the condition that it was only for the children.

A Jesuit priest, the Reverend Arturo Peraza, who had taken part in the opposition march the previous day, went to the embassy about 9:30 P.M. dressed in his clerical collar. He stood on top of a car and tried to calm the crowd and get them to abandon the embassy. Few listened. The embassy staff was in serious danger. "If they came out, they would be killed, I have no doubt," Peraza later stated. He left, came back about midnight, and tried again. There were fewer people. But they were still seething. Some were drunk.

As the mob assaulted the Cuban embassy that afternoon, on the other side of town many of Venezuela's elites flocked to Miraflores Palace. Carmona was preparing to be formally sworn in and announce his first actions as president. International news reports were quickly describing him as "mild-mannered" and "respected." A *Financial Times* story said the "balding, soft-spoken" Carmona had "a reputation for being a safe pair of hands." He was likely to include in his transitional government "other calming influences." *The New York Times* ran a "Man in the News" profile on Saturday, April 13, titled "Manager and Conciliator." It described Carmona as "slight and meek." It added, "Mr. Carmona, experts said, is a level-headed manager who is also known as a conciliator."

But Carmona's first actions as "president" of Venezuela that Friday were hardly meek, conciliatory, or levelheaded. In one fell swoop he wiped out nearly every democratic institution in the country and installed a dictatorship. Carmona shut down the National Assembly, eliminated the Supreme Court, tore up the constitution, and fired every public official from the attorney general to state governors to local mayors. He said new presidential elections would be held — in a year. He even changed the name of the country back to the Republic of Venezuela, eliminating the constitutional reference to Bolívar, and ordering the Liberator's portrait removed from the presidential palace's walls.

As Daniel Romero, the former aide to Carlos Andrés Pérez who was with Carmona in Fort Tiuna the previous night, read off each of Carmona's decrees, the assembled elites in Miraflores Palace erupted into wild, Orwellian cheers of *"Democracia! Democracia!"* Romero floated a rationale for the draconian measures. "As President Chávez has offered his resignation to the military chiefs of staff" and as "Vice President Diosdado Cabello has abandoned his post, we must fill the power vacuum and for that reason we decree a democratic, national unity government," he told the assembled elites.

After Romero read Carmona's decree, representatives of business, the media, the church, and other sectors came forward to sign the document. They included Archbishop Ignacio Velasco and Rocio Guijarra, whose business organization, CEDICE, was the recipient of a National Endowment for Democracy grant. Carmona named other NED beneficiaries to his cabinet including Leonardo Carvajal as education minister and Leopoldo Martínez as finance minister. Also signing a list of four hundred people who came to Miraflores that afternoon and evening to support Carmona's decree was María Corina Machado, the head of the NED-funded "electoral monitoring" organization Sumate. Machado later contended she had come to visit Carmona's wife, an old family friend, and thought the paper she was signing was merely a sign-in sheet typically used at government offices. She claimed she had no idea Carmona had assumed dictatorial powers and eliminated all democratic institutions even though the decree-signing ceremony was broadcast live all over the country on nearly every major television and radio station. It was almost impossible to miss.

Carmona also named several key leaders of the military revolt against Chávez to high-level posts. He appointed Rear Admiral Carlos Molina Tamayo head of security at Miraflores Palace. He returned Guaicaipuro Lameda to his post at the head of PDSVA. He also named Vice Admiral Héctor Ramírez Pérez, the officer who made the taped announcement renouncing support for Chávez, his defense minister. Notably absent from the junta was Carmona's co-leader of the opposition movement, union boss Carlos Ortega, and General Efraín Vásquez Velasco, the head of the army who on Thursday evening as the streets of Caracas were bathed with blood had quit as he uttered the devastating phrase to Chávez: "Mr. President, I was loyal to you until the end." Carmona was to pay for the slights.

After he took the oath of office, Carmona gave a short speech to supporters that was Kafkaesque given he had just installed a dictatorship. "We must go about returning to the rule of law," he said. "Strongman rule will be left behind."

Back at Fort Tiuna, Chávez could hear the commotion of a small group of his supporters gathering outside on the street and protesting his disappearance. News was spreading by word of mouth, cell phone, and alternative media radio stations and Web sites that Chávez had not resigned and was being held by the rebels in the military headquarters. Locked in a room at the fort, he was watching the scene at Miraflores on television. He was aghast. "I saw on the television Carmona's self–swearing-in," he recalled later. "I saw all that and I saw the faces that were in the Salon Ayacucho and the shouts, 'Democracy! Democracy!' while they were stabbing the Constitution."

The rebels decided to move him. As darkness fell, they transferred him to a couple of different buildings, and then took him outside and ordered him to get into a helicopter. Chávez was apprehensive.

> The idea began to grow, the idea I had in the morning of the possibility of killing me, of an assassination. However, since I had already given myself over, I think given myself over to God, like someone who lets himself be taken by the current, I didn't ask where we were going. Nothing. I got into the helicopter and we took off. We passed over Caracas. I remember silently asking myself where are they taking me. Could it be we are going to Maiquetia [international airport]? They're taking me to Maiquetia, maybe they are going to take me out of the country by force. I looked at Caracas from above, but no, we continued west, along the coast.

> On that flight, I had that sensation, that feeling, that I was being taken toward my death . . . I had a cross in my hand. I was very relaxed. I was ready to die.

The cross was the small blue one that his old military academy professor, General Pérez Arcay, had given him as he left Miraflores Palace to turn himself in. Now Chávez thought about his children, his wife, his

parents, his friends, and the Venezuelan people in general. It seemed
like an eternal flight. Eventually they landed at the remote naval base
of Turiamo near Puerto Cabello on the west coast.

He thought they might do it by shooting him and then claiming
he killed himself or tried to flee. He felt like Che Guevara in the final
moments of his life, trapped in the forests of Bolivia. Turiamo was desolate and dark. It seemed like good place to "eliminate" Chávez.

> We arrived at Turiamo in a dark place by the sea. They took me to
> a small house, I imagine a storage deposit, in semi-darkness. They
> left me alone in the house, under guard but a few meters away,
> five or ten meters from me, when I see a vehicle come up from
> beyond the helicopter. They turn off the lights and get out. I hear
> a noise in the darkness, and suddenly fifteen or twenty soldiers
> appear in the dark lined up, dark figures, with weapons, of course.
> I thought there they were going to "suicide" me. There was a lot of
> tension among the officers and the troops.
>
> Later an officer arrives and tells me, "OK, we are going to take
> you to the presidential residence." . . . They put me in a truck, and
> we go very slowly along a road. The helicopter takes off and the
> soldiers are walking on both sides of the road. We stop once for a
> few minutes, in a place where to me there was no reason to stop,
> on the dark road. The officer gets out and talks with the others.

Chávez had noticed conflicts among some of the soldiers. He believed
some came with orders to kill him, while others wanted to stop it.

> Two of them were there to kill me, but the others no, they were
> constitutionalists. In the moment in which they were going to
> carry out the order, I was standing up like this. One of those mer-
> cenaries walked around me and stood behind. I think to myself,
> "This one is going to give it to me in the back." I turn around and
> look at him in the face. "Look at what you are going to do," I tell
> him. And at that moment another young officer jumps to my side
> and says, "If you kill the president here we'll all kill one another."
> That neutralized those two mercenaries and saved my life.

The group continued on to the presidential residence on the base,
but no one could find the key. They had nothing prepared for Chávez,

not even a clean room. Finally they brought him to the nurses' station, where they gave him a bed, a chair, a small table, and a bathroom. Most of the nation still had no idea where he was. It was nearly twenty-four hours after he was last seen walking into Fort Tiuna. The president was missing.

Pedro Carmona showed at up Miraflores Palace early on the morning of Saturday, April 13. It was to be his first full day as "president" after swearing himself into office late Friday afternoon and eliminating democracy. He planned to swear in his "cabinet" in the early afternoon. His first visitor of the day was Charles Shapiro, the US ambassador to Venezuela.

The two men along with the Spanish ambassador shared break-fast together at about 9 A.M. By Shapiro's account, he urged Carmona to restore the National Assembly and call elections as soon as possible. Carmona didn't remember it that way. He said Shapiro never brought it up. Whatever the case, the presence of the US ambassador in the pres-idential palace a day after Carmona seized power was interpreted by many as an endorsement.

After Shapiro finished his breakfast with Carmona, the country's media moguls pulled onto the palace grounds in black limousines for a meeting with Carmona, who asked them to do everything they could to support the regime. They included Venevisión's Gustavo Cisneros, Radio Caracas Television's Marcel Granier, Globovision's Alberto Ravell, and Televen's Omar Camero. The editors of two of the nation's leading newspapers also came — Miguel Henrique Otero of *El Nacional* and Andrés Mata of *El Universal*. Around the same time, other power elites started arriving for the swearing-in. Bishop Baltazar Porras offered bear hugs to friends. Archbishop Ignacio Velasco came, too.

In the United States, Carmona was winning the support of newspaper editorial pages across the country. They condoned the coup, blamed Chávez for the massacre, and welcomed the "restoration" of democracy. "With yesterday's resignation of President Hugo Chávez," *The New York Times* said, "Venezuelan democracy is no longer threatened by a would-be dictator." The newspaper called Chávez a "ruinous demagogue," avoided the word *coup*, and said the former paratrooper "stepped down after the military intervened and handed power to a respected business leader, Pedro Carmona." Venezuela, it added, needed a "leader with a strong democratic mandate to clean up the mess."

Long Island's *Newsday* carried an editorial with the headline, "Chávez's Ouster Is No Great Loss." The *Chicago Tribune* called him an "elected strongman" and declared, "It's not every day that a democracy benefits from the military's intervention to force out an elected president."

Support flowed in from business, too. US-based BellSouth and its Venezuelan affiliate, Telcel, took out a full-page ad in the Caracas daily *El Universal* offering customers free long-distance calls to celebrate Venezuela's new "FREEDOM and the brilliant future that awaits us."

But that morning as Carmona prepared to formally install his provisional government, events outside the palace were shifting the balance of political power. Word was spreading in the barrios that Chávez had never resigned and was being held incommunicado against his will. The protests outside Fort Tiuna on Friday night grew larger on Saturday morning. They also spread to the streets near Miraflores presidential palace. People streamed into the city center, carrying signs that said, DONDE ESTA CHÁVEZ? — where is Chávez? Others held large photographs of the missing president. Opposition-controlled police fired tear gas canisters and rubber bullets. They also moved into barrios throughout the capital, repressing protests and looting with real bullets.

Hospitals overflowed with victims. One man, Edgar Paredes, told a US reporter, "They are gunning us down out there." Another pro-Chávez demonstrator, Juana Chirinos, had tears streaming down her face as she watched ambulance after ambulance pull in. "While we bring in our dead one after the other," she said, "the rich people in the east are having drinks and fanning themselves."

If the rich people fanning themselves turned on their televisions, they would have had no idea of the protests and bloodshed sweeping the barrios as people demanded Chávez's return. The media's news blackout was running full force. As one the biggest stories in Venezuela's modern history unfolded, they refused to report on the groundswell demanding Chávez's return, the repression in the streets, or even that the president was missing. Instead the television networks showed cartoons, cooking shows, and Hollywood movies like *Pretty Woman*.

The new regime sought to suffocate the one place people without cable television or the Internet could get news about the uprising — the alternative media. Police raided and shut down community radio and television stations that often operated out of people's houses and that the Chávez government had encouraged as a small counterbalance to the media giants.

The unrest over Chávez's disappearance was not only spreading in the streets — it was growing in the barracks. General Raúl Isaías Baduel, one of the founders of the MBR-200 and now the head of Chávez's old paratrooper unit in Maracay, was trying to make his opposition to the new regime public. No Venezuelan commercial media outlet would interview him. So he drafted a manifesto declaring he would not support Carmona's regime. He hoped it would somehow get out. Other high-ranking military officers signed it, too. Meanwhile thousands of pro-Chávez demonstrators gathered outside his paratrooper's regiment, clamoring for Chávez to return.

Baduel got on the telephone with several loyalist commanders, including Colonel Jesús Del Valle Morao Cardona, who was in charge of the honor guard at Miraflores Palace. After Carmona took over, the troops along with other palace personnel continued fulfilling their functions for the new regime. They served them coffee, and Morao's honor guard band played the national anthem for the new head of state, even though some cried as they did. Carmona and his cronies thought the soldiers supported them. In reality they were waiting for a chance to help overthrow him.

Morao Cardona's troops were stationed in barracks across the street from Miraflores. They could enter the palace through tunnels. With the crowds outside Miraflores growing, another loyalist officer called Morao from Fort Tiuna. "Colonel, today is the 13th," he told Morao. "It's now or never."

Morao responded, "Come here. I can't take this situation any more."

Morao called Baduel, who told him to go ahead with the plan to recapture Miraflores and take Carmona prisoner. They believed they had the support of most of the barracks in the country. The officers who overthrew Chávez had high ranks, but almost no direct command of troops.

Late that morning Morao's troops marched through the underground tunnels and ran into the palace. The soldiers grabbed nearly two dozen people — including Daniel Romero — who were in the cabinet meeting room. Carmona, Molina Tamayo, Lameda, and others escaped. The coup leaders made their way to Fort Tiuna to reunite with other plotters. Cameras captured the humiliating scenes of well-coiffed women from Venezuela's upper class running from the palace in high heels as they fled the loyalist troops. They left behind whiskey, champagne, and a presidential sash. It had an adjustable band, to fit any size.

Not long after Carmona fled the palace, some of the military plotters convoked a meeting in Fort Tiuna. Some lower-level officers were questioning what was happening, since Chávez had not presented a resignation letter and no one knew where he was. They had watched the scenes of the violence on Avenida Baralt on Thursday and the television commentaries blaming Chávez for the killings. But now some were doubtful. They thought they'd been lied to about Chávez's resignation. They were also angry about Carmona's dismantling of democratic institutions and the dissolution of the constitution.

Some higher-ranking officers who had played important roles in the revolt were dismayed, too. General Efraín Vásquez Velasco, the head of the army, was one of them. Carmona had appointed him to nothing.

Chávez ally General Luis Jorge García Carneiro managed to get into the meeting, which started about 1 P.M. It was a confusing scene. Officers were yelling back and forth at one another. Outside, they could hear the sounds of Chávez supporters shouting for the president and banging sticks and pipes on a metal rail.

The officers agreed to draft a declaration recognizing Carmona as head of state but demanding the restoration of the constitution and the country's democratic institutions. Vásquez Velasco was to read it. Before he did, García Carneiro grabbed the document while Vásquez Velasco was talking to other officers, edited it, and crossed out the section where they recognized Carmona as head of state. Amid the confusion, Vásquez Velasco did not notice.

The Venezuelan media would not broadcast Vásquez Velasco's statement, so he had to read it by telephone to CNN's studios in Atlanta. It was a bombshell. The man who had made the dramatic pronouncement against Chávez on April 11 saying he was "loyal until the end" now was reversing himself. The coup was collapsing. Chávez's wife, Marisabel, also spoke with CNN. She told the network her husband had not resigned.

In Turiamo the night before, Chávez had been visited by a nurse assigned to check on him. After barely escaping what he believed was an assassination attempt, Chávez had momentarily fallen into a depression. "I had my doubts in Turiamo, looking at a star, whether it was worth living, for a few minutes," he later told a National Assembly panel investigating the coup. "I had come to the conclusion it was not worth living." The idea receded when he thought about the soldiers who supported him, and the Venezuelan people. Now the nurse brought him some moral support. "I always wanted to meet you, but not like this," she told Chávez, her eyes welling with tears. "My mother adores you."

The encounter triggered something in Chávez. "I had a lot of things bottled up inside me," he said in April 2007. "I had in my heart I don't know how many feelings of pain, of frustration, of hopelessness. And that girl with her tears caused a dam inside me to burst. The flood came in tears. I cried a lot. She left and I went in the bathroom and cried and cried and cried. But this crying spell was like getting things out of my system and I came out like a bull, like I was alive again. But there had been moments when I felt like I was dead."

He slept a few hours and by the next morning, Saturday the thirteenth, started to feel that *el pueblo* was going to react to his disappearance. "Only I never thought it was going to occur with the magnitude that it did," he said in April 2007. "When I woke up I had regained hope and the desire to not die, and moreover, to return to power. I said, no, we will return, I don't know if in one month, or six months, or six years, but we will return. Only I never thought that the following day I would be back again in the palace."

That morning a soldier brought Chávez breakfast and spoke to him quietly. He asked Chávez if he had resigned. Chávez told him he hadn't. "Then you are the president and these people have violated the constitution," the soldier said. "They are deceiving us."

The soldier gave Chávez his first information about what was happening in the country. He told him the paratroopers in Maracay under Baduel's command were rising up and refusing to recognize Carmona as the nation's president. People were massing outside Baduel's barracks. The soldier told Chávez he believed Baduel and other commanders were planning an operation to rescue him.

Even at Turiamo, the situation seemed to be changing. The soldiers were treating Chávez with respect, like he was still the president. They asked if he wanted to go jogging. They lent him a white T-shirt, and he started running with a couple of sergeants assigned to guard him. As they jogged, the sergeants called him "president" and said the plotters were creating a "disaster." After they finished, they sat around talking with some other soldiers. Chávez was feeling at home. He asked about their families, their lives as soldiers, the decrepit installations they had to put up with at Turiamo.

He went inside to take a shower, put on another white T-shirt and a pair of shorts the soldiers lent him, and was brought lunch by the same soldier he'd spoken with in the morning. He asked the soldier if he would be willing to take a written message and somehow distribute it. The soldier agreed. Chávez wanted to alert the world that he had not quit. As he started to write, they heard a helicopter arriving outside. The soldier had to leave. He told Chávez to hurry and place the paper in the bottom of a garbage can in the room. He would get it later.

Chávez quickly finished the note. It stated: "Turiamo, 13 April 2002, at 14:45. To the Venezuelan people . . . (and whoever else may be interested). I, Hugo Chávez Frías, Venezuelan, President of the Bolivarian Republic of Venezuela, declare: I have not renounced the legitimate power that the Venezuelan people gave me." He ended with, "Forever!" — Che Guevara's famous phrase.

Chávez had to go outside to meet the military officers who had arrived in the helicopter. They had a new plan. They were going to take him to La Orchila, an island off the Caribbean coast. Chávez resisted, saying they could not force him to leave. He told them he was the constitutionally elected president of the country, was incommunicado, and had been denied a lawyer. The officers told him they were there to guarantee his safety. Chávez procrastinated, but eventually they took off. The loyal soldier, meanwhile, snuck back to the nurses' station, grabbed the note out of the garbage can, and set off trying to get it to General Baudel in Maracay.

Outside Miraflores Palace that afternoon, the throng of Chávez supporters was growing. They were streaming into central Caracas not only because Chávez was missing, but because their dream was dying. Chávez was much more than a president. To them, he was a symbol of hope. He truly believed in his people, they thought, and made them realize a better life was possible. He had asked them to help build the country of their dreams, and they were embarking on that road together.

His disappearance was something like the assassinations of John F. Kennedy and Martin Luther King Jr. in the United States — it was not just the man who was vanishing, but the hope, the ideals, and the dreams that he inspired. And it was all going to be taken away by the same people who had blocked them from realizing those aspirations in the past. The impoverished masses felt that, along with Chávez and the constitutional assembly, they had written the constitution themselves. The document clearly stated that even if the president resigned, as the opposition claimed, the vice president was to succeed him in office. The *golpistas* did not just take out Chávez. They destroyed the constitution and removed everyone in his administration. To top it off, they put in a figurehead of the oligarchy to run the country.

After a day of feeling hopeless and lost, of crying and sinking into despair over their fallen leader, the masses were fighting back now. In the barrios, word spread by megaphone and cell phone: *Todos a Miraflores!* — Everyone to Miraflores! People streamed out of their homes and packed buses and cars, or even walked miles to the palace. "It was like a human river going down the mountainsides," recalled one protestor.

The opposition-controlled police had backed off much of their repression as the coup began to falter. The crowds pressed up against the black rails surrounding the palace. Some took a white bed sheet and spray-painted a message: *Donde Está Chávez? Que Hable!* — Where's Chávez? Let him speak! They hung the sheet on gates near the palace grounds. One protestor climbed up a pole that held a traffic light by the entrance. Others clambered up a white cement pillar. Thousands of people held up photographs of Chávez, pumped their fists in the air, and chanted, "Chávez! Chávez!" One man shouted, "We voted for Chávez. We don't want a dictatorship."

After Morao and his soldiers took control of the palace, three of them climbed on top of the roof of Miraflores and pumped their fists in the air. One made a V for victory sign with his fingers. The crowd went crazy. On top of another nearby building, soldiers waved a huge Venezuelan flag and pumped their fists, egging the throng on. The crowd pushed their arms through the metal rails and shook the hands of some of the soldiers inside. Some of the Chavistas had tears of gratitude in their eyes. The tide was turning. The *golpistas* were running scared.

But none of it was appearing on Venezuelan television networks. About the only way people could get news about what was happening in their country was by watching international news channels like CNN, if they were affluent enough to have cable television. By Saturday afternoon groups of Chavistas — livid that the Venezuelan networks refused to broadcast news of the huge demonstrations — surrounded some of the stations on motorcycles and demanded that their side of the story be aired. Television workers cowered inside, afraid the crowds were going to kill them. They all but begged for their lives on the air. Protestors broke windows at one station, but no one was attacked.

By early afternoon, as word spread that the coup was collapsing, some of Chávez's ministers started returning to the palace. Aristóbulo Istúriz had been holed up in his house not far from the palace. It turned into an informal command center for high-level government officials. Istúriz did not have to go into hiding, because he had natural protection in the barrio where he lived. If the *golpista* authorities tried to detain him, the people in the barrio would come to his defense.

He was one of the first to arrive at Miraflores. He clambered atop a car with other officials and led the crowd in chants for Chávez. Eventually soldiers ushered him into the honor guard barracks across the street, and took him through the tunnels into Miraflores. They were still not certain the palace was safe from attack by the coup forces, and wanted to ensure he was not shot. It was about 2 P.M. As other ministers, including Ana Elisa Osorio, made their way to Miraflores, the euphoric crowd swept them up and practically carried them to the palace gates. A ruffled attorney general, Isaías Rodríguez, arrived, his untucked buttondown shirt hanging out of his pants. Chávez's chief of staff, Rafael Vargas Medina, came with a new look — he had dyed his gray hair black to disguise himself.

Across town at Fort Tiuna, after Vásquez Velasco read his statement to CNN, General Jorge Luis García Carneiro went outside to talk to the growing throng. He climbed atop a tank, told the crowd the armed forces did not recognize Carmona as president, and said the army was going to fight until Chávez was returned to power. "It is very important that you stay here," García Carneiro told the demonstrators. "We aren't leaving here until Hugo Chávez appears!" The protestors had a loudspeaker system set up and were playing music by Alí Primera. Every ten minutes or so García Carneiro and others interrupted the music with the latest news of another barrack reporting in that they supported the president.

That evening they received a copy of the note Chávez wrote in Turiamo. Congresswoman Iris Varela, a red MVR bandanna wrapped around her head, read it out loud. The crowd exploded in wild cheering. The private at Turiamo had taken it off the base and brought it to General Baudel in Maracay. Using a flashlight to see in the night, the general read it out loud to the crowd in Maracay, provoking pandemonium there, too.

With the coup falling apart, García Carneiro decided to arrest Carmona and other coup leaders. They were meeting in Fort Tiuna, desperately trying to figure out their next move. At about 7 P.M. several officers went to the fifth floor of the army headquarters, cut off the electricity, broke down the door to the army commander's officer, and detained several coup leaders from the military, including Molina Tamayo. They also grabbed Carmona, who was hiding in an adjacent bedroom.

With Carmona under arrest, Chávez's ministers wanted to reconstitute the legitimate government. But they needed the man who should succeed him according to the constitution, since the president was missing. That was the vice president, Diosdado Cabello. One of Chávez's MBR-200 recruits from the military academy in the 1980s, Cabello had gone into hiding the afternoon of April 11 when it became apparent a coup was under way. He spent the next two days moving from place to place, from an apartment of a friend to a farm in nearby Vargas state that had no electricity or cell phone coverage.

By Saturday afternoon, Cabello had managed to communicate with CNN en Español, where he told newscasters, "I am the president in this moment. The president [Chávez] is not in office. So I am in control." He added, "I can't go out in the street because my life is in danger."

Cabello had gotten word about 1 P.M. that loyalist soldiers had retaken Miraflores Palace, but they told him to wait before going there. They wanted to see if the coup leaders launched a counterattack first. By late afternoon the situation seemed under control. Cabello had to reach Caracas from the Caribbean coast in Vargas, but the highway was blocked by barricades of trucks, garbage, and sticks set up by angry Chavistas demanding the president's return. Cabello and another government official had to walk, run, and change cars to get through the barricades. When the people saw who it was, some started running behind him to offer protection.

By the time he got to Caracas, crowds were looting stores in anger over Chávez's disappearance. Bullets were flying through the air. Cars were on fire in the streets. Cabello had to change routes. Guards at Miraflores said they would meet him at a market at the foot of Avenida Baralt. They showed up in an ambulance with its sirens wailing, wrapped a bulletproof sheet around Cabello, and threw him on the floor of the vehicle. Then some guards sat on top of him for extra protection.

When Cabello arrived at Miraflores about 9 P.M., the ministers and other allies shouted with joy. Some cried. In Fort Tiuna, Carmona was writing his resignation as president. At about 10 P.M. he read it to a radio station. A few minutes later Cabello took the oath of office in the palace. Across town loyalist troops helped the staff of channel 8 retake the state-run television channel, which was slowly coming back to life. Congressman Juan Barreto went on the air and declared that "the tyrant has been deposed."

In Maracay a plan to rescue Chávez was under way. By Saturday afternoon Baduel and other loyalist officers knew the rebels were holding Chávez on La Orchila. They organized a mission to bring him back to the mainland, dubbing it Operation Rescue National Dignity. Three helicopters carrying a team of elite commandos along with a doctor and a military lawyer took off around midnight. They had received word that an airplane with US insignias was parked on the small island. General Alí Uzcátegui Duque, who was leading the mission, feared the rebels were going to put Chávez on the plane, take off, and then blow it up or crash it — claiming the president had died in an accident. The loyalists were racing against the clock. They were also prepared for combat — they did not know what to expect on the island.

They landed without incident, though, and to their surprise one of the first people they saw was a priest: Cardinal José Ignacio Velasco. The archbishop of Caracas had come to La Orchila in a last-ditch effort to persuade Chávez to sign the resignation letter. Another coup leader was with him, Colonel Julio Rodríguez Salas. Chávez spent several hours on the island with the archbishop. According to the president's account, they sat on the beach together, prayed, looked at the stars, and even held hands for a time. Chávez asked for forgiveness and spoke of the need for all sectors of society to work together. He had no idea a rescue team was on the way.

When Uzcátegui and the others arrived, Chávez was stunned. They embraced. Many of the rescuers cried. The doctor examined Chávez to make sure he was not injured. The lawyer read a prepared statement declaring that with his relocation Chávez was once again legally the president. Then the helicopters took off for Caracas. Chávez said little during the flight. He was exhausted. His head was spinning. He needed time to think.

As they entered the airspace over Caracas, he saw columns of smoke rising out of Catia and other barrios. He asked what was going on. He was worried the city was erupting the way Bogotá had in 1948 when the popular political leader Jorge Gaitán was assassinated, setting off bloody riots that later led to a civil war that still raged. In Caracas, thousands of angry Chávez supporters were looting stores, some of which were on fire.

Outside Miraflores Palace the throng had stayed through the night, waiting for Chávez. Word spread that he was in La Orchila, but was coming back. When a light appeared in the night sky, the crowd exploded with joy. As the helicopter hovered in the air and its spotlight broke through the fog, it seemed like a surreal scene out of a Pink Floyd concert. The crowd sang, "He's back! He's back!" People hugged and cried and danced. The aircraft touched down at 2:45 A.M. Chávez climbed out wearing a blue windbreaker and tennis sneakers. He looked tired but elated. A throng of soldiers and allies swarmed around him as he walked off the heliport landing pad and down a set of stairs that led to the palace grounds, now packed with his supporters. He smiled broadly and held his left fist in the air. The crowd went crazy. They shouted. They sang. They prayed. Some fainted. They were delirious. It was as if Chávez had risen from the dead. "Jesus rose on the third day, and Chávez rose in two," one Caracas resident remarked. "They thought they could kill him, but they could not."

An hour after he landed Chávez gave a nationally broadcast speech from the palace. The country had seen three presidents in two days. For forty-seven hours, millions of people did not know where Chávez was or even if he was alive. "To God what is God's, to Caesar what is Caesar's, and to the people what is the people's," were his first words. He was still stunned by the turn of events, still trying to assimilate it all. He was shaken, but confident. "I was certain, absolutely certain, that we would return," Chávez said. "I just didn't think it would be so soon."

**22**

# The Aftermath

Within hours of Chávez's return to the presidency, the United States was lecturing him. Appearing on NBC's Sunday morning news program *Meet the Press*, national security adviser Condoleezza Rice issued a warning about respecting democratic norms. Remarkably, it was aimed not at Carmona, but Chávez. "I hope that Hugo Chávez takes the message that his people sent him that his own policies are not working for the Venezuelan people," Rice said. "He needs to respect constitutional processes . . . We do hope that Chávez recognizes that the whole world is watching and that he takes advantage of this opportunity to right his own ship, which has been moving, frankly, in the wrong direction for quite a long time."

White House spokesman Ari Fleischer followed with comments of his own. "The people of Venezuela have sent a clear message to President Chávez that they want both democracy and reform," he said. "The Chávez administration has an opportunity to respond to this message by correcting its course and governing in a fully democratic manner." President Bush weighed in four days later, admonishing Chávez for interfering with Venezuela's "free press" when he cut off television transmissions of the violence on April 11. "When things got hot in Venezuela, he shut the press down," Bush said. "I've always believed in a free press. I don't care how tough the questions are or, as significantly, how they editorialize in their news stories. But nevertheless — because I respect the press, and so should President Chávez."

The United States was almost alone in the world in all but openly endorsing the coup. Yet Chávez initially was careful of accusing it of any role in his ouster. Speaking to the nation on Monday, April 15, he appeared to give the United States the benefit of the doubt regarding their multiple accusations that he ordered the killings outside Miraflores Palace and wrought his own downfall. "I think they were victims of mis-information," he said. His position shifted within a month, when he told *The Washington Post* that "worrying details" were emerging that a foreign hand may have played a role in the coup. The details consisted mainly of radar detection of US ships, airplanes, and helicopters oper-ating in and over Venezuelan territory during the coup. As time passed and relations deteriorated, Chávez openly accused the United States of assisting in his overthrow. The United States dismissed the reports. It said its military was off Venezuela's coast for routine exercises.

The public US bumbling of Chávez's overthrow provoked a storm of criticism that ricocheted around a continent still leery of US inter-vention. Many analysts blamed two of the old Iran-contra figures for the policy debacle: Otto Reich and Elliot Abrams, head of Democracy, Human Rights and International Organizations at the National Security Council. Democratic senator Christopher Dodd of Connecticut quipped that Reich required "more adult supervision."

Reich shot back that the administration had nothing to regret. "Apologies for what?" he said. The government's statements about Chávez resigning and ordering the killing of marchers "reflected the best information that we had at the time." At Dodd's request, the State Department conducted an internal review of US government and National Endowment for Democracy actions related to the coup. It found that while the NED, the Department of Defense, and other US agencies provided assistance to organizations and individuals involved in the coup, there was no evidence the support "directly contributed to or was intended to contribute" to the the putsch.

While the State Department cleared itself of intentional wrong-doing, it was not without casualties. By late November, Reich was forced out of his position as the top official for Latin America. In a sudden job reshuffling, he became a special adviser to Secretary of State Colin Powell for Latin American affairs. Officials asked him to move out of his spacious sixth-floor State Department office.

Back in April, less than a week after the coup, *The New York Times* had broken the story that the United States was pumping hundreds of thousands of dollars into Venezuela through the National Endowment for Democracy. It reported that in the year leading up to the coup, the NED nearly quadrupled its funding in Venezuela, to $877,000. Some of the money went to Carlos Ortega's CTV, the labor organization whose protests helped lead to Chávez's ouster.

After the *Times*'s article appeared, Long Island lawyer Eva Golinger and Washington, DC, investigative reporter Jeremy Bigwood filed Freedom of Information Act requests for thousands of documents detailing the work of the NED, USAID, and other US agencies in Venezuela. The requests revealed that much of the NED's money was going to opposition groups, including some whose leaders backed the coup or were named ministers in Carmona's cabinet. In the aftermath of the putsch, the State Department also issued a special $1 million grant to the NED on top of its regular budget for Venezuela.

In August 2002, USAID opened an Office of Transition Initiatives in Caracas. The name itself suggested Venezuela needed to transition to a new government, and that the US government was there to "help" the transition. The announcement of a job opening for the OTI's Caracas office sent out by USAID the same month as the coup said Venezuela's president "had been slowly hijacking the machinery of government and developing parallel non-democratic governance structures . . . Chávez has demonstrated increasing disregard for democratic institutions and intolerance for dissent."

By USAID's own description, the OTIs were intended to be two-year initiatives in conflict-prone zones. But four years later the OTI was still operating in Venezuela. An examination by the Associated Press and other news outlets revealed that USAID was pumping far more money into Venezuela than the NED — some $26 million overseen by OTI between 2002 and 2006. USAID refused to reveal where much of the US taxpayers' money was going. It censored out many recipients' names from documents released through FOIA requests.

While the United States came out of the coup with its reputation battered in Latin America, Chávez emerged stronger in many ways. Some polls said his popularity rating jumped immediately by 10 percentage points. To supporters, his survival and return to the presidency took on mythic proportions. It was a story straight out of Hollywood.

Chávez took a conciliatory approach after the coup. He toned down his rhetoric, announced he was creating a "national roundtable" to sit down with opposition leaders, and shifted some of his more controversial cabinet ministers to other posts. He replaced Gaston Parra as head of PDVSA with Alí Rodríguez, Venezuela's OPEC representative, and reinstated several of the PDVSA dissidents he had fired from the board of directors.

While some military officers were detained, most were released eventually. Few spent significant time in jail. Carmona was placed under house arrest, but slipped out of his luxury apartment in late May and made his way to the Colombian embassy, where he sought political asylum. Colombia granted it, and Venezuela let him fly out of the country on May 29, even though he was wanted by authorities.

Rear Admiral Carlos Molina Tamayo eventually sought political asylum in El Salvador, a close US ally and the only country in Latin America that recognized Carmona's regime. Other suspected coup participants ended up in the United States: Isaac Pérez Recao, a reputed arms dealer and heir to a Venezuelan oil fortune who allegedly plotted alongside Carmona, fled to South Florida, the press reported. His family owned several homes in Key Biscayne, including a $2.4 million beachfront penthouse where he was said to live with his wife.

Four high-ranking military officers including General Efraín Vásquez Velasco and Vice Admiral Héctor Ramírez Pérez were charged for their role in the coup. But on August 14 the Supreme Court dismissed the charges by an eleven-to-eight vote, citing insufficient evidence. Chávez accused the court of succumbing to the influence of the opposition and denying the existence of the coup, but he accepted the ruling. "It's a totally absurd decision," he said. "But it's a decision . . . we have to swallow it like a fish with bones." He said the magistrates' names would be "stained for the next five thousand years."

One official who did eventually end up in jail for four months was Henrique Capriles Radonski, the mayor of Baruta who appeared at the Cuban embassy the day of the mob attack. His jailing in 2004 turned him into a cause célèbre for the opposition and much of the international media. They contended that he was a political prisoner and had gone to the embassy to try to calm the crowd. But to the government, he did nothing to stop the outrageous assault even though he was the highest-ranking local authority and in charge of public order.

Capriles's case was unusual. Most opposition leaders and military rebels implicated in the coup went free — a sign that many in the opposition interpreted as weakness on the government's part. Suspected coup leaders were walking around town freely, entering and leaving Fort Tiuna as they pleased and denouncing the president.

Hatred was in the air. "Opposition leaders openly long for Chávez's death," one journalist wrote in July. A *Los Angeles Times* reporter who spent a week interviewing people in Venezuela wrote that opponents "used the following words to describe Chávez: Hitler, assassin, psychopath, terrorist, messianic, Stalinist, communist, fascist, authoritarian, country bumpkin and several other epithets not fit for breakfast reading." A leading historian wrote a front-page article with the headline, "It's OK to Kill a Leader Who's Not Following the Laws."

Chávez took the threats seriously. Long known for thrusting himself into adoring crowds, he eliminated most public appearances for months and kept his schedule secret until the last minute. When he did go out, he took to wearing a bulletproof vest under his clothes. In late June he installed ground-to-air missile batteries around Miraflores after intelligence agencies uncovered reports of a possible aerial attack.

The elites' hatred of Chávez stemmed from a variety of factors, including frustration, paranoia, classism, and a fear of being left out of Chávez's project. All of it was reinforced by a twenty-four-hour-a-day bombardment of vitriolic anti-Chávez propaganda on television that brainwashed a segment of the population and stoked something bordering on mass hysteria.

Chávez was not a diplomatic politician and had a way of bullying his opponents, whom he likened to enemies in a war. He insulted them publicly and by name, belittling, humiliating, and depicting them as worthless scum. For their part, the elites could not accept that an uncouth country bumpkin type like Chávez whom they were more accustomed to seeing in a tuxedo serving them at their clubs was now in charge of them. On a larger scale his political program and his plan to redistribute the country's oil wealth was a clear threat to their interests.

In the end, some believed the elites' visceral hatred of Chávez stemmed from two basic things: racism and loss of power. While Venezuela's moneyed classes denied it, racism was alive and well in Venezuela. As former Catholic missionary and longtime Venezuela resident Charles Hardy noted, there has been "prejudice in Venezuela for ages, but no one talks about it. If they do, they deny it. There are no well-known black commentators on Venezuela television. There have been no black Miss Venezuelas. The major beer commercials present an almost naked blond."

Chávez was the country's first dark-skinned president. His followers largely shared his skin tone.

Chávez's rise represented the first time in the country's history that the dark-skinned impoverished majority was seizing power. After decades, even centuries, of running the country like their own personal hacienda, the elites' grip on the corruption-riddled and exploitative system was suddenly undone. From the time Chávez took power, he demonstrated that — to the surprise of many elites, who hoped to strike a bargain with him — he wasn't going to play the typical populist game but rather was going to truly shake up the system. The moneyed classes were trying everything they could to get rid of him, and as they failed their frustration and vitriol grew. As Hardy said, "An old and evil way of life is dying and those who enjoyed it so abundantly are fighting its death all the way."

He likened them to a person suffering a terminal disease and going through the five stages of denial: anger, bargaining, depression, and acceptance. Except they showed few signs of being anywhere near the peaceful acceptance stage.

Many of the facts about the episode that brought the conflict to a head — the April 11–14 coup — remained a mystery. No serious investigation was conducted into the killings or the coup plot. Four of the Chavista shooters on the bridge were arrested and held in jail for a year, but eventually they were acquitted. The judge said there was no evidence they had killed any of the marchers. By 2006 prosecutors charged and put on trial several leaders of the Metropolitan Police whose officers allegedly killed some of the Chavistas. The trial lingered on into 2007.

While Chávez survived the coup, his marriage did not. Tensions stemming from the political tumult, along with other conflicts within their marriage, became too much for his wife, Marisabel. In early June, less than two months after the coup, she announced that the presidential couple was getting divorced. She cited a "contrast of personalities" as the main reason, but added that she and her children were forced to flee the presidential mansion three times because of political upheaval. "That's no life for anyone," she said. Their marriage had lasted five years.

Chávez was alone again, and more trouble was on the horizon.

**23**

# Oil Strike

In the early 1970s when the United States was trying to overthrow President Salvador Allende, Richard Nixon instructed the CIA to "make the economy scream" in Chile. The idea was that by fomenting economic chaos and making the country "ungovernable," Allende would be forced out of office — either by voters or by a military coup. In Venezuela the opposition pursued the same strategy after the April putsch failed. They attacked the lifeblood of Venezuela's economy: the oil industry.

On Monday, October 21, 2002, opposition leaders called yet another national strike — the third in less than a year. Factories, stores, and malls across the nation closed their doors, prompting traffic in normally chaotic Caracas to slow to a trickle. Airlines canceled many domestic flights for lack of passengers. Most newspapers refused to publish. Television networks suspended regular programming and provided wall-to-wall coverage of the shutdown. More than reporting on it, they promoted it.

The walkout had a clear goal: getting Chávez to leave office. The opposition proposed three ways out. He could resign, agree to early elections, or permit a nonbinding referendum on his presidency. Opponents believed that if he lost the referendum, he would be embarrassed into resigning. Chávez wasn't interested in any of the options. He contended that the constitution allowed for a binding recall referendum halfway through his term, which would be the following August. But that was not acceptable to the opposition. Chávez had to go. Now.

The one-day strike, which did not affect the oil industry, was barely over when a new protest erupted. The next day fourteen dissident military officers occupied a plaza in the upscale Altamira neighborhood, declared it "Liberated Territory," and called for a rebellion against Chávez. They claimed they were not trying to provoke a coup but were employing Article 350 of the constitution, which allowed citizens to rebel against a government they considered undemocratic. Many of the officers had helped lead the April revolt and were cashiered by Chávez. Leading them was General Enrique Medina, the former military attaché at the Venezuelan embassy in Washington.

Medina and the other military rebels in the Plaza Altamira became instant heroes to the opposition. By the next afternoon, several thousand people flocked to the plaza after work. More officers came, too. By Friday, October 25, a total of one hundred had joined the protest. Fedecámaras, the business chamber of commerce once led by Pedro Carmona, announced its support for the officers. So did Carlos Ortega's union, the CTV. The country's three leading opposition parties, Democratic Action, Primera Justicia, and COPEI, also endorsed the military dissidents.

The plaza turned into a twenty-four-hour-a-day symbol of resistance to Chávez. People set up Coleman tents and slept there overnight. A banner declared, WE ARE IN LIBERATED TERRITORY. A massive balloon bore the Orwellian legend, THIS IS NOT A COUP. A large digital time display marked the occupation to the second. Organizers erected a stage that the military dissidents mounted to give speeches. In between, cheerleaders and folk dancers kept the crowd worked up. It was like a high school pep rally.

The throngs treated the officers like rock stars. Middle-aged women crowded up to the stage and blew them kisses. Others screamed in delight. "We have been having the most entertaining coup in the world here for the past month," commented Vice Admiral Daniel Comisso Urdaneta, one of four officers cleared by the Supreme Court in August when it threw out the coup charges.

The dissident officers accused Chávez of turning the country into a Cuba-style dictatorship. But this was a strange dictatorship. Military rebels who overthrew a democratically elected president were out on the streets free, wearing their uniforms and openly calling for rebellion against him. Fidel Castro thought Chávez was crazy. "In what country could there be a coup and then have all the perpetrators meet in a plaza to spend fifty days agitating through the television networks, proposing another coup?" he said. "Not in any country in the world."

General Medina, who showed up at the plaza still waving a general's baton, believed the dissidents had "a lot of support in the barracks right now. The United States now seems to understand the serious crisis in this country, that a crazy eccentric is running it."

But Medina was wrong. The dissidents did not have a lot of support in the barracks. After the coup, Chávez cleansed the armed forces of many of his enemies. He was also handling the plaza protest skillfully. He ignored it. It continued for weeks but eventually fizzled, at the end attracting mainly a handful of elderly ladies walking their dogs.

After the occupation of Plaza Altamira failed to dislodge Chávez, the opposition moved to its next plan: another strike. It was to turn into the most serious challenge to Chávez's presidency since the coup. It kicked off on Monday, December 2, with mixed results. While most shops shuttered in affluent eastern Caracas, many streets in downtown and western Caracas bustled with pedestrians, and many stores opened. In the sprawling barrio of Catia, life was near normal. Many business owners supported Chávez or did not want to risk their livelihoods for somebody else's politics.

The next day the walkout lost momentum in some regions. Chávez declared that "this strike, like all the others, has a hidden agenda: another coup attempt." He insisted that the protestors would not "paralyze" the crucial oil industry. But they were already trying. Strikers in small boats attempted to block a navigation canal in Lake Maracaibo that oil tankers used to export a million barrels of crude a day. The navy chased the strikers away. PDVSA administrative employees and executives also joined in the strike and started trying to shut down the industry, although thousands of workers stayed on the job. In Caracas protestors outside PDVSA offices clashed with National Guardsmen, who fired tear gas to break up their demonstration. The conflict helped pump life into the anti-Chávez protests.

Amid the clashes, the National Electoral Council produced what might have been a solution to the conflict. It voted four-to-one to hold a nonbinding national referendum on February 2 asking Venezuelans whether Chávez should continue as president. Opposition leaders decided to press on with the strike anyway. Against Chávez's wishes, the council was approving one of the ways the opposition had proposed for ending the crisis, but their leaders chose to ignore it.

On Wednesday the walkout seemed to further weaken, with more stores opening. But thousands of protestors marched through Caracas to the glitzy Melia Hotel, where they delivered a letter to César Gaviria asking for new elections. The former Colombian president was leading an Organization of American States delegation trying to negotiate a settlement to the conflict.

That evening the captain of a huge oil tanker named the *Pilín León* (for a Venezuelan beauty queen) stunned the nation. Appearing on television, he announced he was joining the strike. He anchored the eight-story-high ship and its 280,000 barrels of refined gasoline in the middle of the Lake Maracaibo shipping channel and refused to move. "This government is pushing us into a situation like Cuba," declared the captain, Daniel Alfaro. The rest of PDVSA's thirteen-ship fleet quickly followed suit, anchoring at sea or refusing to leave ports. Within days another two dozen internationally owned tankers joined in.

Combined with the walkout by PDVSA management, the anchoring of the ships threatened to paralyze Venezuela's oil industry. If that happened, it would be hard for any Venezuelan president to survive. Oil accounted for a third of Venezuela's $100 billion gross domestic product, half of government revenue, and 70 percent of exports. Moreover, if gasoline dried up, transportation would come to a halt, provoking food shortages. Without food, the hungry population would rise up to overthrow any government — Bolivarian or not.

Inside Miraflores Palace, Chávez huddled with his ministers and scrambled to find a solution to the crisis. They were caught off guard by the captains' walkout — they had not anticipated it. Chávez called the strike by the *Pilín León's* captain an "act of piracy" and warned of military action if the crew did not return to work. "It's as if the doctor who's supposed to be looking after your heart suddenly starts trying to stop it," he said.

Alfaro and the other captains became the latest instant heroes to the opposition. Hundreds of supporters gathered on the shoreline of Lake Maracaibo with the *Pilín León* in sight. Others circled the vessel with yachts, motorboats, canoes, and even kayaks to "protect" it if soldiers tried to board. León herself, a Miss World 1981 who was now in her forties, eventually made her way out to Lake Maracaibo to support the strikers. The ship turned into an emblem of the opposition's resistance against Chávez. Many of Venezuela's massive oil tankers were named for some of the country's most cherished beauty queens, including Miss

Universe or Miss World winners Susana Duijm, Barbara Palacios, and Maritza Sayalero.

Two days after Alfaro anchored his ship in Lake Maracaibo, another shocking event galvanized the opposition to Chávez. At about 7:15 P.M. on Friday, minutes after Carlos Ortega and Fedecámaras's new leader Carlos Fernández announced on national television in their nightly appearance that they were extending the walkout again, a gunman opened fire on the crowd in Plaza Altamira. He killed three people, including an eighteen-year-old girl who'd just graduated from high school, and injured twenty-eight as protestors hit the ground and the military dissidents on the stage pulled out their guns.

The opposition immediately blamed Chávez for the bloodshed, although they had no proof. In the end, it turned out the gunman was a deranged Portuguese taxi driver named Joao de Gouveia who confessed to the shootings and did not bother fleeing the scene of the crime. But the killings energized and radicalized the opposition movement. Leaders extended the strike indefinitely, declared three days of mourning, and said the only solution to the standoff now was Chávez's immediate resignation.

The strike quickly succeeded in inflicting severe damage on the oil industry. By Monday, December 9, PDVSA president Ali Rodríguez went on national television to announce that the industry was in serious condition. "We are threatened with a national disaster," he said. The country's two largest refineries, Paraguana and El Palito, were paralyzed. Rodríguez warned that gasoline shortages and electricity blackouts were imminent.

Panic was setting in. People rushed to supermarkets to stock up on food and water. Motorists had to wait up to four hours at some service stations for gasoline. Lines stretched as long as a mile. Waits of twenty-four hours or more later became common, with lines as long as three miles. Scarcities of drinking water and cash at automatic tellers spread. Airlines canceled dozens of domestic flights. Striking banks limited business to three hours a day. Eight of the Supreme Court's twenty justices joined the walkout, too, restricting their work to urgent cases only. It was the peak Christmas shopping season, yet many stores and businesses were shut down. The Democratic Coordinator, the opposition umbrella group, "canceled" Christmas. They instructed Chávez opponents to sacrifice now so they could achieve the "final victory" later. They adopted a slogan: "2002 Without Christmas, 2003 Without Chávez."

Protest marches became a nearly daily occurrence, at times attracting hundreds of thousands of people. Each night at eight o'clock, opposition supporters opened their windows and banged pots to call for Chávez to resign. Even Chávez's former wife, Marisabel, joined in the criticism. "President, please, in the name of your daughter, in the name of your family, in the name of the country, listen to the people," she said in a television interview as their daughter Rosinés sat beside her. She had joined the critics who believed Chávez was too arrogant and all-knowing to accept others' advice and seek compromise.

Television networks broadcast the rallies and strike activities nearly nonstop. They canceled regular advertisements and ran pro-strike, anti-Chávez spots around the clock. News talk shows featured one-sided commentators. Even news anchors blasted Chávez. Each evening, the networks broadcast rambling, triumphant updates by Ortega and Fernández. The president of Gustavo Cisneros's Venevisión openly acknowledged that the network hoped to see Chávez go. "We are united with the strike," Victor Ferreres said.

With the oil industry grinding nearly to a standstill, political analysts believed Chávez faced "a nearly impossible situation," *The New York Times* reported. Few thought he could survive. Venezuela defaulted on its international petroleum contracts, including those with its principal customer, the United States. It was the first time since the discovery of oil nearly a century earlier. Not even World War II, the Arab oil embargoes of the 1970s, the 1989 Caracazo riots, or the 1992 coups had caused that.

The Venezuelan opposition thought Chávez would fall within a week or two of the strike's commencement. PDVSA executives who walked off the job left their offices intact, figuring they would be back shortly in a nation no longer under Chávez's rule. They were willing to risk it all because so much was at stake. PDVSA was the "hen that lays the golden egg," as one of Chávez's ministers had put it. Control of it was crucial to where the money — billions of dollars — went. For decades the company had operated as an independent entity almost untouched by government oversight. Its executives lived the high life, traveling to the United States and Europe for vacations. They dictated company policy. Many hoped to privatize the company, bringing huge profits to themselves.

But now Chávez was threatening to undo it all. He wanted to seize control of PDVSA, divert the company's profits to the majority poor, shut down the chalets in the Andes, sell off the fleet of jets, end the plans for privatization, and bring in his own people to run the oil giant. If that happened, the elites' access to the hen with the golden eggs would be over.

Chávez was not about to surrender easily to the strikers. The government analyzed three possible scenarios stemming from the walkout. They could negotiate with the opposition for early elections — a possibility the government rejected. They might also face another coup — something Chávez was far more alert to now than in April. A final scenario was letting the strike simply wear itself out like the protest in the Plaza Altamira by the military rebels. Chávez thought that was the best strategy. "Let's fight them," he said at one high-level meeting. "We've got the support of the people, of the armed forces and of the workers" at PDVSA.

The "strike" at PDVSA was really more of a management lockout, since many mid- and low-level employees ignored the walkout and reported to work. The strikers and their supporters tried to stop them, surrounding installations and intimidating them as they arrived. The protestors also sabotaged the industry, destroying electrical lines, paralyzing refineries, dumping water into the ships' fuel tanks, and hacking into PDVSA's computer system to create havoc.

Chávez moved quickly to try to regain control of the installations. He dispatched troops to secure service stations, oil wells, refineries, and gasoline distribution centers. Then, on December 13, he called on his supporters to surround key oil installations. They would form human chains to protect them.

The situation was desperate. Gasoline supplies were dwindling, and service stations were closed. So Chávez did something else previously unthinkable in a nation with some of the world's largest oil reserves — he imported gasoline. He contacted Brazil, Trinidad and Tobago, Mexico, Russia, and other countries to ask them to send what they could. When basic foods grew scarce, he cobbled together another informal supply network, persuading Colombia, the Dominican Republic, and others to send rice, flour, milk, meat, and other products.

With PDVSA, he took a hard line. On December 12 he fired four executives — including Juan Fernández — who were leading the strike. Chávez had dismissed them and several others in April just before the coup, but reinstated them after the revolt to ease tensions. Now he decided to clean out the company wholesale. Day by day he dismissed more striking executives and managers, until some three hundred were gone by early January. Thousands more followed. Industry experts and dissident PDVSA executives predicted the government would be unable to restart the company or get it back to its normal production levels without the fired employees' expertise.

During much of December, it seemed like they were right. PDVSA had suffered a devastating blow. Production plummeted to as little as 150,000 barrels a day, compared with normal output of 3 million a day. Exports typically averaging 2.5 million barrels a day dropped to next to nothing. The Supreme Court ordered striking PDVSA managers and executives back to work, but they simply ignored the order. Oil production, the lifeline of the economy, slowed to a trickle. The country was gasping for breath.

The government believed the critical period for defeating the strike and ending the sabotage was December 16–21. If they could not make progress by then, they would be in serious trouble. They came up with a strategy they called Plan 1621.

Chávez desperately needed gasoline. The *Pilín León* was sitting in Lake Maracaibo with nearly twelve million gallons of it. So he ordered soldiers to take over the ship and arrest the captain. Navy troops scaled up the side of the tanker with ropes and held the crew at gunpoint. But the sailors refused to leave, saying they were protecting the ship and would not hand it over to an unqualified crew. Chávez was having trouble finding a replacement team. Ultimately the government convinced a number of retired seamen including Captain Carlos López to assume the mission.

López and the others climbed aboard the vessel on December 19, protected by soldiers as opposition supporters circled the tanker in boats. They spent two days working nonstop to prepare to restart the *Pilín León*. It was a dangerous mission. The tanker was a gigantic floating bomb. If something went wrong — an engine overheated, a spark flashed in a gas tank — it could set off a cataclysmic explosion. The ship also had to navigate underneath the massive Maracaibo Bridge to reach port. If it went off course, it could smash into the pillars and tear down the bridge, the longest in Latin America. Complicating their efforts, the departing crew had sabotaged the ship, leaving behind hard-to-notice traps in the computer system and elsewhere that could set off an explosion.

The media was full of reports that Chávez had brought in Cubans or other unqualified foreigners to run the tanker. The reports merely infuriated López and the others, shoring up their resolve to take on the risky mission.

Most of the nation was glued to their television sets around noon on December 21 as López and the others attempted to restart the *Pilín León*. If something went wrong, Chávez could be blamed for irresponsibly sending an unprepared crew on a suicide mission to serve his political needs. The president was in Miraflores, nervously watching along with the rest of the country. He knew the fate of the strike and perhaps his presidency was on the line.

Suddenly a puff of smoke came out of the ship's chimney. The monster was running again. López ordered the ship to move ahead, but as it did the engines started overheating dangerously. He sent the ship in a circle to avoid heading to the bridge while engineers tried to bring the temperature under control. They did, and the tanker headed for Maracaibo. When it was three hundred yards from the bridge, the crew let out a cheer. Even if something went wrong, the ship had too much momentum now to change course before passing under the bridge safely. It was going to make it. Soldiers guarding the bridge pumped their fists into their palms while holding their arms over their heads in a gesture made famous by Chávez. In Miraflores the elated president shouted with joy. "There goes the *Pilín León*!" he said and, in a soccer reference, added, "Gooooal!"

The ship's return to port was a major and daring victory for Chávez. With gasoline supplies drying up, creating the specter of food shortages, he had taken control of the central symbol of the strike. That night he flew to Maracaibo to congratulate the crew. Alejandro Gómez — who'd helped organize the *Pilín León* mission and was in the cabin with the captain as it restarted and passed under the bridge — later became head of the oil company's marine division.

While Chávez struggled to get the ships moving again, he was also trying to revive oil production. Executives and managers hadn't just walked off the job when they left, according to Chávez and other government officials. They'd also sabotaged the company to make restarting it difficult and dangerous. They'd damaged pipes, stolen files, and, most seriously, taken with them elements of PDVSA's automated system. That allowed them to use remote computers to block reactivation. For months the company had to operate completely or partly manually as it tried to resume normal production. In a speech in January 2003, Chávez explained one method of sabotage:

> You know that all these systems — all the industry — are computerized and systemized . . . The sabotage consisted in changing the adjustment points in the control systems. A variable has been introduced into the computers of the control systems so that the temperature in the boilers does not rise above six hundred degrees, which is the temperature ceiling. Above six hundred degrees, the plant reaches a dangerous level.
>
> Well, these gentlemen not only abandoned their posts but changed the adjustment points before leaving. That is, they raised the ceiling from six hundred degrees to eight hundred degrees centigrade. What would have happened if our patriotic and well-trained technicians had not checked these control systems and adjustment points well? What would have happened if they had started the systems and valves and all the operating system? When the temperature had gone above six hundred degrees and reached eight hundred, there would have been a disaster — an explosion.

To try to regain control of PDVSA's computer system, Chávez's government had to bring in its own "hackers" to combat the striking PDVSA technicians who were hacking in from the outside. Amid the strike Chávez told reporters:

> I didn't know anything about that. I'm learning a lot now. I was in an office with the minister, it's an electronic bombardment on the computers, the system goes crazy, it goes crazy, by remote control. So a young guy arrived, a hacker, with an apparatus, and I joked, "Are you a witch doctor?" Because he arrived with this apparatus. He said, "There's an electronic war going on." So it was hackers against hackers, some shooting here, others shooting there. It was an impressive thing. I had studied war tactics during a number of years, but I never imagined it was going to come down to this electronic war.

Complicating Chávez's efforts to regain electronic control of PDVSA — and raising suspicions in the government of covert United States involvement — was a contract the oil giant had signed with a US-based technology services company named Intesa, and its associated company SAIC (Science Applications International Corporation). SAIC's roster of high-ranking officials included former US military officers and CIA officials. Among them were General Wayne Downing, appointed by President George W. Bush to head the White House Office for Combating Terrorism; General Jasper Welch, a former coordinator for the National Security Council; and Admiral Bobby Ray Inman, former director of the NSA and deputy director of the CIA. Eventually PDVSA cut its ties with SAIC.

Just as Chávez had to hunt for hackers and for new teams to staff the tankers, he also had to find people to operate PDVSA since he was in the process of firing thousands of employees. He looked to mid- and lower-level workers to take over operations previously run by higher-level supervisors and managers, or brought in retired employees like the captain who steered the *Pilín León* to port. Like Venezuelan society in general, PDVSA was polarized between a well-heeled elite who despised Chávez and lower-paid workers who supported him or at least did not want to use PDVSA as a political weapon.

The Puerto La Cruz refinery was a typical example and became a showcase for the government's efforts to restart the industry. Almost all the plant's high-level executives walked off the job, but fewer than 20 percent of the operators, mechanics, and technicians did. Using skeleton crews working extensive overtime, they brought the plant back to life. "We are prouder now than ever," one seventeen-year veteran stated. "We have shown our supervisors we can run the plant without them." By late December, the plant was producing sixty thousand barrels of gasoline a day. That was about 70 percent of its capacity and one-seventh of the nation's normal daily consumption of four hundred thousand barrels.

PDVSA president Ali Rodríguez himself acknowledged that the company faced enormous obstacles in regaining its previous production. The institutional knowledge and expertise the fired employees took with them was considerable. As part of the government's plan to revive PDVSA, it decided to split the company into two regional entities based in the east and west of the country where the oil actually lay. It gutted the central headquarters in Caracas, where many of the striking executives worked.

By late December, Rodríguez claimed production was up to seven hundred thousand barrels a day — a figure dissident PDVSA executives disputed. But Chávez was keeping the country afloat — barely. On December 28 the first foreign shipment of gasoline arrived: Brazil sent 525,000 barrels. It was another shocking milestone. One of the world's largest petroleum producers was importing gasoline.

Still, the Brazilian gasoline was a drop in the bucket for Venezuela. Most service stations remained closed. When one opened people waited in line for up to two days to slowly make their way to the pump. Some organized shifts, arranging for friends, neighbors, and relatives to take turns sitting with their cars. In preparation for long trips, Venezuelans spent weeks stockpiling plastic jugs of gasoline at home. They could not count on finding a station open along the way.

Propane cooking gas also became scarce. On December 26 about three hundred people blocked a highway in Caracas for two hours to demand more of it. Some said they had been using charcoal and kerosene to cook for two weeks. Others in the city were burning their furniture. On street corners a surreal sight appeared — people selling wood.

The protest was one of the first signs of unrest, although in the barrios most of it was aimed at the opposition leaders who organized the strike. Other isolated demonstrations broke out at empty service stations. The situation was critical. Store shelves were increasingly bare, especially of drinks like milk, bottled water, and beer. People trying to carry on with their lives by holding events such as a girl's fifteenth "coming out" birthday party had to spend days scouring their cities or towns to round up enough soda.

But much to the opposition's surprise, Chávez was still in power. He was proving to be far more tenacious and resourceful than they expected. He found he had friends. Trinidad and Tobago, off Venezuela's Caribbean coast, pitched in to help stave off the crisis, sending four hundred thousand more barrels of gasoline. The Dominican Republic shipped rice. On January 8 a Venezuelan navy ship arrived in Colombia to take on five hundred tons of food and supplies including flour, corn, wheat, soft drinks, tomato sauce, butter, toilet paper, and diapers. Another two ships from Venezuela were on their way, too, to pick up more food. When some of the supplies came in, Chávez made sure they got to his power base in poor neighborhoods.

The strike was failing to dislodge him for another reason. Forced to wait on long lines for gasoline, Venezuelans did what they do best: they socialized and turned it into a party. People pulled out dominos, gathered under trees, and shared *empanadas* and coffee. They spent hours gabbing, telling jokes, and trading war stories about surviving the strike. Waiting on long lines was nothing new for the average Venezuelan: working-class people did it every day waiting for the bus to take them to work. The opposition leaders, out of touch with the masses, failed to foresee the patience many poor Venezuelans would exhibit in confronting the hardships the opposition was inflicting. Even many in the middle-class started to feel the strike was ridiculous.

By the start of the New Year, it was showing signs of fraying. More and more businessmen were unwilling to destroy their livelihoods in a quest to oust the president. Increasingly desperate, the opposition leadership tried to step up the pressure and pry Chávez out of Miraflores. They called for a tax boycott and organized a march to the federal tax agency. Television networks ran "public service announcements" encouraging citizens to stop paying the sales tax. The government reminded them that tax evasion was a crime, punishable by up to seven years in prison.

The banks, which had been operating for three hours a day, shut down completely for two days. Carlos Ortega, who two weeks earlier declared he would not call on protestors to march to Miraflores because it "would be irresponsible" after the violence in April, now reversed himself. He threatened another march if Chávez did not permit the nonbinding referendum, which by now was tied up with court challenges. "I say, let's go," Ortega said on New Year's Eve. "And if they are going to kill us, let them kill us once and for all."

Chávez invoked some audacious moves of his own. On January 17 National Guardsmen raided two privately owned bottling plants to seize bottled water, soda, and beer in the city of Valencia. The owners of the plants were Cisneros's Panamco, the Coca-Cola bottler in Venezuela, and Pepsi bottler Empresas Polar, the country's largest brewer and food producer. They claimed they had been unable to distribute the products because of fuel shortages and striking workers. The government contended they were hoarding them to help starve the population and spark Chávez's overthrow.

National Guard general Luis Felipe Acosta Carles, the brother of Felipe Acosta Carles, the MBR-200 founder who was killed during the Caracazo, led the raids. He had to battle through a ring of protestors to get inside the plants. After he did, he appeared on television. "Taking into account that collective rights preside over personal rights, we are proceeding to distribute these products to the population," he said. "It's for the people." He grabbed a warm soda and drank it. Then he promptly belched into the opposition television cameras.

Chávez's opponents were horrified. They thought it was a disgusting display that symbolized the vulgarity of the Chavistas and the illegality of Chávez's assault on private property. But in most barrios, Venezuelans were delighted by the raid and even the burp. To them, it was an act of in-your-face justice against elites who were trying to sabotage the economy and force Chávez out.

By now clear signs were emerging that the strike was backfiring. Graffiti appeared on banks: BANKER THIEVES! COUP PLOTTERS! Many small businesses never joined the walkout in the first place. In January many of those that had quietly reopened, although large transnational companies remained shut. Traffic increased in Caracas as more shops, restaurants, and markets opened their doors. The strike was turning into a form of economic suicide or cannibalism. Many business owners wanted nothing more to do with it.

By the middle of January strike leaders were quietly signaling to some hard-hit businessmen that it was all right to reopen their doors, although publicly they maintained the walkout was still in effect. Weakened, they dropped their demand that Chávez resign before new elections could be held. Instead they focused on the February 2 non-binding referendum, which in the end was suspended by the Supreme Court on a technicality.

By the last week in January the opposition leadership was publicly telling schools, restaurants, and malls they could reopen in February, at least part-time. Many tanker pilots were also returning to their jobs. A risk management expert at Energy Merchant LLC in New York called their decision "the first chink in the armor."

On January 23 hundreds of thousands of Chavistas took to the streets of Caracas in a massive rally to support the president. They chanted, "Ooh! Ah! Chávez isn't leaving!" Residents of middle- and upper-class sectors where private militias were forming braced behind the gates of their homes, fearing an invasion that never came. Four days later, on January 27, the Caracas Stock Exchange opened for the first time in nine weeks. It operated for two and a half hours a day to continue showing support for the walkout. The next day Chávez scored another victory: Oil production passed the one-million-barrel-a-day mark. It was a milestone even dissident PDVSA executives reluctantly acknowledged.

A week later, as Chávez marked the eleventh anniversary of the February 1992 coup attempt, the strike all but collapsed outside the oil industry. Private schools, businesses, restaurants, franchises, and banks opened their doors full-time. The walkout was over. Chávez had achieved what many observers believed was impossible: He had survived a strike by the oil industry.

He came out of the crisis even stronger than after the April coup, when he felt compelled to make concessions to the opposition. Now his opponents were proving increasingly inept. "They have an 'F' for failure on their foreheads," Chávez quipped. This time he did not reinstate any of the dissident PDVSA executives or managers; instead he fired a total of eighteen thousand of them by the end of March. It was close to half of the oil giant's thirty-eight thousand employees.

Leaders of the strike were not allowed to walk the streets freely to continue conspiring or occupying plazas they declared "liberated territory." Instead judges issued arrest warrants for them. DISIP political police seized Fedecámaras president Carlos Fernández on February 19 as he left a restaurant in trendy Las Mercedes. His counterpart in the CTV, Carlos Ortega, went into hiding and later fled for Costa Rica, where he gained political asylum. He and others contended they were victims of political persecution. Some even called Fernández a "political prisoner."

But Chávez saw the strike leaders as nothing more than "terrorists" and "coup plotters" who had tried to oust him by wreaking economic chaos. It was a repeat of the CIA-backed coup in Chile in 1973, only in Venezuela it didn't work. The military stood by Chávez. If the April 2002 revolt was a "media coup," this one was an "economic coup."

While Chávez survived, the walkout inflicted devastating economic damage on Venezuela. The economy nearly collapsed, contracting by 27 percent in the first four months of 2003. In total, it cost the oil industry $13.3 billion.

Despite the economic damage, Chávez was now freer to pursue his radical reform program and spend less time fending off attempts to topple him. "The coup-mongering, fascist opposition had their turn at bat and they have struck out three times," he said. "Now it's our turn to bat." He turned his attention to his social programs. They were in their infancy in his first four years in office. Now they were to become the centerpiece of his administration.

At the suggestion of Alejandro Gómez, the man who'd helped organize the rescue of the *Pilín León*, Chávez made one final move to mark the end of the disastrous strike. He changed the names of the PDVSA tankers that had refused to deliver their contents. Instead of beauty queens, they took on the names of heroines of Venezuela's independence. The *Susana Duijm* became the *Manuela Sáenz*, for Bolívar's longtime companion and fellow revolutionary. The *Barbara Palacios* was renamed the *Luisa Caceres de Arismendi*, for the woman who — while imprisoned by the Spanish on Margarita Island — delivered a baby girl who died at birth.

Two more ships were honored with the names of two black women who played a crucial role in Bolívar's early life. The *Maritza Sayalero* became the *Negra Hipólita*, in honor of the wet nurse who helped raise Bolívar and whom the orphaned Liberator once referred to as both his mother *and* his father. And the *Pilín León*, the ship that helped turned the tide for Chávez, was rebaptized the *Negra Matea* for the governess who helped raise Bolívar. In the aftermath of the devastating oil strike, Chávez wanted to remind the country of Venezuela's revolutionary roots as his own revolution prepared to take off.

**24**

# The Social Missions

Dilia Mari Davila grew up in rural Venezuela and never went to school to learn to read and write. When she was eight years old her impoverished family sent her off to work as a live-in maid, since they could barely afford to feed her. It was a childhood of deprivation not uncommon among millions of people in Venezuela's lower classes.

Nearly three decades after leaving her family, Davila finally got a chance at an education. She signed up for one of Chávez's signature social programs, Mision Robinson. She learned to read and write, and within a year was even mastering division and multiplication. By 2004, at the age of thirty-four, she had reached a fourth-grade level of education. Before, she could not help her elementary-school-aged son with his homework because she didn't understand the words on the paper. Now she could. She even started dreaming of going to college.

Davila was among a million and a half Venezuelans who took part in Mision Robinson, one of the first of several social programs that marked a new, more radical phase of Chávez's presidency in the post-coup, post-oil-strike era. Initiated in 2003, the missions were a more elaborate and organized version of the makeshift Plan Bolívar 2000 that Chávez started early in his presidency to meet immediate needs for food, medical care, roads, and schools. Offering everything from subsidized food markets to literacy classes to health services, the missions became wildly popular in the teeming barrios of Caracas and other urban centers and in the impoverished countryside. They were so successful that even Chávez's opponents eventually declared that if they took power, they would continue funding the programs.

Davila lived in the Sector A, La Casita (little house), section of La Vega, a sprawling mountainside barrio in Caracas that turned into one of the showcases of Chávez's social experiment. It attracted visitors and journalists from around the world, although Venezuela's media ignored it and up until the middle of 2004 no journalist from the United States had visited. The barrio was a collection of simple cinder-block homes including some packed into narrow, winding streets barely the width of a person's outstretched arms.

One of the first and most dramatic missions to arrive in La Vega was Barrio Adentro — Inside the Neighborhood. Starting in 2003 Chávez and Caracas mayor Freddy Bernal sent hundreds of Cuban doctors into barrios in Caracas such as La Vega, and thousands more into other poor neighborhoods throughout the country. The program stemmed from Chávez's agreement in 2000 to provide energy-starved Cuba with cut-rate oil. In return Castro sent doctors, teachers, sports trainers, and other experts.

When Chávez took office, Venezuela's public health system, which most of the population relied on for care, was collapsing. In the barrios and impoverished countryside, medical attention was pitiful and in some cases nonexistent. "Pregnant women in these neighborhoods have never been to the doctor for prenatal care, and give birth at home on the floor," noted Rafael Vargas, who was Chávez's chief of staff during the coup and later managed the Cuban doctors program. "There are ten-, fourteen-year-old kids who have never been to the dentist."

Barrio dwellers had to leave their homes before dawn to make the long trek to a clinic or a hospital to be seen. If they weren't far ahead enough in the line, they were sent home. Those undergoing surgery had to supply everything on their own: gauze, medicines, sheets, even Band-Aids. The joke in Venezuela was that the only thing patients didn't have to supply was the doctor. Sometimes even that was missing. Patients commonly languished in hospitals for weeks waiting for a doctor to become available or broken surgical equipment to get fixed. Some in urgent need of emergency care simply died.

Cuba was a different story. The island had a health system recognized by the World Health Organization as a model for Third World nations, although economic troubles in the 1990s after the collapse of its main benefactor, the Soviet Union, deprived it of some basic supplies. It sent doctors all over the world, from Haiti to Honduras in Latin America and the Caribbean to Gambia and Angola in Africa, as part of its revolutionary solidarity with other Third World nations. Venezuela became its largest operation, with twenty thousand doctors and health workers eventually. By some accounts, the fourteen thousand doctors amounted to one-fifth of all Cuba's physicians. While previous governments had tried to bring some health care to the barrios, by now that was a distant memory and was nothing like the scale of Chávez's project.

The physicians were greeted like heroes in the barrios. Neighbors fought with one another to offer them dinner invitations. Hosting them was an honor. In some areas neighbors dropped off so much donated food, the doctors had to tell them to stop. Initially the Cubans lived in people's homes and ran makeshift clinics out of everywhere from living rooms to the backs of bodegas. Eventually the government constructed hundreds of two-story, hexagonal brick buildings; the doctors provided medical service on the first floor and lived on the second. They usually served two-year stints, and received a $250 monthly stipend from the Venezuelan government.

They focused on preventive medicine, hoping to head off ailments before they turned more serious and required extensive medical intervention. Along with local volunteers they conducted surveys of the communities, walking house-to-house to take down medical histories, find out who was ill, and try to obtain the necessary medicines. They trained community volunteers to give workshops on nutrition and preventive medicine. By the program's second year dentists and ophthalmologists were joining them, bringing advanced equipment into the barrios that included new Chinese- and Brazilian-made dentists' chairs, eye-testing and lens-making machines, and fully equipped Pap smear units.

It was not always an easy assignment. In some barrios, neighbors convinced gang members to escort the doctors as they made their rounds or were passed off from one gang-controlled area to another. The safety measures didn't always work; a few Cuban physicians were attacked and killed by common criminals.

Nor was the program universally hailed. The physicians' lobby criticized it, saying the Cubans were not needed — eight thousand unemployed Venezuelan doctors could take their place. They criticized Chávez for failing to improve public hospitals, where most Venezuelans went for more intensive medical treatment the Cubans could not provide in the neighborhood clinics. They also questioned the credentials of the Cubans, and accused some of malpractice. Douglas León Natera, president of the Venezuelan Medical Federation, went so far as to allege that the Cubans weren't doctors at all. "We're not xenophobes," he said. "We have information that these people, almost one hundred percent of them, are not doctors. These are people masquerading as doctors, wearing white robes with stethoscopes around their necks."

While that accusation was simply laughable to Chávez's supporters, León's other arguments were undercut by some simple facts. When the government placed ads in newspapers offering housing and jobs in the barrios, few Venezuelan doctors showed up. Hailing mainly from the middle class, they were more interested in treating affluent patients at lucrative private clinics, where business was booming in elective procedures, breast enlargements and other "touch-ups," in the beauty-queen-crazy country. Many doctors were simply afraid to set foot in the barrios. The allegations of malpractice also seemed unfounded — the Cuban health system was widely respected.

As for the notorious public hospitals, they did not miraculously turn into models of efficiency under Chávez overnight, but they did improve, with supplies becoming more abundant, care getting better, and more buildings going up. Social spending per capita on health rose a whopping 74 percent between 1999 and 2005 alone, according to government figures. It jumped an estimated 10 percent more in 2006, and kept rising in 2007. Most of the money came from PDVSA. Chávez set up a special fund at the oil giant to finance the social programs. Booming world oil prices helped make it all possible.

Thousands of poor patients who could not be treated in Venezuela flew to Cuba for advanced treatment and surgery for strokes, back injuries, and other ailments in another part of the medical program that became immensely popular. One of the programs, Mision Milagro — Miracle Mission — flew patients to Cuba for free eye surgery. Many impoverished people considered it a godsend, although some Cubans resented their special treatment. Eventually Chávez expanded the program, flying people from Jamaica, Bolivia, and other countries in Latin America to Cuba for eye surgery. He even floated the idea of bringing in poor people from Africa and impoverished communities in the United States. Cuba provided the medical expertise; Venezuela provided the money.

Many of the patients suffered from cataracts and were blind or badly impaired. After the operations, they could see. "This is an example of integration and south–south cooperation," said Elinor Sherlock,

Jamaica's ambassador to Cuba. "You see them, especially poor people who cannot afford care, staring in awe for hours out the window after their operations. It really is miraculous."

Some of Chávez's opponents claimed he was using Cuban doctors to win votes, but in the end it was hard to argue that putting full-time doctors in slums was a bad thing, no matter where they came from. "If it's necessary to go to Mars or the moon to help the poor, then we'll get doctors from Mars," said program head Rafael Vargas. Chávez claimed that in the first few months of the program alone, the Cuban doctors saved three hundred lives.

Eventually the government moved into a second phase of the Mission Inside the Neighborhood program, going beyond community-based preventive health care initiatives to focus on improving or creating facilities to treat more serious illnesses. It spent $52 million building a state-of-the-art children's cardiac hospital. It spent another $1 billion to repair forty-four hospitals, build about six hundred diagnostic or reha-bilitation centers, and open more than twenty-one hundred neighbor-hood clinics for Mission Inside the Neighborhood. Doctors conducted a growing number of surgeries in Venezuela as the government resur-rected the long-decaying public hospital system. It also sent hundreds of young people to Cuba to attend medical school for free, returning home to serve impoverished sectors.

The medical missions had an overwhelmingly positive impact on barrio residents. By some estimates, by 2006 some fourteen and a half million people — 54 percent of the population — was receiving free health care through the Barrio Adentro program.

One typical beneficiary, sixty-three-year-old Margarita Mendez, had been a prisoner in her small cement home for years. A severe case of varicose veins had swollen her lower legs, which were covered with pink, raw blisters. To leave her house in the grim San Pablito shanty-town, relatives had to carry her down a steep, dizzying outdoor staircase leading to a main road below. To get back, she had to climb the flight of stairs. She could barely make it. She had scaled the staircase only half a dozen times in a decade to make the thirty-minute trip to the nearest general hospital. In her last visit doctors told her they would have to amputate. She never went back.

Her life changed when Cuban doctor Roberto Hernández arrived on the scene. Burly and mustachioed, Hernández had served in Haiti and Angola as part of Cuba's international medical missions. In Caracas's

San Pablito, he started making house calls to Mendez three times a week, climbing the staircase and ducking under clotheslines. Gang members escorted him and passed him off from one territory to the next. The visits helped. Mendez's condition improved. She made her first tentative steps through the unpaved streets outside her house, and hoped to make it down the treacherous staircase within a few months more. "Doctor Hernández," she said, "has been a godsend."

While Cuba excelled at health care despite its lack of democratic freedoms and its morose state-controlled economy, it also boasted of a strong educational system. One of the great achievements of the early years of Castro's revolution was a literacy campaign in which thousands of volunteers headed out into the streets and the countryside to teach the illiterate to read and write. They wiped out illiteracy and, along with an enhanced higher education system, turned Cubans into arguably the best-educated populace in Latin America. Cuba had a higher literacy rate than the United States, according to the United Nations and other independent organizations. Poor black Cubans who never dreamed of going to college during the Batista dictatorship now could.

Chávez borrowed the Cuban model for his literacy campaign, with some twists adapted to the Venezuelan reality. Cuba sent hundreds of literacy trainers to Venezuela to teach a hundred thousand Venezuelan volunteers how to give the classes. And while the Cubans a generation earlier had gone out into the fields with pencils and notebooks to teach people to read, this time they brought television sets, video recorders, and reading glasses.

Volunteers gave classes in schools after regular classes got out, in church basements, and in community libraries. In the Caracas barrio of Coche one afternoon, twenty-two-year-old university student Rosana Alviarez was teaching four elderly women who were enrolled in Mision Robinson. They sat in a stifling hot converted cement garage on the grounds of a local convent as a fan tried fruitlessly to cool off the room. The women repeated words Alviarez said to illustrate the difference in Spanish between the regular r and the rolling double-r sound. Afterward they praised Chávez for allowing them to learn to read, write, and master basic math. "He's a good president for all Venezuelans," said sixty-eight-year-old Maria Barrio. "He's done very good programs that were never seen here before."

The literacy program was named for Simón Rodríguez, Bolívar's tutor who — when he went into exile — gave himself the pseudonym Samuel Robinson to honor Robinson Crusoe. Chávez created another educational program, Mision Ribas, named for independence hero José Félix Ribas, who married one of Bolívar's aunts. Eventually a slave betrayed him to the Spanish, who severed his head, boiled it in water, and displayed it in a cage in Caracas.

Mision Ribas was aimed at allowing young dropouts to complete their high school education. It had plenty of potential participants: Huge numbers of Venezuelans had never finished their secondary or even elementary education. The first year six hundred thousand students signed up; eventually the number reached 1.4 million. They studied mainly at night, focusing on mathematics, advanced grammar, geography, and English as a second language. Some students received small stipends to make up for time they could have spent working or to provide for child care or bus fare. The compressed course was designed to be completed in two years.

Finally, Chávez created another program for those who had a high school diploma but needed financial assistance to go to college. Named for General Antonio José de Sucre, who helped conquer Bolivia, the program provided aid to one hundred thousand students each year. Chávez also created a new university for low-income students: the Bolivarian University of Venezuela. Symbolically, it was opened in the PDVSA office building in Chuao emptied after Chávez fired thousands of striking oil executives and managers. It later opened campuses across the nation, offering majors that included public health, architecture, medicine, computer science, and environmental management, along with activities such as dance and soccer.

While the educational programs received widespread praise from Venezuela's lower classes, they were not without critics. Some questioned the quality of the classes, especially in Mision Ribas, where they doubted a proper high school education could be compressed into two years. Others complained that the Bolivarian University of Venezuela was more about pro-Chávez political indoctrination than the pursuit of higher education.

To Venezuela's poor, however, the missions were revolutionary. Flaws and all, they were a genuine and massive effort to help lift the underclass the likes of which the country had never seen. By some estimates, by 2006 some three million people had enrolled in one of the educational missions since their initiation in 2003.

The programs didn't stop at health care and education. Chávez also created thousands of subsidized food markets across the country called Mercals. They offered flour, pasta, bread, rice, beans, meat, and other products at steep discounts to shantytown dwellers and peasants. By 2006 an estimated 40 to 47 percent of the population shopped at the Mercals, which sold food at discounts that averaged between 41 and 44 percent. The government also created thousands of soup kitchens in low-income areas such as La Vega. It donated the pots, dishes, and food to small groups of neighborhood women who set up a kitchen in one of their homes and cooked a nutritious hot lunch each day for about 150 people in extreme poverty.

While the government focused on improving education and health care — at the most basic level getting food into hungry people's stomachs — it also initiated projects aimed at job creation. Mision Vuelvan Caras, or Mission About-Face, was designed to reduce unemployment and foster community development by creating thousands of small-scale cooperatives in agriculture and other areas. It was based on a concept called endogenous development, or development "proceeding from within."

Eschewing traditional Marxism-Leninism, the concept envisioned using local cooperatives to make Venezuela self-sufficient by favoring domestic products as opposed to imports brought in by what one government official called a "parasitic oligarchy" that then resold the products at vast profit. Items like baby strollers or computers often sold for two or three times the price consumers paid in the United States, where Venezuelan businessmen bought them. On trips to Miami, Venezuelan tourists with money loaded everything from air conditioners to stereos onto airplanes for the return trip. Chávez wanted to take Venezuela's raw materials and, instead of shipping them to the United States and other industrialized nations, keep them at home to make the country's own products. As Carlos Lanz, the aging university professor who helped lead the effort, put it: "We hand over cheap raw material to The Empire [the United States] and the multinational corporations, and they sell us very expensive goods. So who benefits? People in the North."

Chávez's government set up one example of its new economic model on a hill overlooking the sprawling working-class barrio of Catia, creating a manufacturing and agricultural cooperative in the neighborhood of Gramoven. It was built on the site of an old PDVSA plant where delivery trucks once filled up with gasoline. The plant had been abandoned more than a decade earlier, but large empty tanks were still sitting on the hillside.

The government restored a huge storehouse on the site and turned it into a plant where workers manufactured shoes. Another converted warehouse was devoted to producing T-shirts and other clothing. The site also included a shining new health clinic, a "Bolivarian" school that offered free meals and Internet-connected computers, and a large gazebo where residents held weekly community meetings. Off to the side, co-op members planted tomatoes and other crops on a small mountainside urban farm. In a poor community where past governments were nearly invisible, the project was a source of great hope and pride to residents.

Beyond Mision Vuelvan Caras, one of the government's most important and most overlooked efforts was a program to hand out land titles to barrio dwellers. Many of the barrios in Caracas and elsewhere were started by poor Venezuelans who simply "invaded" the land, set up makeshift houses of cardboard or even tents made of plastic bags, and eventually constructed simple cinder-block homes, many of them stacked on top of one another. Some of the barrios sprang up on dangerous mountainsides prone to the kind of mudslides that had killed thousands in December 1999. Chávez's government initiated a program to give the residents of areas that were not in disaster zones titles to their homes. It was a milestone for the residents, opening up myriad possibilities such as obtaining bank loans to start small businesses.

The list of missions went on. Mision Identidad was a voter registration drive aimed at bringing all eligible residents onto the electoral roll. Thousands of Venezuelans had long ago lost their national identification cards, seen them expire, or never received them in the first place. Now they could get a new one quickly without going through the typical nightmarish bureaucracy. Skeptics charged it was a ploy by Chávez to pack the voting rolls with supporters, but others compared it to the voter registration drives in the United States in the 1960s aimed at bringing disenfranchised blacks into the political system. The program also allowed hundreds of thousands of foreigners who had lived in Venezuela for years but never became nationalized to receive legal papers and gain voting rights.

The identification card, the *cedula*, was also critical in Venezuela because without it, it was impossible to obtain government licenses, apply for government programs, or in many cases get a job. Gaining the card made people full citizens for the first time in their lives.

Other missions addressed everything from the indigenous population to gold miners. Mision Zamora sought to assist peasants. Mision Guaicaipuro targeted the Indian tribes and their five hundred thousand members in some of the remotest corners of the country. Mision Piar reached out to the miners who used high-pressure water hoses to blast through the dirt in the Amazon rain forest looking for gold, and often lived in miserable conditions.

The missions came under attack from Chávez's critics, who accused him of pandering to the poor and engaging in "populism" — a pejorative term in Latin America associated with government handouts and cheap short-term gimmicks to win votes. They criticized his endogenous economic model as nothing but a poor imitation of the import-substitution policies that had swept Latin America in the 1960s and 1970s, with limited success. They thought the missions were poorly run and failed to get to the root of the major systemic problems plaguing Venezuela such as a corrupt judicial system, one of the most bloated government bureaucracies in Latin America, rising crime and poverty rates, and widespread unemployment.

Luis Pedro España, a professor at the Andrés Bello University in Caracas who studied poverty, contended that "the government does not really have a social policy. What they have is social theater." He and other critics predicted that Chávez's social missions would all come tumbling down — along with his presidency — when oil prices dropped.

That argument posed a legitimate question. Yet Chávez's supporters asked: What's wrong with spending oil money on the majority poor while it lasts? Chávez was merely following the IMF-endorsed formula that had turned South Korea, Singapore, and other nations into the "Asian Tigers" by boosting spending on health and education, which in the long run helped send economic growth soaring at record rates. Venezuelan political scientist Edgardo Lander wondered if there was a double standard when it came to presidents like Chávez redirecting state resources to the poorest sectors of their countries. "Why is that populist?" he said. "Why isn't that the state fulfilling its responsibilities?"

Chávez's missions, in reality, were more than government handouts. They were serving to stimulate, excite, and organize communities like no other government program before. Neighbors who'd barely said hello to one another on the streets were coming together to form land committees, which the government required before handing out titles. They were working together in soup kitchens and studying side by side at night in Mision Robinson or Mision Ribas. They were launching grassroots community projects to fix decrepit water systems, put up guardrails to keep children off busy streets, or tack up posters to advise residents how to combat dengue fever — often with little or no government assistance.

The infectious hope that was spreading through the barrios was coming not only from services people were receiving from the government for the first time in their lives, but from their own participation as catalysts in the process. While previous governments didn't give much, they didn't ask much either. Chávez was challenging people to give back as much as they received. The thousands of volunteers cooking meals, teaching literacy classes, and organizing land committees were gaining a new sense of identity and dignity that no one could take away.

It was possible Chávez's entire project might collapse when the day came that he departed or oil profits vanished. But it was more likely that he had awakened the majority poor in a way there was no turning back from. After decades of submission, the underclass had risen up and taken power. Venezuela would never be the same, with or without Chávez.

To some followers it did not matter whether Chávez's programs succeeded immediately. He was their president — the first to truly represent them. People hung portraits of him on the walls of their homes next to pictures of Jesus Christ. Women slept with posters of him above their beds. Men vowed to defend him to the death. "I would prefer to be hungry with Chávez than have the opposition return," said Julio César, a Caracas shantytown dweller. He lost both legs to amputation after he was shot during a robbery, but when Chávez visited his barrio and heard his story, the president got him fitted with prostheses. "Chávez is the only president who came here to the barrios. He loves the people."

To Chávez's supporters, the complaints about his government were driven by one basic fact: The poor had taken power in Venezuela for the first time in the country's history, and the wealthy elites who lived in gated mansions and maintained second residences in Manhattan or Paris didn't like it. "For the affluent sectors of the country the problem is not that there is poverty," stated the Harvard-educated political scientist Lander. "The problem is that the poor are organizing and mobilizing. And that signifies a threat of the 'dangerous classes.'

The dangerous classes are dangerous if they mobilize, if they act, if they demand."

He likened the situation to a high-society party of "the white people, the refined people, the people who know how to speak well, who know how to hold the crystal cups to drink wine. Suddenly, into the party barge some people who don't have manners, who are poorly dressed, who haven't taken a bath and smell bad. They grab the food with their hands. They create the sensation they are taking over the country."

Chávez's mission — and his missions — sparked growing interest outside Venezuela. "Revolutionary tourism" became a booming business. Academics, activists, students, civil rights leaders, church workers, and union heads flocked to the country. Venezuela turned into the new mecca of the left. The newcomers were the latest incarnation of the activists who'd visited Cuba in the 1960s or 1970s or Nicaragua and El Salvador in the 1980s. Many distrusted mainstream media accounts of the Bolivarian Revolution. They wanted to see for themselves.

When they visited the barrios, the atmosphere was electric. Some watched women and men in their seventies learn to read their first words. "You've got a nation and a leader trying to provide an alternative to neo-liberalism and the policies that have ravaged Latin America for twenty years," one Australian student told *The New York Times*. "That's why people are coming here. There's a sense that it's a moment in history." Another visitor, New York City union leader Brenda Stokely, said that "President Chávez is trying to provide poor people with health care, education and decently paid jobs. Anyone opposed to that either has their head under a rock or has no respect for human beings that live in poverty."

Groups such as Global Exchange in San Francisco organized tours to Venezuela where visitors saw everything from cooperatives to the medical missions. Skeptics dismissed the pilgrimages, arguing that the visitors got a skewed view of Venezuela that left out the critiques of those who opposed Chávez. Sociologist Amalio Belmonte likened the ideological tourists to "nineteenth century anthropologists who travel the world looking for primitive cultures. Then they return to their comfortable lives in the First World and repeat Chávez's revolutionary discourse, but with no interest in finding out the other side of the story."

In reality, many of the tour groups did meet with opposition leaders to hear the other side of the story. They came away with a deeper understanding of the dynamics of the Bolivarian Revolution than many in the opposition — who had never set foot in a barrio.

The newcomers included Chesa Boudin, the son of Katherine Boudin and David Gilbert, former members of the 1970s radical group the Weathermen. A graduate student at Oxford, Chesa Boudin interned briefly in the Venezuelan government's international affairs section. The best-known American visitors to throw their support behind Chávez were African American leaders including Jesse Jackson, singer Harry Belafonte, and *Lethal Weapon* and *The Color Purple* star Danny Glover. Another visitor, Princeton University professor Cornell West, said one reason for the trips was to get beyond the mainstream media portrayal of Venezuela. "We in the United States have so many lies about President Hugo Chávez and the Bolivarian Revolution," he said.

On one trip organized by the African American group TransAfrica Forum, Belafonte, Glover, and others stood by as Venezuela dedicated its first Bolivarian school in honor of Martin Luther King Jr. The school was located in the predominantly black town of Naiguata on the Caribbean coast that was hard hit by the 1999 floods and mudslides. Aristóbulo Istúriz, the first Venezuelan of African descent to serve as education minister, oversaw the ceremony. In a rousing speech, TransAfrica president Bill Fletcher noted the parallels between Chávez's Bolivarian Revolution on behalf of Venezuela's majority poor and King's leadership of the 1960s civil rights movement:

> Dr. King was not a man who was fundamentally concerned with changing laws. He was fundamentally concerned with social justice. He was a man who abhorred the oppression of billions of people on this planet and despised the vampires who absorbed wealth for a small number of people. He was a man who abhorred war and who had the courage to speak against the war in Vietnam . . . Any movement that advances that kind of politics is a movement consistent with the legacy of Dr. King.

While most upper-class Venezuelans retained a bitter hatred of Chávez, a few followed his path, if not completely embracing him. When 457 pro-Chávez families invaded an estate owned by one of Venezuela's wealthiest families and home to one of the country's oldest rum distilleries, the owner, Alberto Vollmer, did not have them arrested or hire gunmen to kick them off. Instead he made a deal: He offered them some of the land to build houses on if they would provide the labor and respect the rest of his property.

Vollmer, in his thirties, was a scion to one of Venezuela's oldest families. His father, Alberto J. Vollmer, went to prep school with the first President Bush and was once Venezuela's ambassador to the Vatican. His mother, Christine de Marcellus, was a Palm Beach socialite and anti-abortion activist in high-level Roman Catholic circles. The family bought Santa Teresa Rum in 1885. The hacienda where it stood was founded in 1796. Two centuries later, in 1996, the factory was on the verge of bankruptcy when the younger Vollmer, a former student at Valley Forge Military Academy near Philadelphia, joined it and helped revive it.

In February 2000 the families invaded, but Vollmer's response turned into a model of cooperation between Venezuela's wealthy elites and the impoverished masses. They built one hundred homes on sixty acres of land in a project that won recognition from experts in conflict resolution at Harvard University, among other institutions. The government pitched in, too, providing roads and installing public services including electricity and telephone lines. The families were required to pay mortgages to a government housing agency.

The project didn't end there. When street gangs from a nearby slum started harassing company workers, and two were arrested for stealing a gun from guards, Vollmer made another deal. He offered not to press charges if the gang members provided three months' labor on the estate, receiving weekly rations of food in return. The gang members agreed. Eventually the program grew to include seventy-five young men from three rival gangs. After three months' labor, the gang members received schooling and psychological counseling. Vollmer also helped them find jobs with local businesses. He dubbed the program "Alcatraz" after the prison off San Francisco. Eventually he flew one of the rehabilitated gang members first-class to Sarajevo to attend a World Bank conference on social programs.

Chávez took to mentioning Vollmer's program in speeches as a model of what Venezuela could be. Vollmer, who did not vote for Chávez, even appeared on television with him, provoking dozens of angry e-mails from people who considered him a class traitor. Some customers vowed never to buy from him again. But to the project's inhabitants, it was a godsend in the same way Chávez's missions were changing their lives. "If one quarter of the rich people were like Alberto," one said, "this would be a different country."

# The Recall

As Chávez's missions solidified and his popularity strengthened, the opposition was running out of options to oust him. The strikes failed. The 2002 coup did not achieve it, either. The December 2002 to February 2003 oil shutdown devastated the economy but left Chávez ensconced in Miraflores — with the opposition more discredited than ever after "canceling" Christmas and wrecking thousands of businesses.

The oil walkout was barely over when the opposition seized on a fresh tactic to push Chávez out of office. The 1999 constitution drafted by the pro-Chávez constitutional assembly and approved overwhelmingly by the public in December 1999 contained a clause that was unique in the Western Hemisphere and perhaps the world: It allowed for a binding referendum on whether the president should be recalled from office.

To hold one, opponents had to gather the signatures of 20 percent of registered voters, or about 2.4 million people. The recall election could take place only after the midway point of the president's six-year term — in this case August 19, 2003. To win it, opponents had to obtain more votes than the number originally cast electing the president — here nearly 3.8 million. And of course they had to gain more votes to oust him than those who voted for him to stay. If the opposition won the recall, a new election would be held within thirty days to choose a new president. While the laws were not entirely clear, it appeared Chávez could run again.

With tensions still high between the government and the opposition, the two sides signed a landmark agreement in May 2003 pledging to find a constitutional solution to the crisis. The pact was the result of six months of arduous negotiations by the two sides overseen by former president Jimmy Carter's Atlanta-based Carter Center, among others. The mood was hopeful. The opposition was confident it would easily win a recall vote. Polls backed them up. One by Greenberg Quinlan Rosner Research and Public Opinion Strategies, which did work for both the Democratic and Republican Parties in the United States, predicted in April that Chávez would lose by a two-to-one margin. News articles routinely reported that Chávez's policies have, as one said, "turned a majority of Venezuelans against him."

Venezuela still did not have an organization to oversee the recall. In late August the Supreme Court broke a deadlock between the government and the opposition by naming the five members of the National Electoral Council. Both sides along with the United States hailed the appointments, saying the council was balanced — two members supported by the opposition, two by the government. Board president Francisco Carrasquero was a left-leaning university professor.

The board's first decision went against the opposition. It ruled that the petitions handed in by them in August and purportedly containing three million signatures were not valid. The council said they were gathered without any official oversight starting back in February 2003 — before the midway point of Chávez's term. The opposition claimed that the government was trying to head off a recall and that it was intimidating people from signing petitions by publishing on the Internet a list of signers and denying them government jobs, passports, national identification cards, or student grants. The government countered that private companies were forcing employees to sign or lose their jobs.

In the end opposition leaders agreed to a new petition drive. It took place the last weekend in November. Citizens stood in long lines at schools, plazas, and churches to sign their names. A week earlier Chávez supporters had held their own petition drive to try to recall thirty-eight opposition Congress members. The process seemed a far better alternative to coups and oil strikes. An elated César Gaviria, secretary general of the Organization of American States, declared that Venezuela was "finding a democratic way of solving the problem."

At the end of its two-day petition drive, the opposition claimed it had the signatures needed to trigger the recall. But it refused to immediately release the number. Then it took three weeks to hand in the petitions. The actions raised suspicions among Chávez and his followers. Calling the opposition's efforts a "mega fraud," the president held up scores of petitions at a rally on December 6 and claimed that they contained the names of people who were not registered to vote, had signed two or more times, or were dead. He also charged that signature gatherers entered hospitals, homes for the elderly, and mental institutions to pressure people to sign.

After an intense review, in late February the electoral council announced that the opposition had handed in about three million signatures, not the 3.4 million they claimed. It ruled that 1.83 million were valid. The council rejected 375,000 signatures outright as fakes. Another 876,000 were in doubt because of similar handwriting on the petitions. The council said they could be accepted if citizens came forward to confirm their signatures. They needed about 530,000 to be confirmed to convoke the referendum.

The opposition exploded in anger, accusing the council of fraud and of siding with Chávez. They launched street protests with a new tactic of "civil disobedience" they dubbed Operation Guarimba. They instructed supporters to set up roadblocks on key avenues near their homes or other safe locations, and then retreat inside when the police or other authorities came. After they left, the protestors could return to the streets. The idea was to create chaos and prevent people from going to work, school, stores, and hospitals. Robert Alonso, the brother of Venezuelan actress Maria Conchita Alonso and owner of a Web site that announced the day, place, and time of each Operation Guarimba, believed the turmoil would provoke the intervention of the armed forces and that Chávez would fall within a matter of days.

Operation Guarimba quickly triggered violent clashes with security forces. Protestors burned tires, vehicles, and bags full of garbage as they blockaded streets, especially in wealthy eastern Caracas. Some threw rocks and Molotov cocktails at soldiers, and tried to break through lines of National Guardsmen called into the streets to control the crowds. Some troops fired at the protestors. Opposition mayors in wealthy areas where the protests broke out refused to send in police to restore order. Henrique Capriles Radonski, the mayor of Baruta who failed to control rioters at the Cuban embassy during the April 2002 coup, defended the rights of the Operation Guarimba demonstrators. He said they were doing "nothing less than exercising their legal right to protest."

The weeklong demonstrations came at a sensitive moment — leaders of the Group of 15 developing nations were beginning a summit in Caracas. The government warned the protestors against storming the meeting at the Hilton Hotel, although some tried. The riots forced private banks to close twenty branch offices, halted garbage collection, shut down gasoline stations, caused massive traffic jams, and hampered transit by emergency vehicles. In the first week, they caused $1 million in street damage in Caracas alone.

Human rights groups including Amnesty International accused security forces of using excess force to put down the protests, including reports of torture and beatings. Ten people were killed and up to three hundred injured. Another four hundred were arrested illegally, according to the opposition, who contended that they were exercising their constitutional right to protest. Critics seized on the clashes to depict Chávez as a major human rights violator reminiscent of Latin America's bloodiest dictators. Venezuela's ambassador to the United Nations, Milos Alcalay, resigned, saying the crackdown "closely resembles" the methods of Latin America's right-wing military dictatorships of the 1970s.

But to the government, Operation Guarimba was nothing but another CIA-style attempt to topple Chávez by creating street chaos and violence, provoking the authorities into a reaction, and spurring the military to step in to remove the "human rights abuser" president.

The opposition charged that Chávez was trying to derail the recall referendum. They contended the National Electoral Council, which they had previously praised as balanced, was now under his control. They argued that any procedural violations in the petition signings were minor. The Venezuelan and international news media reported the council had thrown out hundreds of thousands of signatures because of "technicalities."

But it was a little more than "technicalities" that prompted the council to reject the signatures. The electoral council had set down and publicized specific rules for the petition process. They included the requirement that all signers other than those with a handicap must fill in the information including name and national identification card number themselves. But when the council received the petitions, tens of thousands of the forms appeared to have been filled in with similar handwriting. Even some signatures appeared the same. The opposition conceded that volunteers at some booths had filled out the forms, but insisted the signatures were legitimate.

In the end the electoral council did not throw out the questionable signatures wholesale. It offered a compromise. During a five-day "repair period," citizens could confirm they had signed the petition.

Chávez's supporters were suspicious of the recall effort partly because of who was running it: the NED-financed group Sumate. In early 2004 mounting evidence of NED interference in Venezuela had of course emerged as Freedom of Information Act requests filed by two North Americans, Eva Golinger and Jeremy Bigwood, produced thousands of pages of internal documents detailing the group's activities. Much of the organization's funding of about $1 million a year in Venezuela was going to opposition groups, including some whose leaders signed the Carmona Decree wiping out democracy during the April 2002 coup or showed up in the palace that day. One of them was Maria Corina Machado, a founder and leader of Sumate. Machado, the attractive, English-speaking, fashion-plate daughter of one of Venezuela's wealthiest families, insisted Sumate was an "independent" pro-democracy organization dedicated to "voter education."

As the recall effort picked up momentum, the Venezuelan government counterattacked. Prosecutors opened an investigation against Machado and Sumate co-leader Alejandro Plaz for conspiracy to commit treason. If convicted, they faced up to sixteen years in prison.

The investigation set off a firestorm of international protest. Machado's defenders depicted her as a brave pro-democracy activist battling the evils of a dictatorial government out to crush the smallest sign of dissent. "Hers is a heroic fight," a *Washington Post* columnist wrote. "Maria Corina Machado smiles bravely but admits she is terrified. They are after her, she explained; the machinery of the state." Moisés Naím, the editor of *Foreign Policy* magazine and one of the technocrats behind Carlos Andrés Pérez's 1989 economic "shock package," cast Machado's activities in a religious light. "This is God's work," he said. By November 2004 more than seventy major figures had signed a letter endorsed by the NED calling the prosecution of Machado and others a "grave threat to democracy." The signers included former secretary of state Madeleine Albright and Senator John McCain, who sat on NED boards.

To Chávez and his followers, Machado was hardly an innocent freedom fighter struggling to save Venezuelan democracy. Rather, they saw her as a tool of the United States and its campaign to unseat him. The NED approved a grant of $53,400 for her group. Chávez and his supporters didn't question Sumate's right to organize a recall referendum. They did question their right to receive funds from a foreign government to do so. They put it this way: What would be the reaction in the United States if a foreign government helped finance a campaign to remove President Bush from office? Would *that* be legal?

The NED funding played into Chávez's hands. He cast the recall campaign as a plot by Bush and the United States to overthrow him. David was trying to fend off another attack by the gringo Goliath. At a rally February 29, organizers erected a huge papier-mâché piranha representing the United States. Nearby was a small fish representing Venezuela.

The haggling between Chávez and the opposition went on for weeks more until late May when the opposition finally held its "repair period" to validate the signatures in doubt. The National Electoral Council ruled that they had obtained enough signatures — barely — to hold the recall. The opposition was thrilled. They were convinced the results of the recall were a foregone conclusion in their favor. Chávez was equally confident. In June he predicted he would take five million votes and easily walk away victorious.

The conventional wisdom among analysts, diplomats, and the mainstream media was that Chávez was in serious trouble and likely to lose, or that at a minimum the race was too close to call. Just one week before the August 15 vote, two of Venezuela's "leading" pollsters, Luis Vicente León and Alfredo Keller, who were also Chávez critics, called it a dead heat. *The Washington Post* reported that "Chávez's popularity has clearly diminished since he was first elected."

Besides the standard critiques that he was running an inept, authoritarian government that was crushing free speech and heading the way of Castro's Cuba, Chávez was under attack on other fronts. The National Assembly passed a new law in June allowing it to expand the Supreme Court from twenty to thirty-two members and nullify the appointments of sitting judges. Human Rights Watch and other groups accused Chávez of packing the court to help determine the outcome of the referendum if disputes arose.

Chávez had reason to be wary of the Court. Some magistrates appointed with the help of his former political mentor Luis Miquilena turned against him and openly assumed an antigovernment stance after the two men fell out in early 2002. After the April 2002 coup, the court let all the suspects go free and declared there was no coup.

While no one could argue that Chávez was not the legitimately elected president of Venezuela, some critics asserted he was a "fake democrat," as suggested by the title of an op-ed piece in *The New York Times* by Bernard Aronson. A former assistant secretary of state for inter-American affairs, Aronson was by now involved in Venezuelan investments. A day before the referendum, he wrote that Chávez "represents a new breed of Latin autocrat — a leader who is legitimately elected but then uses his office to undermine democratic checks and balances and intimidate political opponents." He pointed to the Supreme Court packing, the case against Sumate's Maria Corina Machado, and the detention in May of Mayor Henrique Capriles Radonski, who after Operation Guarimba was put in jail as part of the investigation into the riot at the Cuban embassy during the 2002 coup. Aronson said he was detained "on a clearly fraudulent charge of fomenting a riot." The Cuban ambassador disagreed. He'd remained trapped in the embassy that day and night with his staff and some of their children, with food, water, and electricity cut off. Outside was an angry mob that the mayor and his police failed to disperse.

Aronson's piece was similar to another *Times* op-ed article written a year earlier by Naím, Carlos Andrés Pérez's former minister of trade and industry: "Hugo Chávez and the Limits of Democracy: How Free Elections Led to Tyranny in Venezuela." Citing one of Venezuela's infamous polls, Naím claimed that two of every three Venezuelans living below the poverty line opposed Chávez. Coupled with the overwhelming sentiment against Chávez in the middle and upper classes, it meant the vast majority of Venezuelans opposed the president, Naím asserted. All they needed was an election to boot the tyrant out.

Aronson argued in the *Times* that "a new agenda is needed that offers upward mobility and political empowerment to the hemisphere's poor. This would require not only a deepening of structural economic reforms and fiscal discipline, but a new focus on giving the poor title to their land, credits for micro enterprise, easing the transition for small enterprises from the informal to the formal economy, cracking down on tax evasion and official corruption, and ending the subsidization of higher education at the expense of primary and secondary education."

Yet with the major exception of Chávez's failure to significantly crack down on endemic corruption, many of the steps Aronson outlined were exactly what Chávez was pursuing. His educational programs and land reform were prime examples. Crackdowns on alleged tax evasion including by multinational companies such as Coca-Cola, McDonald's, and Chevron were soon to increase.

While most of the media downplayed or ridiculed it, Chávez was redirecting vast sums of Venezuela's oil wealth to the most impoverished sectors. Education Minister Aristóbulo Istúriz estimated that the government was spending $4.5 billion, or 20 percent of its budget, on education. That amounted to 6.1 percent of Venezuela's gross domestic product, about twice the percentage of the previous year. For its part, PDVSA was pumping $1.7 billion of its $5 billion capitalization budget into the government's social programs such as Mision Robinson. It included $600 million on education and health care programs, $600 million on agriculture, and $500 million to build homes, highways, and other infrastructure projects. While most of the media and elites like Naím and Aronson focused on the complaints of the opposition, a grassroots revolution — however flawed — was breaking out in the barrios and countryside. The opposition's bubble prevented them from seeing it.

Chávez transferred the widespread popularity of his social missions to his campaign to defeat the referendum. Turning to his penchant for historical references, he dubbed his anti-recall campaign "The Battle of Santa Inés." That was the site of a famous nineteenth-century battle won by Ezequiel Zamora in Barinas, where he lured the unsuspecting Spaniards into an ambush. Chávez personally directed the anti-recall campaign, appointing a new team to run the electoral effort. He called them the Comando Maisanta after his great-grandfather. The team, which included few political cadres, was dominated by artists, academics, and social communicators with little previous participation in politics. Untainted by the past, they lent prestige and freshness to the campaign.

With his presidency on the line, Chávez and his supporters came up with a novel idea. They organized thousands of small UBEs or Electoral Battle Units in the barrios. Each UBE was made up of ten people who were responsible for convincing ten other people to vote against the referendum and making sure they got to the polls. Each unit, then, was to secure one hundred votes. Rather than working with assigned electoral lists, many UBEs organized themselves street by street or building by building. Others focused not on where they lived but where they worked. They proved to be an effective electoral tool: An estimated 1.2 million people, or 4 percent of the population, joined a UBE. Many were activists in long-standing social movements or land and health reform committees that were springing up in barrios amid the Bolivarian Revolution. But for the majority it was their first experience in political activism. Chávez called on them to get to the polls early.

They listened. On Sunday, August 15, hundreds of thousands of shantytown dwellers woke up to the sounds of fireworks and "reveille" bugle calls blasted from loudspeakers. The UBEs were summoning their followers to action. It was three A.M. The polls did not open until six. In wealthy eastern Caracas and other pockets of affluence, residents were equally charged up. They were finally getting their chance to vote. They were ecstatic and convinced the national nightmare was about to end.

The turnout was stunning. Thousands of people were lined up an hour before the polls opened. As the election got under way, lines stretched for blocks around polling places — up to 1.2 miles. People waited patiently in the scorching sun. A typical wait lasted seven hours. The voting was mostly peaceful and orderly.

International observers who had monitored elections around the globe were taken aback. They had never seen anything like it. Jimmy Carter said it was the biggest turnout of any of the dozens of elections he had monitored, from Nigeria to Indonesia to Mozambique. The recall referendum was turning into an impressive, beautiful celebration of democracy. The people were having their say. When Chávez went to cast his ballot in the impoverished 23 de Enero barrio of high-rise apartment buildings, he commented, "All those who were saying the dictator Chávez wouldn't agree to a vote . . . Well, here's the proof." Carter and his team were greeted with loud cheers everywhere they showed up.

By late afternoon it was clear there would not be enough time for all the voters still in line to cast their ballots. The National Electoral Council extended the 6 P.M. voting deadline to 8 P.M. That still wasn't enough, and they extended it again, to midnight. Even then, people were still voting. Balloting in some neighborhoods went on until three A.M., mainly in poor sectors. The election marathon lasted twenty-one hours. In the end, nearly ten million of fourteen million registered voters went to the polls. It was a record in Venezuela.

By 4 A.M. authorities were ready to release the first official results. As Francisco Carrasquero, president of the National Electoral Council, appeared on television to make the announcement, much of the nation was still awake and watching intently. Both sides were convinced they were going to win. Chávez supporters were gathered outside Miraflores. Opposition leaders came together in affluent eastern Caracas. They were totally unprepared for what Carrasquero was about to declare. Television was part of the reason why.

The nation's major networks, controlled by media moguls who opposed Chávez, had spent the day showing long lines of people waiting to vote in anti-Chávez neighborhoods such as Altamira. They did not bother going into the far more numerous low-income barrios where the lines were at least as long and the sentiment in favor of Chávez ran strong. The networks, which had played a leading role in the 2002 coup and the economic strikes, created a false impression that the anti-Chávez forces were winning an overwhelming victory in the recall referendum. Their distortion was so great that at one point, leading Chávez critic and newspaper editor Teodoro Petkoff called the owner of one station to urge him to send cameras into the slums in the interest of a more accurate and balanced account of what was happening. According to Petkoff, the owner refused.

The slanted television coverage, the media-reported polls showing a close race, and the opposition's preconceived conviction that it spoke for the majority of the country made Carrasquero's 4 A.M. announcement all the more shocking and unbelievable to the president's opponents. Chávez, he declared, had won in a landslide. His margin of victory was overwhelming — 58 to 42 percent, Carrasquero said. As more results came in later, Chávez's margin of victory grew, increasing to 59–41. The results even surpassed Chávez's margin of victory in 1998, when he had won by a 56 to 44 percent margin. He surpassed the 5 million votes he predicted in June he would obtain, attracting a record 5.6 million. The opposition garnered 3.9 million, losing but still making a notable impact: Four of every ten Venezuelans opposed Chávez.

Carrasquero's announcement set off a fusillade of fireworks in Chavista neighborhoods that shook the city. An hour later as dawn approached, the beaming president walked out onto the second-floor balcony at Miraflores Palace to greet a cheering throng of supporters. He had triumphed — again. Including congressional and gubernatorial elections, it was his eighth straight victory since 1998, when he'd won the presidency. It was also the third major defeat for the opposition in two years, following the failed April 2002 coup and the failed oil shutdown. Chávez told the ecstatic crowd that the anti-recall success was the equivalent of hitting a mammoth home run that rocketed out of Caracas, sailed over Cuba, and landed on the grounds of the White House occupied by George W. Bush. "Venezuela has changed forever," he said. "There is no turning back. The country will never return to the false democracy of the past where the elites ruled." He added that "this is a victory for the opposition. They defeated violence, coup-mongering and fascism. I hope they accept this as a victory and not as a defeat."

But the opposition was not about to accept the results so easily. Within an hour of Carrasquero's announcement, they were appearing on television and claiming fraud. They based their allegations largely on an exit poll conducted by the New York–based polling firm Penn, Schoen & Berland Associates. The poll showed Chávez losing by the same margin the electoral council declared he had won by. Breaking a law against releasing exit poll results before the balloting ended, Penn, Schoen & Berland Associates sent out a fax and e-mail at 8 P.M. to the media and opposition offices. Its headline read, "Exit Poll Results Show Major Defeat for Chávez." News of the poll spread earlier during the afternoon by cell phone, contributing to the widespread impression among the opposition that they were on their way to a smashing and inevitable victory.

Besides breaking the law against releasing polls while people were still voting, there was another problem with the survey: It was conducted not by neutral observers who were trained poll takers but by volunteers from Sumate, the anti-Chávez group that led the recall drive and was funded by the NED. Exit polls are notoriously unreliable — as the 2000 US presidential race proved — but Sumate's participation cast even more doubt over the poll's legitimacy. As Communications Minister Jesse Chacon put it, "If you use an activist as a pollster, he will eventually begin to act like an activist."

Jimmy Carter believed the opposition used the discredited poll to try to tilt the vote their way and create the impression of a victory that was imminent and unstoppable. "There's no doubt some of their leaders deliberately distributed this erroneous exit poll data in order to build up, not only the expectation of victory, but also to influence the people still standing in line," Carter later told reporters.

But none of that mattered to the opposition. They did not question the poll. Instead, they took it as evidence that the government was committing massive fraud. They insisted they had won. Headlines in the opposition-controlled press blared "Catastrofe," "El Fraude Permanente," and "Serias Dudas."

It was a minority opinion. Carter endorsed the results of the vote as free, fair, and accurate. So did César Gaviria of the Organization of American States. Even the US government declared Chávez had won, although it declined to congratulate him. "The people of Venezuela have spoken," State Department spokesman J. Adam Ereli said. Even a "quick count" sampling of votes conducted by Sumate that was separate from the Penn exit poll showed that the government had won. The opposition chose to ignore it and keep it quiet.

Carter and Gaviria met with media owners and opposition leaders early that Monday in Carter's hotel suite before Carrasquero's announcement to try to calm them and convince them to accept the results. The two men had been present in the electoral council headquarters at about 12:30 A.M. to witness the disclosure of the first electronic tabulations, which showed Chávez well ahead with 6.6 million votes counted. Now, in the hotel suite, Carter and Gaviria said they believed the vote count was just and that their own polling samples confirmed the results of the electoral council. Some of the leaders became "extremely irate," according to Carter's account. "Their faces were white, and they were very condemnatory of our lack of objectivity and fairness." Other opposition leaders such as Miranda state governor Enrique Mendoza were "clearly astonished and remained quiet," one news report said.

The opposition also alleged that Venezuela's new touch-screen electronic voting system was vulnerable to fraud, and that the government had manipulated it to turn a crushing defeat into an overwhelming victory. But election experts including the Carter Center's Jennifer McCoy — hardly a Chávez devotee — were convinced that this was virtually impossible. McCoy said the machines created "the most technically advanced election we have observed." When people voted, the machines took their thumbprints, transmitted them by satellite, and compared them almost instantaneously to prevent multiple voting. Besides that, the machines also produced paper ballots that voters stuffed into boxes. To alter the final results, someone would have to intervene with the machines electronically. The military — historically the custodians of election material in Venezuela — would have to reprogram "19,200 voting machines to print out new paper receipts with the proper date, time and serial code and in the proper number of Yes and No votes to match the electronic result, and to have reinserted these into the proper ballot boxes," McCoy later wrote in *The Economist*. "All of this in garrisons spread across twenty-two states, between Monday and Wednesday, with nobody revealing the fraud. We considered this to be supremely implausible."

The opposition looked especially silly because they had participated in a pre-election check of the machines after tamper-proof software was installed following controversy over the Florida-based companies that were to provide the machines and software. It was the first election for the companies, which were run by Venezuelans and had offices in Caracas. A Venezuelan government-run credit agency had given the small software company, Bizta, a $150,000 loan, but the company quickly repaid it after critics complained of a potential conflict of interest since Bizta put up a 28 percent share in the company as collateral. The pre-election check showed the machines to be working perfectly. The opposition and acerbic Chávez critics such as Teodoro Petkoff agreed to accept them and the outcome of the vote.

Now, in the wake of defeat, the opposition demanded an audit of the vote. The electoral council agreed to a partial one. They proceeded to conduct it under the eyes of the Carter Center and other respected international observers. But then the opposition dropped out of the very audit it had demanded, claiming to have unearthed new evidence of fraud that the review would not detect.

The opposition was beginning to look like something of a lunatic fringe. They refused to accept reality. They lost. In an editorial *The New York Times*, which was generally critical of Chávez, wrote that "It is time for President Hugo Chávez's opponents to stop pretending that they speak for most Venezuelans. They do not." Some analysts believed a type of "collective neurosis" or "hysteria" was overtaking a large segment of the opposition. They were fed by a twenty-four-hour-a-day bombardment of harsh, mocking, and often false anti-Chávez propaganda on television. "They can't see reality," concluded the Central University of Venezuela sociologist Margarita López Maya. "There is a mental block . . . It's almost a pathology." Jesuit priest Arturo Peraza, the human rights lawyer and critic of Chávez who took part in the opposition march on April 11, 2002, believed the opposition leadership's refusal to acknowledge the referendum results was creating a perception to the outside world that "they are a bunch of crazy people." He compared them to an eight-year-old child who throws a tantrum when he doesn't get his way. "All the credibility they've had they've thrown away," he said. "It's an act of suicide."

Peraza and others feared that with their loss in the referendum, followed by the failed coup and economic strikes, radical right-wing elements in the opposition might resort to the only option seemingly left: assassinating Chávez. The worst nightmare of Peraza and others was a Venezuelan version of "El Bogotazo" in Colombia, where the assassination in 1948 of popular Liberal Party leader Jorge Eliécer Gaitán set off three days of bloody riots. The resulting civil war still rages.

Chávez shared the fears of physical attack — and not without reason. Two months after the referendum, self-exiled Venezuelan actor Orlando Urdaneta appeared on a Miami television talk show and called for Chávez's assassination. Speaking on the program *Maria Elvira Confronta*, Urdaneta said, "There's no room for doubt. There's no other way out. Physical disappearance, definitely." When he was asked how this would happen, he replied, "This happens with a few men with rifles and telescopic sights that do not miss . . . It's an order I am giving right now, let's go, hurry up."

Venezuelan officials were astonished that the United States let Urdaneta take to the airwaves to publicly call for the assassination of a democratically elected head of state. If he had called for Bush's death, he would be under arrest. Chávez's new information minister, Andrés Izarra, the television news producer who resigned during the April 2002 coup when his bosses at RCTV ordered "zero Chávez on the screen," said: "At this time, we want the US government to explain to us how Orlando Urdaneta could call for murder without any type of sanctions against him."

Chávez's nemesis, Carlos Andrés Pérez, also joined the calls for the president's physical elimination. Shortly before the referendum, he said Chávez "must die like a dog, because he deserves it. I am working to remove Chávez [from power]. Violence will allow us to remove him. That's the only way we have." Pérez, whom the conservative *Washington Times* called a symbol of the "kleptocracy and incompetence that originally gave rise to Chávez," also said: "We can't just get rid of Chávez and immediately have a democracy . . . we will need a transition period of two to three years to lay the foundations for a state where the rule of law prevails."

The opposition and much of the media dismissed Chávez's repeated references to assassination plots against him as paranoia. But clear signs existed — and common sense dictated — that it was a real possibility as his hold on power strengthened and the opposition's chances of returning to power by democratic means faded. In November 2004 prosecutor Danilo Anderson, who was investigating four hundred suspects in the April 2002 coup including some who received funding from the National Endowment for Democracy, was killed when a two-bomb explosion set off by remote control blew apart his car. His murder shocked a nation unaccustomed to high-level political assassinations, unlike its neighbor Colombia or even the United States, where in recent decades alone the Kennedy brothers, Martin Luther King Jr., and Malcolm X succumbed to bullets while Ronald Reagan, Gerald Ford, and George Wallace survived assassination attempts.

With a physical attack against the president obviously a genuine possibility, Chávez beefed up his security. He got some assistance from the Cubans, whose leader Fidel Castro had survived dozens of assassination plots over four decades. By the time Chávez came to New York in September 2006, bodyguards in civilian clothes stood near him on stages at Cooper Union in the East Village and Mount Olivet Baptist Church in Harlem. They held sinister-looking thin black "briefcases" that actually opened into bulletproof shields.

Despite the increasing threats to his physical safety, Chávez emerged from the recall referendum stronger than ever politically. His opponents got what they wanted — a vote — and they lost, big-time. They failed to present an attractive alternative to Chávez. Their only platform seemed to be a hatred of everything he did. Now Chávez was the undisputed democratically elected president of Venezuela, supported by the majority of Venezuelans in election after election. Segments of the US-backed opposition leadership looked increasingly like they did not want to play by the democratic rules of the game. They clamored for democracy, but only when it gave them the results they wanted.

With the opposition all but obliterated, Chávez was free to turn his attention not only to strengthening the social missions that had catapulted him to victory in the recall referendum, but also to securing his place on the world stage as the modern-day heir to Simón Bolívar. He had turned one of the biggest challenges of his presidency into an even broader mandate for his Bolivarian Revolution, and proven the pollsters and the media that predicted his political demise to be wrong. His dream of trying to unite Latin America and spreading the Bolivarian quest for social justice to other continents was poised to take off, although it would meet resistance and stumble over some of its own mistakes as Hugo Chávez grabbed the attention of the world.

**26**

# Striking Back

Officially the Bush administration accepted Chávez's overwhelming victory in the recall referendum. But in practice nothing changed. It still wanted to see him gone. It tried to discredit him any way it could. A month after the vote, the government announced that it was "decertifying" Venezuela in the global fight against human trafficking. It imposed sanctions that put in jeopardy hundreds of millions of dollars in loans from international financial institutions including the Inter-American Development Bank. Venezuela could lose up to $1 billion in loans earmarked for a $750 million hydroelectric plant and other projects aimed at clean drinking water, Amazon rain forest preservation, judicial reform, school improvement, and tax collection.

The allegation was absurd and obviously born of the administration's hostility toward Chávez. It charged that Venezuela was among the six worst human-trafficking offenders in the world. Yet just a year earlier, Venezuela was not even among the five worst offenders in the Western Hemisphere alone, according to the State Department's own annual report. Now it was suddenly catapulted into a group of countries that happened to include major enemies of the Bush administration — Cuba, North Korea, Sudan, Myanmar (formerly Burma), and Equatorial Guinea. Human rights experts saw nothing to back up the Bush administration's allegations against Venezuela.

The campaign against Chávez didn't end with human trafficking. A year later the Bush administration "decertified" Venezuela again, this time for alleged lapses in the drug war. The only other nation in the world decertified along with Venezuela was Myanmar. But again, the government's accusations against Venezuela didn't match reality.

The US offensive against Chávez was moving forward despite the absence of one of its key architects, Otto Reich. The hard-line anti-Castro Cuban American stepped down in May 2004 as Bush's special envoy to Latin America after two years in the administration. Reich didn't abandon the fight, though. He soon published a cover story in the *National Review*: "The Axis of Evil . . . Western Hemisphere Version." The cover showed a photograph of Chávez and Fidel Castro.

Reich's replacement as assistant secretary of state was hardly more enlightened. Roger Noriega was a longtime aide to Senator Jesse Helms and had played a key role in drafting the Helms-Burton Act of 1996 tightening the US embargo on Cuba. He kept Reich's hard-nosed approach to Chávez intact. The US hostility was underscored in May 2005 when Bush received leading Chávez opponent Maria Corina Machado in the Oval Office for a fifteen-minute meeting. A photograph of Bush and Machado conversing in the White House was front-page news in Venezuela.

A month later Secretary of State Condoleezza Rice singled out Machado for a private meeting during an Organization of American States general assembly in Fort Lauderdale. Venezuela's ambassador to the United States, Bernardo Álvarez, had been waiting for two months without success to meet with Rice. At her confirmation hearings the previous January, Rice called Chávez a "negative force in the region."

Chávez had publicly held back much of his criticism of the US government, even immediately after the 2002 coup when it all but endorsed the putsch and Rice lectured *him* to respect democratic norms. But by now he was holding back no longer. He lashed out at the attacks by Rice and others with some of his typical personal invective and Venezuela-style humor that played big with the home crowd but seemed offensive to outsiders. In Venezuela, with its obsession for beauty pageants and its stunning women walking the streets in skintight outfits that barely covered their breasts, seemingly every other joking comment included a double meaning pregnant with sexual innuendo. At a rally before thousands of supporters, Chávez suggested that the problems with Rice, a single woman, might stem from a lack of male companionship. Moreover, maybe she fantasized about him. But "I will not make that sacrifice for my country," he added, sending the crowd into titters, but hardly amusing feminists overseas.

He also called the former Stanford University provost "illiterate" in her understanding of Latin America and referred to her as Condolencia, which means "condolence." In one of his most famous barbs, he called Bush a *pendejo*. The international media incorrectly translated the word as "asshole." More precisely, in Venezuela it meant "fool" or "a person of whom others are taking advantage." But it was still a strong term. Chávez also proclaimed Bush a "drunk," a "donkey," and a "coward." He regularly referred to him as "Mr. Danger," a blue-eyed American character in Rómulo Gallegos's classic 1929 novel *Doña Bárbara* who robbed land from unwary Venezuelan peasants.

The mud slinging went both ways. Secretary of Defense Donald Rumsfeld compared Chávez to Adolf Hitler. (That prompted Chávez to shoot back that "Hitler would be like a suckling baby next to George W. Bush.") The Pentagon's head for Latin America, Rogelio Pardo-Maurer, likened Chávez to a "hyena." Evangelical minister Pat Robertson, who enjoyed close ties to the Bush administration, even called for Chávez's murder. "If he thinks we're trying to assassinate him, I think we ought to go ahead and do it," Robertson proclaimed in August 2005 on his cable television show *The 700 Club*, setting off an international uproar. "It's a whole lot cheaper than starting a war."

Robertson was not arrested or even questioned by authorities after he made the widely publicized comment. That amazed Chávez. He accused the United States of abetting "international terrorism." "The only place where a person can ask for another head of state to be assassinated is the United States, which is what happened recently with the Reverend Pat Robertson, a very close friend of the White House," Chávez said. "He publicly asked for my assassination and he's still walking the streets."

Robertson's call for Chávez's death and the US attacks initially did little to dim his popularity at home or slow the spread of other leftist leaders in Latin America. All around him, like-minded opponents of the neoliberal Washington Consensus were rising to power as the "free-market revolution" endorsed by Wall Street, the International Monetary Fund, and others failed to decrease mass poverty.

It started with the election in October 2002 of Luiz Inácio Lula da Silva, the first president in Brazil's history from the working class. He was followed by Néstor Kirchner in Argentina and in November 2004 by Tabaré Vázquez, the first socialist elected president in Uruguay.

The most stunning victory came in December 2005 when Evo Morales became the first indigenous person elected president in Bolivia. Of the new leaders, whose opposition to the Washington Consensus came in varying hues, Morales was the closest in outlook to Chávez. He grew up in a family so poor that as a boy he ran behind buses to pick up the orange skins and banana peels passengers threw out the windows. At times that was all he had to eat.

The roll to the left continued as Chile elected the first female socialist president in its history. By November 2006 Nicaragua brought the Cold War icon Daniel Ortega and his Sandinistas back into power. Less than a month later Ecuador elected Rafael Correa, a leftist econo-mist with a doctorate from the University of Illinois who lambasted the Washington Consensus, pledged to throw the Americans off a military base in Ecuador, and invoked Chávez's guiding light, Simón Bolívar. "The dream of Bolívar in the 21st century is more than a dream," he said. "It's a decision of survival."

Correa's opponent, billionaire Alvaro Noboa, tried an increasingly popular tactic to defeat his opponent — he linked him to Chávez. Not surprisingly, the strategy helped Noboa to a degree. The United States and the international media demonized Chávez so much that many in Latin America believed he was the devil incarnate.

While ultimately the Chávez strategy failed in Ecuador, it worked in other countries. In Peru cashiered lieutenant colonel Ollanta Humala was an Inca Indian version of Chávez who praised aspects of General Juan Velasco Alvarado, the leftist Peruvian dictator whose 1968–1975 social experiment Chávez saw firsthand as a cadet. Humala even led a failed coup against the corrupt government of Alberto Fujimori. In the end he lost the presidential election. Many people blamed his associa-tion with Chávez.

Chávez's biggest defeat came in Mexico, where former Mexico City mayor Andrés Manuel López Obrador lost by a razor-thin margin in July 2006 to conservative Felipe Calderón. Obrador was leading the polls until Calderón pulled out his secret weapon — Hugo Chávez. He started running TV ads linking Obrador and Chávez. Obrador had never met or spoken to Chávez. He insisted he was not going to re-create a Mexican-style Bolivarian Revolution. But it didn't matter. The ads worked. Obrador's poll numbers dropped.

Chávez's detractors charged that he was trying to sway races from Mexico to Uruguay to Nicaragua and generally trying to win influence around the world by dishing out some of his country's oil largesse. He was openly backing some candidates such as Humala and Ortega. In Nicaragua he signed a deal offering ten million barrels of oil a year at preferential rates to fifty-one communities allied with the Sandinistas. Elsewhere he distributed billions of dollars in aid, bond purchases, and subsidized oil deals. He sent $260 million to Jamaica to repave a highway, $17 million to upgrade airports in Antigua and Dominica, and $3 million in emergency food aid to Burkina Faso, Mauritania, and Niger.

To Chávez, he was simply doing what the United States and other countries did all the time — building goodwill and winning allies. It was all part of his plan to enact a modern-day version of Bolívar's dream of a united Latin America, and to spread it beyond to encompass developing nations around the world that could provide a multipolar alternative to United States hegemony. Besides, the United States, which enjoyed far more resources than Venezuela, was also intervening directly in elections in Latin America. When Evo Morales first ran for president in Bolivia in 2002, the US ambassador, Manuel Rocha, warned Bolivians that electing the coca leader could result in a cutoff of US aid. The threat backfired, and Morales came soaring out of fourth place in polls to lose the election by just 1.5 percent. He jokingly referred to Rocha thereafter as his "campaign manager." US officials were more discreet in 2005, but their opposition to Morales was no secret.

In Nicaragua the United States openly vowed to cut off aid if Daniel Ortega won. Two years earlier in El Salvador, Otto Reich had warned that electing former Marxist guerrilla leader Schafik Handal as president would be a "radical change" that could adversely affect bilateral relations. While his intervention wasn't the only reason for it, Handal lost.

Despite efforts by Reich and the US government to sideline him, Chávez's popularity in some sectors simply grew. Once shunned by the left because of his history as a soldier and coup leader, he increasingly became the most prominent figure in a worldwide antiglobalization movement hungry for a charismatic leader.

At the January 2005 World Social Forum in Porto Alegre, Brazil, admirers greeted him like a rock star. The forum was a yearly event mounted to protest against the simultaneous World Economic Forum in Switzerland organized by political and business elites. Sporting a red shirt embossed with a picture of Che Guevara, Chávez provoked a roar of appreciation from fifteen thousand activists who packed a sports stadium and greeted him with cries of "Here comes the boss!" Chávez responded with a denunciation of corporate-sponsored capitalism and declared that a free trade agreement the United States hoped to enact from Alaska to Argentina was "dead."

The day before, Brazil's Lula had drawn jeers at the forum. Some participants accused him of failing to fulfill promises to eradicate Brazil's mass poverty and of caving in to corporate interests, the IMF, and the United States. Chávez had to defend him. "I love Lula!" he yelled at the stadium. "I respect him. Lula is a good guy."

While Chávez's popularity was rising among millions, his image in the mainstream media remained mostly negative. It frequently emphasized the elites' version of events and never fully explained *why* he was so popular at home, winning election after election. It often turned into not only a mouthpiece for the elites but also a weapon. Chávez knew he had to do something to bring the domestic media under control.

His efforts accelerated after the 2002 coup. The National Assembly passed a Law of Social Responsibility for Television and Radio that aimed to establish limits on the media. The law banned "vulgar" language and many images of sex and "psychological" or physical violence from 7 A.M. to 11 P.M., times during which television networks routinely broadcast scenes of blood, guts, and flesh that went far beyond that permitted on noncable US stations at any hour. It also increased criminal sentences from eight days to one year for slander or statements that impugn "the honor, the reputation, the respect" of a person, including public officials. Violations could lead to heavy fines or revocation of broadcasting licenses.

Critics dubbed the measure the Gag Law. After its passage in December 2004, television networks initially edited explicit sexual scenes and graphic violence out of often steamy soap operas or action-filled sitcoms. Some news programs "self-censored" — in some cases to an exaggerated degree to make a political point — such as stating that there was a tragic car accident in Caracas today, but because of the gag law details couldn't be reported until after 11 P.M. A couple of fiercely anti-Chávez hosts including Venevisión's Napoleón Bravo (who celebrated Chávez's overthrow by hosting some of the coup leaders on his program *24 Hours*) were taken off the air by the network. Detractors warned that the law amounted to another crackdown on freedom of the press by Chávez. They noted that many Venezuelan journalists had come under physical attack by Chávez supporters in the streets, although government television reporters also were attacked by the opposition and Chávez spoke out against all the assaults.

To him, the Venezuelan corporate media was out of control and needed to be reined in. Advocates of the media law pointed out that many of the provisions differed little from US Federal Communications Commission regulations that sought to protect children during normal viewing hours. Above all, they hoped the law would lead to more balanced coverage by a media that not only was ferociously critical of Chávez but also participated in efforts to overthrow him — not all of them legal.

It wasn't hard to find examples. When the government and opposition groups held huge competing demonstrations in March 2002, for example, the station manager at RCTV channel 2 ordered news operations manager Andrés Izarra to give blanket coverage to the opposition march. Izarra sent ten television crews. But he was ordered not to cover the pro-Chávez march at all. It was the same at the other major networks.

Some journalists admitted they had stopped being journalists presenting both sides of the story and instead had turned into political activists trying to destroy a president. "The common attitude has been that we can leave aside ethics and the rules of journalism," Laura Weffer, a political reporter for *El Nacional*, confessed to a writer for the *Columbia Journalism Review*. But the consequence of that was fomenting an intense hatred among people in the mountainside barrios who now viewed once respected journalists as prostitutes for the media moguls and wealthy elites. "Before, when we went up to the hills, we were welcomed as if we were the Red Cross," a reporter for *Ultimas Noticias* told the *CJR*. "Afterward, reporters were showered with rocks and bottles at the bottom of the hill." Another female reporter, in tears, told Weffer how she was called a *puta*, a whore, when she tried to enter a poor neighborhood wearing a press pass.

International media outlets were not quite as bad as the Venezuelan media, occasionally providing fairer coverage of important events such as the mobilization of Chávez supporters in the streets calling for his return during the coup. In general, though, they followed the lead of the locals.

They slanted their coverage to highlight the point of view of Chávez's opponents and downplay the opinion of his supporters, who happened to be a majority of the population. One way they did so was by the sources they chose. The vast majority of "analysts" cited by major US outlets were Chávez critics as opposed to more neutral observers or those who tended to view Chávez sympathetically. In one study, Latin America specialist Justin Delacour tracked the "independent" analysts most often cited by five major US newspapers: *The Miami Herald*, *The New York Times*, *The Washington Post*, the *Los Angeles Times*, and the *Chicago Tribune*. Delacour found that the four analysts most often cited were critics of Chávez — Michael Shifter of the Inter-American Dialogue in Washington, DC, Venezuelan historian Alberto Garrido, newspaper editor Teodoro Petkoff, and "pollster" Luis Vicente León. Only the fifth most cited analyst, Larry Birns of the Washington-based Council on Hemispheric Affairs, "could be described as somewhat sympathetic to Venezuela's government." And he was a distant fifth — he was cited 16 times, while the others were cited a total of 107.

In contrast, eight Venezuela scholars whose articles appeared in the March 2005 issue of the journal *Latin American Perspectives* and who had a moderate or favorable view of Chávez were not quoted a single time during the nearly two-year period studied. They included Steve Ellner, a respected American political scientist who has lived in Venezuela for nearly three decades. The others were Pomona College professor Miguel Tinker-Salas, Edgardo Lander, Dick Parker, Jesús Maria Herrera Salas, Margarita López Maya, Luis Lander, and Maria Pilar García-Guadilla.

Many of the foreign correspondents had probably barely heard of these experts, since they were so immersed in the world of the opposition. Many simply "parachuted" in to the country for periodic reporting assignments, checked in at five-star hotels, and spent much of their time hobnobbing with the elites and trading observations with one another. Venezuela expert Julia Buxton called it the "Hilton Hotel" brand of journalism. Even many of those stationed full-time in the country were more connected to the upper and middle classes than to the working class in the barrios, where some rarely ventured. Instead they hung out in upscale neighborhoods at trendy restaurants and bars. One wire service journalist's antipathy to Chávez was so blatant, she sported a button above her desk that said SAQUEMOS AL LOCO — let's get rid of the crazy one.

Foreign correspondents regularly ridiculed Chávez among one another and complained about his long speeches. They would groan when he came on television and mock his statements. Some hoped he would lose the presidential election or get thrown out of office so they would not have to listen to his hours-long talks any more. They openly stated that his programs amounted to craziness and seemed to be in lock-step with the opposition's thinking. Most of their sources, of course, were linked to the opposition. At one point, one even repeated in conversation an opposition slogan, opining that Chávez "has to go."

In one news bureau, shouting matches occasionally broke out between journalists who wanted to present a more balanced portrait of Chávez and those who were clearly on a mission to destroy him. The debate about how to cover the president turned into a constant battle. In the end, the anti-Chávez journalists won out, overwhelming in sheer numbers those who favored a more neutral approach. It wasn't far off from Andrés Izarra's experience working at RCTV.

To many foreign correspondents, Chávez was a laughingstock and a nut. And their copy reflected it. In one typical story sent around the world in February 2003 as the oil strike died, Reuters wrote that Chávez's opponents "accuse him of ruling like a dictator, ruining the economy with anti-capitalist policies, threatening media freedom and trying to make Venezuela a copy of communist Cuba." In normal journalism, that loaded sentence would be followed by an immediate rebuttal giving the other side of the story and what Chávez's supporters thought of him: namely, that his government was the most democratic in the nation's history; that the opposition's coup and oil strike was what was destroying the economy; that the media was arguably the freest in the world, publishing and broadcasting outrageous attacks against the president and encouraging his overthrow; and that Venezuela was a far cry from communist Cuba, with a free press, a largely free-market economy, and a multiparty political system with regular free and fair elections. It even had a recall mechanism to remove the president and other elected officials halfway through their terms.

But the writer didn't provide that information. It was standard operating procedure at Reuters and many international or US news outlets. The opposition to Chávez was highlighted, placed high up in stories, and described in fine detail. The other view favoring him was mentioned lower down or not at all, with little or none of the extensive detail and supporting evidence given to the often spurious opposition charges. The overall impression was that Chávez was a crazed dictator bent on destroying one of Latin America's oldest thriving democracies. As the media watchdog group FAIR put it, "Hugo Chávez never had a chance with the US press."

Delacour, who sympathized with Chávez, also found the anti-Chávez bent extended to the op-ed pages of US newspapers. In fact, it was even worse. When he tracked the opinion pages of the twenty-five largest-circulation newspapers in the United States during the first six months of 2005, he found that "95 percent of the nearly one hundred press commentaries that examined Venezuelan politics expressed clear hostility to the country's democratically elected president." The views of op-ed writers such as progressive economist Mark Weisbrot, who criticized US policies toward Chávez and viewed some of his programs favorably, rarely appeared. Instead, rabid anti-Chávez critics such as Mary Anastasia O'Grady at *The Wall Street Journal* and Jackson Diehl at *The Washington Post* had their own regular columns in which they could constantly bash Chávez from the podium of two of America's most powerful newspapers with little rebuttal to their often specious arguments. No one had a regular column in any newspaper defending Chávez. Newspaper editorial writers across the United States seemed almost universally contemptuous of him. Delacour concluded that

> In spite of the fact that recent polls indicate that Chávez's domestic approval rating has surpassed 70 percent, almost all the commentaries about Venezuela represent the views of a small minority of the country, led by a traditional economic elite that has repeatedly attempted to overthrow the government in clearly anti-democratic ways.
>
> In presenting opinions that are almost exclusively hostile to the Chávez government, US commentaries about Venezuela serve as little more than a campaign of indoctrination against a democratic political project that challenges US political and economic domination of South America. The near absence of alternative perspectives about Venezuela has prevented US readers from weighing opposing arguments so as to form their own opinions about the Chávez government.

Some North Americans wanted to see for themselves what was happening in Chávez's controversial Bolivarian Revolution. So they traveled to the country and went on "reality tours" where they visited barrios and other projects that journalists, columnists, and analysts often ignored or had never been to even as they excoriated Chávez. What the visitors found often contradicted the one-sided version provided by much of the media. "All I had heard about Chávez was that he was a dictator," stated Donna Santiago, a Philadelphia beneficiary of a Venezuelan program providing discounted home heating oil. "The man is far from that. He's a really warm person. I wanted to bring him home and stick him in the White House." The coordinator of a Venezuelan community radio station noted that the experience of Santiago wasn't unusual. "People go back to the USA and say, 'I went to Venezuela and saw something totally contrary to what CNN is telling me.'"

Chávez did not accept the one-sided media coverage passively. If the mainstream media would not report on his political project in a more balanced way, he had a solution. He would create his own media outlets.

During the 2002 coup, Chávez was left with only one media source — small community radio stations often run out of people's apartments in barrios and a handful of low-budget independent community television stations. These alternative media outlets were virtually the only ones sending out word about Chávez's kidnapping, and played an important role in organizing resistance to the coup. They were also among the first targets of repression during Pedro Carmona's brief reign. Pro-coup police raided the stations, confiscated equipment, and detained and sometimes beat staff.

After Chávez's return to power, he moved to expand and strengthen the alternative media. The government granted broadcasting licenses to scores of "pirate" radio stations. It also provided $2.6 million in 2004 for radio and television stations including Catia TV in the sprawling barrio of Catia in western Caracas. The number of alternative radio and television stations jumped from about fifty nationwide before the coup to three hundred by early 2004.

They were hardly media powerhouses. Radio Perola, one of those raided during the coup, transmitted from a thirteen-kilowatt station in the former storeroom of a housing project. Its message reached barely a few hundred homes. Another station, Radio Un Nuevo Dia, had just five kilowatts. Its transmitter was set up in the corner of a bedroom in a cleaning lady's two-room cinder-block house. She hung bedsheets from the ceiling to separate the equipment from the cots where her two children slept. Operating mainly with volunteers, the alternative stations played salsa music and focused on community problems like trash pickup or potholes.

In November 2003 the government decided to move beyond merely funding the alternative stations. It set up one of its own — Vive TV. The idea was to present a different version of Venezuela, Latin America, and the world than the one depicted by big corporate stations like Venevisión or RCTV, which preferred steamy soap operas and American-style consumer-oriented programming such as *Quien Quiere Ser Millionario* (*Who Wants to Be a Millionaire*). Vive TV aimed to focus on the lives not of beauty queens and movie stars but of the vast Latin American underclass. By late 2004 its transmission was capable of reaching between 60 and 70 percent of the Venezuelan population.

But the big corporate networks still dominated in Venezuela and throughout Latin America. Chávez came up with another idea to counter their control. He proposed a twenty-four-hour regionwide television news network to be run cooperatively by various countries. It would be Latin America's answer to CNN. Its "reason for being is the need to see Latin America with Latin American eyes," stated its general director, veteran journalist Aram Aharonian. Chávez also hoped it would be a counterweight to the largely negative image of him created by the mass media that dominated international news programs in Latin America. They included CNN en Español, Spain's Televisión Española, and Gustavo Cisnero's Univisión.

They called the new station Telesur — Television of the South. Initially it was a joint effort by Venezuela, Argentina, Cuba, and Uruguay. Bolivia later also joined. Brazil offered up its state-run television network for collaboration. Venezuela footed most of the bill, providing the majority of the $2.5 million in seed money. It opened bureaus around the region and in Washington, DC.

Even before it went on the air, critics attacked Telesur as a mouthpiece for Chávez. They dubbed it "TeleChávez" and compared it to Al Jazeera, the Arabic-language satellite news channel designed to bring a non-Western perspective to events in the Middle East and beyond. Republican congressman Connie Mack of Florida went so far as to propose beaming US government radio and television signals into Venezuela to counter the new station. He made the absurd charge that Venezuela's press was muzzled. "In Hugo Chávez's Venezuela," he told Congress, "there is no free press — just state-controlled anti-American propaganda."

Mack's ravings aside, whether Telesur would become a mere cheer-

leader for its main benefactor was a legitimate question. It did have something of a leftist bent, showing images of Che Guevara and Salvador
Allende in a promotional video introducing the network. Its president
was Andrés Izarra, who had quit RCTV in disgust during the 2002 coup
and become Chávez's information minister. Recognizing the conflict of
interest, he soon stepped down from the government post.

But Izarra, who once worked at CNN in Atlanta, along with
Aharonian and other directors also realized the network would have to
go beyond mere pro-Chávez rhetoric to attract and maintain audiences.
If it only broadcast speeches by Chávez and other presidents, "we would
have to take it for granted that no one would watch," Aharonian said. "If
this were to turn into a propaganda tool, we would all leave." He added
that "this is not a channel where we'll be saying, 'Viva Chávez.'"

Less than a year after Telesur went on the air, Chávez's government
proposed expanding the idea to include radio stations. They called it
Radiosur, and envisioned existing radio stations from across the region
joining in a single network. Compared with mounting Telesur, creating
an integrated regional radio network would be comparatively easy.

Chávez also went on the offensive inside the United States itself.
He created the Venezuelan Information Office in Washington, DC,
to combat what he called widespread misinformation put out by the
corporate media about Venezuela. Its goal was to present what Chávez
and his allies considered a more accurate version of the Bolivarian
Revolution. The VIO, as it was known, created a Web site, compiled
background reports, and sent out action alerts to supporters to contact
media outlets. The office, though, was no match for the massive corporate media.

Chávez's efforts to counteract the corporate news media extended to
trying to rescue indigenous Venezuelan and Latin American culture
from the US-dominated mass media. Faced with an onslaught from
Britney Spears, the Backstreet Boys, and other icons of the US music
scene, Chávez wanted to preserve the quaint traditional Venezuelan
music that originated in the llanos, the Andean highlands, and the
steamy streets of oil-rich Maracaibo. The December 2005 media
responsibility law included a provision requiring at least 50 percent of
the music played on local stations to be Venezuelan, and at least half of
that to have a "traditional aspect to it such as using the *llanero* harp."

The law sparked a boom among traditional Venezuelan musicians who played harps, maracas, flutes, fiddles, and the famous *cuatro*, a four-string bandola. Suddenly the mournful, bawdy, or humorous songs and ballads from Chávez's native llanos and elsewhere that commemorated fast horses, romantic sunsets, or love lost were hotter than ever. Simón Díaz, a troubadour in his late seventies who enjoyed international fame, found his songs back on the airwaves again. The Traditional National Orchestra, which had previously been lucky to sell one CD at their concerts, now sold two hundred at a single performance.

Chávez set his sights on another icon of the US mass media: Hollywood. In June 2006 he created a film studio complex in Caracas called Cinema Town. It was aimed at offering an alternative to films that often emphasized sex and violence and depicted Latinos as gang members or drug barons. "It's a Hollywood dictatorship," Chávez complained as he toured movie sets and sat in a director's chair. "They inoculate us with messages that don't belong to our traditions . . . [about] the American way of life, imperialism."

Chávez also extended his "cultural revolution" to literature. Books were hard to come by in Venezuela — they were expensive, and public libraries were scarce. So Chávez instructed the government to print some and hand them out for free. On the four hundredth anniversary of the classic tale *Don Quixote* by Miguel de Cervantes Saavedra, he ordered up one million copies. He also distributed five hundred thousand copies of another personal favorite, Victor Hugo's *Les Misérables*.

Internationally he was still widely seen as a "brutal Marxist dictator," as the head of the Christian Civic League in Maine put it. Chávez had a serious image problem. To try to counteract it, he came up with an ingenious idea. In the midst of record oil prices, he decided to distribute discounted home heating oil to low-income people in the United States.

The program started in the winter of 2005–2006 with the Venezuela-owned Citgo Petroleum Corporation pledging to provide twelve million gallons of home heating oil to residents in Massachusetts and eight million gallons to people in the Bronx. The recipients would get a 40 percent discount. Former congressman Joseph P. Kennedy II, the son of the late Robert Kennedy who now ran the nonprofit Citizens Energy Corporation, helped broker the Massachusetts deal.

The plan was a masterstroke that even Chávez's fiercest critics could not effectively attack, especially after no other oil companies responded to a plea from a group of US senators to donate some of their record profits to poor people. One analyst called it "shrewd political theater." Even the US government grudgingly saluted it. Venezuela did not fail to capitalize on the positive PR. It took out full-page advertisements in *The Washington Post* and *The New York Times*. The headline was: "How Venezuela Is Keeping the Home Fires Burning in Massachusetts."

As word of the program spread, requests flooded in. Before winter was over, it expanded to Maine, Vermont, Rhode Island, Connecticut, Delaware, and the Philadelphia area. In Maine the beneficiaries included members of four Indian tribes. Citgo flew some of them and others to Venezuela in April 2006 to meet Chávez. Donna Santiago, the single mother from Philadelphia, broke down in tears. "You have treated the American people like brothers and sisters," she said. "This has saved lives, and that has no price . . . In times of desperation, God sent us an angel. And you, President Chávez, are our angel."

Chávez managed to throw away much of that goodwill five months later when he called Bush "the devil" during his speech at the United Nations General Assembly. He had planned to triumphantly announce during his visit to New York that the oil program was going to more than double in 2006–2007, from forty to a hundred million gallons. Some 400,000 families — up from 181,000 — were going to benefit in sixteen states or cities, including Michigan, Minnesota, Wisconsin, Virginia, Maryland, Pittsburgh, and Washington, DC. Indian tribes as far away as Alaska who paid $8 a gallon for home heating oil were going to take part.

But the personal attack, something Chávez seemed incapable of resisting in general, provoked a backlash even among some of the home heating oil beneficiaries. Linda Kelly, a resident of Quincy, Massachusetts, said Chávez "stepped over the line" with his comments, which also included calling Bush an "alcoholic" and a "sick man" during an appearance in Harlem. A seventy-five-year-old neighbor, Agnes Crosson, said, "I'm not a Bush person, believe me. But I really resented that." The governor of Maine said he was dropping out of the program. Even some of the Indian tribes in Alaska backed away. Citgo ran full-page ads in major newspapers again. But this time it was trying to clean up the mess as lawmakers and citizens proposed boycotting the company and its thirteen thousand gas stations.

Back in Venezuela most people were barely fazed by Chávez's attack on Bush. Many thought he wasn't far off the mark about a man they viewed as a buffoon. Chávez forged ahead undaunted. Another presidential election was a couple of months off. He was dominating the polls. He was still hugely popular in Venezuela and in many parts of Latin America. With a new six-year mandate on the way, he was poised to head into a more radical phase of his presidency. He planned to implement his most advanced plan yet for remaking the country.

It was something he called twenty-first-century socialism.

**27**

# Twenty-First-Century Socialism

Hugo Chávez stood before twenty-five thousand cheering fans in a soccer stadium in Mar del Plata, Argentina. It was November 2005, and the presidents of thirty-three Latin American nations along with George W. Bush were gathering for the fourth Summit of the Americas. It was aimed partly at cementing support for the US goal of a free trade pact stretching from Alaska to Argentina. But the summit had hardly begun and Chávez was upstaging Bush. Standing next to him in the stadium for a "counter summit" was the greatest soccer legend in Argentina's history, Diego Maradona. Demonstrators carried signs that compared Bush to Adolf Hitler and chanted in unison as they entered the stadium, "Bush, the fascist! Bush the terrorist!" Polls showed he was the most unpopular US president ever among Latin Americans.

Chávez provoked roars of approval as he declared that Bush was wasting his time trying to implement the Free Trade Area of the Americas, a key component of the Washington Consensus. "Every one of us has brought a shovel, because Mar del Plata is going to be the tomb of the FTAA," Chávez said during a two-hour speech. "FTAA is dead, and we, the people of the Americas, are the ones who buried it." In an initiative he compared to John F. Kennedy's Alliance for Progress, Chávez announced a $10 billion decade-long assistance program to eliminate hunger in Latin America.

While Chávez was talking, anger toward Bush and US-backed policies that had helped plunge Argentina into the worst economic debacle in its history turned violent in the streets. Demonstrators tried to breach steel barriers and reach summit sites including the Sheraton Mar del Plata. They tossed rocks, smashed windows, looted stores, and set a bank on fire with a Molotov cocktail. Police fired tear gas and rubber bullets. By evening fifty people were in jail.

The next day Chávez landed on the front pages of *The New York Times* and other major newspapers after stealing the show from Bush. *The Washington Post* described him as assuming "the role of gleeful outside provocateur."

Even rabid critics such as *Miami Herald* columnist Andrés Oppenheimer acknowledged that Chávez was "having a field day" as he eviscerated Bush, who seemed lost as he took a "public relations pounding." His visit to Latin America, meant to be a moment of triumph, ended with riots and tear gas in the streets. He left the summit before it was over, with no trade agreement in hand. "The great loser today was George W. Bush," Chávez boasted. "The man went away wounded. You could see defeat on his face."

The day before the summit began Venezuela staged a mock invasion of its territory by the United States. The exercise was part of Chávez's efforts to prepare for a possible attack by American troops. Camouflaged soldiers jumped from boats into the surf off Venezuela's coast as hundreds of residents who confronted them on the beach shouted "Gringo go home!" and "Freedom!" While US officials laughed off Chávez's fears as paranoia, the region's recent history of invasions was not forgotten by the Venezuelan leader and his allies. The interventions included Panama in 1989 to depose Manuel Noriega, Grenada in 1983 to dethrone the radical successors to leftist Maurice Bishop, the Dominican Republic in 1965 to overthrow Juan Bosch, and Cuba in the failed 1961 Bay of Pigs attack to oust Fidel Castro. Sometimes the rationales offered by the Americans for the invasions were risible. In Grenada the Reagan administration claimed it was rescuing American medical students. In Panama the first Bush administration demonized Noriega as a drug trafficker, even though for years he was on the payroll of the CIA, which Bush once headed.

Chávez also remembered how the United States stood by and let armed right-wing rebels, including former CIA operatives, run democratically elected President Jean-Bertrand Aristide out of Haiti in February 2004. The biggest recent US invasion was in Iraq, where the Bush administration falsely argued that Saddam Hussein possessed weapons of mass destruction and played a role in the 9/11 attacks. If the United States demonized Chávez enough, it might create an environment where the world would support and even cheer a US intervention.

Chávez made other moves to prepare for an invasion. He created a civilian reserve militia he hoped would number at least two million people. Housewives, teachers, students, and taxi drivers spent weekends learning about first aid, firing automatic weapons, and marching in formation. Critics charged Chávez was forming a Cuba-style militia to spy on opponents, stifle internal dissent, and defend his presidency at all costs. But little evidence of that emerged, and the possibility of the Bush administration launching an attack was not entirely far-fetched. "The United States went to war in Iraq over lies, and now it is telling lies about the Venezuelan government, so we must be prepared," said retired general Alberto Müller Rojas, Chávez's national security adviser.

Moreover, the Bush administration was making moves to soften Chávez's military defenses. It refused to sell Venezuela spare parts for its North American–made F-16 fighter jets. Then, in May 2006, it declared that Venezuela was not cooperating with the war against terrorism. That was on top of Venezuela's alleged failure to cooperate in the war on drugs and in the war on human trafficking. The latest condemnation meant the United States was imposing a ban on all arms sales to Venezuela. No more spare parts for any of the North American–made airplanes that Venezuela's military owned would be sent. It was no small matter. By some estimates, of the 277 aircraft in Venezuela's air force, 177 had been made in North America.

If the United States would not sell arms to Venezuela so it could defend itself, then Chávez would look elsewhere. He tried making deals with Spain and Brazil, but the United States helped block them by refusing to sell spare parts. So he turned to Russia. Chávez signed a deal to provide one hundred thousand Kalashnikov assault rifles to replace the Venezuelan military's aging Belgian FALs, which would be passed on to the civilian reserves. He bought a license from the Russians to build the first Kalashnikov factory in South America. In addition, he ordered twenty-four sophisticated Sukhoi-30 fighter jets and fifteen helicopters.

The United States called it an alarming arms buildup, and warned that some of the weapons could end up in the hands of Colombian guerrillas. But Venezuela's military spent less than neighboring Colombia, for instance, which expended $6.3 billion on defense in 2005, or Chile, which laid out $3.9 billion the same year. And it spent far less than the United States, whose defense bill in 2006 was estimated at $500 billion including for the wars in Iraq and Afghanistan. Chávez vowed to use every means at his disposal to resist a US invasion. The Venezuelan military even enlisted the help of five hundred Indians with poison-tipped arrows. "If they had to take a good shot at any invader," Chávez said, "you'd be done for in thirty seconds, my dear gringo."

Besides an invasion by the United States, about the only real option left for Chávez's domestic opponents to remove him from power was assassination. It was not implausible. But the opposition may have also realized that assassinating Chávez would not end Chavismo; it would merely send the country into a cataclysmic civil war. Hundreds of thousands of enraged Chávez supporters, many of them armed, would take to the streets. "Venezuela will never go back to being governed by The Squalid Ones," one Chavista told a reporter. "We won't go back to being a country where the petrol money is used for a minority and not for the barrios. So what will happen if Chávez is killed? Civil war. We are ready."

The Bush administration's antipathy to Chávez was driven by many factors, although he believed the principal one was access to oil. Chávez often warned that Venezuela would cut off supplies or blow up oil fields Iraqi-style if the United States invaded his country or if he was assassinated, presumably with the Americans' blessing. He was forging an alternative economic model that bucked the Washington Consensus free-market approach. He was setting a "dangerous" and "radical" example that other Third World countries might follow by challenging US hegemony. Like the Sandinista experiment in Nicaragua in the 1980s, the Allende experiment in Chile in the 1970s, the Bosch experiment in the Dominican Republic in the 1960s, the Arbenz experiment in Guatemala in the 1950s, and virtually every other left-wing or progressive project in Latin America since the dawn of the Monroe Doctrine in 1823, the Bolivarian Revolution in Venezuela had to be crushed. The North Americans had learned nothing from nearly two centuries of history in their "backyard" or even John F. Kennedy's famous observation to Latin American diplomats in 1962: "Those who make peaceful revolution impossible will make violent revolution inevitable." Chávez was doing his best to keep his revolution peaceful in the face of relentless US hostility.

• • •

He first mentioned the phrase *twenty-first-century socialism* at the Fifth World Social Forum in Porto Alegre, Brazil, in January 2005. It was a still-undefined ideal and alternative to the neo-liberal model that had wrought havoc in Latin America. It was something between "savage capitalism" and failed communism. Whatever it was, it would not be a repeat of the state socialism of the Soviet Union, Eastern Europe, and even his beloved Cuba. Chávez knew they were flawed, and that most Venezuelans would not abide a clone of Castro's communism. But he was no fan of unbridled capitalism, whose results he had seen firsthand in Venezuela and throughout Latin America. "The capitalistic model is perverse," he said. "It favors a minority and expropriates from the majority." His mission, he added, was a "search for social justice, for equality."

The implementation of his new economic model did not always follow a linear pattern. One state oil company manager compared it to "changing a tire when the car is moving." But some clear elements emerged as Chávez prepared for a reelection run in December 2006. The most obvious ones were the social missions. The state was taking a direct role in improving education, health care, food supplies, housing, and other basics.

Another key element was the "endogenous development" model aimed at making Venezuela self-sufficient. It was on display in the Gramoven section of Catia, where PDVSA had converted an abandoned oil storage facility for the cooperative where men and women made shoes, T-shirts, and other items, and ran the business collectively. Mission About-Face also included instruction that encouraged cooperative solidarity over cutthroat capitalistic competition. The government fostered the creation of thousands of similar cooperatives that produced everything from corn to yogurt.

It also implemented something called "cogestion," or "co-management." The idea was to help workers purchase shares and assume management duties in sometimes failing companies. One of the most prominent models was the obsolete state-owned Alcasa aluminum plant in the industrial powerhouse of Ciudad Guayana. Workers elected their own managers and transformed a top-down management style into a roundtable format where laborers provided more input. The state-owned electricity company Cadafe, which provided 60 percent of Venezuela's energy, also implemented co-management.

Chávez extended the model to several failing or idle factories, which the government expropriated to keep alive. Among the best known was the Venepal paper mill, a major paper and cardboard producer. At its height it employed sixteen hundred workers and reigned over a sprawling complex that included thousands of acres of land, houses, a school, a baseball stadium, a hotel with a swimming pool, and its own airfield.

Venepal's owners shut down the complex during the December 2002 to February 2003 oil strike, sending the company into a tailspin. After a series of tumultuous reopenings and closings that included one stint in which the workers occupied and ran the mill for seventy-seven days, it went bankrupt for good in late 2004. Weeks later, in January 2005, Chávez announced that the government was nationalizing Venepal. It paid the owners market value, helped restart the bankrupt company with $6.8 million in credit, and handed over half the shares to the workers. Chávez noted that the expropriation, while heralding a new direction in the Bolivarian Revolution, was not the start of mass nationalizations. "The expropriation today is an exception, it's not government policy," he said, although his detractors were skeptical. The workers ran the plant in "cogestion" style and envisioned using it to benefit the revolution by producing paper or notebooks for the educational missions. They dreamed of turning over the sports stadium and other facilities to the community.

If Chávez was going to go after idle factories, he was also going to go after idle land. As part of his twenty-first-century socialism, he announced he was stepping up the land reform program that started haltingly after the November 2001 decrees that led to the coup in April 2002. Just as Chávez wanted to use Venezuela's natural resources and labor to manufacture its own goods, he wanted the country to become self-sufficient in food. Despite having vast arable lands, Venezuela imported 70 percent of its food. Landownership was wildly out of kilter. By one government estimate, 5 percent of farmers and ranchers possessed 75 percent of the arable land. "Any self-respecting revolution cannot permit such a situation," Chávez said. "It is a sign of feudalism, it is pre-history."

One of the first targets could hardly have packed more symbolic weight. Government investigators descended on a thirty-two-thousand-acre ranch owned by Lord Vestey, an English aristocrat and meat tycoon. Government authorities questioned whether the lord's ancestors obtained the vast swath legally since land acquisition in Venezuela was rife with corruption. Vestey's representatives swore they could produce all the necessary legal papers, and depicted themselves as victims of a misguided government reform program. Chávez's heated rhetoric about land reform had long ago prompted hundreds of peasants to invade El Charcote (the puddle), set up shanties, and start farming the land. Government officials insisted they would expropriate only land that was idle and pay its owners. They would seize property outright only if it had been obtained illegally.

Critics contended that Chávez was on a far-fetched, quixotic mission that was doomed to failure —just like numerous other land reform efforts throughout Latin American history. Some suggested he was even flirting with the same fate as other leaders who had tried land reform and been overthrown in CIA-backed coups, including Salvador Allende in Chile in 1973 and Jacobo Arbenz in Guatemala in 1954. The message seemed to be: Don't bother trying.

Environmentalists also criticized Chávez for attempting to break up prized conservation centers such as the whopping 195,000-acre Hato Piñero ranch in Cojedes state. The ranch was home to endangered or unusual species including the jaguar, the yellow-knobbed curassow, the capybara — the world's largest rodent — and tapirs, which looked like a cross between a pig and an anteater. The ranch also raised nearly eleven thousand head of cattle, hosted scientists conducting investigations, and attracted ecotourists from around the world who paid $100 a day or more to see some of South America's most exotic wildlife. Ecologists warned that carving up the ranch into small holdings would ruin its conservation value and destroy one of the last relatively untouched examples of the wild llanos.

But to some of Chávez's supporters, Hato Piñero was little more than a walled-off fortress that only dollar-bearing foreign tourists and affluent Venezuelans could afford to enjoy while many Venezuelans could barely eat. They questioned the owners' claims that they were preserving the environment, and pointed to allegedly widespread deforestation on the property. Chávez portrayed Piñero's owners as part of Venezuela's out-of-touch and insensitive landowning elite.

He was determined to push forward with his land reform. He made efforts to rectify past mistakes, providing credit and technical assistance to the new landowners and requiring 15 percent of bank loans to go toward agriculture. Despite widespread fears, the government generally respected private property. Expropriations were limited. In the end it reached an agreement with El Charcote's owners. The company agreed to sell the ranch in Cojedes state for $4.2 million, and another 106,000-acre ranch it owned in Apure state for $4.7 million. The company kept eight others whose 638,000 acres represented the vast majority of its holdings. Chávez praised the agreement as a model for other large landowners. The government itself also owned vast swaths that could be distributed.

If Chávez could achieve a lasting land reform in Venezuela, it would be a monumental achievement. By early 2007, the government had distributed nearly nine million acres to one hundred eighty thousand families. The price was not cheap: some one hundred seventy campesino leaders were assassinated in the struggle.

Beyond land reform and the cogestion movement, Chávez acted to create state-owned businesses in telecommunications, air travel, and petrochemicals. He founded state companies that produced everything from tractors to "Bolivarian computers." He reined in PDVSA, bringing it back under government control and raising taxes on foreign oil companies. A new study initiated in 2006 indicated that Venezuela's proven oil reserves, previously calculated at 80 billion barrels, might be 316 billion when heavy crude in the east was counted. That would make them the largest in the world, surpassing Saudi Arabia's 260 billion barrels.

Chávez's emerging economic model was not greeted with unanimous acclaim. Critics said it was not only a work in progress — it was a piece of work. They contended that "endogenous development" and "cogestion" were little more than warmed-over versions of the import-substitution policies that had swept the region in the 1960s and 1970s and in their view had limited success. They doubted Chávez's plans would lead to long-term prosperity, and believed his entire project would collapse once oil prices dropped.

The overdependence on oil was a valid point, although Chávez argued that the cooperatives were aimed precisely at developing alternative sources of income. He was convinced that unfettered capitalism had failed the region. His allies pointed to the dismal economic record of the region since the advent of the "free-market revolution." From 1980 to 2005 income per person grew just 10 percent, according to the IMF. But it grew 82 percent between 1960 and 1980 before the reforms were adopted. "The past twenty five years have been an unprecedented failure for Latin America," concluded economist Mark Weisbrot, who called it the region's worst long-term economic performance in a century.

Meanwhile, after suffering through the upheavals of the 2002 coup and the oil strike, Venezuela's economy was rebounding. Growth skyrocketed by 28 percent in 2004 and 2005, the best rate in the region. The boom continued in 2006 with 10.3 percent growth. Even *The Economist*, while noting some "worrying" trends, concluded that Chávez's economic policies "do not remotely add up to Cuban communism." By some accounts, the private sector actually held a *larger* share of the economy than before Chávez took office. While he talked up twenty-first-century socialism, many economists considered his policies "gradualist reform" that had far more in common with European-style social democracy than Cuban communism. Former Marxist guerrillas such as Douglas Bravo even thought their onetime ally was a sellout. Rather than a revolutionary, Bravo said, Chávez was a neo-liberal.

Chávez's idea of a new economy did not rely on traditional notions of trade among nations based simply on extracting the most profit for oneself. He introduced the idea of solidarity. Instead of competition, he fostered cooperation. The most obvious example was the oil pacts he signed with countries throughout Latin America. Some agreements offered discounted financing that allowed countries to pay up to 40 percent of the bill over periods as long as twenty-five years. Interest rates were as low as 1 percent. In return, Chávez received everything from Cuban doctors to Argentine cows to Caribbean rice. He was not simply giving the oil away. As he said, "How much would 20,000 Cuban doctors cost?"

He used the oil deals to foster his vision of a united Latin America as his hero Simón Bolívar had proposed nearly two centuries earlier. He created regional alliances through pacts including PetroCaribe, which offered fourteen Caribbean nations a total of 198,000 barrels of oil a day with "soft financing." PetroSur united Brazil, Uruguay, and Argentina with Venezuela. PetroAndina brought together Colombia, Ecuador, Peru, and Bolivia. Chávez envisioned uniting them all through a massive joint endeavor he called PetroAmerica.

One of the most ambitious projects to unite the region was a proposed natural gas line that was to stretch fifty-six hundred miles from Venezuela through Brazil and down to the southern tip of Argentina. Branch lines would connect to Uruguay, Paraguay, and Bolivia. The cost of the project was estimated at $20 billion, although some experts believed complications might double the price. It would be twice as long as the US border with Mexico and possibly the longest gas pipeline in the world. Chávez dubbed it the "pipeline of the south." He depicted it as a symbol of a new era of regional cooperation and diminishing US influence in Latin America. "This is the end of the Washington consensus," he declared. "It's the beginning of the South American consensus."

Some energy experts dismissed the project as a pipe dream. They believed it was driven more by Chávez's political ambitions than by economic common sense. They noted the difficulties in traversing the vast and delicate ecosystems of Venezuela's and Brazil's Amazon rain forests. Environmentalists warned of damage not only to the exotic bird and animal species that inhabited the region but to isolated indigenous tribes as well. Groups such as Greenpeace were not impressed by Chávez's track record, although he had begun to show greater sensitivity toward their concerns, issuing warnings about global warming, urging emissions controls, exhorting his followers to drive less and use public transportation, distributing millions of energy-saving fluorescent light bulbs, and even installing solar-powered streetlights. But the Venezuelan leader continued to insist that the natural gas project was feasible. He noted that Russia had built a gas pipeline stretching thousands of miles to Europe. Brazil's Lula and Argentina's Kirchner supported the idea. Some experts believed it could be completed in five to seven years, while Chávez asserted it would pay for itself within five to eight years of completion.

He devised other plans to foster regional unity. He proposed a "Bank of the South" that would serve as a Latin American version of the IMF. He suggested a common Latin American currency like Europe's euro. He joined a trade pact known as Mercosur that included Brazil, Argentina, Paraguay, and Uruguay. He even proposed sending a Latin American satellite into space and creating a Latino version of NATO. That idea attracted little support in a region plagued by a history of bloody military dictatorships.

Still, the common theme of all these initiatives was to foster unity among Latin American nations — a unification that was part of Bolívar's vision — and to promote a multipolar world. It wasn't based just on opposition to the US empire, but on a belief that there would be more stability in a world with a number of power centers.

Acting on that belief, Chávez extended his geopolitical economic project beyond the region and across the globe. Faced with increasingly hostile relations with a Bush administration that was trying to iso-late him internationally, he sought allies wherever he could find them. His biggest international initiative outside of Latin America involved China. The Asian giant was emerging from decades of communist con-trol and increasingly embracing elements of capitalism. In search of new markets, its trade with Latin America was soaring. Chávez decided to get in on the boom. China's starving energy market made it a perfect match for Chávez's plans to divest himself as much as possible from the United States and foster a "multipolar world." He struck a deal to send China oil.

It started with a commitment in 2005 to supply thirty thousand bar-rels a day. By 2007 that was to jump to three hundred thousand, with an ultimate goal of half a million barrels a day by 2009 or 2010. It was part of a plan to increase from 15 percent to 45 percent the amount of its crude and other oil products Venezuela sent to Asia.

Chávez needed more tankers to get the oil to China and other parts of Asia where he was expanding distribution, so he struck a $1.3 billion deal with the Chinese to buy eighteen ships. He signed other deals with Brazil for ten more tankers and Argentina for four, including one to be named the *Eva Perón*. In total, he hoped to triple Venezuela's fleet to fifty-eight tankers by 2012. He also signed accords with China for everything from building computer and cell phone factories to off-shore drilling platforms in Venezuela. In August 2006 he made his fourth trip to China as president. By then PDVSA was operating an office in Beijing.

Skeptics dismissed Chávez's oil plan as unrealistic, given the vast distance between Venezuela and China — forty-five days by ship, according to some estimates. Experts calculated that the transportation alone would cost Chávez $5 to $10 a barrel. They contended Venezuela's natural market was the United States, where it was sending 60 percent of its oil. Chávez responded that he could get around the transportation problems by striking swap arrangements with new allies such as Russia, Indonesia, and Australia to deliver the oil to China so he could avoid sending it all across the Pacific Ocean himself.

The most stunning member of Chávez's expanding international alliance of developing nations was Iran. Chávez first cultivated the Middle Eastern oil giant early in his presidency when he successfully pushed for the OPEC cartel to decrease supplies and boost prices. By 2006, with the Bush administration openly agitating for his demise,

Chávez accelerated ties with Iran, which made up part of George W. Bush's "axis of evil" along with Iraq and North Korea. Chávez figured he had nothing to lose. The US government was showing it was no friend of his, and he needed allies in high places. He signed a range of accords with Iran that called for setting up joint Venezuelan-Iranian factories in the South American nation to churn out everything from shiny red tractors to cement, surgical tools, bricks, bicycles, cars, and buses. The countries also agreed to produce oil and petrochemical products together, start a student exchange program, and establish a direct airline flight between Caracas and Tehran.

Beyond the trade agreements, Chávez turned into Iran's most vociferous supporter of its right to develop nuclear energy, which Iran insisted was intended only to produce electricity despite allegations by the United States to the contrary. When Chávez visited Tehran in July 2006, he was awarded the country's highest state medal, the golden High Medallion of the Islamic Republic. Iranian president Mahmoud Ahmadinejad made his own visit to Venezuela several weeks later in September, and in return Chávez gave him a medal in honor of Simón Bolívar. The two referred to each other as "brother," and made common cause in denigrating their common enemy, the US government led by Bush, and the main US ally in the Middle East, Israel. "Let's save the human race," Chávez said. "Let's finish off the US empire."

His alliance with Iran had other benefits. After the overthrow of the shah and the hostage crisis of 1979, Iran remained in possession of American-made military aircraft including F-111s, F-14s, and F-5 fighter jets purchased when the shah was in power. Iran figured out how to keep the jets flying by jury-rigging them. Now it might share the tips with Chávez to keep Venezuela's F-16s and other jets in the air despite the US refusal to sell it replacement parts.

Venezuela's blossoming alliance with Iran set off alarm bells in the Bush administration. Unfounded allegations swirled that Venezuela might send uranium from its Amazon jungles to Iran to help develop nuclear power. Nightmare scenarios emerged of Islamic radicals and terrorists establishing a beachhead in Venezuela. In reality, close relations between Venezuela and Muslim countries were nothing new, dating to the formation of OPEC in Baghdad in 1960 largely through the efforts of Venezuelan oil minister Juan Pablo Pérez Alfonso. Chávez's alliance with Iran differed little from the close relationships of the United States with controversial regimes as part of what Henry Kissinger called "realpolitik."

Still, Chávez's growing friendship with Ahmadinejad underscored his radicalization fostered by the Bush administration's antagonism. If it had followed the more moderate approach of the Clinton administration, it seemed reasonable to ask whether Chávez would be courting some of the most openly anti-US regimes on the planet. The reign of Otto Reich and his cohorts made that a moot question. Their ultraconservative left-over Cold War fanaticism helped radicalize and alienate Chávez. Reich's successor, Roger Noriega, was replaced by career diplomat Thomas Shannon in October 2005, but the policies toward Venezuela changed little. One regional expert dubbed it "harpoon diplomacy."

Even as the United States got bogged down in the war in Iraq and oil prices skyrocketed, it did not seek to ease tensions with Chávez. Secretary of State Condoleezza Rice referred to Venezuela and Cuba as Iran's "sidekicks." She announced the United States was pursuing an "inoculation strategy" in other countries in Latin America to limit Venezuela's influence. In August 2006 the Bush administration appointed longtime CIA official J. Patrick Maher to oversee intelligence-gathering operations on Venezuela and Cuba. Previously, it had similar posts only for Iran and North Korea. Venezuela was now absurdly considered a threat on the level of the "axis of evil."

Escalating US hostilities toward Chávez and his government did not go unnoticed by ordinary Venezuelans. When Ambassador William Brownfield, the replacement to Charles Shapiro, visited a barrio in Caracas in April 2006 to donate baseball equipment, Chávez supporters gathered outside the stadium chanting "Go home! Go home!" As he left they showered his vehicle with eggs, tomatoes, and onions. A dozen motorcyclists pursued Brownfield's car down a highway, pelted it with food, and pounded on it when the ambassador got stuck in traffic. It was a repeat of 1958, when Venezuelans enraged by US support for the dictator Marcos Pérez Jiménez nearly dragged Vice President Richard Nixon out of his vehicle. The United States had learned little from past mistakes.

Since Chávez was considered a threat to democracy and stability in Latin America and was, with dubious evidence, included in the 2005 US Country Report on Terrorism for "providing haven" to terrorists, the United States moved to investigate his allies — even ones on American college campuses. In March 2006 two Los Angeles County sheriff's deputies working with an FBI anti-terrorism task force showed up at the office of Pomona College professor Miguel Tinker-Salas. The Venezuelan-born Tinker-Salas, a professor of Latin American history, was generally sympathetic toward Chávez. The deputies questioned him for twenty-five minutes, asking about his possible ties to the Venezuelan government and the local Venezuelan community. They even questioned some of his students who happened to show up for office hours, and examined cartoons on his office door.

The university's president, David Oxtoby, said the interrogation had a "chilling effect," while Tinker-Salas said his students felt "intimidated." For some people, the grilling carried eerie overtones of J. Edgar Hoover's FBI investigations of civil rights leaders such as Martin Luther King Jr. and antiwar artists including John Lennon during the 1960s COINTEL program of covert domestic spying, blackmail, and intimidation.

Despite the US efforts to discredit Chávez and intimidate his supporters, he rolled to victory in the December 2006 presidential election. He racked up a record 63 percent to 37 percent landslide victory in an election that was a foregone conclusion for months. His main opponent, Zulia governor Manuel Rosales, was a former Democratic Action member who signed the infamous Carmona Decree wiping out democracy during the April 2002 coup. Still living in its bubble, the opposition was convinced they were going to win a stunning victory with Rosales. When they lost, some pulled out the same card they'd used in the 2004 recall referendum — fraud.

But to his credit Rosales accepted his defeat, and for the first time some of the opposition acknowledged that Chávez was the legitimately elected president of the country, while they were the minority. It opened the possibility that Venezuela could move beyond the coups and economic sabotage that marked Chávez's first term and enter into a new era of normal electoral politics.

Emboldened by his crushing triumph, Chávez's plans for a twenty-first-century socialism took a sharp, defining turn after the election. As he was about to be sworn in to start his second six-year term in January 2007, he announced that the government would nationalize several utilities in the telecommunications, electricity, and natural gas sectors. He also said that on May 1 it would take a majority share in four multibillion-dollar oil projects in eastern Venezuela where international companies had a stake. At the same time, Chávez said he was dissolving the MVR and forming a single socialist party, the United Socialist Party of Venezuela, to meld the disparate groups that supported him. He also announced the government would not renew the license for RCTV television network when it expired in May 2007. He sought to rule by decree for eighteen months on certain issues including the economy. He shook up his cabinet again, bidding farewell to two of his closest allies — Vice President José Vicente Rangel and Aristóbulo Istúriz, who was replaced as education minister by Chávez's brother Adán.

It all climaxed when Chávez was sworn in on January 10 and repeated Fidel Castro's famous phrase, "Fatherland, socialism or death — I swear it."

The phrase and the machine-gun-fast delivery of the announcements over the course of a couple of weeks set off alarm bells in the establishment, the media, and the Bush administration. They declared it was proof positive Chávez was finally moving to install a Castro-style dictatorship. Critics claimed he was eliminating free speech by refusing to renew RCTV's license, crushing political dissent by forming a unified party, and moving to a state command economy by nationalizing key industries.

The critics, of course, told only part of the story. Chávez was nationalizing only one telecommunications company, CANTV, which had been privatized in 1991 and which held a monopoly on landlines in Venezuela. While CANTV had improved some services in a country where the phones were so bad companies employed full-time secretaries simply to dial all day long, it was also far from perfect. It often took two years and a bribe to get a landline installed. The attacks on Chávez also left out the fact the government generally planned to compensate at fair market rate any companies it bought. That had been its track record to date, although in the case of CANTV it said it was also going to take into account debts the company owed to workers and an unspecified "technological debt" it owed the state. After the opposition nearly drove him from office in 2003 by shutting down the crucial oil industry, Chávez believed it prudent to take control of the country's key strategic economic sectors.

The refusal to renew the RCTV license was not simply bare-faced censorship but based on the network's history of refusing to pay taxes and fines to the government and, most damningly, its blatant support for and participation in the April 2002 coup against Chávez and the oil strike later that year. The network conducted itself in a manner — inciting people to overthrow a democratically elected president — that would not last two minutes with the FCC in the United States. It took Chávez's government five years to shut it down, although it was still free to operate on cable or by satellite dish.

His move to form a single party also was misconstrued. He wasn't outlawing any political parties. He was calling for those that supported him to unite into one. The opposition was still free to operate. They, too, were trying to form a new unified opposition party. Chávez had no reason to shut them down. He could easily beat them in free and fair elections.

Still, there was no doubt Chávez's revolution was moving into its most radical phase yet, and the jury was out as to where it would end. Even some supporters questioned why he needed to rule by decree on certain issues when the National Assembly was controlled entirely by Chávistas. They also were disturbed by the loss of respected cabinet members such as Aristóbulo Istúriz and José Vincente Rangel, who had stood by him — literally — during some of the most difficult moments of his presidency.

It was certainly possible Chávez would move to replicate Castro's revolution in Venezuela, creating a totalitarian state where the government controlled everything from oil production plants to ice cream parlors. But it seemed more likely he was moving in the direction of a mixed economy and social democracy, nationalizing some key strategic industries, unifying his political base to move his new socialist project forward, and keeping free speech and democratic avenues open.

As Chávez launched into another six-year term in 2007, the critical question was whether his Bolivarian Revolution was improving people's lives in a sustainable way, or whether it was just a lot of archaic leftist hot air. Another was whether Chávez was going to deepen the revolutionary process by instilling more power in grassroots movements, or entomb himself as an irreplaceable one-man show whose revolution would collapse the day he left office. If he opened and included others with critical points of view in the power circle, the revolution would last. If his ego ran away and he retreated into a bubble of adulation and "yes men," it might well collapse.

Like any government, his was a mixed bag. His opponents could point to clear shortcomings. One of the biggest was the war on corruption. Chávez had taken office pledging to attack corruption that was among the worst in the world. But eight years into the battle, he had little to show. Corruption remained a way of life in Venezuela. Allegations of wrongdoing even reached into a huge government sugar cooperative in his home state of Barinas. Chávez argued that corruption was not simply a *problem*. It was a *culture* in a country where many people thought only fools did not grab what they could. Chávez called it a "monster with a thousand heads." Slaying it was not easy. It might take years, even generations. To the government's credit, it arrested several military officers implicated in the Barinas sugar factory scandal. But even some of Chávez's allies acknowledged that he needed to attack corruption more aggressively.

His critics pointed to soaring crime rates as another failure. Murder rates that were high throughout the 1990s did not decrease under Chávez's reign and by some accounts got worse. One report by the United Nations asserted that Venezuela had the highest number of deaths by gunfire per capita in the entire world. The government insisted it was making progress in the battle against crime by fighting one of its causes, mass poverty, and reforming notoriously corrupt, ill-trained, and underpaid police forces. But like the rest of Latin America, in Venezuela the rule of law remained limited and the judicial system weak, with judges vulnerable to financial and political pressures.

Chávez's detractors and even some supporters also criticized him for failing to dismantle the country's culture of patronage. In Venezuela *palanca* (connection) was often more important in landing a job in the public or private sector than education or qualifications. So was loyalty to the two ruling parties, Democratic Action and COPEI. Critics claimed Chávez did little to change the *palanca* mentality, and that it pervaded his own government. The most notorious example was the "Tascón List." Obtained by pro-Chávez National Assembly member Luis Tascón, it was a list of more than three million people who'd signed the petitions calling for a recall against Chávez. Tascón originally posted the list on a Web site to allow Chávez supporters to make sure their names were not fraudulently included. But eventually people in the government used it to deny Chávez opponents everything from jobs to driver's licenses and passports. Opponents called it the kind of political discrimination that plagued the old Venezuelan regimes Chávez was elected to dismantle. Chávez's supporters responded that concern about opposition sympathizers holding public sector jobs wasn't unwarranted. Many had helped destabilize or sabotage the government during the oil strike.

In the end Tascón was suspended temporarily from Chávez's Fifth Republic Movement, and the president himself called on the country to "bury the list." But the episode raised questions about how much the Bolivarian Revolution had transformed Venezuela's political culture. Government incompetence, a perennial problem in Venezuela and throughout Latin America, did not vanish.

Critics also complained about a concentration of power in Chávez's hands. They alleged that he "controlled" the government, the courts, the attorney general, the military, the National Electoral Council, and just about everything else. It was true Chávez wielded tremendous influence in Venezuela as the leader of the Bolivarian Revolution. But it wasn't all his doing, or all that different from other countries. In the United States, the president appointed judges to the Supreme Court — George W. Bush named like-minded conservatives. The US president also appointed his own attorney general — John F. Kennedy, for instance, named his brother Bobby. Venezuela's opposition initially accepted the makeup of the electoral council. Even if it was politicized, no one could seriously argue that Venezuela's elections were not free and fair. It was true Chávez had an overwhelming majority in the National Assembly — by December 2005 Chavistas held all 167 seats. But that was because the opposition boycotted the vote that month after realizing they would suffer an overwhelming defeat. The complete dominance of the assembly by Chavistas gave the opposition what they wanted — ammunition to charge they were living in a dictatorship.

One of the biggest weaknesses of the Bolivarian Revolution was the cult of personality surrounding Chávez. He was a one-man show when it came to leading the movement, and it was a serious question what would happen when the day came for him to depart from the scene. One Caracas-based analyst sympathetic to Chávez, former Fulbright scholar Gregory Wilpert, did not predict a rosy picture:

> If Chávez were to disappear from one day to the next, the entire movement would fall into a thousand pieces because it would have lost its unifying glue. This extreme dependence on Chávez also means that it is extremely difficult for Chávez supporters to criticize Chávez because every criticism threatens to undermine the project because it gives rhetorical ammunition to the opposition. A further consequence is that the lack of criticism insu-

lates Chávez and makes it very difficult for him to test his ideas and policies against the outside world. Criticism from within the ranks is rarely present and criticism from outside the ranks is easily dismissed. The result is a strong potential for wrong-headed policies.

One example, Wilpert concluded, was the media responsibility law that increased maximum penalties for insulting government officials. He called it "anti–civil rights" and believed it "did not serve any useful purpose." The polarized political scene in Venezuela was creating an unhealthy environment among Chavistas where anyone with anything critical to say was "against the revolution." Some people wondered whether in the end Chávez would suffer Simón Bolívar's fate as the Venezuelan president's populist project (and oil prices) came crashing down of its own weight, and the masses who adored Chávez just as quickly turned to despising him.

Yet while it was possible Chávez was going to turn into just another stereotypical tin-pot dictator and prove Simón Bolívar's adage that "those who serve the revolution plough the sea," he also had the potential to go down as the greatest president in Venezuela's history. His supporters believed his social missions were the country's first serious and massive effort to redirect the oil resources to the majority poor. It was a Venezuelan version of FDR's New Deal.

Cynics dismissed the programs as populism, contending that they did little to improve people's lives in the short or long term. They declared they were not part of a viable economic model offering sustainable growth and breaking Venezuela's dependence on fluctuating world oil prices and its people's dependence on the state. Some journalists and analysts claimed that despite the billions of dollars of oil revenue that rained down on Venezuela, Chávez had been unable to make a dent in poverty. It seemed like irrefutable proof of his folly. It turned out to be another example of misinformation.

The poverty rate when Chávez entered office in 1999 was 42.8 percent, and it had indeed surged to 55.1 percent by the second half of 2003. That wasn't surprising. The April 2002 coup and the December 2002 oil strike sent the economy into a tailspin. But once the opposition's efforts to create turmoil ran out of steam, the economy boomed. It grew by 17.9 percent in 2004 and 9.3 percent in 2005 — the best rates in Latin

America. Poverty plummeted, falling to 37.9 percent by the second half of 2005, nearly 5 percentage points lower than when Chávez began. And it only counted cash income. If the food subsidies and free health care were included, the rate would be substantially lower. The rate kept dropping as Chávez's social programs expanded. By 2006, not including the subsidies it was 33 percent.

Other indicators also showed that life really was improving for millions of impoverished Venezuelans. The United Nations Human Development Index for Venezuela improved from 0.765 to 0.772 between 1999 and 2005. And that data was based largely on figures from 2003, when the economy was still in deep recession. The numbers would likely only get better as more data came in from subsequent years with the economy on the rebound. "The Chávez government has only had three years of stability and control over the oil industry," economist Mark Weisbrot stated in November 2006. "In that time they have dramatically increased access to health care and education . . . I don't know of anywhere else in the hemisphere that has made these kinds of gains."

Chávez embarked on or completed a series of major public works projects that culminated in late 2006 just before the presidential election. They included everything from high-technology health centers to petrochemical plants to a cable car system to ferry denizens of Caracas's mountainside barrios down to the underground subway. He cut the ribbon on a $1.2 billion, two-and-a-half-mile bridge that spanned the Orinoco River and took five years to build. He celebrated the completion of an $850 million subway line between the bedroom community of Los Teques and Caracas. He sat in the driver's seat as the country's first new railroad in seventy years made its inaugural trip to another bedroom community, Cua. He even proposed a transcontinental railroad stretching all the way south to Argentina.

To deepen the process of participatory democracy, he encouraged the formation of thousands of neighborhood communal councils empowered to implement health, education, transportation, housing, and agriculture projects at the local level. The government planned to pump at least $1.8 billion into the councils in 2007.

The new spirit was symbolized by millions of people who proudly walked around with pocket-sized copies of the 1999 constitution, the blueprint for the Bolivarian Revolution. Many could cite specific articles and claimed credit for certain sections their barrios suggested to the constitutional assembly. Quotations from the constitution appeared on packages of rice, beans, flour, and other foods in the Mercal markets. One Manhattan College religious studies professor visiting Venezuela on a "reality tour" noted that the constitution's human rights agenda bore "a strong resemblance to Catholic social teachings," including the recently released "Compendium of Social Doctrine of the Church." Despite allegations of a dictatorship, Venezuela was alive with politics at the grassroots level.

Leading it all, Chávez barely had time to sleep; he was intensely engaged in his presidency and curious about every detail down to the arcane. At his cabinet meetings, there was no doubt who was in charge. While debate might be open, in the end it was clear he was the man making the decisions.

Five years after his divorce from his second wife, Chávez was still an unmarried man. He didn't have the time or the lifestyle for a conventional marriage. He contended his great love was the Venezuelan people and his revolution. Often late at night after most people had left the presidential palace, he would stay on, poring over reports and reading books until 2 or 3 A.M. He would keep a television turned on with the volume low. When a talk program caught his attention, it wasn't unusual for it to be interrupted by a special phone call — the president was on the line.

Chávez's old military academy mentor, General Jacinto Pérez Arcay, had once told him he shouldn't complain about being alone. Bolívar lived the same way after his wife died shortly after their wedding, leaving him with the time and the drive to liberate Latin America. "If she hadn't died," Pérez told him, "Bolívar would have been nothing more than the mayor of San Mateo," the small village where he had his hacienda.

Still, a tough-talking, hard-core Chávez street leader named Lina Ron wrote a newspaper column in January 2007 urging Chávez to get married — and to pick fellow revolutionary and former vice foreign minister Mari Pili Hernández as his bride. "We need a First Lady now!" Ron wrote. "My comandante [Chávez] is alone and he can't continue that way." She added that Hernández should leave her jealousies at the door, because Chávez "is the man most loved by the women of this country."

Married or not, even if Chávez's run as president were to end immediately, he would have left his mark on Venezuela. The country would never be the same. He had broken the back of a privileged light-skinned minority that for decades had run the country almost like a mafia. The old order was dying. A new one was being born. Some believed that with or without Chávez, the process would continue. He was simply the symbol of a historic shift of power to the long-exploited brown-skinned majority poor, who were now in control of their country for the first time since the Spanish conquest five centuries ago.

With Fidel Castro suffering a major health crisis in August 2006, Chávez was his heir apparent as the chief leader of the left in Latin America and perhaps in the world. In ways, he already surpassed Castro as he trotted the globe and preached the revolution that began with Bolívar nearly two centuries earlier. He turned fifty-three in July 2007, still a relatively young man. With Venezuela's opposition self-destructed, Chávez just kept getting stronger. He vowed to hold a referendum on eliminating term limits so the Bolivarian Revolution's indispensable man could keep governing. Even his old comrade in arms, Francisco Arias Cárdenas, who helped lead the 1992 coup and later turned against him, abandoned the opposition and returned to the fold. He became Venezuela's ambassador to the United Nations in 2006 and led the fight for a seat on the Security Council.

On Election Day, December 3, 2006, thousands of Chávez's supporters streamed out of their homes at 3 A.M. and blasted tapes of reveille from loudspeakers mounted on trucks to wake their neighbors and head to the voting booths before dawn. The turnout nationwide broke a record — nearly 75 percent of eligible voters. The combination of Chávez's social programs and charisma — and the billions of petrodollars raining down on the country — was too much for any opponent to overcome. That night after his crushing 26 percentage point victory, Chávez stood on the balcony at Miraflores Palace and addressed a screaming throng who had waited hours in a torrential downpour. "This is another defeat for the empire of Mr. Danger. This is another defeat for the devil who wants to dominate the world," Chávez thundered. Venezuelans, he declared, had "voted for 21st century socialism, this new era of Socialist Democracy."

A new, more radical phase of the revolution was about to begin. Chávez was a figure unlike any other in Venezuela's history. He was a role model to millions, a teetotaling, history-loving, book-addicted, fire-spewing workaholic from the underclass who was fighting to overturn decades of injustice. "This is the real thing," stated Juanita Ortega, an

American nun and nurse with fifty years' experience in barrios in the country. "The revolution will last as long as there is no outside interference." Chávez's supporters vowed to defend him at any cost. Even their lives. He was giving hope to millions of Venezuelans, and that was something they had not felt in a long, long time.

# Afterword

Like most of the world, I first heard of Hugo Chávez in February 1992 when he launched his failed coup attempt. I was in the process of moving to Venezuela, initially as a Catholic Peace Corps–style worker with a group called Maryknoll, the foreign mission branch of the US Catholic Church.

I was in language school in Cochabamba, Bolivia, when Chávez led the coup, and arrived to stay in Venezuela that July. By October, I moved into a barrio in Barquisimeto, where I spent the next eighteen months.

The experience gave me a face-to-face view of life among the poor majority in Venezuela, an invaluable lesson for a journalist. Many of my neighbors in the *parte alta*, or upper part, of El Trompillo inhabited shacks made of corrugated tin sheets or even, as in the case of my neighbor across the street, the kind of mud hut that Hugo Chávez grew up in.

One day the neighbor told me she had not eaten in two days, had had only coffee to drink, and had no food for her three children. I bought her a bundle of groceries.

The barrio of dusty dirt roads lacked running water and indoor toilets. Like many residents, I bathed with a bucket in an outdoor "shower" that consisted of four walls of corrugated tin. A water truck came by a couple of times a week and filled barrels we kept in our front yards.

Six weeks after my arrival, the sun had not yet risen one morning when I heard what sounded like someone banging a pole into the ground somewhere outside my small concrete house. It turned out the noise was from people shooting off fireworks. Another coup attempt was underway. It was November 27, 1992. Civilian collaborators in another part of the barrio were heralding the rebellion. Before long, my neighbors gathered on the dirt street. We all watched as security forces stormed houses in the hillside barrio where the fireworks originated. Frightened, the neighbors ran back inside their homes. I figured I'd better do the same.

By later that day we could see rebel and loyalist jet fighters engaged in dogfights above the city. Some pilots ejected from their planes, landing in another barrio on the other side of the city. I wasn't sure what to make of it all. I was helping a neighbor with English lessons that day, and more experienced Maryknollers swung by in a jeep to instruct me to stay indoors. By that evening, the shaken government of President Carlos Andrés Pérez declared martial law. Anyone caught on the streets after dark faced the possibility of being shot.

I first met Chávez in 1994, shortly after he was released from prison. By then I had fully resumed my career as a journalist, joining the Caracas bureau of the Associated Press, which was certainly no bastion of Chávez supporters and where I worked until 2000. I soon moved into the upscale Altamira/Los Palos Grandes neighborhood, which in time was to become an intense hotbed of opposition to Chávez, with people furiously banging pots from their windows at night to call for his ouster. The neighborhood sat at the foot of the lush Avila mountain range, and featured elegant apartment buildings, trendy restaurants, and well-stocked grocery stores. Diplomats, international businessmen, and other high-powered people inhabited the area. It was the polar opposite of El Trompillo. It was my home for the next five years.

I met El Comandante in a Chinese restaurant in the trendy Las Mercedes section of Caracas a few days after his release, landing one of the first post-prison interviews granted to a foreign correspondent. His entourage that day included his son, Hugo, and lawyer Manuel Quijada. There wasn't much time for questions. His cell phone wouldn't stop ringing, and well-wishers kept coming by.

A year or so later I interviewed him again in the offices of an architect in the Chuao section who was lending him the space. After Chávez laid out some elaborate plans for the country, an aide and former military officer, Luis Alfonso Dávila, asked what I made of it all. I wasn't quite sure what to say. By then Chávez was being dismissed by the establishment — including the media to which I belonged — as a semi-crazed has-been who was little more than a passing fad.

By 1998, when he was running for president, we sat down again. He was surging in the polls and stood a real chance of winning; the establishment had misjudged what was happening at the grassroots level. The majority poor had never really forgotten El Comandante. As his brother Adán, one of his closest collaborators, told me in April 2007, "That was really a hurricane, a hurricane that has not stopped."

After chronicling Chávez's rise to power and the early part of his presidency, I returned to the United States but kept close tabs on Venezuela, making regular visits. In 2003, I began researching this book.

Several years had passed since I last had a chance to speak with Chávez personally, and I wanted to visit with him again.

However, getting to him was no longer easy. I spent months trying to arrange an interview. I lobbied aides, Venezuela's ambassador to the United Nations, its ambassador to Washington, friends who had friends who were supposedly connected, anyone I could think of. Most of it got me nowhere. Some of the aides came and went. But by April 2007, I was summoned to Caracas. I was finally getting close.

Chávez stood me up on the appointed day of our interview, so I headed over to see his longtime vice president, José Vicente Rangel, who had recently left the government.

Sitting in a living room filled with artwork and statues at his home in the Alta Florida neighborhood, Rangel recounted for me the events of the 2002 coup. He had been at Chávez's side for most of the night of April 11. He said one of the most remarkable things was Chávez's controlled, methodical demeanor, which was in sharp contrast to the chaos, tension, and bomb threats that surrounded him. At one point the president asked to be left alone to contemplate what he ought to do. Rangel said it was characteristic of Chávez to ask for privacy whenever he had a major decision to make.

"He was very serene, unbelievably serene," Rangel said. "He is very contradictory in this aspect, because he is a very hyperactive, emotional man. But in special circumstances he acts with an incredible serenity, coldly. That's why the decisions he's taken until now have been very good. I think one of the reasons that he removes himself is precisely to avoid letting the pressures of the moment mark the path he is going to take."

Later, in the evening, I met Adán Chávez at his spacious office at the Education Ministry he now headed. The president's brother was not known for giving interviews, much less to journalists from the United States. He said he had a half-hour window. We ended up speaking for an hour.

I recounted some of his history of joining the MIR and Douglas Bravo's PRV, and then his role as a link between Bravo and his brother Hugo. I asked if it was all true. He seemed surprised that I was familiar with details of his past that even many Venezuelans were not aware of, and said that it was all indeed accurate. Hugo, he said, "was immediately ready to make contact" with Bravo when he suggested the idea. They finally met in early 1979, he said, adding, "It was important, because it was the beginning of this process of constructing a civilian-military movement."

He spoke a little about their childhood in Sabaneta, about how his parents traveled between there and Los Rastrojos in the early years, about his birth and that of Hugo in Rosa Inés's mud hut. He denied a report that surfaced in a book originally published in Venezuela that claimed Hugo and his mother had at one point not spoken for at least two years. He talked about the Bolivarian movement's evolution in the 1990s, and Chávez's crucial decision in 1997 to run for president.

As we got up to leave, I asked Adán to put in a word with his brother for me, since I still wasn't convinced an interview would actually happen. He said he would, but I didn't know if he was just being polite.

A few days later, after it looked like the interview with the president would fall through, I was aboard the presidential jet with Hugo Chávez sitting in front of me. His office was smaller than I had expected, given his critics' uproar over his purchase of the $65 million Airbus 319. The aircraft in general seemed relatively modest for a presidential jet that took Chávez around the world. It was certainly nowhere near the size of Air Force One. It contained around forty seats for passengers. The gold faucets and other objects lambasted by his opponents turned out to be simply gold-colored.

Chávez was still wearing the trademark red shirt he'd worn on the final day of the summit he had arranged that weekend in Barquisimeto with Bolivan president Evo Morales, Nicaraguan president Daniel Ortega, and other leaders. He was accompanied by his oldest daughter, Rosa, who sat on a sofa in the room.

Chávez said he was glad to see me again. He was friendly but slightly reserved, a bit more formal than usual. There was no trademark bear hug. I wondered if he was wary of talking to a US journalist, given the lambasting he regularly received in the international media.

We sat down at a table in his office. Chávez had certainly changed in the years since I had covered him in the 1990s. He was no longer the *flaquito*, the skinny one, who was so thin and big-footed in his youth that his friends dubbed him *Tribilin*, Goofy. He face was fuller, his body more robust.

I asked him how he had changed as a person and as a government administrator since becoming president eight years earlier — and surviving everything from the coup to the oil strike to the recall referendum. Assassination was a real possibility, and security around him was tight.

With Rosa listening from the couch, Chávez answered that he had not changed at all. Rather, he had resisted great pressures from powerful forces to cave in to the elites and abandon his revolutionary project to transform Venezuela in the name of the poor. "I think I continue to be the same — the same subversive, the same man who has spent years and years thinking about how to help, how to be useful, how to lead a people to a better destiny. . . . I'm a subversive in Miraflores. I'm always thinking how to subvert the old order, how to turn things upside down."

I asked him to discuss the events and experiences that had played the biggest role in his formation, and he started by talking about the Bible and Jesus Christ. When he was an altar boy in Sabaneta the parish priest had him read the Bible. One thing Chávez said he could never understand was "why Jesus was born among animals in a manger, with so many other places and him being the son of God." His grandmother, Rosa Inés, tried to explain, saying that "when the poor die, we are going to heaven." He told me, "But I couldn't understand that, why you had to die to go to heaven. Why couldn't we live better here?"

Later in life, he continued, he began to understand why Jesus was born in such dire circumstances. "Christ came to be born among the poorest of the poor, to look for the road of liberation."

Chávez said books were the other great influence of his early life. From a young age he was a voracious reader. "I'm a reading addict," he told me. "I can't live without it, like someone who is addicted to drugs." One of the first books he embraced was a set of reference books his father brought from Caracas. The first chapter was called "How to Triumph in Life." It ended by saying, "Triumphing in life comes above all else from being useful to society."

Chávez's detractors depict him as a power-hungry demagogue and dictator who is destroying the country, but the president insisted that that simple saying was one of the guiding lights of his life — and that it cut against the grain of capitalist societies' core belief: you are successful if you are rich.

"From when I was very young I learned to be happy helping others," he said. "I am happy when I give a hand to someone to help them pick themselves up. . . . If someone doesn't have a pencil and I break mine in half and give one to them, I'm happy." He crossed his arms across his chest and smiled broadly to show his pleasure at the thought.

He recalled that since his family and neighbors in Sabaneta did not have a television — and in fact he never watched television until he arrived in Caracas as a cadet in the early 1970s, saving himself from the "poison" of TV as a child — he often listened to radio soap operas. One of his favorite characters was El Gavilan — The Hawk — a man who was dressed in black and was a just avenger for the poor.

Later, Chávez said, he discovered Bolívar, Zamora, and Maisanta. He pulled out the century-old medallion that once belonged to Pedro Pérez Delgado and that he had worn around his neck ever since a relative had given it to him while he was in prison.

I asked Chávez how he responded to allegations that he is power-mad and is installing a dictatorship in Venezuela. "What kind of tyrant takes pains to teach the people to read and write?" he said, referring to the social missions. What kind of tyrant hands out weapons to thousands of civilians to form military reserves? "I've never had a vocation for power," he said. "Power for what?" Rather than a dictator, he insisted, "I represent an antipower, a clash with the power of the empire."

If his main goal was simply amassing power for himself, he said, he never would have continued pursuing a project on behalf of Venezuela's majority poor that almost got him killed. "I have been close to the line of death several times," he said. "If I had a concept simply of personal power I never would have come close to that line."

He spoke about the night during the 2002 coup when he was taken from Fort Tiuna to Turiamo. He said word had gone out through the Venezuelan and international media that he had resigned the presidency, and "the only way I could be stopped from denying it was by killing me. . . . The coup leaders didn't know what to do with me. The order arrived from Miraflores that I had to be killed." He charged that Pedro Carmona "gave the order that everything should appear to be an accident" — an allegation Carmona has denied.

When Chávez arrived at Turiamo around midnight he did not know where he was. As they reached some warehouses and a small house by the sea, mercenaries sent by the coup leaders showed up in a helicopter and were prepared to kill him, Chávez said. "I prayed, I asked God's blessing for my children, I looked at a star in the sky, I held my cross. . . . I was ready."

He said he recalled Che Guevara at the moment of his death in the jungles of Bolivia, when the wounded revolutionary told his killer to hold his fire so he could stand up and show him "how a man dies."

"I remembered Che. I said to myself, I'm not going to ask for clemency, I'm not going to turn myself into a coward," Chávez said.

At the moment when he believed the mercenaries were about to kill him, he confronted them, asking what did they think they were going to do the next day, where would they hide, what would they tell the people who asked what had happened to him? When some of the soldiers assigned to the base realized what was going on, one of them intervened and told the mercenaries, "If you kill this man here, we are all going to kill one another." The comment "fell like a bomb in that solitude," Chávez recalled, and ended the standoff. The loyalist soldiers seized control of the situation and whisked Chávez away. The mercenaries were forced to leave in the helicopter. One of the loyalists told Chávez, "Don't worry. Nothing is going to happen to you. We guarantee your life."

Rescued from execution, Chávez was brought to the base's infirmary — the only room with air conditioning — and a military doctor and nurse tended to him, bringing him some medications. When the doctor left momentarily, the nurse — tears streaming down her face — told Chávez she had always wanted to meet him, "but not like this."

That was the encounter that triggered something in Chávez. By the next morning, Saturday April 13, he became convinced that *el pueblo* was going to react to his disappearance and that he would return to power.

By the time Chávez finished telling me about these events, the plane had landed, and his cell phone was already ringing. I wanted to confirm one point quickly before the interview ended. What year did he return to the military academy to start giving classes? He jogged his memory, told me 1981, and then answered another quick question: How exactly did he organize the conspiracy in the academy?

He talked about his activities as an instructor at the academy, how "I started it in silence, with a lot of discipline, with a lot of attention to the boys" — the cadets. He explained how he initially focused his recruiting efforts on the one hundred or so cadets directly under his command. Then he turned to the approximately three hundred he taught in classes. Then he got involved in as many activities as he could to increase contact, from staging historical theater acts to organizing sports teams.

It was time to go. Chávez's ministers and other aides were on the tarmac waiting for him to finish the interview. He stood up, embraced

Rosa, spoke to her softly, and said good-bye. Then, to my surprise, he invited me to accompany him in his car on the ride to Caracas.

I got into the backseat with Chávez. The only other people in the car were the driver and an aide — a colonel who was the only military woman to take part in Chávez's 1992 coup. A couple of vehicles and guards on motorcycles drove in front of us. The rest of the caravan carrying the ministers followed. Chávez offered me some cookies and a small plastic cup of soda. It was close to 11 P.M. None of us had eaten dinner.

The president seemed to warm up to me a bit more, and leaned over as he gave me something of a guided tour on the way up Mount Avila into Caracas. He spoke softly and seemed a bit like a proud father describing the attributes of his newborn.

He pointed out how his government had removed tollbooths that workers heading from the coast up to Caracas had had to negotiate each day. He also noted how the government had taken down light posts located on the highway median and placed them off to the side on a hilltop, where they did a better job of illuminating the road. As we drove through the two tunnels that cut through the mountains on the way to Caracas, he boasted about cleaning the inside walls, which for years were poorly ventilated and had been filthy — "like a cave belonging to wolves."

A minute later he was talking about his grand plans to create a "socialist city" just off the highway in the Avila mountain range. Suddenly he ordered the driver to stop so he could show me the entrance, which set off a flurry of radio calls in the caravan. It turned out to be the wrong spot, and we continued on.

Chávez explained that his vision of a socialist city included a place where human beings and not motor vehicles would reign. People would be required to park their cars outside the city, then walk five hundred yards or so to the town itself. The city would be built to coexist in harmony with nature. Solar and wind energy would be utilized. Cooperatives, farms with animals, tourism, and small businesses would pump the economy.

The idea was to draw people out of the teeming, dangerous barrios of Caracas into an area between the capital and the Caribbean coast where they could live in a new, more humane place. As they left their *ranchos* in Caracas, the government would bulldoze the shacks to reduce density.

Venezuelan and Cuban workers already were busy carving terraces out of the mountainside where the government planned to build thirty to forty thousand homes, Chávez said. "It's a new Caracas." He said work was also underway on another socialist city to the east of Caracas, on the way to Guarenas. About twenty thousand houses were planned for that location. He said he hoped to expand the idea around the country.

Like many of his projects, I thought, this one could be a stroke of genius or a stillborn case of fanciful dreaming.

Not long after we reached Caracas, we drove down the main street of the sprawling barrio of Catia and pulled into Miraflores. I figured that was the end of the interview, but Chávez surprised me again by inviting me to climb a long set of stairs outside the palace that led to a helicopter landing pad and a small garden on a hilltop. It was the same set of stairs he'd descended early in the morning on April 14, 2002, when he returned to the palace at the end of the coup.

The spot atop the hill offered a spectacular view of the Twenty-third of January barrio high-rises constructed by the dictator Marcos Pérez Jiménez in the 1950s. We could also see hundreds of *ranchos* that covered the landscape. Beyond that on another hill stood the Museo Histórico Militar that served as Chávez's base of operations during the 1992 coup. In the middle of the tableau was a Catholic church with a cross atop it and a statue of Christ holding his arms open. Chávez had ordered the church and the museum to be illuminated at night.

He commented that he enjoyed the same view from the "balcony of the people" on the second floor of Miraflores. "If I had not occupied that point during that dawn," he said, referring to the military museum, "I would not be here" in the palace. "From there, '92, six years later, I arrived here. It has tremendous significance for me." He added that the view also summed up some of the key elements of his life: Military, God, and *el pueblo*.

It was close to midnight, and we walked back down the stairs. Chávez promised to see me the next day around noon to finish the interview.

Noon came and went the next day. I heard nothing from Miraflores. Shortly after five my cell phone rang: Be at the palace at 8 P.M. The president will see you.

I showed up at the appointed hour, and then waited three hours. Chávez was not in the palace, but at the Teresa Carreño Theater near the Hilton Hotel. He was making a flurry of announcements on the eve of International Workers' Day, May 1. I watched him on an aide's television.

Chávez said the government was raising the minimum wage to the equivalent of $286 a month, which when free food coupons were added in gave Venezuela the highest minimum wage in Latin America. He also said housewives would be eligible for government pensions when they turn sixty-five, because their labor at home was as legitimate was any worker's.

On top of that, Chávez announced that Venezuela would withdraw its membership from the International Monetary Fund and the World Bank. Other countries, such as Ecuador, which blamed the institutions for the region's economic debacles, were making similar moves. Critics said the withdrawal might not be so simple since it might technically imply a default on some Venezuelan bonds.

The president made yet another arresting announcement: He wanted to reduce the legal work day from eight hours to six by 2010. He noted that the massacred workers of the Chicago Haymarket riots in the nineteenth century had fought to achieve the eight-hour workday more than a century ago, and many nations had not advanced beyond that.

His speech ended sometime after 9 P.M., and he made his way back to the palace. I was finally summoned to the second floor of Miraflores. An aide walked me through his spacious *despacho*, main office, and then turned into a short hallway where a small elevator took us upstairs. We walked down another hall, and onto a semi-enclosed outdoor patio where Chávez was sitting alone at a table. He wore a green shirt and a kind of green safari jacket. He seemed relaxed.

I was struck again by Chávez's demeanor. In contrast to the booming orator that transfixed the masses at public rallies and who, according to his detractors, would not listen to anyone, he was soft-spoken and attentive to my questions. He had a pile of reports on his desk.

A television set was attached to the roof, and Chávez was keeping a close eye on it. After the announcements earlier that evening, he was preparing for another bit of history: the Venezuelan takeover of four major oil projects in the eastern Orinoco River basin. The government was not kicking the foreign companies out, but was taking majority control of the projects — at least a 60-percent share. The companies could continue as minority partners if they wanted.

The move unleashed a wave of criticism; critics accused Chávez of turning Venezuela into a communistic state where the government was going to control all aspects of the economy and life in general. Texas senator Kay Bailey Hutchison, head of the Senate Republican Policy Committee, declared that the seizures were "the latest and most ominous scheme out of Fidel Castro's playbook." US State Department spokesman Sean McCormack said Venezuela's negotiations with the oil companies over terms of the takeover "will proceed as they will," but blasted Chávez's other actions, including the withdrawal from the IMF and World Bank, saying Chávez was digging Venezuela into a hole.

"You can't take the shovel out of the man's hand," McCormack said. "He just keeps on digging. And sadly, it's the Venezuelan people who are victimized by this."

In reality, Chávez's moves were hardly radical. Since the nationalization of Venezuela's oil industry by Carlos Andrés Pérez, in 1976, until the early 1990s, Venezuela enjoyed complete control of its oil operations. The government's oil "opening" in the early 1990s allowed some foreign companies to come back in, but Chávez was now asserting majority control of the projects on behalf of the government. Lost in the debate was the fact that countries such as Mexico and Saudi Arabia allowed no foreign ownership participation of any kind in their oil industries, and that 75 percent of the world's oil reserves were controlled by state companies like Venezuela's PDVSA. Would the United States, for instance, allow foreign companies to have majority control over its strategic natural resources?

Chávez defended the takeover to me, saying that Venezuela was now regaining some of the sovereignty it had surrendered in the 1990s over what new studies indicated might be the largest crude reserves in the world — larger even than Saudi Arabia's. Chávez added that many of the Venezuelan workers involved in the projects "were exploited by the transnationals." He said many were hired on three-month contracts so the companies would not have to pay legally required benefits, and then rehired continually when the contracts expired. "Now the situation will change radically," Chávez said. The nearly four thousand workers would go on the PDVSA payroll, and receive full salaries and benefits.

The oil companies had complained that they had invested some $20 billion in developing the Orinoco heavy tar belt, which requires specialized technology, and were now losing out on their investment. But Chávez said that for years the companies had gotten away with paying almost no taxes. Even with the new arrangement, the situation remained profitable enough that most decided to stay.

There was still time before midnight struck, so I launched into a series of questions we hadn't had time to address the night before. I asked Chávez when he came up with the idea of twenty-first-century socialism. Was this a card he had hidden for years, merely biding time before pulling it out, kind of like when Fidel Castro declared his revolution socialist a couple of years into his reign?

Chávez said that from "a long time ago the socialist thesis had always attracted my attention. I've always been a good student of different currents. I have always believed that it's a perfectly valid alternative, even after the fall of the Soviet Union."

Still, he noted, his military movement in the 1980s never adopted the banner of socialism, even though he met with revolutionaries such as Douglas Bravo and Alfredo Maneiro. His group's focus at the time was on nationalism and Bolivarianism. Socialism was not a widely accepted model.

"In those days even the left hid the socialist banner," Chávez said. "Almost no movement on the left in the Americas, with the exception of Cuba, lifted this banner. The big parties of the left distanced themselves from the socialist project and the word itself disappeared from the political lexicon." Leftists started talking about things like the *Tercer Camino* or Third Way, the name of Bravo's new group in the 1980s and 1990s.

He denied that he was planning to install a socialist government when he was elected president in December 1998. He noted that not one member of his Patriotic Pole was talking about that prospect, and that "not even the Communist Party here was proposing the socialist thesis. . . . You won't find in any speech of mine in the 1998 campaign or in the constitutional proposal" references to socialism. The new constitution, adopted in 1999, "has elements of socialism, but it does not go so far as to propose in an open and clear manner the thesis of socialism."

Chávez said that as president, little by little, he began to embrace the idea of socialism as a result of "political and ideological maturation" and a "deepening analysis." But what pushed him over the edge in particular, he said, was the April 2002 coup in which he was almost killed. "I came to the conclusion above all after the coup . . . that any attempt to reach an agreement with the forces of the old regime here, the old order, would be in vain."

The coup, he said, "accelerated many things. I entered into a very deep process of reflection. For several years I had been moving amid a dilemma . . . of conciliating between the most retrograde forces and the advanced forces. It was like a bridge, at both the internal and international level. But then I realized it was impossible. I realized the Bible was profoundly correct when it says you can't be okay with God and with the devil at the same time. Maybe before I was trying to be okay with God and throw an olive branch to the devil. It's impossible. The devil will stab you."

Around the same time, he added, amid indications the United States endorsed and perhaps even played an active role in the coup, he decided to declare the "anti-imperialist" character of his revolution. The US had long argued that "through free trade the big and good father was going to permit us to live better," Chávez said. "But the world has come to realize that imperialism continues to be the same bloody imperialism as always, more ferocious now than before."

When I asked if he thought, back in 1998, that he could become a radical as president and take his government hard to the left, he responded by saying: "I've always been a radical and I continue to be one."

But how, exactly, did he define twenty-first-century socialism, a proposal which still seemed vague to many people and alarming to his opponents? He offered some of the measures announced earlier in the day as partial examples of what he had in mind — the new minimum wage, the pensions for housewives, the six-hour work day. He noted that he had been working on the six-hour proposal for two years, and that not everyone in his government supported it. "But I'm not going to wait until everyone is in agreement," he said. "The leader is the leader."

Chávez said his socialist project aimed to promote equality, liberty, fraternity, and the fulfillment of basic necessities such as food, education, housing, health, and jobs — in sum, the search for the reign of God, but "here on earth." He referred to a phrase from Bolívar, saying his project aimed to create the greatest amount of happiness possible for the largest number of people. He said it would not exclude private property, although it would seek to promote social property, social production, and social distribution.

Above all, he insisted, he wished to transfer power to the people through mechanisms such as the community councils. "I do not conceive of socialism as anything but a profoundly democratic system, although not the democracy of the elites." Still, he added, "I know I will die and we will not have attained the goal of socialism. . . . Reaching 100 percent? I don't think it is possible."

By now it was several minutes before midnight. Chávez interrupted the conversation to turn his attention to the television and the events in Anzoátegui state, where Venezuela was about to take control of the oil installations. He spoke to PDVSA president Rafael Ramírez for a firsthand account of what was happening, and instructed Ramírez to address the nation.

Ten minutes or so later, with the situation in Anzoátegui under control, Chávez muted the television and returned to the interview. I wanted to ask more about Douglas Bravo: Had the legendary guerrilla leader really played an important role in Chávez's formation, or were he and his colleagues exaggerating their influence? Chávez said, "It would be terribly unjust of me to not recognize the importance that a group of persons had during one stage of my life." He said he had spoken with Bravo by telephone recently, and hoped to see him, although he knew the former guerrilla was extremely critical of his government, which he called "neo-liberal."

"He is very critical but I respect him profoundly because he is an upright man, an integral revolutionary," Chávez said. "Douglas helped me a lot. I learned a lot from him."

We were now on the topic of civilians who assisted him in his conspiracy, and I knew it was time to launch the most delicate question I had — his relationship with Herma Marksman. To my knowledge he had never publicly acknowledged the relationship.

I told him that several of the comandantes I had interviewed — Francisco Arias Cárdenas, Raúl Baduel, Jesús Urdaneta — had mentioned Marksman as an important civilian figure in the conspiracy. They didn't do it to embarrass the president, it seemed, or from any prompting from me, but simply as a point of fact in reconstructing the history of the movement. None spoke of her as a mistress, but rather as a respectable history professor who was loyal to their movement and to Chávez. Anticipating an angry outburst, I asked the president if she had really played an important role.

Chávez reacted calmly and seemed a little surprised by the question. "Everyone had their importance," he said quietly. "I don't want to minimize anyone's role." He continued: "Herma Marksman. A fighter. I was very fond of her," he said, using the Spanish verb *querer*, which could also be translated as "love" but is not as strong as the verb *amar*, which means a much deeper love.

I was a bit taken aback by his frankness, since I was half-expecting him to be more evasive or to even deny the relationship. He didn't, although he also didn't seem anxious to post the news on billboards. I asked if it was valid to compare their relationship to the one Simón Bolívar enjoyed with Manuela Saenz. Chávez laughed and dismissed the notion. "I'm Bolívar?" he said. "It would never be comparable. Bolívar is the giant."

He added, "Manuela Saenz accompanied Bolívar in war, in battle, in the campaign. She accompanied him in his final days, until his death. She was loyal until death."

Marksman clearly was not being loyal to Chávez until death. She was a harsh critic of his government, and actively took part in opposition activities. Chávez later commented that he thought she had been "poisoned" by the opposition. "Herma," he said with a sense of melancholy, "should be with us."

As long as we were on the terrain of quite personal matters, I thought I should ask the president about the assertion in the biography *Hugo Chávez Sin Uniforme* (published in the US as *Hugo Chávez*) that he and his mother had not spoken for two years — even ignoring each other on the streets when they passed.

Chávez said that was false. He added that the effect of one cause of the alleged falling out — his marriage to his first wife, Nancy Colmenares — was being exaggerated. While relations between the two women initially were not good, he said, eventually they visited him in jail together and even worked together at a children's foundation in Barinas.

I also wondered about an account in the book that depicted the old Communist leader in Barinas, José Esteban Ruíz Guevara, indoctrinating Chávez in Marxism and communism when he was a teenager. Chávez scoffed at the assertion. He also denied that he entered the military academy in 1971 carrying the diary of Ernesto "Che" Guevara and said it was ridiculous to think he was already planning a coup as a cadet. "It's something totally irrational."

We turned to talking about one of the main "houses of conspiracy," the one owned by Elizabeth Sanchez in Caracas. I asked if it really was a primary meeting place. Chávez said it was one of the main houses they met at, but that for security reasons it was not good to meet repeatedly at any of the locations. Sanchez's house also had a serious defect: It was located in a cul de sac on a dead-end street. You had to come and go through the same spot, and had no avenue of escape.

Chávez noted that he met in the house not only with Douglas Bravo but with military officers including Luis Reyes Reyes. He also recalled that Marksman lived there, and that that was where they met. Since the topic of Marksman came up again, I decided to ask about something she had told me in an interview — that she had become pregnant at one point with their child, but miscarried. Chávez said simply, "She at one time had the desire to have a child. We were never in agreement."

He went on to speak about the five congresses the Bolivarian Group held, recalling the first one at the beach outside Caracas, and the others in Maracay, San Cristobal, and elsewhere. He said that if someone wanted to enter the clandestine organization, the group studied the person carefully — and if just one member objected, the candidate was rejected. By the time of the two coups in 1992, the movement was the largest of its kind in Venezuela's history, Chávez said, incorporating hundreds of officers and soldiers. "I don't know how they didn't discover us," he said.

He recalled how Kleber Ramírez — a close ally of Douglas Bravo — helped edit some of the decrees they prepared for the February 4 coup, and said he still occasionally reviews them. They include some of the ideas he is trying to implement today, including the community councils and the concept of popular power. He thought back to Ramírez and others: "All of them I have here inside of me, with great affection."

It was 1:30 in the morning, and Chávez said he had to go. We had spoken alone for nearly two and a half hours, on top of the time spent together the night before. Chávez still had work to do. Later he would fly east to mark the takeover of the oil projects with a May Day speech. Before his day ended he had to study reports laying out details of the operation.

We walked toward the small elevator. Chávez commented that he was following the 2008 US presidential race, and that he hoped someone like Barack Obama would win. "Someone we can at least talk to," he said, in an obvious reference to the breakdown in communications with George W. Bush and his administration.

I entered the elevator, and El Comandante stood at the end of the hall waving good-bye. I waved back, and when I got downstairs his chief of staff was huddled with aides, still working. The revolution that never rests was marching on, to a destiny yet to be determined.

# Updated Epilogue to the UK Edition

Seven months after I interviewed Hugo Chávez, he suffered the political defeat of his life. On December 2, 2007, voters narrowly rejected a national referendum aimed at pushing forward his Twenty-First-Century Socialism project. A key part of the proposal was to abolish presidential term limits, which would have allowed him to keep running for re-election. The defeat was a political earthquake in Venezuela. After annihilating the opposition a year earlier in the presidential election, taking 63 percent of the vote — his highest percentage yet — Chávez lost the referendum with about 49 percent of the vote. He had suddenly lost his aura of invincibility — defeated for the first time in a major election. It appeared he might now have to leave office by February 2013 after fourteen years in power.

After their remarkable victory, opposition members took to the streets to party until dawn, dancing in the Plaza Altamira and swigging from bottles of rum. A glum Chávez appeared on national television and acknowledged his defeat.

His constitutional reform package was a hodgepodge of sixty-nine measures that dealt with everything from banning discrimination against gays and lesbians to lowering the voting age from eighteen to sixteen. One key proposal focused on institutionalizing the community councils that were a pillar of Chávez's plan to install participative and direct democracy. In 2008, the government hoped to pump between three and four billion dollars into the grassroots groups, which could decide what to do with the money — bring electricity to their neighborhood, install water systems, fix potholes.

But Chávez's proposed reform was fatally flawed. Some measures set off alarm bells for many Venezuelans, even some of his supporters. The media focused on the most obvious one — abolishing presidential term limits. Under the current constitution, Chávez was limited to the single re-election he had already won. Under the proposed reform, he could keep running for more six-year terms as long as he kept winning.

His opponents screamed that the move would allow Chávez to install himself as a "perpetual president" or even a "dictator for life." At a minimum, it underscored one of the central weaknesses of the Bolivarian Revolution: it had aspects of a one-man show and was overdependent on

Chávez as its central figure. There was a sense that if Chávez left the scene tomorrow, the whole Bolivarian project might collapse.

Chávez's supporters argued that the United States had elected Franklin Delano Roosevelt to the White House four times. Other nations, including France and England, had no limits at all on re-electing their leaders. They also noted that approving the reform would not automatically make Chávez president for life; he would have to run for re-election. He could also be removed from office at any time after the halfway mark of a term through the recall referendum, a mechanism the Chavistas themselves had installed in the 1999 constitution. It was unique in the Western Hemisphere.

Beyond the term-limit debate, the most contentious aspect of the proposed reform was Chávez's central thrust to bring Twenty-First-Century Socialism to the country. The reform would have officially declared Venezuela a socialist nation. After winning his landslide victory in December 2006, Chávez had stepped up his rhetoric and actions in this direction. He took more and more to citing Ernesto "Che" Guevara as an icon, even adopting Che's famous saying, "Homeland, Socialism or Death! We will triumph!" He insisted members of the armed forces repeat it.

But in pushing for a twenty-first-century version of Che's vision of socialist utopia, Chávez was badly misreading public sentiment. Many Venezuelans, including some of his supporters, wanted nothing to do with socialism or Che Guevara or Fidel Castro's Cuba. They wanted social justice, but they weren't looking for a Cuban-style system or anything that remotely resembled it.

When the votes were counted, Chávez managed to get only 4.4 million — compared to 7.3 million a year earlier. The opposition vote, meanwhile, stood steady at about 4.5 million. It appeared many of Chávez's supporters simply stayed home. The outcome shocked him and his allies — they actually lost in barrios in Caracas such as Petare, La Vega, and Caricuao, formerly undisputed Chávez territory.

Beyond his fundamental judgment error, Chávez had also committed tactical ones. He didn't consult the Venezuelan people, but rather drafted his proposal with a small team of close confidants, and then presented it to the National Assembly for initial approval.

Chávez never clearly explained the proposal to the public, either. Wide-spread confusion existed about some items, such as a new "geometry of power." The opposition took advantage of these doubts. It pushed a slick, misleading propaganda campaign that terrified millions by telling them the government would be able to take their homes — even their children — away from them if the reform passed. Many people believed it.

The defeat nonetheless raised a central question about Chávez: As he grew in power and fame, was he becoming too isolated from the people, too all-knowing and powerful? For a man who was famous for his ability to sense the pulse of the country at the street level, he had badly misinterpreted the sentiment on this one. Some observers believed he had surrounded himself with yes-men; advisors who failed to give him an unvarnished account of how people were reacting and led him to believe his ideas enjoyed massive support. For years the well-heeled opposition had lived in a bubble, failing to comprehend what was happening in the impoverished barrios. Now it seemed possible Chávez had created his own bubble.

Perhaps the Bolivarian Revolution itself was becoming too insulated — a movement where healthy internal debate even among supporters failed to exist and where anyone who questioned anything about the government was condemned as "counterrevolutionary." Before the vote, Chávez had called anyone who said they supported him but would vote against the reform a traitor. That didn't seem to leave much space for healthy criticism.

He suffered a major setback when General Raúl Isaías Baduel, one of the four founders of the MBR-200 in 1982 and the man who engineered the countercoup that brought Chávez back to power during the April 2002 putsch, defected. Baduel denounced Chávez's proposed constitutional reform as a "coup," and campaigned against it.

Adding strength to the opposition were new actors — university students. Tens of thousands, many of them from Venezuela's monied classes, took to the streets to protest the reform. They presented a fresh image for an opposition movement that had for years featured many of the same old tired faces of Venezuela's discredited political parties. The students pumped new life into the opposition movement, for the first time in years giving it hope that it could defeat Chávez. Many other students supported Chávez, but they did not receive the same media coverage.

Even though he lost the referendum vote, Chávez initially came out of it looking good. The international and Venezuelan media, along with the Bush administration, had charged for years that Chávez was a dictator or a dictator-in-the-making, yet the president accepted his loss. It went a long way in bolstering Chávez's democratic credentials. The country had conducted a free and fair vote, Chávez narrowly lost, and he accepted the results. That is not the type of thing dictators do. The vote also disproved the widespread allegation that the National Electoral Council was controlled by Chávez and rigged elections in his favor.

But Chávez quickly proceeded to throw away much of the goodwill he earned from his gracious acceptance of defeat, illustrating the paradox of a man who could be both brilliant and obtuse in the same day, the same hour, the same sentence.

After taking the moral high ground, Chávez started to denigrate the opposition's triumph. At a press conference a few days after his loss he called it *"una victoria de mierda"* — a "shit victory," repeating the word "shit" four times during the conference.

He also indicated the battle over the reforms — and even provisions allowing him to run again — was not over. In his concession speech the night of his defeat, he stated that he and his allies had lost "for now" — repeating his famous phrase from the failed 1992 coup. He also proclaimed he was "not withdrawing a single comma of this proposal . . . This proposal is still alive."

In subsequent days he spelled out what he meant. He began to insist the proposals could be put up to a vote again, even though the 1999 constitution appeared to state that was not permitted during the same presidential term. Chávez insisted certain proposals could be voted on again in a referendum called either by citizens signing petitions or by the National Assembly itself.

While that seemed a matter of debate, the one unmistakable hot button issue was abolishing presidential term limits. If Chávez and his allies tried to do so, they risked seeing Caracas and other parts of the country erupt with the opposition violently taking to the streets. They felt they had voted on the issue as part of the referendum package, had won fair and square, and that it could not legally be voted on again.

After the referendum, the key question became how Chávez would react, long-term, to the first major loss of his political life. Would he take the opportunity to step back, reflect on what went wrong, and adjust course? Would he abide by the voters' will and step down in 2013? Giving up the presidency clearly would not be easy for Chávez — from as far back as his days in the military academy in the early 1970s, he had devoted his life to his mission of transforming Venezuela.

While the electoral loss represented a devastating setback, it also presented important opportunities for Chávez and his movement to grow and progress. It now seemed clear to some people that the Chavistas needed to focus on developing other leaders in the movement who could replace the president when the day came for him to step down. The vote also appeared to be a message that Chávez had to begin concentrating more on bread-and-butter issues at home rather than traveling the world to promote and spread his Bolivarian Revolution. Crime and corruption were serious problems that were threatening to spiral out of control and which Chávez had done little to combat.

He was also facing problems on the economic front. The bolivar was badly overvalued, trading on the black market in late 2007 at around 6,000 bolivars to the dollar, as opposed to the official rate of 2,150. As gross domestic product continued to grow at a breakneck pace, inflation for 2007 jumped to more than 22 percent. Basic staples such as milk, rice, and chicken were scarce. Producers cut output or simply hoarded products, claiming government-imposed price controls meant they could not turn a profit, while demand shot up because many Venezuelans had more money in their pockets thanks to the oil boom and Chávez's social programs.

By late December 2007 and throughout the first half of 2008, he gave signs he was listening to the unrest. During Christmas week he declared he was reflecting on where his government was headed and was adjusting course. "We are going to make this year one of truly deep revision, of rectification and of revitalizing the revolutionary process," he said. He called them the "three Rs."

He shook up his cabinet again, replacing officials including the vice president. His government lifted price controls on certain types of milk, quickly boosting its availability. Chávez also ordered up massive food fairs, distributing tons of cheap or free food to counteract the shortages. He made moves to bring the black-market bolivar into line with the official rate. He declared a crackdown on crime, corruption, inefficiency in the social missions, and the most basic of problems — mounds of garbage that were accumulating in Caracas during Christmastime.

In one of his most remarkable moves, on New Year's Eve he announced an amnesty for many of the people allegedly involved in the April 2002 coup against him. They included the four hundred who signed the infamous "Carmona decree," which wiped out democracy. The amnesty also extended to those involved in the takeover and sabotage of oil tankers during the two-month oil strike that nearly strangled the economy later that year. "It's a matter of turning the page," Chávez said. "We would like a country that moves toward peace."

Despite Chávez's decision to accept his loss in the referendum and play by the democratic rules of the game, his image in the United States and elsewhere remained poor. He was still widely depicted as a power-mad, delusional dictator — a threat to the civilized world. Instead of taking a balanced, realistic, and sane look at Chávez, much of the media and the public continued to feed hysteria about him. Often they concocted an impression of a ruthless tyrant, rather than presenting a more accurate picture of a strong, even authoritarian president who, like any leader, had his flaws and attributes but certainly was not imprisoning people for their political beliefs, or torturing or killing opponents.

It was not uncommon to see his name lumped in with Castro, Hitler, Mussolini, or bin Laden, although his sins were nowhere near those committed by real dictators and terrorists. Venezuela really did have legitimate elections with a multiparty system. Its press was generally free — people went on television and called Chávez a dictator, and nothing happened. Tens of thousands protested freely against him in the streets — something unimaginable in Castro's Cuba.

In Venezuela's neighbor Colombia, evidence surfaced of links between US-backed President Alvaro Uribe's government and right-wing paramilitary death squads that had murdered hundreds of union leaders, peasants, and others. Uribe's foreign minister, campaign manager, cousin, and more than two dozen other political allies were arrested or forced to resign. Few people seemed to care. Instead, it was Chávez who was the international pariah, even though he was not the one with blood on his hands.

In a post-referendum piece, *The Chicago Tribune* contributed to the hysteria with an editorial titled, "Hugo Chávez — Scarier than Hell." *The San Francisco Chronicle* called him a "global blowhard." *The Kansas City Star* gushed that Venezuela had just avoided allowing Chávez "to become dictator for life."

Chávez's only chance for improved relations with the United States seemed to be if Barack Obama defeated John McCain in the November 2008 presidential election. During the primary campaign Obama largely bought into the simplistic stereotype of Chávez the brutal dictator, but indicated he might at least converse with the Venezuelan leader and seek a more realistic view of the Bolivarian Revolution. McCain gave few signs of changing the Bush approach; he referred to Chávez as a thug, dictator, and charlatan.

The Venezuelan leader, of course, gave his critics ammunition to dismiss him as a leftist buffoon. One commentator noted that his vitriol often "seems more befitting a professional wrestler than a head of state." In the weeks leading up to the December 2007 referendum he got into a typical public spat with the leaders of Spain when he denounced former prime minister José María Aznar as a "fascist," adding that "a snake is more human." Chávez was outraged that Aznar's successor, José Luis Rodríguez Zapatero, was defending Aznar during a summit of Latin American and Iberian leaders held in Santiago, Chile. Chávez kept interrupting Zapatero. Finally, the king of Spain, Juan Carlos, told Chávez *"Por qué no te callas?"* (Why don't you shut up?).

The phrase became a hit among Chávez opponents. They printed it on T-shirts and put it on their cell phones as a ring tone. The media, of course, never fully explained the source of Chávez's rage against Aznar — during the April 2002 coup when Chávez was kidnapped for two days and by his account nearly executed, Spain supported the revolt. On Pedro Carmona's first morning in office following the coup, two men joined him for breakfast in Miraflores presidential palace — the ambassadors from the United States and Spain. To Chávez, Aznar had officially endorsed the coup.

Chávez also flirted with moments of brilliance that could have burnished his public image if they reached fruition. In late August 2007, the right-wing Uribe invited his left-wing Venezuelan counterpart to conduct negotiations with Colombia's leftist FARC guerrillas to release dozens of hostages. They included three military contractors from the United States and a former Colombian presidential candidate, Ingrid Betancourt.

Relatives of the hostages said they felt their loved ones might finally, after years, be freed. But in November, just as Chávez seemed close to making progress, Uribe pulled the plug and removed him as a negotiator. It was a few weeks before the referendum vote in Venezuela. Uribe cited Chávez's alleged violation of protocol — a brief telephone contact with Colombian military leaders. To Chávez's supporters, it appeared

Uribe and his major sponsor — the US government, which seemed to pressure the Colombian — did not want to see Chávez succeed.

The FARC then made a surprise announcement, saying they would release directly to Chávez three hostages, including a three-year-old boy said to be born to one hostage in captivity. The Venezuelan president brought in a glittering array of international figures including former Argentine president Néstor Kirchner to accompany the rescue mission in late December. Even the filmmaker Oliver Stone showed up. It seemed like a Christmas miracle was about to happen.

But the FARC suspended the operation, saying Colombia's military was engaging in attacks that made the release impossible to conduct safely. Uribe called the FARC "liars." An angry Chávez charged that Uribe had "torpedoed" an operation that would have embarrassed the Colombian — whose own efforts up until then to free hostages were largely unsuccessful — and would have turned Chávez into a hero. Instead, to some he ended up looking like a fool.

Chávez won back some prestige a couple of weeks later, when the FARC finally released two female hostages on January 10, 2008. The three-year-old, it turned out, had long ago been sent by the guerrillas to a foster home in Bogotá — as Uribe had claimed. By now the women's release was almost anticlimactic, as most of the international observers summoned by Chávez had gone home and the media paid less attention.

But the FARC burst back into public view with a dramatic series of events starting on March 1, 2008. That night Colombian troops, apparently aided by US military intelligence, illegally crossed into Ecuadorean territory. They bombed a FARC camp, and killed one of its leaders, Raúl Reyes, along with twenty-four others. Reyes was the rebels' second-in-command. He had been leading negotiations to free the hostages, arranging the latest release to Venezuelan officials just a week earlier.

The Colombian government said it retrieved three of Reyes's laptop computers, two external hard disks, and three USB thumb drives that somehow survived the bombing. All told, the computers and hardware contained what Interpol later stated was the equivalent of 39.5 million pages in Microsoft Word. The agency calculated that at a rate of one hundred pages a day, it would take a thousand years to read.

Yet within hours after the bombing, Colombian officials declared the documents contained a treasure trove of information linking Chávez and Ecuador's president, Rafael Correa, to the guerrillas. They asserted

Chávez had even provided money and arms to them and was involved in all kinds of schemes, including shipping uranium to the FARC for use in dirty bombs.

The allegations were explosive. If it was proved Chávez was aiding an organization deemed "terrorists" by the United States and the European Union, he could end up even more of an international outcast than he already was.

Both Chávez and Correa heatedly denied the allegations. They cast the computer evidence as the latest trumped-up, US-backed scheme to smear them. Correa cut off diplomatic relations with Colombia. Chávez dispatched troops to the border and warned Uribe against invading. War seemed possible. It was one of the worst regional crises in Latin America in years.

Despite the tensions and blowback against Uribe, the computer allegations served him well: they managed to divert attention from Colombia's illegal, deadly incursion into Ecuador, and from the mounting scandal of his government's links to paramilitary death squads.

Chávez, in fact, not Uribe, became the target of media criticism. He was attacked for "provoking" the crisis by sending troops to the border even though, according to Chávez's detractors, Venezuela was not involved in the dispute. Chávez argued that if Uribe had invaded Ecuador, he could also easily invade Venezuela. Dispatching the troops, he said, was a defensive measure.

Responding to Correa and Chávez's denials, Uribe announced he was turning over the computers to Interpol so the international police agency could examine them. Meanwhile, as the weeks passed, Colombia's government selectively leaked to the news media some of the seemingly incriminating documents supposedly found in the computers. But they refused to release the entire package, which could have contained embarrassing information about the Uribe government, too. The media generally ran with the story that Hugo Chávez appeared to be supporting terrorists.

On May 15, 2008, Interpol released its much-awaited findings — and backed up Colombia's government. It asserted it could find no evidence Colombia had improperly tampered with the computers. Interpol head Ronald K. Noble, a former US Treasury Department official, went so far as to declare the computers indeed belonged to FARC leader Reyes. "We are absolutely certain that the computer exhibits that our experts examined came from a FARC terrorist camp," Noble said at a press conference. "No one can ever question whether or not the Colombian government tampered with the seized FARC computers." He added, "Mr. Reyes is now dead. But they were definitely his computers, his disks, his hardware." The media largely reported that Chávez now seemed to be a confirmed terrorist sympathizer.

However, there were some problems with the story. Some people questioned whether Noble and Interpol had politicized their findings. Interpol never investigated where the computers came from. So Noble's declaration that they belonged to Reyes was hard to explain. The agency was simply supposed to determine whether Colombia improperly handled or altered the laptops and hardware. Interpol declared that it had not — except for the first two days, when the military did not follow established international norms for handling such evidence. The agency's investigation also made no determination about the authenticity, accuracy, authorship, or significance of the information supposedly on the laptops. The two agents from Singapore and Australia who handled the examination could not read Spanish, so had no idea what the documents said.

As it turned out, most of the documents on the laptops were simply copies of e-mails, allegedly written by guerrillas, who were isolated in the jungle giving their own, perhaps embellished or distorted, accounts. The computers provided some information that indicated they may have been genuine — Colombian officials said the files helped them recover $480,000 from a safe house in Costa Rica.

But it was possible they had this and other information already available from other sources. The validity or accuracy of the information said to be contained on the computers also was called into question. Some of the thousands of files, for instance, had erroneous creation dates — 2009 or 2010. In others, the guerrillas allegedly spoke about the involvement of Bill Clinton and Colombian writer Gabriel García Márquez in Colombian peace negotiations — statements with little connection to reality. In the end, while it was possible Chávez was aiding the guerrillas, there was no definitive proof, certainly nothing that would stand up in a court of law.

But that did not stop the onslaught of accusations against him, or the widespread perception he was guilty. Allegations based on e-mails of questionable origin and accuracy turned into an accepted truth: Hugo Chávez was aiding terrorists. *The Wall Street Journal* declared he was "a proven supporter of terrorism in our own hemisphere." *The*

*Christian Science Monitor* called him "the rebels' rich funder" and said he was "caught red-handed."

As the drumbeat grew louder, some members of the US Congress proposed adding Venezuela to the United States' official list of state sponsors of terrorism, which would have led to economic sanctions against Venezuela. Although the US was bogged down in Iraq, in Chávez's eyes the listing still might have given George W. Bush an excuse to invade Venezuela the same way George H. W. Bush invaded Panama in 1989 to overthrow president and former CIA asset Manuel Noriega.

But the US did not add Venezuela to its list of state sponsors of terrorism. If it had, Chávez might have stopped shipping Venezuelan oil at a time when world prices were hitting $140 a barrel and US gasoline prices were skyrocketing past $4 a gallon.

But the computers, whatever their validity, did serve an important purpose for the Bush administration: They helped demonize Chávez once again.

By early June 2008, the FARC controversy took another turn when Chávez made his own dramatic announcement. He called on the guerrillas to lay down their guns, release all their hostages in exchange for nothing, and surrender. "The guerrilla war is history," he said. "At this time in Latin America, an armed guerrilla movement is out of place."

It was a remarkable statement. As recently as early 2008, Chávez had been calling on the world to recognize the FARC not as terrorists but as a belligerent force waging a legitimate rebellion. Shortly after Raúl Reyes's death on March 1, Chávez proclaimed him a "good revolutionary." During one of the televised hostage releases in the jungles of Colombia, Chávez's interior minister, Ramón Rodríguez Chacín, hugged the guerrillas and urged them to "keep up the struggle."

Critics and the media cast Chávez's latest statement as a surprising and hypocritical about-face. They believed it was fueled by his fears of losing regional elections for state governors, mayors, and other posts in November 2008, and by the alleged laptop evidence linking him to the FARC.

But Chávez's call for the rebels to give up guerrilla warfare should not have been entirely surprising. He had made a similar call in January 2008. Referring to FARC leader Manuel "Sureshot" Marulanda, Chávez stated that "I do not agree with the armed struggle and that is one of the things that I want to talk to Marulanda about." Chávez wanted the FARC declared a belligerent force to help speed negotiations to end the war. The conflict often spilled over to Venezuela, where hundreds of thousands of Colombians had fled.

Chávez's stance also seemed propelled by changing events on the ground. Barely a week after Raúl Reyes's death, another guerrilla leader, Ivan Ríos, was assassinated by his own security chief. He delivered Ríos's severed hand to Colombian authorities to prove he was dead. Then a legendary one-eyed female FARC commander, Nelly Ávila Moreno, also known as Karina, emerged from the jungle, surrendered to authorities, and called on her colleagues to give up as well. Finally, in late May, the FARC announced its supreme leader, Marulanda, had died of natural causes a few months earlier.

A weakened FARC was on the defensive. Chávez believed the time of guerrilla warfare in Latin America — although not the fight for social justice — had passed. After all, leftists were rising to power throughout the region not through bullets but through the ballot box.

The FARC's disarray seemed further confirmed when on July 2 Colombia launched an audacious rescue mission in which military spies tricked the rebels into handing over their most prized hostages — French-Colombian Ingrid Betancourt, three US contractors, and eleven others. The Colombian government, aided by US intelligence, said it had infiltrated the FARC's high command with intelligence operatives. Then — without firing a shot — elite commandos disguised as rebels plucked the hostages out of the jungle by helicopter on a supposed humanitarian mission to transfer them to captivity elsewhere.

The made-for-Hollywood rescue was a huge victory for Colombian President Alvaro Uribe. In retrospect, it appeared to explain to Chávez's allies why Uribe torpedoed the Venezuelan's efforts to gain the hostages' freedom in November, just as he appeared to be on the verge of success. Both men wanted to see the captives safely liberated, and to get the credit for it. Uribe and his US-trained counterinsurgency forces had made great strides against the FARC, and they were not about to let Chávez benefit from their efforts. Some of the newly freed hostages, who languished for months in captivity as this risky gambit played out, bitterly decried the Uribe administration within days of their return to society.

Not long after the hostage rescue, Chávez turned his full attention to the regional elections set for November. As the campaign geared up, the new party Chávez and his allies formed in 2007, the PSUV, or

United Socialist Party of Venezuela, tried to organize itself. It had brought together under one umbrella most of the parties that supported the president. On June 1, 2008, it fulfilled a requirement of the 1999 constitution — it held primaries to select candidates for public office. They were the first primaries in the nation's history. Some 2.5 million voters turned out.

The opposition still had no plans for primaries. But it did produce a notable candidate: Chávez's ex-wife, Marisabel Rodríguez. She declared her candidacy for mayor of her hometown, Barquisimeto. She and the president had become involved in a nasty, public custody battle over their daughter, Rosainés. Chávez ultimately dropped a lawsuit demanding he be given more time with his daughter, saying he did not want her to become the center of a public spectacle.

Rodríguez's candidacy, while wrapped up partially in the couple's personal woes, also underscored a disturbing trend among many of Chávez's allies: a significant number over the years ended up deserting him. While some of it could be attributed to jealousies, power struggles, and political differences, some of it also seemed to be Chávez's propensity at times to alienate those close to him, from Herma Marksman to Raúl Isaías Baduel.

His critics were also wondering where all the oil money was going. Billions were flowing into Venezuela. The government's budget had leaped from seven billion dollars in 1999, when Chávez took power, to fifty-four billion in 2007. His detractors thought the country should have been turned into some kind of Switzerland of South America. It wasn't. Corruption, inefficiency, bureaucracy, patronage, and nepotism remained ingrained problems the government had to overcome.

Yet Chávez had without doubt made inroads through his social missions and other projects. By some estimates the poverty rate was cut by more than half, from 54 percent of households to 26 percent, from the first half of 2003 to the end of 2008. And that measured only cash income, excluding increased access to health care and education. Even many impoverished barrios were bursting not only with basics such as food and jobs but new cell phones, cars, cameras, televisions and DVDs amid the oil boom.

Chávez still enjoyed the support of the majority of Venezuelans, who felt his government remained a far better option than a bumbling opposition that offered no real plan to improve the country. The irony of the December 2007 referendum vote was that if he had made it only on the question of abolishing presidential term limits and left out the Twenty-First Century Socialism elements, he might well have won. Rhetoric about Che Guevara aside, many Venezuelans backed the general thrust of Chávez's efforts to redirect the oil wealth to the majority poor.

Still, in the barrios and impoverished countryside, certain doubts were starting to grow. Many felt it was time for Chávez to deliver on issues that were affecting people's daily lives and to spend less time preaching about sometimes nebulous ideals like socialism. They believed he needed to step down from the throne a bit and get back in touch more directly with the people and the themes that originally brought him to power. If he didn't, his Bolivarian Revolution might find even more turbulent waters ahead, and deal a devastating blow to the Latin American Left. If revolution in the name of the poor could not work in oil-rich Venezuela with a powerful and charismatic leader like Chávez, some wondered, where could it?

The results of the November 2008 regional elections seemed to underscore the doubts. Overall, Chávez and his allies won. They took seventeen of twenty-two governorships and 80 percent of mayoral posts including the one his former wife was vying for. But they also suffered some significant, even devastating, setbacks. They lost the state governor races in Miranda (which includes part of Caracas), Zulia (center of the massive oil industry) and Carabobo (a major industrial and manufacturing hub). Moreover, they lost the mayor's race in the sprawling slum of Petare in Caracas – previously undisputed Chávez territory – and the contest for metropolitan mayor of Caracas. Even more shocking was who won and lost that race: Antonio Ledezma, a symbol of the old, corrupt political system, defeated Aristóbulo Istúriz, formerly a respected mayor of Caracas and one of Chávez's confidants when he was education minister.

It all seemed to be a wake-up call – again – for Chávez to hone in on domestic problems and spend less time on the global revolution. It seemed especially true as oil prices plunged from record highs of about $145 a barrel to nearly $30 a barrel during the world economic crisis of 2008 and 2009. That put greater restrictions on Chávez's ability to carry out his international assistance programs.

Still, there was enough good news in the results for Chávez to interpret the elections as a victory, and he decided to push ahead with another referendum on eliminating term limits. He wanted to move fast, capitalizing on the momentum of the Chavistas' victories and the fact the government was still in campaign mode. Opponents attacked the move as more proof Chávez was power mad and unwilling to leave office. Yet his supporters viewed him as a unique figure in Venezuelan history, a kind of indispensable man still needed to push through long-term radical change in the country and break for good the chains of an ossified traditional ruling elite. In their view, he was a charismatic figure like Nelson Mandela or Martin Luther King Jr. whose ability to lead and inspire could not easily be replaced. There was no other Chávez waiting in the wings.

The National Assembly, rather than Chávez himself, introduced the petition this time for a vote on the issue. The date was set for February 15, 2009.

Meanwhile, his chances for a better relationship with the United States improved as Barack Obama was elected president and took office January 20, 2009. During the campaign Obama said he was willing to meet with opponents of the United States including the leaders of North Korea, Iran – and Venezuela. But he still bought into the general demonization of Chávez. Days before assuming the presidency Obama lashed out at him. He called Chávez "a force that has impeded progress in the region," and accused him of "exporting terrorist activities and supporting malicious entities like the FARC" in Colombia.

No proof existed that Chávez was "exporting terrorist activities." He had little patience for Obama's accusations. Harking back to his speech at the United Nations in 2006 when he called George W. Bush "the devil," Chávez shot back that Obama had the "same stench" as his predecessor. He left open the door for improved relations, though, saying Obama still had time to correct his views. But he added "no one should say I threw the first stone at Obama. He threw it at me."

Chávez's mission to transform Venezuela received a major boost weeks later when he easily won the referendum on dropping restrictions against running for re-election more than once. Amid heavy voter turnout, the "sí" vote defeated the "no" by a 55 to 45 percent margin. After he cast his ballot that morning, Chávez acknowledged his political fate was on the line, suggesting he would leave office in February 2013 if he lost. The Bolivarian Revolution – at least with him officially at the helm – would come to an end.

His detractors such as former leftist guerrilla turned Wall Street darling Teodoro Petkoff noted Chávez's support had dropped from the 63 percent he won in the December 2006 presidential vote to 55 percent. He predicted the trend would continue. Chávez would be met with "inevitable defeat" in the December 2012 presidential race.

But the night of his victory, Chávez took to the "balcony of the people" on the second floor of Miraflores palace for the eighth time in a decade to mark another historic moment in his presidency. As the gates opened to let in the throngs from the barrios and floodlights lit up his figure, Chávez declared that "unless God decides otherwise, unless the people decide otherwise, this soldier is already a candidate" for the next race. It opened the possibility Chávez could remain in office until February 2019 - a total of 20 years since he first became president – or even beyond.

It was not an ideal scenario; he remained the indispensable man in Venezuela's transformation. He enjoyed an almost cultlike status among the dispossessed masses, a mythic figure whose smiling image was plastered on huge billboards throughout the country. But as he stated, his victory that Sunday also was a triumph for the movement for change in Latin America and around the world. As global capitalism suffered convulsions that originated in the United States, it seemed likely Chávez's search for a socialistic alternative would attract growing interest in the same way alternatives to capitalism attracted interest during the Great Depression of the 1930s.

"February, February, always February!" he told the cheering crowd, referring to key moments in his life such as the February 1989 Caracazo food riots, his February 1992 coup, and his February 1999 ascension to power. He called the day's vote "the perfect victory," recalled a saying from his grandmother Rosa Inés about serving the people, and pledged to pursue "socialism, the reign of God on Earth, the reign of peace, of justice and equality, that which Christ came to announce two thousand years ago."

Ten years after rising to power and after a lifetime of trying to change Venezuela, Chávez was still seeking utopia – although his search was far from over.

Bart Jones, March 2009

# Acknowledgments

I am grateful to a number of people who helped nurture and make this book possible. A colleague at *Newsday*, Thomas Maier, first suggested to me the idea of writing a book, and served as a valuable, patient, and insightful guide throughout the process. I owe a debt of gratitude to Tom for his many hours of support and advice.

In a way the book's origin can be traced to 1992, when I first arrived in Venezuela and was befriended by a number of people. My greatest guide to discovering the country at the grassroots level was community organizer Xiomara Tortoza, who regularly took me into the barrios of Caracas and exposed me to a world where most of the population lives but commentators rarely venture. In addition to her friendship, Xiomara and her family offered me an invaluable education in what Venezuela is like from the viewpoint of the impoverished majority.

Another great friend, Americo Sanchez, made Los Bucares, his bed-and-breakfast in Mérida, available as a base of operations and provided countless hours of insightful conversation about Venezuela and the Hugo Chávez phenomenon — including some that took place during spectacular biking trips in the Andes.

My longtime journalism mentor, the Reverend Raymond A. Schroth, S.J., whom I had the good fortune to meet and study with as an undergraduate at Fordham University in the late 1970s, helped make it possible for me to tell the story of Venezuela and Chávez by connecting me with Steerforth Press. I thank Thomas Powers and Chip Fleischer at Steerforth for giving a first-time author a chance, and the entire Steerforth team including Christa Demment-González, Kristin Sperber, and Helga Schmidt.

Tom Roberts of *The National Catholic Reporter* was generous enough to send me on a reporting assignment to Venezuela to cover the critical 2004 recall referendum against Chávez, and the story I wrote was one of the seeds from which this book sprouted. The Fund for Investigative Journalism in Washington, DC, generously provided funding that helped me conduct some of the research for the book on subsequent trips back to Venezuela.

A number of people read parts of the manuscript and offered valuable suggestions, or assisted me in other ways, including much-needed encouragement when the project seemed overwhelming. They include my parents, Frank and Claire Jones, Nataly Lucena, Hildebrando Lucena, Lauli Iriarte, Greg Cascione, John Bingham, Lisa Sullivan, Eric Wingerter, William Camacaro, the Reverend Richard Dillon, Ed and Jo Connelly, Marta Harnecker, Daniene Byrne, Stacie Walker, Kathy McNeely, and Matilde Parada.

People in Venezuela were generous in granting their time for interviews and conversations; my thanks to Herma Marksman, Angela Zago, Fernando Ochoa Antich, Mario Ivan Carratú, Agustín Blanco Muñoz, and Francisco Arias Cárdenas, who spent hours talking about the development of the Bolivarian movement and made extensive efforts to arrange an interview for me with an extremely busy President Chávez. Also helpful in that regard were Maximilien Arvelaiz, Alex Main, and Willian Lara.

Special thanks to Charles Hardy, who at one time or another did many of the things mentioned above. Charlie patiently read through the manuscript, made valuable suggestions based on his own long experience in the country and skills as a writer, and was a faithful ally in tracking down information, materials, telephone numbers, and other contacts in Venezuela — never an easy task. He did all this while he was completing his own book about the country, which speaks volumes about the character of this former missionary priest.

My greatest thanks go to my wife, Elba, and my son, Frank, who valiantly put up with the long stretches I spent in the "little office" and offered the kind of support and acceptance that is critical to an undertaking of these proportions. Elba's devotion and love could not have been made clearer by the patience she demonstrated as she cared for Frank on her own during long periods that I was away. I can only hope my own love and adoration for her goes a little way toward making up for the time we spent apart.

# Notes

## Chapter 1: Hurricane Hugo

5    *first shots rang out*   Author's interviews, Aristóteles Aranguren, April 25, 2003; June 7, 25, 28, 2003; and February 3, 2005.

9    *happening in Venezuela*   Bart Jones, "Venezuela: Divisions Harden After Chávez's Victory," *National Catholic Reporter*, September 8, 2004.

14   *for that matter in the United States*   "Michael Skol Discusses Hugo Chávez's Resignation," National Public Radio, April 12, 2002.

14   *ward off evil spirits*   Charles Hardy, "Is Bush a Devil?" www.21stCenturySocialism.com, September 25, 2006.

15   *three times*   "Shocked! By Chávez," *The Wall Street Journal*, September 22, 2006.

16   *cut it off*   Helene Cooper, "Iran Who? Venezuela Takes the Lead in a Battle of Anti-US Soundbites," *The New York Times*, September 21, 2006.

16   *best-sellers chart*   Zach Dowdy, "Fiery Speech Gives Book a Boost," *Newsday*, September 22, 2006; Marc Santora, "A Scholar Is Alive, Actually, and Hungry for Debate," *The New York Times*, September 22, 2006.

16   *made such news*   Eugene Robinson, "Why the Firebrands Get Heard," *The Washington Post*, September 22, 2006.

17   *the uni-polar world*   Peggy Noonan, "The World Is as Hot as the Devil," *The Wall Street Journal*, September 23, 2006.

17   *alcoholic who found Jesus*   Michael Goodwin, "Dem Demagogues," New York *Daily News*, September 24, 2006.

17   *get away with it*   Ibid.

17   *watchdog group* FAIR   Jeff Cohen, "What's Wrong with Calling Bush a Devil?" www.alternet.org, September 23, 2006.

18   *think it was a joke?*   Santora, "A Scholar Is Alive."

18   *coup against him?*   Katrina vanden Heuval, "The Devil and Mr. Bush," *The Nation*, September 25, 2006.

18   *then consolidated power*   "Rumsfeld Compares Venezuela's Chávez to Hitler," Voice of America, February 2, 2006.

19   *to the people in Venezuela*   Cooper, "Iran Who?"

19   *worse, a bullet*   "Venezuela Oil Pimp Can Have UN," New York *Daily News*, September 21, 2006.

19   *No one survived*   James Anderson, "Fidel Castro Honors Victims of 1976 Cuban Plane Bombing," Associated Press, August 1, 1998; Andrew O. Selsky, "Documents: CIA Warned of Plane Bomb Plot," Associated Press, October 10, 2006.

20   *souls of the poor*   Jones, "Venezuela: Divisions Harden."

## Chapter 2: Roots of Rebellion

21   *his grandmother Rosa Inés Chávez*   Eleazar Díaz Rangel, *Todo Chávez*, (Caracas: Editorial Planeta Venezolana, 2006), page 32; Rosa Miriam Elizalde and Luis Báez, *Chávez Nuestro* (Havana: Casa Editorial Avril, 2004), page 21; author's interview, Aníbal Chávez, January 22, 2006; author's interviews, Flor Figueredo, January 22, 2006 and February 10, 2007.

21   *from leukemia*   Rangel, *Todo Chávez*, page 32.

22   *pair of shoes*   Author's interview, Flor Figueredo, January 22, 2006.

23   *spider shapes*   Elizalde and Báez, *Chávez Nuestro*, page 34.

23   *were their bats*   Author's interview Aníbal Chávez; author's interview, Flor Figueredo; author's interview, Narcisco Chávez, January 24, 2006.

23   *but very happy*   Elizalde and Báz, *Chávez Nuestro*, page 317.

24   *an entire universe*   Ibid.

24   *buy him supplies*   Ibid., pages 35–36.

24   *ward off a beating*   Author's interview, Aníbal Chávez.

24   *passed on the street*   Author's interview, Herma Marksman, January 7, 2006; Cristina Marcano and Alberto Barrera Tyszka, *Hugo Chávez Sin Uniforme*, ( Caracas: Grupo Editorial Random House Mondadori, 2004), page 38.

24   *they stopped talking*   Author's interview, Herma Marksman; Marcano and Barrera Tyszka, *Hugo Chávez*, page 322.

25   *did not speak, no.*   Author's interview, Hugo Chávez, April 30, 2007.

25   *on the streets*   Author's interview, Adán Chávez, April 25, 2007.

25   *Hugo's fifth-grade teacher*   Elizalde and Báez, *Chávez Nuestro*, page 24.

25   *became a state governor*   Ibid., page 336; Marcano and Barrera Tyszka, *Hugo Chávez*, page 66.

25   arañas *on the streets, too*   Elizalde and Báez, *Chávez Nuestro*, page 23.

26   *the soul of my country*   Ibid., pages 318, 369.

26   *That never stops*   Ibid., pages 367–369.

27   *one of his slogans declared*   Daniel Charles Hellinger, *Venezuela: Tarnished Democracy* (Boulder, CO: Westview Press, 1991), page 26.

27   *to the homes of the poor*   Ibid.; Richard Gott, *In the Shadow of the Liberator: The Impact of Hugo Chávez on Venezuela and Latin America* (New York and London: Verso, 2000), page 121.

28   *on fence posts*   Elizalde and Báez, *Chávez Nuestro*, pages 21, 30–33, 312–316.

28   *"The truth liberated me," he said*   Aleida Guevara, *Chávez: Un Hombre Que Anda Por Ahí* (La Habana, Cuba: Ocean Press, 2005), page 83.

28     *An agrarian revolution . . .*     Agustín Blanco Muñoz, *Habla El Comandante*, (Caracas: Fundacion Catedra Pio Tamayo, 2005), page 65.

29     *the spirit of Maisanta*     Elizalde and Báez, *Chávez Nuestro*, page 79.

29     *and deep-set eyes, she said*     Ibid., page 60.

30     *higher than Switzerland's Matterhorn*     Bart Jones, "Charming Mérida a Mile-High Gem in Inland Venezuela," Associated Press, March 11, 1999.

30     *toward both leaders*     Elizalde and Báez, *Chávez Nuestro*, page 338.

30     *barely 19 percent of the population was literate*     Hellinger, *Venezuela: Tarnished Democracy*, pages 26–28.

31     *when he died in 1935*     Ibid., page 39.

31     *in this condition*     Ibid., page 37.

31     *three hundred more*     Ibid., page 85.

33     *an impassioned communist*     Marcano and Barrera Tyszka, *Hugo Chávez*, page 55.

33     *Che Guevara's diary*     Ibid., page 63.

33     *political motivation*     Author's interview, Hugo Chávez.

33     *converting Hugo Chávez to communism*     Author's interview, Wladimir Ruíz, January 23, 2006.

34     *Chávez never joined*     Marcano and Barrera Tyszka, *Hugo Chávez*, page 58.

34     *pitching techniques*     Author's interview, Hugo Chávez, April 29, 2007.

35     *a bridge*     Elizalde and Báez, *Chávez Nuestro*, page 332.

35     *I signed the papers*     Díaz Rangel, *Todo Chávez*, page 35.

35     *grasping everything he presented*     Author's interview, Manuel Felipe Díaz, January 23, 2006.

36     *military base in Caracas*     Elizalde and Báez, *Chávez Nuestro*, page 337.

36     *my true vocation*     Documentary film on Chávez's life transmitted by Venezolana de Television, August 13, 2004.

37     *I was liberated*     Elizalde and Báez, *Chávez Nuestro*, page 337.

## Chapter 3: A Revolutionary Is Born

39     *progressive ideas*     Marta Harnecker, "The Venezuelan Military: The Making of an Anomaly," *Monthly Review*, September 1, 2003.

39     *in December 1981*     Mark Danner, *The Massacre at El Mozote* (New York: Vintage, 1994).

39     *reach the higher ranks*     Harnecker, "Venezuelan Military."

39     *fresh social sensitivity*     Michael McCaughan, *The Battle of Venezuela* (New York: Seven Stories Press, 2005), page 61.

40     *he once said*     Marcano and Barrera Tyszka, *Hugo Chávez*, page 147.

41   *with George Washington*   Charles Hardy, *Cowboy in Caracas: A North American's Memoir of Venezuela's Democratic Revolution* (Willimantic, CT: Curbstone Press, 2007), page 83.

41   *he was the Liberator*   Jerome R. Adams, *Latin American Heroes: Liberators and Patriots from 1500 to the Present* (New York: Ballantine, 1993), page 45.

41   *an indulgent lifestyle*   Robert Harvey, *Liberators: Latin America's Struggle for Independence* (Woodstock, NY: Overlook, 2000), pages 61–62.

42   *shut down the schools*   Richard Gott, *Hugo Chávez and the Bolivarian Revolution* (New York and London: Verso, 2005), page 103.

43   *make it obey us*   Harvey, *Liberators*, pages 82–83.

43   *punishment against Chávez*   Yolanda Ojeda Reyes, "Ruegan Al Nazareno Por Un Milagro," *El Universal*, December 19, 1999.

44   *cook in her bed*   Harvey, *Liberators*, page 126.

44   *who were decapitated*   Ibid., page 124.

44   *Liberty or Death*   Ibid., page 176.

45   *battles and skirmishes*   Ibid., page 227.

45   *at his feet*   McCaughan, *Battle of Venezuela*, page 44.

46   *vacillating and autocratic style*   Hellinger, *Venezuela: Tarnished Democracy*, page 19.

46   *met as he fled*   Adams, *Latin American Heroes*, page 52; Harvey, *Liberators*, pages 262–263.

48   *ignorance and disease*   Harvey, *Liberators*, pages 274–278.

48   *national project for Latin America*   Richard Gott, *In the Shadow of the Liberator*, page 108.

49   *Be careful, co-madre, what you say*   Rosa Miriam Elizalde and Luis Báez, *Chávez Nuestro*, pages 126–127.

49   *not fully liberated*   Daniel Hellinger, "Venezuela: Tarnished Democracy," page 23.

49   *many residents*   Author's interview, Hugo Chávez, April 29, 2007.

50   *there is coldness*   Ibid.

50   *the Great Bolívar*   Marcano and Barrerra Tyszka, *Hugo Chávez*, page 32.

50   *belongs to us*   Ibid., pages 73–74.

50   *for those people*   Ibid.

51   *bilateral trade with the Soviet Union*   Richard Gott, *In the Shadow of the Liberator*, page 91.

51   *traveled to Ayacucho*   Agustín Blanco Muñoz, *Habla El Comandante*, pages 42–43.

52   *seventeen years later*   Elizalde and Báez, *Chávez Nuestro*, pages 341–342.

52  *beneficiaries of his reforms*   Gott, *In the Shadow*, page 92.

52  *saw the revolution in action*   Blanco Muñoz, *Habla El Comandante*, page 44.

53  *women use cosmetics*   Gott, *In the Shadow*, pages 89–90.

53  *told interviewer Agustín Blanco Muñoz in 1995*   Blanco Muñoz, *Habla El Comandante*, page 44.

54  *only we knew*   Elizalde and Báez, *Chávez Nuestro*, page 339.

54  *spoke and acted differently*   Blanco Muñoz, *Habla El Comandante*, page 43.

55  *where I was headed*   Elizalde and Báez, *Chávez Nuestro*, pages 343, 349.

## Chapter 4: Testing the Waters

56  *the original class of 375 didn't survive*   Rosa Miriam Elizalde and Luis Báez, *Chávez Nuestro*, pages 337, 348.

56  *as a soldier*   Ibid., pages 343–344.

57  *an organized league*   Ibid., pages 344–345.

58  *I give you permission to play*   Ibid., pages 345–346.

58  *whenever they wanted*   Ibid., pages 346–347.

59  *Martí said about him*   Ibid., pages 347–348.

59  *set up a small library*   Ibid., page 349; Agustín Blanco Muñoz, *Habla El Comandante*, pages 49–50.

59  *he later commented*   Elizalde and Báez, *Chávez Nuestro*, page 349.

60  *cultural life of Barinas*   Ibid., page 348.

60  *the camp went dark*   Eleazar Díaz Rangel, *Todo Chávez*, pages 40–41; Blanco Muñoz, *Habla El Comandante*, page 55; Marta Harnecker, *Understanding the Venezuelan Revolution: Hugo Chávez Talks to Marta Harnecker* (New York: Monthly Review Press, 2005), page 29; Elizalde and Báez, *Chávez Nuestro*, pages 348–349.

60  *no reason to torture them*   Harnecker, *Understanding the Venezuelan Revolution*, page 29.

61  *impoverishes the majority?*   Elizalde and Báez, *Chávez Nuestro*, page 350.

62  *more than $150 billion*   Daniel Hellinger, *Venezuela: Tarnished Democracy*, pages 122–123.

64  *What else?*   Hugo Chávez's unpublished diary, October 28, 1977.

64  *small isolated groups*   Harnecker, *Understanding the Venezuelan Revolution*, page 29.

65  *at that moment*   Blanco Muñoz, *Habla El Comandante*, page 57.

65  *young second lieutenant* Author's interview, Wladimir Ruíz, January 23, 2006; Harnecker, *Understanding the Venezuelan Revolution*, page 29. Accounts vary as to the date of the meeting;

some place it in 1977. Author's interview, Pablo Medina, January 11, 2006; Marcano and Barrera Tyszka, *Hugo Chávez*, pages 78–80.

66    *ten years from now*    Harnecker, *Understanding the Venezuelan Revolution*, page 30

66    *don't fit with theirs*    Blanco Muñoz, *Habla El Comandante*, page 57.

66    *in the army all my life*    Ibid., page 57.

## Chapter 5: A Sacred Oath

67    *and was horrified*    Alberto Garrido, *Testimonios de la Revolución Bolivariana*, (Caracas: privately printed, 2002), page 52.

68    *different social system*    Ibid., pages 55–56.

69    *a socialist system," he stated*    Ibid., page 56.

69    *were entombed*    Ibid., page 59.

69    *overshadowed only by Democratic Action*    Daniel Hellinger, *Venezuela: Tarnished Democracy*, page 72.

70    *according to Bravo*    Garrido, *Testimonios*, page 13.

70    *inevitable in Venezuela*    Author's interview, Douglas Bravo, January 20, 2006.

71    *scant public support*    Hellinger, *Venezuela: Tarnished Democracy*, pages 110–111.

71    *considered Bolívar anathema*    Author's interview, Douglas Bravo.

72    *political and revolutionary education*    www.marxist.com interview with Alan Woods, April 20, 2005; Rosa Miriam Elizalde and Luis Báez, *Chávez Nuestro*, pages 37–38.

72    *we joined another party*    www.marxist.com interview with Alan Woods.

72    *dogmatic and sectarian*    Ibid.

72    *clean-cut cadet*    Elizalde and Báez, *Chávez Nuestro*, pages 38–39.

73    *in a 2004 interview*    Ibid., page 336.

73    *Nights of Hungary . . .*    Ibid.

73    *an area of insurgents*    Ibid.

73    *confessed his frustrations to Adán*    Eleazar Díaz Rangel, *Todo Chávez*, pages 41–42.

74    *religious order in Venezuela*    Author's interview, Nelson Sánchez, January 25, 2006.

74    *talking about him*    Díaz Rangel, *Todo Chávez*, page 42.

74    *That was the power*    Ibid.

74    *according to Adán*    Author's interview, Adán Chávez, April 25, 2007.

75    *not exactly a game*    Garrido, *Testimonios*, page 36.

75    *allowed her onto the base*    Author's interview, Elizabeth Sánchez, January 28, 2006; author's interview, Nelson Sánchez.

76   *a long-term project*   Author's interview, Douglas Bravo.

77   *navigated through those waters*   Author's interview, Jesús Urdaneta Hernández, December 22, 2005.

77   *meet with Bravo at all*   Aleida Guevara, *Chávez, Un Hombre Que Anda Por Ahí*, page 76.

77   *throws you in the garbage*   Agustín Blanco Muñoz, *Habla Jesús Urdaneta Hernández, El Comandante Irreductible*, page 147.

78   *industrial expansion projects*   Hellinger, *Venezuela: Tarnished Democracy*, pages 122–126.

78   *$34 a barrel*   Ibid.

78   *Brazil, Mexico, and Argentina*   Ibid., page 127.

79   *a liar, a demagogue . . .*   Elizalde and Báez, *Chávez Nuestro*, page 352.

79   *Chávez recalled*   Ibid., page 353.

80   *the fighter Ezequiel Zamora*   Ángela Zago, *La Rebelión de los Angeles* (Caracas: Fuentes Editores, 1992), page 58.

81   *how we started to organize*   Blanco Muñoz, *Habla Jesús Urdaneta Hernández*, page 320.

81   *they must be taken*   Agustín Blanco Muñoz, *Habla El Comandante*, page 295.

81   *Zamora in an earlier life*   Author's interview, Jesús Urdaneta Hernández; author's interview, Nedo Paniz, April 11, 2006.

82   *"rings" of security*   Díaz Rangel, *Todo Chávez*, pages 52–53.

82   *we wanted to say*   Ibid.

## Chapter 6: The Conspiracy Deepens

83   *a luckier stroke*   Eleazar Díaz Rangel, *Todo Chávez*, page 43.

83   *defense is preponderant*   Cristina Marcano and Alberto Barrera Tyszka, *Hugo Chávez Sin Uniforme*, page 92.

83   *the cadets*   Author's interview, Hugo Chávez, April 29, 2007.

83   *in the army*   Ibid.

83   *been fatal*   Ibid.

84   *homage to Zamora*   Agustín Blanco Muñoz, *Habla El Comandante*, page 126.

85   *fool higher-ups*   Author's interview, Hugo Chávez.

85   *Chávez once noted*   Blanco Muñoz, *Habla El Comandante*, page 126.

85   *almost all four years*   Díaz Rangel, *Todo Chávez*, pages 43–44.

85   *would not die*   Author's interview, Pedro Carreño, April 21, 2006; Marcano and Barrera Tyszka, *Hugo Chávez Sin Uniforme*, page 92.

86   *get far from mine*   Rosa Miriam Elizalde and Luis Báez, *Chávez Nuestro*, page 304.

86    *the capital and Ciudad Bolívar*   Author's interviews, Herma Marksman, January 7, January 18, March 3, March 20, 2006; Alberto Garrido, *Testimonios de la Revolucion Bolivariana*, page 157.

87    *to implement reforms*   Agustín Blanco Muñoz, *Habla Herma Marksman, Chávez Me Utilizó* (Caracas: Fundación Cátedra Pío Tamayo, 2004), page 63.

87    *get to know each other*   Ibid.

87    *to talk with Hugo*   Blanco Muñoz, *Habla Herma Marksman*, page 64.

88    *little by little*   Ibid., page 65.

88    *away from the house*   Garrido, *Testimonios*, page 159.

88    *prepare the meetings*   Author's interview, Herma Marksman, January 7, 2006.

88    *fall in love*   Agustín Blanco Muñoz, *Habla Jesús Urdaneta Hernández, El Comandante Irreductible*, page 246.

89    *in his free time*   Author's interview, Herma Marksman, January 7, 2006.

89    *betray him and the movement*   Blanco Muñoz, *Habla Herma Marksman*, pages 129–130.

90    *he lacked so much*   Author's interview, Herma Marksman, January 7, 2006.

90    *later broke bitterly with him*   Ibid.

90    *where he was going*   Ibid.

91    *according to Medina*   Author's interview, Pablo Medina, January 11, 2006.

91    *between the two men*   Author's interview, Herma Marksman, March 20, 2006.

92    *held around the country*   Agustín Blanco Muñoz, *Habla El Comandante*, page 126.

92    *for the weekend*   Díaz Rangel, *Todo Chávez*, page 56.

92    *salsa music*   Author's interview, Herma Marksman, March 20, 2006.

92    *fell into enemy hands*   Díaz Rangel, *Todo Chávez*, pages 55–56.

92    *even a coup*   Elizalde and Báez, *Chávez Nuestro*, page 41; Blanco Muñoz, *Habla Herma Marksman*, page 67.

93    *social justice for the poor*   Author's interviews, Francisco Arias Cárdenas, December 17–18, 2005.

93    *prolonged standoff*   Author's interview, Herma Marksman, March 20, 2006; Garrido, *Testimonios*, page 127.

94    *provoke a mass rebellion*   Author's interview, Francisco Arias Cárdenas, December 18, 2005; author's interview, Herma Marksman, March 20, 2006.

95    *of the economy*   Garrido, *Testimonios*, pages 125–126.

95    *time comes for a revolt*    Ibid.

95    *our possibilities of growing inside*    Ibid., pages 127–128.

95    *distance himself from Bravo*    Author's interview, Herma Marksman, March 20, 2006.

95    *his clandestine activities*    Díaz Rangel, *Todo Chávez*, page 61.

96    *I felt this presence*    Marta Harnecker, *Understanding the Venezuelan Revolution*, page 30.

96    *at least to Marksman*    Author's interview, Herma Marksman, March 20, 2006.

97    *word would leak out*    Blanco Muñoz, *Habla El Comandante*, page 128.

97    *Piaroa, Cumanagotos*    Díaz Rangel, *Todo Chávez*, pages 56–57.

## Chapter 7: First Betrayals

98    *Hugo Chávez with conspiracy*    Author's interview, Carlos Julio Peñaloza Zambrano, April 29, 2006.

99    *Arauca River thundered nearby*    Richard Gott, *In the Shadow of the Liberator*, page 42.

100    *the top superior*    Author's interview, Carlos Julio Peñaloza Zambrano.

100    *burned them alive*    Rosa Miriam Elizalde and Luis Báez, *Chávez Nuestro*, page 356.

100    *this wasn't my job," he recalled*    Ibid., pages 357–360.

101    *he told Chávez*    Ibid.

101    *almost hit my head*    Ibid.

101    *shoot arrows, too*    Ibid.

102    *for several days*    Ibid.

102    *for twenty years*    Ibid.

102    *understand their world*    Ibid.

102    *mutual adoration," Chávez said*    Ibid.

102    *living at their side*    Ibid., page 356.

103    *a few days later*    Ibid., pages 355–356.

103    *I finished finding myself*    Ibid.

104    *hoisted the banner*    Author's interview, Herma Marksman, January 12, 2007; Alberto Garrido, *Testimonios de la Revolucion Bolivariana*, page 166.

104    *full-page spread including photographs*    Author's interview, Herma Marksman, January 12, 2007; Garrido, *Testimonios*, pages 165–166.

104    *close to success*    Eleazar Díaz Rangel, *Todo Chávez*, page 45; Garrido, *Testimonios*, page 167.

104    *killing him if he resisted*    Agustín Blanco Muñoz, *Habla Herma Marksman, Chávez Me Utilizó*, pages 77–78.

105   *Chávez and his colleagues*   Ibid.

105   *Cristina and the message*   Ibid.

105   *incriminating documents they possessed*   Ibid.; author's interview, Herma Marksman, March 20, 2006.

106   *didn't find anything*   Díaz Rangel, *Todo Chávez*, page 47.

106   *he was convalescing*   Ibid.

107   *a shack in the llanos*   Ibid.

108   *You want a cup of coffee?*   Ibid., pages 48–49.

108   *I'm a Bolivariano*   Ibid.

108   *a high proportion of it short-term*   Daniel Hellinger, *Venezuela: Tarnished Democracy*, page 128.

109   *$4.4 billion in 1987*   Ibid., page 129.

109   *"Nothing has happened here"*   Ibid., page 144.

110   *an economic time bomb to dismantle*   Ibid.

110   *burned them*   Díaz Rangel, *Todo Chávez*, pages 57–58.

110   *I thought it was going to end*   Ibid., page 61.

## Chapter 8: The Massacre

111   *CAP's appeal is CAP himself*   Merrill Collett, "The Next Liberator? The Pérez Approach to Latin Debt Worries US Bankers," *The Atlantic Monthly*, February 1989.

112   *Let's Get to Work!*   Ibid.

113   *hundreds of Venezuelan soldiers*   George de Lama, "Quayle, Castro Could Make This Some Party," *Chicago Tribune*, February 1, 1989.

113   The New York Times *reported*   Mark A. Uhlig, "Venezuela Unrest: Lesson for Leader," *The New York Times*, March 6, 1989.

113   *down with champagne*   Bart Jones, "Report from Venezuela: Country's Version of Ferdinand Marcos," *Newsday*, October 17, 1994.

113   *Hirohito or something*   de Lama, "Quayle, Castro," *Chicago Tribune*, February 1, 1989.

114   *what was known as the Washington Consensus*   Fernando Coronil, *The Magical State: Nature, Money, and Modernity in Venezuela* (Chicago: University of Chicago Press, 1997), page 375.

115   *in Miami, Mr. President*   Daniel Hellinger, *Venezuela: Tarnished Democracy*, page 130.

116   *monthly salary*   Harold Olmos, "Violence Hits Venezuela Over Transport Price Increases," Associated Press, February 27, 1989.

116   *two cars were ablaze*   Margarita López Maya, "The Venezuelan Caracazo of 1989: Popular Protest and Institutional Weakness," *Journal of Latin American Studies*, February 1, 2003.

116   *what was happening*   Hardy, *Cowboy in Caracas*, page 32.

117   *nerve centers*   López Maya, "The Venezuelan Caracazo of 1989."

118   *sang the national anthem*   Ibid.

118   NO MORE DECEPTION   Ibid.

118   *"collective madness"*   Harold Olmos, "Long Lines Form at Food Stores, Government Tells People to Get Used to It," Associated Press, March 1, 1989.

118   *some stores*   López Maya, "The Venezuelan Caracazo of 1989"; Hardy, *Cowboy in Caracas*, page 27.

118   *the death penalty*   Hardy, *Cowboy in Caracas*, page 27.

119   *the scales, too*   Anthony Caplan, "Dozens Dead in Caracas Riots," Associated Press, February 28, 1989.

119   *die from starvation*   Harold Olmos, "Lines Form at Food Stores."

119   *rifles, pistols, and machetes*   Harold Olmos, "Continent in Crisis: Venezuela — Fabulously Rich, Desperately Poor," Associated Press, May 10, 1989.

119   *caviar, lobster, and salmon*   Ibid.; Don A. Schanche, "Venezuela Riots Not Political, Pérez Says," *Los Angeles Times*, March 4, 1989.

120   *capitalist dream for free*   Author's interview, Xiomara Tortoza, April 30, 2006.

122   *He was dead*   Author's interview, Iris Medina, April 4, 2006.

122   *top of his head was blown off*   Author's interview, Roy Carson, June 23, 2006.

122   *the contagious disease*   Agustín Blanco Muñoz, *Habla El Comandante*, page 182.

123   *perverse from every point of view*   Ángela Zago, *La Rebelión de Los Angeles*, page 89.

123   *unless we are attacked*   Ibid.

123   *twenty-nine hundred nationwide*   Coronil, *Magical State*, page 376; Hellinger, *Venezuela: Tarnished Democracy*, page 3.

123   *$1.5 billion in losses to businesses*   Hellinger, *Venezuela: Tarnished Democracy*, page 3.

123   *dead in Caracas*   Julie Skurski, "Bloody Riots Hit Caracas" and "The Streets Are Quiet but the Crisis Goes On," in *The Guardian* (New York), March 16 and April 5, 1989.

123   *"Yesterday, Caracas was Beirut"*   Fabricio Ojeda, "Beirut en Caracas," *El Nacional*, March 1, 1989.

## Chapter 9: Waiting in the Wings

125   *one foreign economist observed*   Don A. Schanche, "Venezuela Riots Not Political, Pérez Says," *Los Angeles Times*, March 4, 1989.

125   *the misery of the masses*   Harold Olmos, "Continent in Crisis: Venezuela — Fabulously Rich, Desperately Poor," Associated Press, May 10, 1989.

125 *nearly seven years later* Bart Jones, "He Once Tried to Overthrow Government; Now He's Running for Office," Associated Press, October 20, 1995.

126 *turn them over to the* DISIP *political police* Aleida Guevara, *Chávez, Un Hombre Que Anda Por Ahí*, pages 34–35.

126 *not cut out to be in this army* Ibid., page 35.

126 *not prepared to go on killing people* Agustín Blanco Muñoz, *Habla El Comandante*, page 183.

126 *Here there was never democracy* Guevara, *Chávez*, page 35.

126 *and popular movements* Marta Harnecker, *Understanding the Venezuelan Revolution: Hugo Chávez Talks to Marta Harnecker* (New York: Monthly Review Press, 2005), page 32.

127 *gunfire erupted* Anthony Caplan, "Dozens Dead in Caracas Riots," Associated Press, February 28, 1989.

127 *sparked the riots* Don A. Schanche, "Despite Riots, Venezuela Will Stress Austerity," *Los Angeles Times*, March 3, 1989.

128 *They didn't kill you, compadre* Rosa Miriam Elizalde and Luis Báez, *Chávez Nuestro*, pages 281–284.

128 *sick government and society* Blanco Muñoz, *Habla El Comandante*, page 183.

128 *More than a few died* James Brooke, "Caracas Journal: Venezuela's Two-Faced Boom, Riches and Riots," *The New York Times*, January 21, 1992.

129 *delivering information to him* Author's interview, Carlos Julio Peñaloza Zambrano, May 3, 2006.

129 *according to Peñaloza* Author's interview, Carlos Julio Peñaloza Zambrano, April 29, 2006.

130 *posted in the mid-1980s* Blanco Muñoz, *Habla El Comandante*, page 236.

130 *They had tricked us* Author's interview, Fernando Ochoa Antich, November 24, 2005.

130 *have the military force in hand* Blanco Muñoz, *Habla El Comandante*, page 467.

130 *Plan Ezequiel Zamora* Ibid., page 131.

## Chapter 10: Rebellion of the Angels

131 *dissuade the rebels* Author's interview, Mario Ivan Carratú, December 1, 2005.

132 *Arias went anyway* Eleazar Díaz Rangel, *Todo Chávez*, page 81.

132 *flirted with killing Chávez* Agustín Blanco Muñoz, *Habla Herma Marksman: Chávez Me Utilizó*, pages 104–106, 152–161; Blanco Muñoz, *Habla El Comandante*, page 134; Augustín Blanco Muñoz, *La Maisantera Chávez, Habla Luis Valderrama*, pages 171, 173–174, 181.

132 *Chávez told an interviewer* Blanco Muñoz, *Habla El Comandante*, page 138.

132 *threatened to create a rupture* Ibid., page 133.

133 *a hot dog vendor in Caracas told one reporter* John R. Engen, "Venezuela on Edge Amid Fresh Round of Protests and Violence," Associated Press, December 4, 1991.

133 *to even mention the word* Ibid.

133 *late January and early February* Díaz Rangel, *Todo Chávez*, page 86.

134 *General Francisco Visconti Osorio* Blanco Muñoz, *Habla El Comandante*, page 135.

134 *it was too late* Alberto Garrido, *Testimonios de la Revolucion Bolivariana*, pages 277–283.

134 *setting a car on fire* Blanco Muñoz, *Habla El Comandante*, pages 147, 222, 233–234, 482.

136 *determine their own destiny* Ibid., page 120.

136 *political and moral corruption* Michael McCaughan, *The Battle of Venezuela* (New York: Seven Stories Press, 2005), page 68.

136 *make the changes happen* Author's interview, Francisco Arias Cárdenas, December 18, 2005.

137 *So it was very simple* Author's interview, Francisco Arias Cárdenas, December 17, 2005.

137 *finally I left* Blanco Muñoz, *Habla El Comandante*, page 139.

137 *February 3* Ibid., page 140.

138 *the same pitch* Marta Harnecker, *Understanding the Venezuelan Revolution*, page 36.

138 *there was no turning back* Blanco Muñoz, *Habla El Comandante*, page 142.

138 *battle of Carabobo led by Bolívar* Author's interview, Francisco Javier Centeno, January 19, 2006.

139 *don't send me anything* Blanco Muñoz, *Habla El Comandante*, page 143.

139 *details of the plot in Caracas* Ibid., pages 267–268, 327.

140 *they would open fire* Ángela Zago, *Rebelión de los Angeles*, page 105.

141 *construct a real democracy* Author's interview, Francisco Arias Cárdenas, December 17, 2005.

143 *La Carlota military air base* Author's interview, Joel Acosta Chirinos, January 12, 2006.

144 *launching a coup themselves* Author's interview, Antonio Rojas Suárez, November 3, 2006.

145 *fled inside to take cover* Author's interviews, Mario Ivan Carratú, November 28, 2005; December 1, 2005; December 4, 2005; January 10, 2006.

145   *returned fire*   Author's interview, Francisco José Jara Ramírez, January 20, 2006.

146   *prepared to defend himself*   Author's interviews, Mario Ivan Carratú, November 28, 2005; December 1, 2005; December 4, 2005; January 10, 2006.

146   *get me out of here immediately*   Ibid.

149   *It was a terrible confusion*   Blanco Muñoz, *Habla El Comandante*, pages 489 and 222.

149   *It was about 2 A.M.*   Zago, *Rebelión*, page 142.

150   *personal courage to attack Miraflores*   Author's interviews, Fernando Ochoa Antich, November 24–25, 2005.

150   *not to do crazy things*   Blanco Muñoz, *Habla El Comandante*, page 247.

151   *loyalist troops would prevail*   George Gedda, "Bush Rallies to Pérez's Defense After Coup Attempt," Associated Press, February 4, 1992.

152   *like a desperate Kamikaze*   Blanco Muñoz, *Habla El Comandante*, pages 146, 484.

153   *broken promises*   Harnecker, *Understanding the Venezuelan Revolution*, pages 34–36.

153   *have told a different story*   Author's interview, Pablo Medina, January 11, 2006.

153   *or a different opinion*   Alberto Garrido, *Testimonios de la Revolucion Bolivariana*, pages 23–24.

155   *to fight hopelessly, to die or kill, isn't right*   Blanco Muñoz, *Habla El Comandante*, pages 471, 151.

155   *lay down their arms*   Author's interview, General Ramón Santeliz Ruíz, April 20, 2006.

155   *breaking into pieces*   Blanco Muñoz, *Habla El Comandante*, page 473.

156   *he thought to himself*   Rosa Miriam Elizalde and Luis Báez, *Chávez Nuestro*, page 364.

157   *That was live*   Blanco Muñoz, *Habla El Comandante*, page 261.

158   *a barrio in Barquisimeto*   Author's interview, Lisa Sullivan, December 10, 2005.

158   *have the political impact it did*   Author's interview, Fernando Ochoa Antich, November 24, 2005.

159   *the future of events*   Díaz Rangel, *Todo Chávez*, page 17.

## Chapter 11: Jail

161   *prevent suicide attempts*   Author's interview, Francisco Arias Cárdenas, June 17, 2006.

161   *you're a hero*   Cristina Marcano and Alberto Barrera Tyszka, *Chávez Sin Uniforme*, page 146.

162  *didn't fail like we thought*  Ibid., page 163.

162  *should be given a medal*  James Brooke, "Venezuelans Secretly Support Army Coup Plotters," *The New York Times*, February 9, 1992.

162  *victory by the insurgents*  Harold Olmos, "Government, Uneasy After Coup Attempt, Warns News Media," Associated Press, February 6, 1992.

163  *government were pulled*  Harold Olmos, "Newspapers and Magazines Raided; Retired General Arrested," Associated Press, February 8, 1992.

163  *most copies of the supplement*  James Brooke, "Venezuela, Wary After Coup, Censors Press," *The New York Times*, February 10, 1992.

163  *on the verge of perishing," he said*  Olmos, "Newspapers and Magazines Raided."

163  *death and damage*  James Brooke, "Venezuela, Wary After Coup, Censors Press."

163  *supposed to go*  David L. Marcus, "Crackdown on Media Angers Venezuelans," *The Dallas Morning News*, February 10, 1992.

163  *ordered stories removed*  Harold Olmos, "Police Close Newspaper as Media Crackdown Continues," Associated Press, February 10, 1992.

164  *"Democracy with censorship is dictatorship!"*  Steven Gutkin, "Journalists March in Venezuela Demanding Rights Be Restored," Associated Press, February 11, 1992.

164  *a popular hero*  Ibid.

164  *share power with anybody*  John R. Engen, "Venezuelans Make Coup Leader Hero, See Leadership Vacuum," Associated Press, March 11, 1992.

164  *our Saddam Hussein*  James Brooke, "Fiery Nationalism Drove Venezuelan Plotters," *The New York Times*, February 11, 1992.

165  *failed to kill the president*  Brooke, "Venezuelans Secretly Support Army Coup Plotters."

165  *are with you!*  Engen, "Venezuelans Make Coup Leader Hero."

165  *armored vehicles from leaving*  Author's interview, Francisco Arias Cárdenas.

165  *a bookshelf*  Rosa Miriam Elizalde and Luis Báez, *Chávez Nuestro*, page 25.

165  *ruefully noted*  Marcano and Barrera Tyska, *Hugo Chávez Sin Uniforme*, page 146.

166  *movement should take*  Blanco Muñoz, *La Maisantera Chávez*, pages 154, 197.

166  *his political philosophy*  Richard Gott, *In the Shadow of the Liberator*, page 127.

167  *between his sock and his shoe*  Elizalde and Báez, *Chávez Nuestro*, page 43.

167   *of the group*   Marcano and Barrera Tyszka, *Hugo Chávez Sin Uniforme*, page 176.

168   *hot, stagnant air*   Author's interview, Francisco Arias Cárdenas.

168   *according to Francisco Arias Cárdenas*   Ibid.

168   *peppers, tomatoes, and cucumbers*   Elizalde and Báez, *Chávez Nuestro*, page 137.

169   *letters he received*   Ibid.

169   *English classes*   Ángela Zago, *La Rebelión de los Angeles*, page 97.

169   *as Chávez saw it*   Aleida Guevara, *Chávez: Un Hombre Que Anda Por Ahí*, page 12.

169   *Chávez's recorded messages*   Author's interview, Jhannett Madriz Sotillo, January 18, 2006.

169   *amid their clothes*   Ibid; Blanco Muñoz, *La Maisantera Chávez*, pages 154, 197.

169   *taking advantage of the time*   Guevara, *Chávez*, pages 10–11.

170   *out of San Carlos*   Agustín Blanco Muñoz, *Habla El Comandante*, page 317.

170   *Venezuela's independence day*   Ibid., page 320.

170   *chatter of the parrots has grown*   Ibid., page 318.

171   *never had access to them*   Ibid., pages 320, 322.

171   *remain silent with the media*   Author's interview, Francisco Arias Cárdenas.

171   *it was their moment*   Elizalde and Báez, *Chávez Nuestro*, page 109.

172   *the rebellion had already started*   Blanco Muñoz, *Habla El Comandante*, pages 331–332.

172   *ten thousand feet*   Elizalde and Báez, *Chávez Nuestro*, page 110.

173   *rallied loyal units*   James Brooke, "Second Day of Violence Wracks Venezuela," *The New York Times*, November, 29, 1992.

173   *they were next*   Alberto Garrido, *Testimonios de la Revolucion Bolivariano*, page 292.

174   *"Pérez, get out of here!"*   David Beard, "Days After Coup Attempt, Many Still Hope for Democracy's End," Associated Press, December 2, 1992.

174   *comfortable with racist jokes*   David Beard, "Post-Coup Souvenirs, Sales Reflect Discordant Yuletide in Caracas," Associated Press, December 10, 1992.

174   *down to the masses*   James Brooke, "Caracas Journal: New in the Seat of Power: A Two-Fisted Radical," *The New York Times*, March 26, 1993.

174   *imposed by the IMF*   Ibid.

175   *an unjustified manner*   Blanco Muñoz, *Habla El Comandante*, page 331.

176    *responsible for the failure*   Ibid.

176    *he now "incarnated" Maisanta*   Elizalde and Báez, *Chávez Nuestro*, page 69.

176    *I am here*   Marcano and Barrera Tyszka, *Hugo Chávez Sin Uniforme*, page 160.

## Chapter 12: Secret Comandante's Good-Bye

177    *Marksman commented years later*   Agustín Blanco Muñoz, *Habla Herma Marksman, Chávez Me Utilizó*, page 230.

178    *the archive of that time*   Ibid., pages 13–14.

178    *gives him encouragement*   Blanco Muñoz, *La Maisantera Chávez*, page 150.

179    *that referred to her*   Bart Jones, "Long Maligned, Simón Bolívar's Lover Emerging as Heroine," Associated Press, September 17, 1998.

180    *interviewer Agustín Blanco Muñoz*   Blanco Muñoz, *Habla Herma Marksman*, page 284.

180    *lost the baby prematurely*   Ibid., pages 114–115, 174–175.

181    *with other tasks*   Author's interview, Hugo Chávez, April 30, 2007.

181    *never mentioned Marksman once*   Blanco Muñoz, *Habla Herma Marksman*, page 12.

181    *"political cadaver"*   Ángela Zago, *La Rebelión de Los Angeles*, page 27.

182    *congratulating him on his triumph*   Eleazar Díaz Rangel, *Todo Chávez*, page 93.

182    *the president's kitchen cabinet*   Kenneth Freed, "Venezuelan Bank Collapse Threatens Nation's Future," *Los Angeles Times*, February 14, 1994.

183    *that year's entire budget*   Bart Jones, "Judges Dismiss Charges in Major Banking Scandal," Associated Press, September 7, 1999.

183    *eliminated political enemies*   Patricia Márquez, "The Hugo Chávez Phenomenon," in *Venezuelan Politics in the Chávez Era: Class, Polarization and Conflict*, edited by Steve Ellner and Daniel Hellinger (Boulder, CO: Lynne Rienner, 2003).

183    *upper-middle-class scoundrel*   Ibid.

184    *shortage of water*   David Marcus, "No Soft Soaps," *The Dallas Morning News*, July 5, 1993.

184    *they run out*   Ibid.

184    *the myth of Chávez would deflate*   Cristina Marcano and Alberto Barrera Tyszka, *Hugo Chávez Sin Uniforme*, page 169.

185    *not to insist*   Díaz Rangel, *Todo Chávez*, pages 93–94.

185    *I'm ready*   Ibid., page 95.

185    *I cried again . . .*   Ibid.

186    *were a saint," Maduro said*    Rosa Miriam Elizalde and Luis Báez, *El Encuentro* (Havana: Oficina de Publicaciones del Consejo de Estado, 2005), page 26.

186    *Bolívar reincarnated*    Ibid.

186    *he told reporters*    Vivian Sequera, "Top Rebel Leader from February 1992 Coup Attempt Released," Associated Press, March 26, 1994; "Caldera Pardons Chávez, Other Coup Plotters" BBC, March 28, 1994.

## Chapter 13: On the Road

187    *what it is to be alone*    Rosa Miriam Elizalde and Luis Báez, *El Encuentro*, page 37.

188    *he recalled*    Elizalde and Báez, *El Encuentro*, page 34.

188    *strengthening it*    Marta Harnecker, *Understanding the Venezuelan Revolution*, page 42.

188    *crowds went wild*    David L. Marcus, "The Man Is the Message: Venezuelans Flocking to '92 Coup Attempt Leader," *The Dallas Morning News*, June 8, 1994.

188    BOLÍVAR LIVES AGAIN    Gabriel Escobar, "Venezuelan Ex-Plotter Turns Cult Politician; Cashiered Colonel Now Invoking Bolívar," *The Washington Post*, July 24, 1994.

189    *The only way is revolution*    James Brooke, "Freed After Unsuccessful '92 Coup, Rebel to Test Venezuela's Political Waters," *The New York Times*, May 20, 1994.

189    *against the* corruptos    Ibid.

189    *just to watch him walk by*    Marcus, "The Man Is the Message."

189    *not the voice of reason*    Escobar, "Venezuelan Ex-Plotter Turns Cult Politician."

189    *he'll be forgotten*    Ed McCullough, "Coup Leader Seeks Venezuelans' Hearts and Minds, and Maybe Their Votes," Associated Press, May 6, 1994.

189    *Avenida Bolívar today*    Cristina Marcano and Alberto Barrera Tyszka, *Hugo Chávez Sin Uniforme*, page 174.

190    *in the process of divorcing*    Ibid., page 172.

190    *Chávez boasted*    "Venezuela's Chávez Challenges President," UPI, October 21, 1994.

191    *"That's how I operate."*    Author's interview, Nedo Paniz, April 11, 2006.

191    *chicken bones*    Ibid.

192    *waiting to greet him: Fidel Castro*    Elizalde and Báez, *El Encuentro*, page 20.

192    *This man is invincible*    Ibid., page 31.

192    *I do not yet merit*    "Cuba Welcomes Would-Be Venezuelan Coup Leader with Open Arms," Agence France Presse, December 14, 1994.

193    *the average Venezuelan*   Elizalde and Báez, *El Encuentro*, page 40.

194    *refused to meet with him*   Author's interview, Nedo Paniz, June 25, 2006.

194    *rejected and condemned me*   Harnecker, *Understanding the Venezuelan Revolution*, page 61.

195    *because it interviewed me*   Aleida Guevara, *Chávez: Un Hombre Que Anda Por Ahí*, page 22.

195    *wouldn't have to meet with him*   Marcano and Barrera Tyszka, *Hugo Chávez Sin Uniforme*, page 167.

195    *mystique in the barrios*   Marcus, "The Man Is the Message."

195    *he had to go*   Eleazar Díaz Rangel, *Todo Chávez*, page 101.

195    *"Execute them. Now!"*   Gabriel Escobar, "Venezuelan Economy in Crisis," *The Washington Post*, June 27, 1994.

196    *value of the Bolivar*   Richard Sanders, "A Really Big Bank Bust; Venezuela's Crash of the Century Is Still Crashing," *The Washington Post*, March 19, 1995.

196    *any living Venezuelan*   Tim Johnson, "At 81, Venezuela's President Is the Grand Old Man of Politics," *The Miami Herald*, September 10, 1997.

196    *newly elected senator, told reporters*   Katherine Hutt, "New President to Blend Free-Market Reforms and Social Justice," Associated Press, February 2, 1994.

197    *military hospital window*   Bart Jones, "Revolutionary Days Over, Ex-Communists Assume Top Government Posts," Associated Press, March 28, 1996.

197    *"instrument of savage capitalism"*   Ibid.

198    *September 1996*   Fernando Coronil, *Magical State*, page 384.

198    *Antonio Esparragoza*   Humberto Márquez, ""Government Arrests Followers of Coup Leaders," Inter-Press Service, March 14, 1995.

198    *to avoid the DISIP's spying*   Elizalde and Báez, *El Encuentro*, page 35.

199    *would not recognize him*   Ibid., page 44; author's interview, Nedo Paniz, April 11, 2006.

199    *Mars is going behind its moon*   Vivian Sequera, "Astrologer Who Predicted Caldera's 'Death' Released from Custody," Associated Press, October 24, 1996.

199    *1997 looks dark for Caldera*   Ibid.

199    *this kind of statement*   Ibid.

201    *for her daughter*   "Indicated Ex-Venezuelan President Resigns from Party," Associated Press, June 14, 1994.

201    *on a yacht*   James Brooke, "Under House Arrest, Venezuela's Ex-Chief Takes Aim," *The New York Times*, September 22, 1994.

201    *the government could not touch*   "Government Accuses Jailed Ex-President of Controlling Swiss Bank Accounts," Associated Press, June 8, 1994.

201 *by Internet*  Bart Jones, "Home from Jail, Pérez Works to Clear Name, Secure Place in History," Associated Press, August 14, 1994; Bart Jones, "Former President 'Escapes' House Arrest via Internet," Associated Press, December 22, 1995.

202 *they wrote*  Agustín Blanco Muñoz, *Habla El Comandante*, page 178.

202 *would have been crazy*  Harnecker, *Understanding the Venezuelan Revolution*, pages 42 and 37.

202 *to carry out the survey*  Ibid., page 44.

203 *later told an interviewer*  Ibid.

203 *the pickup truck where Arias stood*  Mary Beth Sheridan, "From Coup Leader to Candidate: Many Venezuelans Hail Ex-Officer as Corruption Fighter," *The Miami Herald*, November 30, 1995.

204 *a pit of quicksand*  Harnecker, *Understanding the Venezuelan Revolution*, page 45.

204 *the obvious choice*  Bart Jones, "Failed 1992 Coup Leader Will Run For President," Associated Press, April 2, 1997.

204 *poverty and corruption*  Ibid.

204 *8 percent of the vote*  Raymond Collit, "Coup Leader to Seek Election," *Financial Times*, July 31, 1997.

## Chapter 14: Beauty and the Beast

205 *avoid serious thinking*  Diana Jean Schemo, "A Venezuelan Factory Line That Is Adept at Assembling Beauty," *The New York Times*, December 9, 1997.

206 *bordering on the absurd*  Ibid.

206 *"Not Just Another Pretty Face"*  *People*, September 7, 1998.

206 *John Travolta in a movie*  Jane Knight, "Catwalk Route to the Presidency," *The Independent*, March 26, 1995.

207 *employed as a spokeswoman*  Richard Gott, "The Cracker from Caracas," *The Guardian*, March 16, 1996.

207 *oil-rich but impoverished nation*  Bart Jones, "Miss Venezuela: Inside the World's Top Beauty School," Associated Press, November 18, 2007.

208 *he sniffed*  Bart Jones, "Venezuela's Favorite Politician a Former Miss Universe," Associated Press, January 31, 1996.

209 *"Jewish plot" against the nation*  Richard Gott, *In the Shadow of the Liberator*, pages 131–132.

209 *history of mankind*  Alberto Garrido, *Testimonios de la Revolucion Bolivariano*, page 182.

209 *in the Americas than that*  Ibid., pages 182–184.

210 *ambitious presidential projects*  Michael McCaughan, *The Battle for Venezuela*, pages 107–110.

210 *couldn't find anywhere*  Garrido, *Testimonios*, pages 185–186.

211  *MAS member*  Eleazar Díaz Rangel, *Todo Chávez*, page 100.

211  *an intellectual, a writer*  Ibid., page 101.

211  *alienated Ceresole*  *Venezuelan Politics in the Chávez Era*, edited by Steve Ellner and Daniel Hellinger, pages 45–46.

212  *you should know it*  Bart Jones, "In Venezuela, a Five-Second Kiss Can Land You in Jail," Associated Press, October 21, 1997.

212  *not have a girlfriend*  Ibid.

212  *Blanca Ibáñez*  Tim Johnson, "A Kiss Is Still a Kiss? Not in the Park," *The Miami Herald*, November 13, 1997.

212  *very sexy package*  Doug Camilli, "Trump to Wed? Venezuelan Paper Says The Donald Has Fallen for Beautiful Mayor of Chacao," *The Gazette (Montreal)*, September 6, 1997.

213  *Bolívar and Sucre*  Gott, *In the Shadow*, page 145.

213  *controlled by the MBR-200*  Margarita López Maya, "Hugo Chávez Frías: His Movement and His Presidency," in *Venezuelan Politics in the Chávez Era*, edited by Ellner and Hellner, pages 82–83.

213  *whom he appointed himself*  Ibid.

213  *exercise solidarity*  Margarita López Maya, *Del Viernes Negro al Referendo Revocatorio* (Caracas: Alfadil, 2005), page 170.

213  *with mixed success*  Ibid.

214  *Chávez's political success*  López Maya, in *Venezuelan Politics*, pages 81–83.

215  *the newspaper reported*  Raymond Collit, "Ex-Coup Leader Improves in Polls," *Financial Times*, February 24, 1998.

215  *$17.745 billion*  López Maya, *Del Viernes Negro*, page 214.

215  *5 percent of the GDP*  Ibid.

216  *A sea of hands went up*  Bart Jones, "Venezuelan Poor Praise Coup Leader," Associated Press, August 3, 1998.

216  *"poisoned chalice"*  Gott, *In the Shadow*, page 147.

216  *as an independent*  "Workers Party Withdraws Support for Former Miss Universe," Associated Press, August 2, 1998.

216  *Roman Catholic country*  Ray Collit, "Venezuela's Party Stalwart Eyes Victory Over Flamboyant Rivals," *Financial Times*, June 16, 1998.

217  *without hesitation*  Steve Ellner, "Report from Venezuela," *Commonweal*, October 23, 1998.

217  *going to be democratic*  Todd Robberson, "Venezuelan Front-Runner Worries US," *The Dallas Morning News*, December 5, 1998.

217  *pale in significance*  "Salas Römer Closes Fast on Chávez," *Latin America Regional Reports*, October 6, 1998.

217  *organized by Chávez*  Andrés Oppenheimer and Tim Johnson, "Venezuelan Candidate Had Marxist Rebel Link, Reports Allege," *The Miami Herald*, October 5, 1998.

218    *"shootable" if he won*    Diana Jean Schemo, "Renegade Officer Favored in Venezuela Election Today," *The New York Times*, December 6, 1998.

218    *possibility of violence*    Steve Ellner, "Man of the People: President Hugo Chávez Challenges Venezuela's Political Establishment," *In These Times*, March 21, 1999.

218    *fried babies for breakfast*    "Salas Römer Closes Fast on Chávez."

218    *Gadhafi with a bit of Castro*    Tim Johnson, "Former Coup Leader Emerges as Top Venezuelan Candidate," *The Miami Herald*, May 9, 1998.

218    *propaganda purposes*    McCaughan, *Battle for Venezuela*, page 41.

218    *go to jail*    López Maya, *Del Viernes Negro*, page 222.

218    *sizzling frying pan*    Ibid.

218    *despised the Adecos*    Ibid.

219    *calm their fears*    Bart Jones, "Former Coup Leader, Popular in Presidential Polls, Scares the Rich," Associated Press, April 22, 1998.

219    *any way she could*    Cristina Marcano and Alberto Barrera Tyska, *Hugo Chávez Sin Uniforme*, page 334.

220    *Yalies, too*    Bart Jones, "Venezuelans Hope to Get a New Leader," Associated Press, December 1, 1998.

221    *US bank accounts*    Bart Jones, "Former Venezuelan President Charged with Illegal Enrichment," Associated Press, April 14, 1998.

221    *ran out to greet him*    Steven Gutkin, "Thousands Greet Detained Ex-President as He Arrives in Hometown," Associated Press, October 31, 1998.

222    *gaining fourteen was possible*    López Maya, *Del Viernes Negro*, page 227.

222    *1,096,116 compared with 564,391*    Ibid.

222    *keeps going up*    Jones, "Venezuelan Poor Praise Coup Leader."

222    *the traditional parties*    "Yale-Educated Businessman Rejects Pact to Oppose Ex-Coup Leader," Associated Press, November 18, 1998.

223    *AD's request anyway*    López Maya, *Del Viernes Negro*, page 225.

223    *see if he could do it*    Tim Johnson, "Leader of Failed Coup Leads Venezuela Race," *The Miami Herald*, December 4, 1998; Steven Gutkin, "Venezuelans Try to Prevent Former Coup Leader's Presidential Victory," Associated Press, November 28, 1998.

223    *architecture professor said*    Tim Johnson, "Leader of Failed Coup Leads Venezuela Race."

223    *"but liberty"*    Sebastion Rotella, "Venezuelans Likely to Vote In a Strongman," *Los Angeles Times*, December 6, 1998.

223    *a communist*    Steven Gutkin, "Chávez Elected Venezuelan President," Associated Press, December 6, 1998.

223   *no one can stop it*   Bart Jones, "High Expectations May Haunt Venezuela's President-Elect," Associated Press, December 8, 1998.

224   *widest gap between rich and poor in the world*   Steven Gutkin, "Venezuela's Chávez Presents Agenda," Associated Press, December 7, 1988.

224   *United Nations Development Program*   Raymond Collit, "Chávez Capitalizes on Deep Divisions in Venezuelan Society," *Financial Times*, November 19, 1998.

224   *jets per capita in the world*   Ibid.

224   *for a very long time*   Diana Jean Schemo, "Renegade Officer Favored in Venezuelan Election Today," *The New York Times*, December 6, 1998.

225   *the only antibiotic we have*   Brook Larmer with Victoria Cunningham, "Col. Charming," *Newsweek*, November 23, 1998.

## Chapter 15: To Power

227   *What scientist can explain this?*   Clifford Krauss, "New Chief to Battle Venezuela's 'Cancer,'" *The New York Times*, February 3, 1999; Tim Johnson, "Leader of Failed Coup Leads Venezuela Race," *The Miami Herald*, December 4, 1998.

227   *accept it," he said*   Serge F. Kovaleski, "Venezuelan President Vows 'New' Revolution," *The Washington Post*, February 3, 1999.

227   *most inexcusable basket cases*   Tim Padgett, "Mystery Man," *The New Republic*, January 4, 1999.

228   *this century*   Steven Gutkin, "Venezuela's Hugo Chávez Begins Presidency with Controversy," Associated Press, February 27, 1999.

228   *constitutional framework," Dobbins said*   George Gedda, "President-elect Hugo Chávez Tells Clinton He's Not a Dictator-in-Waiting," Associated Press, January 27, 1999; "'Good Chemistry' at Chávez-Clinton Meeting," Agence France Press, January 28, 1999; Andrés Oppenheimer, "Chávez Says 'Right Things' to US Officials," *The Miami Herald*, January 28, 1999.

228   *on a good footing*   Oppenheimer, "Chávez Says 'Right Things.'"

228   *American–Venezuelan relation*   Bart Jones, "Former Coup Leader Calls for Change to Venezuela's Constitution," Associated Press, February 3, 1999; Krauss, "New Chief to Battle Venezuela's 'Cancer.'"

229   *checks and balances*   Gutkin, "Venezuela's Hugo Chávez Begins Presidency with Controversy."

229   *December presidential race*   "Heightened Criticism of Chávez's Alleged Authoritarianism," Associated Press, February 17, 1999.

230   *a committed democrat*   "Venezuela's Chávez to Convince World He Is Not Hitler, Mussolini," Agence France Press, January 11, 1999.

230   *pacify followers*   Laurie Goering, "Personality to Spare in Venezuela: New President Shows Signs of Jekyll and Hyde — And Both Are Popular," *Chicago Tribune*, March 10, 1999.

231 *the response was really beautiful*   Marta Harnecker, *Understanding the Venezuelan Revolution*, page 74.

231 *exactly what this country needs*   Larry Rohter, "In New Role, Venezuela Army Runs Clinics and Shops," *The New York Times*, April 13, 1999.

232 *enthusiasm and happiness*   Harnecker, *Understanding the Venezuelan Revolution*, page 82.

232 *role of military defense*   Deborah L. Norden, "Democracy in Uniform: Chávez and the Venezuelan Armed Forces," in *Venezuelan Politics in the Chávez Era*, edited by Steve Ellner and Daniel Hellinger, page 105.

232 *emergencies and natural disasters*   Laurie Goering, "Soldiers Take Pride in New Project: In War with Poverty, Venezuela Mobilizes Military to Motivate Change," *Chicago Tribune*, March 3, 1999.

233 *turn to the armed forces*   Harnecker, *Understanding the Venezuelan Revolution*, page 74.

233 *metastasized in all directions*   Ibid., page 63.

233 *repackaged and sold it*   David Marcus, "Chronicle of Corruption: Book of Political Scandals Lures Venezuelan Readers," *The Dallas Morning News*, February 21, 1993.

234 *a national sport*   Tim McGirk, "Hail to the Chief: His Landslide Victory Gives Chávez the Power to Set His Own Political Agenda: What Is It?" *Time*, May 10, 1999; Tim Johnson, "Populist President Stirs Hearts — And Some Fears," *The Miami Herald*, March 1, 1999.

234 *very affectionately*   Johnson, "Populist President Stirs Hearts."

235 *He seduced them all*   "Venezuela's Chávez Plays Ball with US Financiers, Baseball Stars," Agence France Presse, June 11, 1999.

235 *others did, too*   Sergio R. Bustos, "Did Chávez 'Make' It in New York," *Latin Trade*, August 1999.

235 *"President Jekyll and Colonel Hyde"*   Goering, "Personality to Spare"; "Venezuela's President Is Seeking Radical Change in His Country's Institutions. Nobody Is Quite Sure to What End," *The Economist*, June 5, 1999.

235 *Latin American strongman*   Goering, "Personality to Spare."

236 *not anti-communist*   Agustín Blanco Muñoz, *Habla El Comandante*, page 392.

236 *a bit of all of those*   Larry Rohter, "Venezuela's New Leader: Democrat or Dictator?" *The New York Times*, April 10, 1999.

236 *chaos and mismanagement*   Tim Padgett, "Mystery Man," *The New Republic*, January 4, 1999.

236 *arcane details of state spending*   Larry Rohter, "Venezuela's New Leader."

236   *Every human being deserves respect*   Todd Robberson, "Venezuelan President Riding Momentum of Support," *The Dallas Morning News*, June 6, 1999.

237   *escort the protestors out*   Steven Gutkin, "Chávez Supporters Stage Sit-In to Protest Media Coverage," Associated Press, September 23, 1999.

237   *seriously ill daughter*   Bart Jones, "Live from Caracas It's President Chávez — And You Can Talk to Him," Associated Press, July 23, 1999.

238   *Carlos Canache Mata*   Bart Jones, "Critics Say Chávez Wants to Use Assembly to Create Dictatorship," Associated Press, June 30, 1999.

238   *"outright defeat for Chávez"*   Steven Gutkin, "Chávez's Goals for Venezuela May Yet Derail; Mistrust Widespread Despite Vote," Associated Press, April 27, 1999.

238   *"superman"*   Laurie Goering, "Venezuela's Charismatic Leader on a Roll; But Some Worry as New President Adds to Powers," *Chicago Tribune*, April 25, 1999.

239   *15.4 percent*   Margarita López Maya, *Del Viernes Negro al Referendo Revocatorio*, page 338.

239   *in January 2000*   Ibid.

239   *asked what they want*   Bart Jones, "Hundreds Vie to Rewrite Venezuela's Constitution," Associated Press, May 20, 1999.

240   *Many constitutional experts agreed*   Richard Gott, *Hugo Chávez and the Bolivarian Revolution*, page 147.

241   *before it sinks completely*   Steven Gutkin, "Constitutional Assembly Convenes in Caracas, Declares Itself Sovereign," Associated Press, August 3, 1999.

241   *guilty of defamation*   Bart Jones, "Imprisoned Journalist in Venezuela: Bold Critic or Sloppy Reporter?" Associated Press, December 24, 1996.

241   *dismissed at will*   Gott, *Hugo Chávez and the Bolivarian Revolution*, page 182.

242   *often for years*   Steven Gutkin, "Constitutional Assembly Declares Judicial Emergency in Venezuela," Associated Press, August 19, 1999.

242   *James B. Foley said*   Barry Schweid, "Administration Registers Concern Over Curbs on Venezuela's Congress," Associated Press, August 26, 1999.

243   *build them up again*   Laurie Goering, "Personality to Spare."

243   *give birth to another*   Michael McCaughan, *The Battle of Venezuela*, page 88.

243   *being consummated*   Steven Gutkin, "Legislative Emergency in Venezuela," Associated Press, August 25, 1999.

244   *"a worse fate"*   "Chávez's Muddled New World," *The Economist*, November 20, 1999.

245   *believe it is the truth*   Serge F. Kovaleski, "Getting the Word Out; Venezuela's Populist Leader Says Opponents 'Lies' Have Led to US Misperception of His Reform Drive," *The Washington Post*, September 6, 1999.

245   *"verbal shootouts"*   Bart Jones, "Standoff Between Congress and Constitutional Assembly Resolved in Venezuela," Associated Press, September 9, 1999.

245   *tried to block reform*   Steven Gutkin, "Chávez Outlines Plan for 'Revolution' Through New Constitution," Associated Press, August 5, 1999.

245   *get what he wanted*   Steve Ellner, "A Clean Break," *In These Times*, October 31, 1999.

246   *overflowed with 25,000*   Bart Jones, "Venezuela's Prison System a House of Horror," Associated Press, December 26, 1996.

246   *didn't allow it*   Ibid.

247   *worker programs*   Ellner, "A Clean Break."

## Chapter 16: A Birth and a Tragedy

248   *broke the record*   Cristina Marcano and Alberto Barrera Tyszka, *Hugo Chávez Sin Uniforme*, page 222.

248   *I am not a tyrant*   Ibid.

249   *a coal substitute*   Steven Gutkin, "China Gives Full State Honors to Controversial Venezuelan Leader," Associated Press, October 11, 1999.

249   *"a true world power"*   Ibid.; Steven Gutkin, "Controversial Venezuelan President Visits Shanghai," Associated Press, October 10, 1999.

249   *like water to fish*   Gutkin, "Controversial Venezuelan President Visits Shanghai."

249   *beginning to "stand up"*   Richard Gott, *Hugo Chávez and the Bolivarian Revolution*, page 189.

250   *he began pitching baseballs*   Steven Gutkin, "Controversial Venezuelan President Visits Shanghai."

250   *the almost unheard-of gesture*   Marcano and Barrera Tyszka, *Hugo Chávez Sin Uniforme*, page 226.

250   *"I'm a baseball man myself"*   Ibid., page 225.

250   *"Guess who?"*   Ibid.

250   *there is no protocol*   Ibid., page 226.

251   *And it gets results*   Ibid.

251   *on four continents*   Ibid., page 228.

251   *shrieking outburst*   John Rice, "Castro and Chávez Meet on Baseball Diamond," Associated Press, November 19, 1999.

251   *his heir apparent*   Gott, *Hugo Chávez and the Bolivarian Revolution*, page 11; John Rice, "Chávez: Now Batting for Fidel?" Associated Press, November 20, 1999.

252   *Castro laughed from the dugout*   David Gonzalez, "Havana Journal: Game Produces 28 Hits, and Political Home Run," *The New York Times*, November 20, 1999.

252   *More alive than ever*   Ibid.

252   *are marching toward*   John Rice, "Castro and Chávez Meet on Baseball Diamond."

252   *they also had different policies*   Ibid.

253   *no squelching of domestic dissent*   John Rice, "Chávez: Now Batting for Fidel?"

253   *different ways of achieving it*   Ibid.

254   *closet Marxist*   Tim Johnson, "Chávez Puts Hard Edge on His Referendum Drive," *The Miami Herald*, December 5, 1999.

255   *as time passed*   Serge F. Kovaleski, "Venezuelan Voters Make President More Powerful," *The Washington Post*, December 16, 1999.

255   *Benito Mussolini*   Bart Jones, "Venezuela's President Headed for Victory on New Constitution," Associated Press, December 14, 1999.

255   *"devils in vestments"*   Larry Rohter, "Venezuela's New Leader: Democrat or Dictator?" *The New York Times*, April 10, 1999.

256   *for the referendum, he said*   Johnson, "Chávez Puts Hard Edge on His Referendum Drive."

256   *democratic credentials," he said*   Michael McCaughan, *The Battle of Venezuela*, page 94.

256   *to 67 percent*   Steven Gutkin, "Venezuelan Referendum More About Chávez than Constitutional Niceties," Associated Press, December 13, 1999.

256   *normally falls in a year*   Bart Jones, "Once a Palm-Treed Paradise, Caribbean Town a Cemetery After Landslides," Associated Press, March 22, 2000.

256   *840 tons*   Bart Jones, "A Rebuilding Program That Could Bring More Disaster," Associated Press, January 26, 2000.

257   *Many were dismembered*   Fabiola Sánchez, "Authorities Find Dozens of Mudslide Victims Floating in Caribbean Sea," Associated Press, January 6, 2000.

257   *in a cabinet meeting*   Bart Jones, "Chávez Denies Partying During Flood," Associated Press, January 17, 2000.

258   *Alvaro Palache*   Jones, "A Rebuilding Program."

259   *revolutionary government did*   Gott, *Hugo Chávez and the Bolivarian Revolution*, page 152.

259   *back up her allegations*   "Venezuela Official Says Journalist Should Ignore Subpoena from Political Police," Associated Press, January 19, 2000.

259   *nothing new in Venezuela*   "Rights Groups Welcome Venezuelan Shift on Abuses," Agence France Presse, January 20, 2000.

260   *lined people up and shot them*   Steven Gutkin, "Chávez Investigates Human Rights Abuses, Names Vice President," Associated Press, January 23, 2000.

260   *even sworn in*   Marcano and Barrera Tyszka, *Hugo Chávez Sin Uniforme*, page 200.

260   *he later stated*   Agustín Blanco Muñoz, *Habla Jesús Urdaneta Hernández*, page 130.

260   *the old regime*   Ibid., pages 130–131.

## Chapter 17: First Defections

261   *his high-voltage attacks*   Tim Johnson, "Chávez Puts Hard Edge on His Referendum Drive," *The Miami Herald*, December 5, 1999.

262   *more than an hour*   Tim Johnson, "Chávez's Speeches Hog TV, Soaps Pushed Off Screens," *The Miami Herald*, February 18, 2000.

262   *like living in a dictatorship*   Paul Hughes, "Soaps Are Squeezed Out as Chatty President Hogs Television Airtime," Reuters, March 2, 2000.

262   *I can even do surgery!*   Jon Lee Anderson, "The Revolutionary," *The New Yorker*, September 10, 2001.

262   nicknamed The Rifleman   Johnson, "Chávez's Speeches Hog TV."

262   *part statesman*   Kevin Gray, "Venezuela President Hugo Chávez: Loquacious and Proud of It," Associated Press, July 15, 2000.

262   *didn't always listen*   Author's interview, the Reverend Jesús Gazo, January 27, 2006.

263   *World War II*   Steve Ellner, "President Hugo Chávez of Venezuela," December 10, 1999.

263   *a clothing salesman commented*   Johnson, "Chávez's Speeches Hog TV."

263   *happening in Venezuela*   "Chávez Complains About the Media, But Newspaper Says He Talks Too Much," Associated Press, February 17, 2000.

263   *taken over the farm*   Anderson, "The Revolutionary."

263   *maybe their houseboy*   Ibid.

264   *500,000 jobs had been lost*   Steven Gutkin, "Former Comptroller Issues Scathing Report Against Venezuelan President," Associated Press, January 10, 2000.

264   *aren't exactly known for our patience*   Bart Jones, "Venezuela Clashes with US Over Reported Comments by Official," Associated Press, February 1, 2000; Steve Ellner, "Venezuela's Foreign Policy: Defiance South of the Border," Z *Magazine*, November 2000.

264   *as it did with Castro*   Ellner, "President Hugo Chávez of Venezuela."

264   *with the IMF*   Ellner, "Venezuela's Foreign Policy."

265 *old way of doing politics* "Chávez Criticizes Assembly for Lack of Consultation on Appointments," *BBC Summary of World Broadcasts*, January 8, 2000.

265 *were a "mistake"* Ibid.

265 *a national pastime* Steven Gutkin, "With Economy in Doldrums, Venezuela's President Still Rides High," Associated Press, May 9, 2000.

266 *he joked* Ibid.

266 *including Petkoff's operation* Richard Gott, *Hugo Chávez and the Bolivarian Revolution*, page 207.

266 *the Capriles family* Gutkin, "With Economy in Doldrums."

267 *turned into criminals* Tim Johnson, "Chávez Government Hit by Corruption Allegations, Leader Faces Major Crisis," *The Miami Herald*, February 12, 2000.

267 *in my opinion doesn't exist* Bart Jones, "Chávez, Fellow Coup Leaders Feud, Stir Division in Government," Associated Press, February 7, 2000.

267 *leading him to the cliff," he said* Tim Johnson, "Former Army Officers Challenge Chávez on Corruption," *The Miami Herald*, February 21, 2000.

267 *the Fourth Republic," he said* Ibid.

267 *'Yes, master.'* Bart Jones, "Venezuela's President Falls Out with Former Coup Leaders," Associated Press, February 15, 2000.

268 *for the last year* Jones, "Chávez, Fellow Coup Leaders Feud."

271 *Standing Tall in Venezuela* John Maisto, "Democracy Standing Tall in Venezuela," *Rochester Democrat and Chronicle*, April 17, 2000.

271 *"he's a psychopath"* Phil Gunson, "Is Hugo Chávez Insane," *Newsweek*, November 12, 2001.

272 *dangerously unhinged* David Adams, "Venezuelan Leader's Sanity in Question," *St. Petersburg Times*, December 17, 2001.

272 *the rejection permanent* Margarita López Maya, *Del Viernes Negro al Referendo Revocatorio*, page 234.

273 *any questions this afternoon* Alexandra Olson, "Journalists Refuse to Ask Chávez Questions," Associated Press, April 1, 2000.

273 *only doing their job* Luis Cordova, "Media-Venezuela: Chávez Has Stormy Relationship with the Press," Inter-Press Sevice, May 3, 2000.

273 *mental equilibrium* Tim McGirk and Cristina Hoag, "The Battle of the Colonels," *Time*, May 29, 2000; "Chávez Tiene Problemas de Equilibrio," *El Universal*, March 13, 2000.

273 *a traitor for vice president?* "Chávez Supporters Protest Ex-Colleague's Bid for Venezuela's Presidency," Associated Press, March 15, 2000.

274    *a rock knows that," he said*   Tim Johnson, "Chávez Supporters Predict a Landslide Re-Election," *The Miami Herald*, May 25, 2000.

274    *"Venezuelan golden age"*   Ibid.

274    *former personal secretary*   Larry Rohter, "Critics Question Legitimacy of Venezuelan Election Process," *The New York Times*, May 23, 2000.

275    *eighteen of twenty-four states*   López Maya, *Del Viernes Negro*, page 241.

275    *see how Chávez responds*   Timothy Warren, "Opposition Gains Could Force Chávez to Change His Leadership Style," Associated Press, August 1, 2000.

275    *process of revolutionary change*   Steve Ellner, "Renegade or Redeemer," *In These Times*, September 4, 2000.

276    *in concrete ways*   Ibid.

276    *vote for Chávez that Sunday*   Patrice M. Jones, "Venezuela's Chávez Wins Second Term, But Rest of Party Has a Harder Time," *Chicago Tribune*, July 31, 2000.

276    *García Morales said*   Phil Gunson, "In Venezuela, Military Sours on President," *St. Petersburg Times*, July 29, 2000; Phil Gunson, "Chávez's Military Maneuvers," *Newsweek*, July 31, 2000.

276    *the possibility is high*   Gunson, "In Venezuela, Military Sours."

277    *bad days are ahead*   Todd Robberson, "Venezuelan Leader Prevails Amid Unrest," *The Dallas Morning News*, July 31, 2000.

## Chapter 18: Oil Man

278    *at least fifty years*   Bernard Mommer, "Subversive Oil," in *Venezuelan Politics in the Chávez Era*, edited by Steve Ellner and Daniel Hellinger, page 140.

279    *$34.37 a barrel*   Steven Gutkin, "Venezuela Criticizes US House Move to Punish Oil Producers for High Prices," Associated Press, March 24, 2000.

279    *to $16 billion*   Fabiola Sánchez, "Venezuela's Chávez Basking in Spotlight as OPEC Summit Begins," Associated Press, September 26, 2000; Tim Johnson, "Oil Analysts Describe Chávez as a Catalyst in the Price Run-Up," *The Miami Herald*, March 2, 2000.

279    *in fifteen years*   Margarita López Maya, "Hugo Chávez Frías: His Movement and His Presidency," in *Venezuelan Politics in the Chávez Era*, edited by Ellner and Hellinger, page 86.

279    *flowed into the fund*   Richard Gott, *Hugo Chávez and the Bolivarian Revolution*, page 171.

280    *hard working and honest*   Bart Jones, "Oil Riches Curse, Bless Venezuela," Associated Press, January 17, 1995.

280    *Oil rotted it*   Ibid.

280    *drilled in 1914*   Fernando Coronil, *The Magical State*, pages 70, 75, 79.

280    *its top exporter*   Ibid., page 70.

281    *numerous office buildings*   Gott, *Hugo Chávez and the Bolivarian Revolution*, page 168.

281    *sixteen million people*   Daniel Hellinger, *Venezuela: Tarnished Democracy*, pages 122–123.

282    *violated human rights*   Leon Barkho, "Venezuela's Chávez Holds Iraq Talks," Associated Press, August 11, 2000.

282    *see me with Saddam Hussein*   George Gedda, "Iraq-Bound Venezuelan President Angers Washington," Associated Press, August 9, 2000.

282    *suited their purposes*   Steve Ellner, "Venezuela's Foreign Policy: Defiance South of the Border, *Z Magazine*, November 2000.

283    *riding a camel*   Leon Barkho, "Chávez Heads to Iraq, Breaking Isolation and Annoying Washington," Associated Press, August 10, 2000.

283    *worries Venezuelans much*   Steven Gutkin, "Chávez Visit to Iraq Provokes Little Outcry in Venezuela," Associated Press, August 10, 2000.

283    *those who act that way*   Daniel Cooney, "Venezuelan Leader Visits Indonesia," Associated Press, August 12, 2000.

284    *except Fidel Castro*   Larry Rohter, "A Man with Big Ideas, a Small County . . . and Oil," *The New York Times*, September 24, 2000.

284    *to their hotels*   Anwar Faruqi, "OPEC Summit Opens in Spruced Up Venezuelan Capital," Associated Press, September 26, 2000.

284    *prophet Muhammad*   Anwar Faruqi, "With Heavy Security, Venezuela Welcomes Princes and Presidents," Associated Press, September 27, 2000.

285    *Cacique restaurant*   Ibid.

285    *fourteen months or so*   Steve Ellner, "Venezuela and OPEC," *In These Times*, November 3–10, 2000.

285    *is justice*   Traci Carl, "Chávez Rallies OPEC Leaders," Associated Press, September 27, 2000.

285    *filed out of the auditorium*   Ibid.

285    *interest on foreign debt*   Scott Wilson, "Windfall from Rising Prices Unifies and Energizes OPEC," *The Washington Post*, September 26, 2000.

286    *between the two countries since 1997*   Alexandra Olson, "OPEC Members Wrap Up Summit Promising Kinder, Gentler Oil Cartel," Associated Press, September 29, 2000.

286    *against savage capitalism*   Ellner, "Venezuela and OPEC."

286    *twenty-five-year history*   Wilson, "Windfall from Rising Prices."

287   *"Welcome Fidel!"*   Alexandra Olson, "Castro, Chávez Visit Historic Sites, Opposition Parties Protest," Associated Press, October 27, 2000.

287   *where Chávez was born*   Chris Hawley, "Castro Visits Chávez's Old Stomping Grounds in Venezuela," Associated Press, October 28, 2000.

288   *no one who can substitute for you*   Larry Rohter, "Venezuelan Leader Finds a Teammate in Castro," *The New York Times*, October 30, 2000.

288   *a third of its oil needs*   Alexandra Olson, "Fidel Castro Signs Much-Criticized Oil Assistance Pact with Venezuela," Associated Press, October 30, 2000; Larry Rohter, "Venezuela Will Sell Cuba Low-Priced Oil," *The New York Times*, October 31, 2000.

289   *the land of the Liberator*   Fabiola Sánchez, "Cuba's Castro Showered with Praise, Honors in Venezuela," Associated Press, August 11, 2001.

289   *in Venezuela," he'd insisted*   Alexandra Olson, "Castro Applauds Chávez's 'Social' Revolution, Emphasizes Differences with Cuba," Associated Press, October 31, 2000.

290   *Fidel the Communist*   Rohter, "A Man with Big Ideas."

290   *the government of President Chávez*   James Anderson, "Venezuelan Government Extends Hand to Incoming Bush Administration," Associated Press, December 29, 2000.

**Chapter 19: First Revolts and the Return of the Iran-Contra Crowd**

291   *got through elementary school*   Juan O. Tamayo, "Chávez's School Plans Ignite Furor in Venezuela," *The Miami Herald*, February 27, 2001.

291   *or when they're open*   Author's interview, Lisa Sullivan, December 10, 2005.

291   *a total of one million*   Christopher Toothaker, "Chávez Strikes Back at Teachers Concerned About 'Revolutionary' Educational Program," Associated Press, January 21, 2001.

292   *5.2 percent in 2001*   Greg Wilpert, "Collision in Venezuela," *New Left Review*, May–June 2003.

292   *sixteen hundred families*   Larry Rohter, "Caracas Journal: Salutes, Some Skeptical, As Schools Go 'Bolivarian,'" *The New York Times*, November 9, 2000.

292   *extend to private schools*   Author's interview, Héctor Navarro, August 9, 2006.

292   *his teenage students*   Ibid.

293   *supervisor number one*   Cristina Marcano and Alberto Barrera Tyszka, *Hugo Chávez Sin Uniforme*, pages 210–211.

293   *77 percent*   Steve Ellner, "Organized Labor and the Challenge of Chavismo," in *Venezuelan Politics in the Chávez Era*, edited by Steve Ellner and Daniel Hellinger, page 162.

294 *minister of the interior in early* 2002   Daniel Hellinger, "Political Overview: The Breakdown of *Puntofijismo* and the Rise of *Chavismo*," in ibid., page 48.

294 *eventually joined a circle*   Michael McCaughan, *The Battle of Venezuela*, page 108.

295 *endangered harpy*   Bart Jones, "Indians Fight to Save Gold-Rich Amazon Paradise," Associated Press, August 11, 1998.

295 *toppled at least thirty*   Christopher Toothaker, "Chávez to Talk with Indigenous Tribe Blamed for Knocking Down Power Lines," Associated Press, October 22, 2000.

297 *he said in English*   Christopher Toothaker, "Venezuela's Chávez Clarifies His Remarks," Associated Press, November 3, 2001.

297 *watch what you say*   Scott Wilson, "Chávez Turns Caracas from US Ally to Critic; Supporters Urge Venezuelan to Chance Approach," *The Washington Post*, November 22, 2001.

297 *relations with Venezuela*   Christina Hoag and Tim Johnson, "Chávez Testing US Ties," *The Miami Herald*, November 6, 2001.

297 *to November 7*   Conn Hallinan, "The Scent of Another Coup," *San Francisco Examiner*, December 29, 2001.

297 *the meeting was over*   Eva Golinger, *El Código Chávez: Descifrando la Intervención de los Estados Unidos en Venezuela* (Havana: Editorial De Ciencias Sociales, 2005), page 69; Miguel Bonasso, "Anatomia Intima de un Golpe Contado por Chávez," *Pagina* 12, June 1, 2003.

298 *totalitarian trademarks of dictatorships*   William Finnegan, "Castro's Shadow: America's Man in Latin America, and His Obsession," *The New Yorker*, October 12, 2002; Johanna Neuman, "Anti-Communist Reich Given State Department Post," *Los Angeles Times*, January 12, 2002.

298 *"propaganda and disinformation outfit"*   "Back to the Future with Reich," *Chicago Tribune*, May 9, 2001.

298 *pillaged along the way*   Ibid.

299 *without salary*   Ken Guggenheim, "Lawmakers Spar Over Latin America Post," Associated Press, December 3, 2001.

299 *fire extinguisher*   Andrés Oppenheimer, "Bush Makes Recess Appointments, Defies Senate Democrats," *The Miami Herald*, January 12, 2002.

299 *one newspaper columnist wrote*   Mary McGrory, "Bush Brings Back Iran-Contra Affair," *The Washington Post*, July 10, 2001.

300 *set it on fire*   Mark Danner, *The Massacre at El Mozote*.

300 *"were not credible"*   Terry J. Allen, "Scandal? What Scandal? Bush Iran-Contra Appointees Barely a Story," *Extra! Fairness and Accuracy in Reporting*, September–October 2001.

300   *fabulous achievement*   Guy Gugliota and Douglas Farah,
      "12 Years of Tortured Truth on El Salvador; US Declarations During
      War Undercut by UN Commission Report," *The Washington Post*,
      March 21, 1993.

300   *high public office*   Marie Coco, "Bush Turns to Icon of Bloodshed,"
      *Newsday*, July 15, 2001.

301   *Jesuit priest Joseph Carney*   Frank del Olmo, "A Key Nominee's
      Troubling Past," *Los Angeles Times*, October 5, 2001.

301   *Ivy League variety*   Ibid.

301   *they established in Washington, DC*   Daniel Schorr, "History of
      the US Intervening in Latin American Politics in Order to Promote
      Stability Over Democracy," National Public Radio's *All Things
      Considered*, April 17, 2002; Christopher Marquis, "US Cautioned
      Leader of Plot Against Chávez," *The New York Times*, April 17, 2002.

301   *seeking political asylum*   George Garties, "Judge Told Human
      Rights Conditions Have Improved in El Salvador," Associated Press,
      December 5, 1986.

302   *big bully on the block*   Bart Jones, "Latin America's Leftist Tilt
      Roils DC; Three Reagan-Era Hardliners Return to Help Run Bush's
      Foreign Policy Team," *Newsday*, December 1, 2002.

302   *is an insult*   Bart Jones, "Three Tarnished Reagan Figures
      Have Hands in Bush Foreign Policy," *National Catholic Reporter*,
      January 10, 2003.

302   *messed with the media*   Terry J. Allen, "Scandal? What Scandal?"

302   *December 18, 2001, in Washington*   Juan González, "Familiar Fingers
      in Venezuela Mess," New York *Daily News*, April 18, 2002.

303   *preferential trade treatment*   Scott Wilson, "Chávez Regained Power
      While Plotters Bickered; Coup Was Not Planned, Ex-Leader Says,"
      *The Washington Post*, April 18, 2002.

303   *we don't like this guy*   Christopher Marquis, "Bush Officials Met with
      Venezuelans Who Ousted Leader," *The New York Times*, April 16,
      2002.

303   *dissident Venezuelan military officials*   Wilson, "Chávez Regained
      Power While Plotters Bickered."

303   *what would be illegal activities*   Bart Jones, "Like Old Days: US Role
      in Coup Under Scrutiny," *National Catholic Reporter*, May 31, 2002.

304   *in the Western Hemisphere*   Stephen Schlesinger and Stephen
      Kinzer, *Bitter Fruit: The Story of the American Coup in Guatemala*,
      revised and expanded (Cambridge, MA: Harvard University David
      Rockefeller Center on Latin American Studies, 2005).

304   *US covert activities*   Bart Jones, "US Funds Aid Chávez Opposition,"
      *National Catholic Reporter*, April 13, 2004.

304    *NED programs*    William I. Robinson, *A Faustian Bargain: US Intervention in the Nicaraguan Elections and American Foreign Policy in the Post–Cold War Era* (Boulder, CO: Westview Press, 1992), page 17.

305    *to $877,000*    Christopher Marquis, "US Bankrolling Is Under Scrutiny for Ties to Chávez Ouster," *The New York Times*, April 25, 2003.

306    *to 50 percent*    Fabiola Sánchez, "Law Tightens Grip on Venezuela's Oil," Associated Press, November 28, 2001.

306    *the magazine* América Economía    Gregory Wilpert, "Collision in Venezuela," *New Left Review*, May–June 2003.

306    *39¢ by 2000*    Ibid.

306    *the arable land*    Jorge Rueda, "Squatter Invasions, Chávez's Push for Land Title Law Has Venezuela's Farmers on Edge," Associated Press, August 12, 2001; Seth DeLong, "Venezuela's Agrarian Reform: More Like Lincoln than Lenin," *Washington Report on the Hemisphere* (Council on Hemispheric Affairs), February 25, 2005.

306    *owners living in Caracas*    Fabiola Sánchez, "Venezuelan President Warns Ranchers," Associated Press, March 7, 2001.

306    *70 percent of its food*    Karl Penhaul, "Venezuela Land Program Tills the Soil of Class Strife," *The Boston Globe*, March 31, 2002.

306    *importer in South America*    DeLong, "Venezuela's Agrarian Reform."

306    *the previous ratio*    Wilpert, "Collision in Venezuela."

306    *lowest figure in Latin America*    Ibid.

307    *the hands of large landowners*    Rueda, "Squatter Invasions."

307    *most of their land*    DeLong, "Venezuela's Agrarian Reform"; Wilpert, "Collision in Venezuela"; Gregory Wilpert, "Land for People Not Profit in Venezuela," www.venezuelanalysis.com, August 23, 2005.

307    *democracy in the United States*    Seth DeLong, "Venezuela's Agrarian Reform."

307    *the most fertile soil*    Christina Hoag, "Venezuelan Land Reform Raises Ire, Threats from Private Sector," *Houston Chronicle*, December 8, 2001.

308    *Colombian paramilitary organizations*    Sánchez, "Venezuelan President Warns Ranchers."

308    *two young sons*    Penhaul, "Venezuela Land Program Tills the Soil of Class Strife."

308    *were assassinated*    Wilpert, "Land for People Not Profit."

308    *130,000 families*    DeLong, "Venezuela's Agrarian Reform."

308    *other presidents in the region*    Reed Lindsay, "Clash Over Venezuela Land Law," *Newsday*, September 21, 2003.

309    *"Is Hugo Chávez Insane?"*    Phil Gunson, *Newsweek*, November 12, 2001.

310     *ghost towns*   Juan Forero, "Daylong Venezuelan Strike Protests Economic Program," *The New York Times*, December 11, 2001.

310     *completely paralyzed*   Christina Hoag and Nancy San Martin, "Caracas Comes to Screeching Halt in Protest of National Economic Policy," *The Miami Herald*, December 11, 2001.

310     *military intervention is inevitable*   Scott Wilson, "Though Poor Remain Loyal, Opposition to Chávez Grows," *The Washington Post*, November 26, 2001.

310     *his presidential term*   Felix Salmon, "Embattled Chávez Makes a Last Stand," *Euromoney*, January 2002.

310     *daily less important*   David Adams and Phil Gunson, "Chávez Steels Grip, But Hold Slips," *St. Petersburg Times*, December 10, 2001.

## Chapter 20: The Coup

311     *removal from office*   Scott Wilson, "Clash of Visions Pushed Venezuela Toward Coup," *The Washington Post*, April 21, 2002.

312     *these despotic regimes*   George Gedda, "Powell Voices Scorn for Hugo Chávez," Associated Press, February 5, 2002; Steve Ellner and Fred Rosen, "Chavismo at Crossroads," NACLA *Report on the Americas*, May–June 2002.

312     *events in Venezuela*   Peter Slevin, "Political Crisis in Venezuela Worries White House," *The Washington Post*, February 23, 2003.

312     *condemned the idea*   George Gedda, "US Strongly Opposes Venezuelan Coup," Associated Press, February 27, 2002.

312     *remove Chávez from power*   Ellner and Rosen, "Chavismo at Crossroads."

312     *communist government here*   Wilson, "Clash of Visions."

312     *Molina Tamayo recalled*   Ibid.

313     *$180 a month*   Jorge Rueda, "Revolt Rocks Venezuela's Oil Company, Crown Jewel of Its Economy and a Key US Oil Supplier," Associated Press, April 6, 2002.

313     *the whisky runs*   Juan Forero, "Labor Strife of a Different Color," *The New York Times*, March 19, 2002.

313     *the eggs it is producing*   Scott Wilson, "Strike Challenges Chávez; Venezuelan Protest Shuts Stores, Slows Oil Deliveries," *The Washington Post*, April 10, 2002.

313     *worth their time to try*   Author's interview, General Raúl Isaías Baduel, April 17, 2006.

314     *He is an autocrat*   T. Christian Miller, "Venezuelans Are Divided Over Chávez," *Los Angeles Times*, February 9, 2002.

314     *the sake of the country*   John Pilger, "Allende's Ghost," *Morning Star*, March 21, 2002.

314     *questioning Chávez's sanity*   Ibid.

314   *move to overthrow him*   www.venezuelafoia.com.

315   *oil tanker deliveries*   Fabiola Sánchez, "Stand-Off in Venezuela Oil Protest," Associated Press, April 5, 2002.

315   *of their eras*   Alexandra Olson, "Venezuela Leader Fires 7 Oil Execs," Associated Press, April 7, 2002.

315   *return the oil industry to Venezuelans*   Alexandra Olson, "Venezuelan President Moves to Crush State Oil Revolt as Unions, Business Gear Up for New Strike," Associated Press, April 8, 2002.

315   *"committed suicide"*   Ibid.

316   *they were*   Author's interviews, Ana Elisa Osorio, March 11, 2005; Aristóbulo Istúriz, April 15, 2006; Willian Lara, September 20, 2006.

316   *into office buildings*   Juan Forero, "General Strike in Venezuela to Extend Another Day," *The New York Times*, April 10, 2002.

316   *even bringing tents*   Hardy, *Cowboy in Caracas*, page 59.

317   *said nothing and left*   Maurice Lemoine, "Venezuela's Press Power," *Le Monde Diplomatique*, August 2002; Kim Bartley and Donnacha O' Briain, *The Revolution Will Not Be Televised*, documentary film, April 2003; *24 Horas*, Venevisión, April 12, 2002.

317   *leaders discussed it*   Sandra La Fuente and Alfredo Meza, *El Acertijo de Abril: Relato Periodístico de la Breve Caída de Hugo Chávez* (Caracas: Colección Actualidad, 2003), pages 59–60; Eleazar Díaz Rangel, *Todo Chávez*, page 146.

317   *"insurrectionist"*   Jorge Rueda, "Venezuela's General Strike Extended," Associated Press, April 10, 2002.

317   *the official said*   Laura Bonilla, "US Warns It Could Seek Diplomatic Isolation of Venezuela if Rights Violated," Agence France Presse, April 10, 2002.

318   *any part of it*   Author's interviews, Aristóteles Aranguren, April 25, 2003; June 7, 2003; June 25, 2003; June 28, 2003; July 2, 2003.

319   *by the opposition*   Author's interview, José Vincente Rangel, April 25, 2007.

319   *in a bar and talking*   Author's interview, Charles Shapiro, December 20, 2004.

319   *get rid of him*   Larry Rohter, "Venezuela's Two Fateful Days: Leader Is Out, and In Again," *The New York Times*, April 20, 2002.

320   *from reaching Miraflores*   José Vicente Rangel, testimony before Venezuela National Assembly, May 3, 2002.

320   *they could do*   Author's interview, José Vicente Rangel.

320   *the time for dialogue had run out*   General Lucas Rincón Romero, testimony before Venezuelan National Assembly, May 5, 2002.

320   *I don't know if I'm going to return," he said*   Author's interview with Linares's widow, Dalila Mendoza, April 15, 2006.

321   *How can I stop them?*   Angel Palacios, *Llaguno Bridge — Keys to a Massacre*, documentary film, 2004.

322   *combat broke out*   Author's interview, Pastora Peña, April 25, 2006.

323   *overcome the tear gas*   *Llaguno Bridge — Keys to a Massacre*.

324   *covered with blood*   Author's interview, Henry Rodríguez, April 15, 2006.

324   *fainted from the heat*   *Llaguno Bridge — Keys to a Massacre*.

326   *outside the country*   Díaz Rangel, *Todo Chávez*, page 151.

326   *he had joined the coup*   La Fuente and Meza, *El Acertijo de Abril*, page 45.

327   *the Bolivarian Circles*   *Llaguno Bridge — Keys to a Massacre*.

328   *standing on Baralt*   Francisco Olivares, *Las Balas de Abril* (Caracas: Colección Actualidad, 2006), pages 57–58; Sandra La Fuente and Alfredo Meza, *El Acertijo de Abril* (Caracas: Grupo Editorial Random House Mondadori, 2004), pages 116–117, 231.

329   *to that point: at least six*   *Llaguno Bridge — Keys to a Massacre*.

329   *in the Hotel Eden*   Olivares, *Las Balas de Abril*, page 155.

330   *demonstrators in the streets*   National Public Radio's *All Things Considered*, April 11, 2002.

330   *thousands of anti-government protestors*   CBS *Evening News*, April 12, 2002.

330   *"It was an ambush"*   Phil Gunson and David Adams, "Venezuela Nears Chaos, Dictatorship," *St. Petersburg Times*, April 12, 2002.

330   *as his supporters*   Juan Forero, "Uprising in Venezuela," *The New York Times*, April 13, 2002.

330   *the president's resignation*   Juan Tamayo, "Venezuela in Crisis After Deadly March," *The Miami Herald*, April 12, 2002.

330   *reaching his palace*   PBS *NewsHour*, April 12, 2002.

332   *abandoned its functions*   Héctor Tobar and Christopher Toothaker, "President Negotiates the Terms of His Resignation After Deadly Street Protests, Army Says," *Los Angeles Times*, April 12, 2002.

332   *massacred from the rooftops*   Ibid.

332   *This government is criminal*   Jorge Rueda, "National Guard Rebels Take Over Government Television, Reports Chávez Flown Out of Caracas," Associated Press, April 12, 2002.

332   *a peaceful demonstration*   Jorge Rueda, "Venezuelan President Hugo Chávez Resigns Under Military Pressure After Day of Violence in Caracas," Associated Press, April 12, 2002.

333   *never did*   Hugo Chávez, press conference in Miraflores Palace, April 15, 2002.

333   *Don't resign!*   Ignacio Ramonet, *Fidel Castro, A Two-Voiced Biography*, excepts published in *El Nacional*, April 8, 2006.

333 *see better in the darkness*   Rosa Miriam Elizalde and Luis Báez, *Chávez Nuestro*, page 158.

333 *he never got through*   Marta Harnecker, *Militares Junto Al Pueblo* (Caracas: Vadell Hermanos, 2003), page 285.

333 *"until death"*   Hugo Chávez, press conference in Miraflores Palace, April 15, 2002.

333 *and kill us*   Harnecker, *Militares Junto Al Pueblo*, page 289.

333 *factor in a bloodbath*   Ibid.

334 *New Year's Eve*   Ibid., pages 45–46; author's interview, General José Luis García Carneiro, April 17, 2006.

334 *come to fruition today*   La Fuente and Meza, *El Acertijo de Abril*, page 80.

335 *justify the coup against him*   Elizalde and Báez, *Chávez Nuestro*, pages 175–176; Aleida Guevara, *Chávez, Un Hombre Que Anda Por Ahí*, page 139; author's interview, Jorge Luis García Carneiro, April 17, 2006.

335 *against the president*   Guevara, *Chávez*, page 139; Elizalde and Báez, *Chávez Nuestro*, pages 175–176.

335 *probably by a businessman*   Lucas Rincón Romero, testimony before Venezuela National Assembly, May 5, 2002.

335 *provoke an international reaction*   La Fuente and Meza, *El Acertijo de Abril*, pages 139–140.

335 *Colonel Ronald McCammon*   Author's interview, General Jorge Luis García Carneiro, April 17, 2006; Elizalde and Báez, *Chávez Nuestro*, page 176.

336 *Navarro said*   Author's interview, Héctor Navarro, April 17, 2006.

336 *Vásquez, Velasco*   Marta Harnecker, *Understanding the Bolivarian Revolution*, page 179.

336 *without a son*   Elizalde and Báez, *Chávez Nuestro*, page 152.

336 *innocent people to die*   Ibid., page 162.

337 *Castro could offer*   Harnecker, *Understanding the Venezuelan Revolution*, pages 96–97.

337 *by killing himself*   Author's interviews, Aristóbulo Istúriz; Ana Elisa Osorio, August 29, 2006; Willian Lara, September 20, 2006; La Fuente and Meza, *El Acertijo de Abril*, page 48.

338 *I left as a prisoner*   Harnecker, *Understanding the Venezuelan Revolution*, page 97.

338 *"president prisoner"*   Author's interview, Ana Elisa Osorio, August 29, 2006.

339 *it's a coup, Hugo," he said*   Cristina Marcano and Alberto Barrera Tyszka, *Hugo Chávez Sin Uniforme*, page 252.

339 *fists in the air*   Kim Bartley and Donnacha O'Briain, *The Revolution Will Not Be Televised*, documentary film, April 2003.

339   *an airplane accident*   Author's interview, Aristóbulo Istúriz,
      April 15, 2006.

339   *there in the palace*   Harnecker, *Understanding the Venezuelan
      Revolution*, page 179.

339   *not produce a bloodbath*   Author's interview, Héctor Navarro.

340   *"This isn't ending here"*   Díaz Rangel, *Todo Chávez*, page 157.

340   *do without you?*   Ibid.

340   *"We will return"*   La Fuente and Meza, *El Acertijo de Abril*, page 65.

340   *we're going now*   Marcano and Barrera Tyszka, *Hugo Chávez*, page 247.

340   *in the backseat*   Díaz Rangel, *Todo Chávez*, page 158.

340   *soldiers stopped them*   Author's interview, Aristóbulo Istúriz.

## Chapter 21: The President Is Missing

341   *in silence," Chávez recalled*   Eleazar Díaz Rangel, *Todo Chávez*,
      page 158.

341   *inside the building*   Ibid.

341   *on their behalf*   Sandra La Fuente and Alfredo Meza, *El Acertijo de
      Abril*, page 66.

341   *so much as look at it*   Díaz Rangel, *Todo Chávez*, page 158.

342   *began to take notice*   Ibid., page 159.

342   *the room next door*   Ibid.

342   *twist my arm*   Ibid.

342   *according to the bishop*   Cristina Marcano and Alberto Barrera
      Tyszka, *Hugo Chávez Sin Uniforme*, page 252.

342   *the crimes he committed*   Díaz Rangel, *Todo Chávez*, page 159.

343   *whatever you feel is necessary*   Ibid.

343   *just a journalist*   Maurice Lemoine, "Venezuela's Press Power,"
      *Le Monde Diplomatique*, August 2002; Bartley and O'Briain, *The
      Revolution Will Not Be Televised*, 2003.

344   *use of the armed forces*   24 Hours, April 12, 2002, as shown in *The
      Revolution Will Not Be Televised*, 2003.

344   *radio and television*   Roberto Giusti, "El Ultimo Crimen de un
      Dictator," *El Universal*, April 12, 2002.

344   *make it past tonight*   Miguel Bonasso, "Anatomia Intima De Un
      Golpe De Estado Contado Por Chávez," *Pagina* 12, June 11, 2003;
      Díaz Rangel, *Todo Chávez*, page 161.

344   *a slip of paper*   Díaz Rangel, *Todo Chávez*, page 161.

345   *Move quickly*   Ibid.

345   *She could not speak*   Rosa Miriam Elizalde and Luis Báez, *Chávez
      Nuestro*, page 297.

345   *I am not going to resign*   Díaz Rangel, *Todo Chávez*, page 163.

345   *she told one of them*   Elizalde and Báez, *Chávez Nuestro*, page 299.

345  *Fidel would not abandon us*  Ibid.

346  *they are all in hiding*  Ibid., pages 303–304; "Venezuela: Chávez Daughter Denies on Cuban TV That Her Father Resigned," *BBC Monitoring International Reports*, April 12, 2002.

346  *to offer support*  Elizalde and Báez, *Chávez Nuestro*, page 299.

346  *dawn of a new country*  Angel Palacios, *Llaguno Bridge — Keys to a Massacre*, documentary film, 2004.

346  *president of the republic*  Eleazar Díaz Rangel, *Todo Chávez*, page 163.

346  *he has not resigned*  Ibid., page 164.

347  *I wish you all a good afternoon*  *Llaguno Bridge — Keys to a Massacre*.

348  *led by Pedro Carmona*  Larry Rohter, "Venezuela's Two Fateful Days: Leader Is Out, and In Again," *The New York Times*, April 20, 2002.

348  *one reporter wrote*  William Neikirk, "US Offers No Regrets Over Ouster of Chávez," *Chicago Tribune*, April 13, 2002.

349  *nothing to do with it*  National Public Radio's *All Things Considered*, April 12, 2002.

349  *the will of the people*  Neikirk, "US Offers No Regrets."

350  *Napoleón Bravo stated on 24 Hours*  *Llaguno Bridge — Keys to a Massacre*.

350  *dead or alive*  Author's interview, Aristóbulo Istúriz, April 15, 2006.

350  *one news report stated*  Fabiola Sánchez, "Interim Leader Sworn In; Latin Nations, Attorney General, Challenge Appointment, Claim Hugo Chávez Is Still President," Associated Press, April 12, 2002.

350  *looking for you, assassin*  Author's interview, Tarek William Saab, February 5, 2005.

350  *they might all be killed*  Ibid.

351  *allow food to enter*  *Llaguno Bridge — Keys to a Massacre*.

351  *only for the children*  Author's interview, the Reverend Arturo Peraza, January 6, 2005.

351  *Peraza later stated*  Ibid.

351  *"mild-mannered" and "respected"*  Sánchez, "Interim Leader Sworn In."

351  *"other calming influences"*  Richard Lapper and Andy Webb-Vidal, "Venezuelan Officers' Rebellion Forces Chávez Out," *Financial Times*, April 13, 2002.

351  *known as a conciliator*  Juan Forero, "Uprising in Venezuela: Man in the News: Manager and Conciliator — Pedro Carmona Estanga," *The New York Times*, April 13, 2002.

352  *he told the assembled elites*  Ken Dermota, "Venezuela Provisional Junta Announces Chávez Out, Carmona In as Interim President," Agence France Presse, April 13, 2002.

352     *almost impossible to miss*    Bart Jones, "Venezuelan Activist in NY; Chávez Foe Speaks Out," *Newsday*, July 8, 2004.

353     *will be left behind*    Héctor Tobar, "Venezuelan President Resigns," *Los Angeles Times*, April 13, 2002.

353     *stabbing the Constitution*    Eleazar Díaz Rangel, *Todo Chávez*, page 165.

353     *along the coast*    Díaz Rangel, *Todo Chávez*, page 165–166.

353     *I was ready to die*    Greg Palast, "Venezuela President Hugo Chávez: Interview," www.gregpalast.com, May 2, 2002.

354     *forests of Bolivia*    Author's interview, Hugo Chávez, April 29, 2007.

354     *talks with the others*    Díaz Rangel, *Todo Chávez*, page 166.

354     *saved my life*    Miguel Bonasso, "Anatomia Intima De Un Golpe De Estado Contado Por Chávez," *Pagina 12*, June 11, 2003.

355     *about 9 A.M.*    Rohter, "Venezuela's Two Fateful Days."

355     *to support the regime*    Richard Gott, *Hugo Chávez and the Bolivarian Revolution*, page 234; "Coup and Counter-Coup," Economist.com, April 15, 2002.

355     *Otero of* El Nacional    Ibid.

355     *clean up the mess*    "Hugo Chávez Departs," *The New York Times*, April 13, 2002.

356     *that awaits us*    Charles Hardy, *Cowboy in Caracas: A North American's Memoir of Venezuala's Democratic Revolution* (Wilimantic, CT: Curbstone Press, 2007), page 136.

356     *fanning themselves*    Christopher Toothaker, "Screams of Pain, Agony, Sorrow: The Dying and the Dead in Caracas Hospital," Associated Press, April 13, 2002.

357     *would interview him*    Author's interview, General Raúl Isaías Baduel, April 17, 2006.

357     *cried as they did*    Marta Harnecker, *Militares Junto Al Pueblo*, page 150.

357     *I can't take this situation any more*    Ibid.

357     *take Carmona prisoner*    Author's interview, General Raúl Isaías Baduel.

358     *dismantling of democratic institutions*    Elizalde and Báez, *Chávez Nuestro*, pages 178–181.

358     *recognized Carmona as head of state*    Ibid., pages 180–182.

359     *and the Venezuelan people*    Hugo Chávez, testimony before National Assembly, May 31, 2002.

359     *"My mother adores you"*    Díaz Rangel, *Todo Chávez*, page 168.

359     *I was dead*    Author's interview, Hugo Chávez, April 29, 2007.

359     *in the palace*    Ibid.

359     *"They are deceiving us"*    Díaz Rangel, *Todo Chávez*, page 168.

359     *an operation to rescue him*    Ibid.

361  *recalled one protester*   Hardy, *Cowboy in Caracas*, page 64.

362  *come to his defense*   Author's interview, Aristóbulo Istúriz,
      April 15, 2006.

362  *provoking pandemonium there, too*   Elizalde and Báez, *Chávez
      Nuestro*, pages 275.

363  *my life is in danger*   Héctor Tobar, "Venezuelan President Resigns,"
      *Los Angeles Times*, April 14, 2002.

363  *to offer protection*   Elizalde and Báez, *Chávez Nuestro*, page 215.

363  *for extra protection*   Ibid., page 216.

364  *"the tyrant has been deposed"*   Andrew Selsky, "Interim President
      Resigns in Venezuela After Thousands Protest to Restore Chávez to
      Power," Associated Press, April 13, 2002.

364  *what to expect on the island*   Author's interview, General Alí
      Uzcátegui Duque, April 18, 2006; Elizalde and Báez, *Chávez Nuestro*,
      page 289.

364  *was on the way*   Hugo Chávez, nationally broadcast speech,
      Miraflores Palace, April 14, 2002; Hugo Chávez, press conference,
      Miraflores Palace, April 15, 2002.

364  *rescuers cried*   Rosa Miriam Elizalde and Luis Báez, *Chávez Nuestro*,
      page 289.

365  *that still raged*   Hugo Chávez, press conference, Miraflores Palace,
      April 15, 2002.

365  *They were delirious*   Hardy, *Cowboy in Caracas*, page 65.

365  *they could not*   Patrice M. Jones, "Chávez Triumph Spotlights Deep
      Class Divisions," *Chicago Tribune*, April 21, 2002.

365  *didn't think it would be so soon*   Hugo Chávez, nationally broadcast
      speech, Miraflores Palace, April 14, 2002.

## Chapter 22: The Aftermath

366  *quite a long time*   NBC's *Meet the Press*, April 15, 2002.

366  *fully democratic manner*   Patty Reinert, "US Tells Chávez to Heed
      Reform, Democracy Calls," *Houston Chronicle*, April 15, 2002.

366  *so should President Chávez*   George Gedda, "Bush Says Venezuelan
      President Should Respect Democratic Values," Associated Press,
      April 18, 2002; Tim Johnson, "Bush Denies US Role in Venezuela
      Uprising," *The Miami Herald*, April 19, 2002.

367  *victims of misinformation," he said*   Juan Forero, "Chávez Offers
      Words of Reconciliation," *The New York Times*, April 16, 2002.

367  *played a role in the coup*   Scott Wilson, "Chávez Raises Idea of
      US Role in Coup; Interview Suggests Rocky Road Ahead," *The
      Washington Post*, May 5, 2002.

367  *"more adult supervision"*   Christopher Marquis, "Man in the News:
      Combative Point Man on Latin Policy — Otto J. Reich," *The New
      York Times*, April 18, 2002.

367    *we had at the time*    Tim Johnson, "Reich Rejects Call for Apology; US Criticized for Its Handling of Chávez Crisis," *The Miami Herald*, April 23, 2002.

367    *to the putsch*    US Department of State, Office of Inspector General, "A Review of US Policy toward Venezuela: November 2001–April 2002," Report No. 02-OIG-003, July 2002.

368    *intolerance for dissent*    Tom Barry, "Transitioning Venezuela," International Relations Center, Americas Program, December 2005.

368    *between 2002 and 2006*    Ian James, "AP: US Aid Stirs Venezuela's Suspicion," Associated Press, August 27, 2006.

369    *live with his wife*    David Adams, "Alleged Coup Leaders Land in South Florida," *St. Petersburg Times*, April 24, 2002.

369    *fish with bones*    Alexandra Olson, "Venezuela's President Urges Supporters to Accept Court Ruling," Associated Press, August 17, 2002.

369    *the next five thousand years*    Fabiola Sánchez, "Chávez Plans Offense to Indictment," Associated Press, April 19, 2002.

370    *Not Following the Laws*    T. Christian Miller, "Opposition Wishing for Ultimate End to Chávez," *Los Angeles Times*, July 7, 2002.

370    *possible aerial attack*    Ibid.

370    *almost naked blond*    Charles Hardy, *Cowboy in Caracas*, page 153.

371    *fighting its death all the way*    Ibid., page 159.

371    *lasted five years*    "Report: Chávez, Wife to Divorce," Associated Press, June 2, 2002.

## Chapter 23: Oil Strike

372    *coverage of the shutdown*    Juan Forero, "Strike Staged to Force Vote," *The New York Times*, October 22, 2002.

373    *embassy in Washington*    Phil Gunson, "14 Venezuelan Flag Officers Continue Protest Against Chávez," *Voice of America News*, October 23, 2002; Alexandra Olson, "Chávez's Ouster Sought in Venezuela," Associated Press, October 23, 2002.

373    *military dissidents*    Olson, "Chávez's Ouster Sought."

373    *screamed in delight*    Mark Stevenson, "Venezuela's Fate Hangs on Turf Wars," Associated Press, October 30, 2002; David Gonzalez, "In Venezuela's Capital, the Two Faces of a Bitter Divide," *The New York Times*, November 25, 2002; Gary Marx, "In Venezuela, Rebel Officers Now Heroes," *Chicago Tribune*, November 1, 2002; Scott Wilson, "In Two Caracas Plazas, Sides Taken on Chávez," *The Washington Post*, November 26, 2002.

374    *any country in the world*    Justin Delacour, "Can You Believe Venezuela's Pollsters?" *Narco News Bulletin*, February 6, 2003.

374    *a crazy eccentric is running it*    Wilson, "In Two Caracas Plazas."

374    *life was near normal*    Niko Price, "Venezuelan Opposition Launches Strike," Associated Press, December 2, 2002.

374  *the crucial oil industry*   James Anderson, "Venezuelan National Guard Disperses Protest," Associated Press, December 3, 2002.

374  *chased the strikers away*   Ibid.

375  *not anticipated it*   Richard Gott, *Hugo Chávez and the Bolivarian Revolution*, page 251–252.

375  *trying to stop it," he said*   Phil Gunson and David Adams, "Protests Take Toll on US Oil Source," *St. Petersburg Times*, December 6, 2002.

376  *blackouts were imminent*   James Anderson. "Venezuela Strike Ups Pressure on Chávez," Associated Press, December 9, 2002.

377  *news anchors blasted Chávez*   Frances Robles, "Chávez Ratchets Up His War Against Broadcast Media," *The Miami Herald*, February 1, 2003; Jorge Rueda, "More than 100,000 Converge on City Highways to Protest Government in Venezuela," Associated Press, January 18, 2003; Alexandra Olson, "Venezuelan President Threatens to Revoke TV Broadcasting Licenses as Protests Continue," Associated Press, January 13, 2003.

377  *Victor Ferreres said*   Juan Forero, "Venezuelan News Outlets Line Up with Foes of Chávez," *The New York Times*, December 22, 2002.

377  The New York Times *reported*   Juan Forero, "In Venezuela's General Strike, the Pinch Becomes Pain," *The New York Times*, December 10, 2002.

378  *of the workers" at* PDVSA   Eleazar Díaz Rangel, *Todo Chávez*, page 180.

379  *3 million a day*   Christopher Toothaker, "Venezuela Output Slowly Picking Up," Associated Press, January 24, 2003.

379  *Plan 1621*   Díaz Rangel, *Todo Chávez*, page 181.

380  *could set off an explosion*   Alexis Rosas, *El Rescate del Pilín León*, (Caracas: CENAL, 2004), page 63.

380  *going to make it*   Ibid., pages 93–99.

380  *"Gooooal!"*   "'Gooooal' — Chávez Celebrates Taking of Tanker Idled by Strike," Agence France Presse, December 22, 2002.

380  *difficult and dangerous*   Juan Forero, "Venezuela's Lifeblood Ebbs Even as it Flows," *The New York Times*, February 26, 2003.

381  *block reactivation*   Margarita López Maya, *Del Viernes Negro al Referendo Revocatorio*, page 275.

381  *a disaster — an explosion*   Gott, *Hugo Chávez and the Bolivarian Revolution*, page 252.

381  *this electronic war*   Hugo Chávez, *El Golpe Fascista Contra Venezuela* (Buenos Aires: Nuestra América, 2003), pages 295–296.

382  *Among them were*   Hardy, *Cowboy in Caracas*, page 122.

382  *four hundred thousand barrels*   Ginger Thompson, "Trickle of Oil Starts Flowing in Venezuela," *The New York Times*, December 29, 2002.

383  *open along the way*   Author's interview, Lisa Sullivan, February 12, 2007.

383   *for two weeks*   James Anderson, "Opposition Resumes Protests in
        Venezuela," Associated Press, December 26, 2002.

383   *people selling wood*   Author's interview, Lisa Sullivan,
        February 12, 2007.

383   *enough soda*   Ibid.

383   *toilet paper, and diapers*   Juan Pablo Toro, "Venezuelan Navy Ship
        Steams into Colombian Port to Take on Tons of Food, to Alleviate
        Effects of Strike," Associated Press, January 8, 2003.

384   *strike was ridiculous*   Author's interview, Lisa Sullivan.

384   *federal tax agency*   James Anderson, "Venezuelan Opposition March
        on Offices of Federal Tax Agency," Associated Press, January 7, 2003.

384   *stop paying the sales tax*   Frances Robles, "Chávez Ratchets Up His
        War Against Broadcast Media," *The Miami Herald*, February 1, 2003.

384   *once and for all*   Niko Price, "Venezuela Opposition Shuts Down
        Highway," Associated Press, December 14, 2002; Jorge Rueda,
        "Venezuela Bracing for Violent New Year," Associated Press,
        December 31, 2002.

385   COUP PLOTTERS!   Alexandra Olson, "Venezuela's Banks
        Abandon Two-Month Strike Against Chávez," Associated Press,
        January 29, 2003.

385   *opened their doors*   Christopher Toothaker, "Thousands of
        Venezuelan Bank Workers Join Nationwide Strike; Currency Value
        Plummets," Associated Press, January 9, 2003.

385   *still in effect*   Scott Wilson, "Venezuelan Opposition Softening;
        Demands Scaled Back as Government Is Said to Have Little Reason
        to Compromise," *The Washington Post*, January 15, 2003.

385   *chink in the armor*   Christopher Toothaker, "Venezuela Oil Output
        Slowly Picking Up," Associated Press, January 24, 2003.

385   *support for the walkout*   Fabiola Sánchez, "Venezuelan Strike Shows
        Signs of Waning," Associated Press, January 27, 2003.

386   *Chávez quipped*   Frances Robles, "Whatever His Foes Do, Chávez
        Grows Stronger," *The Miami Herald*, February 16, 2003.

386   *first four months of 2003*   López Maya, *Del Viernes Negro*,
        pages 274–275.

386   *$13.3 billion*   Díaz Rangel, *Todo Chávez*, page 180.

386   *our turn to bat*   Juan Forero, "How Venezuelan Outlasted His Foes,"
        *The New York Times*, February 7, 2003.

## Chapter 24: The Social Missions

389   *the United States had visited*   Bart Jones, "Venezuela: Divisions
        Harden After Chávez Victory," *National Catholic Reporter*,
        September 8, 2004.

389    *never been to the dentist*    Frances Robles, "Rise of Cuban Doctors Raises Questions for Venezuela's Chávez," *The Miami Herald*, August 19, 2003.

390    *one-fifth of all Cuba's physicians*    Ian James, "One-Fifth of Cuba's Doctors Working in Venezuela as Oil Flows to Island," Associated Press, July 13, 2005.

390    *Pap smear units*    David Adams, "Help for Poor Sways Voters in Venezuela," *St. Petersburg Times*, August 19, 2004.

391    *stethoscopes around their necks*    Robles, "Rise of Cuban Doctors."

391    *few Venezuelan doctors showed up*    Ibid.

391    *more in 2006*    Venezuela Planning and Development Ministry, www.sisov.mpd.gov.ve; author's interview, Luis Sandoval, Center for Economic and Policy Research, January 18, 2007.

392    *It really is miraculous*    Marc Frank, "Eye Surgeons Bring a Ray of Hope to the Caribbean," *Financial Times*, October 21, 2005.

392    *said program head Rafael Vargas*    Robles, "Rise of Cuban Doctors."

392    *saved three hundred lives*    Ibid.

392    *Mission Inside the Neighborhood*    Elizabeth M. Nunez, "Cuban Doctors, Clinics Don't Cure All Venezuelans," Associated Press, November 25, 2006.

392    *through the Barrio Adentro program*    Mark Weisbrot, Luis Sandoval, and David Rosnick, "Poverty Rates in Venezuela: Getting the Numbers Right," Center for Economic and Policy Research, May 2006.

392    *She never went back*    "Doctors Rouse Suspicions in Venezuela; Chávez Opponents Say Cubans Are Sent to Slums to Bolster President, Not Provide Care," *The Washington Post*, August 23, 2003; Brian Ellsworth, "Cuban Doctors Lend Hand in Venezuela; Chávez Backs Health Program in the Slums," *Houston Chronicle*, August 10, 2003.

393    *been a godsend*    Ibid.

393    *never seen here before*    Author's interview, Maria Barrio, April 11, 2006.

394    *a cage in Caracas*    Richard Gott, *Hugo Chávez and the Bolivarian Revolution*, pages 258–259.

394    *dance and soccer*    Ian James, "Revolutionary University or Political Ploy? School for the Poor Draws Controversy," Associated Press, July 28, 2005.

394    *their initiation in 2003*    Chesa Boudin, "Letter from Venezuela: Land of Chavismo," *The Nation*, November 16, 2006.

395    *between 41 and 44 percent*    Weisbrot, Sandoval, and Rosnick, "Poverty Rates in Venezuela."

395   *People in the North*   Gary Marx, "Chávez Touts 21st Century Socialism," *Chicago Tribune*, July 15, 2005.

397   *social theater*   Juan Forero, "As Venezuela Slides, the Poor Stand By Their Man," *The New York Times*, April 30, 2003.

397   *the state fulfilling its responsibilities?*   "The Essential Lesson of Chávez," *National Catholic Reporter*, September 8, 2004.

398   *little or no government assistance*   Reed Lindsay, "Chávez Gives Hope to Barrios," *Sun-Sentinel*, August 19, 2003; Gary Marx, "Venezuela's Poor Stick By Chávez; Many Still Have Hope Despite Lack of Progress So Far," *Chicago Tribune*, June 14, 2003.

398   *He loves the people*   Marx, "Venezuela's Poor Stick By Chávez."

399   *taking over the country*   Bart Jones, "Venezuela: Divisions Harden After Chávez Victory," *National Catholic Reporter*, September 8, 2004.

399   *a moment in history*   Juan Forero, "Visitors Seek a Taste of Revolution in Venezuela," *The New York Times*, March 21, 2006.

399   *that live in poverty*   Brian Ellsworth, "Chávez's Social Reforms Impress American Liberals; US Visitors Hail Attack on Poverty," *Fort Lauderdale Sun-Sentinel*, October 6, 2004.

399   *the other side of the story*   Ibid.

400   *the Bolivarian Revolution," he said*   Gregory Wilpert, "Delegation of Prominent US Progressive Leaders Visits Venezuela," www.venezuelanalysis.com, January 8, 2006.

400   *oversaw the ceremony*   "Media Misinforms About Situation in Venezuela, According to African-American Activists," www.venezuelanalysis.com, January 9, 2004.

400   *the legacy of Dr. King*   "Venezuela Honors Martin Luther King Jr. with School Named After Him," www.venezuelanalysis.com, January 10, 2004.

401   *the rest of his property*   José de Cordoba, "As Venezuela Tilts Left, a Rum Mogul Reaches Out to Poor," *The Wall Street Journal*, November 11, 2004; David Adams, "Rum Maker Concocts Mix for Social Reform," *St. Petersburg Times*, October 10, 2004.

401   *conference on social programs*   Ibid.

401   *"this would be a different country"*   Adams, "Rum Maker Concocts Mix for Social Reform."

## Chapter 25: The Recall

403   *two-to-one margin*   "US Pollsters: Venezuela President Could Lose Recall Referendum," Associated Press, April 2, 2003.

403   *Venezuelans against him*   Scott Wilson, "Venezuelans Pin Hopes on Chávez Referendum," *The Washington Post*, August 17, 2003.

403   *left-leaning university professor*   Juan Forero, "Chávez Urges Deference to Electoral Board," *The New York Times*, September 1, 2003.

403 *solving the problem* Scott Wilson, "Venezuelan Petition Drive Fair, Observers Say," *The Washington Post*, December 2, 2003.

404 *pressure people to sign* Steve Ellner, "Recall Fever Spreads South; Chávez Faces Third Ouster Attempt," *In These Times*, January 19, 2004.

404 *within a matter of days* Margarita López Maya, *Del Viernes Negro al Referendo Revocatorio*, page 280.

404 *legal right to protest* Steve Ellner, "Chávez Escapes Recall; But the Venezuela Opposition Escalates Its Tactics," *In These Times*, April 12, 2004.

405 *emergency vehicles* Fabiola Sánchez, "Venezuelan Rioting Spreads as Panel Rules Opposition Lacks Signatures Needed for Chávez Recall," Associated Press, March 2, 2004.

405 *in Caracas alone* Steve Ellner, "Chávez Escapes Recall; But the Venezuela Opposition Escalates Its Tactics," *In These Times*, April 12, 2004.

405 *three hundred injured* Francisco Olivares, *Las Balas de Abril*, page 26.

405 *signatures appeared the same* López Maya, *Del Viernes Negro*, page 286.

406 *the machinery of the state* Nora Boustany, "Signing on to Challenge Hugo Chávez," *The Washington Post*, July 9, 2004.

407 *a small fish representing Venezuela* Ellner, "Chávez Escapes Recall."

407 *walk away victorious* James Anderson, "Venezuelan President Hugo Chávez to Face Aug. 15 Recall," Associated Press, June 9, 2004.

407 *a dead heat* Gary Marx, "Chávez Rallying as Recall Vote Nears; Social Spending Boosts Appeal of Venezuelan Leader," *Chicago Tribune*, August 8, 2004.

407 *since he was first elected* Mary Beth Sheridan, "Turnout Massive in Venezuela's Vote on Chávez; Polling Hours Extended for Recall," *The Washington Post*, August 16, 2004.

408 *fell out in early 2002* Marta Harnecker, "After the Referendum: Venezuela Faces New Challenges," *Monthly Review*, November 2004.

408 *fomenting a riot* Bernard Arsonson, "Venezuela's Fake Democrat," *The New York Times*, August 14, 2004.

408 *opposed Chávez* Moisés Naím, "Hugo Chávez and the Limits of Democracy," *The New York Times*, March 3, 2003.

409 *infrastructure projects* Juan Forero, "Free-Spending Chávez Could Swing Vote His Way," *The New York Times*, August 14, 2004.

409 *freshness to the campaign* Harnecker, "After the Referendum."

410 *joined a UBE* Jonah Gindin, "Chavistas in the Halls of Power, Chavistas on the Street," NACLA *Report on the Americas*, March 2005.

410 *here's the proof* Sheridan, "Turnout Massive in Venezuela's Vote."

410 *everywhere they showed up* Jimmy Carter, "Venezuelan Election Trip Report," Carter Center, August 13–18, 2004.

410   *mainly in poor sectors*   Ibid.

411   *the owner refused*   Bart Jones, "Venezuela: Divisions Harden After Chávez Victory," *National Catholic Reporter,* September 8, 2004.

412   *where the elites ruled*   Ibid.

412   *not as a defeat*   Juan Forero, "Venezuela Votes by Large Margin to Retain Chávez," *The New York Times,* August 17, 2004.

412   *Major Defeat for Chávez*   Andrew Selsky, "US Polling Firm Lands in Middle of Venezuelan Referendum Dispute," Associated Press, August 19, 2004.

412   *act like an activist*   Ibid.

412   *Carter later told reporters*   Forero, "Venezuela Votes by Large Margin to Retain Chávez."

413   *"Serias Dudas"*   Carter, "Venezuelan Election Trip Report."

413   *J. Adam Ereli said*   Mary Beth Sheridan, "What Next for Venezuela? Economic Woes, Political Gridlock Are Seen Likely to Linger," *The Washington Post,* August 18, 2004.

413   *the government had won*   Juan Forero, "Opposition Rejects Audit Plans in Venezuela Recall Vote Dispute," *The New York Times,* August 19, 2004; Carter, "Venezuelan Election Trip Report," Carter Center, August 19, 2004.

413   *one news report said*   Forero, "Venezuela Votes by Large Margin to Retain Chávez."

413   *we have observed*   David Adams, "Venezuelan President's Recall Vote Today," *St. Petersburg Times,* August 15, 2004.

413   *to prevent multiple voting*   Carter, "Venezuelan Election Trip Report," Carter Center, August 13–18, 2004.

414   *supremely implausible*   Jennifer McCoy, "What Really Happened in Venezuela," *The Economist,* September 4, 2004.

414   *as collateral*   Sandra Hernandez, "Boca Raton, Fla. Electronic Voting System Maker Gambles on Venezuela Vote," *South Florida Sun-Sentinel,* July 9, 2004.

414   *outcome of the vote*   Gary Marx, "Chávez Foes Seek Wider Audit; Opposition Snubs Partial Review," *Chicago Tribune,* August 19, 2004; Brian Ellsworth, "A Crucial Vote for Venezuela and a Company," *The New York Times,* July 20, 2004.

414   *They do not*   "Hugo Chávez Wins," *The New York Times,* August 18, 2004.

414   *almost a pathology*   Jones, "Venezuela: Divisions Harden."

414   *act of suicide*   Ibid.

415   *hurry up*   Orlando Urdaneta Llama al Magnicidio desde Miami," Temas http://www.temas.com.ve/nodules.php?name:news&new_topic=9, November 2, 2004; Eva Golinger, "US Agression Towards Venezuela: The Rise of Black Propaganda and Dirty War Tactics

(Again)," www.venezuelanalysis.com, March 30, 2005; Phil Gunsun, "Prosecutor's Killing Hikes Fears," *The Miami Herald*, November 20, 2004; Karen Juanita Carrillo, "Political Terror Comes to Venezuela," *New York Amsterdam News*, December 1, 2004.

415   *sanctions against him*   Carrillo, "Political Terror Comes to Venezuela."

415   *the only way we have*   "Back to Venezuela's Future," *The Washington Times*, July 28, 2004.

## Chapter 26: Striking Back

417   *own annual report*   Michael Shifter, "Picking a Fight with Venezuela," *The Washington Post*, September 20, 2004.

417   *Equatorial Guinea*   Bart Jones, "US–Venezuela Rift: Sanctions Stress Relations Further; Bush Accuses Nation of Failing to Combat Human Trafficking, But Chávez Officials Say Move Is Political," *Newsday*, September 26, 2004.

418   *with Venezuela was Myanmar*   Steven Dudley and Pablo Bachelet, "United States Decertifies Venezuela as Ally in War on Drugs," *The Miami Herald*, September 16, 2005.

418   *in Fort Lauderdale*   Jane Bussey, "Rice Talks with Foe of President Chávez," *The Miami Herald*, June 7, 2005.

418   *sending the crowd into titters*   Steven Dudley, "US–Venezuela Relationship Reaches a Low," *The Miami Herald*, January 26, 2005.

419   *others are taking advantage*   Charles Hardy, www.cowboyincaracas. com, March 2004.

419   *"hyena"*   Andy Webb-Vidal, "Washington Crafts Policy to Contain Chávez 'Subversion,'" *Financial Times*, March 14, 2005.

419   *cheaper than starting a war*   Laurie Goodstein, "Robertson Suggests US Kill Venezuela's Leader," *The New York Times*, August 24, 2005.

419   *still walking the streets*   Colum Lynch, "Chávez Stirs Things Up at the UN; Venezuelan Leader Wins Cheers with Rant Against US," *The Washington Post*, September 17, 2005.

420   *a decision of survival*   Simón Romero, "Leftist Candidate in Ecuador is Ahead in Vote, Exit Polls Show," *The New York Times*, November 27, 2006.

421   *allied with the Sandinistas*   Filadelfo Aleman, "Nicaragua Asks Chávez to Stop Interfering," Associated Press, May 5, 2006.

421   *if Daniel Ortega won*   James C. McKinley Jr. and Jill Replogle, "Leftist Headed Toward Victory in Nicaragua," *The New York Times*, November 7, 2006.

422   *"Here comes the boss!"*   Alan Clendenning, "Chávez Blasts 'US Imperialism' as Social Forum Draws to Close," Associated Press, January 31, 2005.

422   *Lula is a good guy*   Ibid.

422  *revocation of broadcasting licenses*   Christopher Toothaker, "Venezuela's TV and Radio Stations Alter Programming as Government Phases in Media Law," Associated Press, January 27, 2005.

423  *pro-Chávez march at all*   John Dinges, "Letter from Caracas," *Columbia Journalism Review*, July–August 2005.

423  *a writer for the* Columbia Journalism Review   Ibid.

423  *wearing a press pass*   Ibid.

424  *Maria Pilar García-Guadilla*   Justin Delacour, "Bias Through the Back Door: Independent Source Selection in US Press Coverage of Venezuela," paper presented at Annual Meeting of the Western Political Science Association, Albuquerque, NM, March 16–18, 2006.

425  *copy of communist Cuba*   Pascal Fletcher, "Chávez Targets Strike Leaders; TV Stations May Be Closed; Venezuela Leader Threatens Jail Terms," Reuters, February 10, 2003.

426  *with the US press*   Steve Rendall, "The Repeatedly Re-Elected Autocrat," *Extra!* FAIR, November–December 2006.

426  *democratically elected president*   Justin Delacour, "The Op-Ed Assassination of Hugo Chávez," *Extra!* FAIR, November–December 2005.

426  *opinions about the Chávez government*   Ibid.

427  *what CNN is telling me*   Andrew Maykuth, "How Chávez Captures Hearts of US Citizens," *The Philadelphia Inquirer*, May 30, 2006.

427  *Catia in western Caracas*   Juan Forero, "Pirate Radio as Public Radio, in the President's Corner," *The New York Times*, March 8, 2004.

427  *by early 2004*   Ibid.

427  *storeroom of a housing project*   Ibid.

428  *(Who Wants to Be a Millionaire)*   Nikolas Kozloff, "Chávez Launches Hemispheric, 'Anti-Hegemonic' Media Campaign in Response to Local TV Networks Anti-Government Bias," *Washington Report on the Hemisphere* (Council on Hemispheric Affairs), April 28, 2005.

428  *the Venezuelan population*   Ibid.

428  *veteran journalist Aram Aharonian*   Ibid.

428  *anti-American propaganda*   Nikolas Kozloff, *Hugo Chávez: Oil, Politics, and the Challenge to the US* (New York: St. Martin's Press, 2006), page 129.

429  *we would all leave*   Humberto Márquez, "Media: Telesur, a Latin American TV Network, Is On the Air," *IPS*, May 24, 2005.

429  *'Viva Chávez'*   Juan Forero, "And Now, the News in Latin America's View," *The New York Times*, May 16, 2005.

429  *using the* llanero *harp*   Monte Reel, "In Venezuela, New Law Has Hip-Hop Now Giving Way to Flutes and Fiddles," *The Washington Post*, July 17, 2005.

430    *back on the airwaves again*    Juan Forero, "Venezuelan Strongman's New Gig: National Disc Jockey," *The New York Times*, October 3, 2005.

430    *at a single performance*    Reel, "In Venezuela, New Law."

430    *the American way of life, imperialism*    "Chávez Inaugurates Venezuelan Film Studio to Counter Hollywood 'Dictatorship,'" Associated Press, June 4, 2006.

430    *Christian Civic League in Maine put it*    John Christoffersen, "Bush Foe Makes Friends with Poor Americans Through Oil Program," Associated Press, February 23, 2006.

431    *"shrewd political theater"*    Mark Clayton, "A Congressman Brings Home the Fuel — from an Unorthodox Supplier," *The Christian Science Monitor*, November 25, 2005.

431    *grudgingly saluted it*    Pablo Bachelet, "Chávez Oil Deal Finds Eager Takers," *The Miami Herald*, December 12, 2005.

431    *you, President Chávez, are our angel*    "Venezuela's Chávez Denies Using Fuel Program as Political Tool," Associated Press, April 25, 2006.

431    *I really resented that*    Pablo Bachelet, "Chávez's Oil Recipients Having Second Thoughts," *The Miami Herald*, September 27, 2006.

## Chapter 27: Twenty-First-Century Socialism

433    *Bush the terrorist!*    Monte Reel and Michael A. Fletcher, "Anti-US Protests Flare at Summit," *The Washington Post*, November 5, 2005.

433    *among Latin Americans*    Larry Rohter and Elisabeth Bumiller, "Protestors Riot as Bush Attends 34-Nation Talks," *The New York Times*, November 5, 2005.

433    *the ones who buried it*    Ibid.

434    *gleeful outside provocateur*    Reel and Fletcher, "Anti-US Protests Flare at Summit."

434    *"public relations pounding"*    Andrés Oppenheimer, "Chávez Having Propaganda Field Day at US Expense," *The Miami Herald*, November 5, 2005.

434    *defeat on his face*    Patrick J. McDonnell and Edwin Chen, "Bush Exits Summit as Trade Talks End in Disagreement," *Los Angeles Times*, November 6, 2005.

434    *"Freedom!"*    Ian James, "As Chávez Warns of US Threat, Venezuelan Troops Stage Mock Coastal Assault to Prepare," Associated Press, November 3, 2005.

435    *Chávez's national security adviser*    Chris Kraul, "Chávez's Personal Militia May Have a Dual Purpose," *Los Angeles Times*, April 16, 2006.

435    *177 were made in North America*    George Gedda, "US Orders Ban of Arms Sales to Venezuela," Associated Press, May 15, 2006.

435    *fifteen helicopters*    Christopher Toothaker, "Chávez Kalashnikov Factory Stirs Fears," Associated Press, June 19, 2006.

436   *my dear gringo*   Fabiola Sánchez, "Chávez Begins Training Civilian Militia," Associated Press, April 19, 2006; Venezuela Information Office, "Venezuela's Defense Spending," http://www.rethinkvenezuela.com/downloads/milspend.htm.

436   *We are ready*   Johann Hari, "Chávez's Miracle Mission," *The Independent*, August 25, 2005.

437   *for social justice, for equality*   Ian James, "Socialism a Hard Sell for Some Venezuelans," Associated Press, September 5, 2005.

437   *when the car is moving*   Gary Marx, "Chávez Touts '21st Century Socialism,'" *Chicago Tribune*, July 15, 2005.

438   *paper and cardboard producer*   Jorge Martin, "Workers Struggle to Take Over a Paper Mill in Venezuela," www.venezuelanalysis.com, October 15, 2004.

438   *his detractors were skeptical*   "Venezuela's Government Expropriates Bankrupt Paper Company," Associated Press, January 19, 2005.

438   *75 percent of the arable land*   Christopher Toothaker, "Venezuela Promises to Grant 100,000 Plots of Land to Poor Farmers," Associated Press, January 4, 2005.

438   *it is pre-history*   Alice M. Chacon, "Venezuelan President Encourages Authorities to Implement Land Reform Law," Associated Press, January 9, 2005; Juan Forero, "'Venezuela Land Reform Looks to Seize Idle Farmland," *The New York Times*, January 30, 2005.

439   *Arbenz in Guatemala in 1954*   Steven Dudley, "Chávez Eyes Idle Lands, Raising Fears," *The Miami Herald*, January 22, 2005.

439   *the wild llanos*   Brian Ellsworth, "A Delicate Balance," *Fort Lauderdale Sun-Sentinel*, June 12, 2005.

439   *insensitive landowning elite*   Ibid.

440   *assassinated in the struggle*   Author's interview, Braulio Álvarez, February 15, 2007.

440   *Saudi Arabia's 260 billion barrels*   Natalie Obiko Pearson, "Chávez Says Initial Drilling in Orinoco Finds Deeper Deposits than Expected," Associated Press, August 11, 2006.

440   *before the reforms were adopted*   Mark Weisbrot, "The Failure of Hugo Bashing," *Los Angeles Times*, March 9, 2006.

440   *economic performance in a century*   Mark Weisbrot, "Populists Aid Poor, Spur Growth," *The Augusta Chronicle*, March 23, 2006.

441   *best rate in the region*   Banco Central de Venezuela, www.bcv.org.ve.

441   *add up to Cuban communism*   "Oil, Missions and a Chat Show — Hugo Chávez's Venezuela," *The Economist*, May 14, 2005.

441   *than Cuban communism*   Mark Weisbrot, "Growth Is a Homerun in Venezuela," Knight Ridder/Tribune Information Services, November 1, 2005.

441 *Chávez was a neo-liberal* Simón Romero, "For Venezuela, as Distaste for US Grows, So Does Trade," *The New York Times*, August 16, 2006.

442 *the South American consensus* Monte Reel, "A Latin American Pipeline Dream; Regional Leaders Put Weight Behind Gas Plan," *The Washington Post*, February 12, 2006.

442 *five to eight years of completion* Alan Clendenning, "Energy Independence Is South America's Pipe Dream," Associated Press, January 20, 2006.

443 *Venezuela sent to Asia* Steven Dudley, "In Ideology, Oil, Two Nations Find Common Ground," *The Miami Herald*, August 15, 2005; "Venezuela to Buy 18 Oil Tankers from China," Associated Press, May 10, 2006; "Venezuela Signs Oil Deal with China," *Voice of America News*, August 24, 2006; Tim Johnson, "Chávez Touts Stronger Ties Between Venezuela, China," *The Miami Herald*, August 26, 2006; "Venezuelan Oil Shipments to China Rise to 200,000 Barrels a Day," Associated Press, September 15, 2006.

443 *fifty-eight tankers by 2012* "Venezuela to Buy 18 Oil Tankers from China"; "Venezuela, Argentina Begin Construction of New PDVSA Oil Tanker Fleet," Associated Press, July 27, 2006.

443 *$5 to $10 a barrel* Dudley, "In Ideology, Oil."

444 *finish off the US empire* Nasser Karimi, "Hugo Chávez Receives Iran's Highest Honor," Associated Press, July 31, 2006.

444 *refusal to sell it replacement parts* Chris Kraul, "US Eyes Venezuela-Iran Commercial Alliance," *Los Angeles Times*, June 24, 2006.

445 *"harpoon diplomacy"* Larry Birns and Julian Armington, "The State Department's Shannon," *Washington Report on the Hemisphere* (Council on Hemispheric Affairs), December 20, 2005.

445 *Iran's "sidekicks"* Steven Dudley, "Chávez's Wooing of Iran Called Troubling," *The Miami Herald*, March 2, 2006.

445 *stuck in traffic* Ian James, "US Envoy's Car Pelted in Venezuela," Associated Press, April 8, 2006.

446 *cartoons on his office door* Richard Winton and J. Michael Kennedy, "Deputies' Questions Unsettle University; 'Chilling Effect' Is Feared After a Pomona College Professor Is Queried on His Links to Venezuela," *Los Angeles Times*, March 11, 2006.

447 *get a landline installed* Eva Golinger, "Confused About Venezuela," www.venezuelanalysis.com.

448 *the oil strike later that year* Ibid.

449 *in the entire world* Gary Marx, "In Venezuela, Crime Runs 'Absolutely Out of Control,'" *Chicago Tribune*, June 12, 2006.

450 *"bury the list"* Fabiola Sánchez, "List of Government Opponents on Web Site Draws Discrimination Complaints," Associated Press, May 13, 2005.

451     *a strong potential for wrong-headed policies*   Gregory Wilpert,
        "The Meaning of 21st Century Socialism for Venezuela,"
        www.venezuelanalysis.com, July 22, 2006.

452     *when Chávez began*   Mark Weisbrot, Luis Sandoval, and David
        Rosnick, "Poverty Rates in Venezuela: Getting the Numbers Right,"
        Center for Economic and Policy Research, May 2006.

452     *still in deep recession*   Ibid.

452     *made these kinds of gains*   Chesa Boudin, "Letter from Venezuela:
        Land of Chavismo," *The Nation*, November 16, 2006.

452     *five years to build*   Gregory Wilpert, "Brazil's President Lula Visits
        Venezuela, Inaugurates Projects," www.venezuelanalysis.com,
        November 13, 2006.

452     *south to Argentina*   Gregory Wilpert, "Venezuela Inaugurates
        First New Railroad in 70 Years," www.venezuelanalysis.com,
        October 16, 2006.

453     *"Compendium of Social Doctrine of the Church"*   Joseph J. Fahey,
        "A Hopeful People," *America*, November 13, 2006.

453     *he had his hacienda*   Miguel Bonasso, "Anatomia Intima de un
        Golpe Contada Por Chávez," *Pagina 12*, June 1, 2003.

453     *loved by the women of this country*   Lina Ron, "Lina Ron: 'No Es
        Bueno Que Chávez Este Solo,'" www.aporrea.org, January 30, 2007.

454     *the process would continue*   Charles Hardy, *Cowboy in Caracas*,
        page 157.

454     *new era of Socialist Democracy*   Patrick Moser, "Venezuela's Chávez
        Celebrates Re-Election, Promises 'Revolutionary Democracy,'"
        Agence France Press, December 4, 2006.

455     *no outside interference*   Joseph J. Fahey, "A Hopeful People,"
        *America*, November 13, 2006.

## Afterword

467     *Fidel Castro's playbook.*   States News Service, "Senator Hutchinson:
        Chavez a Threat to our National and Economic Security," May 4, 2007.

467     *victimized by this.*   Natalie Ibiko Pearson, "Chávez Takes Over
        Venezuela's Last Private Oil Fields, but Seeks to Entice Big Oil to
        Stay," Associated Press, May 2, 2007.

# Index

Note: The subject of this work is indexed *under* Chávez Frías, Hugo Rafael in a main heading. Otherwise, he is identified as *Hugo Chávez*, *Chávez*, and *HC* .

Note: Photo essay page numbers are identified with a *p*.

on recall results, 413, 417
and Romero, Peter, versus HC
administration, 264, 265
2002 coup: garnering Latin American
support, 348, 349; prediction
of, 317; recognition of Carmona
government, 348; reports from
Gustavo Cisneros (Venevisión)
owner, 348; US ambassador breakfast
with interim president, 17, 355
Venezuela statements, 242, 264, 467
visa denial to HC, 217
and World Bank withdrawal by HC,
467
Sullivan, Lisa (Maryknoll Catholic
missionary), 158, 291
Sumate (Join Up) civil society/electoral
monitoring organization
FOIA disclosures on, 406
and NED, 305, 352, 406, 407, 412
and recall, 407, 412
Sumavila, Arelis (sociologist/Indian
expert), 102
Summit of the Americas (Argentina, 2005),
433–34
Supreme Court, 68, 200, 351, 369, 379, 385,
403, 407–8

Táchira state (Venezuelan homeland of
dictators), 112
Tamayo Molina, Adm. Carlos (anti-Chávez
coup planner), 303, 312, 319–20, 326
Tascón list used against Chávez opponents,
449
teetotaling role model of HC, 234, 454
Telesur (CNN–style Latin America station
by HC), 427, 428
Televen, meeting with 2002 coup interim
president, 355
Televisión Española (Spain), 428
Teresa Carreño Theater, Caracas
International Workers' Day HC
speech, 2007, 466
and OPEC summit, 284
Pérez second inaugural celebration, 113
site of HC victory speech, 223
Thatcher, Margaret, 206, 211
Through These Streets/Por Estas Calles
(soap opera), 182–83
Time magazine, HC as among world's one
hundred most influential, 10
The Times of Ezequiel Zamora (Brito
Figueroa), 59
The Times of London on Sáez, Irene, 208
Tinker-Salas, Miguel (Pomona College
professor), 424
questioned by LA sheriffs on
Venezuelan ties, 445–46

Torres, Camillo (Colombian priest-turned
guerrilla), 136
Torrijos, Gen. Omar (Panama leader),
52–53, 135, 209
Tortoza, Jorge (2001 newspaper
photographer). See also main heading
Llaguno Bridge massacre (2002 coup)
2002 coup shooting victim, 324, 328
Tortoza, Xiomara (community organizer)
on austerity package result on poor, 120
on HC military formalities, 194
on solders' economic rebellion
response, 121–22
traditional culture preservation of HC,
429–30
The Traditional National Orchestra, 430
TransAfrica Forum tour to Venezuela, 400
transforming Venezuela dream of Chávez.
See also road to power of Chávez;
socialism for twenty-first century; social
missions of Hugo Chávez
and Bolívar, Simón, 48–49, 61
and Caracas barrios visits, 49–50 (See
also main heading road to power)
and constitutional assembly need, 169
(See also constitutional assembly of
Hugo Chávez)
HC teen wish for national
responsibility, 50
hope for great destiny by HC, 61–62
MBR-200 discussions/goals, 179
and Primera, Alí, protest singer,
49–50, 189
redistributing oil wealth, 370, 378, 409
self-sufficiency, 395, 437–38
Transparency International, 224
Trejo, Col. Hugo (Pérez Jiménez overthrow
leader), 134
Trinidad, 378, 383
24 Hours Venevisión program
arrest warrants report, 350
cancellation, 272, 422
and Carmona putsch witch hunt,
349–50
during 2002 coup, 343, 350
and media as essential to 2002 coup,
343–44
2002 coup, 8. See also Carmona interim
government (2002); 2002 entries under
USA main heading; presidency of Hugo
Chávez (after "mega-election")
as accelerating HC vision, 468–69
aftermath, 366–71 (See also presidency
of Hugo Chávez [after 2002 coup])
ambassadors called by HC, 333
assassination of investigator, 416
bloodbath prevention by HC, 333,
336, 339